CONTEMPORARY MUSICIANS

ISSN-1044-2197

CONTEMPORARY MUSICIANS

PROFILES OF THE PEOPLE IN MUSIC

LEIGH ANN DeREMER, Editor

VOLUME 33
Includes Cumulative Indexes

GALE GROUP

THOMSON LEARNING™

Detroit • New York • San Diego • San Francisco
Boston • New Haven, Conn. • Waterville, Maine
London • Munich

STAFF

Leigh Ann DeRemer, *Editor*
Laura Avery, *Associate Editor*

Mary Alice Adams, Don Amerman, Michael P. Belfiore, Timothy Borden, Gloria Cooksey,
Nicole Elyse, Christina Fuoco, Judy Galens, Lloyd Hemingway, Laura Hightower, Janet Ingram,
Anne Janette Johnson, Ronald D. Lankford, Jr., Brenda Sanchez, Janet Stamatel, B. Kimberly Taylor,
Elizabeth Thomas, Bruce Walker,
Sketchwriters

Bridget Travers, *Managing Editor*

Maria L. Franklin, *Permissions Manager*
Shalice Shah-Caldwell, *Permissions Associate*

Mary Beth Trimper, *Manager, Composition and Electronic Prepress*
Gary Leach, *Composition Specialist*
Dorothy Maki, *Manufacturing Manager*
Stacy Melson, *Buyer*

Robert Duncan, *Imaging Specialist*
Randy Bassett, *Image Database Supervisor*
Dean Dauphinais, *Senior Editor, Imaging and Multimedia Content*
Pamela A. Reed, *Imaging Coordinator*
Michael Logusz, *Graphic Artist*
Cover illustration by John Kleber

Copyright © 2002 by Gale Group, Inc.
27500 Drake Rd.
Farmington Hills, MI 48334-3535

ISBN 0-7876-4644-X
ISSN 1044-2197

10 9 8 7 6 5 4 3 2 1

Contents

Introduction ix

Cumulative Subject Index 237

Cumulative Musicians Index 265

Introduction

Fills in the Information Gap on Today's Musicians

Contemporary Musicians profiles the colorful personalities in the music industry who create or influence the music we hear today. Prior to *Contemporary Musicians,* no quality reference series provided comprehensive information on such a wide range of artists despite keen and ongoing public interest. To find biographical and critical coverage, an information seeker had little choice but to wade through the offerings of the popular press, scan television "infotainment" programs, and search for the occasional published biography or expose. *Contemporary Musicians* is designed to serve that information seeker, providing in one ongoing source in-depth coverage of the important names on the modern music scene in a format that is both informative and entertaining. Students, researchers, and casual browsers alike can use *Contemporary Musicians* to meet their needs for personal information about music figures; find a selected discography of a musician's recordings; and uncover an insightful essay offering biographical and critical information.

Provides Broad Coverage

Single-volume biographical sources on musicians are limited in scope, often focusing on a handful of performers from a specific musical genre or era. In contrast, *Contemporary Musicians* offers researchers and music devotees a comprehensive, informative, and entertaining alternative. *Contemporary Musicians* is published four times per year, with each volume providing information on about 80 musical artists and record-industry luminaries from all the genres that form the broad spectrum of contemporary music— pop, rock, jazz, blues, country, New Age, folk, rhythm and blues, gospel, bluegrass, rap, and reggae, to name a few—as well as selected classical artists who have achieved "crossover" success with the general public. *Contemporary Musicians* will also occasionally include profiles of influential nonperforming members of the music community, including producers, promoters, and record company executives. Additionally, beginning with *Contemporary Musicians 11,* each volume features new profiles of a selection of previous *Contemporary Musicians* listees who remain of interest to today's readers and who have been active enough to require completely revised entries.

Includes Popular Features

In *Contemporary Musicians* you'll find popular features that users value:

- **Easy-to-locate data sections:** Vital personal statistics, chronological career summaries, listings of major awards, and mailing addresses, when available, are prominently displayed in a clearly marked box on the second page of each entry.

- **Biographical/critical essays:** Colorful and informative essays trace each subject's personal and professional life, offer representative examples of critical response to the artist's work, and provide entertaining personal sidelights.

- **Selected discographies:** Each entry provides a comprehensive listing of the artist's major recorded works.

- **Photographs:** Most entries include portraits of the subject profiled.

- **Sources for additional information:** This invaluable feature directs the user to selected books, magazines, newspapers, and online sources where more information can be obtained.

Helpful Indexes Make It Easy to Find the Information You Need

Each volume of *Contemporary Musicians* features a cumulative Musicians Index, listing names of individual performers and musical groups, and a cumulative Subject Index, which provides the user with a breakdown by primary musical instruments played and by musical genre.

Available in Electronic Formats

Diskette/Magnetic Tape. *Contemporary Musicians* is available for licensing on magnetic tape or diskette in a fielded format. The database is available for internal data processing and nonpublishing purposes only. For more information, call (800) 877-GALE.

Online. *Contemporary Musicians* is available online as part of the Gale Biographies (GALBIO) database accessible through LEXIS-NEXIS, P.O. Box 933, Dayton, OH 45401-0933; phone: (937) 865-6800, toll-free: (800) 543-6862.

We Welcome Your Suggestions

The editors welcome your comments and suggestions for enhancing and improving *Contemporary Musicians.* If you would like to suggest subjects for inclusion, please submit these names to the editor. Mail comments or suggestions to:

The Editor
Contemporary Musicians
Gale Group, Inc.
27500 Drake Rd.
Farmington Hills, MI 48334-3535

Or call toll free: (800) 347-GALE

Johnny Adams

Singer

After Johnny Adams had his first local hit in 1959, he remained a fixture of music in New Orleans, Louisiana, for the rest of his life. With an expressive voice and a range that included the beautiful falsetto that led a local disc jockey to call him "the Tan Canary," Adams sang several styles with ease. Starting as a gospel singer, he later expanded his range to include blues, soul, county, and jazz. He often seemed on the verge of breaking out as a national star, but problems with record companies held him back. Still, Adams became a legend in New Orleans, and his vocal style influenced singers working in a wide range of music, from the soulful Aaron Neville to rocker Darius Rucker of Hootie and the Blowfish. Upon his death in 1998, the outpouring of tributes from the music industry and the press revealed the stature that Adams had achieved among his peers.

Born on January 5, 1932, in New Orleans, Adams was the oldest in a family of ten children. He dropped out of school at the age of 15 and began singing in gospel groups. His talent soon made him the lead singer in these groups, although he told Scott Aiges of the New Orleans *Times-Picayune,* "[M]y voice was so loud that it couldn't even blend with the others. They said, 'You have to sing lead.'" But singing in the bathtub, not on stage, gave Adams his first opportunity to record as a solo act. He lived downstairs from songwriter Dorothy Labostrie, who decided she wanted him to sing one of her songs after hearing Adams' rendition of "Precious Lord" through her floor. The 1959 single, "I Won't Cry," produced by a young Mac Rebennack, who would later claim his singing fame as Dr. John, became a local hit.

This promising start, though, did not launch Adams to stardom. Years later, Adams would remember that Joe Ruffino, the owner of Ric Records for which Adams recorded, held up national distribution of the singles. According to Tony Russell of the *Guardian,* Adams said, "I believe we could have gone places with 'I Won't Cry' if Ruffino would have helped and cooperated with major companies." Still, Adams continued to record with Ric, gaining national attention with "A Losing Battle," written by Rebenack, which made the rhythm and blues charts in 1962.

Still, the stories persisted that Ruffino kept holding Adams back. Reports circulated that Barry Gordy, Jr. wanted to sign Adams to his Motown label after the success of "A Losing Battle," but that no deal occurred because Ruffino threatened to sue. Thus, Adams continued to record for Ric until 1968, when he changed labels and produced his largest commercial success. Working with producer Shelby Singleton for SSS Records, Adams turned his vocal skills to a blend of country and soul. His 1968 cover of the country standard "Release Me" became a hit, and 1969's "Reconsider Me" also made the top ten on the rhythm and blues charts. Bill Dahl of *All Music Guide* remarked on the passion in Adams' performance on "Reconsider

For the Record . . .

Born Lathen John Adams on January 5, 1932, in New Orleans, LA; died on September 14, 1998, in Baton Rouge, LA; wife, Judy Adams.

Left school and began singing career at age 15; debut single, "I Won't Cry," 1959; had first national hit with "Release Me," 1968; continued performing in and around New Orleans, 1970s; signed with Rounder Records, 1984; recorded last album, *Man of My Word*, 1998.

Awards: Pioneer Award, Rhythm-and-Blues Foundation, 1999.

Me": "[H]e swoops effortlessly up to a death-defying falsetto range to drive his anguished message home with fervor."

Once again, though, this glimpse of a larger audience did not lead Adams to stardom. While he remained a New Orleans fixture throughout the 1970s, the rest of the world remained largely unaware of him. Even though he signed for a brief stint with a major national record label, Atlantic Records, the collaboration did not lead to much success. Adams himself believed part of the problem lay with the record companies trying to limit his range of music. In an interview recounted in the *Guardian*, Adams said, "In the past, record companies tried to pigeonhole me as a country singer or a ballad singer. But I consider myself able to do it all. Hell, I think I could sing bluegrass if I had to."

Finally in 1984, Adams found a record company and a producer with whom he could have a fruitful relationship. He began working with Scott Billington of Rounder Records, a collaboration that would last for the rest of Adams' career. Billington recognized that Adams' talent extended to a wide range of musical styles. As Tom Surowicz pointed out in the Minneapolis *Star Tribune*, "Adams could sing sophisticated jazz. He could sing sentimental pop, or stirring gospel. He had precious few peers when tackling Southern deep-soul classics. And on the right night, with the right band, he all but owned the blues."

From the Heart, released in 1984, started the upswing for Adams' career. A few subsequent albums would be devoted to the works of a single songwriter, such as *Johnny Adams Sings Doc Pomus: The Real Me* in 1991. Others showcased his talents at exploring specific genres, such as the jazz-oriented *Good Morning*

Heartache in 1993 and *One Foot in the Blues* in 1996, which Kenny Mathieson of the *Scotsman* claimed, "summed up his philosophy as well as any—the blues were always present in his work, but that second foot could be planted in any of several different styles." Along with gaining more control over the material he recorded, Adams also became more well-known outside New Orleans after beginning his work with Billington. He began to tour nationally and even internationally as more people realized the power of his voice and range of styles.

Although he had been diagnosed with prostate cancer, Adams went into the studio to record his final album, *Man of My Word*, released in 1998. The sessions were difficult for Adams. Billington told Keith Spera of the New Orleans *Times-Picayune*, "It's a miracle it was finished. I'm still moved to tears when I listen to his vocal performances on that record." Although he was suffering, Adams put together a strong album. Surowicz wrote, "[I]t lives up to Adams mighty legacy, and easily rates as one of the best roots R&B outings of the year."

Adams succumbed to the cancer and died on September 14, 1998, in Baton Rouge, Louisiana. He continued to receive more recognition for his work after death. In 1999 he received a Pioneer Award from the Rhythm-and-Blues Foundation. Then in 2000, Rounder issued an album sampling the best of his work. Called *There Is Always One More Time*, it featured not only tracks from Adams' previous albums, but also some collaborations with other performers. Reviewer Britt Robson of the *Washington Post* summed up Adams' career by saying that the album "documents an artist consistently in his prime." For almost 40 years, Adams moved audiences with a stunning voice that could grace any genre he chose.

Selected discography

Singles

"I Won't Cry," Ric, 1959.
"A Losing Battle," Ric, 1962.
"Release Me," SSS, 1968.
"Reconsider Me," SSS, 1969.
"I Can't Be All Bad," SSS, 1969.

Albums

Heart and Soul, SSS, 1969.
Christmas in New Orleans, Ace, 1975.
Stand by Me, Chelsea, 1976.
After All the Good Is Gone, Ariola, 1978.
From the Heart, Rounder, 1984.
After Dark, Rounder, 1986.
Room with a View of the Blues, Rounder, 1987.
Walking on a Tightrope: The Songs of Percy Mayfield, Rounder, 1989.

Johnny Adams Sings Doc Pomus: The Real Me, Rounder, 1991.
I Won't Cry: From the Vaults of Ric & Ron Records, Rounder, 1991.
Good Morning Heartache, Rounder, 1993.
The Verdict, Rounder, 1995.
One Foot in the Blues, Rounder, 1996.
Man of My Word, Rounder, 1998.
There Is Always One More Time, Rounder, 2000.

Sources

Books

Graff, Gary, Josh Freedom Du Lac, and Jim McFarlin, *MusicHound R&B: The Essential Album Guide,* Visible Ink Press, 1998.

Periodicals

Guardian (London), October 6, 1998, p. 22.
New York Times, September 16, 1998, p. B11; February 27, 1999, p. B9.
Scotsman, October 14, 1998.
Star Tribune (Minneapolis, MN), September 20, 1998, p. 4FF.
Times-Picayune (New Orleans, LA), January 1, 1993, p. 16; April 25, 1999, p. E1.
Washington Post, December 13, 2000, p. C5.

Online

"Johnny Adams," *All Music Guide,* http://www.allmusic.com (May 9, 2001).
Rounder Records, http://www.rounder.com (June 11, 2001).

—Lloyd Hemingway

Air

Pop duo

Although Air—the diverse electronic French duo of Nicolas Godin, a former architect, and Jean-Benoit Dunckel, a mathematician—are associated with an emerging ambient-dance scene in France for their combining of open-ended pop forms with atmospheric effects, their music stands apart from typical electronica. One might assume that Dunckel and Godin rely heavily on sampling and other high-tech devices because of their connection to the genre, but in reality, the pair prefer to play their own instruments. "We liked playing instruments, you know, it's a pleasure," Godin said, as quoted by the MTV website. "It's a chance to make a record and to hear me playing the piano or the guitar, and I could say to my children later, 'hey, look here, it's me, I'm playing.' So I don't understand why I should program what I play, because, when I wake up in the morning the first thing I'm doing is playing the piano."

Another noble characteristic of Air is their insistence on not duplicating instrumentation or sounds presented in previous work. For example, with their pivotal 1998 album *Moon Safari*, the duo provided the tracks with a retro feel through the use of mini-Moog and vocoder, while the romantic themes of space travel and stargazing gave the recording a futuristic sense. Moving forward to 2001's *10,000 Hz Legend*, a computerized, space-age set exploring vacant pop culture, Godin and Dunckel introduced flutes and gentle rhythms into their repertoire. As former Redd Kross drummer Brian Reitzell, who joins Air for live shows, recorded with the duo their score for the *Virgin Suicides* film soundtrack,

and worked in the studio on *10,000 Hz Legend,* told Corey Moss of Sonicnet.com: "With *Moon Safari,* they use a lot of vocoder and Fender Rhodes [keyboards], and when they did the score they wanted to explore other instruments. They're constantly reinventing themselves."

Dunckel and Godin, both originally from Versailles, France, first united musically while attending university in Paris. At the time, in the early 1990s, Dunckel, a mathematician and teacher, was already a member of the independent rock group Orange with producer Alex Gopher (born Alex Latrobe), who introduced Godin, an architect, to the band. Soon, Godin accepted an offer to join Orange. The trio played together as Orange until the mid 1990s, when Gopher left to begin producing for the influential Paris-based dance music labels Source and Solid; he also released material as a solo artist. Meanwhile, Dunckel and Godin, after a period of concentrating on their respective studies, morphed into Air in 1995.

Upon reuniting, Dunckel and Godin began forging a new electronic direction different from their experiences with Orange. Their trademark would soon become what the press dubbed "ambient-kitsch electric French pop." Also in 1995, the duo signed with Source, a Virgin Records offshoot label based in Paris, and released a handful of singles for both Source and Mo' Wax, another Paris label. Later that year, in November, Air released their first *Modular Mix* EP for Source.

In July of 1996, Air released a second EP on Source called *Casanova '70,* followed in August by a second *Modular Mix* EP for Mo' Wax. Their next EP, *Le Soleil est Pres de Moi,* surfaced in November of 1997 on Source. Previous to this record, though, a cumulative album of their four EPs arrived in July of 1997. Issued by Source under the title *Premiers Symptomes,* the record brought Air to the attention of Europe's most prominent DJs, leading to remixing opportunities for the likes of Depeche Mode and Neneh Cherry. Some sources, however, claim that Godin and Dunckel have since disowned their earlier work compiled on *Premiers Symptomes.* Overall, though, critics received the record favorably, but some nonetheless called the songs a little hesitant and underdeveloped. Still, it was a substantial beginning and offered plenty to admire.

When it came time to record a proper debut album, Godin and Dunckel retreated to an abandoned, eighteenth-century chateau located just outside Paris. Here, on an eight-track console, the duo recorded and produced ten songs of new material. The result, 1998's *Moon Safari,* proved a striking mixture of dance loops and jazzy pop melodies that moved from instrumentals to effortless techno-pop. The album and subsequent tour across Europe and the United States propelled Air to international stardom. In the United Kingdom, the set reached number five on the charts, and the singles

For the Record . . .

Members include **Jean-Benoit Dunckel**, keyboards, piano, clavinet, synthesizer; **Nicolas Godin**, bass, guitar, vocoder, percussion.

Formed in Paris, France, 1995; released *Moon Safari*, 1998; composed original score for the 2000 film *The Virgin Suicides*; released *10,000 Hz Legend*, 2001.

Addresses: *Record company*—Astralwerks, 104 W. 29th St., 4th Fl., New York, NY 10001, phone: (212) 989-2929, fax: (212) 643-5573, website: http://www.astralwerks.com.

"Sexy Boy," "Kelly Watch the Stars," and "All I Need," featuring vocals by Godin and Beth Hirsch, an American singer based in Paris, all became hits. At the end of the year, *Moon Safari* appeared on several "best of" lists; *Select* magazine as well as *Muzik* named it the number one album of the year, the *Oakland Tribune* ranked the album at number seven, and the *Chicago Tribune* listed *Moon Safari* at number ten.

In 1999, after both Dunckel and Godin became fathers within one week of each other (Dunckel had a girl and Godin a boy), Air set out on their next project—composing the original score for the film *The Virgin Suicides,* directed by Sophia Coppola and based on the book by Jeffrey Eugenides. According to Dunckel, Coppola was a big fan of *Moon Safari* and knew Mike Mills, who directed videos for Air and provided all their artwork. Dunckel and Godin, who always wanted to work on a soundtrack, jumped on the opportunity to try something new. "We're big fans of soundtracks—they were my first introduction to classical music," said Dunckel in an interview for *Uncut* magazine. "I like pop songs too, of course, but here you can use more strings, and have a theme you return to." The album soundtrack, released in February of 2000 on the American label Astralwerks and on Virgin overseas, further solidified Air's reputation, and the first single from the record, "Playground Love," received wide airplay in both Europe and the States.

Staying true to their rule about not re-using instruments or past ideas, Air spent much of 2000 working on their follow-up to *Moon Safari*. "It's very different from *Moon Safari* and nothing like the soundtrack," commented Reitzell about *10,000 Hz Legend,* a "masterpiece," hailed the drummer. "*The Virgin Suicides* score was Air working incredibly quickly. There weren't a lot of arrangements. This new record, every song is a contained work of art. But every song is a song. There's no art damage." The sublime, expansive, and intoxicating album, released in May of 2001 on Astralwerks in the United States, also enjoyed critical acclaim, as reviewers compared their journeys into psychedelic panoramas to that of Pink Floyd, Gong, Can, and post-rock groups like Oval, Tortoise, and Radiohead. Notable tracks from the eleven-song set included "Radian," "Electric Performers," "People in the City," "Don't Be Light," and "The Vagabond," with a guest appearance by the abstract funk-rock superstar Beck.

Selected discography

Singles and EPs

Modular Mix (EP), Source, 1995.
Casanova '70 (EP), Source, 1996.
Modular Mix (EP), Mo' Wax, 1996.
Le Soleil est Pres de Moi (EP), 1997.
"Sexy Boy," Source/Virgin, 1998.
"Kelly, Watch the Stars," Source/Virgin, 1998.
"All I Need," Virgin, 1998.
"Playground Love," Virgin, 2000.

Albums

Premiers Symptomes, Source/Virgin, July 1997; reissued, Virgin, 1999.
Moon Safari, Source/Virgin, 1998.
The Virgin Suicides, Virgin, 2000.
10,000 Hz Legend, Astralwerks, 2000.

Sources

Periodicals

Uncut, April 2000.

Online

The Biggest Air Site Online, http://www.airfrenchband.co.uk (May 17, 2001).
MTV, http://www.mtv.com (May 17, 2001).
The Raft, http://www.theraft.com (May 17, 2001).
Sonicnet, http://www.sonicnet.com (May 17, 2001).
Yahoo! Music, http://musicfinder.yahoo.com (May 17, 2001).

—Laura Hightower

Julie Andrews

Singer

Singer and actress Julie Andrews has long been famed for her perfect pitch and impressive vocal range. From her 1954 Broadway debut as Polly in *The Boy Friend*, she has received rave reviews from critics and lasting devotion from music fans. Best known for her roles in stage and film musicals, including *My Fair Lady*, *The Sound of Music*, and *Mary Poppins*, Andrews has concentrated in later years on acting on the screen rather than singing, appearing in husband Blake Edwards films, including *S.O.B.* and *That's Life*. Andrews' latest film, *The Princess Diaries,* was scheduled for release in August of 2001.

Andrews had a somewhat unusual childhood. Born Julia Elizabeth Wells on October 1, 1935, at Walton-on-Thames, England, her parents divorced when she was very young. Her mother, a pianist, married Edward Andrews, who sang in music halls, and the child took her stepfather's last name. The newly made family traveled throughout England, Mr. and Mrs. Andrews performing for a living. Julie, as they called her, first began displaying her own considerable vocal talents during World War II, when she was about eight years old. While hiding in community air-raid shelters, Mr. Andrews led the frightened citizens in singing to keep spirits up. Mrs. Andrews began to notice that her daughter's voice often rose far above those of even the men and women; when examined by a doctor, Julie's vocal chords proved to have already developed to an adult level. As soon as they were able, the Andrewses provided their prodigy with professional singing lessons by Madame Stiles-Allen.

By the time Andrews was 12, she was performing in the same venues as her mother and stepfather; she made her professional singing debut with the *Starlight Roof* revue at the Hippodrome Theatre on London's West End. But she was destined to go further than her parents. After performing in several other pantomimes, Andrews played the featured role in a pantomime of *Cinderella* in 1953, and in this capacity she caught the attention of director Vida Hope, who was working on the London production of Sandy Wilson's musical about the 1920s, *The Boy Friend*. Hope brought this discovery to the United States to shine on Broadway where she won rave reviews portraying Polly Brown, an earnest young British flapper. Critic John Beaufort asserted in the *Christian Science Monitor* that the young singer's interpretation of the part was both "comic and adorable" and that "her solemnly pretty ingenue-ness" was "a triumph of controlled exaggeration"; Wolcott Gibbs agreed, calling Andrews "the season's dramatic highlight" in the *New Yorker*. The New York version of *The Boy Friend* ran for 485 performances.

Andrews moved to an even bigger triumph in 1956, when she became the youngest actress ever to play the part of Eliza Doolittle professionally. She starred in the musical version of George Bernard Shaw's *Pyg-*

For the Record . . .

Born Julia Elizabeth Wells on October 1, 1935, in Walton-on-Thames, England; daughter of Edward C. (a teacher) and Barbara Wells (a pianist); married Tony Walton (a set designer), May 10, 1959 (divorced, 1968); married Blake Edwards (a film director, producer, and screenwriter), November 12, 1969; children: (first marriage) Emma Kate Walton; children: (second marriage; adopted) Jeanna Lynne, Amy Leigh.

Singer, 1947—; actress, 1948—; has appeared in stage musicals including *The Boy Friend*, Royale Theatre, New York, 1954; *My Fair Lady*, Mark Hellinger Theatre, New York, 1956; *Camelot*, Majestic Theatre, New York,1960; has appeared in films including *Mary Poppins*, Buena Vista, 1964; *The Americanization of Emily*, MGM, 1964; *The Sound of Music*, Twentieth Century-Fox, 1965; *Hawaii*, United Artists, 1966; *Torn Curtain*, Universal, 1966; *Thoroughly Modern Millie*, MGM, 1967; *Darling Lili*, Paramount, 1970; *The Tamarind Seed*, AVCO-Embassy, 1974; *10*, Warner Bros., 1979; *Little Miss Marker*, Universal, 1980; *S.O.B.*, Paramount, 1981; *Victor/Victoria*, MGM/United Artists, 1982; *The Man Who Loved Women*, Columbia, 1983; *Duet for One*, Cannon, 1986; *That's Life*, Columbia, 1986; has also written children's books including *Dumpy the Dump Truck*, 2000.

Awards: New York Drama Critics Award, Best Actress in a Musical, 1956, for *My Fair Lady*; Golden Globe Awards, 1964, 1965, and 1967, for *Mary Poppins*, *The Sound of Music*, and as World's Film Favorite, respectively; Academy Award, 1964, Best Actress, for *Mary Poppins*; Woman of the Year Award from *Los Angeles Times*, 1965; Woman of the Year Award from the B'nai B'rith Anti-Defamation League, 1983; Hasty Pudding Woman of the Year Award from the Harvard Hasty Pudding Theatricals, 1983. Honorary D.F.A. from the University of Maryland, 1970; Dame Commander, Order of the British Empire (OBE), 2000.

Addresses: *Agent*—William Morris Agency, 151 E1 Camino Drive, Beverly Hills, CA 90212.

Higgins." In this capacity Andrews garnered a nomination for an Antoinette Perry (Tony) Award and the New York Drama Critics Award for best actress in a musical. Despite her critically acclaimed performance, however, she was passed over for the film version in favor of actress Audrey Hepburn. Andrews received another Tony nomination in 1961 for her portrayal of Queen Guinevere in the smash Arthurian musical, *Camelot*.

Though Andrews was again passed over for the film version of *Camelot*—this time in favor of actress Vanessa Redgrave—her time in films was not long in coming. She made her screen debut in 1964 in *Mary Poppins*. Her appearance as the magical nanny won her both an Academy Award and a Golden Globe Award for best actress. This film and the following year's *The Sound of Music*, in which she played a children's governess who wins the love of her charges' father, began to establish Andrews as a specialist in wholesome family entertainment. As Clive Hirschhorn put it in his 1981 book, *The Hollywood Musical*, *The Sound of Music* was accused of "mawkish sentimentality" by many critics, but "it was Andrews's extraordinarily assured and appealing central performance ... that was largely responsible for the film's enormous success." Her featured songs in the film included the title theme, "I Have Confidence in Me," and "My Favorite Things."

Another musical film featuring Andrews was 1967's *Thoroughly Modern Millie*, which Hirschhorn hailed as "an irresistible mixture of brashness, charm, and nostalgia put together with expertise." Like her first major stage play, *Millie* had Andrews portraying a young woman during the 1920s—a young woman who goes to New York City as a secretary in search of a rich husband and becomes involved in a white slavery ring. During what Hirschhorn describes as a "thoroughly captivating star performance," Andrews sang ditties such as "Jimmy" and "Poor Butterfly."

Not long after filming *Millie,* Andrews divorced her first husband, theatrical designer Tony Walton, and married motion-picture producer and director Blake Edwards, famed for his Pink Panther films. She began working in Edwards' efforts, including 1970's *Darling Lili*. Andrews was also featured as actor Dudley Moore's long-suffering girlfriend in Edwards' *10*. In 1981's *S.O.B.*, Edwards spoofed his wife's wholesome image by making a big production of her character, Sally Miles, baring her breasts for the camera. Andrews perhaps moved even further from her former reputation when she portrayed a singing transvestite in Edwards' 1982 motion picture, *Victor/Victoria*. The critics especially took her seriously in the latter role, and she received nominations for both an Academy Award and a Golden Globe for her part in the film.

During the late 1980s, Andrews concentrated on more serious film roles, ones that did not utilize her talent for

malion—My Fair Lady—and in it warbled songs such as "Wouldn't It Be Loverly" and "Just You Wait, Henry singing. Though Edwards's 1986 effort *That's Life* was a comedy, Andrews' portrayal of Gillian Fairchild was a serious one—Gillian is waiting for the results of a biopsy. Andrews "is the movie's strong, quiet heart," declared reviewer David Ansen in *Newsweek*, "and it is she who devastates us when she finally unleashes her pent-up emotions." Despite some negative comments about the film in general, critics tended to agree favorably about Andrews' performance in *Duet for One*. Playing a famed violinist dying of multiple sclerosis, "Andrews doesn't tear a passion to tatters; she uses it to stitch a coherent soul," according to Richard Corliss of *Time*. And *Maclean*'s critic Lawrence O'Toole asserted that "Andrews gives what may be the performance of her life in *Duet for One*."

But Andrews continues entertaining fans with her voice. In 1987 she released the album *Love, Julie*, which featured her renditions of songs like "Tea for Two," "Come Rain or Come Shine." Though *People* reviewer David Hiltbrand considered the disc a mixed effort, he had praise for the "sensuousness to her tone," and said that her voice was "sweet and clear, often frosted with an appreciable sparkle." Andrews appeared on the short-lived television sitcom *Julie* on ABC in 1992, and she made her first stage appearance after a 30-year hiatus in Stephen Sondheim and Julia McKenzie's musical *Putting It Together* in 1993. Andrews appeared on the Broadway stage to sold-out crowds in *Victor/Victoria* during 1995-97. Though she was nominated for a Tony Award for her role in the musical, she bowed out of the awards because the production was not recognized in other categories. According to *Time*, Andrews told the crowd after a performance of *Victor/Victoria*: "I have searched my conscience and my heart, and I find that I cannot accept this nomination—and prefer to stand with the egregiously overlooked."

Andrews had throat surgery at New York's Mount Sinai Hospital in 1997 to remove noncancerous nodules, an operation which resulted in a significant deterioration of the singer's voice. Andrews filed a malpractice claim against her doctors in 1999; the claim was settled in September of 2000. While continuing rehabilitation exercises to strengthen her voice, Andrews continues to perform. She appeared in the television specials *One Special Night* with James Garner on CBS in 1999 and *On Gold Pond* with Christopher Plummer on CBS in 2001. Andrews also continues to write children's books. Some of her most successful have been *Mandy*, published in 1971, and *The Last of the Really Great Whangdoodles*, published in 1974. Her most recent book is *Dumpy the Dump Truck*, published in 2000.

Selected discography

The Boy Friend, RCA, 1955.
My Fair Lady, Columbia, 1956.
Cinderella, Columbia, 1957.
Julie Andrews Sings, RCA, 1958.
Camelot, Columbia, 1961.
Broadway's Fair Julie, Columbia, 1962.
Julie & Carol at Carnegie Hall, Columbia, 1962.
Mary Poppins, Buena Vista, 1964.
The Sound of Music, RCA, 1965.
Thoroughly Modern Millie, Decca, 1967.
A Little Bit of Love, Harmony, 1970.
TV's Fair Julie, Harmony, 1972.
The World of Julie Andrews, Columbia, 1972.
Julie Andrews, RCA (U.K), 1975.
Victor/Victoria, MGM, 1982.
Love, Julie, USA, 1987.
A Little Bit of Broadway, CBS, 1988.
The King & I, Philips, 1992.
Thoroughly Modern Julie: The Best of Julie Andrews, Rhino/Sony, 1995.
The Sound of Julie Andrews: 22 Classic Songs, Time Life Records, 1996.
Christmas with Julie Andrews, Sony/Columbia, 1999.
Classic Julie: Classic Broadway, Uni/Decca, 2001.

Sources

Books

Hirschhorn, Clive, *The Hollywood Musical*, Crown, 1981.

Periodicals

Christian Science Monitor, October 9, 1954.
Knight-Ridder/Tribune News Service, April 26, 2001.
Maclean's, March 2, 1987.
McCall's, November 1986.
Newsweek, October 6, 1986.
New Yorker, October 9, 1954.
People, January 25, 1988; November 29, 1999.
Publisher's Weekly, September 11, 2000.
Time, September 29, 1986; March 2, 1987; May 20, 1996.

Online

"Julie Andrews," Julie Andrews.tv, http://www.juliean drews.co.uk (June 26, 2001).
"Dame Judy Settles over Op Damages" BBC Online, http://news.bbc.co.uk/hi/english/entertainment/newsid_915000/915932.stm (June 26, 2001).
"Queen Honours Movie Dames," BBC Online, http://news.bbc.co.uk/hi/english/entertainment/newsid_750000/750290.stm (June 26, 2001).

—*Elizabeth Thomas*

Marc Anthony

Singer, songwriter

AP/Wide World Photos. Reproduced by permission.

Though he began riding a wave of popularity among Latin recording artists in the United States in the late 1990s, Marc Anthony has been a mainstay in the salsa genre for years. By blending in pop and spicing up his songs with a healthy dose of romance, he had been a star in Spanish-speaking areas long before the release of his English-language salsa album, *Marc Anthony,* hit the shelves in 1999. His slightly smoky tenor is lush and expressive, and he has been known to start crying on stage during love songs. Women swoon and throw undergarments on stage during his concerts, and his balladeering style has earned him comparisons to Frank Sinatra. In 1998, before Ricky Martin had burst on the scene, Anthony took home the Grammy Award for best tropical Latin performance, for his 1997 album *Contra la Corriente.* A second Grammy win came in 2000 for Song of the Year for "Dímelo (I Need to Know)" from *Marc Anthony* at the first annual Latin Grammy Awards. The singer has started drawing raves for his acting talents as well, most notably with a turn as a deranged transient man in 1999's *Bringing Out the Dead.*

Anthony was born Marco Antonio Muniz on September 16, 1969, in New York City. He was raised in Spanish Harlem, the youngest of five boys and three girls. His father, Felipe, worked in a hospital lunchroom, and Guillermina ("Jenny"), was a homemaker. They are now divorced. Anthony was exposed to jibaro music and salsa beginning at a tender age. His father had moved from Puerto Rico in the 1950s and played guitar; he also enjoyed listening to Ruben Blades, Hector Lavoe, and Willie Colon. Anthony would climb up on the kitchen table and sing along during his dad's jam sessions. By the time he was three, he was able to draw tears from female family members with his soulful renditions.

When Anthony was six or seven, he sang "El Zolsar" at a social club where his father was playing, and a man gave his mother a dollar, telling her that her child would make it big someday. It was the first money Anthony ever earned for his talent. However, like many children, Anthony considered his parents' music and the Latin image uncool. "I couldn't relate to the suits, the chains and the pinky rings, so it didn't interest me," he remarked to Cristina Veran in *Newsday.* Instead, he started getting into rock and roll, rap, and dance music. "I was raised in New York during the Seventies and Eighties," he mentioned to Clark Collis in the *Daily Telegraph.* "So I was exposed to everything. Jimi Hendrix. Motown. Disco. Salsa. You name it." He has also claimed the light-as-their-name pop group Air Supply as an influence.

At age 12, Anthony and his sister began singing background vocals for commercials, including one for Bumble Bee tuna. At 15, he was a water boy for one of his idols, Ruben Blades. "I used to pray for him to be thirsty, just to be onstage," Anthony reminisced to

Collis in the *Daily Telegraph.* By high school, Anthony was writing music, which caught the attention of the dance-pop singer Sa-Fire. He ended up penning two songs, "You Said You Love Me" and "I Better Be the Only One," for her album, as well as singing backup. Another single he wrote, "Boy I've Been Told," became a Top 40 hit. He went on to sing background for The Latin Rascals, who worked with Little Louis Vega. In the meantime, Anthony was also writing songs in both English and Spanish for Menudo, as well as serving as a backup singer and vocal coach for them.

In the early 1990s, Vega became a producer for Atlantic Records and asked Anthony to sing for him. He recorded a dance album in English, *When the Night Is Over,* and had a number one *Billboard* dance hit with "Ride on the Rhythm," but failed to make waves beyond that. Though he was performing house music at clubs in New York City, he found it encouraging if audiences numbered even in the triple digits. Then he and Vega opened for Tito Puente at Madison Square Garden in New York City. Anthony's manager subsequently prodded him to begin recording salsa music, but he resisted. Not long after that, though, he was listening to the radio and heard the Juan Gabriel ballad, "Hasta Que Te Conoci" ("Until I Met You"). Inspired, he came up with an upbeat salsa version of the tune, and it became his ticket to stardom.

In 1993, Anthony released his first salsa album, *Otra Nota,* on Soho Latino/RMM Records. Soon, his manager sent him to perform at Radio y Musica, a Latin-music convention in Los Angeles. Most of the attendees were disc jockeys. Highly intimidated and wearing borrowed clothes because his financial situation was tight, he sang a song backed only by instrumentals from a DAT player. He recalled to Alec Wilkinson in the *New Yorker,* "I'm trembling up a storm.... I walk up to the mike and think, 'Make believe you're in your living room singing to your mom.'" Afterward, he darted off the stage so fast that until his manager grabbed him, he did not notice he was getting a standing ovation. He told Wilkinson that he then heard disc jockeys making calls, saying, "Find this kid's CD. I threw it out this morning—it's in the trash. Find it and play it."

Later that same day, Anthony was booked on a Spanish-language television program called *Carnaval Internacional,* which is broadcast internationally. "That changed my life forever," he stated to Wilkinson, adding, "It seemed like years before I was ever in New York again." He began to tour constantly, playing Puerto Rico, Argentina, Colombia, Ecuador, even Tokyo. Some traditionalists disliked his romantic take on salsa and dismissed it an inauthentic, but many critics delivered accolades. He also won support from fellow musicians like Blades and Placido Domingo, who began to call and ask about doing projects together.

In 1995, Anthony followed up with *Todo a Su Tiempo* ("All in Due Time"). Touring to promote the work, he spent 50 weeks on the road. Though his energy level on stage is cranked up as he struts through his dance moves, unlike salsa stars of old, Anthony projects a more down-to-earth appearance, favoring simple apparel in lieu of the "hot Latin lover" image with sleek suits and slick hair. "It is an appeal that is real, accessible and trustworthy," observed Veran in *Newsday.* Anthony in 1996 was nominated for a Grammy Award in 1996 for *Todo a Su Tiempo,* sharing the category with three of his idols—Blades, Colon, and Celia Cruz.

As his music career was reaching new heights, Anthony was gearing up an acting career as well. He made his debut in 1995's *Hackers,* playing a Secret Service agent in a thriller about cybersleuths trying to foil an evil genius planning to unleash a crippling computer virus. The next year, he was cast as a waiter in *Big Night,* starring Minnie Driver, Isabella Rossellini, and Stanley Tucci, about a family trying to save their Italian restaurant. He also had a minor role as a high school gang member in *The Substitute* that same year.

Anthony's next album, *Contra la Corriente* ("Against the Current") came out in fall of 1997. But he did not have the opportunity to embark on a promotional tour, because he had been cast in Paul Simon's *Capeman,* which opened on Broadway in early 1998. This turned out to be a boon, though, when Anthony's new manager, Bigram Zayas—also his half-brother and best friend—suggested he play an "Off to Broadway" mega-concert at Madison Square Garden. Though no salsa solo act had ever headlined there, Anthony sold out two concerts at the venue. He then took the stage in *Capeman,* a musical about a murder case. In it, he played teenager Salvador Algron, a Puerto Rican who killed two other teens in a New York park in 1959 after a gang misunderstanding. Blades, incidentally, portrayed the killer as an older man. Although *Capeman* was praised for its song sequences and Anthony was applauded for his vocal talents, the play closed after two months.

By this time, Anthony was so famous that an architect refused payment for his work in building a home in Puerto Rico for the singer, claiming that working for him was payment enough, as Wilkinson reported in the *New Yorker.* In fact, he is something of a saint in Puerto Rico for committing to build 100 homes for families displaced by Hurricane Georges. In addition, he sold out a 60,000-seat stadium in Colombia, and is popular throughout Europe, Japan, and Central America as well. He became so well-known in Spanish-speaking areas that he needs escorts to accompany him, and he became the only salsa singer with a gold album in America.

However, Anthony did not get major crossover exposure until fellow Latin crooner Ricky Martin hit the scene and reached number one on the pop charts with his first all-English release. In addition, Jennifer Lopez—with whom he recorded the radio hit "No Me Ames"—was beginning to attract attention as well. Around that time, amid disputes with music mogul Ralph Mercado—with whom he had signed a contract in 1992—Anthony managed to cut his own English album as well, the first since his 1991 dance effort. He signed a deal with Columbia Records estimated to be worth more than $30 million, and in 1999 released *Marc Anthony.* Featuring Latin-tinged pop tunes, it spawned the top ten hit "I Need to Know." But he bristled at the term "crossover," explaining to Chris Willman in *Entertainment Weekly,* "I started out singing in English, so what am I crossing over to? That makes

it sound like I'm trying my hand at someone else's music. But I'm just as American as I am Puerto Rican. This is my music as much as anybody else's."

Also in 1999, Anthony was seen in his biggest film role to date, playing the erratic homeless man Noel in Martin Scorsese's *Bringing Out the Dead.* Though the film stars Nicolas Cage as a troubled New York City ambulance driver, Noel is the centerpiece of the tale. Disheveled and dreadlocked, the character of Noel provides "sort of the backbone of the morality of the story," according to Scorsese in a *People* article. "Ultimately the whole film comes together around him." Critics were receptive to his wild and violent performance, which countered his usual persona of the sensitive, sensual singer.

Though Anthony had been linked with various starlets—including Lopez and actress Mira Sorvino—he announced his engagement to Dayanara Torres, a former Miss Universe, in October of 1999. The couple married in Las Vegas, Nevada, on May 9, 2000. From a previous relationship with police officer Debbie Rosado, which ended in 1995, he has a daughter, Arianna. Anthony and Torres had a son, Cristian Anthony Muiz, on February 5, 2001. Anthony, who favors wearing Prada designs, is about five feet, eight inches tall, with a slender build, black hair, jutting cheekbones, and a strong jaw. He told Mim Udovitch in *Rolling Stone* that he is the tallest in his family, and revealed, "My father is five feet two and weighs, like, 100 pounds wet."

Although *People en Espanol* magazine once named Anthony one of the most beautiful people alive, he was not always such a looker. As he mentioned to Dennis Hensley in *Cosmopolitan,* "I was ugly and skinny growing up, and one time my dad said, 'You look like me, so you better work on your personality.'" His fame and accolades apparently have not affected his ego. As he told Udovitch, "I don't need other people to validate me. I'm pretty hard on myself, so if I feel good, then I know there's something to feel good about."

Selected discography

When the Night Is Over, Atlantic, 1991.
Otra Nota, Soho Latino/RMM, 1993.
Todo a Su Tiempo, Soho Latino/RMM, 1995.
(Contributor) *Carlito's Way* (soundtrack), EMI Latin, 1996.
Contra la Corriente, RMM, 1997.
(Contributor) *Mask of Zorro* (soundtrack), Sony, 1998.
Desde un Principio, Sony, 1999.
Marc Anthony, Columbia, 1999.
(Contributor) *Runaway Bride* (soundtrack), Sony, 1999.

Sources

Books

Contemporary Musicians, volume 19, Gale Research, 1997.

Periodicals

Cosmopolitan, February 2000, p. 204.
Daily Telegraph, January 6, 2000, p. 25.
Entertainment Weekly, October 8, 1999, p. 32.
Interview, February 1999, p. 84.
Latin Beat, December 1997, p. 40.
Newsday, July 20, 1995, p. B3; June 13, 1999, p. D10.
New Yorker, December 8, 1997, p. 96.
New York Times Magazine, August 29, 1999, p. 42.

People, October 4, 1999, p. 45; December 13, 1999, p. 185; May 29, 2000, p. 147.
Rolling Stone, April 27, 2000, p. 33.
Time, September 20, 1999, p. 80.
TV Guide, February 12, 2000, p. 46.
Variety, February 2, 1998, p. 39.

Online

Marc Anthony Official Website, http://www.marcanthonyonline.com (June 21, 2001).
"Marc Anthony," Internet Movie Database, http://us.imdb.com (June 21, 2001).
The Recording Academy, http://www.grammy.com (June 21, 2001).

—Geri Koeppel

Arab Strap

Post-rock group

Arab Strap—the Scottish post-rock duo of vocalist Aidan Moffat and multi-instrumentalist Malcolm Middleton—first came to the attention of British rock fans in the mid 1990s with a repertoire that largely featured observations about bad sexual encounters, bad jobs, dying relationships, and drunkenness. Despite such subjects, Arab Strap has repeatedly won critical praises. The duo's songs—at once irreverent, heart-breaking, inventive, and visceral—have made them a favorite across Great Britain. "We're more original and more honest than most other bands," Middleton proclaimed in an interview for Scotland's *Sunday Herald.* "There's nothing to compare us with." A hallmark of the duo's music, according to longtime observers, has remained the juxtaposition of Middleton's elegant instrumentation aside Moffat's oftentimes sordid observations and conclusions.

Originally, Arab Strap served as the one-man band of Moffat, who started out making up self-indulgent tunes and playing two drums and a kazoo in his bedroom in Falkirk, Scotland. Meanwhile, Middleton, living nearby, was similarly busy playing guitar under the name the Laughing Stock. The two young men, knowing of each other for about five years, during which time they exchanged cassette tapes of their respective "bands,"

Photograph by Martyn Goodacre. © S.I.N./Corbis. Reproduced by permission.

For the Record . . .

Members include **Malcolm Middleton**, guitar; **Aidan Moffat**, vocals.

Formed in Falkirk, Scotland, signed with the Chemikal Underground label, 1995; released debut single "The First Big Weekend," followed by debut album *The Week Never Starts Round Here,* 1996; released *Philophobia,* 1998; signed with Go! Beat Records, released *Elephant Shoe,* 1999; released *The Red Thread* in the U.S. on Matador Records, 2001.

Addresses: *Record company*—Matador Records, 625 Broadway, 12th Floor, New York City, NY 10012, phone: (212) 995-5882, fax: (212) 995-5883. *Website*—Arab Strap Official Website: http://www.arab strap.co.uk.

eventually joined forces in the summer of 1995. They decided to stick with Moffat's Arab Strap alias, a name he took from a sexual device he once saw in a catalog designed to enhance a man's masculinity.

Within a few months, Moffat and Middleton had secured a record deal with the hip Chemikal Underground label based in Glasgow, Scotland. Surprisingly, Arab Strap's sound bore little resemblance to the record company's roster of wall-of-sound guitar bands. Chemikal Underground, in the case of Moffat and Middleton, was relying more upon the fascination with Scottish urban culture as typified in the Irvine Welsh novel *Trainspotting.* Indeed, the pair's debut single, the stark, downcast "The First Big Weekend," about strawberry tonic wine and the Scottish football team losing the 1996 championship to England, featured simply a guitar and drum machine and made numerous references to Falkirk and Glasgow. It also became a huge British hit after airing on the British Broadcasting Corporation's (BBC) Radio One *Evening Session* program. Host Steve Lamacq declared "The First Big Weekend," later used as the soundtrack for a Guinness beer advertisement, the best record of the decade.

The 1996 single also served as a blueprint for the Arab Strap sound. While Middleton played intricate, yet minimal guitar lines and club-influenced beats, his bandmate muttered lyrics filled with invective and regret. His words were "simultaneously incoherent and articulate," according to the *Sunday Herald,* and spoken in an unashamed Scottish accent, providing an instant focus for the press and the public. In fact, the pair was soon dubbed the first post-*Trainspotting* band, a label they understandably loathed to accept because they were not trying to cash in on the book or the popular film adaptation.

In November of 1996 after selective live performances, Arab Strap issued their full-length debut, *The Week Never Starts Round Here,* featuring their prior single and their 1997 single "The Clearing." The album, too, received regular airplay and garnered favorable reviews in publications such as *Melody Maker, New Musical Express (NME),* and *Vox,* who declared: "These songs resonate like stuporous, intoxicated thoughts swimming around drunken heads. Strapping stuff." A few months later, in March of 1997, the duo returned with an EP entitled *The Girls of Summer,* which entered the British charts at number 74.

Later that year, they embarked on a busy three-week national tour, appearing with the likes of Gorky's Zygotic Mynci, labelmates Mogwai, Gene, and Belle and Sebastian. In 1998, following a performance at the *NME* Brat Awards and scoring hits with "Holiday Girl," a reworking of David Holmes' "Don't Die Just Yet," and "Here We Go"/"Trippy," Arab Strap played a headlining gig at the University of London Union, their biggest date up to that point. Around the same time, their "Here We Go"/"Trippy" single reached number 47 on the charts.

In April of 1998, Arab Strap arrived with their second album, *Philophobia,* which entered the British charts at number 37. Filled with melancholy and plaintive loner realism, the recording led to critical comparisons to the Tindersticks and Joy Division. Moffat agreed, commenting, as quoted by *Select* magazine, "I don't think anyone in Britain since Joy Division has known how to make seriously depressing music." The album also garnered attention in the United States, winning a rave review in *Rolling Stone.* "Songwriters Malcolm Middleton and Aidan Moffat obsess over the details of their romantic chaos and drunken stupors, setting their disillusionment to beautiful, uncluttered arrangements of guitar, organ and strings. Their spare, naked songs are majestic as a teary afternoon rainstorm, and invariably sad."

After completing a 20-show tour of Britain, Arab Strap decided to part ways with Chemikal Underground to sign a deal with London's Go! Beat Records. Their first album for the label, *Mad For Sadness,* recorded live at the Queen Elizabeth Hall, was released in January of 1999. Their next album, *Elephant Shoe,* arrived in September of 1999. Unlike their previous releases, the album displayed a newfound tenderness. "*Elephant Shoe* isn't happier, but it's maybe more optimistic," Moffat explained to the *Sunday Herald.* "It's certainly not as bitter. I just don't have the time to be bitter any more. There's a lot of stuff I never used that was just the usual … hate. Aye, there were a few songs of just abject hate, but they all got dumped. Although it's a lot harder to be nice to people than to slag them off, I'll tell you."

Signing with DNA and Matador Records for distribution in the United States, Arab Strap released their fifth album, *The Red Thread,* in February of 2001. The album, whose title refers to an Eastern concept that suggests an invisible red thread links soul mates through time, includes notable tracks such as "The Long Sea" and "Love Detective."

Selected discography

"The First Big Weekend," Chemikal Underground, 1996.
The Week Never Starts Round Here, Chemikal Underground, 1996.
"The Clearing," Chemikal Underground, 1997.
The Girls of Summer, EP, Chemikal Underground, 1997.
"Here We Go"/"Trippy," Chemikal Underground, 1998.
Philophobia, Chemikal Underground, 1998.
Mad For Sadness, Go! Beat, 1999.
Elephant Shoe, Go! Beat, 1999.
The Red Thread, DNA/Matador, 2001.

Sources

Books

Larkin, Colin, editor, *Virgin Encyclopedia of Indie & New Wave,* Virgin Books, 1998.

Periodicals

Melody Maker, October 11, 1997; November 15, 1997; December 13, 1997; February 7, 1998; March 28, 1998; April 4, 1998; April 11, 1998; April 25, 1998; September 26, 1998; October 17, 1998; August 28, 1999; May 8, 1999; September 11, 1999; September 25, 1999; October 2, 1999.
Mojo, May 1999.
New Musical Express (*NME*), September 4, 1999.
Rolling Stone, September 3, 1998.
Select, May 1998.
Sunday Herald (Scotland), September 5, 1999.
Village Voice, August 11, 1998.
Vox, May 1998.

Online

Arab Strap Official Website, http://www.arabstrap.co.uk (May 28, 2001).

—Laura Hightower

Badly Drawn Boy

Singer, songwriter, guitarist, keyboardist

Badly Drawn Boy, given name Damon Gough, never anticipated all of the excitement surrounding his debut album, let alone winning Great Britain's prestigious Mercury Music Prize. The award—set up in 1992 to be roughly analogous to the Booker Prize for fiction—annually honors a deserving album based on artistic qualities alone, regardless of popularity. Like many young artists, Gough, whose music is sparse, atmospheric, and melodic folk-rock with a lo-fi quality and a feeling of essential optimism, pondered over what to make of the critics' comments. Following the 2000 release of *The Hour of Bewilderbeast,* Gough earned rave reviews on both sides of the Atlantic, drawing comparisons to everyone from rock-funk star Beck and legendary folk singer Nick Drake to eighteenth-century poet William Blake.

At one of his shows in New York City during his first American tour, according to *New York Times* reviewer Jon Pareles, Gough admitted to feeling a little "embarrassed" about winning the Mercury Prize. As he told *Magnet* contributor A.D. Amorosi about all of the media attention: "It's difficult to see or feel all that's being said from this angle. My job is to play these gigs, write and meet the people I'm set to…. I don't think an artist—or a person at the middle of this type of storm—should take it at all seriously. All I have to do is my part of the equation. Besides, I've always been willing to challenge or ride whatever hype came my way."

Gough was born on October 2, 1970, in the small English town of Dunstable, but grew up in a close-knit family in nearby Bolton, a suburb located 20 miles north of Manchester. Gough first became interested in music at the age of ten when he discovered the Police, and in high school, he frequently listened to the Smiths. In the 1980s, Gough also became obsessed with Bruce Springsteen, collecting bootleg recordings and reading every article he could find about the American rock star. Springsteen, he says, was the person who inspired him to pursue a career in music, though Gough's own songs only faintly resemble those of his self-professed idol. What Gough—who would later amass a catalog of more than 1,000 compositions—seems to have borrowed from Springsteen is the musician's passion for his craft. Besides Springsteen, Gough lists Frank Zappa, Carole King, Simon and Garfunkel, Guided By Voices, and Sebadoh as his primary influences.

Still, Gough initiated his musical education relatively late in life. In Bolton, where his parents ran a printing factory, he never took private lessons or joined a teen garage band, though he did eventually teach himself how to play guitar and keyboards and joined several local groups after high school. He also attended Leeds College of Music for a brief period. According to Gough, he only learned a few chords and failed miserably as a music student. Returning home, Gough took a job in his parents' factory and started writing songs. "It was a decent job because I was working with my parents," Gough said to *Boston Globe* writer Joan Anderman. "But for years I woke up every day wanting to do music and wondering why I didn't know how to do it. You know, if you're a carpenter you can buy wood. But this was some out-of-the-stratosphere job that seemed unattainable." Even today, despite his accomplishments, Gough remains uncertain about his songwriting abilities.

Hoping to move closer to the music world, Gough—who at the time did not believe performing was in his future—moved on to a job at a recording studio to learn to become an engineer. At the studio, where he worked for about a year, Gough failed to move up in rank, and his progressions were minimal. Nevertheless, he valued the job because it enabled him to experiment with his own recording techniques during off hours. Subsequently, in 1990, Gough decided to pursue his songwriting in earnest, holding out for several years before a significant opportunity came along. Contrary to the popular perception, Gough was not exactly an overnight sensation. "One thing about growing up in a stable home is that it may leave you a little naïve," he said to Robert Hilburn of the *Los Angeles Times*. "You just kinda think things will work out in time. You're in no rush. If your parents break up at an early age, you might have more drive to get out into the world a bit more. In my case, I took my time. I just kind of felt things would turn out well for me … someday."

In 1996, after moving to Manchester from Bolton, Gough met Andy Votel, a designer and deejay. To-

For the Record . . .

Born Damon Gough on October 2, 1970, in Dunstable, England; children: a daughter, born 2001. *Education:* Attended Leeds College of Music.

Moved to Manchester, England, and met Andy Votel, with whom he founded the Twisted Nerve label, 1996; signed with XL Records, 1998; released *The Hour of Bewilderbeast,* 2000.

Awards: Technics Mercury Music Prize, 2000.

Addresses: *Record company*—Beggars Banquet, 580 Broadway, New York City, NY 10012, phone: (212) 343-7010, fax: (212) 343-7030, e-mail: beggars @beggars.com, website: http://www.beggars.com. *Website*—Badly Drawn Boy Official Website: http://www.badlydrawnboy.co.uk.

gether, the pair founded their own label called Twisted Nerve, and Gough recorded a couple of EPs. These early efforts, simply titled *EP1* and *EP2,* followed later by *EP3,* gained the songwriter a cult following and also provoked somewhat of an A&R bidding war among record labels. "I was shocked by the amount of attention that EP [*EP 1*] and subsequent ones gathered," Gough recalled, who took his stage name from a cartoon-strip character he remembered from his childhood, to Amorosi. "All I wanted was a document, something I could keep." Then, in December of 1997, Gough had the good fortune of having his car mistaken for a cab by the Fall's Mark E. Smith. Smith, apparently not realizing Gough was not a taxi driver, jumped into the car, demanding a ride to his home. The chance meeting led to the Fall recording one of Gough's songs, "Tumbleweed." Next, Gough contributed another of his songs, "Nursery Rhyme," to U.N.K.L.E.'s 1998 album *Psyence Fiction* on James Lavelle's Mo' Wax label.

Prior to that record's release, Gough had signed to Prodigy's XL label for a reported six-figure sum. In April of 1999, Gough released a fourth EP, *It Came from the Ground,* followed by another, *Once Around the Block,* in August of that year. These releases were accompanied by live performances in Liverpool and London. His sets, known for their amateurish nature, saw Gough sometimes forgetting songs or playing pieces he had not yet completed. Nonetheless, fans saw his shows as brilliantly original and anxiously awaited the arrival of his full-length debut, which was preceded by two more EPs. "My whole idea has been to build up a solid base of support so that there would be a group of people who really knew what my music was all about before the album was ever released," Gough explained to Hilburn about deciding to hold out a while for his first album.

The Hour of Bewilderbeast, opening with the strings and horns of "The Shining," finally hit store shelves in Britain in July of 2000, and won the support of both fans and the music press. That month, *Pulse!* magazine and the *London Times* both hailed it as the United Kingdom's debut album of the year, while Britain's influential *Q* magazine described it as the "indie rock *Pet Sounds.*" In September of that year, Gough earned validation for the album when he took home the Mercury Music Prize. "The Mercury is the only one people take seriously, because it reflects the art of the album, not how much a thing sold or how much you spent on the pyrotechnics of a video," he said proudly to Amorosi. "And, fortunately, I won it. It's not my fault, really." During the latter months of 2000, Gough brought his live act to the United States for the first time, where he earned the praises of American critics and music fans as well.

Gough, who does not take drugs, says he has learned to follow his thoughts for pleasure and to get through life's up and downs, and he hopes to express this state of mind with his music. As he told *Rolling Stone* writer Gavin Edwards when asked what he wants his listeners to do while listening to his music: "Solve a thousand-piece jigsaw puzzle." Gough and girlfriend Claire had a daughter in 2001.

Selected discography

EPs

EP 1, Twisted Nerve, 1997.
EP 2, Twisted Nerve, 1998.
EP 3, Twisted Nerve, 1998.
It Came from the Ground, Twisted Nerve, 1999.
(With Andy Votel) *Whirlpool,* Twisted Nerve, 1999.
Once Around the Block, Twisted Nerve, 1999.
Another Pearl, Twisted Nerve, 2000.
Pissing In the Wind, Twisted Nerve, 2001.

Albums

The Hour of Bewilderbeast, XL/Beggars Banquet, 2000.

Sources

Periodicals

Billboard, July 29, 2000; August 5, 2000; September 23, 2000; October 21, 2000; November 25, 2000; December 20, 2000/January 6, 2001.

Boston Globe, November 3, 2000; November 4, 2000.
Los Angeles Times, September 29, 2000; November 5, 2000.
Magnet, January/February 2001.
Melody Maker, December 20-27, 1997; January 24, 1998; January 31, 1998; October 24, 1998; November 28, 1998; January 9, 1999.
New York Times, November 11, 2000.
Rolling Stone, October 12, 2000; November 9, 2000; February 1, 2001.
Village Voice, November 14, 2000; February 13, 2001.
Washington Post, November 3, 2000; November 29, 2000; December 31, 2000.

Online

BBC Online, http://www.bbc.co.uk (May 27, 2001).
Sonicnet, http://www.sonicnet.com (May 27, 2001).
Twisted Nerve Records, http://www.twistednerve.co.uk (June 25, 2001).

—Laura Hightower

Beenie Man

Reggae deejay

A child prodigy in Jamaica's ragga scene during the mid 1980s, Beenie Man became the most popular deejay in the country by the mid 1990s. With international tours and distribution agreements for his work, Beenie Man's international reputation and record sales also expanded, culminating in a record-setting seven 1999 International Reggae and World Music Awards and a 2000 Grammy Award for Best Reggae Album for *Art & Life*. Incorporating various styles such as techno, R&B, hip-hop, and Latin rhythms into his work, the artist pushed the boundaries of reggae. As Beenie Man acknowledged in a 1998 *Billboard* interview, "When you have an album now, you have to do a lot of different types of music, 'cause it's not one type of people who listen to music…. But regardless of which place or how far you take reggae, the music all comes back to one thing: the one-drop beat."

Born Anthony Moses Davis in the Waterhouse section of Jamaica's capital, Kingston, the future deejay grew up in an environment that was rich in music. Much of Jamaica's social life revolved around dancehalls, where people would gather throughout the week—and especially on the weekends—to dance, socialize, and listen to the latest records, often with added vocals contributed by the deejay, a practice known as "toasting." From the 1950s onward, as Jamaican deejays bought their own portable sound systems and played records at dancehalls around the country, competition for the sharpest patter over backing tracks helped the dancehall style evolve into a distinct category of Jamaican music. Taking the popularity of dancehall deejays a step further, recording and distributing the best dancehall tunes on single releases was a relatively inexpensive process. Dancehall music could now be enjoyed by expatriate Jamaicans in Britain and the United States.

While dancehall music remained largely oriented to its home in Jamaica, the development of reggae music in the 1970s brought Jamaican music to an international audience. More political in its message than dancehall music, reggae was also more sophisticated in its blend of traditional African and American R&B rhythms with Jamaican popular music. In contrast to dancehall music, which put the deejay at center stage, reggae was usually performed by one or more vocalists with a backing band. Young Davis' uncle, Sydney Wolf, played in one such lineup as a percussionist for reggae artist Jimmy Cliff, best known for his soundtrack for the 1972 film *The Harder They Come*, in which he also starred. With his uncle's encouragement, Davis began toasting as a deejay from an early age. By the time he was eight years old, Davis had won a local talent show, along with the notice and support of older, more established deejays like Barry G. Rechristened as Beenie Man—"beenie" serving as a slang term for "little"—the young deejay completed an album that was released around his tenth birthday, fittingly titled *The Invincible Beenie Man, 10-Year-Old Boy Wonder*. With

Photograph by Mark J. Terrill. AP/Wide World Photos. Reproduced by permission.

clear that Beenie Man had superseded Bounty Killer as Jamaica's top-rated deejay. As the *Village Voice* noted in a review of *Many Moods of Moses*, "The badman ethic that Bounty espoused proved difficult to sustain, while Beenie peppered the dance with tales of the sexually self-assured.... Beenie's microphone charisma comes from his understanding that rhythmic prowess is sexual prowess." Indeed, many of Beenie Man's lyrics emphasized his reputation as a lady-killer, showing the artist as a trickster, not a rebel.

Having released regionally successful albums with 1994's *Defend It* and the following year's *Beenie Man Meets Mad Cobra*, Beenie Man secured wider international distribution with the 1995 compilation *Blessed*, released on Island Records. His next original releases, *Maestro* in 1996 and *Many Moods of Moses* in 1997, continued to build the artist's international reputation, especially in areas with significant Jamaican immigrant populations such as London, New York, and Miami. Mainstream success in terms of the pop charts, however, remained limited, with one reviewer assessing *Many Moods of Moses* more for its potential at crossover success than actual results. Refusing to be caught between reggae purists and the demand for hit records, however, Beenie Man insisted on choosing his own course and experimenting with different musical forms within his ragga style. The success of the track "Who Am I?" from *Many Moods of Moses*, which reached number one on *Billboard*'s reggae singles chart, also went top ten on its rap singles chart and was a pop hit in Britain. The success demonstrated that Beenie Man's appeal was the greatest of any contemporary Jamaican musician. The album had similar success, becoming the top-selling reggae album in the United States for 1998, although it barely cracked the R&B top 40 during its chart run that year. *Doctor*, released the following year, repeated the pattern. A top-selling reggae album worldwide, it made little inroad in the pop market.

Looking to broaden his international profile while retaining his integrity on the reggae scene, Beenie Man signed an innovative deal with Virgin Records in 1999 that allowed the major label to distribute his albums globally save for the Caribbean region, which would be serviced by Kingston-based independent label Shocking Vibes. In contrast to emphasizing the sale of Beenie Man albums in international markets, Shocking Vibes would also continue to release Beenie Man singles in Jamaica in order to maintain his credibility with the singles-driven ragga scene. Beenie Man also signed a publishing deal with EMI Music, which was estimated to be in the six-figure range. With a powerhouse of sophisticated marketing and distribution talent behind him, expectations were high for Beenie Man's first Virgin/Shocking Vibes release, while many waited to see how far he would go in a bid for mainstream success. In the meantime, Beenie Man continued to tour extensively. His concert series in the

it, Beenie Man gained a high profile in the developing world of "ragga" music, named after its "ragamuffin" incorporation of reggae, rap, and just about any other musical form into dancehall music.

The economics of the Jamaican recording industry made it relatively inexpensive to record and release singles instead of albums, and Beenie Man accordingly released a series of singles during his teens, including the local hits "Too Fancy/Over the Sea," "We Run Things," and "Wicked Man." Beenie Man also engaged in one of the traditional rivalries that marked dancehall music, pitting his reputation against that of rival deejay Bounty Killer. Although Beenie Man was subsequently attacked by some rivals at the Kingston airport after returning from an international tour, the two top deejays eventually reached a truce. By 1994, however, it was

United States in 1999 was another success, although the artist encountered trouble when he and his band members were charged with misdemeanor marijuana possession in Virginia after the police found the drug in their hotel rooms. Unable to prove that any of the individuals had actually possessed the contraband substance, the charges were eventually dropped.

Released in July of 2000, *Art & Life* fulfilled its promise by becoming Beenie Man's biggest selling album with about 350,000 copies sold by the end of the year. The artist frankly acknowledged in a June of 2000 profile in *Billboard* that the album's appeal was designed to broaden his audience: "I'm trying to take up the pigskin ball and score a touchdown with the world, not just the American or Jamaican audience." Reviewers such as an *Orange Country Register* critic agreed that the new album was "more accessible than ever," with Beenie Man determined "to contend that the greatest advancement the reggae subgenre can make is to take America by storm." The album also featured contributions by Mya, Wyclef Jean, and Kelis. Although Beenie Man had not achieved the multi-million-selling breakthrough success of fellow reggae artist Shaggy, his popularity as the world's leading ragga deejay remained unchallenged.

Selected discography

The Invincible Beenie Man, 10-Year-Old Boy Wonder, 1986.
Defend It, VP, 1994.
Dis Unu Fi Hear, Hightone, 1994.
Beenie Man Meets Mad Cobra, VP, 1995.
Blessed, Island Jamaica, 1995.
Maestro, VP, 1996.
Many Moods of Moses, VP, 1997.
Doctor, VP, 1999.
Art & Life, Virgin Records, 2000.

Sources

Books

Broughton, Simon, et al., editors, *World Music: The Rough Guide Volume 2,* The Rough Guides Ltd., 1999.

Periodicals

Associated Press Worldstream, March 29, 2000.
Billboard, July 15, 1995; August 1, 1998; December 26, 1998; February 6, 1999; October 14, 2000; June 24, 2000; December 30, 2000.
Music Business International, December 1999.
New York Amsterdam News, May 21, 1998; June 10, 1999; June 29, 2000.
Newsweek, June 22, 1998.
Orange County Register (California), July 25, 2000.
Q, February 1997; March 1998.
Village Voice, March 17, 1998.

Online

All Music Guide, http://www.allmusic.com/cg/amg.dll (April 19, 2001).
Beenie Man Official Website, http://www.beenie-man.com (April 23, 2001).
Info Please, http://www.infoplease.lycos.com/ipa?A0878118.html (April 19, 2001).
Reggae Source, http://www.reggaesource.com/artists/beenie_man/interview2000-3.html (April 23, 2001).

—Timothy Borden

Chuck Berry

Guitarist

The invention of rock 'n' roll was a collaborative effort, yet many music buffs trace its beginnings back to a singer, songwriter, and guitarist named Chuck Berry. Taking what he knew from the blues, big band, swing, country, and pop, Berry developed a style and sound that uniquely spoke to the experience of the American teenager, and that appealed to white as well as black audiences. And he remains, arguably, rock 'n' roll's most influential figure. Among those who admit to having emulated his complex guitar riffs and quick, witty lyrics in their early days are some of the most prominent bands and artists of the past 50 years—including the Beatles, the Rolling Stones, Bob Dylan, and Bruce Springsteen.

Berry has spent a lifetime in the spotlight, but the spotlight has not always been kind to him. Various lawsuits have been filed against the mischievous rock star, and he has served three prison terms. Despite these setbacks, he has held on to his image as one of rock's esteemed founding fathers. Berry was still rocking and still making the news in 2000, at age 74, when he received a Kennedy Center Honor at the White House for his lifelong achievement as a performing artist.

For the Record . . .

Born Charles Edward Anderson Berry on October 18, 1926, in St. Louis, MO; son of Henry (a carpenter and church deacon) and Martha (a schoolteacher); married Themetta ("Toddy") Suggs, 1948; four children.

Led a blues trio in St. Louis in early 1950s; signed by Chess Records, 1955; hit *Billboard*'s top ten and topped R&B chart with "Maybellene," 1955; released first LP, *After School Session,* 1957; topped R&B chart and reached number two in *Billboard*'s pop chart with "Sweet Little Sixteen," 1958; hit top of the charts with "My Ding-a-Ling," 1972.

Awards: Lifetime Achievement Award at 27th Annual Grammy Awards, 1985; Blues Hall of Fame, 1985; Rock and Roll Hall of Fame, 1986; Kennedy Center Honors, 2000.

Addresses: *Agent*—Richard De La Font Agency, 4845 South Sheridan Road, Suite 505, Tulsa, OK.

Charles Edward Anderson Berry was born on October 18, 1926, in St. Louis, Missouri (some sources—Berry himself is not among them—claim that he was born on January 15, 1926, in San Jose, California, where his parents lived before relocating to Missouri). It was in the Ville, one of the few neighborhoods in St. Louis where African Americans could own property, that Berry spent his formative years, honing his musical skills as a choir boy in his Baptist church, and as a bass singer in his high school glee club. At the urging of a music teacher, he bought a four-string tenor guitar (graduating later to a six-string guitar) and taught himself how to play. His introduction to music was an early one, as was his introduction to trouble and running with the law. At age 17, he and two friends were arrested for attempted robbery; Berry was sentenced to ten years in the Intermediate Reformatory for Young Men in Algoa, Missouri. In the reformatory Berry sang with a gospel group; he was released in 1947, on his twenty-first birthday.

Marriage and an upright life immediately followed his reformatory stint: Berry married Themetta "Toddy" Suggs in 1948 and took a job in an auto assembly plant. After completing night courses in cosmetology, he worked as a hairdresser, moonlighting as a guitarist for various bands to bring in extra money.

Berry soon gained a reputation in the St. Louis music scene, and in 1952 he formed the Sir John Trio with pianist and band leader Johnnie Johnson and drummer Eddie Hardy. The connection with Johnson would be a lasting one, and the influence of the pianist's boogie style would become evident in Berry's guitar playing. Berry had a knack for pleasing the crowd, and the band eventually changed its name to The Chuck Berry Trio. The band's repertoire included the blues, ballads, and a number of "black hillbilly" songs that jokingly parodied the country music popular to the city's white audiences. While the trio's hillbilly songs initially provoked laughter, they became popular dance tunes among the predominantly black club-goers.

"Maybellene" Had Broad Appeal

During a visit to Chicago in 1955 Berry befriended his idol, the blues singer Muddy Waters. Taken with Berry's talent, Waters introduced him to Leonard Chess, then the president of Chess Records, an established rhythm & blues label that was looking to expand into other music genres. In his audition, Berry managed to impress Chess not as much with his blues songs as with a black hillbilly tune called "Ida Red." After reworking the song and giving it a new name, Berry recorded "Maybellene" in Chess's studios on May 21, 1955, with Johnson on piano, Jerome Green on maracas, Jasper Thomas on drums, and Willie Dixon on bass. Following its release on August 20, "Maybellene" hit Number 1 on *Billboard*'s R&B chart and Number 5 on *Billboard*'s pop chart, becoming one of the rare singles to reach hit status among both black and white audiences.

Key to the success of "Maybellene" was a promotional effort from Alan Freed, the disc jockey of WINS radio station in New York, then the most important station for rock 'n' roll in the country. Chess had given Freed the single, and in exchange for airplay, the record executive granted the deejay 25 percent of the writing credit for the song. Berry wasn't aware of the bargain until the song was released and published, and he was unable to resolve the issue until 1986. Meanwhile, "Maybellene" sold more than a million copies.

From 1955 through 1960 Berry turned out a string of hit singles, all on the Chess label. In 1956 he climbed the charts with "Too Much Monkey Business," "Brown-Eyed Handsome Man," and especially "Roll Over Beethoven," a youthful anthem celebrating the triumph of low culture over high culture. Another trio of hits came in the following year, with "School Days," "Oh Baby Doll," and "Rock 'n' Roll Music," which the Beatles later covered. "Johnny B. Goode," "Reelin' and Rockin'," and "Sweet Little Sixteen" were among Berry's successes of 1958, and five years later the Beach Boys came out with a thinly veiled replica of "Sweet Little Sixteen" called "Surfin' U.S.A." Recognizing that the Beach Boys had lifted his melody, Berry sued the band and won a songwriting credit.

As a performer, Berry enraptured audiences with his trademark guitar licks and his bent-kneed, rhythmic "duck walk," which he is said to have created during a performance one night to hide the wrinkles in his pants. He toured often, and like many other rock stars of his day he appeared in several motion pictures, including *Rock, Rock, Rock* in 1956, *Mr. Rock 'n' Roll* in 1957, and *Go Johnny Go* in 1959.

After a few years of newfound, whirlwind success, Berry began enjoying the wealth that had come to him. He bought land—upon which he would later build—in Wentzville, Missouri, purchased a mansion for his family in St. Louis, and opened his own St. Louis nightclub, Berry's Club Bandstand.

Embroiled in Scandal

The nightclub was to become the scene of a scandal for Berry that nearly ruined his career. After he fired a hat-check girl, Janice Escalanti, in 1959, Escalanti went to the police claiming that Berry had taken her across state lines for immoral purposes. Berry had met Escalanti, a 14-year-old from Arizona, during a visit to Juarez, Mexico, and had invited her to work for him at Club Bandstand. In a trial against Berry, testimony revealed that Escalanti was a prostitute when Berry had met her, and the star was found guilty of violating the Mann Act, a federal statute that forbade transporting minors across state lines for the purposes of prostitution. In October of 1961, after appealing his original sentence of ten years, Berry was sentenced to three years in prison and fined $10,000. After serving 20 months, he was released on his birthday in 1963.

The ordeal devastated Berry. He had fallen out with his family, and was left with a strong distrust for the legal system as well as for the media that had hounded him. Once jovial and relaxed, he was now bitter and mistrustful. Yet in the end the scandal ruined neither his family life nor his career. Soon after his release from the Federal Medical Center in Springfield, Missouri, he began touring and recording again. While in prison, he had written a spate of new songs, some of which became hits in 1964 and 1965. Among these were "Nadine," "No Particular Place to Go," and "You Never Can Tell."

Berry toured Great Britain—where he had influenced so-called British Invasion bands like the Rolling Stones and the Beatles—for the first time in 1964. Also in that year, he opened Berry Park, an amusement park near Wentzville, and with guitar legend Bo Diddley he recorded the album *Two Great Guitars.*

In 1966 Berry signed with Mercury Records, but his stay with this company was to be brief. After making a few mistakes with Mercury—releasing a greatest-hits album consisting merely of re-recordings of old songs, and attempting to reinvent himself as a more contem-porary performer with the albums *Live at the Fillmore Auditorium,* released in 1967, and *Concerto in B. Goode,* released in 1969—Berry returned to Chess Records in 1969.

Back at Chess, Berry released the appropriately titled *Back Home Again* as well as *San Francisco Dues* in 1970, which both made the national charts. The biggest hit of his career would come in 1972, with the risqué single "My Ding-A-Ling." Originally recorded by Mercury in 1968 as "My Tambourine," "My Ding-A-Ling" was a song that Berry had long been playing in adult nightclubs and that had thrilled his audiences in Great Britain. The single sold more than a million copies and reached the top of the U.S. pop charts on October 21, 1972.

Although Berry continued to record new albums throughout the '70s, including the popular *Rock It,* the musician found himself becoming increasingly contained to the rock 'n' roll revival circuit. Capitalizing on this, he toured with Chubby Checker, Bill Haley and the Comets, and Bo Diddley as part of Richard Nader's 1973 Rock and Roll Festival. Footage from the festival, as well as from 1950s television, comprised *Let the Good Times Roll,* a well-received 1973 motion picture. Another film appearance came in 1978 with the fictional *American Hot Wax,* in which Berry and legendary deejay Alan Freed played themselves.

Legal troubles were once again in store for Berry in 1979, when he served four months in prison for income tax evasion. Ironically, just before going to prison, Berry performed at the White House at the request of President Jimmy Carter.

Career Celebrated with Awards

In the 1980s Berry's career was slowing down, and the music industry bestowed its honors upon the living legend. On February 26, 1985, he received a Lifetime Achievement Award at the 27th Annual Grammy Awards, and the following year he was inducted into the Rock and Roll Hall of Fame at its first ceremonial dinner. In 1987 he published *Chuck Berry: The Autobiography,* a mixture of life stories and personal philosophies. The documentary film *Hail! Hail! Rock 'n' Roll,* released in 1987, celebrated Berry's life and music, but its candid approach revealed a performer who was often controlling and volatile behind the scenes.

Publicity of a more blatantly negative kind came for Berry in 1990, when some 60 women sued him for allegedly videotaping them in the bathroom of his Berry Park restaurant, The Southern Air. Berry denied the antics, but paid a settlement of more than $1 million. That same year, police raided Berry's Missouri home, nabbing marijuana and homemade pornographic videos.

Berry's bad-boy reputation might have harmed him gravely had he pursued another kind of celebrity, but as a rock 'n' roll star, he's generally pardoned for his mischief. Just over two years after the Southern Air incident, he performed at President Bill Clinton's inaugural celebration, and in 2000 he returned to the White House to receive a Kennedy Center Honor. In perhaps his most extravagant tribute, Berry's "Johnny B. Goode" was the only rock song included in the *Sounds of Earth* gold record—an auditory time capsule telling the story of Earth—stowed aboard the spacecraft Voyagers I and II in their journey beyond the solar system. If other intelligent beings exist in the universe, their introduction to rock 'n' roll might come, appropriately, from the father of rock himself.

Selected discography

After School Session, Chess, 1957.
One Dozen Berrys, Chess, 1958.
Chuck Berry Is On Top, Chess, 1959; remastered and reissued, 1987.
Chuck Berry's Greatest Hits, Chess, 1964.
The London Chuck Berry Sessions, Chess, 1972.
Bio, Chess, 1973.
Rock It, Atco, 1979.
(Contributor) *Hail! Hail! Rock 'n' Roll* (soundtrack), 1987.

The Chess Box, Chess, 1989.
Missing Berries: Rarities, Volume 3, Chess, 1990.

Sources

Periodicals

New York Times, August 23, 2000, p. E3.
Rolling Stone, December 3, 1987, p. 71.
St. Louis Post Dispatch, November 15, 1998, p. D1; January 4, 1996, p.7.
Time, October 19, 1987, p. 84.

Online

"Chuck Berry," The History of Rock 'n' Roll, http://www.history-of-rock.com/berry.htm (January 16, 2001).
"Chuck Berry Biography," Sonicnet, http://sonicnet.com/artists/ai_bio.jhtml?ai_id=2757 (January 16, 2001).
"The Kennedy Center Honors: Chuck Berry," Kennedy Center Honors, http://kennedy-center.org/honors/history/honoree/berry.htm (January 16, 2001).
"Rock and Roll Hall of Fame Inductees: Chuck Berry," Rock and Roll Hall of Fame, http://www.rockhall.com/hof/inductee.asp?id=67 (January 16, 2001).

—*Michael P. Belfiore*

Ray Boltz

Singer

Contemporary Christian music singer Ray Boltz has sold more than one million albums, the result of songs and albums which charted repeatedly throughout the 1980s and 1990s. His inspirational songs have been sung by a number of his colleagues, and Boltz in turn has contributed to popular compilations by multiple artists. In the late 1990s, he assembled a rock-flavored band, thus expanding his inspirational repertoire. Boltz has successfully distinguished himself for his sincerity and integrity in the commercially hyped music culture. In his religious zeal, he undertook a regular battery of public concert tours even as he embraced traditional missionary travels beyond the realm of his musical ministry. In his devotion to the Christian ideal, he embarked on a series of expeditions that sent him to Africa and Asia. While on tour, he collected hundreds of thousands of dollars for food to feed starving people in Calcutta, India.

Boltz, a native of Muncie, Indiana, was born in the mid 1950s. He attended Indiana's Ball State University where he studied a business curriculum and graduated with a degree in business and marketing. Even as a teenager in the early 1970s, Boltz embraced a commitment to Christian ministry. He employed his musical talents to bring a Christian message to shut-ins including prisoners, hospital patients, and convalescent home residents. Likewise, he performed concerts for Christian youth groups. A dozen years passed, and by the mid 1980s Boltz's commitment to a musical gospel ministry was firmly entrenched as the basis of his career. When he released his first album, *Watch the Lamb* in 1986, the message of Christian commitment was clearly evident. *Thank You* and *The Altar* followed by the end of the decade, in 1988 and 1989 respectively. He released *Another Child to Hold* in 1991.

Boltz released *Seasons Change* on Word Records in 1992. Also that year, Boltz emerged as a presence on Christian radio. Among his popular recordings that gained distinction were a series of number one airplay hits including "Seasons Change," "The Altar," and "Thank You." He amassed a following of loyal fans through personal radio appearances throughout the early to mid 1990s. He issued a follow-up album, *Allegiance,* accompanied by a re-release of *Thank You* in 1994.

Parallel with the advancement of his musical career, Boltz nurtured his missionary work and eventually combined the two pursuits. When his teen-aged daughter made a six-week missionary visit to Africa in the mid 1990s, Boltz and his wife were inspired to contribute their own talents to the youth organization that sponsored the trip. Ultimately, Boltz penned a spiritual, "I Will Tell the World," which sparked the administrators of the youth group to authorize a video performance of the song to be filmed on location in Africa. The experience of the African shoot left indelible images in Boltz's memory, and he subsequently sought further opportunities to contribute to missionary programs worldwide, both in person and financially. His enthusiasm drove him to step up the glitzy media effects on his live stage shows in order to attract larger audiences. His fund-raising efforts, which occur largely at his concerts, were augmented in the process. Boltz, a natural baritone, transformed his musical bent into a profitable career as well as a full-blown missionary machine. As Boltz incorporated this Christian ministry into his itinerary, his missionary travels landed him beyond Africa and into India.

By 1995, Boltz was an established talent in the Christian recording industry. Indeed, his first five records alone sold more than one million units by 2001. In September of 1995, his *Concert of a Lifetime* album premiered on the *Billboard* Christian music chart shortly after he embarked on a North American tour by the same name. The promotion culminated nearly one year later, on June 22, 1996, with a concert at the Joe Byrne Memorial Stadium in Grand Falls-Windsor, Newfoundland. A video was released soon afterward, and in May of 2001, the video (by that time certified as gold) was released on DVD. The live concert album reigned at the top of the charts for many weeks as well.

Beyond the success of his Concert of a Lifetime tour, 1995 brought Boltz to a sense of new awakening in his non-musical ministry. In the fervor of this epiphany he initiated an affiliation with a worldwide relief agency called Mission of Mercy and successfully raised nearly

For the Record . . .

Born in the mid 1950s in Muncie, IN; married; children: Karen, Philip, Elizabeth, Sara. *Education:* Business and marketing degree, Ball State University, IN.

Singing career began as a ministry to hospitals and convalescent homes; released *Seasons Change,* 1992; released *Allegiance,* 1994; international tour, 1995-96; No Greater Sacrifice Tour (United States and Asia), 1996-97; released *Honor and Glory,* 1998; toured eastern U.S., 1999; released *Moments for the Heart, Vol. 1 & 2,* 2001.

Awards: Dove Awards, Song of the Year for "Thank You," 1990, and Inspirational Recorded Song for "I Pledge Allegiance To The Lamb," 1995.

Addresses: *Website*—Ray Boltz Official Website: http://www.rayboltz.com.

$500,000 for the Colorado Springs-based organization. With the money raised by Boltz, largely through donations solicited at his concerts, Mission of Mercy purchased food in a quantity estimated at between four and five million meals, which were earmarked for the starving population of Calcutta, India. Much of the fund-raising occurred when Reverend Wayne Francis joined Boltz's tour. Francis later assisted Boltz in arranging a trip to Calcutta to witness the charity drive in action.

In 1997, Boltz embarked on No Greater Sacrifice, a tour of the United States and Asia. Venues for No Greater Sacrifice extended from Dallas, Texas, to Hong Kong and Bangladesh. In Asia, where Boltz performed for free, he transported modified high-tech staging paraphernalia complete with video displays and Asian translations of the song lyrics in an effort to simulate the elaborate concert productions that he performs regularly in the United States. At every American venue, in contrast, Boltz arranged for a collection to be taken. He then designated the proceeds from the collections to be donated to Mission of Mercy.

In 2001, Boltz marked his fifteenth year of musical ministry with the re-release of *Moments for the Heart* in a special two-volume compilation of his most popular hit songs. A video and a DVD by the same name accompanied the anthology entitled *Moments for the Heart, Vol. 1 & 2.* The album featured such popular tracks as "The Altar," "Thank You," and "Shepherd Boy," along with Boltz's chart-topping hit, "I Pledge Allegiance to the Lamb." Other popular singles included "What If I Give All" and "The Anchor Holds." An assortment of eleven key selections featured on the associated DVD included "I Pledge Allegiance to the Lamb," "Thank You," and "What If I Give All." Likewise, a series of *Concert of a Lifetime* items for children were released at that time, including a CD, cassette recording, and video under the title *Jesus Real Loud ...The Concert of a Lifetime for Kids.*

Selected discography

Seasons Change, Word, 1992.
Thank You, Word, 1994.
Allegiance, Word, 1994.
The Concert of a Lifetime (live), Word, 1995.
No Greater Sacrifice, Word/Epic, 1996.
A Christmas Album: Bethlehem Star, Sony, 1997.
Honor and Glory, Sony, 1998.
Moments for the Heart, Vol. 1 & 2, Sony, 2001.

Sources

Periodicals

Billboard, November 14, 1998, p. 20.
Dallas Morning News, October 5, 1996, p. 6G; November 30, 1996, p. 6G; April 26, 1997, p. 6G.

Online

"Ray Boltz," Jamsline Archives, http://www.jamsline.com/b_boltz.htm (April 19, 2001).
"Ray Boltz Biography," TodaysChristianMusic.com, http://todayschristianmusic.com/Profile-RayBoltz.htm (April 19, 2001).

—Gloria Cooksey

Barbara Bonney

Opera singer

Photograph by Robbie Jack. Corbis. Reproduced by permission.

"I never wanted to be an opera singer," soprano Barbara Bonney said in an interview with *Opera News*. "It just kind of happened." And happen it did. Called "one of the great sopranos of her generation," Bonney possesses "rare intelligence and powerful expressiveness," according to the *Guardian*. She got her start singing German Lieder, but the power of Bonney's soprano voice helped the singer rise quickly in the world of opera. After years of playing demanding operatic ingenue roles, Bonney has begun to gradually phase herself out of opera, opting instead to sing in concert. With performances in more than 45 operas and 200 songs in her repertoire, Bonney looked forward to retiring as a singer and focusing on her true love—teaching.

Born on April 14, 1956, in Montclair, New Jersey, Bonney inherited her grandmother's love for music. She began piano lessons at age five, but dropped piano for cello at age eight. Her first vocal solo was "The Battle Hymn of the Republic" in her grade school's Christmas concert, but she did not pursue vocal studies until much later. At age 13, she joined the Portland Symphony Youth Orchestra after moving to Maine with her family. She graduated from high school in 1974 and went on to study music and German at the University of New Hampshire. She was there two years before deciding to refine her German language skills by spending her junior year abroad at the University of Salzburg.

It was in Salzburg that Bonney's vocal education blossomed. There, she was accepted in the vocal program at the Mozarteum and became a soloist with several Salzburg choral groups. Previously a dedicated cellist, Bonney had never planned to pursue voice. Regardless, she excelled and became a member of the repertory with the State Theatre in Darmstadt and sang 40 roles with that company during the next four years; her first role was Anna in Otto Nicolai's *Merry Wives of Windsor*. In 1983, she became a member of the Frankfurt Opera. Her days in Germany were not completely glamorous. To support herself, Bonney worked in a vegetable stand, as an *au pair*, and as a cook for Russian immigrants.

Some of Bonney's important debuts with leading conductors included her first role as Sophie in *Der Rosenkavalier* with Carlos Kleiber at the 1984 Munich Summer Festival and her debut at Covent Garden, again as Sophie, later that year with Sir Georg Solti conducting. She then debuted at La Scala as Pamina in *The Magic Flute* with Wolfgang Sawallisch, at the Vienna Philharmonic in the Brahms Requiem, and at the Metropolitan Opera in New York in 1987 as Nyade in Strauss' *Ariadne auf Naxos*. Bonney's classic roles include Pamina, Susanna in *The Marriage of Figaro*, and Sophie, which she has performed more than 250 times. Her first recording was Shoenberg's *Moses and Aaron*; her second was Haydn's *Nelson Mass* in 1984.

For the Record . . .

Born on April 14, 1956, in Montclair, NJ; married Håkan Hagegård (divorced); married Maurice Whitaker. *Education*: Studied music and German, University of New Hampshire, 1974-76; studied vocal technique and Lieder, Salzburg Mozarteum, 1977-79.

Became a member of the Darmstadt Opera and made professional debut in the *Merry Wives of Windsor*, 1979; appeared with the Frankfurt am Main Opera, Hamburg State Opera, and the Bavarian State Opera in Munich, Germany, 1983-84; first recorded album, Shoenberg's *Moses and Aaron*; Metropolitan Opera debut, New York, 1988; signed recording contract with Decca Records, 1996; taught and performed in concert, 2000; released *Gramophone* Award-winning *Diamonds in the Snow*, 2000; released *Fairest Isle*, 2001; has released more than 70 works recorded on the Decca, Deutsche Grammophon, Philips, EMI, Teldec, Sony, and Hyperion labels.

Awards: *Gramophone* Award, Best Solo Vocal Recording for *Diamonds in the Snow*, 2000.

Addresses: *Publicist*—IMG Artists, Lovell House, 616 Chiswick High Road, London, England, W4 5RX, phone: (020) 8233 5800.

Bonney also recorded with composer and pianist André Previn, who conducted her New York Philharmonic debut and composed *Sallie Chisum Remembers Billy the Kid* especially for her.

The multilingual Bonney—fluent in German, Swedish, and English—is known for her "fresh, urgent response to the text," according to Richard Wigmore in *BBC Music* magazine. She pays close attention to the meaning of words and to their sound. The words are as important to her as the music, and she learns them first. "Only when you've thoroughly digested the text can you allow it to wash through you," she told Wigmore. Bonney also said that she appreciated the danger and self-exposure of performing songs she loved in front of an audience that she could make eye contact with, such as a concert performance, rather than at a complete opera, where the audience is too far back behind the orchestra pit to be seen.

In 1996, Bonney signed an exclusive recording contract with Decca Records. In 2000, she released a CD of Scandinavian music called *Diamonds in the Snow*. After living in Sweden for eight years with her first husband, baritone Håkan Hagegård, Bonney fell in love with the place. "I love the country, and love the way the Swedes sing, with their natural, beautiful voices, their directness and lack of artifice," she told Wigmore. "That's the way I've always tried to sing, and I've felt totally at home there." Learning the language also offered Bonney the opportunity to expand her repertoire. She recorded 25 songs by Swedish composers, including Gireg, Sibelius, and Stenhammar on *Diamonds in the Snow,* many of which were previously not often heard outside of Scandinavia. The release won a *Gramophone* Award for Best Solo Vocal Recording. "It would be hard to find a more seductive recital disc than this...," wrote one critic in a *Gramophone* review. *Fairest Isle,* Bonney's recording of sixteenth- and seventeenth-century English songs, was released in 2001. "Her sweet, unblemished tone and refined legato are a pleasure in themselves," wrote a critic in the *Telegraph.* During her career, Bonney has recorded more than 70 releases for various major labels.

The year 2000 saw Bonney at the peak of her career, yet gradually phasing herself out of opera. She claimed age as one of her reasons; she was tired of physically demanding operatic roles and found it silly for a woman over 40 years old to be playing many of opera's girlish roles. She performed no operatic roles in 2000, instead dividing her time between teaching, concert performances, and exploring her long-time love for Lieder, the German song style. "I'm a Lieder singer who happens to do opera," Bonney explained in *BBC Music.* After auditioning for the Darmstadt Opera, she said she got stuck on the "operatic treadmill," torn between her love for Lieder and the living to be made singing opera. Bonney, who lives in London with her second husband, Maurice Whitaker, predicted in 2000 that she would quit singing in ten years to teach. Breakthroughs with students are "so moving for me and so much more important than standing on stage at the Met and having people shout 'Bravo!'" she told *BBC Music.* "Opera is, in a sense, anonymous. Teaching is so personal, so real."

Selected discography

Mozart: *Lieder*, Teldec, 1992.
Mozart: *The Magic Flute*, L'Oiseau Lyre, 1994.
Lehár: *The Merry Widow*, Deutsche Grammophon, 1995.
Schubert: *Lieder*, Teldec, 1995.
Hasse: *Salve Regina/Symphonies/Fuga and Grave*, Archiv, 1997.
Schumann, *Robert & Clara: Lieder*, Decca, 1997.
Barbara Bonney Sings Mozart, Decca, 1998.
Sallie Chisum Remembers Billy the Kid, Decca, 1998.
Nielsen: *Symphonies Nos. 4 - 6*, Decca, 1999.
Pergolesi: *Stabat Mater*, Uni/Decca, 1999.
Strauss, R.: *Four Last Songs*, Decca, 1999.

Diamonds in the Snow, Decca, 2000.
Fairest Isle, Decca, 2001.
The Radiant Voice of Barbara Bonney, Decca, 2001.

Sources

Books

Slonimsky, Nicolas, *Baker's Biographical Dictionary of 20th-Century Classical Musicians,* Schirmer Books, 1992.

Periodicals

BBC Music Magazine, December 2000, p. 38.
Forte, May 1995, p. 52.
Gramophone, Awards Issue 2000, p. 16.

Guardian, January 24, 2001, p. 13.
Opera News, February 14, 1998.
Telegraph, 2001.

Online

"Barbara Bonney," Amazon.com, http://www.amazon.com (June 27, 2001).
"Barbara Bonney," Decca Classics, http://www.deccaclassics.com (March 30, 2001).
"Barbara Bonney," iClassics.com, http://www.iclassics.com (June 27, 2001).

Additional information was provided by IMG Artists publicity materials, 2001.

—Brenna Sanchez

B*Witched

Pop group

Along with BoyZone, Westlife, the Corrs, and Samantha Mumba, the Irish vocal group B*Witched has sold millions of records around the world with its eclectic pop music and wholesome image. Recognized as one of the hardest-working youth-oriented acts to emerge in recent years, the four group members have conducted extensive concert tours and participated in several marketing tie-ins to promote their music, which include a record-setting run of four number-one-charting singles (their first four releases) in Great Britain. In cultivating an international fan base of pre-teens, teen-agers, and young adults, B*Witched has brought its "Irish hip-hop-pop" to audiences far beyond their home base in Dublin, Ireland, all while retaining the resolutely upbeat attitude embodied in their music.

B*Witched attained international acclaim before any of the members had reached her twenty-first birthday. Each grew up in Dublin, where twin sisters Edele and Keavy Lynch had gained a certain amount of fame as the younger sisters of Shane Lynch, a member of the group BoyZone. One of the most successful teen groups of the 1990s, BoyZone was one of the first Irish acts to reach the top of the charts in Britain and Europe since U2 and Sinead O'Connor. The group had a string of number-one hits, usually cover renditions of ballads,

© Photograph by Steve Granitz. Wireimage.com. Reproduced by permission.

For the Record . . .

Members include **Lindsay Armaou** (born Lindsay Gael Christina Armaou on December 18, 1980, in Greece), vocals; **Edele Lynch** (born Edele Claire Christina Edwina Lynch on December 15, 1979, in Dublin, Ireland), vocals; **Keavy Lynch** (born Keavy-Jane Elizabeth Annie Lynch on December 15, 1979, in Dublin, Ireland), vocals; **Sinead O'Carroll** (born Sinead Maria O'Carroll on May 14, 1978, in Dublin, Ireland), vocals.

Group formed in Dublin, Ireland, c. 1995; released debut album, *B*Witched*, in United Kingdom, 1998; toured with 'N Sync in the U.S., 1998-99; joined 98 Degrees for Turn Up the Heat American tour as opening act, 1999; released second album, *Awake and Breathe*, 1999.

Addresses: *Record company*—Epic Records/Sony Music Entertainment, 550 Madison Ave., New York, NY 10022-3211, website: http://www.epicrecords.com. *Website*—B*Witched Official Website: http://www.b-witched.com.

and was for a time the most popular boy band in the world, following the demise of Britain's Take That. Encouraged by Shane's success as well as their family's long-standing love of music, the twin sisters decided to form a vocal group with friends Lindsay Armaou, who was working as an apprentice mechanic in a garage, and Sinead O'Carroll, an all-around performer with experience in acting and dancing as well as music.

BoyZone's domination of the European charts after the mid 1990s showed great acceptance of Irish pop bands outside their native soil. B*Witched, however, struggled to get noticed in the Dublin scene, which was still considered an out-of-the-way territory by the pop music industry. Their first break came when they appeared in a television documentary on the dance studio where they rehearsed, which was noticed by managers Tommy Jay Smith and Kim Glover. Eventually the group's first record would appear on Glover's Glow Worm label, though it was distributed by Epic Records. The group secured a contract with Epic after putting on a memorable performance for its staff: hoping to distinguish themselves from the most popular girl group of the moment, the Spice Girls, B*Witched decided to put on a children's tea party as the setting

for their appearance. Charmed by the energy and innocence of the act, Epic granted the group its contract, and B*Witched entered the studio to record its first album with producers Ray Hedges and Martin Brannigan. The producers also helped the group finalize its name choice, settling on "B*Witched" because they were entranced by the singers' charm. The asterisk was inserted to make the name more distinctive.

Released in late 1998 in Britain and Europe and early the following year in the United States, *B*Witched* contains twelve tracks in a thirty-nine minute collection of diverse musical styles. The album received mostly positive reviews upon its release, with critics singling out the more upbeat, dance-oriented songs as the collection's strong point. *Rolling Stone* welcomed *B*Witched* as "a cheerfully catchy summary of the state of the slumber party—the sound of nice girls acting tough, all in the name of pop," while *People* named the "giddy confection for the preteen at heart" its "Album of the Week." While reviews almost always invoked the Spice Girls in describing *B*Witched*, Keavy Lynch proudly noted in an interview with the *Orange County Register*, "The press can't compare us to any one thing. Our music is totally different because it has so much to it. We've got indie-rock, drum 'n' bass, Irish music, soul, funk. It's all very energetic and very bewitching!"

From the start, B*Witched took aggressive promotional steps to introduce its work to the public. Prior to its debut release, the group went on a tour of British grammar schools, performing in as many as three schools a day. The free school concerts were a tremendously valuable marketing tool. After each show, the record company signed students up for a fan club database, distributing information on the band's upcoming concerts and releases. By the time "C'est La Vie," the first single from *B*Witched,* was released in Britain, thousands of school-age fans were waiting to buy it, and it entered the charts at number one.

Indeed, riding a renewed wave of popular teen-oriented acts on the music scene, B*Witched proved immensely successful with record buyers. Entering the album charts at number three in Britain, *B*Witched* eventually sold over three million copies worldwide and attained platinum status in America. In Britain, the group achieved a feat that no other group up to that time had accomplished: each of the first four singles— "C'est La Vie," "Rollercoaster," "To You I Belong," and "Blame It on the Weatherman"—entered the charts at number one. A global hit, "C'est La Vie" also went into the top ten in America. The group's popularity extended beyond Europe and North America to include Australia and Asia, where the singers toured in 1999.

Building on its successful debut, B*Witched toured extensively throughout 1999. The group appeared as the opening act for 'N Sync and 98 Degrees in the

United States and conducted its own abbreviated concerts and promotional appearances at shopping malls as well. The group also filmed a television special for the Disney Channel that showed them in concert and offstage. Targeting its fan base of teens and tweenies—youngsters between preschool and teenage years—B*Witched secured promotional space in over one hundred Hello Kitty retail stores in malls and signed a contract to endorse the Fetish brand of makeup for young consumers. As one retail executive explained in a *Billboard* profile by Dominic Pride and Tom Ferguson, "The Spice Girls and All Saints are perhaps becoming a bit distant from the very young kids…. I see B*Witched as being their natural heirs. They're very much an upcoming 'just won the talent show' sort of band, and kids really like them." Reinforcing their wholesome and down-to-earth image, B*Witched usually appear in denim outfits and sports shoes in concert and in videos, an image that caused Irish singer Sinead O'Connor to advise in *Q's* November 2000 "Cash for Questions" column: "Take some more clothes off. We need a dirty Irish band. Apart from me."

In addition to its clean, fun-loving image, B*Witched also uses its Irish identity in its promotions to distinguish itself from the growing number of teen-oriented bands on the music scene. For the release of its first album in the United States, the group made a number of appearances around St. Patrick's Day, which helped the album debut at number thirty-eight upon its release. As Sinead O'Carroll explained in a *Chicago Tribune* interview, "There's an Irish element that runs through all of our songs," despite the range of musical styles on the tracks.

With the astounding success of fellow Irish groups the Corrs and Westlife, who pursued similar musical styles and vocal arrangements, and the continued ascendency of boy bands and girl groups like 'N Sync, All Saints, and S Club 7, B*Witched was no longer a singular pop act by the time of its second release, 1999's *Awake and Breathe*. Produced by Hedges and Brannigan, most of the collection features songs co-written by B*Witched itself, featuring "an exhilarating mixture of bounciness, self-help lyrics, and a refreshing lack of salaciousness," as a *Q* review noted approvingly. Charting in the top five in Britain upon its release,

Awake and Breathe did not quite match the group's extraordinary debut, but the single "Jesse Hold On" did give B*Witched its fifth consecutive hit. The album also gave the group the chance to collaborate with renowned African musicians Ladysmith Black Mambazo, who contributed to the track "I Shall Be There."

In 2000 the group recorded a cover of Tony Basil's song "Mickey," which was included on the soundtrack for the film *Bring It On*. Keeping in touch with its young fan base, B*Witched also toured as part of the Nickelodeon channel's All That Music and More concert series. As it prepared for its third release, B*Witched looked forward to working with producer Richard Stannard, noted for his past work with the Spice Girls. B*Witched also hinted that it would change its musical direction for its third album, though the group insisted that its wholesome image would remain in place.

Selected discography

*B*Witched,* Epic Records, 1998.
Awake and Breathe, Epic Records, 1999.
(Contributor) *Bring It On* (soundtrack), Sony Records, 2000.

Sources

Periodicals

Billboard, January 16, 1999, p 13; April 3, 1999, p. 96; June 12, 1999, p. 1.
Chicago Tribune, June 3, 1999.
Daily News (New York), February 9, 1999.
Orange County Register (California), April 7, 1999.
People, March 29, 1999, p. 43.
Q, December 1998, pp. 114-115; December 1999, p. 126; January 2000, p. 32; July 2000, pp. 54-58; September 2000, pp. 72-76; November 2000, p. 12.
Rolling Stone, April 15, 1999, p. 109.

Online

B*Witched Official Website, http://www.b-witched.com (April 16, 2001).

—Timothy Borden

Calexico

Country rock group

From their Southwestern home base of Tucson, Arizona, the duo of Joey Burns and John Convertino create music complimentary to their surroundings in the Sonoran desert. Theirs is a unique blend of Tex-Mex, folk-rock, and rumbling guitars, among other pop elements, that reveals a mysterious, cinematic quality. According to Burns, as he told Adrian Pannett for *Under the Surface* magazine, Tucson is the perfect town for finding mental images to write about: "The downtown is a damn soap opera, characters blow in like tumbleweeds and disappear like ghosts," he said in a discussion of Calexico's 1998 album *The Black Light.* "We just sit there with our instruments all day and score music as all this sh** is going down. It's really slow, so it gives us a chance to try new instruments all the time. When a majority of the music was written it already had this picturesque quality to it. When it came time to sing over the stuff, I just sketched out a story, thinking of some of these characters that live downtown. Some of them are really talented and have multiple personalities."

Prior to forming Calexico, multi-instrumentalists Burns and Convertino, who also live next door to each other in Tucson, spent years as relatively anonymous sidemen playing music of varying styles with different collaborators. Some of their associates include Victoria Williams, Richard Buckner, Vic Chesnutt, and Barbara Manning. The pair first met in the early 1990s while working as the rhythm section of Giant Sand, a band that evolved—under the direction of Tucson-based singer-songwriter, guitarist, and keyboardist Howe Gelb—into a mix of country rock, swing, and beatnik lyricism.

The two continue to record and tour with Giant Sand, participating on the group's acclaimed 2000 release *Chore of Enchantment,* as well as with OP8, another collaboration with Gelb as well as Lisa Germano. "With Giant Sand it has always been Howe. John and [me] following Howe," said Burns for an interview with Lisa Weeks, as quoted by Calexico's official website. "But that's what makes it so great—because we can. That's where we shine. Knowing him as we do, we can sometimes guess where he's going to go ... though he's also full of surprises. That's what's made him so exciting to play with live, more than anyone else we've played with. OP8 is more of an equal split, with an added guest that will change from record to record."

Calexico, however, is not just another name in their long list of side projects, but their main creative focus as songwriters. Upon relocating to Tucson—Convertino from New York via Oklahoma, and Burns from Montreal via Los Angeles—the pair put together a band called the Friends of Dean Martinez and scored a deal with Sub Pop Records. The lo-fi group provided a first opportunity for Burns and Convertino to develop their own ideas, although working relationships from the past and present served as an inescapable influence. "We're lucky to be able to swap recipes with so many friends," Burns told Pannett. "It's a great excuse to get together and hang out."

But both Burns and Convertino do not necessarily identify their music with the phenomenon known as alternative country. "We identify more with people like Victoria Williams, Vic Chesnutt, Will Oldham from Palace, Smog—the meatier songwriters as opposed to a lot of those bands that sound like Son Volt and Uncle Tupelo," Burns explained to Sylvie Simmons, as quoted for Calexico's website. "Those bands are great too, but there's a lot of watered down versions flooding the record stores."

Another apparent inspiration for Calexico came from the people and landscape of Tucson. Their songs—filled with Latin instruments, Western guitars, country atmospherics, and tales about wandering misfits—resulted from retreating to the Arizona desert. "In moving here, I really enjoyed being surrounded by a completely new environment," said Burns to *Billboard* magazine's Chris Morris. "The music here, the culture, it's amazing. It's the closest thing you can get to being in a foreign country while living in the States.... We picked up on some of the Latin rhythms and culture."

In 1996, Calexico released their full-length debut, the low-key, soft-spoken *Spoke,* for the German label Haus Musik. They had connected with the label by chance at a Giant Sand show in Regensberg, Germany. "There's this beautiful table of handmade

For the Record . . .

Members include **Joey Burns** (born in Los Angeles, CA), guitar, bass guitar, cello, mandolin, accordion, vocals; **John Convertino** (born in Oklahoma), drums, vibes, accordion, guitar, marimba.

Duo met while members of Giant Sand, early 1990s; released full-length debut, *Spoke,* as Calexico, 1996; released country-rock concept album, *The Black Light,* on Quarterstick Records, 1998; released *Hot Rail* and *Tete a Tete,* 2000; released *Even My Sure Things Fall Through,* 2001.

Addresses: *Home*—Casa De Calexico U.S.A., 2509 N. Campbell Ave., #335, Tucson, AZ 85719. *Record company*—Quarterstick Records, P.O. Box 25342, Chicago, IL 60625, phone: (773) 388-8888, fax: (773) 388-3888, e-mail: info@tgrec.com. *Booking*—Billions Corporation, Ali Giampino, phone: (312) 997-9999, e-mail: giampino@billions.com. *E-mail*—Joey Burns: joey@casadecalexico.com; John Convertino: john@casadecalexico.com.

records by this guy Wolfgang Petters," Burns recalled to Morris. "He said, 'Well, if you want to do a 7-inch or album, I don't care.'" Taking Petters up on the offer, Burns and Convertino from their Tucson homes recorded an album's worth of original material, which was released in a limited edition of 2,000 copies in Europe. Soon, American labels began to take notice of Calexico, and the duo opted to sign a deal with Touch and Go Records subsidiary Quarterstick Records out of Chicago. Quarterstick re-issued *Spoke* on CD in August of 1997. It featured gentle tracks such as "Glimpse" and "Spokes," as well as occasional rock tunes such as "Scout" and "Mazurka."

The following year saw the release of Calexico's second effort, *The Black Light,* a country-rock concept album about the desert terrain of Arizona and Mexico. The album received excellent reviews—Jim Fusilli of the *Wall Street Journal* listed it as one of the best records of the year, as well as the entire decade—and gained momentum among consumers as a top radio and record store request. Word of Calexico also spread through tours with the likes of Pavement, the Dirty Three, and Lambchop.

In May of 2000, Calexico returned with *Hot Rail,* an album combining elements of the evocative *Spoke* and the cinematic *The Black Light* while also taking their music in a new direction. Here, bursts of intense energy and full orchestration were countered with quieter moments, and Burns and Convertino opted for the addition of horns and violins on the instrumental "El Picador" and distorted Spanish guitar for "Muleta." Tracks such as "Ballad of Cable Hogue" and "Service and Repair" also earned the duo raves for their songwriting abilities.

The fall of 2000 saw the release of *Tete a Tete,* recorded with two French friends, Naïm Amor and Thomas Belhorn, who had recently relocated to Tucson. Calexico's Western tastes remained, yet the newcomers introduced European influences to tracks like the grand and moody "Gilbert" and classically inspired "Orange Trees in the Yard." In May of 2001, Calexico released their fifth album, entitled *Even My Sure Things Fall Through.*

Selected discography

Spoke (Germany) Haus Musik, 1996; reissued, Quarterstick, 1997.
The Black Light, Quarterstick, 1998.
Hot Rail, Quarterstick, 2000.
Tete a Tete, Quarterstick, 2000.
Even My Sure Things Fall Through, Quarterstick, 2001.

Sources

Periodicals

Billboard, August 2, 1997.
Rolling Stone, April 13, 2000; June 22, 2000.
Village Voice, January 25, 2000.
Wall Street Journal, December 11, 1998; December 31, 1999.
Washington Post, May 15, 1998.

Online

Amazon.com, http://www.amazon.com (May 12, 2001).
Casadecalexico—Calexico's Home Page, http://www.casadecalexico.com (May 7, 2001).

—*Laura Hightower*

The Chainsaw Kittens

Rock group

After more than a decade of performing, recording, and surviving lineup changes, the pop/glam-rock/punk-rock group Chainsaw Kittens from Norman, Oklahoma, remains one of the best-kept secrets in rock music. Though not too well known among the mainstream, they repeatedly receive stellar reviews and have toured with some of the biggest names in the business, including Jane's Addiction, the Smashing Pumpkins, and Iggy Pop. To critics, fans, and fellow musicians, the Chainsaw Kittens are fine examples of continual creativity; undoubtedly, they have their own distinct sound, and yet no two Chainsaw Kittens songs ever sound the same.

Whereas so many other groups seem most energetic and inventive at the onset of their career, the Chainsaw Kittens, by comparison, continued to evolve as the years passed, from their 1990 debut *Violent Religion* through their 2000 release *The All American.* As Kurt B. Reighly asserted in a review for *Seattle Weekly:* "At the risk of sounding evangelical, *The All American* unclogged my jaded ears and reminded me why I love rock."

The Chainsaw Kittens' lead vocalist, chief songwriter, and guitarist, the charismatic Tyson Todd Meade, was born around 1963 in Bartlesville, Oklahoma, the youngest of five children. Before settling into retirement, his father worked as an architect, and his mother pursued a career as a nurse. Both parents, according to Meade, instilled in their son the values of treating others with respect, as well as frugality.

Meade, who grew up on a steady diet of Iggy Pop, the New York Dolls, and Marc Bolan, joined his first band, Defenestration, in the mid 1980s. Although they recorded a couple records, the group did not quite take off, thus opening the door for Meade to move forward with something new. In January of 1989 in Norman, Meade founded the Chainsaw Kittens. These were the days before "alternative" rock groups—like Nirvana, the Smashing Pumpkins, or Bush—had infiltrated the mainstream market. As opposed to the popular guitar-based bands at the time like Whitesnake or Skid Row, the Chainsaw Kittens were just four guys playing music without the long hair and wandering groupies. "I wanted to make a change in the music and it was really kind of scary because I didn't know if anybody would take us seriously or if we'd get signed or whatever," Meade stated in an interview with *LMNOP* online.

After holding practice sessions for a month, Meade, along with the other founding Kittens—guitarist Mark Metzger, bass guitarist Kevin McElhaney, and drummer Ted Leader—recorded a demo and, to his surprise, received a contract offer immediately from Mammoth Records. "We were really lucky in that way, and we've been really unlucky in other ways," explained Meade. "We've watched as other bands that opened for us have sold millions of records. Weezer opened for us when they first put out their record. They actually even got stiffed by the club. And Everclear opened for us at one point, the Toadies opened for us at one point."

In the meantime, though, the Chainsaw Kittens held high hopes. In 1990, they released their self-made debut album, *Violent Religion,* introducing the Kittens' knack for creating fragile melodies and catchy pop choruses alongside twisted lyrics and powerful, raw guitars. Unfortunately, the record received little attention, but the band built a reputation through touring and performing with various up-and-coming acts, most notably the Smashing Pumpkins.

Before touring in support of their debut, the Chainsaw Kittens introduced a new member, guitarist Trent Bell. And while on the road, the band witnessed two additional changes to the lineup; Aaron Preston took over drumming duties, while Clint McBay replaced McElhaney on bass. With the new lineup, featuring Meade, Metzger, McBay, Preston, and Bell, the band recorded their sophomore effort, *Flipped Out in Singapore,* for which they employed the services of Nirvana's *Nevermind* producer, Butch Vig. Released on Mammoth in 1992, the album, containing the songs "Connie I've Found the Door" and "High in High School," enabled the group's profile and fanbase to grow.

Apparently, the departures of some of the founding members failed to quiet the Chainsaw Kittens' sound. "Indeed," wrote *Los Angeles Times* reviewer Elena Oumano after attending a concert, "the Kittens reject coifed heavy-metal glamour and self-conscious virtuosity in favor of pallid, poetic looks that belie their nervy plunge deep into the bowels of a song. Kind of like the Ramones on strychnine-laced acid. Meade is one of the more abandoned and accomplished screamers this side of Little Richard."

However, the band's 1993 release, the EP *Angel on the Range,* marked another shift in membership. But with Matt Johnson on bass and Eric Harmon on drums, the Chainsaw Kittens finally found a stable rhythm section that remained the same ever since. At this point and going forward, the group included Meade, Bell, Johnson, and Harmon. In 1994, the Chainsaw Kittens released their third full-length set, *Pop Heiress,* produced by John Angelo, known for his work with Dinosaur Jr. and Buffalo Tom. Because of Mammoth's new partnership with Atlantic Records and a subtle string section backing the Kittens' already solid songwriting, *Pop Heiress* was poised to become the band's big breakthrough. But such expectations never materialized. Still, the album proved a significant critical

success, ending up on several of the year's top ten lists, including that of Smashing Pumpkins leader Billy Corgan.

Afterward, the Chainsaw Kittens left Mammoth and signed with Scratchie Records, a label co-owned by James Iha and D'arcy of the Smashing Pumpkins. In 1995, the group released a preview of their forthcoming new album with an EP entitled *Candy for You.* The following year saw the release of *Chainsaw Kittens,* the band's fourth album. Recorded by the band themselves at Bell's home studio and mixed by Angelo, the self-titled set, now featuring a more extensive use of string instruments, won the approval of fans and critics alike. It included several notable tracks, including the single "Heartcatchthump," "Ballad of Newsman 5" and "Mouthful of Glass." "We had total freedom over recording, packaging and everything," recalled Meade in an interview published in *LiveWire.* "It was so nice to have complete artistic freedom while making this record."

For the next few years, the Chainsaw Kittens took an extended break, during which time the band members explored other musical and personal interests. Then, in 2000, they returned with a new album for Four Alarm Records called *The All American,* complete with a cover version of Iggy Pop's "Nightclubbing." Despite limited exposure, it, too, received critical praise. The Kittens continued to tour thereafter in support of the album, hoping to one day earn the credit their supporters believe they deserve.

Selected discography

EPs

Angel on the Range, Mammoth, 1993.
Candy for You, Scratchie, 1995.

Albums

Violent Religion, Mammoth, 1990.
Flipped Out in Singapore, Mammoth, 1992.
Pop Heiress, Mammoth/Atlantic, 1994.
Chainsaw Kittens, Scratchie/Mercury, 1996.
The All American, Four Alarm, 2000.

Sources

Periodicals

Billboard, January 24, 1998.
Boston Globe, April 17, 1992.
LiveWire, April/May 1997.
Los Angeles Times, March 27, 1992.
Rolling Stone, January 27, 1994.
Seattle Weekly, August 31-September 8, 2000.

Online

All Music Guide, http://www.allmusic.com (April 29, 2001).

The Almighty Chainsaw Kittens, http://www.richd.com/kittens/biography/ (April 29, 2001).

Flagpole, http://www.flagpole.com (April 29, 2001).

Four Alarm Records, http://www.fouralarmrecords.com (April 29, 2001).

LMNOP, http://www.lmnop.com (April 29, 2001).

Slade's Chainsaw Kittens Page, http://www.ionet.net/˜tslade/kittens.htm (April 29, 2001).

Well Rounded Entertainment, http://www.well-rounded.com (April 29, 2001).

—Laura Hightower

Han-Na Chang

Cellist

At only eleven years old, cellist Han-Na Chang made a grand entrance on the classical music scene by winning the prestigious Rostropovich International Cello Competition in Paris in 1994. In 2001, at age 17, she performed as the featured soloist with the Cincinnati Symphony Orchestra in a sweeping European tour through Spain, Germany, and Poland. No typical teenager, young Chang by that time had appeared in debut performances with many world class orchestras including the Berlin Philharmonic, Israel Philharmonic, the London Symphony Orchestra, the National Symphony Orchestra in Washington, D.C., and the La Scala Orchestra of Milan. A student of the premier virtuoso Mstislav Rostropovich, Chang's personal discography with EMI Records features an outstanding repertoire backed by an equally impressive lineup of noted conductors.

Han-Na Chang was born Hanna (pronounced Hannah) Chang in Seoul, Korea, in 1983; she was named after the Biblical mother of Samuel. She was introduced to piano lessons at age three, but grew tired of that instrument and switched to the cello three years later at age six. Barely two years passed again before Chang, who was merely eight years old, performed in a public debut recital in Seoul with Luciano Berio conducting. At age ten, Chang and her family immigrated to the United States where she enrolled at the prestigious Juilliard School of Music in New York City. It was at that time that Chang adopted the hyphenated spelling of her first name, which was the result of a translation error on her passport papers. In America, Chang and her family settled in rural upstate New York where her talent flourished against an idyllic backdrop of forest wildlife and rippling waters.

Yet even as her childhood dreams and emotions were nurtured in this natural setting, the young cellist adhered to a rigorous lifestyle, augmenting her school days with lengthy practice sessions interspersed with homework. In 1994, at eleven years of age and still too short to play a full-sized cello, Chang won the prestigious Rostropovich International Cello Competition in Paris. Chang, playing a fractionally proportioned 7/8-size cello, won not only the Contemporary Music Prize but also the coveted Grand Prize of the overall competition. The contest was adjudged by Maestro Rostropovich himself along with a collection of his musical colleagues. The judging panel, according to Anna Tims in the *Independent*, gave serious consideration before designating the prestigious award to a child musician for fear of the pressures of exploitation. Thereafter, Rostropovich brought the young cellist under his own guidance as a mentor.

Approximately one year after her prize-winning performance at the international competition, young Chang grew into a full-size instrument. In recognition of the occasion, she was given a 1757 Guadagnini, one of the finest cellos in the world, which was acquired in Milan in support and appreciation of her talent by a consortium of well-to-do Korean citizens. She returned to Seoul in March of 1995 for a formal concert debut with the Dresden Staatskapelle, conducted by Guiseppe Sinopoli. Also that year she issued her first commercial recording through EMI Classics. The album, Tchaikovsky: *Variations on a Rococo Theme,* included works by Saint-Saens, Bruch, and Fauré. It was recorded at England's Abbey Road Studios and featured the London Symphony Orchestra under the baton of her teacher, Rostropovich. According to Chang in an EMI interview, the recording studio posed a more intimidating environment by far than performing in the presence of a live audience because of the permanence attached to every note. As with all true prodigies, she displayed an uncanny ability to infuse an extraordinary purity of artistic expression into her music. Critic Lawson Taitte of the *Dallas Morning News* said of her performance on the Tchaikovsky piece that "Ms. Chang responds to the work's poise and freshness with an adroit innocence." Later in 1995, as she appeared for a series of concerts in Tel Aviv with conductor Yoel Levi and the Israel Philharmonic, Levi remarked to Michael Ajzenstadt of the *Jerusalem Post* that "[S]he brings with her this great naivete which does not exist any longer. It's fresh and blossoming and it's really great."

In April of 1996, a 13-year-old Chang appeared with Leonard Slatkin and the International Chamber Orchestra at the Kennedy Center for the Performing Arts in Washington, D.C. The televised concert marked the

For the Record . . .

Born Hanna Chang in 1983 in Seoul, Korea. *Education*: Juilliard School of Music (pre-college division); studied with Aldo Parisot; student of Mstislav Rostropovich; participated on full scholarship in master class program with Mischa Maisky, Siena, Italy.

Recital tours: Korea, Japan; chamber ensembles with Maisky, Gidon Kremer, Dmitry Sitkovetsky; formal debut with Dresden Staatskapelle in Seoul, Korea, 1995; made recording debut with EMI Classics with Mstislav Rostropovich and the London Symphony, 1995; Carnegie Hall debut with Montreal Symphony, 1996; featured soloist with assorted orchestras including the Israel Philharmonic, Boston Symphony, Berlin Philharmonic, Cincinnati Symphony, National Symphony Orchestra of Washington, D.C., and Orchestre de Paris.

Awards: Grand Prize and Contemporary Music Prize, Fifth Rostropovich International Cello Competition, 1994; Young Artist of the Year, ECHO Classical Music Awards, Germany, 1997.

Addresses: *Record company*—EMI Records Group (United Kingdom), EMI House, 43 Brook Green, London, England, W6 7EF, phone: (44) 20 7605 5000, fax: (44) 20 7605 5050.

center's twenty-fifth anniversary gala celebration. Chang later appeared for a debut at Carnegie Hall in October of 1996 with Charles Dutoit and the Montreal Symphony Orchestra. Under the protective eye of Rostropovich, Chang had assumed a limited concert agenda of 15 concerts per year by the age of 15.

In November of 1999, Chang appeared in a debut performance at Davies Symphony Hall in San Francisco, California. *San Francisco Chronicle* critic Joshua Kosman commended the 16-year-old's "magnificent rendition of Haydn's C-Major Cello Concerto. It was a moment to remember.... In an age when teenage performers and even preteen performers are routinely trotted out onto concert stages regardless of their level of ability, it's a joy to encounter an artist who's the genuine article." Also during the 1999-2000 season, Chang performed with the Berlin Philharmonic, L'Orchestre de Paris, and with Myung-Whun Chung and the Santa Cecilia Orchestra of Rome. In the United States in the summer of 2000, Chang appeared in a debut at the Hollywood Bowl with Slatkin and the Los Angeles Philharmonic. She performed again later that summer with Slatkin in conjunction with the Sydney Olympic Games, which marked her Australian debut. Additionally, she has performed in chamber ensembles with Mischa Maisky, who is also among her teachers, and the popular violinist Gidon Kremer.

Early in 2001, Kosman gave an endorsement of "wild applause" to Chang's EMI Classic album *The Swan*, which she recorded with the Philharmonia Orchestra of London. Soon afterward, on January 22 of that year, she performed with the Cincinnati Symphony Orchestra in a sendoff concert, a prelude to a European tour. The itinerary took her to Spain, Germany, and Poland with Jesús López-Cobos conducting. Upon her return to the United States, she performed the Haydn Concerto with the Atlanta Symphony, evoking praise from Pierre Ruhe of the *Atlanta Constitution*. "Her tone is robust, dark-mahogany in color, with a slightly raspy finish; her technique agile.... Her sound rings out brilliantly—yet she finds ways of singing very quietly with her cello, of making the audience do some of the work. One saw a great many people in the audience leaning forward in their seats during the hushed slow movement, where her sculpted phrasing was understated, poignant, frisson-inducing."

Despite her precocious talent, Chang emphasized to Tims, "I don't find it hard to be normal.... I love music, shopping, and roller blading." Normalcy notwithstanding, Chang admitted to having read Dostoyevsky's intense novel, *The Idiot*, at age 13 "to improve my mind." By 2000, Chang was in her final year of college preparatory studies at the Rockland Country Day School in her hometown of Congers, New York. Her demanding musical curriculum included weekend excursions to Juilliard on Saturdays, interspersed with five-hour daily practice sessions after school.

Selected discography

(With Mstislav Rostropovich and the London Philharmonic) Tchaikovsky: *Variations on a Rococo Theme, Opus 33/ Saint-Saëns/Faure/Bruch,* EMI Classics, 1995.
(With Giuseppe Sinopoli and the Dresden Staatskapelle) Haydn: *Cello Concertos,* EMI Classics, 1998.
The Swan, EMI Classics, 2000.

Sources

Periodicals

American Record Guide, January/February 1997, p. 39.
Atlanta Constitution, April 6, 2001, p. E5.
Dallas Morning News, November 10, 1996, p. 11C.
Independent, February 5, 1998, p. 4.
Jerusalem Post, November 28, 1998.

Minneapolis Star Tribune, April 29, 1996, p. 5B.
San Francisco Chronicle, November 12, 1999, p. C6.

Online

Han-Na Chang Biography, http://www.emiclassics.com/art
   ists/biogs/hanb.html (May 7, 2001).
"Han-Na Chang," Kennedy Center—25th Anniversary
   Scrapbook, http://www.kennedy-center.org/history/gala/
   chang.html (April 19, 2001).
"Han-Na Chang, Cellist," Cello Heaven, http://celloheaven
   .com/bios/chang.htm (April 19, 2001).
"Jesús López-Cobos Leads Orchestra … Cellist Han-Na
   Chang joins CSO at Carnegie Hall before Europe," Cincinnati Symphony & Pops Orchestra, http://cincinnatisym-
   phony.org/news54.html (April 19, 2001).
"Sharps & Flats," Salon, http://salon.com/music/music961
   118.html (April 19, 2001).

—Gloria Cooksey

Chanticleer

Vocal group

Begun as a way for musicology student Louis Botto to rediscover music from the Renaissance period and have it heard, Chanticleer, the only independent full-time classical vocal ensemble in the United States, developed into much more. In addition to a mastery of the male-sung Renaissance genre, Gregorian chant, opera, jazz, gospel, and twentieth-century pop became hallmarks of the group's repertoire. Performances worldwide and over 20 successful CD releases helped the group gain international recognition. The 12 men of Chanticleer handle the full range of vocal parts—including soprano and alto, which are sung in a developed falsetto—without the help of a conductor. "They are, to put it directly, one of the world's best," wrote one *San Francisco Chronicle* critic in comments included in Chanticleer promotional materials.

Botto, a graduate student in musicology, found it strange that the music he was studying— vocal music from the Renaissance period—was never performed. In 1978, he gathered some fellow singers around a dining room table and proposed an idea. He had decided to start a group to sing this forgotten music using male voices in the Renaissance tradition. He plucked friends from the San Francisco Symphony Chorus and Grace Cathedral's Choir of Men and Boys to form the first group of nine men. The ensemble began rehearsals for their debut performance at San Francisco's historic Mission Dolores. Named for the "clear-singing" rooster from Geoffrey Chaucer's *Canterbury Tales,* the group performed music that would become part of Chanticleer's repertoire. Before an enthusiastic, capacity audience, the ensemble performed works by Byrd, Isaac, Ockeghem, Morales, Morley, Dufay, and Josquin. After the successful show, the men agreed to commit to Chanticleer with a goal to perform at least three concerts per year.

The group initially performed on arduous tours of the United States for little money. Botto, a proficient cook, often bragged he could cook dinner for the entire Chanticleer ensemble for less than $50. The size of the group fluctuated during its first years, but the group settled on 12 singers, the number which provided the best flexibility to perform their varied repertoire; since its start, more than 65 men have been part of the Chanticleer ensemble. At San Francisco's Festival of the Masses in 1980, esteemed American choral director Robert Shaw heard Chanticleer perform and declared it "one of the most beautiful experiences of my life." In 1983, countertenor Joseph Jennings joined Chanticleer and had such a positive influence on the group as a whole that the other members soon asked him to become Chanticleer's first music director.

Chanticleer's success grew steadily, and the men were invited to their first overseas performance, which took place in Belgium at the International Josquin Symposium in 1984. International travel would become a mainstay for Chanticleer, which became regular fixtures at such European festivals as the Salzburg Festival, Austria; the Schleswig-Holstein Music Festival, Germany; the Brisbane Biennial Festival of Music, Australia; the Taipei International Choral Festival, Taiwan; and the Voices Festival, Netherlands. They have also performed in a variety of venues worldwide, everywhere from the world's finest concert halls to a barn in Canada, a roofless church in Germany, and New York's Central Park.

Though Chanticleer were among the only performers of Renaissance-period music, they found no interest from record labels in recording and releasing their work. As a result, in 1998, the Chanticleer Records label was founded and the first release, *The Anniversary Album,* was a tenth-anniversary celebration recording by the group. Chanticleer released ten records on their own label including *On the Air: Live Radio Highlights, Psallite!: A Renaissance Christmas, Antoine Brumel: Missa Berzerette savoyenne,* and *With a Poet's Eye: New American Choral Music.* In 1994, they signed an exclusive contract with Teldec Classics International, which gave the group the international exposure it needed. Teldec released Chanticleer albums as diverse as Gregorian chant, gospel music, and folk songs to over 60 countries worldwide.

By 1991, Chanticleer was financially stable enough to hire all 12 members as full-time employees. The move freed the group to perform and rehearse more frequently. Chanticleer performs over 100 concerts per year, spending about half its time on the road, and

gospel and pop music became part of the group's repertoire. In 1994, the ensemble performed a fully-staged version of Benjamin Britten's opera *Curlew River*. Chanticleer twice performed and recorded previously unknown work by Mexican composers Manuel de Zumaya and Ignacio de Jerusalem with an orchestra specializing in period-instrument performance. *Mexican Baroque,* was released in 1994, and *Jerusalem: Matins for the Virgin of Guadalupe* was released in 1998. Chanticleer teamed up with the London Studio Orchestra and the Don Haas Trio to record an album of pop and jazz standards called *Lost in the Stars,* released in 1996. An *American Record Guide* critic called 1997's *Wondrous Love,* a collection of folk songs, "brilliant, yet intimate" with "clever arrangements" and "superb musicianship with clean-as-a-whistle vocalism."

Though most Chanticleer concerts are a cappella performances, the group demonstrated its versatility and talent through a number of creative and sometimes unusual collaborations. The group has shared a stage with orchestras such as the New York Philharmonic, the San Francisco Symphony, and the Saint Paul Chamber Orchestra, as well as with Japanese dancers Eiko and Koma and jazz legend George Shearing. The ensemble commissioned many new works from contemporary classical composers including David Conte, Anthony Davis, Morton Gould, Bernard Rands, Steve Sametz, and Augusta Read Thomas. Composer Chen Yi was the group's composer-in-residence from 1993 to 1996. Chanticleer's 1999 release, *Colors of Love,* is a collection of works by these composers which earned a Grammy Award for Best Small Ensemble Performance in 2000.

Selected discography

The Anniversary Album, Chanticleer Records, 1988.
Our Heart's Joy: A Chanticleer Christmas, Chanticleer Records, 1990.
Antoine Brumel: Missa Berzerette savoyenne, Chanticleer Records, 1991.
Psallite!: A Renaissance Christmas, Chanticleer Records, 1991.
With a Poet's Eye: New American Choral Music, Chanticleer Records, 1991.
Josquin des Prez: Missa Mater Patris, Alexander Agricola: Magnificat and Motets, Chanticleer Records, 1992.
On the Air: Live Radio Highlights, Chanticleer Records, 1992.
Cristóbal de Morales: Missa Mille regretz and Motets, Chanticleer Records, 1993.
Giovanni Pierluigi da Palestrina: Missa Pro Defunctis and Motets, Teldec Classics, 1994.
Mexican Baroque: Ignacio de Jerusalem and Manuel de Zumaya, Teldec Classics, 1994.
Out of this World: A Chanticleer Portrait, Teldec Classics, 1994.
Where the Sun Will Never Go Down: Spirituals and Traditional Gospel Music, Teldec Classics, 1994.

rehearses five hours per day, five days a week. Jennings told the *New York Times* how a Chanticleer singer is chosen and how each member flavors the group: "It's a clear sound but one that has lots of color to it," Jennings said. "We choose singers who are flexible vocally and stylistically, and incorporate all the voices into the total fabric. We try to be as authentic as we can to each style, but we color that authenticity with our twentieth-century American existence." Botto's death in 1997 was a great loss to the group. He had sung with Chanticleer from 1978 to 1989 and served as its artistic director until his death.

Though Chanticleer's roots were in Renaissance music, the group came to perform and record a diverse body of work. Jennings' inventive arrangements of

Mysteria: Gregorian Chants, Teldec Classics, 1995.
(With The London Studio Orchestra & The Don Haas Trio) *Lost in the Stars,* Teldec Classics, 1996.
Sing We Christmas, Teldec Classics, 1997.
The Music of Chen Yi: The Women's Philharmonic with Chanticleer, New Albion Records, 1997.
Reflections: An Anniversary Collection, Teldec Classics, 1997.
Wondrous Love: A World Folk Song Collection, Teldec Classics, 1997.
Chanticleer Performs Byrd: Regina Coeli, Harmonia Mundi, 1998.
Jerusalem: Matins for the Virgin of Guadalupe, Teldec Classics, 1998.
Colors of Love, Teldec Classics, 1999.
Ave Maria: The Myth of Mary, Teldec Classics, 2000.
Magnificat: A Cappella Works by Josquin, Palestrina, Titov, Victoria, and others, Teldec Classics, 2000.

Sources

Periodicals

American Record Guide, November/December 1994; September/October 1997.
BBC Music Magazine, September 1999; November 2000.

Billboard, September 30, 2000.
Boston Globe, December 8, 1998.
Chicago Sun-Times, July 21, 1999.
Chicago Tribune, December 4, 1996.
Dallas Morning News, March 23, 1995.
Gramophone, Awards Issue 2000.
New York Times, December 5, 1999.
Plain Dealer (Cleveland, OH), January 23, 2000.
Sacramento Bee, August 8, 2000, p. D3.
Singapore Straits Times, April 1995.

Online

"Chanticleer," *All Music Guide,* http://www.allmusic.com (April 18, 2001).
"Chanticleer," *Teldec Classics,* http://www.warner-classics.com/teldec (April 27, 2001).
Chanticleer Official Website, http://www.chanticleer.org (April 18, 2001).

Additional materials provided by the Chanticleer publicity department, 2001.

—Brenna Sanchez

Gary Chapman

Singer, songwriter

One of Nashville's most successful songwriters for more than two decades, Gary Chapman has also made a name for himself as a performer and radio/television personality. But for Chapman, 1999 brought major losses: the end of his 17-year marriage to singer Amy Grant and the loss of his high-profile job as host of cable channel The Nashville Network's (TNN) *Prime Time Country*. However, the new millennium brought Chapman a new marriage and the promise of new career opportunities.

During the last days of the twentieth century, Chapman told the *Tennessean* (Nashville) that despite the personal and professional difficulties of 1999, "I'm happier now than I've ever been in my life." Pausing to reflect for just a moment, he corrected himself: "Happy's not correct. I'm more joyful. There's a profound difference between happiness and joy. Happiness for me is based on things going the way I think they should. Joy is found in realizing the profound beauty of the mundane. I'm more joyful than I've ever been in my life."

Born on August 19, 1957, in Waurika, Oklahoma, Chapman is the son of a Protestant minister and a homemaker. Shortly after he was born, the family moved to DeLeon, Texas, where he was raised. Even

For the Record . . .

Born Gary Winther Chapman on August 19, 1957, in Waurika, OK; married singer Amy Grant, 1982; children: Matthew Garrison, Gloria Mills, and Sarah Cannon; divorced, 1999; married Jennifer Pittman, 2000.

Played in rock band during high school; moved to Nashville, TN, joined the Rambos, a gospel group, and began writing songs for other performers; Chapman's "My Father's Eyes," recorded by Amy Grant, went to number one, 1979; has released several albums as a performer including *Sincerely Yours,* 1981; *Happenin'...Live,* 1983; *Light Inside,* 1994; *Shelter,* 1996; and *Outside,* 1999.

Awards: Multiple Dove Awards from the Gospel Music Association (GMA) including Songwriter of the Year, 1982; Male Vocalist of the Year and Inspirational Recorded Song of the Year, 1996; and Country Album of the Year, 1998.

Addresses: *Record company*—Reunion Records, 741 Cool Springs Blvd., Franklin, TN 37067. *Booking*—Richard De La Font Agency, 4845 South Sheridan Road, Suite 505, Tulsa, OK 74145-5719. *Website*—Gary Chapman Official Website: http://www.garychapman.net.

though he was encouraged by family to follow in his father's footsteps, he secretly dreamed of becoming an entertainer throughout most of his childhood. In high school, he joined a school-sanctioned rock band. Bowing to family pressures, he headed off to Bible college after finishing high school, but his heart was not in it, and he dropped out. Even at college, he sought out every possible opportunity to perform. Of his brief stay at college, Chapman said in comments at the Richard De La Font Agency website: "I thought I would be a preacher, and I went to Bible school for a year and a half. I jokingly say God called me out of Bible school, but I really think He did." Chapman found that he could spread the message of Christianity through song far more effectively than through the spoken word.

After leaving college, Chapman moved to Nashville and joined the Rambos, a well-established gospel singing group. He also began writing songs and peddling them to other performers around Nashville. In 1979, Contemporary Christian singer Amy Grant recorded Chapman's "My Father's Eyes." The song eventually went to number one, and even more importantly, brought the singer and songwriter together. The couple married in 1982. In 1981, singer T.G. Sheppard had a hit with Chapman's "Finally," which also went to number one on the country charts. Other performers who have recorded Chapman's songs include Alabama, Kenny Rogers, Barbara Mandrell, Steve Wariner, Kathy Troccoli, Vanessa Williams, Lee Greenwood, and Russ Taff. In 1982, the Gospel Music Association (GMA) presented Chapman with a Dove Award for Songwriter of the Year.

Chapman released his first album as a performer in 1981. Entitled *Sincerely Yours,* the album was released on the Lion & Lamb recording label and fell into the genre of Contemporary Christian Music (CCM), which musically sounds very much like pop music but has lyrics of a religious or inspirational nature. Two years later, a second Chapman album—*Happenin'... Live*—was released on the Lion & Lamb label. In 1987, Chapman hit the road as the opening act for a concert tour with Bruce Hornsby and the Range.

In the early 1990s, Chapman switched recording labels, signing with Reunion Records, based in Franklin, Tennessee, just outside of Nashville. His 1994 album for Reunion, *The Light Inside,* won a Grammy nomination as Best Pop/Contemporary Gospel Album and a Dove Award nomination for Chapman as Male Vocalist of the Year. The album featured the hit singles "Treasure," "Sweet Jesus," and "Sweet Glow of Mercy," the last of which hit number one on the gospel music charts. Chapman also won honors in 1994 for his work as co-producer of *Songs from the Loft,* a Dove Award-winning album containing songs by Grant and other Contemporary Christian Music artists including Ashley Cleveland, Susan Ashton, and Michael W. Smith. The album was recorded in the studio Chapman and Grant had had built into a barn on their farm outside Nashville.

Although 1994 had been a particularly productive year for both Chapman and Grant, 1995 brought new opportunities for Chapman. He served as host of the annual Dove Awards ceremony that year and later began hosting a live concert series entitled Sam's Place at Nashville's Ryman Auditorium, one of the original homes of the Grand Ole Opry. Later in 1995, Chapman hosted specials based on the Sam's Place theme for the Nashville Network. The following year, in a hint of things to come, *Nashville Scene,* a local weekly covering the Music City's entertainment scene and lifestyle news, named Chapman Best Future Talk Show Host.

Chapman's next solo album for Reunion, *Shelter,* released in 1996, produced the number one gospel hit "One of Two" and garnered a Grammy nomination as

Best Pop/Contemporary Gospel Album. Chapman also won the Dove Award as Male Vocalist of the Year in 1996 in addition to three other Dove Awards that year—Inspirational Recorded Song of the Year, Special Event Album of the Year, and another for his involvement with the *Songs from the Loft* project. The Nashville Network, impressed with Chapman's performance on the Sam's Place specials the previous year, decided to give him a tryout as host of its popular *Prime Time Country*. After an eight-show, on-camera trial run, the network made it official, naming him the show's new host.

Things were going well for Chapman on the home front as well. At home on their sprawling farm in Franklin, Tennessee, not far from Nashville, he and Grant enjoyed the country life with their three children, Matt, Millie, and Sarah. When he could find the spare time, Chapman went flying. He owns a helicopter and has his pilot's license for fixed-wing aircraft.

Late in 1997, Chapman's Christmas album, entitled *This Gift,* was released on the Reunion label. In 1998, the album won the World of Christian Music's Victory Award as Best Country Album, while its title song received a Victory nomination as Country Song of the Year. On the strength of *This Gift,* Chapman himself was nominated for a Victory Award as Best Country Artist. The album also received a Grammy nomination as Best Pop/Contemporary Gospel Album. For his work on the Sam's Place concert series, *Nashville Scene* readers voted Chapman Best Host of an Event in 1997 and 1998.

Chapman's life changed dramatically in 1999. The year had barely begun when Chapman and Grant announced to the press that they were separating. By mid-year, their divorce was official. Making the breakup even more painful for Chapman was rampant press speculation that Grant had left Chapman for country singer Vince Gill. (Grant and Gill did, in fact, marry in March of 2000). But that was not the end of the bad news for Chapman. In August of 1999, the Nashville Network announced that it was canceling most of its programming in the talk-variety format, including *Prime Time Country with Gary Chapman*. TNN said the show would cease production in September of 1999.

As 1999 came to a close, Chapman was maintaining a positive attitude, telling *USA Today*: "I lost my job and my wife, and I'm happy. Go figure. As hokey as this may sound, I honestly feel so completely held in the center of God's huge and tender hand." Professionally, Chapman was keeping busy, releasing his latest album for Reunion in September of 1999. Entitled *Outside,* the album was "more personal than any I've ever done," Chapman told the *Tennessean*. Listening to the lyrics of one song, "Learning to Love," it is easy to see how the year's events had influenced his writing: "My heart could not bend/So now it's broken/For so long you told me/You'd never say good-bye."

On a personal level, Chapman had a great deal to be happy about. Earlier in 1999, he had met Jennifer Pittman, an animal trainer at Universal Studios Florida in Orlando where *Prime Time Country* was broadcasting on location. Before long, the two were dating, and in June of 1999, Pittman moved to Nashville to be closer to Chapman. On July 1, 2000, with Chapman's father officiating, the couple was married. Of his new bride, Chapman told K99FM's *CountryNotes* newsletter: "She's the kindest person I've ever met. And I am so looking forward to laughing for the rest of my years with her. She is a great, great soul."

Chapman had several projects in the works as of 2001, and he was confident that whatever happened would be for the best. He told the *Tennessean* that he has turned down some offers that would have involved relocating to the West Coast because he is determined to stay close to his children, custody of which he shares with Grant. In a philosophical mood, Chapman told *CountryNotes*: "All I really want is to be able to look back at the end of life … and see a body of work that I am proud of."

Selected discography

Sincerely Yours, Lion & Lamb, 1981.
Happenin'…Live, Lion & Lamb, 1983.
Everyday Man, RCA, 1987.
Light Inside, Reunion, 1994.
Shelter, Reunion, 1996.
This Gift, Reunion, 1997.
Outside, Reunion, 1999.

Sources

Periodicals

Associated Press, August 17, 1999.
CountryNotes, May-June 2000.
Tennessean (Nashville, TN), December 11, 1999; July 4, 2000.
USA Today, January 4, 1999, p. 2D; December 9, 1999, p. 8D.

Online

"Gary Chapman," *All Music Guide,* http://www.allmusic.com/cg/amg.dll (May 7, 2001).
"Gary Chapman," Richard De La Font Agency Inc., http://www.delafont.com/music_arts/Gary-Chapman.htm (May 9, 2001).
"Gary Chapman: Profile," Today's Christian Music, http://www.todayschristianmusic.com/Profile-GaryChapman.htm (May 9, 2001).

Gary Chapman Official Website, http://www.ontariolive.com/garychapman/allaboutgary.html (May 9, 2001).

—*Don Amerman*

Jacky Cheung

Singer

Multilingual vocalist Jacky Cheung of Hong Kong conquered the Asian music market in the mid 1980s, then expanded into the worldwide music arena and into motion picture markets as a popular screen star. His unique personal charm defied critical articulation, yet he captivated fans and held them spellbound. Indeed, Cheung, an airline reservation clerk turned radio singing contest winner, realized sales of 200,000 units from his debut recording alone. In the late 1980s, when he diverged into a film career, Cheung's popularity surged to a level never before achieved in the modern pop culture of Asia. *Kiss and Goodbye,* his Mandarin-language album of 1993, sold three million copies by the end of the calendar year and achieved a sales mark of four million units sold by 1996. The perpetual endurance of his market presence, a rare quality among Asian pop stars, added further luster to the glow of his rising star.

A charismatic crooner, Cheung records in Mandarin, Cantonese, and English. He was born Zhang Xue-You You (Cantonese pronunciation Cheung Hok-Yao) on July 10, 1961, in what was then British-dominated Hong Kong. He was the son of a seaman and grew up in less than opulent surroundings. A small one-room apartment served as a residence not only for Cheung, his parents, and two siblings, but also for handfuls of relatives who passed through on an intermittent basis. Surprisingly, these disheartening domestic conditions failed to dampen Cheung's passion for music, which surfaced early in his childhood. When he was very young, he enjoyed the music of the region, favoring such stars as Kit Kwan and Alan Tam. Cheung's musical interests broadened as he entered his teens, and in high school, he developed a preference for rock and roll, especially for the Beatles. He also reserved a fondness for the mellower crooning styles of pop songwriter Barry Manilow. With a natural bent for singing and with an excess of personal charm, it was no surprise that Cheung became a singer at a karaoke-style bar.

After a time, Cheung settled into a position as a Cathay Pacific Airlines clerk in the mid 1980s. It was in that capacity that he took first prize in the 18th District Singing Competition in his home territory. The contest, sponsored by a local radio station, offered a lucrative prize of a contract offer with PolyGram Records and attracted a field of 10,000 competitors. The contest win by Cheung proved to be as much of an asset for PolyGram as it did for Cheung, whose debut album scored platinum status and won the Golden Song Award from Radio Television Hong Kong (RTHK) in 1987. He established a fan base with little effort, and sales of his records soared into the millions of copies, an unusual feat in Asian music markets.

By 1990, to the dismay of recording executives, Cheung focused his energies increasingly on a budding movie career. He collected a following of fans through his film work as adeptly as he had charmed the public with his singing style. Cheung, as he detoured from so-called Cantopop music into Chinese cinema, earned a Golden Horse Award for his supporting role as a wayward street denizen named Fly in Wong Kar Wai's *As Tears Go By.*

In all, Cheung has appeared in over 50 films, including the popular three-part epic, *Chinese Ghost Story Trilogy,* beginning in 1987. Cheung appeared in each of the three segments of the trilogy, first in the role of a Taoist monk called Autumn in the first two parts, and as a transient named Yin in the final sequence, which took place one hundred years after *Part I* and *Part II.* The story, according to the *San Francisco Chronicle*'s Michael Snyder, was "entertaining as hell ... like a cross between *Pretty Woman* and *Ghost Story.*" In 1990 Cheung appeared in *Curry and Pepper* and also in John Woo's *Bullet in the Head* that year. Woo's *Bullet,* in which Cheung co-starred with Tony Leung and Waise Lee, was described as "powerful, dynamic ... an epic adventure ...," by Kevin Thomas in the *Los Angeles Times.* In 1991 Cheung was seen in *Chinese Legend,* followed by *Once Upon a Time in China* and *Wicked City* in 1992. He appeared in the role of a swordsman named Hong Qi in Wong Kar Wai's well-received movie *Ashes of Time* in 1994.

In the mid 1990s Cheung abandoned acting to refocus on his singing career at the urging of his manager, Michael Au. Cheung's subsequent release, *Uncontrollable Passion,* collected a series of awards largely as a

For the Record . . .

Born Zhang Xue-You on July 10, 1961, in Hong Kong; married to May Law Mei-Mei.

Signed with PolyGram Records after winning a radio-sponsored talent contest, mid 1980s; has appeared in more than 50 motion pictures, 1988—; has released more than 40 albums and sold more than 25 million records.

Awards: Golden Song Award, Radio Television Hong Kong (RTHK), 1987; Golden Horse Award (for film acting), 1988.

Addresses: Record company—Universal Music Group, 825 8th Ave., New York City, NY 10019, (212) 333-8000.

result of the hit song, "Love You a Bit More Each Day." Andrew Tanzer of *Forbes* acknowledged Cheung as the top Chinese pop star in a discussion of the Chinese entertainment industry and cited sales of three million copies for *Kiss and Goodbye,* Cheung's highly popular Mandarin-language release. Tanzer suggested further that due to excessive levels of bootleg recordings in China, sales of illegal Cheung recordings accounted for an estimated ten million additional sales units. Cheung's undisputed popularity in China and throughout Asia moved into worldwide markets. With concert tickets selling at premium prices, he expanded his tour itineraries. At the Brisbane (Australia) Convention Center on September 16, 1995, tickets for a Jacky Cheung concert sold for $148 apiece, far more than for other popular singers. Likewise, at Toronto, Ontario's Air Canada Center in 1999, spectators paid as much as $168.50 to hear Cheung sing a program of 32 songs, backed by an 18-piece instrumental ensemble and six backup singers. Cheung by that time was a seasoned professional with more than three dozen albums to his credit.

Cheung was among the featured performers at a gala celebration hosted by the Chinese government when the colony of Hong Kong reverted to Chinese control on July 1, 1997. In anticipation of the historic celebration, *Time International* named him among the "25 Most Influential People in the New Hong Kong." At that time, Cheung was recognized as the most popular Chinese singer in the world, based on record sales worldwide. According to *Time*, he was "an odd, unlikely heartthrob … [the performer with] the least fanatical supporters. But he has more of them than anyone else." That year he undertook a new career project as a theatrical producer and brought a musical stage play to China entitled *Swan Wolf Lake.* It was the first production of its kind in China and starred Sandy Lam as Swan, opposite Cheung as Wolf.

Cheung released his first English-language album, *Touch of Love,* a PolyGram import, in 2000. He is married to his manager, the former actress May Law Mei-Mei.

Selected discography

Smile, PolyGram, 1985.
Jacky, PolyGram, 1987.
Forget About Him, PolyGram, 1993.
Kiss and Goodbye, PolyGram, 1993.
This Winter Is Not Very Cold, PolyGram, 1995.
Having Friends, PolyGram, 1995.
Wanna Hang with You in the Wind, PolyGram, 1996.
Release Yourself, PolyGram, 1998.
Jacky Cheung's Greatest Hits, PolyGram, 1998.
Best of Jacky Cheung, PolyGram, 1999.
Riding 1999, Universal, 2000.
First Fifteen Years, PolyGram, 2000.
Touch of Love, PolyGram, 2000.

Sources

Periodicals

Courier-Mail (Brisbane, Australia), August 26, 1995, p. 11.
Forbes, December 20, 1993, p. 78.
Los Angeles Times, September 28, 1990, p. 6; October 4, 1991, p. 6; December 13, 1993, p. 2.
Time International, June 23, 1997, p. 22.
San Francisco Chronicle, August 29, 1991, p. E3.
Toronto Star, April 2, 1999.

Online

All Music Guide, http://www.allmusic.com (June 6, 2001).
"All About Jacky Cheung," NBCi.com, http://members.nbci.com/dnk2311/starsinfo/jacky/jackyinfo.html (May 14, 2001).
"Jacky Cheung Heaven," Yahoo! GeoCities, http://www.geocities.com/Tokyo/Towers/2252/jacky12.htm (May 14, 2001).

—*Gloria Cooksey*

Jesse Cook

Guitarist

After 16 years of musical training, classical guitarist Jesse Cook established a serious musical career in composition and production, seemingly incognizant of his own talent for performance. A gifted instrumentalist, Cook's ability as a performer came to widespread public attention in the mid 1990s and only because a cable television company played his recordings as piped in background music for the television channel guide. Accordingly, he released his first album literally by popular demand and in response to the myriad call-in requests from television viewers who enjoyed the background sounds on the channel guide. The album debuted at number 14 on the *Billboard* New Age chart. By 2000, Cook's performances regularly drew sell out crowds, and his recordings sold quickly to an eager public. In 2001, three of his four albums had attained gold certification in his native Canada.

Cook was born in Paris, France, in 1969. He spent his early childhood in Southern France and in assorted Spanish locales with his filmmaker father and his mother, who was a writer. The family returned home to Canada and settled in Toronto before Cook started school. Cook, who was drawn to his toy guitar as a toddler, was enrolled at the Eli Kassner Guitar Academy at age six. The prestigious school was only the beginning of a 16-year progression of formal musical education, with the exception of a brief adolescent detour at age 13 when Cook allowed a typical boyhood fervor for basketball to overshadow his musical aspiration. From the Kassner Academy, Cook went on to study at Toronto's Royal Conservatory of Music. He then went to the United States where he studied at the Berklee College of Music in Boston, Massachusetts, and at New York University.

Cook enhanced his formal music training with ten-hour practice sessions, and he returned to Europe where he traveled throughout Spain and studied informally with the masters of flamenco guitar. In the process, he honed his art and earned respect as an artist. It was during his European jaunt that he recaptured the artistic inspiration of his childhood after revisiting the centers of art and culture in France. In Spain he sought tutorial guidance from guitarists in Cordoba, Granada, and Madrid, and was mentored by the Gypsy Kings, whose artistry in rumba flamenco music is considered legendary.

Despite the exotic backdrop and the sophistication of his musical training, Cook remained modest in his expectations as a musician and harbored only a slight dream of realizing a career in performance. His love for the art of guitar playing drove him to continue to play his music even as he developed a serious career as a composer and as a producer working for media and theater groups in Toronto. In the course of his work, he became involved with many musical genres beyond the limits of his classical training, including rap and pop. In 1994, a Canadian cable television company employed the syncopated sounds of his rumba flamenco guitar music as a background soundtrack on the television guide channel, and the music attracted the attention of the viewing public. By popular request, Cook produced and distributed independently a debut album called *Tempest*. Soon afterward Narada Records, impressed by the critical approval and overall popularity of the album, proposed a lucrative multi-album contract deal to the unassuming Cook.

As part of the Narada deal, the record label snatched up re-release rights to *Tempest,* which settled into the *Billboard* New Age chart for 49 weeks in succession, following an impressive chart debut in fourteenth place. The international gusto of Cook's music quickly brought him recognition at the forefront of the New Age music scene as his recordings surfaced repeatedly at the top of the charts. His follow-up album, *Gravity,* entered the *Billboard* New Age chart at number nine immediately upon its release in 1996. Cook's recordings by that time had found an audience in Europe where the Spaniards enjoyed his records and used them as musak (piped-in music) in cafés and elsewhere.

Cook's collaborations with Stanley "Buckwheat" Dural along with jazzy vocals by Holly Cole served to enhance his *Vertigo* album in 1998. *Playgirl* dubbed the recording a "sassy mix of acoustic guitar and accordions," and the album inspired Cook's Vertigo Tour of 2000. The tour brought him to venues throughout North America, including the Newport Beach Jazz Festival in

For the Record . . .

Born in 1969 in Paris, France. *Education*: Eli Kassner Guitar Academy; Royal Conservatory of Music, Toronto, Ontario, Canada; New York University; Berklee College of Music, Boston, MA.

Composer and musical arranger for Canadian television, early 1990s; debut album, *Tempest*, self-produced, 1995; signed with Narada Records, 1995; appeared at Montreal Jazz Festival and Catalina Jazz Festival, 1996; Newport Beach Jazz Festival, 2000; Jazz City Fest, Edmonton, Alberta, Canada, 1999; Saskatchewan Jazz Festival, 1999, 2001; Ottawa Folk Festival, 2000; North American tour, 2000.

Awards: Juno Award (Canada), Best Instrumental Album for *Free Fall*, 2001.

Addresses: *Record company*—Virgin Music Canada, 3110 American Drive Mississauga, ON L4V 1A9 Canada, fax: (905) 677-9565. *Website*—Jesse Cook Official Website: http://www.jessecook.com.

California and San Francisco's Great American Music Hall. During the course of his travels, he appeared on a number of occasions with a young vocal prodigy, soprano Charlotte Church. Among their many shared venues were Manhattan's Avery Fisher Music Hall and Boston's Wang Center. On the Vertigo Tour, Cook played to sell-out concerts in Ottawa and in Kitchener, Ontario, and Montreal, Quebec. The *London Free Press* acknowledged Cook's concert renditions as a benchmark for performance, yet the guitarist remained reluctant to accept the laurels of a flamenco guitar virtuoso.

Cook appeared at the Canadian Jazz Festival in 1995 as a prelude to his major label debut on Narada. In 1996, he appeared at the Montreal Jazz Festival and the Catalina Jazz Festival in California. In 1999, Cook appeared at Canada's Saskatchewan Jazz Festival and at the Jazz City Fest in Edmonton, Alberta. One year later he appeared on the headline bill at the Ottawa Folk Festival.

In 2000, Cook released his fourth album, *Free Fall*, which debuted at number eight and achieved gold record status (50,000 units sold in Canada) within weeks. The success marked the third gold album release for Cook. A single track from that album, "Fall at Your Feet," soared up the Canadian pop chart to a top ten ranking. *Free Fall* was named Best Instrumental Album at Canada's Juno Awards in 2000. Cook returned to the Saskatchewan Festival in the summer of 2000.

Cook, who recorded *Free Fall* over the course of approximately 18 months at his home studio in Toronto, described himself to the *Calgary Sun*'s David Veitch as a mild mannered and easygoing person who feels dispassionate about most things except for the music. In Toronto, according to Cook, musical inspiration abounds in a unique multicultural atmosphere that characterizes the metropolis, and it is the international flavor of his hometown of Toronto that contributes to the New Age eclecticism that defines his guitar playing. Cook, whose music has been characterized as Spanish flamenco and Cuban rumba, embellishes his trademark sound with touches of African percussion, reggae, zydeco, and pop. The *Calgary Sun*'s Blair S. Watson called Cook a "new exciting hybrid … [a] world beat," and a line in the CD jacket for *Gravity* coined the term RumbaFlamencoWorldBeatJazzPop for Cook's music.

Selected discography

Singles

"Fall at Your Feet," Narada, 2000.

Albums

Tempest, Narada, 1995.
Gravity, Narada, 1996.
Vertigo, Narada, 1998.
Free Fall, Virgin/EMI, 2000.

Sources

Periodicals

Calgary Sun, April 12, 1997; September 18, 1998.
Edmonton Sun, June 30, 1999, p. 44.
Halifax Herald, June 29, 1999.
London Free Press, October 12, 2000, p. C3.
Maclean's, July 17, 1995, p. 44.

Online

"In the Press" (includes press clips from *London Free Press* and *Playgirl*), Jesse Cook Official Website, http://www.jessecook.com (April 19, 2001).

—Gloria Cooksey

Daft Punk

Pop group

Daft Punk's Thomas Bangalter and Guy-Manuel de Homem Christo are longtime friends, but in terms of their public personas, the French duo prefers to keep their identities secret by donning sci-fi costumes and wearing masks to let their music speak for itself—and fans have listened. Daft Punk's debut album *Homework,* "probably the greatest electronic disco record ever made" according an *Entertainment Weekly* critic, has sold more than two million copies, 400,000 of those in the duo's native France.

The duo met at a Paris school as teenagers in 1987 and shared their passion for music, which four years later led to the formation of Darling, an instrumental indie pop band. Joined by Phillipe Zdar, who later created the similar-sounding Cassius, Darling found fleeting fame with a Beach Boys-style tune that was included on a compilation tape released by Stereolab's United Kingdom label, Duophonic. A reviewer for England's *Melody Maker* magazine dubbed Bangalter and Christo "daft punks" after listening to their first single. When Darling disbanded in 1993, Bangalter and Christo began exploring techno and house clubs, along with the rock-based techno of 1980s deejay Andrew Weatherall. Instead of experimenting in an expensive, big-name studio, they purchased recording equipment and, according to the English music newspaper *New Musical Express* (*NME*), "began producing heavy house music based on big hip-hop beats and boasting strange sounds, sirens and guitar-driven samples."

After hearing Daft Punk's music, the Glasgow, Scotland-based Soma Records quickly signed the group and released its debut single "New Wave," called an "acidic mix of beats and basslines" by *NME,* in 1994. The following year, the song "Da Funk" hit BBC Radio 1 airwaves, capturing the attention of breakthrough electronica/trance deejays Chemical Brothers, who played the song during their sets. Three more singles—"Rollin' and Scratchin'," "Indo Silver Club" and "Alive"—followed, and the Chemical Brothers recruited Daft Punk to remix its song "Life is Sweet."

Banking on Daft Punk's future success, Virgin Records inked a deal with the duo in 1996. As a teaser to the first record, Bangalter and Christo offered the track "Musique" to Virgin Records' *Source Lab 2* compilation CD. While recording its debut, Daft Punk spread its musical wings. The duo remixed singer Gabrielle's song "Forget About the World," and rejoined Zdar for regular club appearances at Paris' Respect.

In 1997, Daft Punk released its debut album, *Homework,* on Virgin and started a "U.K. invasion of French club music," according to *NME*. The pre-release hype helped push *Homework* into the top ten in the United Kingdom, but the album was largely ignored in France. In a review for CDNow, Kirsten Terry chalked up the success to Daft Punk's keen sense of humor: "If you're

For the Record . . .

Members include **Thomas Bangalter**; **Guy-Manuel de Homem Christo**.

Group formed in France, c. 1993; signed with Soma Records, 1994; signed with Virgin Records, 1996; released debut album *Homework* on Virgin, 1997; released *Discovery*, 2001.

Addresses: *Record company*—Virgin Records, 138 North Foothill Rd., Beverly Hills, CA 90210; 304 Park Avenue South, 5th Floor, New York, NY 10010. *Website*—Daft Punk Official Website: http://www.daft punk.com.

looking for a real challenge, try to be in a bad mood after listening to a Daft Punk album." Furthering the duo's mysterious identities, Daft Punk did not appear in its videos, instead opting for young directors such as Spike Jonze, Michel Gondry, and Seb Janiak to create the pieces. In April, the single "Around the World" hit radio and clubs and found success in the United States by August of 1997 when it rose to number eight on *Billboard*'s Hot Dance Music/Club Play charts.

Though Daft Punk's popularity has mounted with music fans, the duo found opposition in what they believe are the French government's reactionary policies. "Right now, we've got some friends who are being charged with inciting people to take drugs," Bangalter said in comments included in the group's biography at its website. "They weren't even selling anything. They were just having a party. But in France these days they're saying that having a party is encouraging people to take drugs, booking a DJ is encouraging people to take drugs."

The group spent 1998 creating and releasing the DVD *D.A.F.T.: A Story About Dogs, Androids, Firemen and Tomatoes*, a compilation of six videos from *Homework*, as well as exploring a variety of side projects. The most well known is Bangalter's Stardust which produced the club hit "Music Sounds Better With You" in 1998. For the next two years, the duo worked on its sophomore effort *Discovery*. In an interview with Peter Gaston for CDNow, Bangalter mocked his group's mysterious identity, saying a problem in the studio had turned he and his partner into robots, and therefore, no more masks were required. "In September 1999, we had this small explosion in our studio around the 9/9/99 computer bug where the sampler crashed and there was some accident—and then we just turned out to become

robots. We look like robots, so we don't wear masks anymore."

Discovery proved to be a success even before its release in March of 2001. The first single, "One More Time," which is similar musically to Stardust's "Music Sounds Better With You," was added to pop radio station and nightclub playlists around the United States in November of 2000. The song, which features the vocals of New York house deejay Romanthony, debuted at number one in France, number two in the United Kingdom, and number one on the Eurosingles charts. As with the first album, Daft Punk hired Japanese artist Leiji Matsumoto to design the animated video.

In the same interview with CDNow, Bangalter said that Daft Punk tried to avoid rules about club music as strictly dancefloor or electronic to create a unique mix on *Discovery*: "We wanted to destroy those rules," and find a gap where "there would be maybe a place for electronic music that could have energy, and could mean something different with a lot of emotion and dynamics and energy."

In 2001, Daft Punk decided not to tour in order to concentrate on Daft Club, an interactive website that allows fans who purchase the new record to download technology to read new content and hear remixes. "In order to express ourselves in a much more fun way, and in order for people to read art, listen to music in a more exciting way, because it's not down to just the CD itself," he told CDNow.

Selected discography

Homework (includes "Around the World"), Virgin, 1997.
Discovery (includes "One More Time"), Virgin, 2001.

Sources

Periodicals

Entertainment Weekly, May 23, 1997, p. 64; March 30, 2001, p. 68.

Online

"Daft Punk," *New Musical Express*, http://www.nme.com (May 28, 2001).
"Daft Punk Goes Robotech," CDNow, http://www.cdnow.com (May 28, 2001).

Additional information was provided by Virgin Records publicity materials, 1997 and 2001.

—Christina Fuoco

Vic Damone

Singer

© Jack Vartoogian. Reproduced by permission.

Among the more prominent of the pop-singing crooners of the mid-twentieth century, Vic Damone recorded more than 2,000 songs during an active career that began in 1947 and spanned 54 years. With a lush and mellow baritone, he possessed one of the finest singing voices of his era and was widely acknowledged by critics as one of the best crooner of the times. Even in his later concerts, his voice never faltered nor did it lose its easy tone. Instead, according to critics, the depth of emotion in his singing voice was improved by life experience as he aged. Damone, who announced his retirement in 2000, embarked on a farewell tour that lasted into 2001. With a sold-out concert at Florida's Kravis Center in February of 2001 and his ultimate farewell concert set at Carnegie Hall in May of that year, Damone closed the chapter on one of the most impressive singing careers on record.

Damone was born Vito Farinola on June 12, 1928, in Bensonhurst in Brooklyn, New York, the only son among five siblings. His father, Rocco Farinola, was an electrician; his mother taught piano. Damone quit high school to find work to help support himself and his sisters after a serious industrial accident left his father disabled. Damone, an aspiring singer at age 17, worked as an usher at the Paramount Theater. Because of his open and easy nature he had the good fortune to befriend a string of show-business professionals who helped him along the path to his chosen career. He encountered vocalist Perry Como in an elevator one day and performed a spontaneous audition for Como. Damone's voice spoke for itself, and Como offered referrals along with encouragement. Over time the two developed a lasting friendship. Two years later, on March 8, 1947, Damone landed an opportunity to sing his radio debut, and before long comedian Milton Berle espoused the cause of Damone's career. Berle arranged for Damone to sing "Prisoner of Love" on *Arthur Godfrey's Talent Scouts,* and when Damone won the competition, Berle assisted him in securing a job at a Manhattan nightclub, called La Martinique. Damone signed with Mercury Records and released his early classic, "I Have but One Heart," to a receptive public that same year. He made live appearances at the Copa and at the Paramount and was hired to host a weekly radio program, called *Saturday Night Serenade,* on CBS. It was on the occasion of his first radio appearance on WHN in 1947, that Damone, still known as Vito Farinola, opted to use his mother's maiden name of Damone as a pseudonym.

Damone's work on Mercury Records brought him abundant success during the late 1940s and throughout the 1950s. Among his more popular renditions, he recorded a number of show tunes and a selection of Italian-language folk songs. In 1948 Damone's recording of "Again" sold one million records, and he repeated the feat with "You're Breaking My Heart" in 1949. He performed with prominent popular orchestras, often with bandleader Richard Heyman as well as

For the Record . . .

Born Vito Farinola on June 12, 1928, in Brooklyn, NY; son of Rocco Farinola (an electrician); married Pier Angeli (an actress), divorced; married and divorced two wives; married Diahann Carroll (an actress and singer), 1987, divorced, 1996; married Rena Rowan (a fashion designer), c. 1998; four children, five grandchildren.

Radio debut, March 8, 1947; star of *Saturday Night Serenade*, CBS Radio, 1947; has recorded for Mercury, RCA, Columbia, Capitol, Warner Brothers; film career: *Kismet, Deep in My Heart, Hit the Deck;* farewell tour, 2000-2001.

Awards: Sammy Cahn Lifetime Achievement Award from Songwriters' Hall of Fame, 1997.

Addresses: *Agent*—c/o Rob Wilcox, Wilcox Public Relations, 23734 Valencia Boulevard, Valencia, CA 91335, (661) 260-0810.

Glenn Osser and George Siravo. Damone's warm baritone appealed to film producers and led to a limited career in motion pictures during the 1950s. After a film debut with Jane Powell in *Young, Rich, and Pretty* in 1951, he was seen and heard most notably in the motion picture production of the musical *Kismet* in 1954.

Damone switched labels, to Columbia Records, in the mid 1950s. In 1956 he recorded "On the Street Where You Live," a popular romantic ballad from Lerner & Loewe's hit Broadway musical, *My Fair Lady*. That song by Damone easily worked its way into the top 20 and earned Damone his third gold record and signaled the peak of his career. Soon afterward the rock 'n' roll music craze and the British Liverpool sound invaded America and dominated popular music and the radio airwaves throughout the 1960s. Damone briefly considered adapting his style to accommodate the contemporary fad, but opted instead to shift his venue from the recording studio to the live stage. He cancelled his contract with RCA Victor Records and established a comfortable niche in performing live in clubs and in Las Vegas, where his following of fans never waned. Critics never wearied of complimenting Damone's inherent talent and style, which was completely devoid of gimmicks. He presented instead a repertoire of straightforward and unabashed renditions of easy-listening songs. He never veered from his comfortable singing

range nor did he abandon the comfort and confidence of his relaxed singing style. As David Finkle noted in *Village Voice,* Damone throughout his career retained "... an implicit understanding of precisely how to match swinging musicianship to the emotional truth behind a lyric so that neither obscures the other ... a rare vocal alchemy ..." In an often-publicized remark during Damone's early career, the late singing idol and movie star, Frank Sinatra, paid Damone an exceptional compliment, noting that Damone had, "... the best pipes in the business."

The 1980s witnessed a revival of Damone's recording career, when he signed for a second time with RCA Victor Records. Over the course of the ensuing two decades he expanded his characteristic nightclub repertoire, moving from his old standards and cabaret fare into modern classics, by Irving Berlin, Johnny Mercer, and George and Ira Gershwin. Despite a conservative aura, Damone never stifled the natural amiability of his personality, injecting well-timed winks, ad-libs, and off-the-wall melody inuendos and slight improvisations that successfully breathed freshness into every performance.

Damone's enduring popularity was punctuated on six occasions by performances at the White House, including three performances for President Ronald Reagan during the 1980s. In 1996, as he approached 70 years of age, Damone recorded a popular new album, *Vic Damone Sings the Greatest Love Songs of the Century,* for Q Records. The unconstrained baritone never faded, and as Damone entered his seventies he attracted audiences and retained critical approval. When he embarked on a farewell tour beginning at Long Island's Westbury Music Fair on May 27, 2000, he easily drew sellout crowds. The tour continued for one year, encompassing mainstream venues such as the Kravis Center in West Palm Beach, Florida, in February of 2001 with a final farewell concert set for Carnegie Hall in New York on May 18 of that year. Both "On the Street Where You Live" and "You're Breaking My Heart" had sold more than three million copies by his retirement in 2001.

As the 1990s drew to a close Damone undertook a project to pen his autobiography, called *Singing Was the Easy Part.* According to Damone, the title alludes to sidenotes to his singing career, which included a bout with financial instability and a string of marriages, the first being to the late actress, Pier Angeli, in 1954. He had married twice more by 1984 when he met his fourth wife, singer/actress, Diahann Carroll, whom he divorced in 1996 after four years of marriage and six years of separation.

In the shadow of pending retirement Damone maintained his characteristically active pace both in his professional career and in his private life. He was wed for the fifth time in the late 1990s to designer Rena

Rowan. He is a father of four, including a son, Perry, named after Perry Como. With close family ties to his children and five grandchildren, he moved to Palm Beach County in Florida also in the late 1990s, to be closer to his extended family. Damone, a one-time Catholic, embraced the Baha'i faith during the height of his popularity in the 1960s. He is a part-time inventor of practical gadgets to improve the quality of life, and he likes to golf.

In 1997 he returned to his alma mater, Lafayette High School in Brooklyn, where he completed the necessary schoolwork to earn his long abandoned high school diploma. He graduated proudly from high school at age 68 and was honored to present an address to the student body at the commencement exercise that year. Also that year he was the honored recipient of the Sammy Cahn Lifetime Achievement Award at the Songwriters Hall of Fame annual awards presentation on June 10 in New York City.

Selected discography

Vic Damone, Mercury, 1950.
Rich, Young and Pretty (soundtrack), MGM, 1951.
Christmas Favorites, Mercury, 1951.
Take Me in Your Arms, Mercury, 1952.
Vocals by Vic, Mercury, 1952.
April in Paris, Mercury, 1952.
Athena (soundtrack), Mercury, 1954.
Deep in My Heart (soundtrack), MGM, 1955.
The Stingiest Man in Town (soundtrack), Columbia, 1956.
That Towering Feeling! Columbia, 1956.
The Voice of Vic Damone, Mercury, 1956.
Yours for a Song, Mercury, 1957.
Affair to Remember, Epic, 1957.
The Gift of Love (soundtrack), Columbia, 1958.
Angela Mia, Columbia, 1959.
Closer Than a Kiss, Columbia, 1959.
This Game of Love, Columbia, 1959.

On the Swingin' Side, Columbia, 1961.
Linger Awhile with Vic Damone, Capitol, 1962.
The Lively Ones, Capitol, 1962.
Strange Enchantment, Capitol, 1962.
The Liveliest, Capitol, 1963.
My Baby Loves to Swing, Capitol, 1963.
On the Street Where You Live, Sony, 1964.
You Were Only Fooling, Warner, 1965.
Arrivederci Baby (soundtrack), RCA Victor, 1966.
Why Can't I Walk Away, RCA Victor, 1968.
Stay with Me, RCA Victor, 1976.
Make Someone Happy, Vianda, 1981.
On the South Side of Chicago, RCA Victor, 1984.
Damone Type of Thing, RCA Victor, 1984.
Christmas with Vic Damone, RCA Victor, 1984.
Greatest Love Songs of the Century, Q Records, 1997.

Sources

Periodicals

AP Online, April 17, 2000; June 27, 2000.
Billboard, June 14, 1997, p. 35.
Fox News Transcripts, May 18, 2000.
Palm Beach Post, February 4, 2000, p. 1E; May 26, 2000, p. 1E; February 11, 2001, p. 1B; February 13, 2001, p. 1D.
Record (Bergen County, NJ), June 29, 2000, p. H10.
Village Voice, September 12, 1995, p. 45; January 27, 1998, p. 4; February 10, 1998, p. 116.

Online

"Vic Damone," GetMusic, http://www.getmusic.com/AMG?artist=12681 (May 31, 2001).
"Vic Damone reminisces about his beginnings," *Jam Music*, March 5, 1997, http://www.sunmedia.ca/JamMusic ArtistsD /damone_vic.html (March 29, 2001).
"Vic Damone," Len Triola Promotional Services, http://www.lentriola.com/damone.htm (March 29, 2001).

—Gloria Cooksey

Delirious?

Formed as part of a Christian youth outreach program at a church in Littlehampton, England, in 1992, Delirious? has delivered some of the most innovative Contemporary Christian music. Whereas most faith-oriented artists have remained firmly within the traditional confines of gospel, country, or easy listening, Delirious? has used sparkling, guitar-based Britpop arrangements similar to Travis and Oasis in its music. The band even scored a top 20 hit in Britain with its single "Deeper" in 1997, a rare crossover success for a Christian group. While some in the Christian music community have deemed the band too pop-oriented because of its success with a more secular audience, Delirious? has nonetheless remained committed to emphasizing the messages of faith and salvation through Christ in each of its releases. Now as popular in the United States as in England, Delirious? could be described as the cutting edge of Christian music.

Delirious? had its origins as the Cutting Edge Band, part of a monthly youth program of the Arum Community Church in Littlehampton, a town located halfway between Brighton and Portsmouth on the English Channel. The group was led by singer and guitarist Martin Smith, who worked as an engineer and producer at a recording studio along with Tim Jupp, who contributed keyboards. Working with graphic designer and percussionist Stewart Smith, the group put on monthly shows at the church. Shortly after its formation in 1992, the group was joined by Stu Garrard as lead guitarist and Jonson Thatcher, son of one of the

church's elders, as bassist. Continuing with their regular jobs, the Cutting Edge Band recorded a series of mini-albums, which the group released on cassettes on its own Furious? label. Hesitant to give up the security of each member's day job, the band performed gigs around England on the weekends.

In 1996, however, a serious car accident that injured Martin Smith, his wife, and Thatcher caused the group to rethink its commitment to a career in music. Deciding to take the risk of devoting themselves full-time to music, the members took on a new name, Delirious?, a name demonstrating their awe of Christ's power in their lives. The question mark, as Garrard told *Campus Life* magazine in January of 1999, was added simply for "a bit of fun, really…. What we are trying to do is stay out of the box. We don't want to be predictable. We don't want to be labeled. We want to be free to be who we are." True to this spirit, Delirious? quickly showed its willingness to ignore the long-standing barrier between faith-oriented music and contemporary, innovative musical arrangements. Claiming U2, the Verve, and the Manic Street Preachers as influences, the band also gained a reputation for its live shows as well as its hook-laden songs.

Putting out a concert album, *Live and In the Can* on its Furious? label in 1996, the band soon delivered its first full-length studio album with *King of Fools* in 1998. Surprisingly, a single from *King of Fools,* "Deeper," entered the British top 20 in 1997, a testament to the band's growing popularity as a live act as well as to the song's own catchy chorus and glittering guitar riffs. Considering the song's topic of following Christ and the band's forthright statements about its religious beliefs, Delirious? became a band that was newsworthy not only for its music, but its mission as well. "We are trying to influence people who have never been to a church. We hope Delirious? can be used to help point people to God," Martin Smith told *Campus Life.* "We feel that what really points people to God is not a particular style of music, but the Spirit of God working through what we do, and through how we live."

Based on the success of "Deeper," Delirious? was signed to EMI Records, which released the compilation *The Cutting Edge* of the band's early work. The band also secured deals with Sparrow Records to distribute its work in the Christian music market in the United States and with Virgin Records to work the secular market on its behalf. The group's next release, *Mezzamorphis,* reflected this appeal to a wide audience. Citing its "expansive guitar-pop and rich, hummable—occasionally anthemic—melodies," *Q* magazine predicted that "*Mezzamorphis* will be the album that makes [the group]." A success with reviewers and audiences, the album also marked an ambiguous phase for the band. The title Mezzamorphis itself was a play on the group's "metamorphosis" into a popular

For the Record . . .

Members include **Stuart Garrard** (born on June 7, 1963, in Ipswich, England), lead guitar, backing vocals; **Tim Jupp** (born on May 1, 1966, in Eastbourne, England), piano, keyboards; **Martin Smith** (born on June 7, 1970, in Woodford Green, England), vocals, guitar; **Stewart Smith** (born on January 21, 1967, in Shoreham-by-Sea, England), percussion; **Jon Thatcher** (born on January 7, 1976, in Rustington, England), bass.

Initially formed as the Cutting Edge Band in Littlehampton, England, 1992; released four mini-albums and toured England; pursued full-time career in Christian music as Delirious?, *Live and In the Can* released on the band's Furious? label, 1996; *King of Fools* released, band signed to EMI Records, 1998; signed contract with Virgin Records for American distribution in the secular market and Sparrow Records in the Christian music market, released *Mezzamorphis*, 1999; *Glo* released on Sparrow Records, 2000; toured as opening act for Bon Jovi on British tour, 2001.

Addresses: *Record company*—Furious? Records, P.O. Box 40, Arundel, West Sussex, BN18 0UQ, U.K., website: http://www.furiousrecords.co.uk; Sparrow Label Group, P.O. Box 5010, Brentwood, TN 37024-5010, website: http://www.sparrowrecords.com; Virgin Records, 338 North Foothill Road, Beverly Hills, CA 90210, website: http://www.virginrecords.com. *Website*—Delirious? Official Website: http://www.delirious.co.uk.

act as well as its feeling of being on a "mezzanine" level as it climbed to higher levels of success.

The 2000 release *Glo* reaffirmed the band's position as one of the most innovative Christian music groups while further expanding its reputation with secular audiences. "We've been on a journey," Garrard told the Jesus Freak Hideout website. "We still have a vision to impact the mainstream music world, but we were feeling like it was time again for us to sing songs about how good God is and how good Jesus is. Consequently, *Glo* is a lot more corporate and congregational in nature than some of our past records." Indeed, tracks like "God You Are My God" and "My Glorious"

made effective use of a choir in their arrangements, and the album received a review in *Billboard* upon its October of 2000 release which called it "another collection of well-written songs that display a joyful abandon." The *Los Angeles Times* echoed this sentiment in a concert review that same month which highlighted the band's "rousing, catchy melodies" and connection with the audience.

Through its extensive touring schedule and string of successful releases, Delirious? has become a leading British group on the international Christian music scene. As the opening act for the Bon Jovi 2001 British tour, however, Delirious? once again courted charges that it had gone too far in embracing mainstream success. From the lyrical content of its songs and the public statements of its members, however, it was clear that the band had remained committed to its original mission. "We don't ever want to be seen as better than anyone we play for," Garrard told *Campus Life*. "We believe we are on a journey with our audience. It's a journey that hopefully will lead all of us closer to God, and will help us worship Him better."

Selected discography

Live and In the Can, Furious?, 1996.
The Cutting Edge, Sparrow, 1997.
King of Fools, Sparrow, 1998.
d:tour 1997 Live, Furious?, 1998.
Mezzamorphis, Virgin, 1999.
(Contributor) *Wow 1999,* Word Entertainment/EMI Christian Music Group, 1999.
(Contributor) *Streams,* Word Entertainment/Sony Entertainment, 1999.
Glo, Sparrow, 2000.

Sources

Periodicals

Billboard, October 28, 2000; December 30, 2000.
Campus Life, January/February 1999; January/February 2001.
Los Angeles Times, October 17, 2000.
Q, June 1999.
Today's Christian Woman, November/December 2000.

Online

All Music Guide, http://www.allmusic.com (April 24, 2001).
Delirious? Official Website, http://www.delirious.co.uk (April 24, 2001).
Jesus Freak Hideout, http://www.jesusfreakhideout.com (April 24, 2001).

—Timothy Borden

Destiny's Child

Pop group

Like the female vocal group with whom it's often compared, the Supremes, Destiny's Child has experienced volatile shifts in its lineup while earning and retaining tremendous popularity for the group's blending of musical styles, social commentary, physical beauty, and fashion statements. Initially a quartet comprised of Houston, Texas, natives Beyoncé Knowles, LaToya Luckett, Kelly Rowland, and LaTavia Roberson, Destiny's Child began in the early 1990s as a group of preteen women singing rhythm-and-blues, gospel, and hip-hop harmonies in such acts as Something Fresh, Cliché, the Dolls, and Destiny, before becoming Destiny's Child in 1995. Knowles' father, Mathew, became the group's manager. Tina Knowles, Mathew's wife and Beyoncé's mother, became the group's stylist. The Knowleses met Rowland when she belonged to one of the musical groups that Beyoncé was a member of as a preteen. Rowland's mother, Doris Lovett, was a nanny who often lived in other families' homes and brought her daughter along. She wanted a more stable home for Rowland, so the Knowleses took her in when she was nine years old.

The group began to attract a loyal local following performing around the Houston area. The women

Photograph by Kevorak Djansezian. AP/Wide World Photos. Reproduced by permission.

Members include **Farrah Franklin** (joined group, 2000; left group, 2000); **Beyoncé Knowles** (daughter of Mathew and Tina Knowles); **LaToya Luckett** (left group, 1999); **LaTavia Roberson** (left group, 1999); **Kelly Rowland** (born Kelendria Rowland; daughter of Doris Lovett); **Michelle Williams** (joined group, 2000).

Group formed in Houston, TX, c. 1990; signed with Columbia Records, 1996; contributed to *Men in Black* film soundtrack, 1997; released *Destiny's Child,* 1998; contributed to *Why Do Fools Fall in Love?* and *Life* soundtracks, released *The Writing's on the Wall,* 1999; contributed to *Romeo Must Die* and *Charlie's Angels* soundtracks, 2000; released *Survivor,* 2001.

Awards: Best R&B Soul Single (Group), "Say My Name" and Best R&B Soul Album of the Year (Group), *The Writing's on the Wall,* 6th Annual Soul Train Lady of Soul Awards; NAACP Image Award, Outstanding Duo or Group, *The Writing's on the Wall,* 2000; Hot 100 Singles Artist Of The Year and Hot 100 Singles Duo/ Group Of The Year, *Billboard* Music Awards, 2000; Favorite Band, Duo or Group (Soul/Rhythm & Blues Music) Award, American Music Awards, 2001; Grammy Award, Best R&B Song for "Say My Name", 2000; Grammy Award, Best R&B Performance By A Duo Or Group for "Say My Name", 2000; U.S. platinum certification for *The Writing's on the Wall,* 2000; Sammy Davis, Jr. Award for Entertainer Of The Year, Soul Train Awards, 2001.

Addresses: *Record company*—Columbia Records, 550 Madison Avenue, New York, NY 10022-3211. *Management*—Mathew Knowles, Houston, TX. *Website*—Destiny's Child Official Website: http://www.destinyschild.com.

gained prominence from an appearance on the television show *Star Search* when they were ten- and eleven-year-olds. Although they did not win, the appearance won them opening stints for such acts as Dru Hill and Immature. Signed to Columbia Records in 1996, the quartet released the song "Killing Time" on the soundtrack for the film *Men in Black,* which was released in 1997. The song also appears on the group's self-titled debut release, which features their first hit single, "No, No, No," produced by Wyclef Jean. Similarly, the group recorded the Timbaland-produced "Get on the Bus" for the *Why Do Fools Fall in Love?* film soundtrack. The song became one of the group's biggest European hits. In Europe, they headlined to sold-out arenas, at one point performing 18 shows in 17 days.

Found Breakthrough Success

The group toured extensively throughout 1998 to promote *Destiny's Child,* supporting such acts as Boyz II Men, K-Ci & Jo Jo, and Uncle Sam. But their breakthrough success came after the group's 1999 release, *The Writing's on the Wall.* Debuting at number six on the *Billboard* 200 album chart, the group's sophomore effort sold more than nine million copies worldwide. For the remainder of 1999, Destiny's Child enjoyed sales and chart success. Nine months after its release, the album advanced to number five on the *Billboard* 200 album chart, and the song "Bills, Bills, Bills" spent nine weeks as the number one single on the *Billboard* singles chart. Featuring production and writing contributions from Rodney Jenkins and Kevin "She'kspere" Briggs, the latter who performed similar duties for TLC's hit single, "No Scrubs," *The Writing's on the Wall* generated three top ten hits on the *Billboard* R&B singles chart. Two other singles from *The Writing's on the Wall,* "Jumpin Jumpin" and "Say My Name," became radio staples, topping the Hot 100 and the R&B singles charts. The song "Say My Name," *Rolling Stone* critic Rob Sheffield noted, "was a hypnotic loop of sex and dread, twitching with unbearable lust while the lyrics spilled near-psychotic paranoia, and the whole song simmered until you didn't think you'd ever get out of it alive—no wonder Elvis Costello was a fan." The group also guest-starred on the television situation comedy *The Smart Guy.* The success of their first two efforts resulted in Destiny's Child being awarded a total of 13 gold, platinum, and multiplatinum certifications from the Recording Industry Association of America for "No, No, No" (gold, platinum), *Destiny's Child* (gold, platinum), "Bills, Bills, Bills" (gold), "Say My Name" (gold) and *The Writing's on the Wall* (gold, six-times platinum).

In March of 2000, however, Destiny's Child was wracked with personnel shifts that sometimes caused journalists and listeners to focus on the group's lineup more than their music. Mathew Knowles was considered by Roberson and Luckett to be more concerned with advancing his daughter's career than in the group's future. When the pair reached the age of 18, they exercised their legal right to acquire new management, which resulted in their dismissal from the group. Luckett told *Teen People* that she knew she and Roberson were no longer in the group when she heard that the "Say My Name" video was filmed without their participation. Luckett and Roberson filed suit against Destiny's Child, claiming a breach in the group's partnership agreement. The suit was settled for an undisclosed amount, and Luckett and Roberson subsequently formed another group, Angel. Knowles and Rowland, on the other hand, drafted Michelle Williams and Farrah Franklin the following February to replace Luckett and Roberson. Williams, who had previously sung backup with R&B singer Monica, debuted with Destiny's Child in the "Say My Name" video. Franklin had danced in the group's "Bills, Bills, Bills" video. Within five months, however, Franklin also was out of the group. She had reportedly missed several live performances with the group, which is known for their dedication to long, arduous work schedules. Franklin told *Teen People*: "I never quit Destiny's Child. I actually found out that I was no longer in the group on MTV. No one contacted me and told me that I was out of Destiny's Child." Knowles countered: "It wasn't a management decision; it was a group decision." The group decided to go forward as a trio comprised of Knowles, Rowland, and Williams.

Despite the controversies of the revolving lineup, Destiny's Child continued to promote *The Writing's on the Wall* throughout 2000, touring as a supporting act for Christina Aguilera's summer tour and appearing on the *VH1 Divas 2000 Tribute to Diana Ross*. The trio also recorded "Independent Women, Part I" which appeared on the film soundtrack of *Charlie's Angels*. The song became one of the act's biggest hits, garnering extensive airplay well after the film left theater screens.

New Focus as Trio

Co-opting the title of the Genesis album *And Then There Were Three* (named after the departures of several founding members in the mid 1970s, including lead vocalist Peter Gabriel), the press focused on Destiny's Child's new status as a trio. The threesome performed at the inauguration ceremony for fellow Texan George W. Bush in January of 2001. In the meantime, nearly nonstop touring combined with immense radio and video airplay kept the group's name and faces familiar with music fans. The youth and physical attractiveness of its remaining members also made the group mainstays of youthful fashion and lifestyle magazines. In May of 2001, Destiny's Child released their third full-length musical recording, *Survivor*, to speculation that the recording's title referred to the CBS television series where contestants competing in a remote location vote off other contestants until only one "survivor" remains. *Rolling Stone*'s Jancee Dunn wrote that the album's title was "named after Beyoncé heard a radio DJ chortling that Destiny's Child was just like the TV show." "The lyrics to the single 'Survivor' are Destiny's Child's story, because we've been through a lot," Knowles told Dunn. "We went

through a lot of drama with the members, and everybody was like, 'Oh, well, no more Destiny's Child.' Well, we sold even more records after all the changes. Any complications we've had in our ten-year period of time have made us closer and tighter and better."

Acknowledging its three-woman lineup, *Survivor* features a song entitled "DC-3," which is how the remaining members refer to the group. As if to emphasize the trio's solidarity and downplay rumors that Knowles was preparing for a solo career, the album also features lead vocals performed by all three remaining members. These songs include light-hearted excursions into accepting aspects of an individual's physique, such as "Bootylicious," a song Williams told Dunn is about "If you've got a big booty, then it's OK." "Apple Pie a la Mode" is a female appreciation of a physically attractive young man. On a more serious note, *Survivor* includes a song, "Story of Beauty," that advises the victim of childhood sexual abuse that she is not at fault and can go on with her life. The trio's acknowledged Christian faith is confirmed by the album's inclusion of "Gospel Medley."

Survivors of Personnel Turmoil

Detroit Free Press music critic Kelley L. Carter noted that *Survivor* makes numerous references to the lineup changes: "The title track chronicles the turmoil, struggle and eventual success the group had [in 2000].... The wise listener will easily notice that the lyrics of several of the songs, including 'Happy Face,' 'Fancy,' and 'Gospel Medley,' focus on that DC-3 talent shake-up of 2000. Founding members Knowles and Kelly Rowland have said they felt as if they came out of a bad ten-year marriage." Carter concluded: "It's still music that you can shake to and throw your hands up with." *Rolling Stone* critic Sheffield concurred: "But nobody would care about the backstage drama if the music didn't rock, and as *Survivor* proves, Destiny's Child are the great pop group of the moment, ruling the radio with fluid R&B harmonies, exotic techno beats and more floss than the American Dental Association." Co-production responsibilities for *Survivor* were handled by Beyoncé Knowles, who appropriated the Bee Gee-written, Samantha Sang disco hit "Emotion" and the guitar lead from the Stevie Nicks song "Edge of Seventeen." The recording features another version of the group's hit, "Independent Women, Part I" from *Charlie's Angels*, the new version entitled "Independent Women, Part II." In May of 2001, Knowles also debuted as the lead character in *MTV's Hip Hopera: Carmen*, based on Bizet's opera *Carmen*. Destiny's Child also confirmed their stature as a popular culture phenomenon when *Rolling Stone* magazine selected the group to adorn their May 2001 cover. The group also released a DVD, *The Platinum's on the Wall*, in 2001, featuring six music videos. *Revolver* critic Cheryl Tan acknowledged that all of the videos could have been taped from television and faulted the release for failing to provide live footage, biographical documentary, "or at least one juicy behind-the-scenes morsel."

Plans are under way for the members of Destiny's Child to release solo albums. Knowles told *Teen People,* "We sat down and agreed on what would be best for Destiny's Child, which is to [release the works] all at the same time." Besides her solo album, Knowles planned to write and produce for other musicians.

Selected discography

(Contributor) *Men in Black* (soundtrack), Sony/Columbia, 1997.
Destiny's Child, Columbia, 1998.
(Contributor) *Why Do Fools Fall in Love?* (soundtrack), Elektra, 1998.
The Writing's on the Wall, Columbia, 1999.
(Contributor) *Life* (soundtrack), Interscope, 1999.
(Contributor) *Romeo Must Die* (soundtrack), EMD/Virgin, 2000.
(Contributor) *Charlie's Angels* (soundtrack), Sony/Columbia, 2000.
Survivor, Columbia, 2001.

Sources

Detroit Free Press, April 29, 2001, p. 5G.
Revolver, May/June 2001, p. 118.
Rolling Stone, May 10, 2001, p. 83; May 24, 2001, p. 52.
Teen People, October 2000, p. 120.

—*Bruce Walker*

The Donnas

Rock/pop group

While still in middle school, the Donnas, an all-female quartet from Palo Alto, California, were already living out their rock 'n' roll dreams playing Ramones-styled punk rock music. Although they have grown up a bit since the release of their acclaimed 1998 album *American Teenage Rock 'n' Roll Machine,* released when the girls were seniors in high school, the Donnas—made up of vocalist Brett Anderson (Donna A), drummer Torry Castellano (Donna C), bassist Maya Ford (Donna F), and guitarist Allison Robertson (Donna R)—con- tinued to create loud, fast, and fun rock songs.

The history of the Donnas dates back to the early 1990s when Anderson, Castellano, Ford, and Robertson were eighth graders at Palo Alto's Jordan Middle School. In junior high, with the emergence of groups such as Nirvana and Green Day, many of the girls' peers were inspired to form bands themselves. Supportive of such aspirations, the school allowed students during lunchtime the opportunity to perform before one another, except, as Ford and Robertson quickly observed, only boys were taking to the stage. Consequently, the pair recruited Anderson and Castellano, adopted the band name Ragady Ann, and practiced in the Castellano family garage every day for about a month to prepare for their first school show. Starting out, the girls learned to play songs by other female groups, specifically the Muffs' "Big Mouth," L7's "American Society," and Shonen Knife's "Ride the Rocket." None of the girls had prior experience playing their instruments or singing, but they all shared an enthusiasm for music.

Not many of their classmates reacted favorably to the all-girl band. The boys especially felt that Ragady Ann was interfering where they didn't belong, and the girls at school seemed to agree. "When we first started, it was a cool thing for all the guys to be in the bands," recalled Castellano to Emma Johnston in *Melody Maker.* "If you were a really cool girl, you were invited to come and watch the practice in the garage. I think a lot of the girls saw us and said, 'Oh, those guys are really mean to those girls, but I don't want to be part of anything that they're doing 'cause then the guys won't give me attention.' I think they were happy just to be fans."

Regardless of what other kids thought, the four young girls continued to play cover tunes by their favorite groups and soon caught the attention of a local promoter named Mark Weiss, who gave the band one of their earliest professional gigs. "They were really good, and yet I wasn't sure if they knew what they were doing," he commented to Michael Ansaldo for a Donnas cover in *BAM* (*Bay Area Music*) magazine. "They were kind of trying to act like adults, or trying to act like rock stars, trying to act like people they saw on MTV. They weren't faking anything; they were just being themselves. They were unconscious of how good they were…. It was rare to see such young people kicking a** like that."

While attending Palo Alto High School, the group embraced harder rock bands like Kiss, AC/DC, Metallica, and Motley Crue, as well as R.E.M. and XTC. Eventually, the girls changed their band's name to reflect their new repertoire. Now known as the Electrocutes, more of a speed-metal act, they booked themselves regularly at local community centers. Again, their style and youthful energy made an impression on another member of the Bay Area music scene, musician and Super*teem Records label owner Darin Raffaelli. After seeing them live, he approached the Electrocutes about recording some songs he had written with a female group in mind. The girls agreed and entered the studio under the name the Donnas, a concept developed by Raffaelli. These sessions resulted in the recording of a handful of bubble-gum punk songs, including "A Boy Like You," and "Let's Rab!" Raffaelli also recorded the Donnas' self-titled debut album. Originally released on Super*teem, *The Donnas* was later reissued by Lookout! Records in 1998.

But though the Donnas were putting their own heavier spin on Raffaelli's songs, they nonetheless felt as though his writing was too pop-oriented for them. They even continued to perform as their alter ego, the Electrocutes, going so far as to publicly slag the Donnas as a "goody goody" band. But amid the rivalry with, in fact, themselves, the Donnas name and sideshow eventually won the favor of audiences. "We once played on the same bill at a radio station," Anderson confessed to the *Washington Post*'s Richard Har-

For the Record . . .

Members include **Brett Anderson** (a.k.a. Donna A; born on May 30, 1979, in Bloomington, IN; *Education*: Attended University of California at Berkeley), lead vocals; **Torry Castellano** (a.k.a. Donna C; born on January 8, 1979, in San Francisco, CA; *Education*: Attended New York University), drums; **Maya Ford** (a.k.a. Donna F; born on January 8, 1979, in Oakland, CA; *Education*: Attended University of California at Santa Cruz), bass guitar; **Allison Robertson** (a.k.a. Donna R; born on August 26, 1979, in North Hollywood, CA; *Education*: Attended University of California at Santa Cruz), guitar.

Formed first band, Ragady Ann, early 1990s; played as both the Donnas and the Electrocutes, mid 1990s; released *American Teenage Rock 'n' Roll Machine* after signing with Lookout! Records, 1998; released *Get Skin Tight*, 1999; released *The Donnas Turn 21*, 2001.

Addresses: *Record company*—Lookout! Records, P.O. Box 11374, Berkeley, CA 94712, website: http://www.lookoutrecords.com. *Website*—The Donnas Official Website: http://www.thedonnas.com.

Hot," and "Speed Demon," were originally written by the four girls for the Electrocutes. Not surprisingly, the second album sounded like a merging of the two bands with its catchy pop refrains and heavier guitar riffs. Released in 1998 on Lookout! Records, the original home of bands such as Green Day and Rancid, *American Teenage Rock 'n' Roll Machine* received favorable press and was followed by touring opportunities in the United States as well as Japan and Europe. Meanwhile, they also gave college a try, but decided to take a leave to concentrate on the Donnas.

In 1999, the Donnas returned with a third album entitled *Get Skintight,* featuring a cover of Motley Crue's "Too Fast for Love" and produced by Jeff and Steve McDonald of Redd Kross. It, too, won over the music press, and reviewers pointed out the Donnas' improved songwriting skills, louder guitars, and propulsive rhythms. Highlights from the record included the smash hit "Hyperactive" and the ballad "You Don't Wanna Call."

Two years later, in the spring of 2001, the Donnas released their fourth album, *The Donnas Turn 21.* But despite their age, the group stuck to playing heavy party rock with songs such as the single "40 Boys in 40 Nights" and a re-make of the Judas Priest classic "Livin' After Midnight." Just because the Donnas are grown up, they don't believe it necessary to abandon the same spirit that brought them together as adolescents. "I think that's what we go on, that's our fuel," Anderson said to Harrington. "I don't see why we would want to get solemn or mature in that way, because that's not the point of our music. It would negate the whole purpose of playing rock 'n' roll for us."

Selected discography

The Donnas (reissued), Lookout!, 1998.
(As the Electrocutes) *Steal Yer Lunch Money* (reissued), Sympathy for the Record Industry, 1999.
American Teenage Rock 'n' Roll Machine, Lookout!, 1998.
Get Skintight, Lookout!, 1999.
The Donnas Turn 21, Lookout!, 2001.

Sources

Periodicals

Boston Globe, February 1, 2001; March 16, 2001.
Guitar Player, August 1999.
Los Angeles Times, July 18, 1998.
Melody Maker, October 23, 1999; December 15-21, 1999.
People, February 12, 2001.
Rolling Stone, June 11, 1998; June 24, 1999; December 16-23, 1999; February 1, 2001.
Village Voice, June 29, 1999; July 27, 1999; March 13, 2001.
Washington Post, July 18, 1999; January 31, 2001; March 2, 2001.

rington. "Because you couldn't see us, it was a good little joke."

The Donnas prevailed, yet the girls would not fully abandon the Electrocutes. Indeed, when it came time to begin thinking about a second album, the Donnas insisted on more creative control. "We were writing songs before we ever met Darin, so it's not like we started playing and someone else was writing our songs," added Anderson. "Then we met him and started making this kind of music and after a while, no one was taking us seriously because they saw him and immediately went, oh, they're not really friends, he's telling them what to do, he's the Svengali/Phil Spector to their puppets—as if there wasn't a possibility for anything else to happen!"

Thus, when the Donnas, who graduated from high school in 1997, recorded their breakthrough album *American Teenage Rock 'n' Roll Machine,* the girls took control by collaborating with, rather than relying solely upon, Raffaelli. In fact, some of the most memorable tracks, including "Looking for Blood," "You Make Me

Online

The Donnas Official Website, http://www.thedonnas.com
(May 12, 2001).

Lookout! Records, http://www.lookoutrecords.com (May 12,
2001).

—Laura Hightower

Emerson String Quartet

Chamber music ensemble

During the final decades of the twentieth century, music critics hailed the arrival of the Emerson String Quartet—whose namesake is poet and philosopher Ralph Waldo Emerson—praising the impressive sound of these musicians. The Emerson musicians—Eugene Drucker, Philip Setzer, David Finckel, and Lawrence Dutton—had collected a total of six Grammy Awards by 2001, including two for Best Classical Album of the year. The Emersons, according to critics, came to represent the apex of their art, and they set a new standard for performance of the Bartok String Quartets in 1989. In 1997, their interpretation of the elusive and extremely difficult Beethoven Quartets captured the emotion of the pieces. In 2000, the quartet's recording of the Shostakovich Quartets brought Western music critics to a new appreciation of the Russian composer's work.

Observers have applauded the Emersons for their unique individuality and some have suggested that the underlying personal independence retained by each member of the quartet is a key factor to the success of their collaborations. Emerson String Quartet founders Drucker and Setzer began playing in chamber ensembles as violin students of Oscar Shumsky at New

a bronze medal at the 1976 Queen Elisabeth of Belgium International Competition in Brussels. Additionally, as a winner of the Concert Artist Guild prize that year, he performed in a New York City debut. His instrument of preference is a prized Antonius Stradivarius instrument made in Cremona, Italy, dating back to 1686.

Accomplished Performers

Cleveland, Ohio-born Philip Setzer came from a musical family. His parents were musicians with the Cleveland Orchestra, and young Setzer began his musical studies at age five. Among his early teachers were Josef Gingold and Raphael Druian. Setzer took second prize at the Meriwether Post Competition in Washington, D.C. in 1967, and along with his colleague, Drucker, took a bronze medal at the Queen Elisabeth Competition in 1976. Both Setzer and Drucker have contributed their talents as visiting professors of violin at the University of Hartford's Hartt School of Music. In 1997, Setzer lent his expertise in master classes at the Isaac Stern Chamber Workshop at Carnegie Hall. The following year he contributed his talents to the Isaac Stern Chamber Music Encounter in Jerusalem, Israel. Setzer's instrument of preference is a modern violin by Samuel Zygmuntowicz of Brooklyn. Setzer inspired Paul Epstein's *Matinee Concerto* and premiered the piece with the Hartt Wind Symphony. Despite criticism from conservative traditionalists, Drucker and Setzer regularly switch positions in their performances between first and second violin parts. In fact, by their own admission, they go to great lengths to equalize the lead position between them. In presenting the selections of most composers, the two violinists divide the repertoire evenly, although each performer has a specialty. Drucker takes the lead for pieces by Debussy, and Setzer plays first chair for Ravel's works.

Dutton, on viola, joined Drucker and Setzer in 1977 and the trio added cellist Finckel in 1979. Dutton began his musical studies on both the viola and violin with Margaret Pardee before devoting his studies exclusively to viola at the Eastman School where he studied under Frances Tursi. He later studied with Lilian Fuchs at Juilliard and received both bachelor's and master's degrees from that school. At Juilliard, Dutton distinguished himself as a winner of the Walter M. Naumberg scholarship. Like his colleagues Drucker and Setzer, Dutton is a visiting professor at the Hartt School of Music. His world-class accomplishments include concert performances with noted string players such as Rostropovich and Shumsky, as well as Lynn Harrell, Misha Dichter, and Isaac Stern. His guest performances extend from the Guarneri Quartet to the Beaux Arts Trio. Dutton's instrument of choice is a 1796 Pietro Giovanni Mantegazza viola from Milan, Italy.

Finckel, a rare American student of Mstislav Rostropovich, was born to a family of cellists. After some years

York City's renowned Juilliard School of Music during the early 1970s. Drucker distinguished himself in 1975 with a prize-winning performance at the International Violin Competition in Montreal, Quebec, and then took

of study under the guidance of his father, Finckel made his debut with the Philadelphia Orchestra at age 15, in recognition of a prize-winning performance in that orchestra's junior competition. Two years later, Rostropovich, upon hearing Finckel play, took him as a student for nine years. At the end of his studies Finckel was honored to perform as a soloist with Rostropovich and the Basel Symphony Orchestra. Additionally, Finckel was the first Piatigorsky Artist Award recipient from the New England Conservatory. He has performed in recitals throughout the eastern United States and teaches regularly with the Isaac Stern Chamber Music Workshops in the United States and Israel. He also contributes his time to the summertime master class program at the Aspen Music Festival. Finckel spent three years during the late 1990s as the artistic co-director of SummerFest La Jolla.

Outstanding Repertoire

As the four musicians gelled into a quartet during the late 1970s, their expectation for the future remained undefined. As they completed their studies, they continued to perform in quartet on a limited basis, increasing their repertoire and expanding their performance schedule throughout the 1980s. In 1987, the Emerson String Quartet signed an exclusive contract with Deutsche Grammophon, a relationship which resulted in a wide assortment of recordings, including a number of award-winning albums. By 2000 public performances by the four musicians had increased to approximately 100 per year. The quartet's 1989 recording of the six Bartok String Quartets received a Grammy Award for Best Classical Album of the Year—a rare distinction for a quartet recording. The album, according to critics, set a new standard. On that recording, Drucker and Setzer, as is their habit, each played lead violin on three quartets apiece. The album also received the Grammy Award that year for Best Chamber Music Performance. In 1994, the Emersons' Ives: *String Quartet Nos. 1 and 2/Barber: String Quartet, op. 11* took the Grammy as the Best Chamber Music Performance of 1993.

In the mid-1990s, the quartet undertook a sizable task in recording the entire collection of 16 Beethoven quartets. As was typical, Drucker and Setzer switched off, performing lead violin on eight quartets apiece. David Patrick Stearns in *USA Today* called the recordings "explosive," and the album earned the Grammy Award for Best Chamber Music Performance in 1997. As a follow-up to the release, the Emersons appeared in a series of Beethoven concerts at the Lincoln Center in New York City throughout 1997 and 1998. In a subsequent Beethoven performance at Caruth Auditorium in Dallas, Texas, in 1999, the Emersons rendered "a strongly profiled presentation by a distinguished musical team," according to *Dallas Morning News* critic Olin Chism in describing the Emersons' performance of the Beethoven Opus 132. Similarly, James Wierz-

bicki in the *St. Louis Post-Dispatch* noted that the Emersons' Beethoven Opus 130 and 131 was "awesome music, and the Emerson Quartet gave it its due…. Consistency of approach—along with collective virtuosity and penetrating interpretations—is what makes the Emerson Quartet such a stellar ensemble."

Continued Grammy Success

In 1999, as the twentieth century drew to a close, so too did the Emerson's project to record the 15 string quartets of Dmitri Shostakovich. Because Shostakovich was largely misunderstood by Western audiences, his quartets, according to the Emersons, are extremely unique and cannot properly be appreciated unless heard in live performance. Shostakovich: *The String Quartets,* as a result, was recorded from a series of live performances at the Aspen Music Festival. Justin Davidson in the *Minneapolis Star Tribune* called the collection "gripping, ambitious, and unsettling," in its expression of the odd moods of the pieces. The album earned Grammy Awards for Best Chamber Music Performance and Best Classical Album in 2001. Justin Davidson remarked that the Emersons' interpretation of the third quartet "tempered fury with stylish restraint, [and] offered a more elastic interpretation." The Emersons received additional plaudits for their rendition of the Shostakovich String Quartet No. 15, a piece that was written while the composer remained hospitalized in 1974, shortly before his death. Shostakovich died in 1975, and music historians believe that the composition represents the inspirations of a gravely ill composer as he was subjected to the emotional extremes brought on by sedative medications to ease the pain of his illness.

In 1995, composer and double bass player Edgar Meyer composed a string quintet of four movements expressly for the Emersons, who recorded the piece with Meyer on bass in 1998. Also in the catalog of compositions written expressly for the Emersons is String Quartet No. 2 by Ellen Taaffe Zwilich. According to Tom Cardy in the *Evening Post,* "If there's an equivalent to rock superstar status in classical music today, one contender must be the Emerson String Quartet."

For their noteworthy careers, each member of the Emerson String Quartet received an honorary doctorate degree from Middlebury College in Vermont in 1995.

Selected discography

Bartok: *The Six String Quartets,* Deutsche Grammophon, 1989.
Prokofiev: *String Quartets 1 and 2,* Deutsche Grammophon, 1992.

Ives: *String Quartets Nos. 1 and 2/Barber: String Quartet, Op. 11,* Deutsche Grammophon, 1993.

Barber: *The Songs,* Deutsche Grammophon, 1994.

(With Menahem Pressler) Dvorak: *Piano Quintet and Quartet,* Deutsche Grammophon, 1994.

String Quartets of Debussy and Ravel, Deutsche Grammophon, 1995.

Beethoven: *Complete String Quartets,* Deutsche Grammophon, 1997.

Beethoven: *The Key to the Quartets,* Deutsche Grammophon, 1997.

Meyer: *Quintet/Rorem: String Quartet,* Deutsche Grammophon, 1998.

(With David Shifrin) Mozart/Brahms: *Clarinet Quintets,* Deutsche Grammophon, 1999.

(With Mstislav Rostropovitch) Schubert: *The Late Quartets and Quintet,* Deutsche Grammophon, 1999.

Shostakovich: *String Quartet No. 8,* Deutsche Grammophon, 1999.

Shostakovich: *Complete String Quartets,* Deutsche Grammophon, 2000.

Sources

Periodicals

Dallas Morning News, October 19, 1999, p. 21A.

Denver Rocky Mountain News, April 3, 1997, p. 54A; April 21, 1999, p. 11D.

Dominion (Wellington, New Zealand), June 24, 2000, p. 22.

Evening Post (Wellington, New Zealand), June 21, 2000, p. 13.

Jerusalem Post, June 4, 1996, p. 7.

Minneapolis Star Tribune, April 2, 2000, p. 2F.

Newsday, February 7, 2000, p. B5.

St. Louis Post-Dispatch, February 24, 1994, p. 5G.

USA Today, April 1, 1997, p. 4D.

Online

"Biographies,"ArtistLed, http:// www.artistled.com/html/contact_us.htm (May 20, 2001).

Emerson String Quartet Official Website, http://emersonquartet.com (June 28, 2001).

—Gloria Cooksey

The Fixx

Rock group

Archive Photos, Inc. Reproduced by permission.

In the early 1980s, the Fixx became a fixture on the American pop charts. One of many British New Wave bands that conquered the airwaves in the United States at the time, the Fixx stood out for their echoing vocals, political lyrics, and richly textured production. From 1982 through 1984, they released a string of hit albums and singles, but never endeared themselves to rock critics. Their commercial popularity waned, though, as the decade progressed. Changing labels and producers didn't help, and by the early 1990s, it seemed that the band might be finished. But being close friends, the band members kept in touch and resumed performing. In 1998 they released *Elemental,* their first album after a seven-year break from recording. Appealing to their hardcore fans and surprising some reviewers with its quality, the album showed the Fixx to be a band determined to persevere even if they weren't the chart-toppers they had once been.

The group came together in London during the late 1970s. Lead singer Cy Curnin had come to the city to attend drama school, after having briefly earned his living by winning prize money in fishing tournaments. At school he met drummer Adam Woods, and they became friends while working together on plays. Woods was in a band at the time, and Curnin eagerly joined. In 1979 the two decided to start a band of their own. In order to fill out their lineup, they advertised for members, recruiting guitarist Jamie West-Oram, keyboardist Rupert Greenall, and bass player Charlie Barret through the classifieds. After going through a couple of other names, their manager dubbed them the Portraits.

They found some early success under that name, releasing the single "Hazards in the Home." By the time they released their next single, "Lost Planes," though, they had become the Fixx. They promoted themselves to veteran producer Rupert Hine by sending him a tape that his girlfriend liked. On her advice, he agreed to work with the group. Shortly thereafter MCA Records signed them, and the group went into the studio to record their first album, *Shuttered Room,* released in 1982. Their social and political views permeated the songs, including the singles "Stand or Fall" and "Red Skies," a song about the devastation of nuclear war. Both singles became hits in the United Kingdom, but not in the United States. The album did stay on the American charts for a year, though, even without any hit singles.

The Fixx generated interest in America with their tour to promote *Shuttered Room.* By then, Barret had left the band and Alfie Agius had replaced him. Wanting to capitalize on the buzz they were creating, the group headed back into the studio with their new bass player to work on their next effort, *Reach the Beach,* released in 1983. During the recording, Agius' personality began to wear on the other band members. In an interview with Lisa M. Bell posted on the Fixx's website, Curnin described Agius as "Napoleon meets Satan … in one body." Thus, Agius didn't last for the whole session. The group found his replacement, Dan K. Brown, through the recommendation of mutual friends, and he joined to record the final track for the album.

Reach the Beach took the band to new heights of popularity. In their native country, though, the album produced no hit singles, and the Fixx would never again have a hit at home. But the United States was another story. The album spawned three hit singles, including "One Thing Leads to Another," which peaked at number four. The album itself went platinum. Rock critics did not necessarily share the audience's enthusiasm. In *Rolling Stone,* Errol Somay described the album as "generic New Wave Muzak more suitable for airports and dentists' waiting rooms than dance clubs." But the public disagreed. Boosted by their touring and the frequent appearance of their videos on MTV, which at the time was still a new phenomenon, the Fixx seemed to have conquered America.

The band wasted no time starting work on their next album. *Phantoms,* released in 1984, was successful, but it never approached the heights of their previous effort. With only one hit single, "Are We Ourselves?" the album didn't have the same staying power as their previous albums. *Phantoms* also marked a shift in the focus of the band's lyrics. A reviewer in *People* noted that "Curnin appears less involved with political issues than in the past and more into personal concerns such as alienation and the inability to communicate."

After three albums in three years, the Fixx took a break from recording. The busy recording and touring schedule had taken its toll. As Curnin told the *Toronto Star's* Greg Quill, "There was nothing left to say to one another after three solid years of work. Our vocation was not charming anymore." After spending a year apart, the band regrouped to produce the 1986 album *Walkabout.* The formula that had worked for them so well a few years earlier started to wear thin. Although the single "Secret Separation" reached the charts, it was by no means a smash. According to Woods, this began to lead to problems with the group's label, MCA. Under new management, the label was looking for the hit-making band of *Reach the Beach.* Woods told Mike Stephens of Gannett News Service, "They put everything into that one single. When it didn't do as well as they thought it should have—even though it went top twenty—they gave up. That, for us, is when the problems began."

Indeed, the group seemed to be searching for direction for the next few years. *Walkabout* turned out to be their last recording with Rupert Hines as producer. Hines often received a large amount of credit for the band's lush, textured, synthesizer sound and echoing vocals. The album also marked their last work for MCA. They took their first step into uncharted waters by signing with RCA, the label that released *Calm Animals* in 1988. Besides a new label, the Fixx also unveiled a new sound, featuring West-Oram's guitar much more prominently than on previous efforts. While the album turned out to be their most successful one in England, in the United States, where just four years earlier they had been fixtures in the top 40, sales continued to decline.

When the Fixx went into the studio again, they continued to explore a more raw, guitar-driven sound instead of returning to the lush textures of their biggest hits. According to Woods, their label was wary about this direction, as the first album for RCA hadn't been commercially successful. He told Barbara Jaeger of the *Bergen Record,* "[W]hen they saw how much was lost on that record and then heard how we were continuing on the same path … they made it known that they would have preferred we go back to form."

So the Fixx found themselves without a label, and it took them 18 months to find a new one. They finally ended up back with MCA, indirectly, on that company's imprint label Impact. The resulting album, *Ink,* while keeping the focus more on guitars and less on keyboards, marked another departure for the band. In the past, they had written all their songs themselves. This time, Curnin collaborated with songwriter Scott Cutler for many of the tracks. The collaboration had not necessarily been meant to end up as Fixx music, but Curnin said the combined effort worked well, telling Kira L. Billik of the Associated Press, "[W]e deliver things in a Fixx way, so we can take songs from other places and make them our own."

It turned out that *Ink* would be the Fixx's last foray into the studio for several years. No longer able to top the charts, the Fixx found that major labels didn't want them. The group went into a forced hiatus. While Curnin occupied himself by starting his own clothing company, Cy Wear, which specialized in designing and making hats, the music was never far from the group's mind. They also kept themselves busy writing songs, even though they had no place to record them. Believing that they still had an audience, the band began to perform live again in 1996 after an extended absence from the public eye. Even though they didn't have a new album to support on tour, they had plenty of new songs to play along with their greatest hits.

While the venues were smaller than when they had been the darlings of MTV and the charts, the Fixx hoped to find that their loyal fans were still out there. Curnin explained to Bill Locey of the *Los Angeles Times* what the group hoped to get from their first tour after the layoff: "We want to show people that we're not on life support. We've got a good catalog and we're one of the best live bands out there." In fact, the group obliged their fans by taking requests from the crowd instead of strictly sticking to a playlist.

Heartened by the response to their tours, the band began recording and releasing new material. They decided to showcase their new songs first through a self-released five-song EP titled *Happy Landings* in 1997, instead of waiting for a contract from a label. Shortly thereafter they signed to CMC records and released their first full studio album in seven years, 1998's *Elemental*. Four of the five members from the band's best-known lineup returned for this effort, with Chris Tait replacing Brown on bass. Even though their time in the limelight seemed long gone, the album demonstrated the Fixx's tenacity. In a review for *All Music Guide*, Stephen Thomas Erlewine wrote, "[T]here are moments showing that the Fixx is actually able to mature gracefully, which many naysayers would have hardly believed at the peak of their popularity."

The Fixx followed up this effort with *1011 Woodland* in 1999. This two-CD set included no new material, but rather featured re-recordings of some of their earlier work. Besides giving these old songs a sound more in keeping with the group's later stripped-down approach, Curnin made no secret of his hope that redoing their familiar material would help the band's cash flow. He told Blair R. Fischer of *Rolling Stone,* "It's a great gig if you can get it…. We're gonna hang on tooth and nail."

Selected discography

Shuttered Room, MCA, 1982.
Reach the Beach, MCA, 1983.
Phantoms, MCA, 1984.
Walkabout, MCA, 1986.
React, MCA, 1987.
Calm Animals, RCA, 1988.
One Thing Leads to Another: Greatest Hits, MCA, 1989.
Ink, Impact, 1991.
Happy Landings (EP), self-released, 1997.
Elemental, CMC, 1998.
1011 Woodland, CMC, 1999.
Ultimate Collection, MCA, 1999.

Sources

Periodicals

Associated Press, May 17, 1991.
Bergen Record, May 8, 1991, p. D1.
Dayton Daily News, May 15, 1998, p. 18.
Gannett News Service, May 19, 1989.
Los Angeles Times, May 23, 1991, p. J6; November 14, 1996, p. F18.
People, October 8, 1984, p. 28.
Rolling Stone, September 29, 1983, p. 72; November 22, 1984, p. 62.
Toronto Star, June 27, 1986, p. D11.

Online

"The Fixx," *All Music Guide,* http://www.allmusic.com (April 16, 2001).
"The Fixx," Excite.com, http://music.excite.com (April 16, 2001).
"The Fixx," *Rolling Stone,* http://rollingstone.com (April 16, 2001).
The Fixx Official Website, http://www.thefixx.com (April 16, 2001).

—*Lloyd Hemingway*

Janie Fricke

Singer

It was probably inevitable that Janie Fricke would become a singer, but she took a somewhat circuitous route to get there. Despite growing up in a musical family and spending much of her childhood singing at home, school, and church, it did not occur to Fricke that music might be a profession. While studying for her bachelor's degree in elementary education at Indiana University, she kept active musically. It remained a hobby, though, not a serious career choice. It was only when Fricke started earning extra money by singing commercial jingles that she began to see that music could actually earn her a living. In the years since the revelation, Fricke has performed for presidents and won some of the highest honors in country music.

Fricke was born Jane Marie Fricke on December 19, 1947, in South Whitley, Indiana, the daughter of a guitar-playing father and a mother who taught piano lessons and played the organ in church. Growing up on her family's 400-acre farm in northern Indiana, she was surrounded by music almost from birth. While still quite young, she learned to play the guitar from her father and the piano from her mother. By the time she was ten, Fricke was singing regularly in church and school. Interviewed in 2000 by Gritz, an online magazine covering country music, Fricke recalled: "music was in our family ever since I was a little girl, so I enjoyed music and the art of making music since the age of seven or eight years old. I didn't think I was going to make it a profession, it was just that I enjoyed it and it was fun. It didn't even occur to me that it might *become* a profession...."

Although she grew up in rural Indiana and later won her greatest fame as a country singer, Fricke showed little interest in country music as a child. "My family was always encouraging me to sing all of the pop songs of the time, so we were buying sheet music and I was singing Dusty Springfield and Rita Coolidge—anything that was a strong pop song at the time," she told Gritz. "So I was not your average country singer growing up on the farm and just singing country music. Musically, I was trained to read music and play the piano."

After graduating from high school, Fricke headed to Indiana University at Bloomington to study for her bachelor's degree in elementary education. She had long set her sights on a career as a grade school teacher. Given her musical childhood, it was not particularly surprising that she got involved with the school's famous Singing Hoosiers, a chorale ensemble that has toured widely in the United States and abroad. But music remained just a pleasant way to spend some free time for Fricke. It was only when she started earning money singing commercials that she began to see music in a whole new light. She realized that she could indeed earn a living with her music and became so excited at the possibility that she was seriously tempted to quit college and devote all her time to singing jingles. However, her mother insisted that she continue her studies at Indiana, so Fricke put her dreams on hold while she finished work on her bachelor's degree. She did manage to keep active musically during the remainder of her college career by "singing in little clubs and singing for any event I could because I loved to sing...," she told Gritz. She also developed an interest in studio work and some of the behind-the-scenes elements involved in recording.

After graduating from college in 1972, Fricke headed to Los Angeles, California, to see if she could make a living as a studio singer. Finding it hard to break into the business on the West Coast, she didn't stay long. In 1975, she headed to Nashville, Tennessee, where she joined the Lea Jane Singers, a group specializing in background vocals. The group often recorded as many as three sessions a day, five days a week. In her several years doing studio work, both with the group and solo, she sang background on hundreds of albums. She also continued to work as a jingle singer, recording commercials for such corporate giants as United Airlines, Coca-Cola, 7-Up, and Red Lobster.

After a few years in Nashville, Fricke became one of the city's most sought-after studio singers, supplying background vocals for such stars as Elvis Presley, Crystal Gayle, Ronnie Milsap, Conway Twitty, Tanya Tucker, Al Green, Eddie Rabbit, and Barbara Mandrell. Some of the better known singles on which she sang background include Presley's "My Way," Conway Twitty's "I'd Love to Lay You Down," Crystal Gayle's "I'll Get Over You," and Tanya Tucker's "Here's Some Love." However, it was her work as background vocalist on several recordings by Johnny Duncan that first brought Fricke to national attention. After supplying uncredited background vocals for such Duncan hits as "Jo and the Cowboy," "Thinkin' of a Rendezvous," "It Couldn't Have Been Any Better," and "Stranger," she was finally rewarded when she was given equal billing with Duncan on a single entitled "Come a Little Bit Closer." It was likely her contribution to Duncan's number one hit "Stranger" in 1977 that generated the most interest. In that song, Fricke sang the line, "Shut out the light and lead me...." Thousands of listeners wanted to know the identity of the "mystery singer." Fricke recalled to Gritz how she came to sing the line that was to take her into the limelight: "I was a backup singer in the studio at the time, and during a session they needed a girl to sing a couple of lines, so I happened to get the job of singing the line on that record. There again, fate had it. " Before long she had recorded duets with some of country music's top male singers including Merle Haggard, Charlie Rich, and Moe Bandy.

Soon Fricke released a couple of successful singles— "What're You Doing Tonight?" and a remake of "Please Help Me, I'm Falling." In 1982, Fricke hit number one on the country charts with "Don't Worry 'bout Me, Baby," on which Ricky Skaggs sang harmony. She toured with Alabama, and in 1983, scored another number one country hit with "He's a Heartache (Looking for a Place to Happen)," a single from Fricke's *It Ain't Easy* album. Other big hits from the album included "It Ain't Easy Being Easy" and "Tell Me a Lie."

"A Place to Fall Apart," her duet with Merle Haggard, hit number one on the country charts in 1985. The song was based on a letter Haggard had written about ex-wife Leona Williams. That same year, Fricke established the Janie Fricke Scholarship at Indiana University to benefit gifted students in the School of Music. The scholarships are open to active members of the Singing Hoosiers vocal ensemble who demonstrate financial need.

In 1986, Fricke released *Black and White,* an album that explored her love of the blues. Three years later, in 1989, she worked with producer-songwriter Chris Waters on her album entitled *Labor of Love.* Among the successful singles from that collaborative effort were "Love Is One of Those Words," written by Waters and his sister Holly Dunn, and Steve Earle's "My Old Friend, the Blues." Not long after the album's release, Fricke left the Columbia label. In 1992 she signed with Branson Entertainment and released two albums on the Branson label—*Crossroads* in 1992 and *Now & Then* in 1993.

Fricke's album *Bouncin' Back* was released in 2000 under her own label, JMF Records. In a unique marketing decision, she decided to use the power of the Internet exclusively to sell the album. Fricke continues to tour extensively, but she makes sure to set aside plenty of time to spend with her family on her Texas ranch near Lancaster.

Asked what she saw as the highlights of her career, Fricke did not hesitate. For this farm-bred girl, nothing has been quite as thrilling as performing for three presidents. She performed for President Gerald Ford at the White House, entertained President Ronald Reagan at Camp David, and sang in a show for President George Bush at Washington's Ford Theater. Coming in a close second in the thrill department, she added, was "winning an award and going up to get it," she told Gritz.

Selected discography

Singer of Songs (includes "What Are You Doing Tonight" and "Baby, It's You"), Columbia, 1978.
Love Notes (includes "Playin' Hard to Get" and "Let's Try Again"), Columbia, 1979.
Janie Fricke, Intersound, 1979.
From the Heart (includes "But Love Me" and "Pass Me By"), Columbia, 1980.
I'll Need Someone to Hold Me When I Cry (includes "Down to My Last Broken Heart" and "Pride"), CBS, 1981.
Sleeping with Your Memory (includes "Do Me with Love" and "Don't Worry 'bout Me, Baby"),CBS, 1981.
It Ain't Easy (includes "It Ain't Easy Being Easy" and "He's a Heartache"), Columbia, 1982.

Love Lies (includes "Let's Stop Talking about It" and "If the Fall Don't Get You"), CBS, 1983.
First Word in Memory (includes "Your Heart's Not in It"), CBS, 1984.
Somebody Else's Fire (includes "Easy to Please" and "She's Single Again"), Columbia, 1985.
Black & White (includes "Always Have, Always Will"), CBS, 1986.
After Midnight (includes "Are You Satisfied" and "Baby, You're Gone"), CBS, 1987.
Celebration, CBS, 1987.
Saddle the Wind, Columbia, 1988.
Labor of Love (includes "Love Is One of Those Words"), Columbia, 1989.
Crossroads, Branson, 1992.
Now & Then, Branson, 1993.
Bouncin' Back, JMF Records, 2000.

Sources

Books

Mansfield, Brian, and Gary Graff, *MusicHound Country: The Essential Album Guide,* Visible Ink Press, 1997.

Online

"Fate Loves Janie Fricke," Gritz, http://www.gritz.net/jan ief-ricke.html (May 9, 2001).
"Janie Facts," Janie Fricke Official Website, http://www .janiefricke.com/facts.html (May 9, 2001).
"Janie Fricke," *All Music Guide,* http://www.allmusic.com (May 9, 2001).
"Janie Fricke," Grabow & Associates, http://66.33.9.57/ Janie%20Fricke.htm (May 9, 2001).
"Janie Fricke," iMusic Country Showcase, http://imusic.artist direct.com/showcase/country/janiefricke.html (May 9, 2001).
"Janie Fricke," Richard De La Font Agency Inc., http:// www.delafont.com/music_acts/Janie_Fricke.htm (May 9, 2001).
"Janie Fricke: Biography," Sonicnet.com, http://www.sonic net.com/artists/biography/505343.jhtml (May 9, 2001).
"The Janie Fricke Scholarship," Indiana University School of Music, http://www.music.indiana.edu/som/scholarship/fric ke.htm (May 9, 2001).

—*Don Amerman*

Galaxie 500

Rock group

Influential indie rock group Galaxie 500 had a modest start. Three high-school friends wanted to form a "real" band after attending Harvard University and ended up making music that *Spin* critic Pat Blashill called a "wintry opiate. Sounds like love (lost) in a cold snap." Though Galaxie 500's first album, *Today,* was released in 1987 and the band disbanded four years later, they made a major impact on the indie rock scene. In addition to numerous independent singles, the group released three major-label albums, *Today, On Fire,* and *This Is Our Music,* on British label Rough Trade. Rykodisc continued to release Galaxie 500 material after the band's demise.

Damon Krukowski and Naomi Yang, both New York City natives, met Dean Wareham, a New Zealand transplant from Australia, in high school in New York City. Wareham took on the guitar and Krukowski learned to play drums from the high-school percussion teacher. After graduation in 1981, Krukowski and Wareham went on to Harvard University, with Yang following a year later. Once they arrived in Cambridge, Massachusetts, Krukowski and Wareham started a band called Speedy and the Castanets, which played punk rock covers but was short-lived after the group's bass player quit to pursue religion.

That left Wareham on vocals and guitar, and Krukowski on drums. The two placed an ad in the *Village Voice* for a new bassist, but found no one. They graduated from Harvard, after which Wareham traveled Europe. Originally a "graphics advisor" for Speedy and the Castanets, Yang, with no musical experience, finally stepped in to play bass. After a summer of practice in New York, the group returned to Cambridge in the autumn of 1987. *Spin* magazine's Pat Blashill dubbed the new trio "a hypnotic open loop of gentle drums, a bass that becalms like mother's finger to her lips, and a guitar that drifts purposely from languid to leveling. A voice singing high and strange."

The group took its name from the mid-1960s Ford muscle car, the Galaxy 500, and began playing shows around Boston and New York. A tip from a fellow musician led them to record a three-song demo tape and send it to Kramer, the producer and owner of the independent record label Shimmy Disc and New York's Noise Studio. The three spent eight hours in the studio with Kramer and recorded seven songs, including the two singles "Tugboat" and "Oblivious." The latter was included as a flexi-disc with the magazine *Chemical Imbalance.* It was in those recording sessions that producer Kramer gave Galaxie 500 their signature sound—the guitar effects and heavy reverb he added to the vocals gave the music its soft, billowy, ethereal feel.

Though the three had their roots in punk rock, they shared an affinity for older music. The Velvet Underground guitarist Sterling Morrison's work on *The Velvet Underground '69* was Wareham's favorite. Krukowski played on a vintage drum set from the 1950s or early 1960s, and Yang played an old, semi-hollow Gibson bass, which produced a warm, natural tone.

"Tugboat" was the foundation for Galaxie 500 to start recording its first full-length album, *Today*, again with Kramer. Wareham went into the studio with a vision, he said in an interview with *Chemical Imbalance.* "I'd like to make one of the best albums ever made. I want to do it because I like this sound. I like playing it, I like listening to it. And if you're not going to let me do that, I'll quit, because there are much better ways to make money." Demand for the group grew, especially in England, where the band's label, Rough Trade, was based, and where *Today* was enthusiastically received. The British music magazine *Melody Maker* called *Today* "an astonishing debut by anybody's standards."

In the summer of 1989, Galaxie 500 returned to the studio with Kramer to record its second release, *On Fire,* and its companion UK-only release, *Blue Thunder. On Fire* captured Galaxie 500 at its finest and included the singles "Blue Thunder" and "When Will You Come Home." Critical response to *On Fire* and *Blue Thunder* was overwhelming. Pat Blashill wrote in *Spin* that *On Fire* sounded like "AM radio pop at three in the morning: lost, beautiful, a very loud quiet." *Sounds* declared the album was a work of "utter magnificence," while *Melody Maker* called it "a stunning collection of daydream pop." *Rolling Stone* gave it three-and-a-half stars.

For the Record . . .

Members include **Damon Krukowski** (born on September 6, 1963, in New York, NY), drums; **Dean Wareham** (born in Wellington, New Zealand), vocals, guitar; **Naomi Yang** (born on September 15, 1964, in New York, NY), bass.

Group formed in Boston, MA, 1986; performed live throughout Boston and New York; Shimmy Disc produces singles "Tugboat" and "Oblivious;" released full-length debut, *Today,* 1997; signed to Rough Trade in the United States, issued *On Fire,* 1998; released *This Is Our Music,* 1990; disbanded, 1991; Wareham formed Luna; Yang and Krukowski continued as Pierre Etoile, then as Damon and Naomi, and as members of Magic Hour.

Addresses: *Record company*—Rykodisc, Shetland Park, 27 Congress St., Salem, MA 01970, website: http://www.rykodisc.com.

Krukowski and Yang dropped out of graduate school at Harvard to pursue music full time with Galaxie 500. This freed the band to travel more, touring Europe and the United Kingdom, where they were adored, in 1989 and 1990. In the spring of 1990, Wareham, who called Galaxie 500's music "spacy" in *Spin,* moved back to New York, leaving Krukowski and Yang in Boston. Also in 1990, they released a limited-edition seven-inch single featuring live covers of Jonathan Richman's "Don't Let Our Youth Go to Waste" and the Beatles' "Rain."

Galaxie 500 returned to Kramer's studio to record its third release, *This is Our Music,* whose title was borrowed from Ornette Coleman's classic recording from three decades before. The record was confident and dynamic. It featured the single "Fourth of July" and an eerie cover of "Listen, the Snow is Falling" by Yoko Ono. The record's release garnered the strong reviews Galaxie 500 was used to, and powered the band up for its first extensive American tour and the UK festival circuit.

Rumors of internal upset in the group proved true in 1991. After the tour supporting *This is Our Music* Wareham phoned Krukowski and Yang to announce he was leaving the group. Soon after, Rough Trade went out of business, taking the group's three releases, and any royalties, with it. Wareham launched a successful band, called Luna, and Krukowski and Yang regrouped first as Pierre Etoile, then as Damon and Naomi, and played in the group Magic Hour. In 1991, Krukowski acquired Galaxie 500's original master tapes at an auction of Rough Trade's assets. From those tapes, Rykodisc released a live album recorded in Copenhagen, a Galaxie 500 box set, and the band's albums once again went into print.

Selected discography

Today, Rykodisc, 1988.
On Fire, Rykodisc, 1989.
This Is Our Music, Rykodisc, 1990.
Galaxie 500, Rykodisc, 1996.
Copenhagen (live), Rykodisc, 1997.
Portable Galaxie 500, Rykodisc, 1998.

Sources

Periodicals

Chemical Imbalance, Issue 8, 1988.
Spin, December 1989.

Online

"Galaxie 500," *All Music Guide,* http://www.allmusic.com (March 30, 2001).
"Galaxie 500," Rykodisc, http://www.rykodisc.com (March 30, 2001).

—Brenna Sanchez

Ghostface Killah

Rap musician

© S.I.N./Corbis. Reproduced by permission.

Like many rap and hip-hop artists, Ghostface Killah emerged from a highly successful group act to become a standout success. But Ghostface did not get his start with just any group, he was an original member of the hip-hop supergroup the Wu-Tang Clan, which was lauded as "the most revolutionary rap group of the mid-'90s," according to *All Music Guide* online. Ghostface was first heard on the group's debut, *Enter the Wu-Tang Clan (36 Chambers),* and on the critically and commercially successful subsequent releases *Wu-Tang Forever* and *The W.* The rapper demonstrated his own skills on fellow Wu-Tang Clan member Raekwon's solo album, *Only Built 4 Cuban Linx,* and on his own first solo track, "Winter Warz," which was heard on the film soundtrack to *Don't Be a Menace to South Central While You're Drinking Your Juice in the Hood.* Ghostface came into his own with his highly successful full-length solo releases *Ironman* and *Supreme Clientele,* which both featured cameo appearances and production assistance from his Wu-Tang Clan cohorts.

Raised Dennis Coles on what he calls "Shaolin" or Staten Island, New York, Ghostface joined his neighborhood friends Robert Diggs (a.k.a. Prince Rakeem or The RZA), Gary Grice (a.k.a. The Genius or GZA), Lamont Hawkins (a.k.a U-God), Jason Hunter (a.k.a. Inspectah Deck), Russell Jones (a.k.a. Ol' Dirty Bastard), Clifford Smith (a.k.a. Method Man), and Raekwon to form a collective of nine rappers known as the Wu-Tang Clan in 1991. From the start, Wu-Tang Clan's boundaries were loose. While other rap groups often disbanded when members worked solo, all of the Wu-Tang Clan's members went on to release solo work with support from the rest of the group. The group released its first album, *Enter the Wu-Tang (36 Chambers)* two years later to rave reviews. The release was "rough and rambling," according to *Time,* "combining ragged street beats with lyrical imagery and audio samples" from Kung Fu films. At a time when the focus of hip-hop culture was on the West Coast, the Wu-Tang Clan drew attention to the East Coast with the album.

Ghostface helped Raekwon on his album *Only Built 4 Cuban Linx,* released in 1995. According to *Vibe,* Ghostface proved himself a "superior MC—kicking lyrics of steel" on his friend's record. In February of 1996, Ghostface's first solo track, "Winter Warz," appeared on the *Don't Be a Menace to South Central While You're Drinking Your Juice in the Hood* soundtrack. His contribution to the *Sunset Park* soundtrack, "Motherless Child," and "Who's the Champion" on the *Great White Hype* soundtrack, were also well received. In 1997, Wu-Tang Clan released a double album called *Wu-Tang Forever* which *Time* called "ambitious ... challenging, complex," and "full of energy and promise."

On his 1996 platinum-selling debut, *Ironman,* Ghostface Killah rapped about male bonding, the drug trade, and male-female politics in his songs. His voice raised just above conversational tone as the rapper borrowed the beats of 1970s soul songs. The song "260" is built around a sample of Al Green's peace-and-love anthem "Let's Stay Together"—an ironic choice for a song about murderous street justice. *Ironman* debuted at number two on the *Billboard* Pop Albums chart. The RZA produced the work, and *Ironman* was the first release on Razor Sharp Records, The RZA's imprint on the Epic record label. According to *Rolling Stone, Ironman* became a hit with "the most evangelical Wu fans."

One of several delays in the release of Ghostface's sophomore release was a four-month prison term he served for attempted robbery. The rapper was accused of assaulting a valet and robbing him of $3,000 after a 1995 altercation at the Palladium nightclub in New York City. Because his car's tires were slashed while in the parking attendant's care, a fight ensued, and Ghostface allegedly tried to take money from one of the attendants. Though he maintained his innocence, he plead guilty to avoid a possible 5-to-15-year sentence if tried and convicted. He then had to return to court for a 1997 arrest for possession of a .357-caliber Magnum handgun. The arrest was questioned after police admitted they wrongly claimed that Ghostface fled the scene when in fact he had accompanied officers to a police station.

Supreme Clientele was not released until the spring of 2000. The album received almost unanimously rave reviews and went on to become a certified gold selling record. *Entertainment Weekly* criticized the release for its "tawdry skits" and "exhausting" length, but most critics reviewed it favorably. The release was a rare example of a "sophomore overshadowing its predecessor," wrote one critic in the *Source*. A *Los Angeles Times* critic predicted *Supreme Clientele* would likely turn out to be the "most popular solo collection from a Wu-Tang member" since *Ironman*. *Village Voice* praised Ghostface's "vocal clarity, verbal dexterity, and narrative facility" throughout the release. *Supreme Clientele* was also noted for featuring less of Ghostface's Wu-Tang Clan counterparts rapping and more of Ghostface himself rapping on his own through most of the album, though his Wu-Tang Clan cohorts all lent a hand in the studio, and The RZA produced or mixed at least four tracks. Ghostface pondered the elements of everyday life on the recording, including life on the streets, soul food, and music. *Rolling Stone* critic Anthony DeCurtis wrote that although Ghostface's lyrics were tough to decipher and comprehend, "his urgent, overpowering flow is designed to maintain the unrehearsed immediacy of freestyle rapping, in which cadence, sound, and unconscious association triumph over logic."

The 2000 Wu-Tang Clan release *The W* found the group "at its most focused," wrote Christopher John Farley in *Time*. "*The W* becomes a terrifically varied album," he continued, "full of differing vocal textures and provocative rhythmic and lyrical ideas." The album was recorded over two months while the entire group shared a house in Los Angeles. For the strength of Ghostface's *Supreme Clientele,* The RZA's *Ghost Dog* soundtrack, and *The W, Rolling Stone* named the group "People of the Year" in 2000. *Rolling Stone* critic Mark Binelli wrote *The W* "hearkens back to the explosive group dynamic" of the Wu-Tang Clan's 1993 debut. Ghostface's third release, *Cuban Linx 2: Bulletproof Wallets* was due in the summer of 2001.

Selected discography

Ghostface Killah

Ironman, Columbia, 1996.
(Contributor) *Don't Be a Menace to South Central While You're Drinking Your Juice in the Hood* (soundtrack), Uni/Mercury, 1996.
Supreme Clientele, Epic/Razor Sharp, 2000.

Wu-Tang Clan

Enter the Wu-Tang (36 Chambers), Loud/RCA, 1993.
Wu-Tang Forever, Loud/RCA, 1997.
Wu-Chronicles, Priority, 1999.
The W, Loud/Columbia/Sony, 2000.

Sources

Periodicals

Entertainment Weekly, November 8, 1996, p. 69; March 3, 2000, p. 74.
Melody Maker, January 17, 1998, p. 4.
New York Times, November 5, 1996, p. C18.
Rolling Stone, February 4, 1999, p. 25; March 16, 2000, p. 74; April 13, 2000, p. 48; December 14, 2000, p. 126.
Time, December 11, 2000, p. 83.
Village Voice, March 28, 2000, p. 110.

Online

"Ghostface Killah," *All Music Guide,* http://www.allmusic.com (April 17, 2001).
"Ghostface Killah," ARTISTdirect, http://ubl.artistdirect.com (May 1, 2001).
"Ghostface Killah," *The Source* Online, http://www.thesource.com (April 17, 2001).
Ghostface Killah Official Website, http://www.ghostfacekillah.com (April 17, 2001).

—*Brenna Sanchez*

João Gilberto

Singer, guitarist

© Jack Vartoogian. Reproduced by permission.

Shy and at times reclusive, singer and guitarist João Gilberto nonetheless played a central role in the birth of bossa nova. Together with Antonio Carlos (Tom) Jobim, they tamed the Brazilian samba, injected it with American jazz, and created a new music that took the world by storm in the early 1960s. Gilberto sings in a quiet whisper and accompanies himself on an acoustic guitar with nylon strings. With haunting harmonies and unusual accents, the beat of the bossa nova is enchanting and always fresh. Although success would lead to a long stay in the United States, Gilberto's lifestyle remained the same: he recorded and performed infrequently. In 1998, as bossa nova celebrated its 40th anniversary, Gilberto played a handful of dates, continuing to follow his unassuming path toward making beautiful music.

Born João Gilberto do Prado Pereira de Oliveira on June 10, 1931, in Bahia, Brazil, Gilberto became interested in music early in life. His father, a prosperous merchant, attempted to properly educate his seven children, but only music interested Gilberto. At age 14, his godfather gave him his first guitar, and within a year, Gilberto became the leader of a group of school friends who performed at social functions. He absorbed the sounds of American jazz, from Tommy Dorsey's "Song of India" to Duke Ellington's "Caravan," and listened to popular Brazilian performers like Geraldo Pereira, Orlanda Silva, and Herivelto Martins. At 18, Gilberto moved to Bahia's capital, Salvador, to become a radio singer. Although he was unsuccessful, he was asked to become the lead singer of the group Garotos da Lua (Boys from the Moon) in Rio de Janeiro. His behavior was non-professional, however. Arriving late for performances and sometimes not arriving at all, Gilberto was fired after one year.

After being fired, Gilberto's life took a downward turn for the next seven years. He became depressed and used marijuana heavily. He let his hair grow long, wore old clothes, and could not find work. His girlfriend, Sylvia Telles (later a famous bossa nova singer), left him. With no place of his own, he lived with friends, never contributing to expenses and usually overstaying his welcome. Still, he was well liked. He slept during the day and played music at night. When he returned home from nightclubs, friends would sit up with him for the remainder of the night and chat. Gilberto refused to take jobs that he considered beneath him, including playing music in clubs where the customers were allowed to talk during performances. It seemed as though Gilberto would spend his life as a drifter.

After seven years of aimlessness, singer Luis Telles removed Gilberto from the corrupting influences of Rio and took him to Porto Alegre. He checked him into a good hotel for seven months and got him a job at the Clube da Chave (Key Club). This boosted Gilberto's confidence, but he still wasn't ready to return to Rio. He lived with his sister Dadainha and her husband for six

For the Record . . .

Born João Gilberto do Prado Pereira de Oliveira on June 10, 1931, in Bahia, Brazil; son of a prosperous merchant; married Astrud Weinert (divorced); married singer Miucha; children: Bebel.

Received first guitar from godfather at age 14; led band of school friends at age 15; at age 18 moved to Salvador to become a radio singer, then moved to Rio de Janeiro where he became the lead singer of Garotos da Lua; fired after one year for showing up late to performances or not at all; relocated to Porto Alegre with the help of singer Luis Telles; began working relationship with Antonio Carlos Jobim, 1956; released "Chega de Saudade," starting the bossa nova craze, 1958; moved to United States, 1962; remain in the U.S. until 1980 (with the exception of two years in Mexico); released *Getz/Gilberto* on Verve Records, 1963; recorded infrequent though well-received albums including *João Gilberto,* 1973; moved back to Brazil, 1980; performed several dates in the United States and Europe to commemorate 40th anniversary of bossa nova, 1998; released *João voz e violão* on Verve, 2000.

Addresses: *Record company*—Verve Music Group, 1755 Broadway, 3rd Floor, New York, NY 10019, (212) 331-2064, website: http://www.vervemusic group.com.

months and played guitar constantly. Her bathroom's unique acoustics allowed Gilberto to learn to sing quietly without vibrato and to play his guitar at fluctuating tempos. During this period he also disavowed marijuana use (as well as strong substances). Although a recognizable artist was taking shape, his family worried about his erratic behavior and committed him to a sanitarium in Salvador. During a series of interviews, Gilberto reportedly made the curious statement, "Look at the wind depilating the trees." When the psychiatrist said that the trees have no hair and therefore the wind could not rid them of it, Gilberto replied, "And there are people who have no poetry." He was released after a week.

In 1956 he returned to Rio with two quiet, simple songs that he had written: "Bim-Bom" and "Hô-Ba-La-Lá." He renewed his contact with composer Tom Jobim who listened to the songs and was impressed by the new rhythms of Gilberto's guitar. The two musicians began a collaboration that would give birth to a unique Brazilian hybrid, the bossa nova (new wave). The bossa nova has roots in many cultures. The samba, full of wild rhythms propelled by various percussion instruments, has its origins in African music. American jazz, especially West Coast players like Gerry Mulligan, Chet Baker, and Shorty Rogers, also proved central. First Jobim and Gilberto toned down the samba, added a looping acoustic guitar, and then inserted intricate harmonies and quiet vocals. In July of 1958 their recording of "Chega de Saudade" jump-started the bossa nova movement in Brazil. After a visit to South America, guitarist Charlie Byrd would carry these enchanting sounds back to the United States, helping spread bossa nova fever. The music received international exposure after Gilberto and Luiz Bonfá wrote the soundtrack for the movie, *Black Orpheus,* in 1958.

In 1962 Gilberto came to the United States where he would remain until 1980 (with the exception of two years in Mexico). In 1963 Verve released *Getz/Gilberto*, an album that brought Gilberto to broader critical and popular attention. The album also included "The Girl from Ipanema," sung by his wife Astrud, which became a hit. The album won two Grammys, one for best album and another for best song, beating out the Beatles' *Hard Day's Night.* In 1966 Verve released *Getz/Gilberto, Vol. II,* an album of live performance from Carnegie Hall. All of this attention brought little change to Gilberto's lifestyle or approach to performing. He seldom played live and gave few interviews. In 1964, he was scheduled to play a nine-night gig at the London House in Chicago. He played four short sets on the first night, and then canceled the remainder, saying the club was too noisy. While he recorded infrequently over the next 15 years, he continued to make beautiful albums such as 1973's *João Gilberto.* He also made a concerted effort to preserve earlier songs by Brazilian artists like Dorival Caymmi, Noel Rosa, Geraldo Pereira and others. *New York Times* critic Robert Palmer saw Gilberto at a rare appearance at the Bottom Line in 1977, and reported: "Mr. Gilberto's charms are durable. For one thing, his taste in material is unimpeachable."

In 1998 a number of events were planned and classic CDs re-released to commemorate the 40th anniversary of bossa nova. The music retains its freshness and vitality, and even finds expression in a younger generation. Gilberto's daughter Bebel has become a talented and popular entertainer in her own right. Gilberto continues to quietly pursue the art of his music, regardless of trends. For the 40th anniversary of the song "Chega de Saudade" he played a small number of dates in Europe and the United States. "One didn't need to understand Portuguese to feel the sadness, longing and joy of these songs," wrote Jesse Hamlin of the *San Francisco Chronicle.* "The sound of Gilberto's gentle voice was enough." Verve re-released 1999's *Joao voz e violão* in 2000, and Gilberto, at 69, continues to captivate. With no more than his quiet guitar and whisper of a voice, he confidently surveys both classics and newer material.

Selected discography

Getz/Gilberto, Verve, 1963.
Joao Gilberto, Polydor Brasil, 1973.
The Legendary Joao Gilberto, World Pacific, 1990.
Joao voz e violão, Mercury, 1999; reissued, Verve, 2000.

Sources

Periodicals

New York Times, September 19, 1977, p. 44.
San Francisco Chronicle, July 29, 1998, p. D1.

Online

"Joao Gilbeto," *Slipcue E-Zine,* http://www.slipcue.com/music/brazil/brazillist.html (April 11, 2001).
"The Man Who Invented Bossa Nova," *Best Web,* http://www.bestweb.net/~silkpurs/joao/essay.htm (April 12, 2001).

—Ronnie D. Lankford, Jr.

Evelyn Glennie

Percussionist

AP/Wide World Photos. Reproduced by permission.

Evelyn Glennie is considered one of the world's foremost percussionists and is the first and only full-time solo classical percussionist. The master of more than 1,000 traditional and unconventional percussion instruments from around the world has performed with a range of musical talents, from the Kodo Japanese drummers to Icelandic pop singer Björk, and with every major orchestra in America and Europe. Profoundly deaf (meaning severely impaired but not completely deaf) since the age of 12, the percussionist identifies notes by vibrations she feels through her feet and body; she insists her deafness is irrelevant to her ground-breaking, critically acclaimed work.

Evelyn Elizabeth Ann Glennie was born July 19, 1965, the only daughter of Isobel, a school teacher, and Herbert Arthur Glennie, a beef farmer. Raised outside Aberdeen, Scotland, Glennie and her two brothers helped on the family farm and, though her mother was an organist, didn't grow up in a particularly musical environment. She was a promising student of piano and clarinet as a child, and she was blessed with perfect pitch, the ability to identify or sing a note by ear. At age eight, Glennie started complaining of sore ears and hearing loss. Her condition steadily deteriorated, and by age 11 she needed a hearing aid, which she found distracting and later discarded. She continued to play music and found she could perceive the quality of a note by the level of the reverberations she could feel in her hands, wrists, lower body, and feet. Glennie counts as her major influences cellist Jacqueline du Pré and pianist Glenn Gould.

Percussion "Felt Right"

When she was 12, Glennie saw a schoolmate playing percussion. She started taking lessons, and, she told *People,* "… it felt right." She graduated with honors from London's prestigious Royal Academy of Music in 1985. She claims her deafness kept her from being caught up by social distractions and made her a better student, but she also realized it affected her ability to play in an orchestra, so she set her sights on becoming a soloist. In 1985 she made her professional debut; the following year she left for Japan to study the five-octave marimba for a year. Glennie's first decade as a professional solo performer was filled with milestones: first performance of a new percussion concerto, first time an orchestra had performed with a solo percussionist, first solo percussion performance at a festival or venue. In 1990 she met Greg Malcagni, a recording engineer, and the two wed four years later.

Glennie introduced her rendition of fellow Scot James MacMillan's *Veni, Veni, Emmanual*—described by *Billboard* as "a devoutly celestial concerto"—at London's Royal Albert Hall in 1992. She released a recording of the work the following year. In 1996 Glennie released *Drumming,* which she described to *Billboard* as "quite a

Born Evelyn Elizabeth Ann Glennie on July 19, 1965, in Aberdeen, Scotland; married Greg Malcagni, 1994.

Musically gifted from an early age; profoundly deaf by age 12, when she began playing percussion; graduated from London's Royal Academy of Music, 1985; debuted professionally as world's first full-time solo classical percussionist, 1985; recorded numerous solo albums for RCA/BMG including *MacMillan: Veni, Veni, Emmanuel; Wind in the Bamboo Grove; Drumming; Her Greatest Hits;* and *Shadow Behind the Iron Sun;* has performed with many of the world's best orchestras.

Awards: Scot of the Year, 1982; Hilda Deane Anderson Prize for Orchestral Playing, 1983; Hugh Fitz Prize for Percussion, 1983; James Blades Prize for Timpani & Percussion, 1984; Queen's Commendation Prize for all-around excellence, 1985; Leonardo da Vinci Prize, 1987; Associate of the Royal Academy of Music, 1987; All Music Young Professional Musician of the Year, 1988; Grammy Award for Best Chamber Music Performance for Bartok's *Sonata for Two Pianos and Percussion*, 1988; Royal Philharmonic Society's Charles Heidsieck Soloist of the Year Award, 1991; Best Classical Percussionist, *Modern Drummer* magazine readers' poll, 1990; Scotswoman of the Decade, 1990; the Gulliver Award for the Performing Arts in Scotland, 1993; OBE (Order of the British Empire), 1993; Young Deaf Achievers Special Award, 1993; International Classical Music Awards Personality of the Year, 1993; Outstanding Individual Award, Alexander Graham Bell Association, 1997; Percussionist of the Year Award, *DRUM* magazine, 1998; Best Studio Percussionist and Best Live Percussionist awards, *Rhythm* magazine, 1998, 2000; numerous other awards, scholarships, fellowships, and honorary doctorates.

Addresses: *U.S. Agent*—ICM Artists, 8942 Wilshire Blvd., Beverly Hills, CA 90211, (310) 550-4477. *Website*—Evelyn Glennie Official Website, http://www.evelyn.co.uk.

personal album." She wanted to make a "raw, ... improvised" album using untuned percussion. *Billboard* critic Timothy White called her playing on the record "breathtakingly instinctive."

Glennie's twelfth solo release, *Shadow Behind the Iron Sun,* was released in 2000 and recorded under unusual circumstances. She and veteran pop producer Michael Brauer spent four days in a studio packed with every instrument Glennie played, exploring as many moods as possible, from dark and aggressive to light and happy. The improvised songs, which were all recorded on the first take, were titled after chapters in *Eaters of the Dead,* a Michael Crichton novel that Brauer was reading at the time. "With this project, there were no boundaries, no rules, no limits," Glennie was quoted as saying on her website, adding it was her favorite record so far. *African Sunrise/Manhattan Rave*, released in 2001 on Black Box Records, is a work by British composer David Heath that Glennie and the London Philharmonic Orchestra bring to life. On "Manhattan Rave," Glennie literally plays on trash (an assortment of sticks, oilcans, and bottles and pans) and "does her best percussion freakout. It truly is an amazing work, capable of raising the dead while remaining somehow 'accessible,'" according to *All Music Guide*'s Thom Jurek.

Master of Timpani, Xylophone, Car Muffler

While countless pieces of music have been composed for the piano, violin, flute, or cello, few works have been written for percussion. In an effort to change that, Glennie has commissioned more than 80 new pieces to date, with projects constantly in the works. She actively pursues new composers and commissions more new pieces, on average, than any other solo performer.

Glennie has collected more than 1,000 percussion instruments, and there seems to be no end to what she is able to make music with. She is a master of common percussion instruments from around the world—marimba, xylophone, timpani, chimes, congas, steel pan, djembes, bodhrans, daiko drums, and many more. But she is also wildly inventive. She creates instruments herself, like an adapted car muffler she strikes with triangle beaters. She also has made music on common items such as a hospital bed, camera, wheel hub, garbage can lid, flower pot, and starting gun. Composer Django Bates wrote a piece for Glennie, which she played only with kitchen utensils, called "My Dream Kitchen." She designed a line of cymbals for cymbal company Sabian called "Glennie's Garbage" that are welded from sheet metal. Glennie, who played clarinet as a child, also began to add wind instruments to her repertoire, starting with Great Highland bagpipes.

Glennie tours extensively and exhaustively. She plays more than 100 concerts each year and has appeared across five continents. She plays on 20 to 50 instruments during each performance, "bounding," as Michael Walsch wrote in *Time*, "from instrument to instrument with the grace of a natural athlete." A *Washington Post* critic was almost as impressed by Glennie's physical show in concert—which he called the "Evelyn Glennie Workout"—as he was by "the subtle gradations of sound and color she brings to every phrase." In addition to the details of her music and instruments, Glennie pays attention to the non-musical details of her shows, performing in colorful, theatrical costumes and with thematically designed sets and lights. Because she feels the music through her feet, she prefers to play barefoot. In addition to about two tons of equipment, Glennie travels with her Gameboy video game player.

Did Not Want to Hear about Hearing

In addition to performing, Glennie and her husband have composed award-winning music for British film and television. She also hosted two series of her own television programs for the BBC, including one called *Soundbites,* which featured interviews and performances by musical guests. She has written two books for the marimba and a music education book for schools. Her best-selling autobiography, *Good Vibrations,* was published in 1985.

Glennie believes that her hearing impairment has no bearing on her position as a world-renowned percussionist, and she is reluctant to discuss the subject with interviewers. Although she is active in some 40 organizations for the deaf, such as a program that provides music-based therapy for hearing-impaired children, Glennie downplays her involvement, preferring to concentrate on elevating the art of percussion. She has achieved her goal, according to *Symphony* magazine: "Glennie is the one individual most responsible for the sudden emergence of percussion from the rear of the orchestra to front-and-center stage, both in fact and in public attention."

Selected discography

Rhythm Song, RCA Victor, 1990.
Light in Darkness, RCA Red Seal, 1991.
Dancin', RCA Victor/BMG Classics, 1991.
Rebounds: Concertos for Percussion, RCA Red Seal, 1993.
MacMillan: Veni, Veni, Emmanual, Catalyst, 1993.
Wind in the Bamboo Grove, Catalyst, 1995.
Drumming, Catalyst, 1996.
The Music of Joseph Schwantner, RCA Red Seal, 1997.
Her Greatest Hits, RCA Victor, 1998.
Street Songs, RCA Red Seal, 1998.
Reflected in Brass, RCA Red Seal, 1998.
Shadow Behind the Iron Sun, RCA Red Seal, 2000.
African Sunrise/Manhattan Rave, Black Box, 2001.

Sources

Books

International Who's Who, Europa Publications, 2000.

Periodicals

Billboard, October 12, 1996, p. 7.
People, March 25, 1996, p. 109.
Time, March 21, 1994, p. 73.
Washington Post, October 12, 1996, p. C1.

Online

Evelyn Glennie Official Website, http://www.evelyn.co.uk (April 23, 2001).
"Evelyn Glennie," *All Classical Guide,* http://www.all classical.com (April 23, 2001).
"Evelyn Glennie," *All Music Guide,* http://www.allmusic.com (April 23, 2001).

—Brenna Sanchez

Gomez

Rock group

Although they hail from England, Gomez does not sound like a typical British pop band. Melding blues, folk, country, classic rock, and sometimes psychedelia with a bit of techno, Gomez actually creates music that sounds more American. Admittedly, their influences include 1960s-era heroes like Joni Mitchell, Jimi Hendrix, the Doors, Marvin Gaye, and J.J. Cale, as well as present-day stars such as Beck. Because of their uniqueness, Gomez, a five-piece act featuring three singers, immediately caught the attention of the public and the press. Their self-made debut, *Bring It On,* earned favorable reviews and surprised many by winning the Mercury Music Prize in 1998, beating out records by acts such as the Verve, Massive Attack, and Robbie Williams. The quintet solidified their reputation with a second album, *Liquid Skin,* in 2000.

"We're trying to carve our own little what do you call it—our own niche," Tom Gray said in an interview with *Rolling Stone*'s Pat Blashill. "The music press here is all about 'This week! This week!' And we don't really care about 'This week!' 'This week!' A friend of ours said, 'Every day's the best day for music, because today someone's just going to add something else to the great mass of all that is good.' And we really like that thought."

Most of the members of Gomez—vocalist and guitarist Ben Ottewell; vocalist, guitarist, and keyboardist Tom Gray; vocalist, guitarist, and harmonica player Ian Ball; bassist and vocalist Paul Blackburn, and drummer and percussionist Olly Peacock—were born in the mid to late 1970s and raised in or close to the seaside town of Southport, a fading vacation destination for residents of Liverpool, England. Ball and Peacock first met each other literally at birth. Both were born on the same day in the same Southport hospital, and their mothers became friends. They formed Gomez with Blackburn, Gray, and Ottewell in their late teens.

The group says that missing out on the punk invasion and the rave scene helps to explain why they adopted influences from progressive rock and folk as a foundation for their alternative, art-rock music. Their greatest inspiration came from the music their parents listened to or through other second-hand sources. Ball's father, an accountant and fan of rock from the 1950s through the 1970s, introduced his son early to artists ranging from Chuck Berry to ELO. Ball discovered his all-time favorite artist, though, by chance. One day in a Manchester record store, Ball heard the Tom Waits album *Jockey Full of Bourbon.* Intrigued by the surreal, hazy sound, he went out the very next day and bought every album Waits had recorded.

Ottewell, the son of a psychology professor and a nursery school teacher, grew up in Derbyshire, near Southport. One of his earliest memories is that of his mother singing the Joni Mitchell song "A Case of You" to him at the age of five. During his adolescent years, Ottewell went through a phase of liking heavy metal, and as a teen, his favorite bands included Nirvana and Pearl Jam, until the day his mother introduced him to the songs of Nick Drake, another of Gomez's primary influences. Now, Ottewell's present day favorites include the Beta Band and Beck. In fact, in college, Ottewell wrote his dissertation on post-modern culture and cited Beck's *Odelay* album to illustrate his point.

In 1996, Ball started recording jam sessions he had been hosting at his home with the other members of Gomez. Before long, the sessions took on a more serious tone, leading to a decision to make an album. Still, Gomez never thought much would come of their home-made productions recorded in garages and bedrooms on four-track equipment. "We were making an album," recalled Ottewell to Mark Jenkins in the *Washington Post,* "but it was never an album we thought would be released. Then our manager got to hear it, and he really liked it."

After re-recording some of the tracks, Gomez shopped the album around to various labels. They ultimately opted to sign with Hut, a Virgin Records imprint, out of a concern about retaining artistic freedom over money. Released in April of 1998, their self-produced debut entitled *Bring It On,* featuring the opener "Get Miles" as well as the single "Get Myself Arrested," ignited an unanticipated success story fueled by rave reviews. Without ever having played a live show, Gomez was immediately thrust center stage. Over the course of a couple of months, they honed their skills at smaller

For the Record . . .

Members include **Ian Ball**, vocals, guitar, harmonica; **Paul Blackburn**, vocals, bass; **Tom Gray**, vocals, guitar, keyboards; **Ben Ottewell**, vocals, guitar; **Olly Peacock**, drums, percussion.

Formed in Southport, England, 1996; released *Bring It On,* 1998; released *Liquid Skin,* 1999.

Awards: Technics Mercury Music Prize, 1998.

Addresses: *Record company*—Virgin Records (U.K.), 553-579 Harrow Road, London, England, W10 4RH, website: www.virginrecords.com.

venues, then played major summer festivals such as Glastonbury, V98, and Reading.

On September 16, 1998, Gomez won Britain's prestigious Technics Mercury Music Prize when *Bring It On* was named the Album of the Year. Subsequently, the band earned the *Q* Magazine Award for Best New Band, as well as three BRIT Award nominations for Best Newcomer, Best Album, and Best Artist. Upon its introduction in the United States, *Bring It On* continued to impress. *Rolling Stone* declared Gomez as "brazen, earnest stylists," while *Spin* called the group's debut a "damn beautiful record."

Gomez also came to the attention of mainstream America via a television advertisement for Philips electronic products, for which they performed a snippet from the Beatles tune "Getting Better." While Gomez's own music does not sound very Beatlesque, the band recognizes the legendary group as a significant inspiration in other ways. "I think that's the mistake these Britpop bands made," Ottewell told Jenkins. "They consciously took what the Beatles did and kind of missed the point. For me, and I think for the other guys, the great thing about the Beatles was the way they experimented. And the fun they had, basically. There's a certain freedom that's kind of gotten lost."

In March of 1999, Gomez commenced work on their sophomore effort, *Liquid Skin.* They recorded the eleven tracks for the self-produced album in studios in Liverpool and London, in their home, and in a fifteenth-century mansion in the English countryside. Released later that year in the United Kingdom and in the spring of 2000 in the United States, *Liquid Skin* met expectations with its denser and more ambitious quality achieved through various, sometimes unconventional, means. Some of their experiments included singing through a toilet paper roll, employing an underwater microphone, using a fire extinguisher as a percussion instrument, and recording a drum machine through a small guitar amplifier. The resulting album featured the free-jamming opener "Hangover," the single "Bring It On" (sharing the same name as Gomez's debut), "Rhythm & Blues Alibi," which combines an unconventional drum machine with guitars, the waltzing "Fill My Cup," the organic tune "We Haven't Turned Around," and the epic closing track "The Devil Will Ride."

Selected discography

Bring It On, Hut/Virgin, 1998.
Liquid Skin, Hut/Virgin, 1999.

Sources

Periodicals

Billboard, August 8, 1998; September 26, 1998.
Boston Globe, April 15, 1999; March 23, 2000.
Guitar Player, October 1998.
Los Angeles Times, April 28, 1999; October 4, 1999.
Melody Maker, March 21, 1998; April 4, 1998; August 22, 1998; June 19, 1999; September 4, 1999; October 27-November 2, 1999.
Rolling Stone, September 2, 1999.
Village Voice, October 5, 1999.
Washington Post, March 10, 2000.

Online

Virgin Records, http://www.virginrecords.com (May 29, 2001).

—Laura Hightower

The Grapes of Wrath

Rock group

The punk rock movement of the mid 1970s gave birth to numerous sub-genres and musical off-shoots such as New Wave, goth, alternative, and grunge. Almost every popular musical group that emerged after punk rock invaded the mainstream has owed a debt to this seminal musical force of the late twentieth century.

By 1977 the punk rock phenomenon had infiltrated Canada. Small towns and big cities alike had begun to attract homegrown bands and performers who were steeped in the nascent punk tradition. The tiny western Canadian town of Kelowna, British Columbia, was no exception. In 1977 schoolmates Chris Hooper and Kevin Kane, who were both in their early teens, joined up with Hooper's little brother Tom, who was barely 11 years old, to form a punk band.

The newly formed trio began to jam together at their parents' homes. They covered punk tunes along with staples of the classic-rock canon before they moved on to playing their own songs. They broke up a short while later. According to the 1991 biography of Grapes of Wrath on the Capitol Records website, "the Hoopers continued to pursue their punk fixation with a group called Gentlemen of Horror, while Kane played in an art-rock outfit [called] Empty Set."

In 1983 the Hooper brothers decided to hook up with Kane again. They formed what was supposed to be a one-night-only cover band called Honda Civic. After the show, the Hoopers and Kane realized that, in order for them to achieve their goals and satisfy themselves both musically and creatively, they were going to have to come together for good this time. The creative spark of their collaborations along with their love of cutting-edge music were the forces that initially brought the Hooper brothers and Kane together in 1977; they served to bring them back together some six years later.

The summer of 1983 saw the trio drop the name Honda Civic in favor of something more substantial. They decided on Grapes of Wrath, a name suggested by the film lover, Chris. They soon began practicing at home under their new name.

With money saved up from various part-time jobs and yard sales, among other things, the Grapes of Wrath traveled to Vancouver in 1984 to record their first record—a four-song self-titled EP. *The Grapes of Wrath* was released on the Vancouver-based Nettwerk label. Soon after the EP's release, the band relocated to Vancouver, picking up a new member around the same time: keyboard player Vincent Jones.

The positive regional support that the Grapes of Wrath's debut EP garnered helped to propel their next release into the musical consciousness of the Canadian nation as a whole. The band's second album, *September Bowl of Green,* was released in 1985. It was this album, their first full-length release, that earned them critical acclaim and national interest, helped along by significant radio airplay throughout Canada.

After capturing the national attention of their homeland, the Grapes of Wrath turned their attention toward the United States to see if they could work their magic south of the border. In 1986 *September Bowl of Green* was released in both America and Europe, thanks to a global distribution deal brokered between Nettwerk and Capitol Records. Unlike the situation in Canada, the record did not cause much of a stir in the United States. Undaunted by this, the Grapes of Wrath entered the studio to record their second full-length album, *Treehouse,* which was released in Canada in 1987. The album was not the breakthrough smash hit everyone in the band had hoped for, but it did yield "Peace of Mind," the Grapes of Wrath's first hit single in Canada. The album did not fare well in America when it was released one year later.

Early 1989 saw the Grapes of Wrath return to the United States, specifically Woodstock, New York, to record the sessions that would eventually become their third album, *Now and Again.* This album evokes the melodies of the Byrds along with the jangly sounds of such college and alternative rock stalwarts as R.E.M., the Connells, and Let's Active. *Now and Again* struck a responsive chord in the record-buying and music-listening public in Canada: the album went gold in Canada after less than two months. The Grapes of

For the Record . . .

Members include **Matt Brain** (joined group, c. 2000), drums; **Chris Hooper** (left group, c. 1998), drums; **Tom Hooper**, bass, vocals; **Vincent Jones** (joined group, c. 1985), keyboards; **Kevin Kane**, vocals, guitars.

Group formed in Kelowna, British Columbia, Canada, 1983; moved to Vancouver, British Columbia, and signed with Nettwerk Records; released *Grapes of Wrath* (EP), 1984; signed to Capitol Records, released *September Bowl of Green,*1985; disbanded, 1992; reformed, 1998; released *Field Trip* on Song Recordings, 2000.

Awards: Canadian platinum sales certification, *Now and Again*, c. 1990; Canadian platinum sales certification, *These Days*, c. 1992.

Addresses: *Business*—P.O. Box 57128, 2480 E. Hastings St., Vancouver, BC, Canada V5K 5G6. *Website*—Grapes of Wrath Official Website: http://www.the grapesofwrath.com.

Wrath also scored their first top-ten hit single in Canada, the lilting ballad "All the Things I Wasn't." The success of *Now and Again* helped to push the Grapes of Wrath out of the clubs and into the concert halls as they toured Canada. While *Now and Again* was achieving platinum sales certification in Canada, the Grapes of Wrath began touring Europe and the United States.

Touring in support of *Now and Again* took up most of 1990, and the Grapes of Wrath's fourth album did not see the light of day until 1991. Like its predecessor, *These Days* was certified platinum in Canada. The sales of the album were bolstered by the fact that it yielded two top-ten hit singles, "I Am Here" and "You May Be Right." Concerts sold out all over Canada, and Europe began to warm up to the charms of the Grapes of Wrath. In Europe the Grapes of Wrath began to see their first chart appearances outside their native land.

Unfortunately, the success and accolades were to be short-lived for the Grapes of Wrath. On October 30, 1992, the band dissolved. According to the official Grapes of Wrath website, "though never officially 'breaking up,' the Grapes of Wrath were pretty much over: the Hoopers and Jones attempted to have Kane removed from the band and Kane took legal action against his former band mates." The Hooper brothers and Jones went on to form the band Ginger, releasing two albums in the mid 1990s. Kane pursued a solo career and released an album around the same time.

Almost four years after the band had broken up, Tom Hooper sent Kane a letter about the split. According to the official Grapes of Wrath website, the "letter sugget[ed] that the two of them try and resolve matters once and for all. Meeting at a 'neutral' Vancouver location, the old Grapes business [was] essentially 'put to rest' in barely over an hour, [and] talk turned to playing together again."

They decided to play small shows and began to record some tracks in the studio in the late 1990s. By the summer of 2000, Kane, along with his songwriting partner Tom Hooper and new drummer Matt Brain, had released the fifth Grapes of Wrath record, *Field Trip,* on Song Recordings. Commenting on *Field Trip*—the first Grapes of Wrath record in nine years—on the Chartattack website, Hooper said, "Time goes by. You'd hope that you wouldn't sound exactly the same that you did 15 years ago. It's whatever comes naturally. We're better players now, we're better everything."

Selected discography

The Grapes of Wrath (EP), Nettwerk Records, 1984.
September Bowl of Green, Capitol Records, 1985.
Treehouse (includes "Peace of Mind"), Capitol Records, 1987.
Now and Again (includes "All the Things I Wasn't"), Capitol Records, 1989.
These Days (includes "I Am Here" and "You May Be Right"), Capitol Records, 1991.
Field Trip, Song Recordings, 2000.

Sources

Books

Graff, Gary and Daniel Durchholz, editors, *MusicHound Rock: The Essential Album Guide*, Visible Ink Press, 1999.

Online

"The Grapes of Wrath," *All Music Guide,* http://www.allmusic.com (April 10, 2001).
Grapes of Wrath Official Website, http://www.thegrapesof wrath.com (April 10, 2001).
"Grapes of Wrath's Magic Mushroom Experience," Chartattack, http://www.chartattack.com (April 10, 2001).

Additional information was taken from Capitol Records press materials for *These Days*, 1991.

—*Mary Alice Adams*

Marc-André Hamelin

Pianist

An unusually talented prize-winning pianist, Marc-André Hamelin achieved legendary renown during the 1990s with his penchant for churning out a catalog of astonishingly difficult piano recordings at a breakneck pace. Repertoire notwithstanding, it is the demon speed of his finger work that has ultimately distinguished this internationally acclaimed virtuoso as his career has unfolded. During the 1980s, Hamelin won both the Pretoria International and Carnegie Hall American International music competitions. He spent long hours during the 1990s recording an expansive collection of piano selections with unprecedented fury. His 1996 collection of the complete sonatas of Alexander Scriabin earned the Canadian Juno Award for Best Classical Album, as did his earlier interpretations of the works of composer Charles-Valentin Alkan. In all, Hamelin released more than 50 recordings during the 1990s and more than a dozen additional albums by early 2001.

Hamelin was born on September 5, 1961, in Montreal, Quebec, Canada. His appreciation of piano music took root early in his youth. His father, a pharmacist, was also an accomplished pianist who nurtured Hamelin's interest in the piano. Hamelin began lessons at age five and later attended the elite l'École Vincent-d'Indy de Montréal where he studied under Yvonne Hubert. Interestingly, his school counselors urged him to study science and mathematics instead of music in order to develop backup skills should he fail in his quest to become a professional pianist. At home, Hamelin was keenly intrigued by the complexity of the piano music that his father enjoyed, including recordings of music by Alkan, Nikolai Medtner, and Leopold Godowsky. By the time Hamelin reached his teens, he had developed an appreciation for the power and versatility of the piano as a musical instrument and began at an early age to seek out lengthy and complicated pieces to play. He was only 15 years old when he purchased a copy of the Kaikhosru Shapurji Sorabji composition *Opus Clavicembalisticum,* an obscure and extraordinarily difficult book-length score that was pulled from publication soon afterward.

Hamelin earned both his bachelor's and master's of music degrees at Philadelphia's Temple University under the guidance of Harvey Wedeen and Russell Sherman. By the early 1980s, Hamelin had established a name for himself in international competition by winning South Africa's Pretoria International Music Competition in 1982, followed by the Carnegie Hall American International Music Competition in 1984. He then spent the summer of 1987 as a featured soloist with the Montreal Symphony Orchestra during a European tour. In 1987 and 1989, the Canada Council honored Hamelin with the Sylva-Gelber Foundation Prize and the Virginia P. Moore Prize, respectively.

Born on September 5, 1961, in Montreal, Quebec, Canada; married Jody Karin Applebaum. *Education*: Studied with Yvonne Huber at Vincent d'Indy School of Music; bachelor's and master's degrees in music, Temple University.

Soloist, European tour with Montréal Symphony Orchestra, 1987; professor, University of Alberta, Canada; worldwide tours, including Australia and Japan, 2000; has recorded extensively with Music and Arts, 1990; Doberman-Yppan, 1992; Hyperion, 1993-.

Awards: Winner, Pretoria International Music Competition, 1982; Winner, Carnegie Hall International American Music Competition, 1985; Sylva-Gelber Foundation Prize, Canada Council, 1987; Virginia P. Moore Prize, Canada Council, 1989; Juno Award (Canada), Best Classical Album for Alkan: *Grande Sonate/Sonatine/Le Festin d'Esope*, 1996; Juno Award, Best Classical Album for Scriabin: *The Complete Piano Sonatas*, 1997; Soundscapes Award (Australia), 1997; Preis der Deutschen Schallplattenkritik, 1997-98; Gramophone Instrumental Award, 2000.

Addresses: *Record company*—Hyperion Records Ltd., P.O. Box 25, London, England, SE9 1AX, phone: (0)20 8294 1166, fax: (0)20 8294 1161. *Agent*—Georgina Ivor Associates, 28 Old Devonshire Road, London SW12 9RB, phone: (0)181 673 7179, fax: (0)181 675 8058, e-mail: GIvor@aol.com.

Virtuosity Unleashed

Hamelin released a lengthy discography during the 1990s, beginning on the Music and Arts label with a Schönberg album and two cabaret collections by William Bolcom and Benjamin Britten, respectively. He entered into collaborations with fellow pianist Louise Bessette for a series of two-piano recordings for Doberman-Yppan in 1992, releasing selected works by Hétu, Matton, and Prévost. On a subsequent series of albums released on the Analekta label, Hamelin was accompanied by Sophie Rolland on cello, with violin accompaniment by Angèle Dubeau on featured selections. These recordings included works by Thuille, Strauss, and Martinú.

Under contract with Hyperion beginning in 1993, Hamelin embarked on an extended period of recording that involved a battery of the most difficult selections ever written by various classical and modern composers. By mid-decade, reviewers and critics were paying due homage to Hamelin's rare talent, which bordered on the courageous in terms of his willingness to present—even in live public performances—an uninterrupted sequence of highly difficult musical scores. *Dallas Morning News* critic Olin Chism said of Hamelin's impromptu program of Bach and Godowsky, presented at the Texas Conservatory for Young Artists in 1996, that the "brilliant passage work, blazing chords, extremes of dynamics were all there." On another occasion, the newspaper's Scott Cantrell commented on Hamelin's penchant for "fist-busting" performances. The *Toronto Star*'s Peter Goddard commented on Hamelin's "extraordinary ability to play a million notes," while praising the speed that he turned out new work.

Piano Benchmarks

In 1993 Hamelin, through Hyperion, released the first in an ongoing series of recordings of the works of a little-known nineteenth-century Parisian composer. Commonly known as Alkan, he is also known as Charles-Valentin Morhange. Alkan was a mysterious and sometimes reclusive musician whose identity and works were obscured by those of his better-known cohorts and contemporaries such as Chopin and Liszt. Hamelin successfully brought Alkan's music to prominence by means of his several recordings. Among these, Hamelin's *Grande Sonate/Sonatine/Le Festin d'Esope* of 1995 won the Juno Award for Best Classical Album in 1996.

Hamelin subsequently rescued from obscurity the complex works of a misunderstood composer named Alexander Scriabin. When Hamelin released Scriabin: *The Complete Piano Sonatas* in 1997 on Hyperion, *Billboard* columnist Bradley Bambarger called the release a "latter-day benchmark." The Scriabin collection helped Hamelin earn a second Juno Award as the Best Classical Album of 1997. Bambarger praised Hamelin further for "[His] pioneering set [1996, 1997, and 1998] of the 14 sonatas by … Nikolai Medtner [that] might never be bettered." Likewise, *Billboard's* Paul Verna called Hamelin a "mega-virtuoso" and the "ideal soloist" in reference to the Marx *Romantisches Klavierkonzert* and the left-handed Erich Wolfgang Korngold concerto, each performed by Hamelin in 1997.

By the end of the 1990s, Hamelin's total number of recorded releases had climbed to more than 50 albums, including many obscure selections that were rarely heard in performance because of sheer difficulty. Among his assorted recordings, Hamelin included some of his own writings on a 1998 Hyperion release entitled *The Composer-Pianists,* although he discounted his efforts as a composer as negligible and avered that, unlike many pianists, he does not conduct orchestras. His acclaimed performances and recordings have earned him a collection of distinctive international awards including the Australian Soundscapes Award and two Preis der Deutschen Schallplattenkritik awards. In 2000 he received the Gramophone Instrumental Award.

When Hyperion released Hamelin's Godowsky: *Studies on Chopin's Etudes* in 2000, *American Record Guide*'s Harold Schonberg noted that the etudes in their original state were uncommonly difficult, and in Godowsky's hands the arrangements were made more difficult still. Thus Schonberg reserved nothing but praise for Hamelin and applauded the final product. "More difficult piano music has never been written...." reported Schonberg. "Hamelin plays this music—really plays it. All piano philes have been impressed by many of his recordings, but here he rises to amazing heights." The National Academy of Recording Arts and Sciences nominated the recording for a Grammy Award as the Best Instrumental Soloist Performance (Without Orchestra) in 2000. Also that year, Hamelin's Busoni: *Concerto, op. 39* with Mark Elder and the City of Birmingham Symphony Orchestra was nominated in the Best Instrumental Soloist (with Orchestra) category.

Illustrious Orchestral Performances

Hamelin has performed with the finest orchestras from North America and Europe, including Europe's Royal Concertgebouw, the BBC Philharmonic, the Minneapolis and Houston Symphonies, and with such eminent conductors as Charles Dutoit, Dmitri Sitkovetsky, and David Zinman. Hamelin's recital venues have extended worldwide to Istanbul, Turkey; Frankfurt and Munich, Germany; Vienna, Austria; Amsterdam, Netherlands; Washington, D.C., Tokyo, Japan; Paris, France; Milan, Italy; and elsewhere. Likewise he has graced festivals around the world with his singular mastery of the piano, having performed at Blackheath Halls Pianoworks, La Grange de Meslay en Touraine; Manchester Glories of the Keyboard Festival, Ruhr Piano Festival, Singapore International Piano Festival, Britain's the Proms, and the Valldemosa Chopin Festival. He performed recitals at Wigmore Hall in June of 1994 at the Virtuoso Romantics series and later returned to the Wigmore Hall Masterconcert Series and the Exploration & Celebration Series at Wigmore in 1999.

In addition to his outstanding career in performance, Hamelin taught for a time at the University of Alberta. He lives in Philadelphia with his wife Jody Karin Applebaum, who is a teacher and a talented performer in her own right. Applebaum sings to her husband's accompaniment in intimate cabaret shows on select occasions.

Selected discography

Schönberg: *Brettl-Lieder,* Music and Arts, 1990.
Bolcom: *12 Cabaret Songs,* Music and Arts, 1990.
Britten: *Cabaret Songs,* Music and Arts, 1990.
Hétu: *Sonate pour deux pianos* with Louise Bessette, Doberman-Yppan, 1992.
(With Louise Bessette, piano; J.Grégoire, V. Dhavernas, percussion) Matton: *Concerto pour deux pianos et Percussion,* Doberman-Yppan, 1992.
(With Louise Bessette) Matton: *Danse Brésilienne pour deux pianos,* Doberman-Yppan, 1992.
(With Louise Bessette) Prévost: *Quatre Préludes pour deux pianos,* Doberman-Yppan, 1992.
Wright: *Chamber Symphony for Piano and Electronic Music,* Composers Recordings Inc., 1993.
Wright: *Night Watch,* Composers Recordings Inc., 1993.
Alkan: *Concerto da Camera, op. 10, no. 1,* Hyperion, 1993.
Alkan: *Concerto da Camera, op. 10, no. 2,* Hyperion, 1993.
Henselt: *Piano Concerto in F minor, op. 16,* Hyperion, 1993.
Variations de Concert, op. 11, Hyperion, 1993.
Rimsky-Korsakov: *Mozart and Salieri, op. 48,* Chandos, 1993.
Alkan: *Concerto for Solo Piano,* Music and Arts, 1993.
Medtner: *Danza Festiva,* Hyperion, 1994.
Alkan: *Grande Sonate/Sonatine/Le Festin d'Esope,* Hyperion, 1995.
Martinú: *Madrigal Sonata,* Analekta, 1995.
Martinú: *Madrigal Stanzas,* Analekta, 1995.
(With Angèle Dubeau, violin; Alain Marion, flute) Martinú: *Promenades for flute, violin and Harpsichord,* Analekta, 1995.
(With Alain Marion) Martinú: *Scherzo for flute and piano,* Analekta, 1995.
(With Alain Marion, flute) Martinú: *Sonata for flute and piano,* Analekta, 1995.
(With Angèle Dubeau, violin; Alain Marion, flute) Martinú: *Sonata for flute, violin and piano,* Analekta, 1995.
Grainger: *Piano Music,* Hyperion, 1996.
Scriabin: *The Complete Piano Sonatas,* Hyperion, 1996.
Medtner: *Complete sonatas and Vergessene Weisen,* Hyperion, 1996.
Korngold: *Piano Concerto for the Left Hand, op. 17,* Hyperion, 1997.
Marx: *Romantisches Klavierkonzert,* Hyperion, 1997.
Medtner: *Primavera, op. 39, no. 3,* Danacord, 1998.
R.Strauss: *Enoch Arden,* 1998.
The Composer-Pianists, Hyperion, 1998.
Bouliane: *Douze tiroirs de demi-vérité pour alléger votre Descente,* Sne, 1999.
Ravel, Riche Lieu, 1999.
Honegger: *Saluste du Bartas,* Riche Lieu, 1999.
Debussy, Riche Lieu, 1999.
Poulenc: *Deux poèmes de Louis Aragon,* Riche Lieu, 1999.
Fauré, Riche Lieu, 1999.
Vuillermoz: *Chansons,* Riche Lieu, 1999.
Rzewski: *The People United Will Never Be Defeated!* Hyperion, 1999.
(With Mark Elder and the City of Birmingham Symphony Orchestra) Busoni: *Concerto, op. 39,* Hyperion, 2000.
Godowsky: *Studies on Chopin's Etudes,* Hyperion, 2000.
Poulenc: *Les Chernins de l'Amour,* Danacord, 2000.
Bernstein: *Symphony no. 2, The Age of Anxiety,* Hyperion, 2000.

Bolcom: *Piano Concerto,* Hyperion, 2000.
Holländer: *An allern sind die Juden schuld,* Danacord, 2000.
Sondheim: *Losing my mind,* Danacord, 2000.
Lemaire: *Le Verger,* Kleos, 2001.
Holländer: *Cabaret Songs,* Kleos, 2001.
Bruant: *Cabaret Songs,* Kleos, 2001.
Cuvillier: *Toutou,* Kleos, 2001.
Doucer: *Cabaret Songs,* Kleos, 2001.
Eisler: *Ueber den Selbstmord,* Kleos, 2001.
Heymann: *Abschied von der Boheme,* Kleos, 2001.
Satie: *Cabaret songs,* Kleos, 2001.
Weill: *Cabaret songs,* Kleos, 2001.
Wolpe: *Es wird die neue Welt geboren,* Kleos, 2001.

Sources

Periodicals

American Record Guide, September/October 1996, p. 52;
  May/June 1997, p. 202; July/August 2000, p. 138.
Billboard, March 14, 1998, p. 20; February 5, 2000, p. 59B.
Dallas Morning News, June 23, 1996, p. 33A; November 18,
  2000, p. 45A.
Independent (London), March 15, 1996, p. 13; May 11, 2000.
Maclean's, March 6, 1995, p. 73; May 12, 1997, p. 71.
Toronto Star, January 20, 2001.

Online

"Discography of Marc-André Hamelin," Frazer Jarvis, http://
  www.sheffield.ac.uk/~pm1afj/mah.html (March 30, 2001).
"Marc-André Hamelin," Georgina Ivor Associates, http://
  members.aol.com/GIvor/mahbio.htm (March 30, 2001).

—Gloria Cooksey

Roy Haynes

Drummer

A versatile percussionist who has witnessed more than 50 years of jazz history, Haynes has contributed to various swing, bop, avant-garde, modal-jazz, free-jazz, fusion, and jazz-rock groups. Although he has played in the rhythm sections of practically every major jazz group since the 1940s, Haynes is not as well known as some of his contemporaries, perhaps because he has been overshadowed by the bands he played with. While such artists as Lester Young, Charlie Parker, Sarah Vaughan, Thelonious Monk, and Chick Corea, among numerous others, became legendary figures in jazz, Haynes did not, though he played rhythm for them all. Known as "everyone's favorite sideman," according to the *All Music Guide to Jazz,* Haynes began focusing on his own recordings in the 1980s and 1990s when he was well past the age when most Americans retire.

Born on March 13, 1926, in Roxbury, Massachusetts, Haynes listened to his older brother's records as a kid. His brother's collection included music by Django Reinhardt, Bing Crosby, Glenn Miller, Art Tatum, Count Basie, Duke Ellington, and the popular singers of the time. Growing up amidst Roxbury's mixed ethnic population, Haynes was also exposed to Irish and Jewish music. He was a drum major in his high school band, but after being disciplined for drumming on the classroom desks with his hands, Haynes avoided going to school altogether. Instead, he said in an interview with *Down Beat,* "I went to school with Lester Young and Charlie Parker and Luis Russell." Haynes added that his life as a musician took him around the world and gave him the confidence and knowledge to talk to anyone—from a stranger on the street to the king and queen of Thailand or the president of the United States.

During the early 1940s, Haynes was part of Roxbury's thriving African American subculture. He began his career by playing in swing groups and little-known Dixieland and big bands, including those led by Sabby Lewis and Frankie Newton. Bandleader Luis Russell encouraged the drummer to join him in New York City in 1945, and Haynes lived in Harlem into the early 1950s. Although Russell had never heard of him, the young drummer had come so highly recommended by an alto saxophone player named Charlie Holmes that Russell sent Haynes a one-way train ticket. Haynes started playing with Russell at New York's legendary Savoy Ballroom. "I must've had something back then," Haynes told *Down Beat.* "I knew I could swing. I knew that."

Afro-Cuban music was big when Haynes first arrived in New York, and jazz musicians were listening to orchestras led by Machito, Tito Puente, and Tito Rodriguez. According to the *New York Times,* Haynes' "outgoing, open" sound has fueled comparisons to that of a timbale or conga player. Haynes, however, dismisses the notion, claiming that his style has always been his

Born Roy Owen Haynes on March 13, 1926, in Roxbury, MA.

Played in Boston swing groups, big bands, and Dixieland groups, 1940s; has played with (among others): Luis Russell's orchestra, 1944-47; Louis Armstrong, 1946; Lester Young, 1947-49; Bud Powell and Miles Davis, 1949; Charlie Parker, 1949-52; Sarah Vaughan, 1953-58; Thelonious Monk, 1958; Eric Dolphy, 1960; Stan Getz and Gary Burton, 1960s; founded the Hip Ensemble, 1960; principal substitute for Elvin Jones in John Coltrane's group, 1961-65; played with Duke Jordan, 1975; Nick Brignola, 1977-78; Burton, Hank Jones, and Art Pepper, 1978; Ted Curson, 1978-79; Joe Albany and Horace Tapscott, 1979; Dizzy Gillespie, 1979; Chick Corea's group Trio Music, 1981–; led various bop quartets in New York, 1985-86; played with Pat Metheny, c. 1989; formed Roy Haynes Trio featuring Danilo Perez & John Pattitucci, early 1990s.

Awards: Certified Jazz Master, National Endowment for the Arts, 1994; Danish Jazzpar prize, 1994; Best Contemporary Jazz Recording for *Te Vou!*, National Association of Independent Record Distributors and Manufacturers, 1995.

Addresses: *Record company*—Verve Music Group, 1755 Broadway, New York, NY 10019, website: http://www.vervemusicgroup.com/grp/.

own. Regardless of his influences, many see Haynes as a standout drummer. "It's the way he breaks up time," pianist David Kikoski told the *New York Times*. "The syncopation that he developed influenced all modern drummers. It sounds natural because it is natural." Haynes contended that he just played how he felt. He told *Down Beat*, "As far as introducing things to jazz drumming that were different, I don't know what I did. I just had certain things in my head I wanted to play, and I played those things."

After two years, Luis Russell split up his band to go on tour, and Haynes started working with various young bandleaders who were heading smaller groups. In 1951 he turned down an offer from Dizzy Gillespie to join his big band in order to continue playing with Charlie Parker. "It was fashionable, then, to leave the big bands and play with the small groups," Haynes told the *New York Times*. "That's what we wanted to do—just stay in New York and gig."

Haynes spent the 1940s and 1950s behind his drum kit for such legendary acts as Lester Young, Bud Powell, Miles Davis, and Thelonious Monk. He played with Sarah Vaughan from 1953 to 1958 and toured the world with her. During the late 1950s and early 1960s, Haynes recorded live dates for record labels EmArcy, Swing, New Jazz, Impulse!, Pacific Jazz, Mainstream, and Galaxy. In 1960 Haynes formed his own bop group, which later became the Hip Ensemble and came to play more of a jazz-rock sound. Also in the 1960s, he played with Eric Dolphy, Stan Getz, and Gary Burton, and he was the principle substitute for drummer Elvin Jones in John Coltrane's legendary group. In the late 1970s, Haynes appeared on recordings by Nick Brignola, Burton, Hank Jones, and Art Pepper, among others.

In 1979 Haynes played the famed Newport and Monterey jazz festivals with Dizzy Gillespie. In 1981 he became a member of Chick Corea's band Trio Music in 1981. He toured sporadically with Corea and led various New York bop quartets in the mid 1980s. He also released several well-received records in the 1980s and 1990s, including *Homecoming, When It's Haynes It Roars, Te Vou!,* and *True or False,* which the *All Music Guide to Jazz* declared "easily recommended to hard bop collectors." When asked by Ben Ratliff of the *New York Times* when he first heard bebop music, Haynes flinched, saying he felt like he had been playing it all his life. Ratliff speculated that Haynes was part of the generation that was "young enough to swallow [bebop] whole and make an actual style of it."

Formed in the early 1990s, the Roy Haynes Trio, featuring Danilo Perez on piano and John Pattitucci on bass, released *The Roy Haynes Trio* on Verve/Universal in 2000. At age 75, Haynes headed back out on an American tour with his group. "I never thought I would be this age and touring," he told the *New York Times*. Haynes recalled in *Down Beat* that, in 1949, Bud Powell speculated that musicians would be playing their music ten years down the road. Almost 50 years later that music was still being played; in 1996 Chick Corea toured with Haynes to celebrate Powell's career. "I feel like I've been here a long time ago and I'm back," Haynes told *Down Beat*. "There have been times when they've said I've been overlooked, neglected, but I can't say that about now. I feel like I've been born again…."

Selected discography

Busman's Holiday, EmArcy, 1954.
Jazz Abroad, EmArcy, 1956.

We Three, Original Jazz, 1958.
Just Us, Original Jazz, 1960.
Out of the Afternoon, Impulse!, 1962.
Cracklin', New Jazz, 1963.
Cymbalism, New Jazz, 1963.
People, Pacific Jazz, 1964.
Hip Ensemble, Mainstream, 1971.
Equipoise, Mainstream, 1972.
Senyah, Mainstream, 1973.
Vistalite, Galaxy, 1977.
Thank You, Thank You, Galaxy, 1977.
Live at the Riverbop, EPM Musique, 1979.
True or False, Evidence, 1986.
Homecoming, Evidence, 1992.
When It's Haynes It Roars, Dreyfus, 1992.
My Shining Hour, Storyville, 1994.
Te Vou!, Dreyfus, 1994.
Praise, Dreyfus, 1998.
The Roy Haynes Trio, Polygram, 2000.
Roy Haynes, MCA, 2000.

Sources

Books

Erlewine, Michael, editor, *All Music Guide to Jazz,* Miller Freeman Books, 1996.
Hitchcock, H. Wiley, and Stanley Sadie, editors, *New Grove Dictionary of American Music,* Macmillan Press, 1986.
Kernfeld, Berry, editor, *New Grove Dictionary of Jazz,* Macmillan Press, 1988.

Periodicals

Down Beat, November 1996, p. 18.
New York Times, June 4, 2000.

Online

"Roy Haynes," *All Music Guide,* http://www.allmusic.com (March 30, 2001).

—Brenna Sanchez

Milt Hinton

Bassist

According to the *All Music Guide,* jazz bassist Milt Hinton quite possibly appeared on more recordings than any other musician in history. Known as "The Judge" to friends, fans, and critics alike and celebrated for his rich tone and sense of rhythmic timing, Hinton remained a vital force in the jazz style for more than 70 years, appearing on over 1,000 records, both under his own name and with others. During his prolific career, Hinton, who died on December 19, 2000, played with nearly all the great jazz leaders as well as various pop stars including Louis Armstrong, Cab Calloway, John Coltrane, Miles Davis, Duke Ellington, Dizzy Gillespie, Benny Goodman, Lionel Hampton, Billie Holiday, Thelonius Monk, Bing Crosby, Frank Sinatra, Barry Manilow, Paul McCartney, and Barbra Streisand.

In addition to playing jazz and educating young musicians, Hinton spent his life doubling as a professional photographer who documented the jazz life. He captured hundreds of images of performers on the road and in the studio, during both good and bad times. Many of his photographs, taken from an archive of more than 60,000 negatives, were exhibited throughout the world. Hinton also published two well-received books of such images: *Bass Line: The Stories and Photographs of Milt Hinton* and *Overtime: The Jazz Photographs of Milt Hinton.* "Milt Hinton is a musical icon," saxophonist Jimmy Heath told *Down Beat*'s Alan Nahigian at a 1999 celebration and exhibition honoring Hinton's work at Flushing Town Hall, New York. "He has given us the history of jazz to contemplate and observe by documenting everything onto film, plus he has shown us the beauty of this music through his performances."

Desiring to share his passion for music with a younger generation, Hinton taught jazz courses at Hunter College and Baruch College in New York City during the 1970s and 1980s, and in 1980, he established the Milton J. Hinton Scholarship Fund for aspiring bassists. His other education-based endeavors included serving as the bass chairman for the National Association of Jazz Educators, as a panel member for the National Endowment for the Arts, and as a board member of the International Society of Bassists. Several colleges awarded Hinton with honorary doctorate degrees for his work in music education including William Patterson College, Skidmore College, Hamilton College, DePaul University, Trinity College, the Berklee College of Music, Fairfield University, and the Baruch College of the City University of New York. Some of his numerous other honors include a Eubie Award from the New York Chapter of the National Academy of Recording Arts and Sciences, a Living Treasure Award from the Smithsonian Institution, an American Jazz Master Fellowship from the National Endowment for the Arts in 1993, and a New York State Governor's Award in 1996.

Milton John Hinton was born on June 23, 1910, in Vicksburg, Mississippi, and was just three months old

For the Record . . .

Born Milton John Hinton on June 23, 1910, in Vicksburg, MS; died on December 19, 2000, in Queens, NY; wife, Mona; children: Charlotte Morgan. *Education:* Attended Crane Junior College, 1929-32; Northwestern University, 1933.

Played with legendary jazz artists including Art Tatum, Erskine Tate, Zutty Singleton, Jabbo Smith, and Eddie South, 1920s-early 1930s; played with Cab Calloway's band, 1936-51; worked as freelance studio musician, playing on more recordings than any other bassist, 1950s-70s; jazz lecturer at various universities including the Bernard M. Baruch and Hunter Colleges of the City University of New York, 1970s-80s; published two books of photography: *Bass Line: The Stories and Photographs of Milt Hinton,* 1988, and *Overtime: The Jazz Photographs of Milt Hinton,* 1991.

Awards: Eubie Award, New York Chapter of the National Academy of Recording Arts and Sciences, 1988; Living Treasure Award, Smithsonian Institution, 1989; American Jazz Master Fellowship, National Endowment for the Arts, 1993; New York State Governor's Award, 1996.

when his father, a missionary from Monrovia, and mother separated. Throughout his childhood, Hinton was well aware of racism. His maternal grandmother had been a slave on a plantation owned by the brother of Jefferson Davis, the president of the Confederacy during the Civil War era, and in 1918, at the age of eight, Hinton witnessed a lynching first-hand. More than 60 years after the terrifying event, Hinton recalled, as quoted by Bart Barnes in the *Washington Post,* "seeing a crowd of people, all around, men shooting, a big barrel of gasoline on the ground and a man is on fire, like a piece of bacon with a wire rope around his neck. In Vicksburg, when you lynched a [black person], you cut the tree down and painted the stump red. I walked to school past that stump every day, but I couldn't understand what was happening."

At age 11, Hinton and his mother moved to Chicago, where he began his musical education on the violin, taking private lessons in classical music. He hoped to one day play for silent films in the movie houses. In music, Hinton discovered a place where racial and class differences were nonexistent, where people

could come together. "Music is an auditory art," he told *Down Beat*'s Michael Bourne in 1993. "We go by sound. Not who your daddy was. Not your ethnicity. B-flat is the same in Japan as it is here. We can't speak the same language but we can play together. I praise God every day of my life that God let me be involved in music. This is where I get more freedom, more respect, more dignity from the world. This is what music means to me."

In 1927, following the release of Al Jolson's *The Jazz Singer,* the first feature film with sound, Hinton realized that the days of a live violinist accompanying films were probably over. Thus, while attending Wendell Phillips High School and Crane Junior College, he switched from violin to the bass saxophone, followed by the tuba, cello, and eventually bass. From the late 1920s until the mid 1930s, Hinton worked with several legendary figures such as Art Tatum, Freddie Keppard, Jabbo Smith, Tiny Parham (with whom he made his recording debut in 1930), Eddie South (ironically, another violinist known for his mix of classical and jazz-oriented material), Zutty Singleton, and Fate Marable.

Hinton's big break arrived in 1936 when bandleader Cab Calloway, after losing his bassist to a Hollywood studio orchestra, offered him a position on a temporary basis. Originally, Calloway planned to replace Hinton with a "real" bassist when his tour left Chicago to perform in New York City. However, Hinton immediately proved himself a valuable addition and remained with Calloway's orchestra until 1951. Featured on the bandleader's 1939 set *Pluckin' the Bass,* Hinton also worked with Dizzy Gillespie to help modernize Calloway's style. While performing with Calloway, Hinton also made dozens of recordings with the likes of Benny Goodman, Lionel Hampton, Coleman Hawkins, and Billie Holiday.

After Calloway dissolved his band in 1951, Hinton, now based in New York, performed in clubs with Joe Bushkin, then briefly played with Count Basie and Louis Armstrong's All-Stars. In 1954, with the help of comedian Jackie Gleason, an old friend Hinton met on the club circuit years earlier, the bassist landed a job as a staff musician at CBS. At the time, the industry was still heavily segregated, making Hinton one of the first African American musicians hired for session work. Over the next 15 years, Hinton appeared on countless recordings, playing jazz as well as many other types of music, like Gleason's mood music and polka bands, film soundtracks and commercials, and jam sessions led by Buck Clayton. Other artists Hinton accompanied included Mahalia Jackson, Erroll Garner, Aretha Franklin, Dinah Shore, Johnny Mathis, Eddie Fisher, and Debbie Reynolds, among others. The same period also saw the release of Hinton's first session as a leader in 1955.

In his later years, Hinton worked with Dick Cavett's studio band, taught music, and continued to play concerts and pursue photography, a hobby he took up in the mid 1930s when a friend gave him an old camera. Hinton died at the age of 90 after an extended illness at Mary Immaculate Hospital in Queens, New York. He was survived by his wife, Mona, a daughter, Charlotte Morgan, and a granddaughter.

Selected discography

Milt Hinton Quartet, Bethlehem, 1955.
Basses Loaded, Victor, 1955.
The Rhythm Section, Epic, 1956.
The Trio, Chiaroscuro, 1977.
Back to Bass-ics, Progressive, 1984.
The Judge's Decision, Exposure, 1984.
Old Man Time, Chiaroscuro, 1989.
The Trio: 1994, Chiaroscuro, 1994.
Laughing at Life, Columbia, 1994.

Selected publications

Bass Line: The Stories and Photographs of Milt Hinton, Temple University Press, 1988.
Overtime: The Jazz Photographs of Milt Hinton, Pomegranate Artbooks, 1991.

Sources

Periodicals

Black Enterprise, June 1993.
Boston Globe, February 10, 1989.
Down Beat, December 1993; August 1995; January 1999.
Ebony, January 1992.
Jet, January 8, 2001.
Los Angeles Times, October 2, 1998; August 1, 1991; August 5, 1991; December 21, 2000.
New York Times, June 15, 2000.
People, May 8, 1995.
Rolling Stone, February 1, 2001.
USA Today, March 1998.
Washington Post, December 21, 2000.

Online

All Music Guide, http://www.allmusic.com (March 7, 2001).
Contemporary Authors Online, http://www.galenet.com/serv let/BioRC (June 26, 2001).
NPR Jazz Online, http://www.nprjazz.org (March 7, 2001).

—Laura Hightower

Hoodoo Gurus

Rock group

Darlings of the college and alternative music scenes for more than 15 years, the Australian-based group the Hoodoo Gurus have delighted scores of fans with their catchy, spunky, power pop-laden songs and albums. Little in the vast world of American pop culture was immune from the often irreverent and highly amusing musical observations of the Hoodoo Gurus, but their witty and clever tunes failed to ignite the American pop music charts despite winning over numbers of fans in Australia.

Le Hoodoo Gurus—they would drop the French prefix some two years later—formed in Sydney, Australia, in 1981. The band was a collaboration between singer, songwriter, and guitarist Dave Faulkner, guitarists Rod Radalj and Kimble Rendall, and drummer James Baker. According to *All Music Guide*, the "Hoodoo Gurus were largely a product of their influences; unlike most bands, however, the Hoodoos [drew] their inspiration from the vast entirety of the American pop cultural landscape, drawing on such disparate sources as B-movies, bad sitcoms, and junk food—in tandem with the usual suspects of garage rock, power pop, and surf—to create a distinctly kitschy and catchy sound." The Hoodoo Gurus released their debut single, "Leilani," in 1982, the same year in which two of the band's three guitarists decided to leave the group. Radalj and Rendall were replaced by one guitarist, Brad Shepherd. Clyde Bramley became the Hoodoo Gurus' first bassist.

The following year saw the Hoodoo Gurus sign to Mushroom Records in Australia and A&M in the United States. They also recorded their debut album entitled *Stoneage Romeos*. Inspiration for *Stoneage Romeos* came from some rather unusual sources—most notably 1960s American television sitcom actors Larry Storch from *F-Troop* and Arnold Ziffel, the pig from *Green Acres*. A pair of minor college and alternative hit songs, "I Want You Back" and "I Was a Kamikaze Pilot," emerged from the album.

Their sophomore release, *Mars Needs Guitars*, was released in 1985 by a then-new American label, Elektra. By this time, Baker had left the band and was replaced by Mark Kingsmill on drums. The departure of Baker left Faulkner as the only founding member of the Hoodoo Gurus. *Mars Needs Guitars* was a much more musically diverse offering than its predecessor. *All Music Guide* noted, "[the] album [was] highlighted by the superb single 'Bittersweet' and marked by a widening scope which touched base with demented hillbilly humor ('Hayride to Hell') and crazed surf ('Like Wow—Wipeout')." *Mars Needs Guitars* was the Hoodoo Gurus' first big American college radio hit album.

It would be another two years before the next Hoodoo Gurus album was released. *Blow Your Cool!*, released in 1987, was filled not only with the Hoodoo Gurus' legendary power pop and punk chords and tunes, but it also contained collaborations with mainstream darlings the Bangles on "Good Times" and "What's My Scene." The following year bassist Bramley exited and was replaced by Rick Grossman.

Despite the help from the Bangles, the Hoodoo Gurus failed to make it big in American pop music. They piqued the interest of college and alternative music fans, but they still had not broken out of the underground. The Hoodoo Gurus had hoped to change this with their 1989 release *Magnum Cum Louder*. With a new American label, RCA, supporting them, they were poised to break into the mainstream. *Magnum Cum Louder* yielded three college alternative radio hits including "Another World," "Baby Can Dance," and "Come Anytime." Heavy play on college and alternative music stations, unfortunately, did not translate into crossover mainstream success. Another two years passed before the release of a follow-up to *Magnum Cum Louder*. *Kinky*, sent to stores in 1991, supplied the hit, "Miss Freelove '69," adding another single to the list of near-chart misses by the Hoodoo Gurus. Like the albums it followed, *Kinky* failed to achieve American mainstream success. This may have been because the album "often rocks a bit too hard for its own good," according to Mark Deming of *All Music Guide*. "[W]hile the Hoodoo Gurus always knew how to crank it up, they also knew when to crank it up, and Brad Shepherd's this-goes-to-11 guitar textures … on "Too Much Fun," "A Place in the Sun," and "Something's Coming" tended to drown out the band's poppier and more melodic inclinations, always one of their greatest virtues."

Members include **James Baker** (left group, 1985), drums; **Clyde Bramley** (joined group, 1982; left group, 1988), bass; **Dave Faulkner**, lead vocals, guitar; **Rick Grossman** (joined group, 1988), bass, backing vocals; **Mark Kingsmill** (joined group, 1985), drums; **Rod Radalj** (left group, 1982), guitar; **Kimble Rendall** (left group, 1982), guitar; **Brad Shepherd** (joined group, 1982), lead guitar, backing vocals.

Formed in Sydney, Australia, 1981; signed with A&M Records; released debut album, *Stoneage Romeos*, 1983; signed with Elektra, released *Mars Needs Guitars*, 1985; released *Blow Your Cool!*, 1987; signed with RCA Records and released *Magnum Cum Louder*, 1989; released *Kinky*, 1991; released *Gorilla Biscuits*, 1993; signed with Zoo/Volcano Records, released *Crank*, 1994; released *Blue Cave*, 1996; signed with Mushroom Records, released *Electric Chair*, 1998 signed with Acadia Records, released *Ampology*, 2000.

Addresses: *Record company*—Acadia/Evangeline Recorded Works Ltd., P.O. Box 20, South Molton, EX36 4YW, England, website: http://www.evangeline.co.uk. *Website*—Official Hoodoo Gurus Website: http://www.hoodoogurus.com.

The Hoodoo Gurus' final RCA album, *Gorilla Biscuits*, was released in 1993. It contained B-sides and rarities. Their next studio album, *Crank*, arrived the following year on Zoo/Volcano Records. *Blue Cave* followed in 1996, and like its predecessor, the album mined the pop cultural landscapes of both Australia and the United States. "I think this is the best thing we've done—no holds barred, no apologies," Faulkner said in comments at the iMusic Modern Showcase website. "Speaking for myself, I really feel like I hit my straps on this one. Songwriting-wise, I didn't think of myself off the hook and I think it paid off." Critics noted the group's "no holds barred" approach on *Blue Cave*: "Sarcastic wit and chunky rhythm let these Australian garage-rock journeymen get away with all sorts of tricks: psychedelic arrangements, spaghetti-western guitars, sprinted tempos, party voices...." an *Entertainment Weekly* review said about *Blue Cave*.

In early 1997, the Hoodoo Gurus announced that they were disbanding. According to their official press re-

lease, "The Gurus ... have been regarded as one of Australia's most credible and successful bands.... [T]hey decided that now is the right time to bring the band to its natural conclusion.... The Hoodoo Gurus would like to express their sincere thanks to all of their fans and those who have supported them over the past 15 years. It's been quite a trip."

After the group's demise, Mushroom Records released the 1998 album *Electric Chair*. It was followed by the Acadia release of *Ampology,* a 40-track, 2-CD Hoodoo Gurus anthology, in 2000. Brad Shepherd continued with the Australian group the Monarchs, which released its debut seven-inch single "2001/This Is All I Can Do" in 2001.

Selected discography

Stoneage Romeos (includes "I Want You Back" and "I Was a Kamikaze Pilot"), A&M, 1983.
Mars Needs Guitars (includes "Bittersweet," "Hayride to Hell," and "Like Wow—Wipeout"), Elektra, 1985.
Blow Your Cool! (includes "Good Times" and "What's My Scene"), Elektra, 1987.
Magnum Cum Louder (includes "Another World," "Baby Can Dance," and "Come Anytime"), RCA, 1989.
Kinky (includes "Miss Freelove '69"), RCA, 1991.
Gorilla Biscuits, RCA, 1993.
Crank, Zoo/Volcano, 1994.
Blue Cave, Zoo/Volcano, 1996.
Electric Chair, Mushroom, 1998.
Ampology, Acadia, 2000.

Sources

Periodicals

Entertainment Weekly, August 23, 1996, p. 124.

Online

"Database—Hoodoo Gurus," Evreka, http://hem.passagen.se/honga/database/h/hoodoogurus.html (April 10, 2001).
"Discography: Hoodoo Gurus," CDnow, http://www.cdnow.com/cgi-bi...ic/ArtistID=Hoodoo+Gurus/select=biography (April 10, 2001).
"Hoodoo Gurus," *All Music Guide*, http://www.allmusic.com (April 10, 2001).
"Hoodoo Gurus," iMusic Modern Showcase, ARTISTdirect Network, http://imusic.artistdirect.com/showcase/modern/hoodoogurus.html (April 10, 2001).
"Hoodoo Gurus Biography," Yahoo! Music, http://musicfinder.yahoo.com/shop?d=hc&id=1801922947&cf=11&intl=us (April 10, 2001).
"Hoodoo Gurus—Biography," Australian Music Website, http://www.amws.com.au/h/hoodoo-gurus-b.html (April 10, 2001).
Hoodoo Gurus Official Website, http://www.hoodoogurus.com/misc/over/htm (April 10, 2001).

—*Mary Alice Adams*

Trevor Horn

Producer, musician

Although his face may not grace the cover of many magazines or be recognizable to groups of fans at large, Trevor Horn is a well-known, driving force within the music industry. Launching his career initially as a musician, the inventive producer has been responsible for bringing forth some of the most defining music of the 1980s and 1990s, including ABC's *Lexicon of Love*, Yes' *90125*, Frankie Goes to Hollywood's *Welcome to the Pleasuredome* and Seal's debut album, which transformed the talented British singer into a worldwide success. Recognized for his sophisticated production techniques, insatiable work ethic and impressive credentials (he has worked with everyone from Rod Stewart and Tina Turner to Prodigy), Horn has earned a reputation as one of the most sought-after producers in pop music.

Horn was born on July 15, 1949, in Hertfordshire, England. His father was a dairy engineer by day and musician by night, who played acoustic bass with a local band. Inspired by early-1960s British radio and artists such as the Beatles, the younger Horn developed a strong interest in music, eventually following in his father's footsteps, playing bass and performing in high-school bands. At age 19, after quitting college and an attempt at a day job, Horn embarked on a career as a professional musician. Due to his then-rare ability to sight-read bass music, he was able to obtain a consistent string of gigs as a session player. However, the young bassist quickly realized that his stint as a struggling musician was not going to bring him the success he desired.

In a rather odd move, Horn decided to build a recording studio with a partner from scratch, mainly because they couldn't afford to rent one. Although Drumbeat Studios had one of the first half-inch eight tracks in England, it hardly attracted the superstar clientele Horn later became known for producing. Instead, the majority of his early work involved producing demos for fledgling musicians looking to enter song contests. Nonetheless, his short reign in the studio business did prove instrumental in determining his future direction. As he explained in a 1998 issue of *Billboard,* "I was just drumming up business for the studio and one day somebody said, 'All the things that you're doing are called being a producer.' So I said 'That's exactly what I want to do.' Regardless, within six months Horn's business partnership dissolved and he left his studio behind.

Shortly thereafter, Horn became romantically involved with United Kingdom disco queen Tina Charles. His relationship with the singer developed into a musical liaison when she provided Horn with his first high-profile music job as a backup bassist for her group. Further impressed with his ability, she promoted Horn to musical director, a position he maintained even after their romance fizzled. Notably, the aspiring producer's time with Charles served two purposes. It allowed him

For the Record . . .

Born on July 15, 1949, in Hertfordshire, England; son of a musician; married Jill Sinclair, 1980; four children.

Began playing bass as a child, performed with high school bands and by age 19, launched career as professional musician; served as bass player and musical director for disco act, Tina Charles; joined Camera Club, 1979; formed The Buggles with Geoff Downes, 1979; released *The Age of Plastic*, 1980; joined Yes, 1980; left group, 1981; released second Buggles album, *Adventures in Modern Recording*, 1981; produced British group, Dollar, 1981-82; produced ABC's *Lexicon of Love*, 1982; formed ZTT Records, 1983; co-founded the The Art of Noise and released *Into the Battle with The Art of Noise,* 1983; produced Yes' *90125*, 1983; produced Frankie Goes to Hollywood's *Welcome to the Pleasuredome,* 1984; released *Who's Afraid of The Art of Noise*, 1984; produced first and second Seal albums, 1991, 1994; produced Seal's third effort, *Human Being*, 1997; reunited with The Art of Noise and released *The Seduction of Claude Debussy*, 1999.

Awards: BPI Producer of the Year, 1983, 1985, 1991; Radio One Award for Contribution to Pop Music, 1984; Ivor Novello Award for Recorded Record for "Owner of a Lonely Heart," 1983; Ivor Novello Award for Best Contemporary Song for "Relax," 1984; Ivor Novello Award for Most Performed Work for "Two Tribes," 1984; Ivor Novello Award for Best Contemporary Song and International Hit of the Year for "Crazy," 1991; BMI Award for "Owner of a Lonely Heart," 1984; Grammy Award for Best Instrumental for "90125," 1984; Grammy Award for Record of the Year for "Kiss from A Rose," 1996; *Q Magazine* Award for Best Producer, 1991; *Music Week* Award for Best Producer, 1991.

Addresses: *Record company*—Zang Tuum Tumb (ZTT), The Blue Building, 42-26 St. Lukes Mews, London, England, W11 1DG. *Management*—Sarm Management, The Blue Building, 42-46 St. Lukes Mews, London, England W11 1DG.

to witness how the music industry really worked and introduced him to future collaborator Geoff Downes, whom Horn had initially hired to play keyboards in Charles' backup band.

Horn's attention shifted back toward producing. He was aware that in order to attract quality clients as a producer he would need to establish a track record. Following a brief stint with the band Camera Club (which included Thomas Dolby, Bruce Wooley, Jeff Downes and Hans Zimmer), Horn and Downes formed the Buggles in 1979. As the fledgling producer explained to *Musician* magazine, "All the time we were working for other people. Finally, in a fit of absolute desperation, we decided to become the artists. We tried to put four and a half years into four minutes and had our first hit, 'Video Killed the Radio Star.'" The song, which was inspired by the sci-fi tale "The Sound Sweep" by J.G. Ballard, took an incredible three months to record and eventually topped the charts in 16 different countries. Although it failed to chart significantly in the United States, "Video Killed the Radio Star" earned a special place in the history of pop culture. On August 1, 1981, the infectious song became the first video ever played on the new cable television network, MTV.

The Buggles' first record, *The Age of Plastic* also managed to attract the attention of Yes member Chris Squire whose interest resulted in Horn and Downes joining the progressive rock super group in May of 1980. In retrospect, Horn viewed joining Yes, a band he had long admired, as a mistake. "Looking back now, it was one of the two or three times in my life that I have done something that I knew was wrong." He explained in the 1984 issue of *Musician* magazine, "The experience was in a word, awful." Reportedly, Horn had issues dealing with the immense pressures of performing in front of the large crowds that Yes attracted. "I remember thinking how could I ever be worried about making a record again or getting a mix right after something truly as horrific as this? And I suppose a bit of that has stayed with me ever since. I've put out records that other people would have been quite nervous about."

In early 1981, Yes disbanded. Instead of returning to the Buggles as was originally intended (the group had never broken up), Downes decided to form his own group with Yes bandmate Steve Howe. Asia, Downes' project, achieved a great deal of success in the early 1980s. Horn returned to the studio and with pre- and post-Yes demos in hand, mashed out a second Buggles' album entitled *Adventures in Modern Recording*. As with its predecessor, the record was acknowledged for its excellent production work. However, overall the Buggles sophomore effort was received to little fanfare.

During 1981-82, Horn's work with unremarkable British pop group Dollar, and a then-largely unknown ABC, augmented his reputation as a producer. Dollar approached Horn with the hope of creating a single similar to "Video Killed the Radio Star." The producer in turn jump-started the group's lackluster career. With Horn's assistance, Dollar's "Hand Held in Black and White," became the band's first breakthrough hit single. It was followed by three chart toppers and a successful album, significantly improving Dollar's appeal. Shortly thereafter, Horn further established his business by assembling a group of his own high-quality studios known as SARM (Sound and Recording Mobiles). In 1982, Sheffield natives ABC asked Horn to make an album for them as well. While Horn liked the band's first record, he thought the sound quality was too rough and wasn't certain that they had the same goals in mind. The band assured him that this was not the case, that in fact, they were seeking a high-quality, sophisticated record. As a result, ABC's *Lexicon of Love* featured impressive orchestrations and a magically clear sound. The record proved to be a major success for the group, launching the hit singles "Poison Arrow" and "The Look of Love."

In January of 1983, Horn—along with several partners—launched ZTT, an innovative record label. ZTT stands for Zang Tuum Tumb, a term described in *The Art of Noises,* a book about the Futurist movement in Italy at the beginning of the century. Unlike most producer's labels which are generally used to showcase vanity projects and other small side offering, ZTT became a very successful record label in its own right. It also added another positive dimension to the producer's growing company SARM, which eventually grew to include a string of recording studios and a management company.

Britpop stars Frankie Goes to Hollywood became the first band signed to ZTT. With Horn at the helm, the group released its smash record *Welcome to the Pleasuredome*. The album was the source of several number one singles in the United Kingdom as well as a great deal of controversy for its sexual overtones. What were not controversial were Horn's impressive production efforts, which were highly acknowledged and evident throughout the record. Several months prior to his work with Frankie Goes to Hollywood, Horn surprisingly returned to produce Yes' 1983 album *90125*. The single "Owner of a Lonely Heart" was credited with reviving Yes' career and was a number one hit in America for two weeks in January of 1984. Horn's back-to-back efforts with Yes and Frankie Goes to Hollywood were a week away from resulting in the talented producer having two different number one songs simultaneously on both sides of the Atlantic.

In 1983, despite an increasingly demanding schedule, Horn collected the ZTT house musicians Anne Dudley, Paul Morley, and Gary Langan to form the critically acclaimed The Art of Noise, a group light on live music, high on production. The band's EP *Into the Battle with*

The Art of Noise became the second ZTT project. Their first full-length recording, *Who's Afraid of the Art of Noise,* birthed the popular single "Close (to the Edit)." After two records, The Art of Noise parted ways with ZTT, leaving Horn to concentrate fully on his production efforts.

Throughout the 1980s, Horn continued to work with some of the most notable artists in the music industry, generating a much-respected body of work and some of the most notable albums of the time, including Grace Jones' *Slave to the Rhythm*, Paul McCartney's *Flowers in the Dirt,* and several records by superstar Rod Stewart.

In 1991, Horn achieved one of his greatest successes when he produced British soul singer Seal's debut album. The record, which contained the single "Crazy," reached multiplatinum status and in turn launched Seal as an international superstar. Horn continued to work with the artist on his two subsequent releases. Seal's second album, also entitled *Seal,* produced the single "Kiss from a Rose," which reached number one on the American charts and won a Grammy Award for Record of the Year in 1996. The late 1990s also saw Horn reuniting with Anne Dudley and Paul Morley to produce a new Art of Noise record, *The Seduction of Claude Debussy*.

In 2001, Horn continued to be one of the main purveyors of solid pop music. His tremendous success may be attributed to the fact that despite his impressive credentials, the prolific producer never loses sight of his objective. As he once stated in a 1982 issue *of The Face,* "The point is to make good records that the people out there are going to like and buy. I believe that every single pop record should have some kind of basic message behind it, a record or a single is a form of communication: you're putting across an idea, a statement, but you've got to be prepared to slog it and not accept second best."

Selected discography

As producer

The Buggles, *Age of Plastic*, Island, 1980.
The Buggles, *Adventures in Modern Recording*, EMI, 1982.
ABC, *Lexicon of Love*, Mercury, 1982.
Dollar, *The Dollar Album*, WEA, 1982.
Malcolm McClaren, *Duck Rock*, Charisma, 1983.
Yes, *90125* (includes, "Owner of a Lonely Heart"), Atco, 1983.
Frankie Goes to Hollywood, *Welcome to the Pleasure Dome* (includes "Relax" and "Two Tribes"), ZTT/Island, 1984.
The Art Of Noise, *Who's Afraid of the Art of Noise* (includes "Close (To The Edit)"), ZTT/Island, 1984.
Grace Jones, *Slave to the Rhythm*, ZTT/Island, 1985.
Paul McCartney, *Flowers in the Dirt* (4 tracks), Capitol, 1989.
Rod Stewart, *Storytellers* (compilation), Warner Bros., 1989.
Rod Stewart, *Vagabond Heart*, Warner Bros., 1991.

Seal, *Seal* (includes "Crazy"), Sire, 1991.
Mike Oldfield, *Tubular Bells II*, Warner Bros., 1992.
Seal, *Seal* (includes "Kiss from a Rose"), Sire, 1994.
Tina Turner, *Wildest Dreams* (8 tracks), Virgin, 1996.
Cher, *It's a Man's World* (3 tracks), WEA, 1996.
Barry Manilow, *I'd Really Love to See You Tonight*, Arista, 1997.
Seal, *Human Being*, Warner Bros., 1998.
Charlotte Church, *Charlotte Church*, Sony, 1999.
The Art of Noise, *The Seduction of Claude Debussy*, ZTT/Universal, 1999.
LeAnn Rimes, *I Need You*, Curb, 2001.

As musician

The Buggles, *Age of Plastic* (multiple instruments), Island, 1980.
Yes, *Drama* (bass and vocals), Atlantic, 1980.
The Buggles, *Adventures in Modern Recording* (multiple instruments), EMI, 1982.
Paul McCartney, *Flowers in the Dirt* (keyboards), Capitol, 1989.
Marc Almond, *Jacky* (multiple instruments and producer), Warner Bros., 1991.
Rod Stewart, *Spanner in the Works* (keyboards, background vocals, and producer), Warner Brothers, 1995.
Tina Turner, *Wildest Dreams* (background vocals), Virgin, 1996.
The Art of Noise, *The Seduction of Claude Debussy* (multiple instruments), ZTT/Universal, 1999.

Sources

Books

Kaplan, Mike, editor, *Variety's Directory of Major U.S. Show Business Awards*, R.R. Bowker, 1989.

Periodicals

Billboard, March 21, 1998, p.53.
Keyboard, January 2000, p. 14.

Online

All Music Guide, http://www.allmusic.com (April 17, 2001).
Dollar Shooting Star, http://www.dollarsite.co.uk (April 16, 2001).
Fisonic (articles from *The Face*, 1982, *Musician*, March 1984), http://home.t-online.de/home/fisonic/index.html (April 17, 2001).
Get Music, http://www.getmusic.com (April 15, 2001).
Sarm Management, http://www.sarm.com (April 15, 2001).
The Trevor Horn Worship Hall, http://www.trevor.horn.de/ (April 15, 2001).
The Ultimate Band List, http://www.ubl.com (April 17, 2001).
Yahoo! Chat with Trevor Horn, http://chat.yahoo.com (April 15, 2001).
ZTT Records, http://www.ztt.com (April 17, 2001).

Additional information was provided by Sarm Management press materials, 2000.

—*Nicole Elyse*

Chris Isaak

Photograph by Ken Settle. Reproduced by permission.

Chris Isaak's moody, anachronistic music is an unlikely addition to the pop charts, but after years of near-obscurity the handsome Californian has achieved major stardom. Virtually since his debut album appeared in 1985, Isaak has had a cult following—and the raves of critics—but he broke through to the public's attention in 1991 with the top ten hit "Wicked Game." Since then Isaak has been quite happy to bring his jazz- and rockabilly-influenced sound to large theaters and concert halls.

Success was slow in coming to Isaak because he placed artistic merit before marketability. A number of his early albums failed to sell because his fifties-style rockers and ballads sounded so different from standard pop fare. Isaak told the *Washington Post*: "I heard all those other records that didn't use any guitars and I heard all those guys who couldn't sing at all, and they didn't stick in my mind at all.... I mean, do you think Wynton Marsalis wakes up every morning and says, 'Jazz is never going to sell as much as pop, so I'm going to change what I'm doing?' No, you have to do what you're going to do. I'm always going to make records where the emphasis is on a good song with the voice out front."

Forged His Own Identity

Unlikely as it seems, a singer-songwriter who plays the accordion and calls up images of Roy Orbison succeeded on his own terms. At one time Isaak and his band Silvertone were fixtures on the West Coast rock scene and were favorites of such Hollywood notables as Sean Penn and David Lynch. In fact, Lynch's inclusion of Isaak's music in the soundtracks of *Blue Velvet* and *Wild at Heart* helped launch the rocker on a national level. Critics have praised Isaak's music, however, even his debut album that sold only 14,000 copies on release. "No one else has so successfully drawn from the past, with an artist's eye, reassembling the disparate images, sounds, styles and artifacts of pop-culture history into one persona," wrote Michael Goldberg in *Rolling Stone*. "Of course, Isaak would be just another two-bit Elvis clone if he didn't manage to transcend all the stagy photos, contrived outfits and retro minutiae. Sure, that stuff is fun; it has its charm. But what matters is his music, which is the genuine article."

Isaak grew up with a healthy distrust of fads and trends. He was raised in Stockton, California, a blue-collar town some 65 miles east of San Francisco. Isaak was a radio buff who wired his whole backyard in order to pull in esoteric stations from all over America and Canada. "I listened to tons of stuff as a kid," he told the *Boston Globe*. "I'd listen to the radio very late at night, laying in bed. All through high school, people probably thought I was the world's sleepiest guy or just a dummy. During the first three classes each day, I would just sleep because I'd been up until 4:30 or 5 listening."

For the Record . . .

Born in 1956 in Stockton, CA; son of a forklift operator. *Education*: Bachelor's degree, University of the Pacific, 1980.

Formed band Silvertone with James Calvin Wilsey on guitar, Kenney Dale Johnson on drums, and Rowland Salley on bass, 1981; signed with Warner Bros. Records, released first album, *Silvertone*, 1985; had first top ten hit, "Wicked Game," on multiplatinum-selling *Heart Shaped World*, 1991; released follow-up, *San Francisco Days*, 1993; released *Forever Blue*, 1995; released acoustic-based *Baja Sessions*, 1996; released *Speak of the Devil*, 1998; debut of *The Chris Isaak Show* on Showtime cable television network, 2001.

Addresses: *Record company*—Reprise Records (Warner Bros.), 3300 Warner Blvd, Burbank, CA 91505, (818) 840-2405, website: http://www.repriserec.com. *Website*—Chris Isaak Official Website: http://www .chrisisaak.com.

Despite his interest in music, Isaak never considered pursuing a singing career. Still, he had an instinct for the offbeat style and a stubborn pride in his individuality. After high school he enrolled at the University of the Pacific, where he studied filmmaking, English, and journalism. He also boxed, mostly as an amateur, and had his nose broken seven times. "I was definitely on the outside," Isaak told the *Chicago Tribune* of his college years. "I'd drive across town over to the old Santa Fe Depot on the south side of Stockton and box all day, and it was all blacks and Mexicans and a couple of white trash guys like myself, and then I'd go across town to this university and it was all these upper-crusty guys with that Poupon kind of mustard. I didn't really fit in with either side."

Isaak cultivated an artistic look by dressing in bizarre thrift shop clothing from other eras. He became devoted to music in 1979 while spending a semester in Japan. "There was this Elvis song that really knocked me out called 'I'll Never Let You Go,'" Isaak said in the *Washington Post*. "I liked the song so much that I sang it and sang it. One day, the Japanese lady that lived downstairs from me started singing it too. She couldn't speak English. She had learned it phonetically from hearing me. That's when I decided to give singing a try."

After graduating from college, Isaak moved to San Francisco, California. "When I came down from Stockton, I was pathetic," he told the *Washington Post*. "I had this bright lime green suit with black velvet buttons. I thought that was how musicians dressed; I didn't really know. I kept going down to this nightclub and standing outside the door until they eventually said, 'Do you want to come in for free?' Then I'd go in and look for people who looked like someone who might want to be in my band."

Played Nightclubs

By 1981 Isaak had formed a small band called Silvertone. The group played in the San Francisco nightclubs and bars, alternating fifties hits with more and more of Isaak's original material. They literally began at the bottom but soon became favorites in the Bay Area. Producer Erik Jacobsen became a big Silvertone fan and eventually helped to secure a recording contract with Warner Bros. Records. The debut album, *Silvertone,* was released in 1985.

The nation's pop music critics simply loved *Silvertone*. *Washington Post* contributor Joe Sasfy wrote: "Chris Isaak's *Silvertone* is not only one of the most striking debut albums of the year, it is also one of the few albums of the '80s offering a thoroughly contemporary rock sound fashioned from America's musical roots." Goldberg called the work "terrific," praising its "sparse, Sun Sessions-like production, … twanging Duane Eddy-ish guitar playing and Isaak's romantic, larger-than-life voice."

The accolades notwithstanding, Isaak's first album—and his second, *Chris Isaak*—sold very few copies at first and received almost no radio airplay. Some influential people did notice Isaak, however—Lynch, for one, and rocker John Fogerty, who called Isaak "a skyscraper against the landscape." Even Roy Orbison befriended Isaak and began writing a few songs with him before Orbison's fatal heart attack.

Inevitably Isaak was compared to Orbison, and to Presley, due to his falsetto vocals and moody tunes about love gone sour. Isaak is frankly uncomfortable with the comparison. For one thing, his music has a distinctive contemporary edge, even though its style harks back to earlier years. Furthermore, Isaak is simply unwilling to try to fill someone else's shoes. "When you compare somebody to Roy Orbison or Elvis, it's like parking a speedboat next to the Queen Mary," he told the *Boston Globe*. "What I do is nice, but I'm not trying to compare to those guys, because it makes my work look tiny. I have hopes that if I keep working hard, some day I'll have a couple of songs that'll add something to music. But I'd drive myself crazy if I thought I had to be like Elvis or Orbison, because I just don't think it's possible. Those guys are once in a generation."

"Wicked Game" Led to National Fame

Isaak's third album, *Heart Shaped World,* seemed destined to follow its two predecessors into obscurity. Fortunately for Isaak, a disc jockey in Atlanta heard the instrumental version of the rocker's "Wicked Game" in the soundtrack of Lynch's film *Wild at Heart* and decided to track down the original song. The deejay then added "Wicked Game" to his station's playlist, and before long, requests for the tune were pouring in. A single was released, and it slowly climbed into the *Billboard* top ten, pulling the album along after it. Two years after its release, *Heart Shaped World* emerged as Isaak's first gold album, and "Wicked Game" became his first hit. The album has since achieved multiplatinum sales.

Isaak then moved from nightclubs to large theaters and the realms of MTV. "After years of playing to avid fans and very few others, Isaak is pleased as punch," wrote Sam Wood in the *Philadelphia Inquirer.* "He's finally found his audience. Several different audiences, actually." Those audiences responded warmly to Isaak's wild rockers and his heart-rending ballads. Isaak has had his share of broken romances, and he explores his own personal pain in his lyrics. "A lot of times it's just stuff that I can't say to anybody," he told the *Chicago Tribune* of his songs. "Those ideas get stuck in my head and the only way I can say 'em is in music. The way I write, I sit down with a guitar, and usually it's in the dark, and I just start singing like I'm talking to myself. It all comes out at one time, the melody and the words."

Isaak followed the success of his third album with *San Francisco Days* in 1993. Again working with Jacobsen as producer, Isaak explored emotional highs and lows that "move from cautious joy to haunting heartbreak within seconds," according to *Billboard*'s Melinda Newman. Isaak's 1995 follow-up, *Forever Blue,* echoed more of his characteristically melancholy moods in a collection of what Andrew Abrahams of *People* magazine deemed "tender odes for the lovelorn." *Baja Sessions,* released in 1996, included acoustic-based versions of earlier work along with new songs "I Wonder" and "Return to Me." *Speak of the Devil,* released in 1998, originated in studio sessions, a departure from Isaak's usual songwriting method of lying in bed with his guitar and recording the songs in his garage. "I wanted to be very experimental this time, use lots of different sounds and be more rockin'," Isaak said in comments included at his official website. The success of *Speak of the Devil* was driven by the single "Please."

Success Beyond the Stage

Now that stardom has found him, Isaak has branched into film and television work. He has appeared in such films as *Wild at Heart* in 1988, *Silence of the Lambs* in 1991, *Twin Peaks: Fire Walk With Me* in 1992, *Little Buddha* in 1993, *That Thing You Do!* in 1996, and *Blue Ridge Fall* in 1999, and he has also made guest appearances on such popular television series as *Melrose Place* and *Friends.* His own television show, *The Chris Isaak Show,* debuted on cable's Showtime network on March 12, 2001. The show is a loosely factual take on Isaak's life as a rock star with a comedic bent.

Though Isaac has found success beyond music, he told the *Philadelphia Inquirer* that he is not at all interested in changing careers. "I'd never give up music, because I like to sing more than anything," he said. "More than *anything.* People always ask me, 'What do you do on your time off?' I tell 'em I sing, 'cause that's what I like to do. Call me a one-dimensional shallow person, but if I got time off, I grab my guitar and play some more."

Selected discography

Silvertone, Warner Bros., 1985.
(Contributor) *Blue Velvet* (soundtrack), Varese, 1986.
Chris Isaak, Warner Bros., 1987.
Heart Shaped World, Reprise, 1989.
(Contributor) *Wild at Heart* (soundtrack), Polydor, 1990.
San Francisco Days, Reprise, 1993.
(Contributor) *A Perfect World* (soundtrack), Reprise, 1993.
(Contributor) *It's Now or Never: The Tribute to Elvis,* Mercury, 1994.
Forever Blue, Reprise, 1995.
Baja Sessions, Reprise, 1996.
(Contributor) *Tin Cup* (soundtrack), Sony, 1996.
(Contributor) *Beautiful Girls* (soundtrack), Elektra, 1996.
Speak of the Devil, Reprise, 1998.
(Contributor) *Eyes Wide Shut* (soundtrack), Warner Bros., 1999.

Sources

Periodicals

Billboard, April 3, 1993.
Boston Globe, July 6, 1989; March 3, 1991; May 10, 1991.
Chicago Tribune, April 28, 1991; May 19, 1991.
People, June 12, 1995.
Philadelphia Inquirer, May 17, 1991; May 20, 1991.
Rolling Stone, June 20, 1985; May 21, 1987.
Washington Post, August 15, 1985; May 12, 1987; May 17, 1991.

Online

"Chris Isaak," *All Music Guide,* http://www.allmusic.com (June 8, 2001).
Chris Isaak Official Website, http://www.chrisisaak.com (June 8, 2001).

Internet Movie Database, http://www.imdb.com (June 7, 2001).

Recording Industry Association of America, http://www .riaa-.com (June 8, 2001).

—*Anne Janette Johnson*

Sharon Isbin

Guitarist

With a repertoire ranging from the Classical period to jazz, folk, and beyond, Sharon Isbin has been called "the pre-eminent guitarist of our time"—high praise for a guitarist who aspired to be a scientist when she was young. Isbin's innate artistry with the instrument paired with her technical mastery has impressed audiences and critics worldwide. "Her brilliantly crisp articulation and her fine sense of sustained line are no less impressive than her sheer virtuosity," wrote one critic in *Gramophone* magazine. Isbin has commissioned and premiered more new pieces for guitar than any other guitarist, and she created the Guitarstream festival at Carnegie Hall and founded the guitar department of the Juilliard School. Her critically acclaimed releases include *Journey to the Amazon, American Landscapes, J.S. Bach: Complete Lute Suites, Nightshade Rounds, Concerti by Christopher Rouse and Tan Dun,* and *Dreams of a World,* for which she won the first Grammy awarded to a classical guitarist in nearly 30 years.

Isbin had no intention of becoming a guitarist. Rather, she wanted to follow in the footsteps of her father, a former professor of chemical engineering. Her mother's side of the family was rife with musical and theater talent, but Isbin planned to be a scientist who spent "hours dissecting anything that leaped or crawled," she told Richard Dyer of the *Boston Globe.* But while living in Italy with her family, her oldest brother requested guitar lessons, then changed his mind when he found out they were for classical guitar. Age nine at the time, Isbin volunteered to take them instead, though she had no idea what classical guitar was. She told the *Boston Globe* that she "loved it immediately." Though she had some experience on the piano, she was taken by the guitar. "The resonance spoke to me right away, the contact of fingers against the strings—there was something very sensual about it."

Born on August 7, 1956, in Minneapolis, Minnesota, Isbin was an award-winning guitarist before she reached college. She was a student of Jeffrey Van in Minneapolis, Oscar Ghiglia at the Aspen Music School in Colorado, Alirio Diaz at the Banff Music Festival, and the legendary classical guitarist Andres Segovia. At age 14, she won a competition that gave her the chance to play with the Minnesota Orchestra, which diverted her from her scientific aspirations. She played Vivaldi's D major Concerto in front of 10,000 people, "which was even more exciting than launching my own spaceship," she told *BBC Music* magazine. That was when Isbin "decided to give up rockets and concentrate on music instead," she continued. She won first prizes in the Toronto International Guitar Competition in 1975, the Munich International Guitar Competition in 1976, and the Queen Sofia International Guitar Competition in 1979. She earned her bachelor's degree from Yale University in 1978 and her master's from the Yale School of Music the following year.

In 1978, Isbin began studying with pianist Rosalyn Tureck, a leading interpreter of Bach. The two worked together to create the first performance editions of the Bach lute suites. After nearly ten years of study with Tureck, Isbin recorded them all on a release called *J.S. Bach: Complete Lute Suites.* Another of her pet projects was *Nightshade Rounds,* a collection of twentieth-century British and American solo works for guitar. The release is anchored by two pieces Isbin regards as the "major landmarks in contemporary music," she told *Gramophone*—Sir William Walton's *Bagatelles* and Benjamin Britten's *Nocturnal after John Dowland.* On the release, wrote *New York Times* critic Allan Kozinn, Isbin created "a mysterious, changeable atmosphere, sometimes alluring and meditative, sometimes charged with prickly energy." Isbin has recorded concertos written for her by John Corigliano, Lukas Foss, and Joseph Schwantner on *American Landscapes,* which was the first-ever recording of American guitar concertos. *American Landscapes* also ended up in space. Astronaut Chris Hadfield, a fan of Isbin's, brought the release with him on the space shuttle *Atlantis* as a gift to Russian cosmonauts during a rendezvous with the Russian space station Mir.

As a beginning guitar player in the late 1960s, there were few places for Isbin to study the instrument in the United States, and she often had to fight for the right to enter classical music competitions that had never before considered guitar. After receiving her master's degree, Isbin began teaching at New York's Manhattan School of Music and later at Mannes College of Music.

For the Record . . .

Born on August 7, 1956, in Minneapolis, MN. *Education*: Bachelor's degree, Yale University, 1978; master's degree, Yale University School of Music, 1979.

Began studying classical guitar at age nine; played with Minnesota Orchestra at age 14; won first prizes at Toronto International Guitar Competition, 1975; Munich International Guitar Competition, 1976; and Queen Sofia International Guitar Competition, 1979; founded guitar department at the Juilliard School of Music, 1989; released *J.S. Bach: Complete Lute Suites*, 1989; released *Nightshade Rounds*, 1994; released *American Landscapes*, 1995; released *Journey to the Amazon*, 1997; released *Dreams of a World*, 2000; released *Concerti by Christopher Rouse and Tan Dun*, 2001.

Awards: Grammy Award, Best Instrumental Soloist for *Dreams of a World: Folk-Inspired Music for Guitar*, 2001.

Addresses: *Record company*—Teldec Classics International, Schubertstraße 5-9 22083 Hamburg, Germany, website: http://www.warner-classics.com/teldec/home 2.html. *Publicist*—Jay K. Hoffman & Associates, 136 E. 57th St., New York, NY 10022, phone: (212) 371-6690, fax: (212) 754-0192. *Website*—Sharon Isbin Official Website: http://www.sharonisbin.com.

In 1989, she was asked to found and head the guitar department at New York's Juilliard School, which had been Segovia's dying wish to do himself. Isbin has also initiated a number of events that have helped bring the guitar into greater prominence as a classical instrument in the United States. Though the guitar is the most commonly owned musical instrument in the United States, it doesn't often appear on a classical concert stage. Isbin created Guitarstream, a festival at Carnegie Hall, and *Guitarjam,* a critically acclaimed series on National Public Radio (NPR). "Persistence and determination and conviction have always taught me that I can go where I want to go," Isbin said in an interview with *Gramophone*'s Patricia Reilly, "and that you just have to take a chance, leap forward, and know that you can prepare yourself to meet that challenge."

Isbin, who has been described as "the Monet of the guitar," is both artistically gifted with the instrument and technically astute. In a *Washington Post* concert review, critic John Pitcher praised her artistry: "She doesn't so much execute her phrases as lovingly caress them...." *Chicago Tribune* critic John von Rhein noted her technical prowess: "She gets nuances out of the classical guitar few guitarists ... have matched. Everything she performs bespeaks perfect technical control yet suggests spontaneous improvisation—the art that conceals art." Isbin is also at the height of technology in concert. She was the first guitarist to use a specially designed wireless sound system that filled concert halls with the intimacy and the wide, dynamic range of her music captured just as the listener would hear it in a living room or on a recording. Despite the technology, though, *San Francisco Chronicle* critic J. Kosman called Isbin "one of the more musically sensitive ... younger guitarists now performing...."

Isbin enjoys playing a range of music from around the globe. On her 1997 album, *Journey to the Amazon,* she explored music from Latin America, particularly Brazil. The collection, wrote a critic in *Stereo Review,* "is delicately balanced between traditional and contemporary, classical, and popular music." Her *Dreams of a World,* released in 2000, is a collection of folk music from around the world that includes technically demanding pieces from the Appalachian Mountains, the British Isles, Spain, Greece, Cuba, Israel, Venezuela, and Brazil. Isbin "taps the timeless power of traditional melodies, yet delivers these sounds with the refined execution of an experienced concert performer" wrote one critic in *Guitar Player.* The release topped the *Billboard* classical charts, and Isbin won the Grammy Award for Best Instrumental Soloist for *Dreams of a World* in 2001, becoming the first classical guitarist to win a Grammy in 28 years.

Isbin has toured Europe annually since she was 17 years old, and has played in Canada, Japan and the Far East, New Zealand, South America, Mexico, and Israel. She has played at countless international festivals and has appeared as a soloist with more than 100 orchestras in the United States alone. She has appeared on the *St. Paul Sunday* and *All Things Considered* radio programs, and on *CBS Sunday Morning* and A&E's *Breakfast with the Arts* on television.

Selected discography

J.S. Bach: *Complete Lute Suites,* EMI/Virgin Classics, 1989; reissued, Virgin, 2001.
Rhapsody in Blue/West Side Story, Concord Concerto, 1990.
Brazil with Love, Concord Picante, 1990.
Love Songs and Lullabies, EMI/Virgin Classics, 1995.
Nightshade Rounds, EMI/Virgin Classics, 1994.
American Landscapes, EMI/Virgin Classics, 1995.
Journey to the Amazon, Teldec Classics, 1997.

Wayfaring Stranger, Erato, 1998.
Aaron Jay Kernis: Double Concerto, Argo/Decca, 1999.
Dreams of a World, Teldec Classics, 2000.
Rodrigo: *Latin Romances* (two-CD set), EMI/Virgin Classics, 2000.
Concerti by Christopher Rouse and Tan Dun, Teldec New Line, 2001.

Sources

Books

Slonimsky, Nicolas, *Baker's Biographical Dictionary of 20th-Century Classical Musicians,* Schirmer Books, 1992.

Periodicals

BBC Music, December 1996.
Boston Globe, February 14, 1999, p. N2.
Chicago Tribune, June 5, 2000.
Elle, June 1996.
Gramophone, July 1994, p. 23; March 1996.
Guitar Player, April 2000.
New York Times, June 13, 1994.
San Francisco Chronicle, April 24, 1994.
Stereo Review, April 1998.
Washington Post, October 3, 2000.

Online

"Sharon Isbin," Decca Classics, http://www.deccaclassics .com (March 30, 2001).

Additional information was provided by Jay K. Hoffman & Associates publicity materials, 2001.

—Brenna Sanchez

Jeru the Damaja

Hip-hop musician

Few hip-hop or rap artists have been as outspoken about the genres' commercialism as Jeru the Damaja. He is known for his open criticism of such heavy hitters as the group the Fugees and famed producer, performer, and Bad Boy label head Sean "Puffy" Combs. But critics and fans have lauded Jeru for the hard-core style, outspoken lyrics, and skillful rhyming on which he has relied. Although he started off with high school chums in Gang Starr, Jeru soon broke out on his own with hit underground singles like "Come Clean" and the full-length releases *The Sun Rises in the East, Wrath of the Math*, and *Heroz4hire*.

Jeru the Damaja: D Original Dirty Rotten Scoundrel—which is his full stage name—was born Kendrick Jeru Davis in Brooklyn, New York, c. 1972. His father was a Rastafarian and the name Jeru means "first god," referring to the son of Egyptian gods Osiris and Isis. His favorite musical artists growing up were Chuck Berry, with the single "Ding-a-Ling," and Jimmy Castor and his song "King Kong." Jeru began rapping at age seven, inspired by his aunt, Sweet G, who was also a rapper. By the age of ten, he was writing his own rhymes.

It was in high school that Jeru first met Guru and DJ Premier of the seminal hip-hop group Gang Starr, "one of hip-hop's greatest groups" that "thrives on that fine line between underground and mainstream," according to hip-hip magazine *Insomniac*. Jeru first appeared on Gang Starr's single "I'm the Man," from the 1992 album *Daily Operation,* and performed live with the group on tour in 1993. He was considered Gang Starr's protégé, but he quickly emerged from the group.

With DJ Premier producing, Jeru released his solo debut single, "Come Clean," on Gang Starr's Illkids label. His style reflected the old-school sound of rap; it was Jeru's clear, enunciated style and focus on rhyming skill that set him apart from hip-hop contemporaries who focused on gangs and guns. "A long time ago rhyming was about having some skills, and what I tried to do is say, 'Let's bring it back to the skills and forget about the guns,'" he was quoted as saying by Yahoo's Musicfinder online. "Come Clean" became an underground hit and earned him a recording contract with Payday Records/ffrr. In 1994, he released his first full-length album, *The Sun Rises in the East,* which DJ Premier produced. The album, which included his single "Come Clean," and showcased Jeru's "molasses-smooth, metaphoric flow," according to one *Billboard* review.

The same year, Jeru appeared on Digable Planets' second album, *Blowout Comb,* and Gang Starr's *Hard to Earn,* and recorded his own sophomore effort, *Wrath of the Math*, which was released in 1996. Lauded as Jeru's masterpiece, *Wrath of the Math* featured Jeru openly professing his disinterest for mainstream success. He took jabs at the Fugees and Sean "Puffy" Combs, and was seemingly "at war with the industry," according to *Insomniac* magazine online. "He's the type of guy who is truly admired," *Insomniac* publisher Israel Vasquetelle said in an interview with the *Orlando Weekly.* "He speaks out against the false people in hip-hop."

DJ Premier once again worked with Jeru as a producer on *Wrath of the Math.* The two enjoyed a rare and thriving artist-producer relationship. "The chemistry that Premier and I have—that a lot of artists and producers don't have—is that he gives me the beat, then I write the rhyme to fit the beat," he was quoted as saying at iMusic.com. Jeru's goal with *Wrath of the Math,* aside from making a "dope" record, was "to provoke thought," he told iMusic.com. "That's all my music is here to do: provoke thought. By provoking thought, I switch and change the order of things."

As a result of a falling out, DJ Premier did not have a hand in Jeru's 1999 release *Heroz4hire*, which featured the single "99.9%." Instead, Jeru took charge of everything on the release including the studio work and production. He even released it himself. After his deal with Payday Records fell by the wayside, he started his own record label, KnowSavage Productions. Jeru's protégé, Afu-Ra, debuted his own release in 2000. As a rule, cameo record appearances are common between hip-hop artists, but Jeru did not appear on Ra's *Body of the Life Force,* and Ra was absent from Jeru's 1999 release, *Heroz4hire.* "Man, money and fame change [things] up," Jeru said in an interview online at

For the Record . . .

Born Kendrick Jeru Davis, c. 1972, in Brooklyn, NY.

Began rapping at age seven and writing rhymes at age ten; met Guru and DJ Premier of Gang Starr in high school; appeared on Gang Starr's "I'm the Man," from the album *Daily Operation,* 1992; toured with Gang Starr, 1993; released his solo debut, "Come Clean," an underground hit, on Gang Starr's Illkids label, 1993; released the well-received *The Sun Rises in the East*, on Payday Records, 1994; appeared on Digable Planets' second album, *Blowout Comb,* 1994; released *Wrath of the Math* on Payday, 1996; released *Heroz4hire* on own KnowSavage label, 1999.

Addresses: *Website*—Jeru the Damaja Official Website: http://www.dirtyrotten.com.

Angelfire.com about the strained relationship between he and Afu-Ra. "I taught [him] how to rhyme and all that, but now I don't see [him] anymore. It's basically the same thing with Gang Starr. We still cool and all that, but brothas ain't on the same level right now, nah man?"

Handling everything himself as he did on *Heroz4hire* brought Jeru to another level, he said. I just want to remain self-sufficient in everything …." he said in the Angelfire.com interview. "I'm like the book of Revelation—I'm the beginning and the end!" In addition to becoming a better producer, he was looking forward to starting an organization called Ghetto Relief Organization (GRO) with friends. GRO would teach inner-city children to record music, giving them the skills and opportunity to express themselves, no matter what kind of music they wanted to make.

Jeru's records never received significant radio play, his videos didn't appear on MTV, and his face wasn't on the covers of many magazines. But the rapper enjoyed a consistent level of respect from critics and hard-core fans, a rarity in the fickle world of hip-hop. Jeru had a lot to tell *Insomniac* magazine on the subject. It is "because I am real," he said, "and I am not really concerned about what people think of me. Fame is not my goal. My goal is to put out dope hip-hop…. I am going to stay Jeru everyday and do my thing, and that's real hip hop."

Selected discography

The Sun Rises in the East, Payday, 1994.
Wrath of the Math (Clean), ffrr, 1996.
Wrath of the Math, Payday/London, 1996.
Heroz4hire, KnowSavage, 1999.

Appears on

Gang Starr, *Daily Operation,* 1992.
Digable Planets, *Blowout Comb,* 1994.
Gang Starr, *Hard to Earn,* 1994.

Sources

Periodicals

Entertainment Weekly, July 29, 1994, pg. 59; January 10, 1997, pg. 58.

Online

Damainion's Exclusive: Jeru the Damaja, http://www.ang elfire.com/ca6/dawriter2000/jeruinterview.html (April 18, 2001).
"Jeru the Damaja," *All Music Guide,* http://www.allmusic.com (March 30, 2001).
"Jeru the Damaja," *Billboard,* http://www.billboard.com (April 18, 2001).
"Jeru the Damaja," iMusic Urban Showcase, http://imusic .artistdirect.com/showcase/urban/jeruthedamaja.html (April 16, 2001)
"Jeru the Damaja," *Insomniac,* http://www.insomniac maga-zine.com (April 16, 2001).
"Jeru the Damaja," *Source,* http://www.thesource.com (April 16, 2001).
"Jeru the Damaja," Yahoo Musicfinder, http://musicfinder.ya hoo.com (March 30, 2001).
Orlando Weekly, http://www.orlandoweekly.com/music/tba/ index.asp?tba=125 (April 18, 2001).

—Brenna Sanchez

Joe

Singer

Helped by the major hit songs "I Wanna Know" and "Stutter," R&B vocalist Joe's third album, the 2000 release *My Name Is Joe,* fulfilled the promise that the artist had developed over several years in the music industry. From his early signing to a record deal right after high school to a personally disappointing first outing in the recording studio, Joe branched out into writing, producing, and offering background vocals for the work of other artists. Gradually building his public profile by contributing songs to several successful soundtracks, Joe's strategy finally paid off. Going double platinum within a year of its release, *My Name Is Joe* established the performer in the top league of R&B singers, writers, and producers, and earned him a reputation as one of the hardest-working artists in the music industry.

Joe Lewis Thomas, Jr. grew up surrounded by music. His parents were both ministers in the Pentecostal Church and made sure that their five children took an active role in church activities. During his childhood in Georgia and Opelika, Alabama, as Joe recalled in a 1997 *Ebony* interview, "[The church] was my whole life. I did nothing else. In high school and growing up, [my parents] weren't having it any other way. 'Forget about parties and hanging out. You're going to church.'" Fortunately, church-going gave Joe an opportunity to develop his musical talents, giving him an appreciation for Christian acts such as the Winans and Vanessa Bell Armstrong. From an early age, he played guitar and piano, and directed the gospel choir in his parents' church as well. By the time he was a teenager, Joe also found the time to perform with a band around Opelika, taking as his inspiration contemporary acts such as Bobby Brown, Babyface, and Keith Sweat in addition to classic Motown artists like Stevie Wonder and Marvin Gaye. After completing high school, Joe decided to forge ahead with a career in music.

Taking a job at a gospel music store in New Jersey and continuing his musical training with a Newark church, Joe enlisted the support of producer Vincent Herbert, who helped him compile a demo tape of three songs. With the tape in hand, Joe reached a publishing deal with Jive Records and a recording contract with Mercury/Polygram Records in 1992. Joe's first professional efforts from these deals came with his writing and producing credits for Toni Braxton and Hi-Five, but by 1993 he had also completed his first album, *Everything,* which was released by Mercury Records in August of that year. Despite his growing list of production and writing credits for other artists, Joe's debut was a disappointment. "I understand a lot of things that went wrong with the writing, production, and vocals on the album," he told *Ebony* in 1997, adding, "I've grown a lot just by listening to the things that I've done before."

Joe was also disappointed by Mercury's promotional efforts behind his first outing, which proved to be only

For the Record . . .

Born Joe Lewis Thomas, Jr. in 1972 in Georgia; son of Pentecostal ministers.

Joined bands while in high school and moved to New Jersey after completing high school; completed record demo and secured publishing deal, 1991; *Everything* released on Mercury Records, 1993; signed by Jive Records; contributed "All the Things (Your Man Won't Do)" to the *Don't Be a Menace to South Central* film soundtrack; released *All That I Am*, 1997; released *My Name Is Joe*, 2000.

Addresses: *Record company*—Jive Records, 11 West 19th Street, 3rd Floor, New York, NY 10011, website: http://www.jiverecords.com. *Website*—Joe Official Website: http://www.joescrib.com.

a minor success despite airplay for the tracks "I'm in Love" and "All or Nothing." Deciding to put more effort into working for other artists, including SWV, Usher, and Tina Turner, Joe let his contract with Mercury expire without recording another full-length album. He closed out his contract, however, with a major hit contribution to the *Don't Be a Menace to South Central* soundtrack in 1996, "All the Things (Your Man Won't Do)," which reached number two on *Billboard*'s R&B singles chart. Quickly signing to a recording contract with Jive Records, where he already had a publishing deal, Joe followed his first hit soundtrack song with another successful movie track, "Don't Wanna Be a Player," from 1997's *Booty Call*. A top 40 hit on *Billboard*'s Hot 100, the song also drew critical praise in *Billboard*'s review of its April 1997 release, proclaiming Joe "among the R&B community's most viable contenders for Luther Vandross's 'King of Soul' throne." The song also projected Joe's image as a romantic and sophisticated singer, in contrast to singers that relied on crude sexual come-ons in their lyrics.

Released in 1997, *All That I Am* concentrated on ballads that reinforced Joe's approach as a sensitive crooner. "I want to bring back the romance to R&B," the singer told *Billboard* in anticipation of the album's June 1997 release, "I talk about relationships from a female and male perspective—how they work, the good times and the bad times—I talk about it all." Discussing his music with *Ebony* later that year, he reflected, "I believe in respect. I look back and wouldn't want anybody to disrespect my mother or my sisters. I want them to be in the best relationship or be in the best situation possible." Helped by Joe's success with "Don't Wanna

Be a Player," *All That I Am* eventually turned platinum, a great improvement over his debut effort. Joe also scored a success with his collaboration on Mariah Carey's "Thank God I Found You" remix, which further enhanced his reputation as a singer and raised expectations for his next album.

Looking forward to the release of his third full-length album, Joe was once again helped by the inclusion of his work on a movie soundtrack. "I Wanna Know," a romantic ballad included on the soundtrack for the 1999 film *The Wood,* hit the top five on *Billboard*'s Hot 100 early in 2000.

While Joe continued to emphasize the romantic nature of his songs on *My Name Is Joe,* released on Jive Records in April of 2000, he commented on his website that "this album is a lot more sexual than anything I've done in the past," with franker expressions of sexual themes. As he related to *Billboard,* "I've had a lot of freedom to express how I feel about certain things, especially sexual content. With this album, I was really comfortable to say what I wanted to say and still have the same amount of respect for women." Indeed, the album was welcomed by a *Times* reviewer as "ideal seduction music," while the *Los Angeles Times* agreed that *My Name Is Joe* was "mood-enhancing background music." Other reviews were not as kind. Spence Abbot of the Wall of Sound website admitted that "Joe's slick, slow-dance-inducing, candles-in-the-dark mood music will be a perfect fit for your sensual activities," but nevertheless insisted that "his brand of soul lacks authenticity and sincerity, not to mention the grit of a Sam Cooke or a Marvin Gaye." An *Entertainment Weekly* review went even further, dismissing *My Name Is Joe* as "boilerplate pop-soul production" that veered into "cruel hostility toward women" on some of its tracks. However, critics agreed that "Stutter" was the collection's standout track; the public agreed, sending the song to the top of *Billboard*'s Hot 100 early in 2001. The international success of "Stutter" also helped make inroads on sales charts outside of the United States.

Joe's mainstream success had taken advantage of Jive's ability to market its artists across a number of musical formats, as he performed with labelmates Britney Spears on her television special and collaborated with 'N Sync on the track "I Believe in You." Describing himself as an all-around entertainer, Joe commented on his website that "I guess you could say I'm sort of old-fashioned in my approach because trends can come and go and my goal is to write songs that last. Good songs don't age, and my objective each time out is to write and sing good songs." Although he built his reputation on romantic ballads with his first three releases, the singer looked forward to exploring social issues in his future songwriting. In addition, Joe planned to continue his work as a producer and songwriter for other artists, including projects with the Temptations, Babyface, Usher, and BeBe Winans.

Selected discography

Everything, Mercury, 1993.
(Contributor) *Don't Be a Menace to South Central* (soundtrack), Island, 1996.
All That I Am, Jive, 1997.
(Contributor) *Booty Call* (soundtrack), Jive, 1997.
(Contributor) *Rush Hour* (soundtrack), Def Jam, 1998.
(Contributor) *The Wood* (soundtrack), Jive, 1999.
My Name Is Joe, Jive, 2000.

Sources

Periodicals

Billboard, April 5, 1997; April 26, 1997; August 16, 1997; May 20, 2000; December 23, 2000.

Ebony, August 1997; October 2000.
Entertainment Weekly, April 21, 2000.
Los Angeles Times, May 12, 2000.
Q, August 2000.
Times (London), February 23, 2001.

Online

All Music Guide, http://www.allmusic.com (April 19, 2001).
Hollywood Stock Exchange, http://www.music.hsx.com (April 19, 2001).
Jive Records, http://www.getmusic.com/artists/001/joe (April 18, 2001).
Joe Official Website, http://www.joescrib.com (April 18, 2001).
Rnation, http://www.rnation.com (April 19, 2001).
Wall of Sound, http://www.wallofsound.comartists/joe/home .html (April 19, 2001).

—Timothy Borden

J.J. Johnson

Trombonist, composer, bandleader

AP/Wide World Photos. Reproduced by permission.

Considered by many as the finest jazz trombonist of all time, J.J. Johnson was a visionary force on his instrument. His developments for the bebop and improvised style on trombone placed him on a par with Charlie Parker on alto saxophone and Jimi Hendrix on the electric guitar. "J.J. elevated the trombone to a higher status," said trombonist Curtis Fuller, according to *Down Beat* magazine writer John Murph. "As a jazz soloist, you had your Trummy Youngs and your Dicky Wells, but in the vernacular of bebop, he was the trombonist for that language. J.J. was a genius; he was no fly-by-night sensation. He was the man for all seasons, and I was drawn to that." After battling cancer and a muscular-skeletal disorder, Johnson took his own life on February 4, 2001. He left behind a legacy of groundbreaking work, with his own groups and recordings with Kai Winding, as well as on the recordings of Miles Davis, Dizzy Gillespie, Charlie Parker, Illinois Jacquet, Sonny Rollins, Ellla Fitzgerald, and others.

Born James Louis Johnson on January 22, 1924, in Indianapolis, Indiana, the future trombonist began his musical studies on the piano, taking lessons at a local church. During his early teens, concurrent with his discovery of jazz, Johnson switched his focus to the saxophone. In high school, however, Johnson was only able to obtain a baritone saxophone, and because he could not make the instrument resemble the caressing tones of his childhood idol, saxophonist Lester Young, the young musician switched to the trombone.

Early Professional Start

Johnson graduated in 1941, but instead of continuing on to college, he opted to turn professional right out of high school. Leaving Indianapolis, the trombonist found work immediately in Midwestern bands led by Clarence Love and Snookum Russell, touring with them during 1941 and 1942. While traveling and performing with Russell's group, he met trumpeter Fats Navarro, whose improvisational style made a lasting impression on Johnson.

In fact, Johnson claimed that trumpeters, as well as saxophonists such as Young, Gillespie, Parker, and Roy Eldridge, influenced him to a greater extent than did trombonists. Consequently, when he applied the bebop technique to the trombone, Johnson played in clear tones and short notes, and some listeners wrongly assumed that he was playing the valve trombone, which lends itself more easily to articulation, instead of the slide trombone. "Making that adaptation to the trombone was very demanding," explained *Los Angeles Times* jazz writer Don Heckman. "It took a decade before other trombonists on the whole began to master what Johnson was doing."

However, Johnson acknowledged to writer Ira Gitler in *The Masters of Bebop: A Listener's Guide* that his

Born James Louis Johnson on January 22, 1924, in Indianapolis, IN; died on February 4, 2001, in Indianapolis, IN; first wife, Vivian, died in 1991; second wife, Carolyn; children: two sons (from first marriage), Kevin and William; stepdaughter, Mikita Sanders.

Toured with bands led by Clarence Love and Snookum Russell, 1941-42; played with Benny Carter's big band, 1942-45; member of Count Basie's Orchestra, 1945-46; formed two-trombone quintet with Kai Winding, 1954; composed "Poem for Brass," "Perceptions," and "Lament," mid 1950s through the early 1960s; wrote scores for film and television, 1970s and 1980s; saw rebirth of career in jazz with the release of albums such as *Brass Orchestra,* 1996, and *Heroes,* 1998.

reinventing of the traditional trombone sound was not entirely original. Another trombone player, Fred Beckett, who played with Harlan Leonard and Lionel Hampton during the 1930s and 1940s, inspired Johnson to take the trombone—previously thought of as a melodic, light-sounding instrument during the era of swing bands—and apply it to the bebop style with rapid phrasing, complex harmonies, and offbeat rhythms. Beckett, said Johnson, as quoted by Ben Ratliff in the *New York Times,* "was the first trombonist I ever heard play in a manner other than the usual sliding, slurring, lip-trilling or gutbucket style."

"Definitive Trendsetter"

Although still a teenager, Johnson, with his unique style, was already gaining a reputation as one of the finest trombonists around among bandleaders, composers, and critics. As the late jazz critic Leonard Feather once wrote, as quoted by *Los Angeles Times* contributor Jon Thurber, "J.J. Johnson was to the trombone what [Dizzy] Gillespie was to the trumpet— the definitive trendsetter who established beyond a doubt that bebop was not beyond the technical possibilities of the instrument."

From 1942 until 1945, Johnson played with Benny Carter's big band, making his recording debut with the group playing a solo on Carter's "Love for Sale" in 1943. The following year, Johnson performed at the first Jazz at the Philharmonic concert at the Los Angeles Philharmonic Hall. Led by the now-legendary impresario Norman Grantz, the event—billed as the city's premiere full-scale jazz concert—proved a huge success, fostering nationwide tours and a popular series of albums. During 1945 and 1946, Johnson performed with Count Basie's Orchestra. Here, too, Johnson was awarded plenty of solo space. Also in 1946, Johnson recorded his first session as a bandleader for the Savoy label.

Thereafter, Johnson balanced his solo career with work as a much-sought-after sideman. Throughout the remainder of the decade, he performed with leading bebop musicians, including Charlie Parker, with whom he recorded in 1947 to become the only person to guest with the original Charlie Parker Quintet. Other affiliations included playing and/or recording with Dizzy Gillespie's big band, Illinois Jacquet, from 1947 until 1949, and Miles Davis, with whom he played on the trumpeter's landmark *Birth of the Cool* recording of 1949. On his own records as a bandleader, Johnson likewise enlisted top players, among them Bud Powell and a young Sonny Rollins.

In the early 1950s, Johnson played with Oscar Pettiford and again with Davis in 1952. But despite staying active, he found that music was not enough to support his family. Thus, from 1952 until 1954, Johnson, who had always held a curiosity about electronic equipment, worked as a blueprint inspector for the Sperry Gyroscope Company. Fortunately, Johnson's fortunes brightened when, in August of 1954, he formed a two-trombone quintet with Kai Winding. Known as Jay and Kai, the format proved a commercial success, and in turn allowed Johnson to quit his day job. The group enjoyed a great amount of popularity through 1956. Afterward, Johnson and Winding disbanded in order to pursue other interests, though they would reunite occasionally over the years.

Made Priority of Own Work

Johnson next formed another quintet, which often featured Bobby Jasper. His primary focus, however, began to lean increasingly toward creating his own music. Beginning in the mid 1950s, Johnson undertook the writing of ambitious compositions, including his first large-scale work, "Poem for Brass." The four-part piece was featured on the 1956 Columbia Records album *Music for Brass,* conducted by noted composer, educator, and jazz historian Gunther Schuller. In 1959, the Monterey Jazz Festival commissioned Johnson to compose two pieces: "El Camino Real" and "Sketch for Trombone and Orchestra." Subsequently, the emerging composer penned his most challenging work for Gillespie, who was so impressed upon hearing "Poem for Brass" that he commissioned Johnson to compose an entire album's worth of material. The result, "Perceptions," recorded in 1961, was a 35-minute long suite that featured six trumpets, four French horns, and two harps.

During the 1950s, Johnson also toured and recorded frequently with his quintet. Then, in the fall of 1960, he decided to break up the band. His reason for ending the group, he remarked years later, was that "it suddenly occurred to me that I needed a change," as quoted by the *Washington Post*'s Adam Bernstein, "and I even began to wonder, was it possible that a musician or artist could be much too dedicated—so much so that he lived in a very narrow world." Although he continued to perform, Johnson's appearances grew more selective. During a period in 1961 and 1962, Johnson returned to work with Davis and continued to perform on occasion with saxophonists Rollins, Jimmy Heath, and Sonny Stitt. From time to time, he formed other small groups of his own, but devoted himself almost entirely to composing.

In 1967, through the support of film composer Elmer Bernstein, Johnson secured a position as staff composer and conductor for M.B.A. Music in New York, a company providing music for television commercials. In 1970, he moved to Los Angeles to embark on a career in film and television. Throughout the decade, he scored music for television series such as *Starsky and Hutch*, *Mayberry, R.F.D.*, and *That Girl*. In the 1970s and 1980s, he also wrote and orchestrated music for films like *Barefoot in the Park*, *Scarface*, *Trouble Man*, *Sea of Love*, and the "blacksploitation" movies *Cleopatra Jones* and *Shaft*.

Stayed Focused on Music

Despite his success in Hollywood, Johnson remained focused on jazz and his trombone. He practiced every day to keep his skills sharp—as evident on *Quintergy* and *Standards*, albums recorded live at the Village Vanguard in 1988. Even while not recording much at all, he kept winning *Down Beat* polls year after year. In the 1990s, under contract with the Verve label, Johnson recorded some of his most ambitious work, including 1994's *Tangence*, a collaboration with film composer Robert Farnon; 1996's *Brass Orchestra*, featuring work in the bebop style and selections from "Perceptions"; and 1998's *Heroes*, his final album, a straight-ahead jazz set. *Heroes*, wrote a *Down Beat* reviewer, as quoted by Bernstein, "leaves a general impression of solid craftsmanship, if not breathtaking artistic significance. The main news is that J.J. Johnson can always assemble a sturdy ensemble, and he's still a hero to trombonists everywhere."

In 1987, Johnson returned to his hometown of Indianapolis with his first wife, Vivian. Following her death in 1991, he recorded an album in her name in 1992. In 1997, Johnson decided to retire from performing in public because of ill health. He had survived a battle with prostate cancer and spent the years prior to his death in 2001 in his home studio learning new technology available for composing and recording.

Johnson's profound influence was made apparent by the wealth of family, friends, and members of the jazz community who attended his funeral. Nine trombonists filled the alter, among them Slide Hampton, Steve Turre, and Robin Eubanks, to perform Johnson's standard piece "Lament." Also making an appearance to pay tribute to Johnson was the legendary Max Roach. "He was a genius, always a great instrumentalist," Roach said at the funeral, as quoted by *Down Beat*'s Matthew Socey. "Even at a young age, he was a rare person to have.... [H]e left us so much."

Selected discography

Mad Bebop, Savoy, 1946.
Modern Jazz Trombone Series, Vol. 1, Prestige, 1949.
Trombone By Three, Prestige, 1949.
Modern Jazz Trombone Series, Vol. 2, Prestige, 1949.
The Eminent Jay Jay Johnson, Vol. 1, Blue Note, 1953.
Jay Jay Johnson All Star, Blue Note, 1953.
The Eminent Jay Jay Johnson, Vol. 2, Blue Note, 1954.
Nuf Said, Bethlehem, 1955.
Kai + J.J., Columbia, 1956.
Jay and Kai Octet, Columbia, 1956.
Blue Trombone, Columbia, 1957.
At the Opera House, Verve, 1957.
The Great Kai & J.J., Impulse!, 1960.
Proof Positive, GRP/Impulse!, 1964.
Stonebone, A&M, 1969.
Concepts in Blue, Pablo, 1980.
We'll Be Together Again, Pablo, 1983.
Things Are Getting Better All the Time, Pablo, 1983.
Quintergy, Antilles, 1988.
Standards, Antilles, 1988.
Vivian, Concord Jazz, 1992.
Tangence, Gitanes, 1994.
Brass Orchestra, Verve, 1996.
Heroes, Verve, 1998.

Sources

Books

Gitler, Ira, *The Masters of Bebop: A Listener's Guide*, Perseus Books Group, 2001.

Periodicals

Billboard, February 17, 2001.
Down Beat, June 2001.
Los Angeles Times, February 6, 2001.
New York Times, February 6, 2001.
Washington Post, February 7, 2001; March 31, 2001.

Online

All Music Guide, http://www.allmusic.com (May 2, 2001).
J.J. Johnson Homepage, http://www.jjjohnson.org (June 22, 2001).
NPR Jazz Online, http://www.nprjazz.org (March 7, 2001).

—Laura Hightower

John Kander

Composer

John Kander is a composer who has produced award-winning work for theater, film, and television. He is best known for his collaborative efforts with lyricist Fred Ebb. For almost 40 years the partners have produced hits for Broadway, such as *Cabaret, Chicago,* and *Kiss of the Spider Woman.* In television they are best known for their musical productions with actress, singer, and dancer Liza Minnelli.

John Harold Kander was born on March 18, 1927, in Kansas City, Missouri, to Harold and Berenice (Aaron) Kander. He was exposed to music at an early age. Kander believed that a bout of tuberculosis as a baby, which had kept him isolated from other people, had actually helped him develop his sense of sound. At age six he began taking piano lessons from a woman in the neighborhood. Kander spent many evenings with his parents and brother playing and singing.

Kander's formal musical training began at Oberlin College. While still a student he composed his first theater scores for *Second Square* and *Opus Two* in 1950 and *Requiem for Georgie* in 1951. In that same year Kander received his Bachelor of Arts degree from Oberlin. He went to attend Columbia University where he earned a Master of Arts degree in 1954. During the summers of 1955 to 1957 he worked as the choral director and conductor of the Warwick Musical Theatre in Rhode Island. Kander began to work steadily as a pianist in 1956 when he landed a job for the pre-Broadway run of *The Amazing Adele* and *An Evening with Beatrice Lillie* in Florida.

The Big Break

Kander believed that his big break in New York came by accident. He went to a club in Philadelphia after seeing a performance of *West Side Story.* By chance he happened to meet the pianist who asked Kander to substitute for him while he went on vacation. The stage manager for *West Side Story* then asked Kander to play the auditions for her next show, *Gypsy.* During the auditions Kander met the choreographer, Jerry Robbins, who then suggested that Kander actually write the dance music for the show in 1959. After that experience he wrote dance arrangements for *Irma la Douce* in 1960.

Kander made his Broadway debut in 1962 with a score for the musical *A Family Affair,* which was produced at the Billy Rose Theatre. While the show was not a success, it nonetheless led to future successes for Kander. The producer of this show, Harold Prince, would work with Kander again. A year later, in 1963, Kander was introduced to lyricist Fred Ebb by the legendary music publisher Tommy Volando. Ebb had been writing songs for nightclub acts and television shows. He had also had an unsuccessful Broadway debut with *Morning Sun.* Kander and Ebb began to

Born John Harold Kander on March 18, 1927, in Kansas City, MO.

Composed first theater scores, 1950; worked as choral director and conductor of the Warwick Musical Theatre, 1955-57; began working as a pianist, 1956; wrote dance music for *Gypsy*, 1959; wrote dance music for *Irma la Douce*, 1960; made Broadway debut with score for *A Family Affair*, 1962; began working with lyricist Fred Ebb, 1963; had a hit with *Cabaret*, 1966; scored *The Happy Time* and *Zorba*, 1968; scored *70, Girls, 70*, 1971; scored *Chicago*, 1975; scored *The Act*, 1978; scored *Woman of the Year*, 1981; scored *The Rink*, 1984; scored *The Kiss of the Spider Woman*, 1990; scored *Steel Pier*, 1997; scored *Over and Over*, 1999; scored *The Visit*, 2000. Wrote film scores for several films, including: *Kramer vs. Kramer*, 1979; *Places in the Heart*, 1984; and *Billy Bathgate*, 1991. Collaborated with Ebb on several films and television specials.

Awards: Grammy Award, Best Score from an original cast show album for *Cabaret*, 1967; Tony Award, Best Composer and Lyricist for *Cabaret*, 1967; Drama Desk Award, Best Composer and Lyricist for *Cabaret*, 1967; New York Drama Critics' Circle Award, Best New Musical for *Cabaret*, 1967; *Emmy Award, Best Music, Lyrics, and Special Material for Liza with a 'Z'*, 1973; Tony Award, Best Score for *Woman of the Year*, 1981; Tony Award, Best Original Score written for the theatre for *Kiss of the Spider Woman*, 1993; Emmy Award, Best Music Composition for *Liza Minnelli Live! From Radio City Music Hall*, 1993; President's Award, Society of Stage Directors and Choreographers, 1996; John F. Kennedy Center for the Performing Arts Honoree, 1998; Oscar Hammerstein Award for Lifetime Achievement in musical theater, York Theatre Company, 2000.

work together and their first song, *My Coloring Book*, was nominated for a Grammy award.

Broadway Success

Kander and Ebb's first theatrical collaboration, the *Golden Gate*, never opened on Broadway. However, the score convinced Harold Prince, the producer from *A Family Affair*, to hire the pair for his next production called *Flora, the Red Menace*. The show opened at the Alvin Theatre in 1965. While it was not a hit, the experience solidified the team of Kander and Ebb. The show was the Broadway debut for the young Liza Minnelli, who would also work with Kander and Ebb again.

Kander and Ebb worked with Prince the following year on the production that brought the pair fame. On November 20, 1966, *Cabaret* opened at the Broadhurst Theatre and ran for 1,166 performances. The story about a relationship between a German cabaret performer and an American writer in pre-Nazi Berlin was based on the book *Berlin Stories* by Christopher Isherwood and the play *I Am a Camera* by John Van Druten. The show won the 1966 Tony Award for best musical and Kander and Ebb won for best score. In 1972 *Cabaret* was adapted to film starring Liza Minnelli and won several Oscars. The play was revived at the Imperial Theatre in 1987 with some of the original cast returning to their same roles. It was revived again in 1998 when it won another Tony for best revival.

After the success of *Cabaret* the partnership of Kander and Ebb was strengthened and they continued to work together on Broadway. In 1968 they wrote the music for *The Happy Time*, produced at the Broadway Theatre, and for *Zorba*, produced at the Imperial Theatre. In 1971 the team wrote music for *70, Girls, 70* at the Broadhurst Theatre.

Their next big Broadway success came in 1975 with the help of Bob Fosse and *Chicago*. This musical was based on a 1926 play written by Maurine Dallas Watkins, a reporter for the *Chicago Tribune*. It was a story about a chorus girl who murdered her husband and then used the ensuing trial to boost her show business career. The show opened on June 3, 1975, at the 46th Street Theatre and ran for 898 performances. It starred Gwen Verdon, Chita Rivera, and Jerry Orbach and included the popular songs *All That Jazz* and *Razzle Dazzle*. While the musical was nominated for 11 Tony awards, it did not win any because of the overwhelming success of *A Chorus Line*. However, the show was revived again in 1997 and won six Tony awards, including best revival, best choreography, and best direction.

Kander and Ebb continued their collaboration with *The Act* in 1978. They received their second Tony award in 1981 for *Woman of the Year*. That production won three other Tony awards, including one for actress Lauren Bacall. In 1984 the duo worked on *The Rink* for the Martin Beck Theatre, which starred Minnelli and Rivera. While *The Rink* did not do well on Broadway, Kander considered it one of his favorite musicals because the songs were very emotional.

Success returned to Kander and Ebb with *The Kiss of the Spider Woman,* a play based on the novel *El Beso de la Mujer Arana* by Manuel Puig about two men in a Latin American prison. The show was produced in Toronto, Canada, in 1990 and then at the Shaftesbury Theatre in London in 1992. It made its Broadway debut on May 3, 1993, at the Broadhurst Theatre where it ran for 906 performances. Kander and Ebb won a Tony award for best musical score and actress Chita Rivera also won for her role. The show also won a New York Drama Critics award for best musical.

Kander and Ebb's next two productions were not as critically acclaimed. In 1997 they wrote the music for *Steel Pier,* a play about a dance marathoner during the depression. In 1999 they wrote the music for *Over and Over,* a play based on the book *The Skin of Our Teeth* by Thornton Wilder. In 2000 Kander and Ebb were working on a new musical together called *The Visit* based on a play by Friedrich Durrenmatt.

Film and Television Scores

Kander's career has not been limited to theater. He has written scores for several films. These include: *Something for Everyone* (1969), *A Matter of Time* (1976), *Kramer vs. Kramer* (1979), *Still of the Night* (1982), *Blue Skies Again* (1983), *Places in the Heart* (1984), *I Want to Go Home* (1989), and *Billy Bathgate* (1991). He also collaborated with Ebb for one of their most famous accomplishments, *New York, New York* (1977). The duo also wrote music for *Cabaret* (1972), *Funny Lady* and *Lucky Lady* (1975), and *French Postcards* (1979).

Kander and Ebb also collaborated on music for several television specials. In 1974 they won an Emmy award for their work on *Liza with a 'Z'* and the soundtrack also won a Grammy Award. They won another Emmy in 1993 for *Liza Minnelli in London, Steppin' Out*. The partners also worked with Minnelli on *Goldie and Liza Together* (1980), *Standing Room Only: Liza in London* (1986), *Liza Minnelli: A Triple Play* (1988), and *Liza Minnelli Live! From Radio City Music Hall* (1992). Additionally, the duet created music for Shirley MacLain's *Gypsy in My Soul* (1976), *Baryshnikov on Broadway* (1980), *Breathing Lessons* (1995) and *The Boys Next Door* (1995). Kander and Ebb also wrote music for two Academy Awards presentations in 1988 and 1993.

Awards and Impact

In addition to his Tony, Grammy, and Emmy awards, Kander has received other public acknowledgments for his contributions to music. He received honorary doctorate degrees from Oberlin College in 1988 and Niagara University in 1994, where he is also a guest lecturer. In 1996 he received the President's Award from the Society of Stage Directors and Choreographers. In 1998 both Kander and Ebb were Kennedy Center Honorees and in 2000 they were awarded the Oscar Hammerstein Award for Lifetime Achievement in musical theater by the York Theatre Company of New York City.

For almost four decades Kander and Ebb have been writing music together for theater, film, and television. Their collaboration is a true partnership. As Kander explained, the two always work together in the same room at the same time when they are writing. In a February 1997 article in *American Theatre,* Marilyn Stasio wrote that "The two artists who do not always agree with each other have nevertheless maintained a perfect balance in their work. They complement each other as Kander's lyricism sweetens Ebb's wit and Ebb's cynicism toughens up Kander's raging romanticism."

While the two artists have been successful in many endeavors, they have left the biggest impression on Broadway. As Kander stated in a February 1997 article with Marilyn Stasio in *American Theatre,* "if you're going to write on a canvas of some size, the Broadway theatre is still the only place that offers you that opportunity." They have created a unique style of musical theater that is characterized by youthful joy and romanticism. In an April 1997 article in the *New York Times,* Ethan Mordden wrote, "Mr. Kander and Mr. Ebb celebrate the Big Break, the American love of show biz, making it, performance. Their musicals may be set in Germany, Greece, or South America, may defy Fascism or flirt with death. But at the center of their art lies a love of the talent-take-all wonder of entertainment."

Selected discography

Flora, the Red Menace, RCA Victor, 1965.
Cabaret (original cast recording), Columbia, 1967.
The Happy Time (original cast recording), RCA, 1968.
Zorba (original cast recording), Capitol, 1969.
70, Girls, 70 (original cast recording), Sony, 1971.
Chicago (original cast recording), Arista, 1975.
New York, New York (film soundtrack), EMI, 1977.
Woman of the Year (original cast recording), Arista, 1981.
The Rink (original cast recording), TER, 1984.
And the World Goes 'Round (original cast recording), RCA Victor, 1991.
An Evening with John Kander and Fred Ebb, DRG, 1992.
Kiss of the Spider Woman (original cast recording), RCA Victor, 1993.
Steel Pier (original cast recording), RCA Victor, 1997.

Selected scores

Stage; with Fred Ebb

Flora, the Red Menace, 1965.
Cabaret, 1966.

The Happy Time, 1968.
Zorba, 1968.
70, Girls, 70, 1971.
Chicago, 1975.
The Act, 1978.
Woman of the Year, 1981.
The Rink, 1984.
And the World Goes 'Round, 1991.
Kiss of the Spider Woman, 1993.
Steel Pier, 1997.
Over and Over, 1999.

Film

Something for Everyone, 1969.
(With Fred Ebb) *Funny Lady*, 1975.
(With Fred Ebb) *Lucky Lady*, 1975.
(With Fred Ebb) *New York, New York*, 1977.
Kramer vs. Kramer, 1979.
Still of the Night, 1982.
Blue Skies Again, 1983.
Places in the Heart, 1984.
I Want to Go Home, 1989.
Billy Bathgate, 1991.

Television; with Fred Ebb

Liza with a 'Z', 1974.
Gypsy in My Soul, 1976.
Goldie and Liza Together, 1980.
Baryshnikov on Broadway, 1980.
Liza Minnelli in London, Steppin' Out, 1993.

Breathing Lessons, 1995.
The Boys Next Door, 1995.

Sources

Books

Contemporary Theatre, Film, and Television, volume 13, Gale Research, 1995.
Guernsey, Otis J., *Broadway Song and Story: Playwrights/Lyricists/Composers Discuss Their Hits,* Dodd, Mead, and Co., 1985.

Periodicals

American Theatre, February 1997, p. 10.
New York Times, April 13, 1997, p. 4.
Variety, September 27, 1999, p. 157.

Online

"John Kander," http://www.niagara.edu/theatre/faculty/kander.html (February 17, 2001).
"The Kennedy Center Honors," http://kennedy-center.org/honors/history/honoree/kander-ebb.html (February 17, 2001).
"The Music of Kander and Ebb: Razzle Dazzle," http://www.wnet.org/gperf/features/html/meet_meet.html (February 17, 2001).

—Janet Stamatel

Khaled

Singer

© Jack Vartoogian. Reproduced by permission.

Known as the "king of rai," Algerian-born Khaled (he dropped Cheb from his stage name in 1992) became a star of Arabic pop music while still a teen. Political and religious unrest led Khaled and many other artists to flee Algeria for France where Khaled recorded his biggest hit, "Didi," in 1992. Khaled became the standout among his fellow expatriates and a star on the French world music scene by incorporating a range of international influences and genres into his music. He included funk, hip-hop, salsa, and reggae, and sang in Arabic and French, giving rai a truly international sound. Khaled enjoys employing diverse producers on his recordings and scored another hit single in 1996 with the love song "Aicha," produced by famed American funk and rock producer Don Was. Khaled's 2000 release, *Kenza,* is a showcase of his global rai interpretations.

Born Khaled Hadj Brahim in Sidi-El-Houri on February 29, 1960, in Oran, Algeria, Khaled sang and learned to play guitar, bass, accordion, and harmonica as a child. He enjoyed the sounds of Moroccan music and Elvis Presley. Though his uncle played the accordion, Khaled's family looked down on his musical aspirations. His father, a policeman, disapproved of it entirely. Khaled's debut recording, *La Route De Lycee,* came out when he was just 14 years old. After that, he dropped out of school, left home, and formed a group called the Five Stars, and started to perform at local weddings, parties, and clubs.

Rai music was originally heard in seedy Algerian bars in the 1920s. This "sinner's music" was sung to the beat of light percussion and an ancient rosewood flute called a *gasba.* Khaled released a handful of self-produced rai cassettes before he teamed up with producer Rachid Baba Ahmed, who had a greater pop sensibility. Under Ahmed's influence, Khaled's sound increasingly began taking on more of a Western sound, incorporating such Western instruments as synthesizers and guitars. Khaled became the most well-known singer of the revived "pop rai" trend that first became popular during the 1960s. Excite online likened his stage presence and effect on Algeria's youth to that of Elvis Presley on American teenagers in the 1950s. Though Khaled was embraced by Algeria's disenchanted youth during the 1980s, not all of Algeria shared the same enthusiasm for rai, which offended the sensibilities of Islamic fundamentalists.

Until 1983, Khaled's music was censored by the Algerian government for both his candid lyrics about romance and his lyrics against Islamic fundamentalism. The Algerian government attacked what it considered to be outspoken hedonism, and Khaled's music was banned from Algerian radio and television. In 1985, though, he was crowned the "king of rai" at Algeria's National Rai Festival in his hometown of Oran. In the late 1980s, sensing trouble in Algeria, Khaled fled to Paris, as did many other Algerian artists, journalists,

For the Record . . .

Born Khaled Hadj Brahim in Sidi-El-Houri on February, 29, 1960, in Oran, Algeria.

Released debut, *La Route De Lycee*, at age 14; left home and formed band, the Five Stars, released several self-produced cassettes; was declared the "king of rai," 1985; left Algeria for France, late 1980s; dropped "Cheb" from his stage name, 1992; had a hit single with "Didi," 1992; scored another major hit with "Aicha," from his Don Was-produced album *Sahra*, 1996; released *King of Rai*, 1999; released *Kenza*, 2000.

Addresses: *Record company*—Ark 21 Records, 14724 Ventura Blvd, Penthouse Suite, Sherman Oaks, CA 91403, website: http://www.ark21.com.

musicians, and intellectuals. The 1992 Algerian elections were clearly going to be won by Islamic fundamentalists, so the military government canceled the elections and violence broke out. Terrorists targeted and killed many artists, including the popular "prince of rai," singer Cheb Hasni.

The mass exodus of rai musicians to France resulted in a change in the traditional rai sound. Used to shoddy equipment and a strict government, the Algerian singers suddenly had creative freedom and access to France's high-tech recording studios. Exposure to European and other emigrant cultures influenced the sound as well, though "with mixed results" for many artists, according to critic Peter Margasak in the *New York Times*.

In 1992, Khaled was the first Algerian expatriate to break out in France with his love song "Didi," a crossover hit for his French record label Cohiba. On his album *Khaled*, the singer continued to globalize the rai sound and even began to incorporate funk, hip-hop, reggae, and the French chanson—a song style from the Middle Ages and the Renaissance. Though his songs had taken on an international flavor, Khaled remained true to the Arabic sound with his "seductive phrasing and nasal, soulfully gruff voice," wrote Margasak. Khaled's records became popular in France, the Middle East, and India. In the mid 1990s, Khaled dropped "Cheb" from his stage name, a term meaning "kid" that was given to singers like Khaled to make them distinct from older, more traditional artists.

Khaled's subsequent albums, including *N'ssi N'ssi, Hada Raykoum,* and *Young Khaled,* did not match the success of "Didi," but Khaled came back with an album, *Sahra,* and a major hit, "Aicha," in 1996. Khaled hired two very different producers for *Sahra,* which he named for his first daughter. Phillipe Eidel brought out an Asian sound on *Sahra,* while famed American rock and funk producer Don Was added a touch of funk. The album reached a new "hip" audience, according to record label Ark 21.

For his fifth studio album, *Kenza,* which he named for his second daughter, Khaled again employed two distinctly different producers. Briton Steve Hillage—who had produced for Simple Minds, Charlatans UK, and founded the 1970s group Gong—took on half the record, and Lati Kronlund, founder of the New York acid-jazz music collective Brooklyn Funk Essentials, produced the rest. The two worked independently, recording with Khaled in studios in London, Cairo, New York, Paris, and the South of France. On *Kenza,* Khaled continued to explore global influences, from the Indian pop sound on "El Harba Wine," a duet with 19-year-old Hindi film star Amar, to "Gouloulha-Dji," with its salsa-like beat. A critic in *Glass Eye* called the release "as infectious as it is diverse." Some of the songs, like "Raba Raba" and "Trigue Lycée," were songs Khaled had released before he left Algeria, but found a fuller, more dynamic sound the second time around. On the Hillage-produced tracks, Khaled is backed by a full Egyptian string orchestra, which brought grace to his funky songs and gave his voice "more elegance and profundity than the rock instruments" Khaled had formerly been backed with, according to Margasak. He also noted that Kronlund's tracks accomplished the "brassy funk" Khaled's previous producers had tried to "fake," while still managing to emphasize "the music's Arabic nature."

Selected discography

Kutche, Stern's, 1989.
Khaled, Cohiba, 1991.
N'ssi N'ssi, Cohiba, 1993.
En Algerie, Vol. 1, Club Arabe, 1994.
En Algerie, Vol. 2, Club Arabe, 1994.
Hada Raykoum, Stern's Music, 1994.
Young Khaled, MDE, 1994.
Sahra, Barclay, 1996.
Together, Terrascape, 1998.
Best of Cheb Khaled, Vol. 1, Blue Silver, 1998.
Best of Cheb Khaled, Vol. 2, Blue Silver, 1998.
King of Rai, NYC Music, 1999.
Monstres Sacres du Rai, Sonodisc, 2000.
Aiysha, Movie Play, 2000.
Hafla (live), Polygram, 2000.
Kenza, Ark 21, 2000.

Sources

Periodicals

Dirty Linen (Baltimore, MD), October/November 2000.
Glass Eye (Toledo, OH), August 2000.
New York Times, July 9, 2000.
Pulse, October 2000.

Online

"Cheb Khaled," *All Music Guide,* http://www.allmusic.com (April 16, 2001).
"Cheb Khaled," Excite, http://music.excite.com/artist/biography/-8641 (May 2, 2001).
"Cheb Khaled," Wled El Bahdja, http://www.bahdja.com (May 2, 2001).
"Cheb Khaled," Yahoo! Music, http://fr.music.yahoo.com/biographies/khaled.html (May 2, 2001).

Additional materials were provided by the Ark 21 Records publicity department, 2001.

—Brenna Sanchez

Chantal Kreviazuk

Singer, pianist, songwriter

AP/Wide World Photos. Reproduced by permission.

Classically trained Canadian pianist Chantal Kreviazuk has become one of Canada's most prized singer/songwriters. Introspective and challenging lyrics based on tough life experiences filled her late 1990s releases *Under These Rocks and Stones* and *Colour Moving and Still*. Kreviazuk's emotionally deep songs may have seemed a little too heavy in comparison with the sugary-sweet pop songs and angry rock that ruled the radio airwaves, but the songstress has maintained a contingent of dedicated fans both in the United States and her native Canada.

Kreviazuk's parents, Jon, owner of a swimming pool business, and Carole, played the violin and harmonica to their only daughter while she was still in the womb. Once born, Kreviazuk started banging on the piano as a toddler. Born on May 18, 1973, in Winnipeg, Manitoba, Canada, the tot wanted to take lessons like her two older brothers, Trevor and Michael, but was told she was too young. At age three, she was picking out songs one note at a time on the piano. "It was like she was a prodigy," her mother recalled in *Chatelaine*. At five, her mother gave in and Kreviazuk began studying piano. Kreviazuk went on to win competitions and study voice. She also took after her brothers in that she was drawn to sports, and took up horseback riding. As a teenager, Kreviazuk felt insecure, misunderstood, and unpopular, feelings she later claimed kept her from openly writing and performing her songs. But while studying at the University of Manitoba, Kreviazuk began singing publicly. She sang jingles for local commercials and the Canadian national anthem at hockey games. She also worked as a singer in Winnipeg hotels.

In 1996, about 100 demo tapes per week from hopeful artists were landing on the desk of Mike Roth, a head talent scout for Sony Music Canada. Roth was "floored" when he heard Kreviazuk's and flew immediately to Winnipeg to meet her. Roth told *Chatelaine* that most new artists require a certain amount of work before they are ready to record for a major label. With Kreviazuk, he recalled saying, "Wow, this is a diamond here, totally ready. Just open the door and let her go." Despite her lack of performing experience, Kreviazuk signed one of the most generous contracts Roth had ever offered a young, unknown talent, reportedly worth $1 million. While most new artists take one or two years to record their first record, Kreviazuk's debut album, *Under These Rocks and Stones,* came out seven months after signing with Sony. The single "God Made Me" pushed record sales to more than 200,000 copies in Canada and another half-million worldwide.

The singer's first major songwriting effort was the result of a 1994 moped accident in Italy that nearly killed her. After major reconstructive surgery to her femur and face, which included the insertion of four plates and 16 screws to repair her shattered jaw, she spent a month in the hospital. Back home, her rehabilitation and

For the Record . . .

Born on May 18, 1973, in Winnipeg, Manitoba, Canada; daughter of Jon and Carole Kreviazuk; married Raine Maida, 1999. *Education*: Attended University of Manitoba.

Began playing piano at age three; signed by Sony Music Canada, 1996; released first album, *Under These Rocks and Stones,* 1997; released *Colour Moving and Still,* 1999.

Awards: Juno Awards (Canada) for Best Female Artist and Best Pop/Adult Album for *Colour Moving and Still,* 2000.

Addresses: *Record company*—Sony Music Canada, 1121 Leslie St., North York, Ontario, Canada M3C 2J9, (416) 391-3311. *Website*—Official Chantal Kreviazuk Website: http://www.chantalkreviazuk.com.

recovery took a year. During this time, she devoted herself to songwriting and found solace in the task. She never regained feeling from her bottom lip to her chin and has scars on her body.

"When people have suffered, and when they've been through stuff, I know what it feels like," the songwriter told *Time International.* Kreviazuk writes challenging and introspective lyrics that explore some of the more difficult times in her life. On *Under These Rocks and Stones,* the song "Surrounded," which was about the suicide of her "friend-slash-love interest" Samuel, went on to be the album's breakthrough single. "That song was like therapy for me," she recalled in *Chatelaine.* The song "M," on her second release, *Colour Moving and Still,* was about a friendship she developed with a girl who died of a brain tumor shortly after her thirteenth birthday. In concert, Kreviazuk will joke and laugh with her audience, and then belt out songs about death or homelessness. The singer's words to live by, according to *Chatelaine,* are "God will never give you more than you can handle."

Colour Moving and Still was a success in Canada and garnered Kreviazuk comparisons to fellow introspective Canadian pop superstar Alanis Morissette. The album explored issues of mortality and spirituality, and the songs "Before You" and "Until We Die," were "unabashed love songs," according to *Maclean's.* "They say that with death comes life," Kreviazuk said in an interview with the magazine. "I think it means that

death changes the living. It can bring us closer together and be an incredible learning experience."

Maclean's also declared, "As Kreviazuk's star continues to shine, recognition will come as surely as winter in her hometown." But she found it tough to get her songs played on United States radio stations. The backlash against female singer/songwriters from Lilith Fair, an all-female music festival, and the rise in popularity of such angry male stars as rapper Eminem made it difficult for her to get airplay. And compared to the wildly popular, but sugary pop tunes of stars like Britney Spears, Kreviazuk came off as heavy and introspective. "People don't really want to hear introspection right now," the singer lamented in *Time International.* But she didn't foresee selling out and writing bubbly top 40 pop hits anytime soon. "Once you've written something of meaning, it's hard to go back."

In December of 1999, Kreviazuk married fellow singer and labelmate Raine Maida, of the Canadian rock band Our Lady Peace. The relationship between the Canadian rock darlings was highly publicized in Canada, but Kreviazuk was hesitant to discuss the relationship in the press until after the marriage. Although she insisted the two had separate careers, Maida co-wrote two songs with her on *Colour Moving and Still* and produced a third.

In addition to her album releases and concert tours, Kreviazuk contributed to television and film soundtracks. Her cover of John Denver's "Leaving on a Jet Plane" appeared on the hit soundtrack for the 1998 action movie *Armageddon.* For television, she recorded Randy Newman's "Feels Like Home" for the WB network's *Dawson's Creek* soundtrack, and the Beatles' "In My Life" for the NBC series *Providence.*

Though mostly unheard in the United States, Kreviazuk's second release was a hit in her native Canada, and she did maintain a dedicated throng of fans in the States. In March of 2000, she won two Juno Awards, which is the Canadian equivalent to the American Grammy Award. Kreviazuk won out over pop diva Celine Dion and alternative rock favorite Alanis Morissette in the Best Female Artist category. *Colour Moving and Still* beat out releases from Bryan Adams, Morissette, and Joni Mitchell for Best Pop/Adult Album.

Selected discography

Under These Rocks and Stones, Columbia, 1997.
(Contributor) *Armageddon: Music Inspired By The Film* ("Leaving On A Jet Plane"), Big Ear Music, 1998.
(Contributor) *Songs from Dawson's Creek, Vol. 1* ("Feels Like Home"), 1999.
Colour Moving and Still, Columbia, 1999; reissued with import bonus tracks ("Leaving On A Jet Plane," "Feels Like Home," "In My Life"), Sony, 2000.

Sources

Periodicals

Chatelaine, September 2000, p. 95.
Maclean's, November 15, 1999, p. 136.
Time International, July 17, 2000, p. 57.

Online

"Chantal," Chantal Kreviazuk Homepage, http://www.chan
talkreviazuk.com (March 30, 2001).
"Chantal Kreviazuk," *All Music Guide,* http://www.allmusic.
com (March 30, 2001).

—Brenna Sanchez

La Ley

Rock group

The world of *rock español* took a highbrow turn with the evolution of a Chilean ensemble called La Ley in the late 1980s. This group (whose name means "the law") originated as a trio, initially featuring keyboard, guitar, and vocals. A bass player and a new vocalist joined the group within two years, and the turnover proved to be only the first in a succession of new iterations of La Ley that transpired throughout the 1990s. The band regenerated persistently as a result of members who quit or were rehired, as well as management shifts. In 1994, the untimely death of La Ley founder and songwriter Andrés Bobe created a more serious quandary for the surviving group members, yet La Ley maintained a dynamic stance in the face of continual tribulation. Even as random group members continued to shift allegiance, the band likewise withstood an international relocation of its home base from Chile to Mexico in 1996. At that time, La Ley diverged into techno-rock and emerged as a stronger presence still in the international music arena. Mainstream music organizations recognized the band's hard-earned efforts and showered awards on the group. Not only had the band released a series of hit albums during its initial decade together, but its songs

AP/Wide World Photos. Reproduced by permission.

also generated a keen intellectual awareness and provocative attitude.

La Ley originated in Santiago, Chile, in 1987 under the guidance of Bobe. He collaborated initially with vocalist Shia Arbulu of Spain and Rodrigo Aboitiz on keyboards to create an experimental recording. Positive feedback from that album inspired Bobe to expand La Ley into a quintet and subsequently to release an independently produced full-length debut album called *Desiertos* in 1989. The expanded personnel lineup on *Desiertos* included a new lead vocalist, Alberto "Beto" Cuevas. Also heard on that album were drummer Mauricio Claveria and bassist Luciano Andrés Rojas. The album featured two hit singles, "Desiertos" and "Que Va a Suceder," and brought La Ley to local prominence.

Ironically, the album's independent producer recalled *Desiertos*—even as it picked up momentum in the marketplace—due to a dispute that ultimately led to severed relations between La Ley and management. Soon after the managerial split, La Ley released a music video, which effectively helped to maintain La Ley's media presence and contributed to the group's rising popularity. The band received an invitation to perform at the prestigious Viña del Mar Festival in 1991, and a follow-up release appeared on Capitol Records in 1991. The Capitol release, *Doble Opuesto,* met with a receptive Chilean audience and brought the band recognition in Latin America beyond its native Chile; La Ley fans emerged in both Mexico and Argentina. *Desiertos* meanwhile remained in metaphorical mothballs and resurfaced as a rare cult classic some years later as the band came to international attention.

There followed for La Ley a string of discouraging happenstance involving personnel turnovers, legal wrangling, and even death, beginning with the departure of Aboitiz, who quit the band shortly before the release of *Doble Opuesto*. The band continued successfully nonetheless, and released its self-titled *La Ley* album on Philips Records in 1993. *La Ley* was distributed internationally, and a hit video from that album, "Tejedores de Ilusion," earned a nomination from MTV for Best Latin Video. La Ley accepted an invitation for a return appearance at Viña del Mar in 1994.

As Mexicans and Argentineans joined the ranks of La Ley fans in the wake of the band's early albums in the 1990s, La Ley was in the midst of mounting success when tragedy struck. In 1994, Bobe died in a motorcycle accident, an event that brought the group to a major crossroad. It was Cuevas who ultimately figured most prominently in the group as it weathered the disaster. He assumed the dual function of bandleader and spokesperson, steering the band through the catastrophe. Some months passed before the band regenerated in the form of a quintet once again, featuring Cuevas, Rojas, and Claveria. The members brought in a new guitarist, Pedro Frugone, and La Ley's former keyboard player, Aboitiz, rejoined the group at that time.

Soon after the resurrection of La Ley, the band, under the guidance of Chilean producer Humberto Gatica, traveled to the Record Plant studio in Los Angeles, California, to record a new album, *Invisible*. The recording, a tribute to Bobe, featured an eclectic selection of tracks, ranging from acoustic to hard rock selections, and served to emphasize the band's versatility. Upon their return to Chile, however, the group encountered daunting legal snafus both with its distributor, PolyGram, and with Bobe's family, regarding the copyrights to his compositions. An out-of-court settlement ensued, resulting in the demise of La Ley's relationship with PolyGram.

The band remained in Santiago and signed a contract with Warner Music Mexico, which in turn released *Invisible* in 1995. In September of that year, La Ley undertook a tour of Mexico, taped a segment of *House of Blues* for TBS, and made a subsequent stop in Buenos Aires on the Chilean-Argentinean border. Soon afterward, during a Chilean tour, the band announced a pending relocation to Mexico City, a move that was complete in 1996. *Invisible,* having realized 40,000 units sold by that time, had well surpassed the platinum level (25,000 units) in Chile, with European releases scheduled for England, France, Germany, and Spain.

For three years after moving to Mexico City, La Ley worked under the direction of manager Julio Galman of Argentina. With Galman as manager, La Ley released two albums by the end of the decade. In search of an explosive new sound, La Ley turned to a modern, avant-garde, techno sound. The band traveled to New York City to produce and record a new album called *Vertigo,* which appeared in 1998. It was the band's fifth release. The album, with its haunting "Guerrillero" track and assorted reflections on urban chaos, was billed as a concept album, according to Cuevas. A commentary in *Hispanic* praised the La Ley musicians and described their output as "visionary." A promotional tour ensued, during which the band lost its bass player, Rojas, who quit the group after ten years of participation. A replacement musician, J. C. Cumplido, was called in to complete the tour, after which La Ley reverted to a foursome. A follow-up album, called *Uno,* was recorded in Los Angeles, produced by Gatica, and released on WEA in 1999. *Uno* met with particular success and won several awards.

In April of 2000, the members of La Ley were honored to appear at the eleventh-annual *Billboard* International Latin Music Conference in Miami, Florida. La Ley—minus keyboard player Aboitiz at that time—appeared on the bill as a trio including Claveria, Cuevas and Frugone. The event is renowned for its history of catapulting Latin artists further into the media spotlight. In 2000 La Ley shared the program with other popular stars including Los Lobos and Charlie Bravo. La Ley toured extensively for the duration of 2000 and into 2001 in promotional efforts for *Uno.* Appearances included a Central Park concert in August of 2000, which served as a promotional opening attraction for the first annual Latin Alternative Music Conference.

Jon Pareles in the *New York Times* compared La Ley's headline performance in Central Park to Depeche Mode and likened Frugone's guitar styles to those of Irish band U2.

In July of 2000, *Uno* received four nominations at the Latin Grammy Awards; the categories were Best Rock Song, Best Rock Album, Best Rock Performance by a Duo or Group with vocal, and Best Video. At the mainstream Grammy Award ceremonies in March of 2001, the Recording Academy honored La Ley with the award for Best Latin/Rock Alternative Album for *Uno.*

Selected discography

Desiertos (independent release), 1989.
Doble Opuesto, Capitol, 1991.
La Ley, Philips, 1993.
Doble Opuesto, PolyGram, 1993.
Invisible, WEA Latina, 1995.
(Contributor) *Red Hot + Latin: Silencio=Muerte,* PolyGram Latino, 1989.
Vertigo, WEA Latina, 1998.
Los Clasicos del Rock en Espanol (compilation), PolyGram, 1998.
Uno, WEA Latina, 2000.

Sources

Periodicals

Billboard, April 30, 1994, p. 32; August 5, 1995, p. 34; September 2, 1995, p. 72; December 9, 1995, p. 36; April 29, 2000, p. LM-10; November 11, 2000, p. 47; March 24, 2001, p. 44.
Hispanic, July-August 1998, p. 98.
New York Times, August 6, 2000, p. 2.

Online

"La Ley," *All Music Guide,* http://allmusic.com/cg/amg.dll?p=amg&sql=Bjmkxu3y5an4k (April 19, 2001).
"La Ley," Eritmo.com, http://www2.eritmo.com/eritmoclubs/laley/biography.htm (April 19, 2001).

—Gloria Cooksey

Mary Jane Lamond

Singer

The music of Mary Jane Lamond resists a neat fit into any specific genre. The Canadian-born artist sings not in English, but in the Gaelic language, uniting the rich, pastoral culture of the Scottish who settled in Nova Scotia hundreds of years ago with current pop trends. Thus, her unique approach to Celtic folk music is not easily identified as pop, world beat, or rock. Lamond's music instead sounds like a mixture of all these styles.

Despite not performing the types of songs commonly associated with the mainstream, Lamond—celebrated for her captivating soprano—has gained worldwide attention, received numerous Canadian Juno Award and East Coast Music Award nominations and garnered favorable reviews in the press. But Lamond insists that fame and fortune are not her main objectives. Songs, stories, and spirit are meant for sharing with others, according to the singer, to create a sense of community and uphold tradition. "I think people tend to equate music with performers, but that's not really what this kind of music is about," Lamond told Jon Roos in the *Los Angeles Times*. "It's more about exchanging songs between your peers. There's no star system. It's just such a different idea than … say, being a Spice Girl. So many people where I live grew up on this music…. They play the fiddle or sing Gaelic songs in homes, on porches and in the streets."

Born in Kingston, Ontario, Canada, where her parents resided at the time, Lamond, the youngest of five children, moved often as a child and grew up in more urban areas. Her mother was originally from Halifax, Nova Scotia, while her father, an engineer, was a native of Albert Bridge, near Sydney, Nova Scotia, on Cape Breton Island. Lamond lived in several cities including Pointe Claire, Quebec; Sarnia, Ontario; Sydney, Ontario; and Brockville, Ontario, before settling with her family in the major city of Montreal, Quebec, at the age of 15. Though she never experienced rural living until her adult years, Lamond spent school vacations with her grandparents in Sydney, who both spoke Gaelic fluently, and became fascinated with Gaelic music early on. Later in her teens, she developed an interest in the language as well and learned a few phrases from her grandfather.

Lamond did not pursue the study of Gaelic in earnest until she moved back to Nova Scotia in 1989. Upon her return, she joined the Antigonish Gaelic Choir and learned several songs, then attended a milling frolic in the town of North River on Cape Breton that further awakened her interest. Here, she heard older, more traditional vocalists singing Gaelic songs; their performances featured heavy, wool cloth beaten against a table to keep time. "It was like no Gaelic singing I had ever heard," she recalled in a *Billboard* feature by Larry LeBlanc. "I'd heard a lot of very pretty Gaelic singing from Scotland, but what I saw [in North River] was so down-to-earth, so powerful. I felt I had to learn how to sing these songs."

Following her experience in North River, Lamond, who wanted to learn the language proficiently, decided to enroll in the Celtic studies program at Saint Francis Xavier University in Antigonish, Nova Scotia, which, in addition to an extensive Gaelic library, maintains access to some 350 field recordings collected by Dr. John Shaw of Scots-Gaelic songs. "I spent a lot of time listening to [Shaw's] collection," said Lamond. "It helped me immensely to understand the [Gaelic] repertoire as a whole in a way that would have taken me years if I was living in Cape Breton and going to events." She graduated with a bachelor of arts degree from the college in 1995.

Meanwhile, Lamond, who never intended to embark upon a musical career, received a chance opportunity. After taking her third-year college exams in 1994, she was invited by B&R Heritage Enterprises of Iona, Cape Breton, to record a traditional collection of Gaelic songs. The sparse album, *Bho Thir Nan Craobh,* which translates to mean "From the Land of the Trees," surprisingly drew a great amount of local attention, and Lamond garnered nominations for female artist of the year and roots/traditional artist at the East Coast Music Awards in 1995. Also asked to open the event, Lamond performed a Gaelic song a cappella.

Despite this taste of success with singing, Lamond planned to remain in the academic world by pursuing a doctorate degree in Celtic studies. Then, just before completing her undergraduate studies, she accepted

Born in Kingston, Ontario, Canada. *Education:* Bachelor of arts degree in Celtic studies, Saint Francis Xavier University, Antigonish, Nova Scotia, Canada, 1995.

Released the traditional Scottish Gaelic album *Bho Thir Nan Craobh,* 1995; toured with fiddler Ashley MacIsaac and the Chieftans, 1996; released *Suas e! (Go For It),* a Gaelic/contemporary pop album, 1997; released *Làn Dùil,* 2000; released *Òrain Ghàidhlig (Gaelic Songs of Cape Breton),* 2001.

Addresses: *Record company*—BMG Classics, 1540 Broadway, Times Square, New York City, NY 10036, phone: (212) 979-6410, fax: (212) 979-6489. *Management*—Jones & Co. Canada, phone: (902) 429-9005. *Booking*—S.L. Feldman & Associates, phone: (902) 429-9005 or (416) 598-0067. *Website*—Mary Jane Lamond Official Website: http://www.maryjanelamond.com.

an offer to tour with fiddler Ashley MacIsaac, who had been taken by Lamond's voice ever since he first saw her perform with a local band in Antigonish in 1991. He also appeared on Lamond's well-received traditional Gaelic album. "What I got from seeing her that night was this punk attitude, as she was singing in Gaelic," he recalled to LeBlanc. "I'd never seen anybody in a Celtic vein do anything other than straight-ahead Celtic music."

Accepting the offer, Lamond toured with MacIsaac and the Chieftans, then recorded with MacIsaac the 1996 hit song "Sleepy Maggie." From there, Lamond recorded a second album entitled *Suas e!,* which translated loosely means "Go For It." A combination of classic Celtic music and pop elements, the 1997 recording was picked up by the Wicklow Entertainment label, a joint venture between BMG Classics, Chieftans leader Paddy Moloney, and Chieftans managers Sam Feldman and Steve Macklam. The album went on to earn several Juno and East Coast Music Award nominations, as well as a MuchMusic Global Groove Award for the video for "Bog a'Lochain." "It's kind of like you're living in two worlds, and trying to bridge a gap between

them," Lamond said to Roos about uniting the two different styles in her music. "I do like to experiment [and] move the music forward. I feel like as long as I'm singing true to the tradition—if the songs still have a voice of their own—I can bring a more contemporary soundscape in behind them."

For her next album, 2000's *Làn Dùil,* Lamond further explored the possibilities of arranging traditional songs in different ways. She recorded with a variety of instruments, including the fiddle, bagpipes, and the Indian tabla. On her fourth recording, *Orain Ghàidhlig,* or "Gaelic Songs of Cape Breton," released in 2001, Lamond opted to focus on a selection of songs and poetry that are central to the Gaelic tradition. The album was recorded in a church in North River and featured fiddler Joe Peter MacLean and some of Cape Breton's best traditional singers.

Whether performing contemporary or traditional music, however, Lamond's underlying purpose always prevails. "This is a huge oral literary tradition that is being lost at an alarming rate, and I am involved with community things that help conserve it for younger people," she stated for her official website. "But I'm also an interpreter, a singer and musician and in my music the challenge is to create something new and exciting that doesn't destroy the heart of it."

Selected discography

Suas e! (Go For It), Wicklow, 1997.
Làn Dùil, Wicklow, 2000.
Òrain Ghàidhlig (Gaelic Songs of Cape Breton), turtlemusik, 2001.

Sources

Periodicals

Billboard, November 16, 1996; April 5, 1997; November 28, 1998.
Los Angeles Times, November 6, 1998.
Maclean's (Toronto), April 7, 1997; September 13, 1999.
Saturday Night (Toronto), April 1997.
Washington Post, November 20, 1998.

Online

Mary Jane Lamond Official Website, http://www.maryjanelamond.com (May 26, 2001).
NPR Online, http://www.npr.org (March 7, 2001).

—Laura Hightower

Ottmar Liebert

Guitarist

As a newcomer on the international music scene during the early 1990s, Ottmar Liebert traveled through much of Eurasia in search of his muse, bringing a fresh new sophistication to the art of flamenco guitar as a result. During this expansive quest for a musical style to reflect his true emotion, Liebert's music rarely fell on deaf ears; his sounds and melodies immediately captured the attention of listeners. From his first self-produced recording to later albums and compilations by major record labels in the United States, Liebert attracted new fans wherever his music was featured. Along with his perennial backup orchestra, Luna Negra, Liebert spent much of the 1990s touring worldwide.

Liebert was born in Cologne, Germany, to a Hungarian mother and Chinese-German father. Except for early guitar lessons beginning at age eleven and some classical guitar training during his adolescence, Liebert's style evolved from his travels and experiences in his late teens. After spending some time in art school investigating his potential for a career in design or photography, he ultimately found inspiration in the indigenous music that he encountered during an extended excursion through Russia and Asia. After returning to Germany where he worked with various blues and funk bands, Liebert moved to the United States where he molded his musical niche in the late 1980s, following a decade of experimentation with pop, funk, jazz, and blues.

In America, Liebert settled initially on the East Coast in Boston, Massachusetts, and again became involved with assorted bands. After moving to Santa Fe, New Mexico, in 1985, his style evolved rapidly into a form of New Age fusion based largely in flamenco rhythms. According to critics, Liebert expresses an inherent international flavor in his music. Some have suggested that Liebert unwittingly inherited an exotic attitude and appearance to match his parents' mixed ethnicity. Well in keeping with his newfound mood, Liebert established a contingency of sidemen in 1988. His band, Luna Negra (Black Moon), is comprised of an impressive group of avant-garde musicians, including his brother, percussionist Stefan Liebert. Ottmar Liebert led Luna Negra to embrace the inspirational atmosphere of magic associated with the nighttime, infused a decidedly happy spin on those nocturnal emotions, and defined his own musical persona in the process.

Liebert's debut album, which he recorded and self-produced under the title *Marita: Shadows and Storms,* an artistic rather than a commercial endeavor, was completed c. 1990. He recorded the album in response to his contingency of fans and colleagues who were eager for a recorded session of his music. Liebert at that time worked largely in local venues, especially in Santa Fe near his home. His album, which was distributed through an art gallery, came to the attention of executives at Higher Octave Music in California. Higher Octave, acutely aware of the commercial potential of the music, signed Liebert to a contract within a year of the initial self-published released. The commercial label reissued the *Marita* album in quantity. Liebert, along with label executives, was gratified at the result of the remastered album, which was released under the title of *Nouveau Flamenco* and remained on the *Billboard* New Age chart for more than three years, achieving platinum status. The album was described by Mike Alexander in New Zealand's *Dominion* as "a gypsy-tinged affair that mixed Spanish, Indian and Anglo cultures." Liebert's debut album resurfaced a third time in 2000 in special edition from Higher Octave entitled *Nouveau Flamenco 1990-2000 Special Edition.* Additionally, 13 flamenco works composed by Liebert that appeared on that album were published in a musical score (folio) by Creative Concepts Publishing Corporation of California in 1997.

After the original issue and reissue of his debut album, Liebert recorded two follow-up titles, *Poets & Angels* and *Borrasca,* which appeared in 1990 and 1991 respectively on Higher Octave. Soon after the release of the Grammy Award-nominated *Borrasca,* Liebert signed with Epic Records. His debut album on the new label, *Solo Para Ti* in 1992, topped 500,000 in worldwide sales by early 1994. It soared to number one on the *Billboard* New Age chart and made further impact as a crossover hit among the top 100 albums on the pop music chart.

Liebert introduced electric guitar styles into his next album, *The Hours Between Night and Day,* which he

For the Record . . .

Born in Cologne, Germany.

Worked with East Coast bands, late 1970s-early 1980s; established recording studio Spiral Subwave in Santa Fe, NM, and self-published during the late 1980s; formed Luna Negra band, 1988; signed with Higher Octave Music and played local New Mexico venues, c. 1990; signed with Epic Records, early 1990s; toured extensively, 1990-94.

Awards: New Age Artist of the Year, *Billboard* magazine, 1991-92.

Addresses: *Record company*—Higher Octave Music, 23852 Pacific Coast Highway, Suite 2C, Malibu, CA 90265, (310) 589-1515. *Website*—Ottmar Liebert at Sony Classical: http://www.sonyclassical.com/artists/liebert.

recorded in 1992 and released in 1993. *The Hours Between Night and Day* was shipped by the hundreds of thousands of units and topped the *Billboard* adult alternative/New Age chart for more than three months. Also in the early 1990s, with a bent toward innovation, Liebert gave license for remix of his work to British electronica colleagues Steve Hillage, DJ Slip, and Aki Nawaz in a project that spawned Liebert's 1995 release, *Euphoria.* Liebert's *Viva* album—a live recording of a 1994 concert—also appeared in 1995. Additionally, much of Liebert's time from 1990 to 1994 was spent on tour with Luna Negra. By the end of the 1990s, Liebert's travels had taken him to New Zealand, among other venues, on three occasions—in 1994, 1996, and again in 1999. Liebert, in fact, amassed an admiring contingency in New Zealand, and took praise from Irene Chapple in *Dominion* during his 1999 New Zealand tour when she commented on Liebert's ability to play with a "fluidity that disguised the technical difficulty of what he was playing," calling him a "consummate, modest and laid-back musician."

In 1996, Liebert released a double-CD set called *Opium.* The two CDs, entitled *Wide-Eyed* and *Dreaming* respectively, were recorded at his Spiral Subwave studio in Santa Fe. There followed a video, *Wide-Eyed and Dreaming,* recorded live in Calgary, Canada. According to the multi-ethnic Liebert, *Opium* was inspired by a postcard from his paternal grandfather, who had worked on the Manchurian railway. The release of

Opium spawned a 1996 tour featuring bassist Jon Gagan, drummer Carl Coletti, and New Age percussionist Ron Wagner on Indian tabla drums and the Arabian dumbek. This exotic album also features Liebert on fretless lute, electric guitar, and his prized flamenco instruments, which include a cedar-topped guitar, fashioned at the back and on the sides from Brazilian rosewood and an Eric Sahlin Flamenco Bianca instrument with cypress back and sides.

Liebert recorded his 1997 album *Leaning into the Night* with an orchestra in a separate sound studio. He maintained contact through a closed-microphone connection, thus achieving an extraordinary purity of sound. On this album, Liebert turned to arrangements by Oscar Castro-Neves to create a top-selling collection featuring works by Ravel, Puccini, and Satie, along with selected tracks of his own. Despite the sultry sophistication conjured by Liebert's typically serene and nocturnal imagery, he in fact lacked the intensive tutorial training that is deemed a prerequisite for the true Flamenco classicist. Although critics have downplayed Liebert's classical guitar skills, *Leaning into the Night* resulted in a classical crossover hit. The album, released on Sony Classical, lasted eight weeks at the top of the classical crossover chart, thus fueling critical theories that Liebert's music, regardless of genre, attracts fans spontaneously. It is this quality that prompted the comment from an agent of a major retail record outlet, who noted, "[I]t is Liebert's irresistible music—not the marketing weight behind it—that has seduced hundreds of thousands of fans," as quoted by *Billboard*'s Paul Verna. Perhaps to prove that point, Liebert released the unique *Rumba Collection* in 1998.

In the late 1990s, Liebert found a wealth of inspiration while on a family excursion in the scenic environs of Italy's Tuscan countryside. There he experienced the emotion for *Innamorare,* which he recorded with Luna Negra and released through Epic (U.S.) in 1999. The album, his eleventh major release, was his first compilation to make significant use of brass instrumentation. *Innamorare* featured what some came to regard as Liebert's signature song, "Summer Flamenco." Even before the album's appearance in the United States, Liebert's "2 the Night" became a favorite in Italy when it was incorporated into the film *Il Ciclone.* The composition later topped music charts in Italy when recorded by Italian group La Fuertezza.

After an extended residency of more than a decade in the United States, Liebert continued to retain his German citizenship as of 2001. He professed to discount national boundaries with the philosophical purity of an artist, deeming citizenship to be a broader, planetary concept. Early in the summer of 2000, Liebert appeared among the headline acts at the Calgary Jazz Festival. A barefooted, reverie-like performance at Edmonton's Jubilee Auditorium during the festival prompted *Edmonton Sun* writer Fish Griwkowsky to comment that "Liebert plays with intensity and humour. Each of his songs, like Santa Fe, bringing visions of distant roads and travels. His music is ambient, escapist...."

Managed by Luna Negra Music, Liebert has performed as an accompanist to many of his popular musical colleagues including Diana Ross, Celine Dion, Kenny Loggins, and members of the hip-hop generation, among others. Liebert has published with both Sony/ATV Songs LLC and Luna Negra Music Incorporated. When he is not touring, Liebert typically works at his personal recording studio at his home in Santa Fe.

Selected discography

Marita: Shadows and Storms, self-produced; reissued as *Nouveaux Flamenco,* Higher Octave, 1990; reissued in special edition, 2000.
Poets & Angels: Music 4 the Holidays, Higher Octave, 1991.
Borrasca, Higher Octave, 1991.
Solo Para Ti, Epic, 1992.
The Hours Between Night and Day, Epic, 1993.
Viva! Epic, 1995.
Euphoria (EP), Epic, 1995.
Opium, Epic, 1996.
Leaning into the Night (Inclinado en la Noche), Epic, 1997.
Rumba Collection 1992-1997, Epic, 1998.
Innamorare: Summer Flamenco, Epic, 1999.
Christmas and Santa Fe, Epic, 2000.
Barcelona Nights: The Best of Ottmar Liebert, Higher Octave, 2001.

Sources

Periodicals

Billboard, January 29, 1994, p. 1; April 17, 1999, p. 10.
Dominion (Wellington, New Zealand), April 8, 1995, p. 22; April 10, 1999, p. 24; April 19, 1999, p. 8.
Edmonton Sun, July 2, 2000, p. 41.
Evening Post (Wellington, New Zealand), April 17, 1999, p. 19.
Guitar Player, September 1995, p. 119; May 1998, p. 50.
Press (Canterbury, New Zealand), April 16, 1999, p. 23.
Sunday Star Times (New Zealand), January 21, 1996, p. 8.

Online

"iMusic Contemporary Showcase-Ottmar Liebert," Artist Direct Network, http://imusic.artistdirect.com/showcase/contemporary/ottmarliebert.html (April 2, 2001).
"Ottmar Liebert," *All Music Guide,* http://allmusic.com (April 2, 2001).
"Ottmar Liebert," Sessions at West 54th, http://sessionsatwest54th.com/artists/liebert03/index.html (April 2, 2001).

—*Gloria Cooksey*

Metallica

After 20 years, ten albums, and five Grammy Awards, Metallica has more than proven its staying power as rock's preeminent metal group. The group paid its dues during the hair band era of the 1980s, but Metallica's 1991 release addressed the decidedly adult topics of nuclear holocaust, mental illness, suicide, and the dangers of drug addiction. Yet despite these grim themes, Metallica's music runs contrary to heavy metal's one-dimensional image; their sound involves more than just bone-breaking chords and fire-and-brimstone lyrics. The band has distinguished itself with a grungy sophistication well beyond the work of its predecessors to become the seventh largest selling act in the history of American music as of 2001. Members of Metallica are rude and cheeky, but they're proficient. *Bass Player's* Coryat attested, "Their famous 'Metal Up Your Ass' T-shirt ensured Metallica a notorious place in rock-and-roll history." Taste in merchandising notwithstanding, *Spin* magazine's Alec Foege called Metallica "a burnished black gem."

Metallica coalesced in 1981 with singer-guitarist James Hetfield, drummer Lars Ulrich, bass player Cliff Burton, and lead guitarist Dave Mustaine. Mustaine, who had taken over for early collaborator Lloyd Grant, was replaced in 1983 by Kirk Hammett. Their first

Photograph by Steve Granitz. Wireimage.com. Reproduced by permission.

album, *Kill 'Em All,* attracted droves of "head-banging" fans. The follow-up releases *Ride the Lightning* and *Master of Puppets* were greeted with even more enthusiasm by the world's heavy metal constituency, which enabled the band to strut their stuff with fellow "metalheads" on the enormous Monsters of Rock Tour. That outing featured a free concert in Moscow that was attended by 500,000 Soviet metal fans. Infamous spitoon in tow for this tour and others—band members needed a place to deposit their chewed tobacco—Metallica was increasingly credited with single-handedly revitalizing heavy metal music, paving the way for other thrash bands like Slayer and Megadeath.

Tragedy struck Metallica on September 27, 1986, when the band's tour bus went into a ditch in Sweden, killing bassist Cliff Burton. After a brief hiatus the band reassembled and began looking for a replacement for Burton. Attempting to fill the bass player's shoes and duplicate his eccentric, unbridled style seemed impossible. Burton had never been a particularly smooth player, but other band members had not attempted to reign him in. They did try once, however, to persuade him to forego his bell-bottom jeans in favor of more traditional heavy metal garb, but quickly realized the attempt was futile; Burton was set in his ways and

rarely influenced by others. In truly bizarre heavy metal fashion, one of his dreams had been to invent a gun that shot knives instead of bullets.

To refurbish their lineup, the members of Metallica decided to settle on someone completely different from Burton: Jason Newsted, then with the Phoenix band Flotsam & Jetsam. Newsted was raised in Niles, Michigan, and had decided to turn professional after playing in bands throughout high school. He told Coryat, "I heard Cliff (Burton) had died the day after the accident.... I was a huge Metallica fan at the time. When I was looking at the blurb in the paper, I was sad, but things started flashing through my mind.... I just thought if I could play 'Four Horsemen' once with those guys, I'd be really happy."

Burton had been a remarkable soloist, but Newsted provided Metallica with a more cohesive sound. Burton's sound had not been well-defined, particularly when he played low on the guitar's neck. Newsted chose to mirror the band's guitar riffs precisely instead, producing a newly unified guitar effect. This sound dominated the new band's 1988 double album. Titled ... *And Justice for All,* the record went multiplatinum by 1989 and earned a Grammy Award nomination, despite a dearth of radio airplay. The release of *Justice* coincided with Metallica's return to its musical roots: the groundbreaking metal stylings of 1970s rock giants Led Zeppelin and Black Sabbath. This resolve became the cornerstone for the 1991 release, *Metallica,* also known as the 'Black' album.

Still steely, but a little slicker, *Metallica* was produced by Bob Rock, who had also worked with metal acts Motley Crue, Loverboy, and Bon Jovi. Buoyed by the dark, driving single "Enter Sandman," *Metallica* sold 2.2 million copies in its first week and has sold more than 15 million copies worldwide since its release. Metallica's hard-won versatility is showcased on the record with guitarist Hammett's winsome wah-wah, and open-throated, more melodic vocals from Hetfield. The band earned Grammys in both 1990 and 1991 and effectively ascended to a new strata of heavy metal superstardom. Featured on the covers of both *Rolling Stone* and *Spin,* Metallica's popularity seemed to know no bounds. With increased media coverage, it became clear that the band's appeal was not narrowly bohemian, political, or reflective of any trend—except perhaps anger. *Village Voice* contributor Erik Davis wrote that "Metallica's 'image'—dark shades, frowns, and poorly conceived facial hair—allies them with a musical culture of refusal. They haven't stopped dragging mud onto the carpet and slamming their bedroom doors without saying hello. 'Enter Sandman' has touched the brains of fry cooks and Bud guzzlers across the land."

Analysis of Metallica's lyrics reveals the band's unique penchant for conjuring up the timeless grandiosity of myth by placing the object of a line before its subject:

"This fight he cannot win," and "Off the beaten path I reign" are two examples. The band's head-banging thrash metal songs are short, but not sweet; they're delivered with grim, tight expressions, and a minimum of emotion, which gives the impression that the entire band is grimacing. Metallica's albums have few tender spots; songs range from the brutal "Sad But True" to the sweet and gritty "Ride the Lightning," from the praised pagan slant found on "Of Wolf And Man" to the metaphysical musings of "Through the Never." Commenting on their larger musical style—"Metallica's riffs crack like glaciers"—the *Village Voice*'s Davis said of the band, "They hew thrash to a rigorous minimalism."

Worn from touring during the early 1990s and a contract suit against Elektra, Metallica's next release was not to come until 1996. The album *Load*, the longest of the group's work with 14 songs, was a marked change in style and sound from the 'Black' album. As described in the group's biography at its official website, the material was "loose, powerful and eclectic, the sound thick and punchy and the image one which screamed out change and freedom from the enslavement to the Black album era." The group built on the critical success of the album and released an additional set of *Load* session tracks as *Reload* in 1997. Instead of simply revisiting *Load*'s eclecticism, *Reload* offers "enough left curves to make it a better record," according to *All Music Guide*'s Stephen Thomas Erlewine.

The late 1990s and early 2000s brought new challenges for the group, both inside the studio and out. The group toured in support of *Load* and *Reload* in 1997 and 1998, and ventured into new musical territory in 1999 with *S&M*, a two-disc collection of concert performances with the San Francisco Symphony. The innovative collaboration between the groups featured orchestral arrangements behind Metallica classics such as "Master of Puppets," "One," "For Whom the Bell Tolls," "Sad But True," and "Of Wolf and Man." On April 14, 2000, the group, along with rapper Dr. Dre, filed suit against Napster, the website that facilitated the sharing of music files between personal computers for free, alleging violation of copyright laws. During a prolonged battle against the site by Metallica, Dre, and the Recording Industry Association of America (RIAA), the group managed to block 300,000 users who had downloaded copies of Metallica songs. The group and Dre settled their suit against Napster for an undisclosed amount in July of 2001. Metallica said it would allow some of its music to be swapped on the site after the scheduled start of subscription service in the late summer of 2001.

In January of 2001, Jason Newsted announced that he planned to leave Metallica after 14 years "due to private and personal reasons, and the physical damage that I have done to myself over the years while playing the music that I love….. This is the most difficult decision of my life, made in the best interest of my family, myself, and the continued growth of Metallica," according to comments at the Elektra Records website. The group planned to search for a replacement for Newsted.

Spin's Foege waxed mathematic in his assessment of Metallica, writing, "At turns algebraically elegant and geometrically raucous, present-day Metallica can stop and start on a dime." With their popularity showing no signs of flagging, their musical and lyrical virtuosity on the upswing, and their fans more crazed than ever, Metallica is a speeding bullet surely headed for continued success.

Selected discography

Kill 'Em All, Elektra, 1983.
Ride the Lightning, Elektra, 1984.
Master of Puppets, Elektra, 1986.
… And Justice for All, Elektra, 1988.
Metallica, Elektra, 1991.
Live Sh**: Binge and Purge, Elektra, 1993.
Load, Elektra, 1996.
Reload, Elektra, 1997.
Garage, Inc., Polygram, 1998.
S&M, Elektra, 1999.

Sources

Periodicals

Bass Player, September/October 1991.
Newsweek, September 23, 1991.
PC Magazine (United Kingdom), July 2000.
Rolling Stone, November 14, 1991; March 19, 1992.
Spin, October 1991; December 1991.
Village Voice, September 18, 1991.
Washington Post, July 12, 2000, p. A23.
Wilson Library Bulletin, January 1992.

Online

All Music Guide, http://www.allmusic.com (June 6, 2001).
Grammy.com, http://www.grammy.com (June 6, 2001).
"Metallica, Dre Settle with Napster," Netscape, http://daily news.netscape.com/mynsnews/story.tmpl?table=n&cat=5 0880&id=200107130714000120526 (July 15, 2001).
"Metallica News," Elektra Records, http://www.elektra.com (June 6, 2001).
Metallica Official Website, http://www.metallica.com (June 6, 2001).
"Napster, MusicNet Forge Deal With Strings Attached," *Billboard.com*, http://www.billboard.com (June 7, 2001).

—*B. Kimberly Taylor*

Jane Monheit

Singer

Jane Monheit became the retro darling of the jazz world after the release of her debut album, *Never Never Land,* in May of 2000. At the time only 22 years of age, Monheit possessed a voice and lyrical presence well beyond her years, as well as a sultry physical appeal reminiscent of singers from the 1930s and 1940s. "Her high, sweet voice is pure (with hints of a rich, budding lower register)," wrote Stephen Holden for the *New York Times.* "Her sense of swing is steady; her taste in popular standards is impeccable; her interpretations of songs like 'Blame It on My Youth,' 'Young and Foolish,' and 'The Folks Who Live on the Hill' are imbued with a precocious wisdom." Monheit, whose career sprung from winning the runner-up prize at the 1998 Thelonius Monk Vocal Competition, is poised, say many, to become a pop star as well as a favorite among standard jazz enthusiasts.

In addition to her *Never Never Land* album reaching the *Billboard* Top Ten soon after its release, Monheit made several high-profile appearances, including a week in July of 2000 at the Village Vanguard, regarded as a place of pilgrimage for jazz where singers are rarely granted the stage, as well as two shows later that year for the Lincoln Center's Great American Songbook series. After this, she played the New Year's Eve show at the Blue Note in Manhattan and gave a recital at the end of January of 2001 at Steinway Hall with pianist Tommy Flanagan, one of his first engagements of this kind since working with Ella Fitzgerald decades ago.

Fittingly, Fitzgerald herself served as Monheit's primary role model. "My main influence was Ella," Monheit said, as quoted at the jazzsingers.com website. "No one else even comes close." She also gained insight from other legendary jazz singers like Sarah Vaughan and Carmen McRae, as well as contemporary vocalists and vocal groups such as Joni Mitchell, Take Six, and New York Voices.

Born on November 3, 1977, Monheit took to singing the standards made popular decades before her birth quite early. Growing up in the suburban town of Oakdale on Long Island, New York, she was a mere two years of age when she began performing tunes such as "Somewhere Over the Rainbow" and "Honeysuckle Rose" in a nearly perfect pitch about the family home. However, Monheit's innate gifts probably came as no surprise, given the fact that other members of her family likewise displayed a talent for music. Both Monheit's grandmother and aunt worked as professional singers, while just about everyone else played various instruments or sang for pleasure, including her father, David Monheit, who owns a machine-tool business but plays bluegrass guitar and banjo in his spare time. Thus, music always played a prominent role in Monheit's day-to-day life.

Monheit received her earliest musical education at her grandparents' home in nearby Bellmore, Long Island.

For the Record . . .

Born on November 3, 1977, in Oakdale, Long Island, NY. *Education*: Studied voice at the Manhattan School of Music; graduated, 1999.

Received first runner-up prize at the Thelonius Monk Institute Vocal Competition, 1998; signed with N-Coded Music and the Jazz Tree, 1999; released *Never Never Land,* 2000; released *Come Dream With Me,* 2001.

Addresses: *Record company*—Warlock Records/N-Coded Music, 126 Fifth Avenue, 2nd Floor, New York, NY 10011, phone: (212) 206-0800, fax: (212) 206-1949, email: e-mail@warlockrecords.com.

Part home, part studio, and filled with various musical instruments (including an amplifier and guitars for Monheit's younger brother, David), as well as hundreds of CDs and albums, mostly from the jazz swing era, Monheit began learning songs and making tapes under the tutelage of her grandfather, Ernest Newton, a retired science teacher, at the tender age of 28 months. "I heard most of the jazz I ever heard in my life, before college, in this house," she informed *New York Times* writer David Hajdu. However, Monheit added, her grandfather's tastes were more traditional than adventurous. "I didn't know what Coltrane sounded like until I went to college."

Aside from the support of her family, Monheit also had the good fortune of attending a school that placed great importance on education in the arts. Her public school district, Connetquot, offered an extensive program in jazz, beginning in the elementary grades. "The district had the greatest music teachers ever," she told Robbie Woliver of the *New York Times.* "I never studied with anyone outside of school." Her primary teacher, John Leddy, instructed Monheit from the fourth grade through high school.

Inspired by legendary vocalists such as Fitzgerald, Vaughan, and McRae, Monheit, who also played clarinet, pursued her studies in music with zeal. Then, at Connetquot High School, her abilities blossomed, and she became the school's theater star. "I played the lead in all the plays, and I loved it," she recalled to Hajdu. "Musical theater—I mean, don't even get me started. The first time I saw 'The Music Man' on Broadway, I could hardly stop crying through the whole thing, because I was just so overjoyed to be sitting in the theater watching a wonderful production of that show. Rebecca Luker has been one of my idols forever." As a

teen, Monheit also performed at weddings and picked up club dates wherever she could on the South Shore of Long Island.

After graduating from high school, Monheit left Long Island for New York City to study voice at the Manhattan School of Music, where she enrolled specifically to take instruction from Peter Eldridge, a founding member of the New York Voices. Upon her arrival, she gravitated toward the cabaret scene and performed show tunes at piano bars in Greenwich Village. Eventually, her college boyfriend and future husband, jazz drummer Rick Montalbano, steered her away from cabaret toward a concentration on jazz. She soon joined the group that Montalbano played in, a swing quintet featuring Joel Frahm on saxophone and David Berkman on piano. The group toured several New England colleges and performed regularly at small Manhattan clubs.

Monheit's big break occurred when Eldridge suggested she enter the Thelonius Monk Institute Vocal Competition, to be held on September 25, 1998, in Washington, D.C. The Thelonius Monk competition is a prestigious annual contest that previously introduced such names as saxophonist Joshua Redman and trumpeter Ryan Kisor, yet Monheit knew nothing of the event's importance. "I had no idea what I was getting into when I entered the Monk competition," she admitted to Eliot Tiegel in *Down Beat.* "I didn't know it could start a career, and now every day there seems to be new, big things happening. It's like a continuous chain of surprises."

During the semi-finals, however, when she saw Wayne Shorter enter the room, Monheit immediately realized the significance of the Monk competition. Joining Shorter for the finals the following evening were other distinguished musicians, as well as record executives, agents, managers, the music press, concert promoters, and jazz fans all hoping to discover new talent. Monheit, feeling relaxed and filled with a sense of purpose, gave a stunning performance singing the number "Detour Ahead" before an esteemed panel of judges that included Dee Dee Bridgewater, Nneena Freelon, Diana Krall, Dianne Reeves, and the late Joe Williams. She earned the first runner-up prize and a $10,000 scholarship. The top honor in the vocal category went to 64-year-old Teri Thornton, the legendary singer and pianist who announced during her performance that she had been diagnosed with cancer. (Thornton succumbed to the disease 20 months later.)

Although she took second prize, Monheit's voice nevertheless instantly caught the attention of several record executives, including Carl Griffin, president of N-Coded Music, who introduced himself to the young singer at the reception following the competition and offered her a contract upon completing college. "I heard the element of Ella that struck me—very unusual for a girl 20 years old, especially a white girl," recalled Griffin, one of the few African American executives in a top position at a jazz label, to Hajdu. "I said 'O.K.— she's in touch with the tradition, and she's young and beautiful. She's the best of both worlds. This is it!'"

Also at the reception, Monheit met Mary Ann Topper, a personal manager who helped shape the careers of Diana Krall, Joshua Redman, Christian McBride, and Michael Petrucciani. Monheit graduated from the Manhattan School of Music in June of 1999 and immediately signed with the N-Coded label for two records, with an option to record three more. She also signed with Topper's agency, the Jazz Tree, on undisclosed terms. Shortly thereafter, plans got under way for her debut album.

Released in 2000, *Never Never Land* featured Monheit singing standards in the company of some of the world's premiere jazz players—Kenny Barron, Ron Carter, Lewis Nash, Bucky Pizzarelli, Hank Crawford, and David "Fathead" Newman. "It was incredible luck to get to work with that band," said Monheit, as quoted by Woliver, "a dream come true." For the album, Monheit chose a classic repertoire, including such sophisticated compositions as Antonio Carlos Jobim's "Dindi" and Duke Ellington's "I Got It Bad (and That Ain't Good)," as well as the effective ballads "Detour Ahead" and "Never Let Me Go." Monheit's sophomore effort, *Come Dream With Me,* released in May of 2001, also concentrated on standard songs such as "Blame It on My Youth" and "Something to Live For." Here, Barron returned in his role as pianist alongside a group comprised of younger talent.

While her star continued to rise, Monheit, who lives in New York but returns to Long Island often to visit her family, is still shocked by her popularity. "I'm just this young girl from Long Island," she confessed to Woliver. "I'm the last person this should be happening to. I thought people would be saying, 'Hey, who's that little white girl?' But everyone's really embracing me."

Selected discography

Never Never Land, N-Coded, 2000.
Come Dream With Me, N-Coded, 2001.

Sources

Periodicals

Billboard, December 2, 2001.
Boston Globe, May 19, 2000; March 22, 2001.
Down Beat, September 2000; January 2001.
Los Angeles Times, September 15, 2000.
New York Times, June 18, 2000; September 20, 2000; November 23, 2000; December 31, 2000; January 16, 2001; March 16, 2001; March 23, 2001.
People, May 22, 2000.
Village Voice, July 25, 2000.
Wall Street Journal, August 9, 2000.
Washington Post, September 28, 1998.

Online

"Jane Monheit," jazzsingers.com, http://www.jazzsingers .com/JaneMonheit (May 5, 2001).

—*Laura Hightower*

The Moonglows

Rock/R&B group

The Moonglows may not have invented rock 'n' roll, but they played an instrumental role in its early development. Working closely with legendary Cleveland, Ohio, disc jockey Alan Freed, one of the early promoters of rock 'n' roll, they had several rhythm and blues hits in the 1950s before reaching the pop charts regularly later in the decade. Known for their four-part doo-wop harmonies, group members also wrote their own songs. By the end of the 1950s, the original lineup had disbanded, and although several reunions throughout the years featured one or two original members, the Moonglows' popularity was behind them. Still, they had left their mark on the history of American popular music, a fact recognized by their induction into the Rock and Roll Hall of Fame in 2000.

The original Moonglows consisted of lead singer Bobby Lester, vocalists Harvey Fuqua, Prentiss Barnes, and Alexander Graves, and Billy Johnson on guitar. Lester and Fuqua had grown up together in Louisville, Kentucky, before going their separate ways upon joining the military. Stories vary about how they came together to form the Moonglows. The group formed in 1951, by which time Lester had already begun to make a name for himself as a rhythm and blues vocalist. One version of the group's origin has

Photograph by Ed Betz. AP/Wide World Photos. Reproduced by permission.

him looking to form a quartet and inviting his childhood friend Fuqua to join him. Although Fuqua had not performed professionally, he had plenty of experience singing in choirs. Another version has it that Fuqua had started a jazz vocal trio in Cleveland and invited Lester to join him. But as Fuqua remembered it in an interview with John Soeder in the Cleveland *Plain Dealer,* no one person really started the group: "We wouldn't have gotten together if I hadn't relocated to Cleveland.... We started singing around town and then we picked up a couple of other guys."

Whoever may have started the group, there is no dispute that they found good fortune by forming in Cleveland. Originally called the Crazy Sounds, the group's name changed when they came to the attention of Freed, who dubbed them the Moonglows, perhaps in reference to his own radio show, *The Moondog Rock 'n' Roll Party*. He became their manager and producer, and he also shared songwriting credits with Fuqua and Lester, although he probably had little input in that part of the process. Freed did back the group wholeheartedly, though, signing them to his own record label, Champagne. They recorded their first single on that label. "I Just Can't Tell No Lie" became a regional hit, but before it could be more widely distributed, Champagne went out of business.

Undaunted, the Moonglows moved to Chance Records, where they recorded singles that gave them a national presence on the rhythm and blues charts.

Their output showed their ability to tackle a wide variety of styles, recording the ballad "Baby Please," a cover of Doris Day's hit "Secret Love," and the rocker "Ooh Rockin' Daddy." But in the middle of 1954, Chance Records went out of business, too. Instead of a setback, this proved to be an excellent opportunity for the Moonglows, who moved on to the Chess label, the Chicago-based powerhouse of rhythm and blues recording.

It was at Chess that the Moonglows had their biggest success. Here they took their sound to the growing rock 'n' roll audience. Robert Hilburn of the *Los Angeles Times* described their appeal as blending "elements of pop/R&B tradition with a sense of the raw, teen-directed urgency that characterized '50s rock." Their first Chess single, "Sincerely," captured a sense of teen desperation. While Paul Simon would later call the song "perfect" at the Rock and Roll Hall of Fame induction ceremonies, for the Moonglows it was a hit only on the rhythm and blue charts. As with many songs originated by black rock 'n' roll artists at the time, the big hit version of "Sincerely" was recorded by a white group, the McGuire Sisters.

Their next single, "Most of All," brought them to the white rock 'n' roll audience in their own right. This hit and their relationship with Freed led the group to even more exposure. The disc jockey had branched out into movie production, and the Moonglows appeared in his films *Rock Rock Rock* in 1956 and *Mister Rock 'n' Roll* in 1957. Meanwhile, the hits continued to come. The year 1956 saw the release of "We Go Together" and "Over and Over Again." In spite of the success, some internal dissension began to surface. Lester's role as lead singer translated into his receiving top billing and resulted in a name change for the group to Bobby Lester and the Moonglows on their 1957 hits "Don't Say Goodbye" and "Please Send Me Someone to Love."

By 1958 Lester had left, but Fuqua stayed and took over top billing. The group released one of their most enduring songs that year, "The Ten Commandments of Love," as Harvey and the Moonglows. Fuqua was the only original member to appear on the single. Joining him were Reese Palmner, James Knowland, Chester Simmons, and a young Marvin Gaye, who would later become one of the leading figures in soul music. This song marked the end of the Moonglows' run as hit makers and popularizers of rock 'n' roll. It also essentially ended the group, as Fuqua followed Lester's lead and struck out on his own.

While both Fuqua and Lester spent their first years after the Moonglows performing as solo acts, both moved into production during the early 1960s. Fuqua found notable success in this field, founding two labels of his own. He also produced several records for the predominant soul label Motown, working with the company's founder and owner (and his brother-in-law) Barry Gordy. While these two group leaders went their separate ways, Graves attempted to revive the Moonglows. As the only original member in the group, he and his three new partners started recording and performing in 1964. While they lasted for awhile, this incarnation had none of the success of the original group.

The revival that came closest to reuniting the original Moonglows came in 1972, when Fuqua and Lester rejoined Graves to record *The Return of the Moonglows*. Aside from a minor hit with a funky remake of "Sincerely," the album had little impact and turned out to be a one-time reunion. The legacy of the Moonglows' pioneering rock 'n' roll would not be forgotten, however, and in 2000 the group was inducted into the Rock and Roll Hall of Fame. By this time Lester and Johnson had passed away, leaving only Fuqua, Graves, and Barnes to accept the honor. The group had been eligible for induction for several years, leading to Fuqua's comment, reported in *Jet* magazine, "I want to know why it took so long." Even though the honor may have been delayed, it gave an official acknowledgment to the Moonglows' status as pioneers who played a key role in the creation of rock 'n' roll.

Selected discography

Singles

"I Just Can't Tell No Lie," Champagne, 1952.
"Baby Please," Chance, 1953.
"Secret Love," Chance, 1953.
"Ooh Rockin' Daddy," Chance, 1953.
"Sincerely," Chess, 1954.

"Most of All," Chess, 1954.
"Ten Commandments of Love," Chess, 1958.

Albums

Look, It's the Moonglows, Chess, 1959; reissued, MCA, 1990.
The Moonglows, Chess, 1964.
The Return of the Moonglows, RCA, 1972.
Sincerely, Huub, 1991.
Blue Velvet—The Ultimate Collection, Chess, 1993.
Moonglows Acapella, Starr Digital, 1996.
Their Greatest Hits, Chess/MCA, 1997.

Sources

Books

Graff, Gary, Josh Freedom du Lac, and Jim McFarlin, *Music-Hound R&B: The Essential Album Guide,* Visible Ink, 1998.
Stambler, Irwin, *Encyclopedia of Pop, Rock & Soul,* St. Martin's Press, 1989.

Periodicals

Jet, March 27, 200, p. 32.
Los Angeles Times, February 4, 2000.
Plain Dealer (Cleveland, OH), March 6, 2000.

Online

"The Moonglows," *All Music Guide,* http://allmusic.com (May 9, 2001).
"The Moonglows Biography," *Rolling Stone,* http://rollingstone.com (May 9, 2001).

—*Lloyd Hemingway*

Shawn Mullins

Singer, songwriter

A young man who has been making music since the tender age of four, Shawn Mullins is hardly what would be considered an overnight success. He had been singing professionally for about a decade when his recording of "Lullaby," a song he wrote himself, started getting heavy airplay across the country in 1998. Half spoken and half sung, the song's lyrics tell the all-too-familiar story of a lonely soul adrift in cold-hearted Hollywood, wary of the future but fundamentally sure that "everything's gonna be all right" in the end. Although the song's story line may have been somewhat formulaic, Mullins' lyrics and the song's melody struck a responsive chord with millions of listeners across North America. In no time at all, *Soul's Core,* the album on which "Lullaby" first appeared, went platinum in the United States and gold in Canada.

Born on March 8, 1968, in Atlanta, Georgia, Mullins is the son of a railroad man and an elementary school teacher. His grandfather, Tom Brown, who had played bass in a big band from the 1930s through the 1950s, got him hooked on music at the age of four when he gave the youngster a miniature set of drums. Brown played a major role in Mullins' musical development. Before long he had mastered the piano, bass, cello, and guitar. Since his childhood and early school years were made difficult by bouts of depression and attention deficit disorder, music provided a welcome escape for Mullins. By the time he was 12 years old, he had formed a rock band and soon was writing his own songs and recording them on tape.

When he was a freshman in high school, Mullins met Amy Ray, who was later to become half of the Indigo Girls duo. At the time, Ray was studying at nearby Emory University and performing in the duo of Saliers and Ray. She visited Mullins' ninth-grade career class to discuss music as a career choice. After listening to her formal presentation, Mullins stayed after class to talk to her privately. After Ray's visit, he seemed more determined than ever to make music his life.

Fed up with school and somewhat discouraged by report cards bearing mostly Cs and Ds, Mullins dropped out of high school during the spring semester of eleventh grade and headed for the local recruiting office of the U.S. Marine Corps. But as it turned out, the Marines didn't want him without his high school diploma. Enrolling in an open-campus alternative school, he finished his junior and senior years of high school in about three months. But instead of heading back to the Marine recruiter, he decided to continue his schooling, having been newly motivated by his most recent learning experience. He enrolled at North Georgia College in Dahlonega, where he studied music. Also known as the Military College of Georgia, North Georgia is one of only four senior military colleges in the United States. When he graduated from college, Mullins was commissioned in the U.S. Army Airborne Infantry. While based at Fort Benning, Georgia, he played local acoustic

For the Record . . .

Born on March 8, 1968, in Atlanta, GA; married Kelly Hobbs, 2000. *Education:* Attended North Georgia College.

Formed his own rock band at the age of 12 and started writing songs when he was in seventh grade; studied music at North Georgia College, and after graduating, enlisted in the U.S. Army; formed own label, SMG Records, 1990; released *Better Days,* 1992; released *Big Blue Sky,* 1994; released *Jeff's Last Dance, Volume 1,* 1995; released *Eggshells,* 1996; released *Soul's Core* and *Jeff's Last Dance, Volume 2,* 1998; released *Beneath the Velvet Sun,* 2000.

Addresses: *Record company*—Columbia Records, 550 Madison Avenue, New York, NY 10022, (212) 833-8000; SMG Records, 2103 North Decatur Road, Suite 124, Decatur, GA 30033. *Management*—Russel Carter Artist Management, 315 West Ponce de Leon Avenue, Suite 755, Decatur, GA 30033. *Website*—Shawn Mullins Official Website: http://www.shawnmullins.com.

music venues in Columbus, Atlanta, and Athens. He also released his first two albums, both of which were self-produced, and distributed them on cassette on his own SMG label.

In the early 1990s Mullins left the military and began focusing all his energies on a career in music. After three frustrating years of sending out demo tapes in the hopes of putting together a record deal, he decided to launch a recording label of his own. Thus, in 1994 SMG Records was born. The label, headquartered in Decatur, just outside Atlanta, continues to operate, providing a launch pad for new and promising artists. Josh Joplin and Matthew Kahler are two of the artists presently recording for SMG. Mullins runs the label with assistance from his wife, Kelly Hobbs, who serves as president of SMG. Mullins himself handles production chores and A&R (artists and repertoire).

Even before founding SMG Records, Mullins released two albums: *Better Days,* which came out in 1992, and *Big Blue Sky,* released in 1994. He followed these in 1995 with *Jeff's Last Dance, Volume 1,* a collaborative effort with Kahler, recorded live.

In 1996, Mullins released another solo album, *Eggshells,* on his SMG label. But his breakthrough came in the latter half of 1998, shortly after the release of *Soul's Core.* "Lullaby," the first single released from the album, caught the attention of music fans all across the country, and before long record sales were going through the roof. Interviewed by *Entertainment Weekly* in January of 1999, not long after "Lullaby" had soared to the top of the charts, Mullins said, "I was hoping to get enough Americana, rootsy airplay to move my record sales up to 20,000 a year. We're doing 30,000 a week right now. I can't even fathom it." After playing second- and third-rate venues across the country for nearly a decade, the arrival of success on such a grand scale was very sweet indeed. With it came a flurry of offers from major record labels eager to sign the folksy singer-songwriter.

Mullins told *Entertainment Weekly* that he was approached by more than 25 major labels in the days immediately following the dizzying climb of "Lullaby" to the top of the charts. He eventually signed with Columbia Records, which less than two months later re-released *Soul's Core,* the album he'd produced and released on his own SMG label for less than $10,000. At first he and Hobbs, who was then his fiancée and co-owner of SMG Records, resisted the call of the majors, but in the end, Columbia's offer was simply too good to turn down. "I was broke and couldn't make enough records to keep up with all the requests," Mullins recalled.

As lucky as "Lullaby" had already been for Mullins, the magic was not yet finished. The single spent several weeks at the top of *Billboard*'s Adult Top 40 chart, while *Soul's Core,* the album on which the single first appeared, went gold and later platinum. Additional excitement—not to mention record sales—was generated by the video of "Lullaby," which starred actress Dominique Swain, best known for playing the title role in the 1997 remake of Vladimir Nabokov's controversial *Lolita.* As if all that were not enough, the song received a Grammy Award nomination.

Over the years Mullins' songwriting style has evolved gradually from an emphasis on love songs, almost all of which were sung in the first person, to character-based story songs. As he travels around the country, encountering characters whose stories appeal to him, he jots down notes in his journal and later browses through the journal when he's looking for inspiration for a song. His story of how "Lullaby" came to be written is fairly typical. Performing before a tiny audience, "I could tell that one of the five people in the audience was moved by my music. She told me her story over Chinese food. I wrote down a few lines in my journal—'she grew up with the children of the stars.' Her story was sad, but I wanted to give her some hope. A week later, driving home through the desert, the hook came to me—'everything's gonna be alright, rock-a-bye.'"

Mullins toured widely in support of *Soul's Core,* an album loaded with troubadour-type songs relating the stories of some of the men and women the singer has observed in his travels across the country. Although their circumstances often seem uniformly dreary and grim, the characters in Mullins' songs somehow manage to maintain an optimistic and upbeat outlook on the future. Some critics found this unrelieved optimism in Mullins' lyrics a bit much to take. Other critics complained about the songwriter's "strict commitment to rhyming couplets." Writing in the *Washington Post*, Dave McKenna observed: "On 'Joshua,' for example, Mullins tells of a young boy from a mountain community who spends his days with an old man playing guitar, singing, and smoking. The kid in this otherwise touching song is just 10, and one could surmise that Mullins rejected more credible ages, like 15 or 16, only because they don't rhyme with 'again.'"

In October of 2000, Mullins released *Beneath the Velvet Sun,* his follow-up to the successful *Soul's Core.* But, despite guest appearances by the likes of Shawn Colvin and Shelby Lynne, the album showed few signs of catching fire in the same fashion as its predecessor. Sales were generally slow. Mullins, in Canada for a benefit in December of 2000, told the *Toronto Sun,* "Singer-songwriters, we're in a weird time right now. People that are writing their own songs are not really on the radio a whole lot. I feel overwhelmed by all that. But at the same time, I feel a lot of faith and hope that people want to hear what we do."

Selected discography

Shawn Mullins, SMG, 1989.
Everchanging World, SMG, 1991.
Better Days, SMG, 1992.
Big Blue Sky, SMG, 1994.
Jeff's Last Dance, Vol. 1, SMG, 1995.
Eggshells, SMG, 1996.
Soul's Core (includes "Lullaby," "Shimmer," and "Gulf of Mexico"), Columbia, 1998.
Jeff's Last Dance, Vol. 2, SMG, 1998.
The First Ten Years, Columbia, 1999.
Beneath the Velvet Sun (includes "Everywhere I Go," "Up All Night," and "Something to Believe In"), Columbia, 2000.

Sources

Periodicals

Entertainment Weekly, January 15, 1999, p. 62.
Rolling Stone, April 1999.
Toronto Sun, December 20, 2000, p. 66.
Washington Post, February 8, 2001, p. C14.

Online

"Shawn Mullins," *All Music Guide,* http://www.allmusic.com/cg/amg.dll (April 25, 2001).
"Shawn Mullins," Artist Information.com, http://www.artistinformation.com/shawn_mullins.html (May 8, 2001).
"Shawn Mullins," iMusic Modern Showcase, http://imusic.artistdirect.com/showcase/modern/shawnmullins.html (May 8, 2001).
"Shawn Mullins," SMG Records, http://www.smgrecords.com/artists_mullins.cfm (May 8, 2001).
"Shawn Mullins Bio," Shawn Mullins: *Beneath the Velvet Sun,* http://www.shawnmullins.com/biof.html (April 29, 2001).
"Shawn Mullins Biography," *RollingStone.com,* http://www .rollingstone.com/artists/bio.asp?oid=6102 (April 29, 2001).

—Don Amerman

MxPx

Punk rock group

One of several pop-punk bands to emerge in the wake of the grunge scene of the early 1990s, MxPx delivered two albums for Seattle's Tooth & Nail Records before its members had even graduated from their Bremerton, Washington, high school. Like the Offspring, Green Day, and Blink 182, their music featured clever and sometimes cartoonish lyrics, tight, guitar-driven arrangements, and an attitude of good-natured unconventionality. While most of their songs dealt with typical adolescent themes such as school, parents, and other authority figures, some of them delivered messages inspired by the group's Christianity. As singer Mike Herrera told *Campus Life* early in the band's career, "It's pretty much, like, feel-good punk rock. It's happy and melodic, but it's fast at the same time…. Kinda something for everyone."

Growing up in Bremerton, just across the Puget Sound from Seattle, Washington, the three members of MxPx met while in the ninth grade. Originally known as Magnified Plaid, the group changed its name to avoid confusion with another area band, and came up with MxPx. Singer and bassist Mike Herrera had already written dozens of songs on his own, and with the addition of drummer Yuri Ruley and guitarist Tom Wisniewski, the three band members began rehears-

Photograph by Karen Mason Blair. Corbis. Reproduced by permission.

ing and playing around the Bremerton area. As Herrera recalled in an interview with the *St. Paul Pioneer Press* in 1998, "I was totally into punk, but I was so new playing my instrument and writing my songs, I just kinda wrote what I could. There were maybe ten bands in the area, and about half of them would regularly play shows in the area." In contrast to the distortion and feedback that dominated grunge music around the Pacific Northwest in the early 1990s, however, MxPx included some pop-oriented punk songs in its repertoire. "They used to make fun of us because we didn't have as much distortion," Herrera remembered. The band also was distinctive for its inclusion of Christian themes in its lyrics, another contrast to the darker orientation of grunge bands like Nirvana and Pearl Jam.

MxPx soon became more than just another garage band in Bremerton. In 1994, while they were completing their junior year of high school, the band released its first album, *Pokinatcha,* on Tooth & Nail. The label specialized in releasing Christian-oriented music, and many of the songs on *Pokinatcha* reflected the band's Christian beliefs. In "Weak," Herrera wrote that "Jesus pulls me back together, my soul will be with him," while in "Think Twice" he sang, "We are a brotherhood and we all know it, bonded by the son of God is how we live." Other songs, such as "PxPx," noted "He's the one true center of our lives" in its social commentary, while

"Jars of Clay" carried its religious theme throughout its lyrics. With Herrera's vocals as much shouted as sung over the steady drumming and intense guitar riffs of his bandmates, however, MxPx sounded like a punk band, not a Christian rock group.

While completing their senior year of high school, MxPx completed another album for Tooth & Nail, 1995's *Teenage Politics.* Like the band's first release, *Teenage Politics* contained songs that included Christian references in their lyrics. In songs like "False Fiction," Herrera sang that "Unless you know Christ you won't know how I feel," while in "Different Things" he wrote, "Jesus Christ, God, Son, and Sacrifice, believe in Him, He'll open up your eyes." Other songs covered more typically adolescent themes such as problems with dating, parents, and employers. Although the band did not shy away from acknowledging its Christian orientation in its music, it nevertheless played to a broader audience, playing concerts around the United States with other punk-rock groups during the members's last year in high school. Despite their out-of-town forays, each band member graduated on schedule in 1995.

After releasing one more album on Tooth & Nail Records, 1995's *On the Cover,* MxPx signed a new contract with A&M Records, which agreed to allow the band to continue recording for Tooth & Nail but take advantage of A&M's more extensive resources for promotion and distribution. The deal between the small, independent Tooth & Nail and the larger A&M was a rarity in the music industry; the arrangement allowed A&M to re-release the band's 1997 offering, *Life in General,* which had sold well despite Tooth & Nail's limited promotional budget. A&M hoped that the single "Chick Magnet," whose video had received some airplay on the MTV network, would bring the band crossover success. Indeed, *Life in General* hit the top 30 on both the Contemporary Christian chart as well as the Heatseekers album chart for up-and-coming acts in *Billboard.* Taking advantage of this breakthrough, MxPx also toured as an opening act for No Doubt and Face to Face in the summer of 1997, as well as appearing on the Warped Tour.

In 1998, MxPx joined the Warped Tour again to support its 1998 release, *Slowly Going the Way of the Buffalo.* Although the album contained a couple of Christian-oriented songs, such as "Tomorrow's Another Day," the band by now was seen as firmly within punk-rock territory. A 1998 profile in *Rolling Stone* even noted that the band's work with Tooth & Nail "created the misimpression that MxPx are a Christian-rock band." Indeed, in contrast to the content of their first releases, *Slowly Going the Way of the Buffalo* largely put aside explicit references to the band's religious beliefs. And, although most of the songs carried social critiques, the album also developed the band's lighthearted side with tracks such as "Party, My House, Be There."

While the band's musicianship had improved with each release, production on its albums remained as sparse as ever, with Herrera's frantic vocals competing for notice over the band's straightforward and energetic playing. Typical of the reviews were *Ride BMX's* approval of MxPx's 1998 compilation *Let It Happen:* "It's great, high-energy stuff that will make you run as fast as you can until you get cramps and then fall over wanting more." On the other hand, in the wake of multi-million selling albums by Blink 182 and Green Day, with whom they were often compared, MxPx's bid for wider crossover success disappointed some critics. A *Los Angeles Times* review of a 2001 concert dismissed MxPx as "Punk Lite"; Despite "optimistic lyrics shouted across rapid beats and loud-fast electric guitar … the band has yet to add anything meaningful to the punk genre, unless you count the Christianity of its members."

Now in his early twenties, Herrera defended his band's direction as he promoted the band's 2000 release, *The Ever Passing Moment.* Retaining Christian lyrics on some tracks, such as the reference on "It's Undeniable" to "giving God control," most of the songs covered the familiar territory of struggling with authority issues. The single "Responsibility," a top 30 hit on *Billboard's* Modern Rock Tracks in the summer of 2000, was about "how I don't want to grow up right now," said Herrera in an interview with the magazine's Jill Pesselnick. He added that the new album was inspired by the realization that "you've got to live each moment or life will pass you by. You'll never get it back." With a couple of hits under the trio's belt, Herrera added that he was pleased by MxPx's success, but that mainstream acceptance would never cause the band to abandon its integrity and creativity. "I want the radio to play us because we wrote a good song. But I don't want to write a song just so radio will play it."

In 2001, MxPx recorded *The Renaissance EP,* a production for the band's own label, Rock City Recording Company, which had also released its concert album, *At the Show,* in 1999. MxPx also continued to tour extensively, making a point to ask concert promoters to make tickets available at outlets that avoided service charges and handling fees such as those charged by Ticketmaster. While MxPx now recorded for a major label and toured on corporate-sponsored concerts around the world, and Herrera appeared in a *Rolling Stone* fashion layout sporting a $320 Versace shirt, it remained at least in part true to its origins. With the return to its roots for *The Renaissance EP,* which the band promoted on its website as: "What our first three records may have sounded like if we had recorded the songs at the present time," MxPx continued its prodigious musical output, making it the band's ninth album in just eight years.

Selected discography

Pokinatcha, Tooth & Nail, 1994.
Teenage Politics, Tooth & Nail, 1995.
On the Cover, Tooth & Nail, 1995.
Life in General, Tooth & Nail/A&M, 1997.
Slowly Going the Way of the Buffalo, Tooth & Nail, 1998.
Let It Happen, Tooth & Nail/A&M, 1998.
At the Show, Tooth & Nail/Rock City Recording Company, 1999.
The Ever Passing Moment, Tooth & Nail/A&M, 2000.
(Contributor) *The Real Slim Santa,* KROQ-FM compilation, 2000.
The Renaissance EP, Rock City Recording Company, 2001.

Sources

Periodicals

Billboard, August 9, 1997, p. 9; October 4, 1997, p. 18; September 9, 2000, p. 97.
Campus Life, February 1996, p. 18.
Los Angeles Times, December 9, 2000; March 23, 2001.
Ride BMX, July 1999, p. 50.
Rolling Stone, July 9, 1998, p. 117; August 17, 2000, p. 100.
Saint Paul Pioneer Press, June 18, 1998.

Online

MxPx Official Website, http://www.mxpx.com (April 16, 2001).

—Timothy Borden

Old 97's

Country group

The Old 97's began their musical career as the darlings of the early alternative-country scene. The band's lineup—guitarist/singer Rhett Miller, bassist/singer Murry Hammond, lead guitarist Ken Bethea, and drummer Philip Peeples—has remained constant since its founding. Like many other alternative country bands, the Old 97's did not want critics and fans to box them into one musical style. Their participation in the 1997 Lollapalooza Tour proved that as they jammed with some of the best groups on the alternative rock scene. The Old 97's included a number of pop songs on 1999's *Fight Songs* as well. Since their beginning, the Old 97's have followed their muse regardless of the consequences.

The Old 97's formed in Dallas, Texas, in 1993. Miller and Hammond had met in the mid 1980s and played together in several bands. The duo later left Texas to work on other projects. Hammond eventually persuaded Miller to move back to Texas to form Sleepy Heroes, a band that covered 1960s British rock. The band stayed together long enough to release one album. Hammond left Texas again, this time opening himself up to music that would have a profound effect on the Old 97's' sound. "It was probably really on that trip more than anything else that I rediscovered roots music—rediscovered the country background, rediscovered bluegrass," Hammond told Peter Blackstock of *No Depression*. He eventually returned and reunited with Miller. In early 1993, Bethea entered the scene, and it was his lead guitar work that gave the fledgling band the country twang it needed. They played for a

short time as an acoustic trio but filled out their sound and went electric in late 1993 with the addition of drummer Peeples. Hammond, a train buff, suggested the name Old 97's, which was drawn from Henry Whitter's 1923 ballad about the 1903 Virginia railroad disaster: "The Wreck of the Old 97."

In 1994 the Old 97's played locally and self-released their debut album, *Hitchhike to Rhome*. Their new sound failed to find a footing in Texas soil, however, so the band traveled north to Chicago. There, they were astounded by the lively reception they received during their first gig, not realizing that they were practically in the backyard of similar-sounding bands like the Bottle Rockets and Jason and the Scorchers. "It was such a shock for us to go to Chicago," Peebles told Shayla Thiel of the *Washington Post*, "because there was a group of listeners who actually liked us. We had never even heard of Uncle Tupelo before then." Bloodshot Records signed the band in 1995 and they recorded the song "Por Favor" for the *Insurgent Country, Vol. II* compilation. In 1996 they recorded *Wreck Your Life*, an album that solidified their status as "the" alternative country band to watch. The five-song EP, *Early Tracks*, would be released by Bloodshot in 2000, reminding everyone of the band's energetic, cow-punk roots.

In 1996 the band began a busy touring schedule that included performances at the South By Southwest music festival in Austin and the Gavin Convention in Atlanta. The band also began to consider changing its record label and musical direction. "We were in Wilmington, N.C., at some horrible gig," Miller told Jon Johnson of *Country Standard Time*, "and we came out afterward and said, 'Okay, tomorrow we're going to get a lawyer and ask the lawyer to call major labels and see if any of them would be interested in having us.' Because this sucked!" They signed to Elektra in September of 1996 and released *Too Far to Care* in 1997. This album, and the group's subsequent performances with the 1997 Lollapalooza Tour, would lead to accusations within the alternative-country community that the group had sold out. Critics said that the "twang" had been toned down on *Too Far to Care* and Lollapalooza's alternative-rock orientation did not fit the group's style. The band, however, continued to move forward. "Sure, we made a rock record," Miller told Andy Langer of the *Austin Chronicle*, "but we didn't necessarily set out saying we're not going to do any country either. We just wanted to make a record that didn't pander."

In 1999 the Old 97's would once again buck the trend by releasing *Fight Songs*, an album filled with pop tunes. Two of the songs, "Nineteen" and "Murder (Or a Heart Attack)," received radio play, and the band began to sell out 1,500-seat auditoriums on tour. While the stylistic shifts—from alternative country to rock to pop—probably puzzled some fans, it seemed a natural shift to the band. "I'm really glad that we kept what we kept," Miller told Blackstock, defending *Fight Songs*,

For the Record . . .

Members include **Ken Bethea**, lead guitar; **Murry Hammond**, bass, vocals; **Rhett Miller**, rhythm guitar, vocals; **Philip Peeples**, drums.

Group formed in Dallas, TX, 1993; released debut *Hitchhike to Rhome* independently, 1994; signed to Bloodshot Records, 1995; recorded *Wreck Your Life,* 1996; extensive touring, 1995-96; appeared at the Gavin Convention in Atlanta and South By Southwest (SXSW) music festival in Austin, TX, 1996; signed to Elektra Records, 1996; recorded first album for that label, *Too Far to Care,* 1997; played several dates with the Lollapalooza Tour, 1997; recorded *Fight Songs,* 1999; *Early Tracks* released by Bloodshot, 2000; *Satellite Rides* issued by Elektra, 2001.

Addresses: *Record company*—Bloodshot Records, 3039 W. Irving Park Rd., Chicago, IL 60618, (773) 604-5300, website: http://www.bloodshotrecords. com; Elektra Records, 75 Rockefeller Plaza, New York, NY 10019, (212) 275-4000. *Website*—Old 97's Official Website: http://www.old97s.com.

"and didn't get scared to put on whatever." While 2001's *Satellite Rides* would rock harder, the shift in themes continued. Two of the band members were now fathers, and wives and girlfriends—barred from early recording sessions—were invited to the studio. The irony that drenched earlier songs no longer seemed appropriate to group members who had fallen in love, had children, and grown a little older.

The growth and changes in the music of the Old 97's are also representative of the trends within the alternative-country community. Bands like Wilco have also traveled the same road, starting with Gram Parsons influences and steel guitars, and then moving to the Beatles and hook-laden pop songs. Songwriters like Miller and Hammond place more importance on crafting good songs than trying to fit into a precon-

ceived genre. The band is also quick to point out that despite a change in record labels and a change in the band's sound, it has yet to become famous. In other words, they haven't sold out. Still, the band has high hopes for the future. Miller, who has residences in New York and Los Angeles, returned to Texas for three months and lived with the band while making *Satellite Rides.* "It just made us a lot closer as a band," he told Wes Orshoski of *Billboard.* "So, it's different from the last record in that respect—we're a lot more of a band. I think that comes across." This harmony and openness to change guarantees that the Old 97's will continue to make music that will perk up listeners' ears—no matter what musical category it happens to be in.

Selected discography

Hitchhike to Rhome, self-released, 1994; reissued, Elektra, 1999.
Wreck Your Life, Bloodshot, 1996.
Too Far to Care, Elektra, 1997.
Fight Songs, Elektra, 1999.
Satellite Rides, Elektra, 2001.

Sources

Periodicals

Billboard, March 24, 2001, p.18.

Online

"Alternative Country, Indy Scene Grows," *Country Standard Time,* http://www.countrystandardtime.com (April 2, 2001).
"Old 97's: Too Far To Care?" *Washington Post,* http://www.washingtonpost.com (April 4, 2001).
"Old 97's' Rhett Miller Ponders Radio, Plant Closures, and the Bi-coastal Life," LiveDaily, http://livedaily.citysearch.com/news/2928.html (April 12, 2001).
"The Old 97's Ride New Track," *Country Standard Time,* http:// www.countrystandardtime.com (April 2, 2001).
"Wreck Your Image," *Austin Chronicle,* http://www.week lywire.com (April 4, 2001).
"You Can't Please Everyone, So You've Got To Please Yourself," *No Depression,* http://www.nodepression.net (April 2, 2001).

—Ronnie D. Lankford, Jr.

OutKast

Hip-hop duo

Upon its release in the fall of 2000, *Stankonia* ushered OutKast—the Atlanta-based duo of Andre "Dre" Benjamin (who also answers to the name "Andre 3000") and Antwan "Big Boi" Patton—into the center of the hip-hop world. In the rap business, where risk-takers rarely reap the rewards of commercial success, OutKast stand as true music mavericks. Not only did they succeed in creating something different to satisfy their own need for self-expression, they also found fans willing to accept their sound. The double-platinum album, which appealed to college kids and urban youth alike, has received much more than popular acceptance. Critics and peers likewise praised *Stankonia*, featuring the quasi-political hit "B.O.B." ("Bombs Over Baghdad"), for its inventiveness and creativity, over-whelmingly calling it the best hip-hop album of the year and crediting OutKast for taking the rap genre to a new level. "'B.O.B.' was maybe the most exciting thing I heard [in 2000]," stated former Rage Against the Machine singer Zack de la Rocha, as quoted by *Spin* magazine's Sacha Jenkins. "It defies definition, and that's the dopest kind of music. They're an incredible group."

Rather than relying on samplers during recording sessions, OutKast instead opted for live instrumentation, along with a varied range of influences that included everything from funk to rock to electronica. "It's like a picnic," explained Benjamin to *Rolling Stone* contributor Mark Binelli. "Your auntie might bring peas; somebody else might bring collard greens. You gotta sit back and say, 'What can I bring to the table that's gonna make this whole meal right?' And we felt like, in hip-hop, there wasn't no driving type music. Everything was real chill and laid-back. We're trying to crank it back up. I like a lot of techno music, but some of it sounds soft, so I'm trying to make our own American style—harder, like hip-hop, instead of ambient and pretty." OutKast call their music "slumadelic," a sort of dance music for the slums.

Benjamin and Patton, who share a love of artists such as George Clinton, Sly and the Family Stone, James Brown, Jimi Hendrix, and Prince, became friends after a chance meeting at a mall in the early 1990s. At the time, both were new students in the tenth grade at Tri-Cities High School—also the alma mater of R&B groups TLC and Xscape—in the East Point neighborhood of Atlanta, Georgia. Despite different backgrounds, the two hit it off immediately. Benjamin, an only child, lived with his mother during his early years before moving in with his father at age 15. In contrast, Patton grew up with several brothers and sisters in Savannah, Georgia, before settling in Atlanta with his family as a teen.

The two friends began rapping together soon thereafter. At school, Benjamin and Patton held impromptu competitions during lunchtime in the cafeteria to try to out-rhyme one another. As their skills progressed, the

Photograph by Jeffrey Mayer. Wireimage.com. Reproduced by permission.

duo set out to break into the hip-hop industry. They met their future producer, Rico Wade, in a parking lot where they rhymed their own version of "Scenario" by A Tribe Called Quest for him. "Them cats was about sixteen and took the bus up to this little plaza where I owned a beauty supply shop and video store," Wade, who made his name as one-third of the Organized Noize production team and has produced for the likes of TLC, Eric Clapton, and En Vogue, recalled to Anthony Bozza of *Rolling Stone*. "They came out with an instrumental of 'Scenario.' And for seven minutes them cats went back to back. I didn't even stop them, I was so in awe. I closed the store, we got in my Blazer and went straight to the Dungeon."

Although Patton and Benjamin planned to visit several producers that day, the Dungeon, a pre-production studio in the basement of an old house, was their first and only stop. According to Benjamin, as quoted by Bozza, "the beats they had were some of the most original music from Atlanta we'd ever heard." After that day, the two teenagers began frequenting the studio on a regular basis to learn from beat makers like Raymon Murray, also of Organized Noize, as well as other local hopefuls such as Big Gripp and Khujo, who would later form the group Goodie Mob. Benjamin and Patton also formed their own group called 2 Shades Deep. During his junior year, Benjamin dropped out of high school to devote himself entirely to music, while Patton completed his education, graduating with a 3.68 grade point average.

Meanwhile, just prior to Patton's graduation and with the help of Wade, the duo inked a record deal with the L.A. Reid and Kenneth "Babyface" Edmonds LaFace label. Their first single, "Player's Ball," arrived in 1993.

An instant hit, the song topped the rap charts for six weeks that year and earned gold status. The following year saw the release of OutKast's debut full-length set. *Southernplayalisticadillacmuzik,* recorded when Patton and Benjamin were 18 years old and largely produced by Organized Muzik, proved another commercial as well as critical success.

Unlike other rap groups outside Los Angeles or New York, the duo presented themselves as simply who they were, highlighting their Atlanta roots, filtering their lives through their music, and implementing rich, live production techniques. OutKast also struck a balance between positive messages and street stories, a hallmark of their music ever since. The album spawned two hits in addition to "Player's Ball": the title track and the song "Get Up and Get Out." Eagerly soaking in the duo's tales about life as they saw it and image of self-empowerment, the hip-hop community embraced OutKast. By the end of 1994, *Southernplayalisticadillacmuzik* reached the platinum sales mark.

In 1996, OutKast's second album, *ATLiens,* reached the number two position on the rap charts and sold over one-and-a-half million copies, cementing the duo's status as the soul-bearers of a new, regional style of hip-hop known as the "Dirty South." The album, an illustration of the pair's fascination with space travel and the raising of consciousness, spawned another gold single, "Elevators (Me and You)." Around this time Benjamin introduced the outrageous image that he is famous for—wearing large wraps or dresses and platinum wigs and turbans, an appearance that often led to frequent rumors about his sexual identity. But like Parliament's Bootsy Collins or Jimi Hendrix, Benjamin simply wanted to look like his music. "You gotta know Dre," Patton said to writer Isaac Guzman in the *Los Angeles Times.* "Dre could put up some Levi's and some Jordans in a minute. You never know. It just depends on how he's feeling. When you're on stage, you want to look like the music feels."

OutKast's ascent continued with the release of their 1998 album *Aquemini,* which sold over two million copies. Despite rave reviews in publications such as *Rolling Stone* and the *Source,* the multiplatinum album was not without controversy. The Grammy-nominated single "Rosa Parks" angered the civil rights matriarch, and her attorneys levied a lawsuit against the group, accusing the duo of exploiting her name for commercial purposes. Although a federal court judge ruled that OutKast had not misused Rosa Parks' name, her attorneys, who additionally retained the services of attorney Johnnie Cochran, famous for defending former football star O.J. Simpson in his murder case, promised to appeal the decision.

The OutKast/Rosa Parks case remained unresolved as of early 2001, yet Patton and Benjamin insist that they did no wrong. "We won the first decision, so they're appealing it," Patton told Jenkins, as stated in *Spin*'s March 2001 issue. "But everybody knows that there was never any disrespect meant at all. If you know anything about OutKast—if you listen to the song, it's not about Rosa Parks. When we sing 'everybody move to the back of the bus,' we're just using that as symbolism."

OutKast returned with their fourth album, the critically acclaimed *Stankonia,* in the fall of 2000. "*Stankonia* is this place I imagined where you can open yourself up and be free to express anything," Benjamin told Sonia Murray in the *Atlanta Journal-Constitution*. Indeed, the album departed from typical rap through the inclusion of varied musical elements. The song "B.O.B.," a political declaration of sorts about not doing anything halfway, prominently featured organs, guitar, and vocals by the Morris Brown College Choir. Other tracks of note included soul jams like "Stanklove" and "Slum Beautiful," a keyboard-laden song about how money, for better and for worse, changes everything titled "Red Velvet," and "Humble Mumble," featuring the vocals of R&B singer Erykah Badu, Benjamin's former girlfriend with whom he had a son, Seven, in 1997. Although Badu and Benjamin split earlier in 2000, their relationship inspired the lyrics for the track "Ms. Jackson," an open letter from Benjamin to Badu's mother in which he promises to take an active role as a father.

Benjamin and Patton, who also started their own label, Aquemini, as well as a line of clothing called OutKast Clothing, attribute their success to enjoying what they do creatively and remaining fans themselves of all types of music. "It's about learning and paying attention," Benjamin pointed out to Bozza. "When we listen to records, we sit down and listen to everything from blues to bluegrass to the people that really inspire us, like Jimi Hendrix, Funkadelic and Sly Stone." Patton added, "We truly love what we do. That's one thing I can say about us as a team."

Selected discography

Southernplayalisticadillacmuzik, LaFace/Arista, 1994.
ATLiens, LaFace/Arista, 1996.
Aquemini, LaFace/Arista, 1998.
Stankonia, LaFace/Arista, 2000.

Sources

Periodicals

Atlanta Journal-Constitution, November 4, 1999; November 5, 1999; October 30, 2000; October 31, 2000; January 4, 2001.
Billboard, January 23, 1999; April 17, 1999; September 23, 2000; November 4, 2000.
Boston Globe, December 7, 2000.
Jet, April 16, 1999.
Los Angeles Times, September 27, 1998; October 22, 2000; October 28, 2000.
New York Times, October 29, 2000.
People, November 27, 2000.
Rolling Stone, December 10, 1998; December 24, 1998-January 7, 1999; February 4, 1999; May 13, 1999; April 13, 2000; November 23, 2000; December 14-21, 2000; December 28, 2000-January 4, 2001; January 18, 2001.
Spin, March 2001.
USA Today, October 31, 2000; November 3, 2000.
Village Voice, November 7, 2000; December 5, 2000.
Washington Post, December 4, 1998; November 8, 2000; November 10, 2000; December 31, 2000.

Online

Wall of Sound, http://wallofsound.go.com (April 21, 2001).

—Laura Hightower

Paul Overstreet

Singer, songwriter

Called "one of the most successful songwriters in Nashville" by the Knight-Ridder News Service, Grammy winner Paul Overstreet came from a modest background in Mississippi but found major success as a songwriter with more than 25 of country music's biggest hits to his name. Randy Travis, the Forester Sisters, Tanya Tucker, the Judds, Glen Campbell, Mel Tillis, Travis Tritt, and Marie Osmond are just some of the singers to perform Overstreet's material. The artist performed his own songs on albums like *Sowin' Love, Heroes,* and *Love Is Strong* before broadening his horizons as a producer, exploring the Christian country genre, and publishing a book, *Forever and Ever, Amen,* in 2001.

Overstreet was born on March 17, 1955, in Newton, Mississippi, the youngest of five children born to William, a Baptist preacher, and Mary Overstreet. Musical talent ran in the Overstreet family. The entire family sang, his sisters and mother played piano, and one of his brothers played guitar. When Overstreet was six years old, his parents divorced, and his mother and siblings survived on prayer and government assistance until his mother remarried. As a child, Overstreet listened to country radio and the songs of Marty Robbins, Charlie Pride, Hank Williams, Sr., Jim Reeves, Johnny Horton, Merle Haggard, Elvis Presley, and Ricky Nelson. He also loved old Motown and R&B music by Sam Cooke and Otis Redding. As a teenager, Overstreet's tastes leaned more to the rock music of the time—the Doobie Brothers, Janis Joplin, Three Dog Night, Grand Funk Railroad, and Bread. After spending a few summers in California with his father, he had taught himself to play most of Creedence Clearwater Revival's songs. Inspired by the story of country legend Hank Williams, Sr. in the 1964 film *Your Cheatin' Heart,* Overstreet aspired to make a living writing and playing country songs.

Ambitious, Overstreet pressed three hundred 45s of a song called "The Wanderer" and sold them at a local grocery store for $1 each. After picking up a single, former Grand Ole Opry performer Walter Bailes contacted Overstreet. Nothing came of their meeting in Nashville, Tennessee, but Overstreet had developed an interest in the city. After graduation from high school in 1973, he went to Texas where he worked as a mechanic. After a concert by country singer Tanya Tucker at a local dance hall, Overstreet approached the country star and got her picture. Little did either of them know that Tucker would later score hits with the then-unknown country songwriter's work. Inspired by Tucker, he quit his job the next day and drove to Nashville in his brother's 1968 Ford Fairlane with a laundry basket full of clothes, ten songs he had written, and a guitar. Country stardom was still a long way off, so Overstreet got a job in a Nashville water heater factory. He worked blue collar jobs by day and played in country bands at night.

Over time, Overstreet began to get more attention as a songwriter than as a singer. He would eventually write more than 25 top ten songs for other artists, his first being "Same Ole Me" for George Jones in 1982, which went to number five. Other country artists who have recorded his songs include Randy Travis, who scored hits with "On the Other Hand," the Grammy-winning "Forever and Ever, Amen," and "Diggin' Up Bones," Travis' first number one hit; the Forester Sisters, who went to number one with "I Fell in Love Again Last Night;" and Tucker, who topped the charts with "One Love at a Time," "My Arms Stay Open All Night," and "I Won't Take Less Than Your Love." The late Keith Whitley recorded the hit "When You Say Nothing At All," which was later re-recorded by Alison Krauss and again by the British pop group Boyzone for the soundtrack to the film *Notting Hill.* Overstreet won a Grammy Award in 1992 for "Love Can Build A Bridge," performed by the Judds.

Overstreet released his first charting single in 1982 with "Beautiful Baby," which made it to number 76. Four years later, he teamed with Thom Schuyler and Fred Knobloch to form SKO and released the number one hit "Baby's Got a New Baby." Overstreet's debut solo album, *Sowin' Love,* was released in 1989. It made it into the top 40 and spawned a few hits. Overstreet stayed on the charts for almost a year with his 1991 album *Heroes,* which *Los Angeles Times* critic Randy Lewis noted for its movement away from country music's "overwhelming dependence on dysfunctional relationships." His third release, 1992's *Love is*

For the Record . . .

Born on March 17, 1955, in Newton, MS; married Julie; children: Nash, Summer, Chord, Harmony, Skye, and Charity Joy.

Moved to Nashville, TN, after graduation from high school, 1973; first top ten song, "Same Ole Me," performed by George Jones, 1982; scored number one hit with "Baby's Got a New Baby" with SKO group, 1986; wrote major hit for Randy Travis, "For Ever and Ever, Amen," 1987; released debut solo album, *Sowin' Love*, 1989; released *Heroes*, 1991; released *Love is Strong*, 1992; released *Living by the Book*, 2001; published book, *Forever and Ever, Amen*, 2001.

Awards: ACM (Academy of Country Music) Song of the Year Award for "On The Other Hand," 1986; ACM Song of the Year Award for "Forever And Ever, Amen," 1987; BMI Songwriter of the Year, 1987-91; CMA (Country Music Association) Song of the Year Award for "On The Other Hand," 1987; CMA Song of the Year Award for "Forever And Ever, Amen," 1988; Grammy Award for "Forever And Ever, Amen," 1988; Grammy Award for "Love Can Build A Bridge," 1992; Dove Award, Country Recorded Song of the Year Award for "Seein' My Father In Me," 1991; Dove Award, Country Recorded Album of the Year Award for *Love Is Strong*, 1992; Christian Country Music Association (CCMA) Country Songwriter of the Year, 1993; CCMA Mainstream Artist of the Year, 1994; Dove Award, Country Recorded Song of the Year Award for "There But For The Grace Of God Go I," 1994.

Addresses: *Record company*—Scarlet Moon Records, P.O. Box 320, Pegram, TN 37143, (615) 952-3999. *Website*—Paul Overstreet Official Website: http://www.pauloverstreet.com.

Strong, was not commercially or critically successful. *Entertainment Weekly* critic Alanna Nash called the album "saccharine and simplistic." After its release, Overstreet turned to Christian songwriting, performing, producing, and book writing. He produced, co-wrote, and sung a duet on an album that topped the Christian country charts and launched the career of Susie Luchsinger, sister of country star Reba McEntire.

After recording with Luchsinger and working with her label, Integrity, a modest Christian imprint, Overstreet turned down an offer to record with a major country label. A devout Christian, the artist chose to record with Integrity instead. "I enjoyed working with Integrity," Overstreet told *Billboard*. "It was fun, and at that point I was really tired of having a corporate decision made on my life. I liked the way these people treated their artists." Integrity created a sub-label with Overstreet called Scarlet Moon Records, which promoted Overstreet's brand of "positive country," a term given by *Billboard*, to both country and Christian markets.

A committed family man, Overstreet's songs are known for being family-values oriented. He turned away from some of the temptations he faced as a successful country singer and songwriter. Instead, he chose to stay close to his family and farm in a rural town outside Nashville where he also has a recording studio. Overstreet has six children whom he and his wife, Julie, chose to home school. When he is not on the farm or performing, Overstreet gives his time to a charity called Samaritan's Purse, an international relief ministry that tends to the spiritual and physical needs of people in crisis worldwide. Samaritan's Purse is run by his good friend Franklin Graham, son of evangelist Billy Graham, with whom he regularly performs.

Overstreet is featured as songwriter, singer, musician, and producer on his own 2000 release, *A Songwriter's Project, Vol. 1.* The album features Overstreet singing and playing the hits he has written for other artists and includes a few new tracks as well. In 2001, he issued the Christian CD *Living by the Book*. Also that year, Overstreet debuted as an author. His book, *Forever and Ever, Amen*, features the fan-inspired stories behind some of his hits.

Selected discography

Sowin' Love, RCA, 1989.
Heroes, RCA, 1991.
Love Is Strong, RCA, 1992.
The Best of Paul Overstreet, RCA, 1994.
Time, Integrity/Scarlet Moon Records, 1996.
A Songwriter's Project, Vol. 1, Scarlet Moon Records, 2000.
Living by the Book, Scarlet Moon Records, 2001.

Sources

Periodicals

Billboard, January 6, 1996, p. 76; February 3, 1996, p. 14; April 6, 1996, p. 95; May 18, 1996, p. 70.
Entertainment Weekly, October 30, 1992, p. 87.
Knight-Ridder/Tribune News Service, March 24, 1994.
Los Angeles Times, August 25, 1991, p. 67.

Online

"Paul Overstreet," *All Music Guide,* http://www.allmusic.com (April 24, 2001).

Paul Overstreet Official Website, http://www.pauloverstreet .com (April 24, 2001).

Additional information was provided by the Scarlet Moon Records publicity department, 2001.

—*Brenna Sanchez*

Pernice Brothers

Pop group

Although singer-songwriter and guitarist Joe Pernice first made his mark as the leader of the rough-edged, country/pop band the Scud Mountain Boys, his style shifted into classic pop recordings for the Pernice Brothers, signaling a profound departure from his previous work. With the Scud Mountain Boys, Pernice kept the music relatively simple and traditional. But in his role with Pernice Brothers, the songwriter opted for arrangements filled with grand orchestrations, piano, and horns, leaving behind his no-frills approach. Pernice transcended the initial label of alternative country, turning instead toward a kind of bittersweet pop in the same vein as Alex Chilton and Elvis Costello. "I just wanted to make a pretty and mellow pop record," Pernice said about the group's 1998 debut album *Overcome By Happiness,* as quoted by his booking agency. "And I'm not afraid to use the word 'pop.' There's nothing shameful about it."

The underlying purpose of Pernice's work—from his time with the Scud Mountain Boys through the Pernice Brothers and solo recordings—has always remained a very personal one. "I always try to make sure I am honestly putting something of myself into the songs," he remarked in an interview posted on NBCi.com. "I never want to feel like I'm putting one over on the listener. If I'm not emotionally connected to the song, and if it wasn't a ton of fun writing the song, it's not worth it. For me, writing and recording songs is an unbelievable pleasure. I think I write so often because I want to repeat the feeling.... Obviously I want people to like my music or I wouldn't release records. Whether or not I continue to release records, I will continue to write and record until it is no longer fun."

Before taking a giant leap into the world of pop-influenced music, Pernice fronted the Scud Mountain Boys on guitar and vocals. Also featuring Stephen Desaulniers on bass and vocals, Bruce Tull on lap steel guitar and vocals, and Tom Shea on drums and mandolin, the Scud Mountain Boys played a hybrid of country and rock that favored traditional American songwriting values over stylistic trends, somewhat akin to the Band. The quartet formed in 1991 in Northampton, Massachusetts, and started out mainly as a rock-oriented group. However, their repertoire soon became more rooted in country, encompassing simple, acoustic songs. Playing local shows, the Scud Mountain Boys, within the span of a few years, found a niche for their music among a growing number of neo-country outfits such as Uncle Tupelo, the Bottle Rockets, Son Volt, and Wilco.

The first recording by the Scud Mountain Boys, "Two Weeks Past," appeared on a 1994 Swedish compilation titled *Hit the Hay.* The following year, the band released their debut album, *Pine Box,* as well as their second full-length set, *Dance the Night Away,* on the small, independent label Chunk Records. In 1996, the Scud Mountain Boys signed with Sub Pop Records and released the single "Knievel" followed by a third album, the highly-acclaimed *Massachusetts.* Their new label then negotiated for the release of the 1997 two-CD set *The Early Years: Pine Box and Dance the Night Away,* comprising the first two Chunk albums as well as a handful of rarities. By now, critics were hailing the Scud Mountain Boys as the "real deal." Unlike the so-called alternative or neo-country bands, the quartet appeared committed to writing poignant, traditional American songs that remained free of historical irony.

Despite the Scud Mountain Boys' success, Pernice felt it necessary to try something new. Thus, in the summer of 1997, he left the band. "I think we went as far as we could go stylistically and it became very limiting," Pernice said about his departure, as quoted on the Pernice Brothers website. "It was just time to move on. I'm not knocking that kind of traditional country music we were doing, but for me it was getting a little boring. I was thinking that a lot of the songs I was writing at the time [of the Scuds breakup] were suited for things like strings and piano. Really, I just wanted to expand the sound a bit and try different instruments and to really indulge myself, which I couldn't do in the Scud Mountain Boys."

In order to bring his new songs to life, Pernice gathered a group of local musicians—including his guitar-playing brother Bob Pernice, guitarist Peyton Pinkerton from New Radiant Storm King, bassist/producer Thom Monahan (who played bass for the Lilys and engineered and/or produced albums for the likes of J

Mascis, Silver Jews, Chamber Strings, Jubilee Allstars, and Beachwood Sparks), drummer Aaron Sperske, pianist/string arranger/producer Mike Deming, and a mini orchestra of strings and horns—to record the Pernice Brothers' debut album at Studio .45 in Hartford, Connecticut. Upon its release in May of 1998, *Overcome By Happiness* drew rave reviews as critics likened Pernice's work to that of the Beach Boys, Big Star, Nick Drake, and the Zombies.

Prior to moving forward with the next Pernice Brothers album, Pernice put out two albums as side projects. The first, *Chappaquiddick Skyline*, released in January of 2000, contained songs that did not quite fit with those appearing on *Overcome By Happiness*. "I wrote those songs pretty much right next to each other, but they just felt different to me," he explained to Joshua Klein of the Onion A.V. Club online. "I wanted to do them a different way. I didn't want full string arrangements, horns, and stuff like that. I also wanted to make a record I could do at home, and I did." For the album, Pernice enlisted the help of Monahan on bass, orchestral samples, loops, keyboards, vocals, and percussion; Pinkerton on electric guitars, slide, and vocals; Laura Stein, an original member of the Halifax, Nova Scotia-based band Jale, on piano, keyboards, and vocals; and Boston native Mike Belitsky, also from Jale, on drums and percussion.

In July of 2000, after leaving Sub Pop to form his own Ashmont Records with friend Joyce Linehan, Pernice released the resonant album *Big Tobacco*. Along with some of the Pernice Brothers lineup—including Monahan, Pinkerton, and Stein—the recording featured additional help from Mike Daily of Whiskeytown, David Reid from Sea of Cortez, Gordon Zachasias from Fan Modine, Matt Hunter from New Radiant Storm King, Jeremy Smith of the New Harmful, and Anne Viebig from Tappan Zee.

With a stable lineup consisting of Joe and Bob Pernice, Monahan, Belitsky, Stein, and Pinkerton, the Pernice Brothers and other guests recorded *The World Won't End* at Rockland Heights in Northampton from May until October of 2000. The album was released in June of 2001 and was followed by an extensive tour of the United States and Europe. Despite a lack of major-label support, the Pernice Brothers have continued to experience a growing fanbase, especially in Great Britain and Japan. Still, Pernice knows that he will probably never become a pop star—but that's fine with him. "You've got to be on a major label to become a star," he told Klein, "but who wants that? To me, I couldn't think of anything more deplorable. I couldn't think of a worse way to live my life."

Selected discography

Scud Mountain Boys

Pine Box, Chunk, 1995.
Dance the Night Away, Chunk, 1995.
Massachusetts, Sub Pop, 1996.
The Early Years: Pine Box and Dance the Night Away, Sub Pop, 1997.

Pernice Brothers

Overcome By Happiness, Sub Pop, 1998.
e.p., Ashmont, 2000.
The World Won't End, Ashmont, 2001.

Joe Pernice

Chappaquiddick Skyline, Sub Pop, 2000.
Big Tobacco, Ashmont, 2000.

Sources

Books

Larkin, Colin, editor, *Virgin Encyclopedia of Indie & New Wave,* Virgin Books, 1998.

Periodicals

Boston Phoenix, February 21, 2000.
Esquire, September 1999.
New York Times, January 6, 1999; December 15, 2000.
Village Voice, June 9, 1998.
Wall Street Journal, November 10, 2000.
Washington Post, May 29, 1998.

Online

Billions Corporation, http://www.billions.com (April 2, 2001).
iVenus, http://www.ivenus.com (April 2, 2001).
NBCi, http://www.nbci.com (April 2, 2001).
Onion A.V. Club, http://www.theavclub.com (April 2, 2001).
Pernice Brothers Official Website, http://www.pernicebroth ers.com (April 2, 2001).
Sub Pop Records, http://www.subpop.com (April 2, 2001).

—Laura Hightower

P.O.D.

Rock group

Both in appearance and sound, P.O.D. belies the stereotype of the mild-mannered Contemporary Christian rock band. By combining a blistering sonic attack and streetwise attitude with fervent spiritual messages, they have reached out from their Christian fan base to attract a growing secular audience. In the process, they have earned considerable interest from the mainstream media through their ability to churn out hard-driving rock/hip-hop without losing their Bible-based message. The gold sales-level success of their 1999 CD, *The Fundamental Elements of Southtown*, confirmed the strength of P.O.D.'s genre-transcending appeal.

In the early 1990s, Marcos Curiel and Noah "Wuv" Bernardo, Jr. started their band in a gritty section of San Diego, California, known as South Bay or Southtown. Only a few miles from the United States-Mexico border, Southtown was populated by a mixture of Hispanics, Filipinos, blacks, and whites, and was considered to be a tough place, filled with drugs, gangs, and violence. Wuv and his cousin Sonny Sandoval grew up next door to one another in Southtown. They both experienced a harsh childhood. "Our dads were 15, 16 when they had us," Wuv explained to *Rolling Stone*'s Mark Binelli. "They were still kids, still doing their partying, and me and my cousin grew up in that scene. People used to break in and put my mom and dad down with a gun, looking for drugs." Wuv's parents separated and his father lived on the streets for three years, homeless and addicted to drugs. His dad finally turned his life around after attending a Christian music concert and converting to Christianity. Eventually the whole family converted. "We didn't grow up religious, in Christian homes. We came to find God later in life and we're grateful for it, so that's what we sing about," Wuv told Randy Lewis of the *Los Angeles Times.*

Sandoval turned to Christianity after his mother died of cancer. He had witnessed the comfort Christianity gave her and his other family members and decided it was time for him to change his life as well. Sandoval played hip-hop music with friends before his cousin, Wuv, invited him to join his group. But Sonny was a shy kid and not very comfortable in front of people. "He's one of those guys who'd take a lower grade on a paper just because he didn't wanna go in front of the class and read it," Wuv told Binelli. "At the band's first show, Sonny sang his lyrics from a sheet of paper with his back to the audience." Singing became the perfect outlet for Sandoval's grief. Such tracks as "Full Color" (on P.O.D.'s 1996 CD *Brown),* in particular, dealt with his mother's death and his spiritual conversion in powerful terms.

By 1993, the band had added bassist Traa (Mark Daniels), a Cleveland native who had been playing in a funk band led by Wuv's uncle. As its lineup solidified, the group adopted the name P.O.D., an acronym for Payable On Death. Wuv recalled in an interview with *CCM* writer Lou Carlozo that his wife-to-be had suggested the moniker: "She was working at a bank and she said, 'Why don't you call it Payable on Death? That's a banking term—it's a document that appoints everything left behind to another person, like a will.' We said, 'Yeah, that's just like what Jesus does with our sins.'"

P.O.D. quickly began to develop a local reputation for playing ferociously energetic live shows. Wuv's father financed their first three independent albums—*Snuff the Punk, Brown,* and *Live at TomFest.* The band performed almost anywhere they were invited—YMCAs, church basements, skate-parks, beds of pickup trucks, and even farms. They made a point of spending time with fans after their concerts and built up a loyal legion of devotees who took to calling themselves "The Warriors." "I'll spend hours talking after a show," Sonny stated on the group's official website. "That's what this band is about—we're just honored to have that kind of opportunity to connect with young people."

Although P.O.D. was growing in popularity, it was sometimes hard to see where fans were coming from. "When they started out, [Christian music audiences] absolutely hated them," Tim Cook, P.O.D.'s manager, told Lewis. "It was a group of multiethnic guys playing this Latin, reggae, hip-hop, real hard music, and people just hated it." On the other hand, they were losing gigs on the indie rock circuit because they pushed their religious beliefs too fervently on stage. The band began to change their approach in order to reach more

---

For the Record . . .

Members include **Marcos Curiel**, guitar; **Sonny Sandoval**, vocals; **Traa** (born Mark Daniels), bass; **Wuv** (born Noah Bernardo, Jr.), drums.

Group formed in San Diego, CA, 1992; released debut *Snuff the Punk* on own Rescue label, 1993; released *Brown* on Rescue, 1996 and *Live at TomFest* on Rescue, 1997; signed with Tooth & Nail and released EP *The Warriors*, 1999; signed with Atlantic and released *The Fundamental Elements of Southtown*, 1999.

Addresses: *Management*—Tim M. Cook/Cook Management, LLC, P.O. Box 1413, Bartlesville, OK 74005-1413. *Website*—P.O.D. Official Website: http://www.payableondeath.com.

people. "Every song might not say 'Jesus' in it," Marcos told *CCM* writer Gregory Rumberg. "It might not have a spiritual overtone, but the passion and emotion behind it, the chords—I'm playing that to the higher power above, which is God...."

P.O.D. got its big break in 1997 when the group captured the attention of John Rubeli of Atlantic Records while performing at a West Hollywood, California, showcase. Steadily building their grassroot support and word-of-mouth sales, they released *The Warriors* EP on the independent Tooth and Nail label before signing with Atlantic in 1999. With the release of *The Fundamental Elements of Southtown*, P.O.D. received accolades from both the rock community and such Christian music publications as *HM* and *7ball*. Band members pushed hard to have "Southtown" as their first single off the album, although the label preferred "Rock The Party (Off The Hook)," seeing it as more radio-friendly. As the single was building, Pat Martin, assistant program director of mainstream rock station KRXQ in Sacramento, California, remarked to *Billboard* writer Carla Hay about "Southtown's" staying power: "The song is hard and edgy, and it generates good phones. More than anything else, this band is getting popular because they've been generating a great street buzz."

Others recognized the band's growing popularity as well. "P.O.D. has had a strong word-of-mouth following from the beginning," Natalie Waleik, music buyer for Boston-based retail chain Newbury Comics told *Billboard*'s Hay. "Sales really started to take off for P.O.D. when they were on [nationally syndicated radio program] *The Howard Stern Show* in February, and sales have increased since then because there's more awareness for the band at radio and MTV."

P.O.D. signed on with a number of high-profile concert packages during 2000, including the Primus "Anti-Pop" tour and the Ozzfest 2000 tour. The latter concert engagement raised some controversy—Ozzfest's namesake, Ozzy Osbourne, was the former lead singer of Black Sabbath and had been associated with demonic imagery in rock music for nearly 30 years. Christian radio talk show host Dr. James Dobson accused P.O.D. of forsaking their religious beliefs; concerned evangelicals approached them at concerts and questioned their integrity. "A lot of Christian kids have a hard time understanding how we can go out into the world and play our music and get along with all these bands," Wuv told *CCM*'s Rumberg. "It's because of our love for God. God has been so real in our lives that we are enabled to do that. There is no way any band is going to rub off on P.O.D. more than P.O.D. is going to rub off on another band because ... we've already been there."

Winning comparisons with such mainstream rock acts as Rage Against The Machine, Limp Bizkit and Korn, P.O.D. increased its visibility by contributing to soundtracks for such films as *Blair Witch 2: Book of Shadows*, *Little Nicky,* and *Any Given Sunday*. Appearing on everything from MTV to Jay Leno to the *Howard Stern Show*, P.O.D. remained true to their beliefs no matter what the setting. "We play concerts full of [other bands'] acts telling kids to put their middle finger up in the air, sleep with women, and do all the drugs they can," Sandoval told *Revolver*. "When you get up and talk about love, people say, 'What do you mean? Rock and roll is about anarchy.' They say there's no room for God in rock. So you look at it and tell me who's the rebel. Who's the one looked down upon because of what he believes?" In his *Rolling Stone* interview with Binelli, Sandoval expanded on this theme, pointing out that "Ninety-five percent of Bob Marley's lyrics are straight Scripture. There's people walking around singing 'One Love,' and they have no idea it's Scripture. We come from the streets ... and we bring it to the kids tastefully. We don't come off all TV-evangelistic. That's how the world stereotypes Christians. We're just real people who love God."

In 2001, P.O.D. received several Dove Award nominations, including ones for Artist, Group, and Rock Recorded Song of the Year. Such recognition hasn't altered their priorities. "The most important thing, man, is my love and respect for God and what I believe to be true," Traa told *CCM*'s Rumberg. "My love and my respect for my wife and my family and the fact that P.O.D. is even out here is a privilege. All that keeps me straight." As their popularity continued to spread, the group affirmed its desire to testify to their personal faith rather than aggressively evangelize. "When I talk to someone who's not a Christian, they shouldn't feel automatically alienated," Sandoval told *Billboard*'s Hay. "We're not ashamed of our faith in God, because our faith is what motivates us to write music. We're not here to judge people or to say we're role models. We just say that this is what works for us, and if it works for you, that's great."

Selected discography

Snuff the Punk, Rescue, 1993.
Brown, Rescue, 1996.
Live at TomFest, Rescue, 1997.
The Warriors (EP), Tooth and Nail, 1999.
The Fundamental Elements of Southtown (includes "Southtown" and "Rock the Party"), Atlantic, 1999.
(Contributor) *Blair Witch 2: Book of Shadows* (soundtrack), Emd/Priority, 2000.
(Contributor) *Little Nicky* (soundtrack), Maverick, 2000.
(Contributor) *Any Given Sunday* (soundtrack), Wea/Atlantic, 2000.

Sources

Periodicals

Billboard, March 18, 2000; October 28, 2000, p. 27; February 24, 2001, p. 47.
CCM, March 2000, pp. 38-39; January 2001, pp. 24-29.
Christianity Today, January 8, 2001, pp. 90-91.
Los Angeles Times, August 27, 2000, p. 56.
Rolling Stone, March 30, 2000, p. 31; December 14-21, 2000, pp. 101, 103.
Wall Street Journal, February 28, 2001, p. B1.

Online

P.O.D. Official Website, http://www.payableondeath.com (April 21, 2001).

—*Janet Ingram*

Powderfinger

Rock group

Long before arriving on the music scene in the United States, Australia's Powderfinger made a huge impression on fans in its home country. Since forming in 1990, the multiplatinum rockers have brought home armfuls of awards, and in early 2001, Australian *Rolling Stone* named the quartet its Band of the Year, *Odyssey Number Five* as Best Album, and "My Happiness" as Best Single.

Success has not come easily for the group, however. Powderfinger, which hails from the musical melting pot of Brisbane, Australia, began its career as a three-member group in 1990 with John Collins on bass, Ian Haug on guitar, and Steven Bishop on drums. At the University of Queensland, the threesome met Bernard Fanning and Jon Coghill (who replaced Bishop), and later connected with Darren Middleton. The do-it-yourself work ethic was strong within the group. Its members paid for the 1,500 copies of *Powderfinger Blue* EP, all of which quickly sold out. The success of *Powderfinger Blue,* as well as that of the group's sophomore EP effort *Transfusion,* led to a deal with Polydor Records.

The band's debut EP, *Parables for Wooden Ears*, was not met with as much praise. Produced by Tony Cohen, who has worked with Nick Cave and the Bad Seeds, and The Cruel Sea, the album was panned by critics as well as the band members themselves who called it pretentious and unfocused. Nevertheless, Powderfinger toured Australia relentlessly with large American acts, namely the Screaming Trees, Soundgarden, and one-hit-wonder Urge Overkill.

To make amends, of sorts, for the *Parables for Wooden Ears*, Powderfinger released a much-improved second album, *Double Allergic*, which debuted at number seven on the Australian album charts. Real Groove online critic Kevin Byrt described it as proof of "a band trying to learn from past mistakes, showcasing a selection of more melody-based tunes with arrangements that suggest commercial leanings from within the band." Powderfinger produced the album itself with the help of Tim Whitten.

The first single, "Pick You Up," was picked up by the Australian radio youth network, Triple J. The follow-up single, "D.A.F."—which stands for the first three chords of the song—was also a radio hit. Adhering to its usual touring practices, Powderfinger traveled throughout Australia playing headlining gigs and big-name festivals such as the Big Day Out, Livid, and Homebake. The group's ultimate tour achievement, however, was a performance at the Crowded House Farewell Concert on the steps of the Sydney Opera House in front of more than 150,000 people in 1996.

Powderfinger then took a break to recuperate from touring and rethink its musical mission. The band members wrote on their own and then headed to Melbourne's Sing Sing Studios with American producer Nick DiDia, whose credits include work with Brad, Rage Against the Machine, Pearl Jam, Local H, and Ben Folds Five. The result was *Internationalist*, which dabbles in surf ("Don't Wanna Be Left Out") and even acoustic rock ("Trading Places"). Fanning explained in Powderfinger's biography on Sonicnet that the group's album, which debuted at number one, was "worth the wait. It always seems to come from a natural, organic progression.... Because everything was written over such a long time, there is no real theme to the album, except for making sure it had space."

The plan worked. Polydor called *Internationalist* "more than a leap forward for the five-piece, it's a horizontal stretch outward, a musical exploration of the sounds and times that surround us." *Internationalist* earned critical acclaim at the Australian Record Industry Association Awards (ARIA), winning Album of the Year, Best Rock Album, Best Cover Artwork, and Record/Single of the Year for "Day You Come." In May of 2000, ARIA dubbed Powderfinger Best Group for 1999, and "These Days" was awarded Song of the Year at the 2000 Music Industry Critics' Awards. Later that month, Powderfinger also received an Australia Performing Rights Association Award for Song of the Year for "Passenger." The group received the same award in 2001 for "My Happiness" from its fourth studio album, *Odyssey Number Five*.

While recording *Odyssey Number Five* at Sing Sing Studios, Powderfinger avoided the use of high technol-

For the Record . . .

Members include **Steven Bishop** (joined group, 1989; left group, 1992), drums; **Jon Coghill** (joined group, c. 1992), drums; **John Collins**, bass; **Bernard Fanning** (joined group, c. 1992), vocals; **Ian Haug**, guitar, vocals; **Darren Middleton** (joined group, c. 1992), guitar, keyboards, vocals.

Formed in Brisbane, Australia, 1990; self-released debut EP *Powderfinger Blue*, 1993; signed with Polydor, released *Parables for Wooden Ears*, 1994; released *Double Allergic,* 1996; released *Internationalist,* 1998; released *Odyssey Number Five* in Australia, 2000, and in the U.S., 2001.

Awards: Australian Record Industry Awards (ARIA) for Album of the Year, Best Rock Album, Best Artwork for *Internationalist*, and Song of the Year for "The Day You Come," 1999; Music Industry Critics' Awards for Best Group and Song of the Year for "These Days, " 2000; Australia Performing Rights Association Award (APRA), Song of the Year for "Passenger," 2000; Australian *Rolling Stone*'s Band of the Year, 2001; Australia Performing Rights Association Award, Song of the Year for "My Happiness," 2001.

Addresses: *Record company*—Universal Music Group, 1755 Broadway, New York, NY 10019, phone: (212) 373-0600, fax: (212) 373-0660, website: http://www.umusic.com. *Website*—Powderfinger Official Website: http://www.powderfinger.com.

ogy. The group, who again teamed with producer DiDia, chose analog sounds over computer-enhanced music. The album debuted at number one on the ARIA charts. "We thought, 'What are the best 11 songs that are going to make this a really good album?'" Coghill explained at the group's official website. "We weren't thinking whether each song was going to be a great song, we just wanted to make it a full album of really good listening, that you could listen to all the way through and not have anything stick out like it's out of place." The first single, "My Happiness," is a reflection of the band's years on the road. "We spend a lot of time away from home because we're a touring band. You're kind of absent from the thing or the people you love. It's really hard on you mentally and physically in a lot of ways. It's that feeling where you know you're going to

be home soon, but it just keeps taking another couple of days, and you're counting it down," Fanning told *Billboard* magazine.

The album immediately struck a chord with the public. "These Days," which was voted number one on Australia's youth radio network Triple J's Hottest 100 Poll in 1999, was on the soundtrack to the movie *Two Hands*, and "My Kind of Scene" appeared on the *Mission Impossible II* soundtrack. Mitch Braund, the assistant music director at Brisbane, Australia's top 40 station Triple M, told *Billboard*, "When listeners fax in their requests, there's usually a Powderfinger song in there somewhere."

Despite all the success, Fanning told Australia's *Rolling Stone* that Powderfinger is not in it for the celebrity. "We're a band. We write songs. We're not celebrities. We don't go out of our way to get publicity. I admit that it's not really possible to be in a rock band without being some kind of personality, but the whole concept for us is about writing songs," he said. "We like touring and playing in front of people, but it's not as much fun as writing songs, it's just part of the job."

Selected discography

Parables for Wooden Ears, Polydor Records (Australia), 1994.
Double Allergic, Polydor Records (Australia), 1996.
Internationalist, Polydor/Grudge (Australia), 1998.
(Contributor) *Two Hands* (soundtrack), Festi, 1999.
(Contributor) *Mission Impossible II* (soundtrack), Hollywood, 2000.
Odyssey Number Five, Grudge (Australia), 2000; Republic/Universal Records (U.S.), 2001.

Sources

Periodicals

Billboard (Australia), April 2001.

Online

Australian Broadcasting Corporation, http://www.abc.net.au/rage/guest/2000/powderfinger.htm (May 29, 2001).
"Double Allergic," Real Groove, http://www.realgroove.xtra.co.nz/47-197/reviews/197-powderfinger-double_allergic.html (May 29, 2001).
The Odyssey, http://web.one.net.au/~stooch/albums/albums.html (May 29, 2001).
"Powderfinger," Sonicnet, http://www.sonicnet.com/artists/ai_bio.jhtml?ai_id=509597 (May 29, 2001).
"Powderfinger," Yahoo! Music, http://au.travel.yahoo.com/music/profiles/mono181.html (May 28, 2001).
"Powderfinger, Killing Heidi Top Oz APRA Awards," *Billboard.com*, http://www.billboard.com (June 6, 2001).

Powderfinger Official Website, http://www.powderfinger.com (May 29, 2001).

Additional information was provided by Universal Records publicity materials, 2001.

—*Christina Fuoco*

Riders in the Sky

Western music group

Every time they step on stage, Riders in the Sky give their audience an enthusiastic greeting: "Mighty fine and a great big Western 'Howdy,' all you buckaroos and buckarettes!" Dressed like singing cowboys from the Saturday morning serials of the 1930s and 1940s, their music honors the tradition of such movie heroes as Roy Rogers and Gene Autry. While their respect for the genre has earned Riders the appreciation of Western music aficionados, their sense of humor has spread their appeal to other audiences, especially children. Their talent for sketch comedy has earned them several stints as hosts of radio and television series. All their audiences have amply awarded them. Besides several awards from Western music associations, they won a Grammy Award for Best Musical Album for Children in 2000 with *Woody's Roundup, Featuring Riders in the Sky,* an album that grew out of their work on the soundtrack for the film *Toy Story 2.*

Musical cowboy may not have been the first career choice for any of the Riders. All three members had earned graduate degrees in other fields before turning to music. When he was merely Doug Green, vocalist and guitarist Ranger Doug earned a master's degree in literature. Vocalist and bass player Too Slim did the

Photograph by Sam Mircovich. Archive Photos, Inc. Reproduced by permission.

same in the study of wildlife management when he was only known as Fred LaBour, and Woody Paul, King of the Cowboy Fiddlers, was just Paul Chrisman, Ph. D., having received a doctorate in theoretical plasma physics from the Massachusetts Institute of Technology (MIT). Ranger Doug described the trio as "the most needlessly educated guys in America" to Michael Vaughn of *Metro Santa Cruz*. All three left other pursuits behind, though, to join the music scene in Nashville, Tennessee. Green worked as a writer, editor, and historian for the Country Music Foundation, while LaBour played with country singer Dicky Lee's band before they teamed up to start Riders in the Sky.

Champions of Traditional Western Music

Riders in the Sky formed at a time when traditional Western music had almost disappeared from a Nashville scene that had become dominated by the outlaw country commonly associated with Waylon Jennings and Willie Nelson. The group made their debut performance in 1977 at a Nashville night spot called Herr Harry's Phranks 'n' Steins. Soon they were performing weekly at Wind in the Willows, a bluegrass club. While Green and LaBour were mainstays, the group didn't have much luck keeping a fiddler until 1978 when Chrisman stepped in. After catching a performance, he approached the other members and told them, "You boys really need me to help you out," according to Craig Havighurst in the *Wall Street Journal*. They accepted his offer, and with his transformation into Woody Paul, the Riders' lineup was set.

Shortly thereafter, the trio signed a recording contract with the Rounder label. Their 1979 album *Three on the Trail* exhibited the mix of music and humor characteristic of Riders in the Sky throughout their history. According to reviewer Thom Owens of *All Music Guide*, "[T]he music is often quite good and they never deviated from this formula—slightly ironic covers, affectionate jokes and made-to-order originals." The track "How the Yodel Was Born" showed how they could give a great musical performance while making a joke. The song attributes the origins of yodeling to a cowboy who landed the wrong way on his saddle horn, but this simple joke provided Green with the opportunity to run through a series of intricate, up-tempo yodels while Chrisman accompanied him on the fiddle with snippets from the *Popeye* theme, a jig, and even a little Mozart.

While active in the recording studio during the 1980s, the full Riders in the Sky experience emerged in their live performances. Wearing their B-movie cowboy outfits, the trio freely interspersed their music with comic skits. Each member developed characters beyond his Riders' persona. For instance, besides being Too Slim, LaBour, the main skit writer, also developed the characters of Too Jaws, a talking horse skull, and Side Meat, a camp cook who would become infamous for his inedible biscuits. Their unique performances brought Riders in the Sky opportunities to perform in new venues. In 1982 they became members of the Grand Ole Opry, making them a staple of the legendary showcase of country and western music. Their music and humor fit well with the atmosphere of Garrison Kieler's *Prairie Home Companion* on National Public Radio (NPR), where they became frequent guests. Even Hollywood caught on to Riders in the Sky, leading to movie roles, most notably in *Sweet Dreams*, the 1985 film biography of country singer Patsy Cline. They even became hosts of a television series, *Tumbleweed Theater*, a daily showing of classic cowboy movies that ran on The Nashville Network (TNN) from 1983-1986.

Comedy Appealed to Children

While all these various programs had primarily adult audiences, Riders in the Sky's comedy also endeared them to children. According to Sheila Daughtry of *Dirty Linen* magazine, "Kids laugh at the silliness and slapstick while their parents chortle at political and cultural zingers whizzing over the kids' heads." In 1985 the trio rewarded their young fans with an album just for them, *Saddle Pals.* It subsequently earned an award as the Independent Children's Album of the Year.

With their exposure on radio, television, and film, along with their nearly perpetual touring—around 200 live performances per year—the Riders finally caught the attention of a major record label. When they released *The Cowboy Way* on MCA in 1987, it was the first album of Western music that the label had released in 20 years, and the first Western album to be recorded digitally. Their next album, *Riders Radio Theater,* took the form of an old-time radio show, mixing skits and commercial parodies with the music. They then took this format to start an actual radio show with the same name, which ran on NPR from 1988-96. For this endeavor they brought on board accordionist Joey Miskulin, better known as Joey The Cowpolka King. He became a regular performer on their recordings, too, even working as their producer.

Riders in the Sky also kept busy performing for children during this time. In 1991, their Saturday morning show *Riders in the Sky* premiered on CBS. According to *Country Music: The Encyclopedia,* Green said at the time, "There's going to be three middle-aged, non-mutant singing cowboys on TV." The show only lasted for one season, and it put Riders in the Sky in the unusual situation of performing scripts that they didn't write themselves. Still, it led to the release of the compilation album *Saturday Morning with Riders in the Sky.*

Explored New Musical Territory

Throughout the 1990s, Riders' albums continued their mix of homage to their musical forebears and their trademark humor. Always working within the tradition of Western music, they continued to explore new territories. *Cowboys in Love,* released in 1994, consisted entirely of Western ballads and love songs, with guests such as Emmylou Harris and Western swing band Asleep at the Wheel joining them on traditional numbers. But the Riders couldn't resist a few humorous originals, such as "You're Wearing Out Your Welcome, Matt," a song addressed to the hero of the long-running Western television series *Gunsmoke,* reprimanding him for never marrying saloon-keeper Miss Kitty. Released in 1996, *Public Cowboy # 1: The Music of Gene Autry,* though, maintained its dignity throughout, as the group performed nothing but songs made famous by

the legendary singing cowboy on their first album without any original compositions. In 1999 *Christmas the Cowboy Way* featured such diverse selections as a twelfth-century hymn, a song entitled "The Prairie Dog's Christmas Ball," and a version of "Let It Snow, Let It Snow, Let it Snow" that incorporated a medley of Christmas songs to show that all holiday songs derive from this one.

Riders in the Sky's next big success started out as one song and turned into an album. A fan of theirs working for Disney studios recommended them to sing the Western song "Woody's Roundup," written by Randy Newman for the animated film *Toy Story 2.* Impressed with the result, Disney commissioned Riders to do an entire album based in part on the cowboy toys that were characters in the movie. The result was the Grammy Award-winning *Woody's Roundup, Featuring Riders in the Sky,* produced by their long-time sideman Miskulin.

The Grammy Award was a crowning achievement for Riders in the Sky, who for years had lobbied for the creation of a separate category for Western music. Although frequently nominated in the country music category, they had never been able to win in a category dominated by the Nashville sound. But in true Riders fashion, the band didn't rest on its laurels. While still performing together, they started on side projects. Green released a solo album, *Songs of the Sage,* in 1997, and Chrisman and Miskulin made plans to release *A Pair of Kings,* backed by Green and LaBour. In addition, the group was slated to appear in *TWANG,* an IMAX movie celebrating country music.

Selected discography

Three on the Trail, Rounder, 1979.
Cowboy Jubilee, Rounder, 1981.
Prairie Serenade, Rounder, 1982.
Weeds & Water, Rounder, 1983.
New Trails, Rounder, 1986.
Saddle Pals, Rounder, 1987.
The Cowboy Way, MCA, 1987; reissued, MCA, 1991.
The Best of the West, Rounder, 1987.
Riders Radio Theater, MCA, 1988.
Horse Opera, MCA, 1990.
Riders in the Sky, Live, Rounder, 1991.
Harmony Ranch, Columbia, 1991.
Merry Christmas from Harmony Ranch, Columbia, 1992.
Saturday Morning with Riders, MCA, 1992.
Cowboys in Love, Columbia, 1994.
Always Drink Upstream from the Herd, Rounder, 1995.
Public Cowboy # 1: The Music of Gene Autry, Rounder, 1996.
Yodel the Cowboy Way, Easydisc, 1998.
A Great Big Western Howdy from Riders in the Sky, Rounder, 1998.
Christmas the Cowboy Way, Rounder, 1999.
Woody's Roundup, Featuring Riders in the Sky, Disney, 2000.
(Contributor) *Toy Story 2* (soundtrack), Disney, 2000.

Sources

Books

Kingsbury, Paul, editor, *The Encyclopedia of Country Music: The Ultimate Guide to the Music,* Oxford University Press, 1998.

McCloud, Barry, *Definitive Country: The Ultimate Encyclopedia of Country Music and Its Performers,* Perigee, 1995.

Stambler, Irwin, and Grelun Landon, *Country Music: The Encyclopedia,* St. Martin's Press, 1997.

Wolf, Kurt, *Country Music: The Rough Guide,* Rough Guides Ltd., 2000.

Periodicals

Billboard, November 13, 1999, p. 34; July 29, 2000, p. 35; December 2, 2000, p. 44.

Dirty Linen, June/July 1997.

Metro Santa Cruz, March 28, 1996.

People, December 13, 1999, p. 58.

USA Today, February 22, 2001, p. 1D.

Wall Street Journal, January 18, 200, p. A24.

Online

"News from Harmony Ranch," Riders in the Sky Official *Website,* http://www.ridersinthesky.com (April 3, 2001).

"Riders in the Sky," *All Music Guide,* http://www.allmusic.com (April 3, 2001).

"Riders in the Sky," iMusic, http://imusic.com (April 3, 2001).

—Lloyd Hemingway

Wallace Roney

Trumpeter

Trumpeter Wallace Roney began playing in top-notch bands in 1979, recorded with jazz legends Tony Williams and Art Blakey in the mid '80s, and received critical accolades for his performance with Miles Davis at the 1991 Montreux Jazz Festival in Switzerland. "I think the thing I like the most about Wallace's playing," Wynton Marsalis told Ed Enright of *Down Beat,* "is the incorruptibility that's in his sound." Like trumpeters Marsalis, Terence Blanchard, Roy Hargrove, and Philip Harper, Roney came to the jazz scene in the 1980s and became known as one of the "young lions." This articulate and well-dressed group of young men drew their inspiration from earlier styles of jazz, especially hard-bop and post-bop. While the world of jazz sometimes appears seamy to outsiders, the professional demeanor of these young men helped to clean up this negative image. Being a young lion didn't translate into critical or monetary success for Roney, however. Only after endless hard work and a number of lean years would Roney begin to receive wider attention.

Wallace Roney was born in Philadelphia, Pennsylvania, on May 25, 1960. By the age of five, he had picked up his first trumpet; at seven, his father bought him his first horn and made sure that he had lessons; at 12, he performed with the Philadelphia Brass Ensemble at the Philadelphia Settlement Music School. In the early '70s he moved with his father and siblings to Washington, D.C., where he was enrolled in the Duke Ellington School for the Performing Arts. He developed a love for Miles Davis, wearing out his 45 RPM record of "Filles de Kilimanjaro" and practicing the master's solos while still in his teens. Upon graduation, Roney declined an opportunity to attend the prestigious Juilliard School, choosing Howard University instead. In 1979 he joined pianist Abdullah Ibrahim's big band for a summer European tour; he toured Europe again in 1980, with Art Blakey. He returned to Boston in 1981, attending the Berklee School of Music until he read in the *Village Voice* that Marsalis was leaving Blakey's Jazz Messengers. Roney wanted his position. He knew the Messengers would be playing a stint at the Bottom Line in New York City, so for Roney there was only one thing to do: sell everything. "My television, my comic books, school books, my trumpet," he told James McBride of the *Washington Post.* "I had to get to New York that day."

While he did get a job touring with Blakey for a few months, followed by a year-long job with Chico Freeman, Roney also spent years scrounging for work. He lived frugally, sleeping on the floors of friends' apartments and generally "wearing out my welcome," he recalled to McBride. In 1983 his future began to look brighter—at least temporarily. While taking part in a tribute to Miles Davis at the Bottom Line in Manhattan, he actually got to meet his idol. "He [Davis] asked me what kind of trumpet I had," Roney told *Time,* "and I told him none. So he gave me one of his." Throughout two dismal years in '84 and '85 he was forced to play in

For the Record . . .

Born on May 25, 1960, in Philadelphia, PA; father, Wallace Roney Jr. (a police detective); brother, Antoine Roney (a saxophonist); sister, Crystal; married pianist Geri Allen, 1995. *Education*: Attended Howard University, 1978, and Berklee College of Music, 1981.

Began playing trumpet at age five; performed with the Philadelphia Brass Ensemble at 12; attended Duke Ellington High School for the Performing Arts as a teenager, graduated, 1978; toured Europe with Abdullah Ibrahim and Art Blakey, 1979-80; played and recorded with Tony Williams Quintet, mid 1980s; recorded debut, *Verses,* for Muse, 1987; performed Montreux Jazz Festival in Switzerland beside Miles Davis, 1991; signed to Warner Bros., released *Misterios,* 1994; recorded *No Room for Argument* for Concord, 2000.

Awards: Named Best Young Jazz Musician of the Year by *Down Beat,* 1979; won the *Down Beat* Critic's Poll for Best Trumpeter to Watch, 1990.

Addresses: *Record company*—32 Records, 250 West 57th Street, Suite 620, New York, NY 10107. *Record company*—Concord Jazz, P.O. Box 845, Concord, CA 94522, (925) 682-3508, website: http://www.concord records.com.

invitation to tour with Herbie Hancock, Wayne Shorter, Ron Carter, and Tony Williams in the Miles Davis Tribute Band in 1992 and to his involvement in a recreation of the "Birth of the Cool" sessions the same year.

While these opportunities certainly raised Roney's profile, they also led to a certain typecasting. The tone and color of Roney's horn has often—perhaps too often—been compared to Miles Davis's. Other jazz musicians have faced similar dilemmas: Sonny Stitt was labeled as another Charlie Parker, John Faddis as another Dizzy Gillespie. "I'm never going to run from Miles," Roney told Fred Shuster of *Down Beat.* "But writers don't have to introduce me and my music to the audience in the context of Miles every single time." To better understand Roney's music, one has to listen to it against the backdrop of the musical innovations that took place in jazz during the mid 1960s. With the style generally referred to as post-bop, a number of musicians began inserting open structures and new chord progressions into their music. They utilized unusual time signatures, allowing drummers and bass players to take prominent roles. This shift allowed talented musicians like Ron Carter and Tony Williams to come forward and form their own bands. While these innovations had endless possibilities for exploration, many musicians moved on as fusion began to dominate the jazz scene in the late '60s. From early in Roney's career, he has sought out musicians who have deep roots in hard-bop and post-bop. Roney has simply made the choice, as many of the young lions did, to return to that golden era of the mid '60s in order to further explore its myriad ideas.

In 1994 Roney received a multiple album contract from Warner Bros. *Misterios,* his debut for the label, found him stretching boundaries by including Brazilian rhythms and strings. He maintained a busy touring schedule, playing dates at the Village Vanguard in New York, Scullers in Boston, and the Jazz Showcase in Chicago. He also traveled to Italy, France, and Portugal for a number of summer festivals. Between recording dates and touring he found time to marry his longtime musical partner, pianist Geri Allen, on May 12, 1995. On 1997's *Village,* and even more so on 2000's *No Room for Argument,* Roney began to incorporate ideas from late-'60s fusion. These albums include synthesizers and electric pianos along with saxophone, piano, and trumpet, creating a spacious and layered sound. "We are trying to play in a way that will open up the music," he told Roberta Penn of the *Seattle Post Intelligencer* concerning his current experiments. His willingness to push boundaries and surround himself with the best contemporary jazz musicians guarantees that Wallace Roney will continue to be a fresh and vital artist.

Latin dance and reception bands. The New York clubs, once a prominent part of the jazz scene, had mostly disappeared. The skies began to clear in 1986 when Roney received two calls—within one month—to tour with two jazz legends: drummers Tony Williams and Art Blakey.

Roney recorded his debut, *Verses,* for Muse in 1987. He also became a central part of the Tony Williams Quintet, touring and recording with the group until it broke up in the early '90s. For Roney, 1991 and 1992 proved to be watershed years. First, he received an invitation from Miles Davis to play at his side during the 1991 Montreux Jazz Festival. "I was soloing on 'Springsville,'" Roney told Zan Stewart of the *Los Angeles Times,* "and after I finished, he [Davis] tapped me on the arm and said, 'Play this tomorrow on the gig.'" The music was later issued as *Miles and Quincy, Live at Montreux,* won a Grammy Award, and let the jazz world know that Roney had arrived. It led to an

Selected discography

Verses, Muse, 1987.
Crunchin', Muse, 1993.
Misterios, Warner Bros., 1994.
Village, Warner Bros., 1997.
No Job Too Big or Small, 32 Jazz, 1999.
No Room for Argument, Concord Jazz, 2000.

Sources

Down Beat, August 1996, p. 48; May 1, 1998, p. 30.
Los Angeles Times, August 16, 1992, p. 6.
Seattle Post Intelligencer, April 10, 1998, p. 7.
Time, September 19, 1994, p. 76.
Washington Post, December 12, 1987, p. D1.

—Ronnie D. Lankford, Jr.

Royal Crown Revue

Swing group

Photograph by Michael Farr. © Warner Bros. Records. Reproduced by permission.

Royal Crown Revue debuted in 1989 and ignited a full-on swing revival—a music-and-fashion fad that recalled a "time gone by." The group laid the groundwork for the swing revival of the 1990s that was epitomized by vintage 1940s clothes and energetic musical blends of traditional swing, jump-boogie, hot jazz, bebop, and rock. Swing revival bands Big Bad Voodoo Daddy, the Cherry Poppin' Daddies, Squirrel Nut Zippers, and the Brian Setzer Orchestra all rode the wave that filled clubs with jumping, jiving, jitterbugging fans, and for a time, inspired film, fashion, media, and advertising.

Former punk vocalist Eddie Nichols and guitarist James Achor first met in a Los Angeles, California, rockabilly band called the Rockomatics. By the late 1980s, Los Angeles punk and rockabilly were dead, Achor said in an interview with the *Washington Post.* So he and Nichols teamed up with tenor saxophone player Mando Dorame who was a fan of "screaming" saxophone players like Big Jay McNeely. The three "decided it was time for something completely different," according to Side 1 Records publicity materials. The trio developed a hybrid of musical styles from the past and present, and added bassist Veikko Lepisto, baritone saxophonist Bill Ungerman, trumpeter Scott Steen, and drummer Daniel Glass. The group would pioneer the new swing, or neo-swing, revival. By the time they started playing in 1989, the group had a ready-made audience at the Club Deluxe, the "first retro-swing hangout in the nation," according to Michael Moss, publisher of *Swing Time* magazine, in the *Washington Post.* In 1991, Royal Crown Revue released its debut album, *Kings of Gangster Bop,* on the independent record label Better Youth.

In 1993, Royal Crown Revue began a residency at a newly renovated nightclub in Hollywood, California. The Derby was a stylish setting for the group's high-energy stage show, and for two years, the house was regularly packed. It was at the Derby that Royal Crown Revue was discovered by the makers of the 1994 comedy *The Mask* starring Jim Carrey and Cameron Diaz. The band performed their swinging "Hey Pachuco!" in the film, "providing neo-swing's first mainstream break," according to Richard Harrington in the *Washington Post.* Young writer and actor John Favreau was also taken by the jumping revival action at the Derby, and used the club as inspiration for his 1996 film *Swingers.* Royal Crown Revue appeared in the film, as did fellow neo-swing band Big Bad Voodoo Daddy.

After being discovered at the Derby, the band was signed to Warner Bros. Records in 1995 and released their major-label debut, *Mugzy's Move,* in 1996. "Hey Pachuco!" appeared on the record, alongside songs about Hollywood street life, gangsters, and a "time gone by—when women were sultry, men cool, and cars and music hot," according to Royal Crown Re-

Members include **James Achor**, guitar; **Mando Dorame**, tenor saxophone; **Daniel Glass**, drums; **Veikko Lepisto**, bass; **Eddie Nichols**, vocals; **Scott Steen**, trumpet; **Bill Ungerman**, baritone saxophone.

Released debut album, *Kings of Gangster Bop*, on independent label Better Youth, 1991; signed to Warner Bros. Records, 1995; released *Mugzy's Move*, 1996; *Caught in the Act*, a live record on the Surf Dog label, produced cult hit "Barflies at the Beach," 1997; second album for Warner Bros., *The Contender*, featured single "Zip Gun Bop (Reloaded)," 1998; released *Walk on Fire*, 1999.

Addresses: *Record company*—Side 1 Records, 6201 Sunset Blvd. Ste. 211, Hollywood, CA 90028, (323) 951-9090. *Website*—Royal Crown Revue Official Website http://www.rcr.com.

vue's press materials. The album peaked at number four on *Billboard*'s Top Jazz Albums chart.

Donned in the sharp, flashy, double-breasted zoot suits, high-waisted pants, gabardine shirts, fedora hats, loud ties, and spectator shoes of the swing era, Royal Crown Revue was a sight to behold. Singer Nichols and the rest of the band "are walking homages to the tough guys of '40s film and that era's jazz musicians of Harlem and Los Angeles," according to critic Ben Ratliff in the *New York Times*.

If their vintage fashions came directly from the swing era, the music was a bit more diverse in its roots. Like that of other neo-swing bands, wrote Steve Appleford in the *Los Angeles Times*, Royal Crown Revue's sound was "a closer cousin to rockabilly than to the visionary likes of Duke Ellington and Benny Goodman." The group's self-described "hard-boiled swing" was less like the smooth, melodic dance tunes of the 1930s and early 1940s, and more like the more aggressive jump blues played by Cab Calloway, Louis Jordan, and Louis Prima during the 1940s and 1950s. Though they freely mixed "traditional swing and jump blues, hot jazz and bebop, honky-tonk and western swing, boogie-woogie, blues, and rock," Harrington wrote, the result fit Count Basie's definition of swing as anything "you can really pat your foot by."

It was with their live shows that Royal Crown Revue really wowed fans. They were a "hard-touring band radiant with professionalism," Ratliff wrote. They played with a "contagious enthusiasm," according to *People,* that infected their fans. Their sets were consistently aggressive, energetic blends of mostly original jump-boogie songs and some bebop standards. Revival swing fans flocked to see them, first in Los Angeles and San Francisco, then as they toured across the United States. In addition to touring relentlessly, they performed live on *Late Night with Conan O'Brien,* the *Today Show,* and the *Billboard Music Awards.* They appeared on the Warped Tour and at the Playboy, Concord, and Saratoga jazz festivals. In 1997, they landed a six-night-per-week residency at the Las Vegas Desert Inn. The group released a live record, *Caught in the Act,* which generated the cult hit, "Barflies at the Beach," in 1997.

Though called "the godfathers of the current swing renaissance" by Harrington, the band did not receive as much radio airplay or media attention as the Cherry Poppin' Daddies, Squirrel Nut Zippers, or the Brian Setzer Orchestra. A popular television spot for clothing merchant the Gap, set to Louis Prima's swinging classic "Jump, Jive, and Wail," really got the revival rolling. The Cherry Poppin' Daddies scored the only top 40 radio hit of the revival. MTV helped push the Daddies' "Zoot Suit Riot" and Squirrel Nut Zippers' "Hell" to the forefront, and VH1 promoted the Brian Setzer Orchestra.

In 1998, Royal Crown Revue released *The Contender,* which featured the single "Zip Gun Bop (Reloaded)." With the record, the group finally received the credit it deserved, according to Bill Holdship in the *Los Angeles Times.* But the critic also noted that certain aspects of the record seemed "too campy to transcend mere faddism." Shortly after, the revival began to fade. Like countless music-and-fashion fads before it, the neo-swing explosion finally petered out, though some hard-core fans remained.

Selected discography

Kings of Gangster Bop, Better Youth, 1991.
(Contributor) *The Mask* (soundtrack), MCA, 1994.
Mugzy's Move, Warner Bros., 1996.
Caught in the Act (live), Surf Dog, 1997.
The Contender, Warner Bros., 1998.
Hay Santa, Better Youth, 1998.
Walk on Fire, RCR/Side 1, 1999.
(Contributor) *Three to Tango* (soundtrack), Atlantic, 1999.

Sources

Periodicals

Billboard, November 1, 1997, p. 18.
Los Angeles Times, September 6, 1998, p. 58; October 3, 1998, p. 6.
New York Times, June 29, 1999, p. 5.

People, July 8, 1996, p. 23.
Washington Post, October 26, 1998, p. B1; October 31, 1998, p. B3.

Online

"Royal Crown Revue," *All Music Guide,* http://www.allmus ic.com (March 30, 2001).
Royal Crown Revue Official Website, http://www.rcr.com (May 14, 2001).

Additional information was provided by the Side 1 Records publicity department, 2001.

—Brenna Sanchez

Don Sebesky

Composer, arranger

With 22 Grammy Award nominations and three Grammy wins to his credit, composer and arranger Don Sebesky has made his mark on music from the big jazz bands of the 1960s and some of the classic jazz recordings of the 1970s, to stage, film, and television. A wildly prolific artist, Sebesky gave up the trombone to dedicate himself fully to composing and arranging, specializing in orchestra music, particularly swing, big band, and jazz. The "versatile and quite often moving" composer-arranger, according to *Down Beat,* has released more than eight albums, including the Grammy-winning *I Remember Bill: A Tribute to Bill Evans* and *Joyful Noise: A Tribute to Duke Ellington.* He also authored the book *The Contemporary Arranger*, published in 1975.

Born on December 10, 1937, in Perth Amboy, New Jersey, Sebesky was voted "Most Musical" and "Ideal High School Boy" in high school. He studied trombone in high school and played on weekends in New York City with Warren Covington. His first composition, arrangement, and trombone solos were recorded in 1954 with Covington. After graduating from high school in 1955, he attended the Manhattan School of Music on scholarship where he studied music composition. In 1958, he joined the Kai Winding Septet, replacing Carl Fontana. Also that year, he joined the Maynard Ferguson Orchestra, with which he recorded many of his compositions, arrangements, and solos until 1964. It was with Ferguson that Sebesky was first noticed as a writer. He became part of the Stan Kenton Orchestra in 1959, recording three albums with the group. In 1960,

he played with the Claude Thornhill Orchestra and Gerry Mulligan Concert Jazz Band.

Sebesky gave up playing trombone and devoted himself completely to composing and arranging in 1960. Among the vocalists and instrumentalists he worked for during the early 1960s were Hugo Montenegro, Carmen McRae, Andre Kostelanetz, and the Tommy Dorsey Orchestra. He broke into television in 1965 when he joined the writing staff of the *Jimmy Dean Show* on ABC-TV. He composed the show's theme and all its arrangements and was music director from 1967-68.

Sebesky would go on to write extensively for television and film. He composed music for *Allegra's Window* on Nickelodeon, the soap operas *Guiding Light* and *Edge of Night,* the Emmy-nominated *Irving Berlin 100th Birthday,* and the Public Broadcasting System (PBS) special *A Sondheim Celebration at Carnegie Hall,* among others. In addition to composing for television programs, he was called on heavily for his award-winning commercial arrangements and jingles. He has written the jingles behind television ads for Hanes, Hallmark, Ford, Nike, Hershey's, Duracell, and Cheerio's, and won Clio advertising awards for tunes composed for Corning, General Electric, and Calvin Klein. Sebesky enjoyed taking on short-term commercial projects, he said in an interview with *Shoot.* "The good part about it is that I'm always working on [other] long-term projects," he said. "Commercials are relatively short-lived. I definitely like the variety."

Sebesky got his start in film by composing the score for Muppet-creator Jim Henson's Academy Award-nominated short film, *Time Piece,* in 1968. Among the many films he would later score or arrange for were *The Rosary Murders,* starring Donald Sutherland, in 1988, *The People Next Door,* starring Eli Wallach and Julie Harris, and the Chet Baker documentary *Let's Get Lost.*

The year 1968 marked the beginning of what arguably was Sebesky's most notable musical affiliation. Sebesky joined producer Creed Taylor and ended up composing, arranging, conducting, and co-producing a score of albums by legendary jazz artists on the Verve, CTI, and A&M labels. During that period, Sebesky composed and arranged recordings by Wes Montgomery, Hubert Laws, Freddie Hubbard, Buddy Rich, Grover Washington, Quincy Jones, Nancy Wilson, Doc Severinsen, Ron Carter, Airto Moreira, Paul Desmond, Chet Baker, Patti Austin, Astrud Gilberto, George Benson, Milt Jackson, Dizzy Gillespie, Roberta Flack, and Earl Klugh, among many others.

Though well-respected as a man behind the scenes, Sebesky was presented front and center on 1973's *Giant Box,* an ambitious two-album release on CTI. Creed Taylor rounded up every major artist on the label

Born Donald J. Sebesky on December 10, 1937, in Perth Amboy, NJ; married, 1959; four children; divorced, 1975; remarried, 1986; two children. *Education:* Studied music composition at the Manhattan School of Music, 1955-58.

Worked with jazz and big bands including the Kai Winding Septet, Stan Kenton Orchestra, and the Claude Thornhill Orchestra, 1953-60; first composition, arrangement, and trombone solos recorded, 1954; first recognized as a writer for the Maynard Ferguson Orchestra, 1958-59; ceased playing trombone, 1960; wrote music for numerous films, television shows, and commercial jingles, 1965—; greatest success arose from writing and arranging for producer Creed Taylor's projects for Wes Montgomery, Buddy Rich, Paul Desmond, Freddie Hubbard, Astrud Gilberto, and others on the Verve, A&M, and CTI labels, 1968-80; released *Giant Box*, 1973; wrote book, *The Contemporary Arranger*, 1975; began composing for Broadway, 1984; released Grammy Award-winning *I Remember Bill: A Tribute to Bill Evans*, 1998; released Grammy Award-winning *Joyful Noise: A Tribute to Duke Ellington*, 1999.

Awards: Grammy Awards for Best Instrumental Arrangement for *Waltz for Debby*, 1998; Best Instrumental Composition for *Joyful Noise Suite* and Best Instrumental Arrangement for *Chelsea Bridge*, 1999; Drama Desk Award for Outstanding Orchestrations for *Parade*, 1999.

Addresses: *Record company*—RCA Records, 1540 Broadway, Times Square, New York, NY 10036.

to perform Sebesky's work, and put the house composer-arranger's name on the package. The *All Music Guide to Jazz* called the lineup a veritable "gathering of the gods" that included Hubbard, Desmond, Washington, Jackson, Benson, Carter, Moreira, Laws, Randy Brecker, Joe Farrell, Bob James, Jack DeJohnette, Billy Cobham, Jackie Cain, and Roy Kral. Sebesky received 12 Grammy nominations for the work. His book, *The Contemporary Arranger*, was published in 1975.

The year 1980 marked the end of Sebesky's work with Taylor and the release of a recording of *Three Works for Jazz Soloists and Symphony Orchestra*. The recording, with soloists Jon Faddis, Bob Brookmeyer, and Alex Foster and the London Royal Philharmonic, garnered two Grammy nominations. Sebesky was also nominated for Grammy Awards for *Rape of El Morro* in 1975, *Moving Lines* in 1984, and *Joyful Noise* in 1999.

Another of Sebesky's releases to garner a Grammy nomination was *Full Cycle*, released in 1982. The record reflected "subtle changes" to Sebesky's sound, according to *All Music Guide to Jazz* writer Richard S. Ginell. Sebesky assembled a big band to record five jazz standards and one "should-be standard"—Freddie Hubbard's "Intrepid Fox"—according to Ginell. Sebesky moved away from his usual use of strong trombones, trumpets, and saxophones, and added an electric rhythm section. The result was a "mellow mutation" of Sebesky's work with Creed Taylor, Ginell wrote.

Sebesky hit Broadway in 1984 with his debut, *Peg*. He proceeded to compose *Sleight of Hand*, with Carly Simon in 1987, *The Prince of Central Park* in 1989, *Stepping Out* in 1991, *Will Rogers Follies* and *Tommy Tune Tonite* in 1992, *The Goodbye Girl* in 1993, and *Cyrano* in 1994. His hit Broadway show *Parade* earned both a Drama Desk Award and a Tony Award nomination in 1999. While his orchestration of *Kiss Me Kate* was running in 2000, Sebesky was working on *Rhythm Club*. Beginning in 1991, he has composed and arranged for such artists as Liza Minnelli, the Boys Choir of Harlem, Michael Feinstein, Sinead O'Connor, Prince, Tony Bennett, and Barbra Streisand.

In 1999, Sebesky won a Grammy Award for *I Remember Bill: A Tribute to Bill Evans*, his nod to the legendary pianist who made his mark on the jazz sound of the fifties and sixties. Long influenced by Evans, Sebesky tackled the labor of love, recasting Evans' originals and tunes he liked to play. Sebesky matched the Evans' "musical personality" by employing the softer side of the "orchestral palette," according to *Down Beat*, and using soprano saxophones, flutes, clarinets, and muted trombones and trumpets. *Entertainment Weekly* noted "occasional missteps" in the work, but found it at times to be "thoughtful and daringly conceived," and an altogether heartfelt tribute. Sebesky's next tribute album, to Duke Ellington, was even more successful than *I Remember Bill. Joyful Noise: A Tribute to Duke Ellington* won two Grammy Awards in 2000. Sebesky interpreted Ellington's tunes and included his own Ellington-inspired works. *Entertainment Weekly* noted that Sebesky's arrangements were more "brassy, boppish, and blatant" than Ellington's, but nonetheless satisfying.

Selected discography

Don Sebesky and the Jazz-Rock Syndrome, Verve, 1968.
Distant Galaxy, Verve, c. 1969.
Giant Box, CTI, 1973.
The Rape of El Morro, CTI, 1975.
Three Works for Jazz Soloists and Symphony Orchestra, Gryphon, 1979.
Moving Lines, Doctor Jazz, 1984.
Full Cycle, Crescendo, 1984.
I Remember Bill: A Tribute to Bill Evans, RCA, 1998.
Joyful Noise: A Tribute to Duke Ellington, RCA, 1999.

Selected writings

The Contemporary Arranger, Alfred Music, 1975.

Sources

Books

All Music Guide to Jazz, Miller Freeman Books, 1998.
Feather, Leonard and Ira Gitler, *Biographical Encyclopedia of Jazz,* Oxford University Press, 1999.
Feather, Leonard and Ira Gitler, *Encyclopedia of Jazz in the '70s,* Horizon Press, 1976.
Kernfeld, Barry, *New Grove Dictionary of Jazz,* Macmillan Press Ltd., 1998.

Periodicals

Down Beat, October 1998, p. 54; September 8, 2000, p. 48.
Entertainment Weekly, May 1, 1998, p. 66; October 22, 1999, p. 90.
SHOOT, March 3, 2000, p. 7.

Online

"Don Sebesky," *All Music Guide,* http://www.allmusic.com (April 27, 2001).
"Don Sebesky," Get Music, http://www.getmusic.com (April 27, 2001).
Drama Desk Awards, http://DramaDesk.Theatre.com/contents.htm (June 25, 2001).
The Recording Academy, http://www.grammy.com (June 25, 2001).

Additional material was provided by Crushing Music, 2001.

—Brenna Sanchez

Shakira

Singer, songwriter

Although she is one of the biggest stars on the Latin music scene, Shakira, a native of Colombia, doesn't think of her sound as typically Latin and has always considered herself first and foremost a "pop-rock" artist. And it may not be too long before fans of pop and rock across the United States and other English-speaking markets around the world are singing her praises. Early in 2001, the Miami-based recording artist was putting the finishing touches on a new album that will contain English translations of some of her biggest hits, and she is widely seen as the next potential crossover star.

Born Shakira Isabel Mebarak Ripoll on February 9, 1977, in Barranquilla on Colombia's Caribbean coast, Shakira is the daughter of a Colombian mother and a Lebanese father. The Arabic background of her father, a writer and jeweler, greatly influenced young Shakira, as can be heard in listening to some of the songs she's written. In Arabic, her first name means "woman full of grace," and it is how she has chosen to be known professionally. While still quite young, she showed a love for music and a talent her parents considered quite remarkable for a child so young. She entered a number of local and national talent and beauty contests, and by the time she was ten years old, she had won several.

At the age of 13, Shakira left Barranquilla for Colombia's capital of Bogota to take a modeling job. Unfortunately the modeling job never materialized, but perhaps it was for the best. Instead she signed her first recording contract with Sony Music Colombia and shortly thereafter released her first album. Entitled *Magia,* Shakira's debut was made up entirely of songs that she had written between the ages of 8 and 13. Although the album never achieved great success, it did bring the young songstress to the attention of her country and led eventually to her selection to represent Colombia at the annual Festival OTI, scheduled to be held that year in Spain. Her participation in the festival was barred at the last moment when officials realized that she was under the minimum age of 16.

At age 15, Shakira graduated from high school. Shortly thereafter she released her second album entitled *Peligro,* which failed to win much more attention than her debut effort. Soon after the disappointing release of *Peligro,* Shakira signed on as an actress in the Colombia television soap opera *El Oasís,* and she remained with the cast for about a year before returning to her first love—music.

Shakira's breakthrough came with the 1996 release of *Pies Descalzos* (Bare Feet), an album that has sold more than four million copies worldwide and one that produced no fewer than six smash singles. However, it was not an immediate success, and at first sales were disappointingly slow. Several months after the album first went on sale, "Estoy Aqui," the first single to be

For the Record . . .

Born Shakira Isabel Mebarak Ripoll on February 9, 1977, in Barranquilla, Colombia.

Moved to Bogota, Colombia, at the age of 13 to model but ended up instead with a recording contract for Sony; released debut album *Magia*, 1991; released *Peligro*, 1994; acted on the Colombian soap opera *El Oasis*, 1994; returned to recording music, 1995; released *Pies Descalzos*, 1996; released *Los Donde Estan Ladrones?*, 1998; released *MTV Unplugged*, 2000.

Awards: Latin Grammy Award, Best Female Pop Vocal Performance for "Ojos Así" from *MTV Unplugged*, 2000; Latin Grammy Award, Best Female Rock Vocal Performance for "Octavo Día" from *MTV Unplugged*, 2000.

Addresses: *Record company*—Sony Music Latin America, 605 Lincoln Road, Miami Beach, FL 33139.

released, started catching fire with disc jockeys at radio stations throughout Latin America and elsewhere in the Spanish-speaking world. The single soon made its way to number one on the Latin charts, a feat that was later matched by a follow-up single entitled "Donde Estas Corazon?" Four other singles from the album—"Antologia," "Pienso en Ti," "Un Poco de Amor," and "Se Quiere, Se Mata"—all reached the top ten on the Latin charts. The album itself managed to hit number one in sales in eight different countries. So popular was *Pies Descalzos* in Brazil, where sales topped 900,000, that Shakira recorded remixes of several songs in Portuguese.

What made Shakira's success with *Pies Descalzos* all the more impressive was the singer's decision to abandon her light pop format and establish for herself a distinctive and somewhat daring new style—a distinctive blend of pop and rock unlike anything being done by Colombian singers at the time. To get the album done the way she wanted, she had to overrule her label's recommendation that she stick to a format with more commercial appeal.

In support of *Pies Descalzos,* Shakira toured widely throughout the Spanish-speaking world, including cities in the United States with large Hispanic populations. The album and tours helped to make her one of the most visible musical performers in Latin music. Her tours crisscrossed the globe and lasted nearly two years.

After the phenomenal success of *Pies Descalzos,* despite its slow start, the big question for Shakira, her recording label, and the critics was whether she could produce another hit her next time out. Ably assisted by record producer Emilio Estefan, husband of Cuban-born singer Gloria Estefan, Shakira released *Donde Estan los Ladrones?* (Where are the Thieves?) in 1998. Critics hailed the spirit and integrity of Shakira's music, showcased beautifully by the high production standards for which Estefan is known. Of her work on *Ladrones,* Shakira said: "My music is sincere, everyday music. It is music that stems from a completely genuine source."

Critics hailed *Donde Estan los Ladrones?* as a breakthrough album for Shakira. Its title track was a none-too-veiled reference to the corruption found at all levels in her native country. One of the first big singles from the album was "Ojos Así," which roughly translates as "Those Eyes." In it one can clearly hear some of the Arab influences that are so dear to Shakira's heart, blended masterfully with the best of Western pop. Estefan was full of praise for Shakira. "It is totally refreshing for me to work with an artist who knows exactly what she wants, both at a musical and a personal level," he said. "Her music is Shakira. It's real music." Even Shakira seemed genuinely pleased with the album. Speaking to an interviewer for *Time International,* she said all the album's tracks have a "real, organic sound. The whole core is rock, even the dance songs." She allowed that the resulting sounds might not please some of her earlier fans but said that "the most important thing is to be honest."

During the summer of 1999, the MTV Network, which broadcasts in markets around the world, including much of Latin America, taped Shakira in one of its MTV Unplugged concerts. Performing in the Grand Ballroom of MTV's Manhattan Center Studios in New York City, the Colombian singer sang almost all of the songs for which she had become well known. MTV's editors then took all of the taped footage and distilled it down into an hour-long program that focused largely on the most important and influential songs of her repertoire. Beginning in 2000, the program was aired throughout Latin America, as well as in the United States. An album of the songs performed on the hour-long show was also released in 2000.

In September of 2000 at the first Latin Grammy Awards, Shakira won Grammys for Best Female Pop Vocal Performance for "Ojos Así" and for Best Female Rock Vocal Performance for "Octavo Día." She also performed at the awards show. Only a week earlier she had won an MTV Video Music Award for her video of "Ojos Así." News of the Grammy Awards gave a big lift to sales of Shakira's albums. In the weeks immediately following the awards ceremony, sales shot up by as much as 30 to 40 percent in the Los Angeles metropolitan area, one of the major Latin music markets in the United States.

Just to prove that into each life some rain must fall, Shakira got the answer to the question posed in the title of her 1998 album *Donde Estan los Ladrones?* (Where are the Thieves?) in November of 2000. The mansion in Punta del Este, Uruguay, in which Shakira had been staying for a couple of months, was robbed, although little of value was taken. The singer, her mother, and Antonio de la Rua, son of Argentine President Fernando de la Rua, stayed in the Punta del Este house while Shakira recorded a number of songs for her new album. Shaken by the break-in, Shakira's party left abruptly for Colombia.

Estefan, who continued to work with Shakira on her upcoming English-language album, told *Entertainment Weekly* late in 2000 that he fully expected Shakira to be the next big Latin crossover star, creating a sensation on the same scale as Selena or Ricky Martin. He further predicted that "Middle Eastern combined with Latin music is the next big sound." Of her work on the English-language album, Shakira said: "I'm working day and night writing, but I'm also taking my time. I want this album to put a big smile on my face."

Selected discography

Magia, Sony, 1991.
Peligro, Sony, 1994.
Pies Descalzos (includes "Estoy Aqui," "Donde Estas Corazon?" and "Pienso en Ti"), Sony, 1996.
Donde Estan los Ladrones? (includes "Ojos Así"), Sony, 1998.
Shakira, MTV Unplugged, Sony, 2000.

Sources

Periodicals

Entertainment Weekly, September 29, 2000, p. 129.
Hispanic, March 31, 1999, p. 75.
Time, February 15, 1999, p. 80.
Time International, August 3, 1998, p. 36.

Online

"Shakira," *All Music Guide,* http://allmusic.com (April 25, 2001).
"Biography," Shakira: MTV Unplugged, http://www.shakira.com/main.html (May 8, 2001).
"International Beat: Shakira, Celia Cruz, Ricky Martin," Sonicnet.com, http://www.sonicnet.com (May 8, 2001).
"International Beat: Valerie Belinga, Shakira, Gloria Trevi," Sonicnet.com, http://www.sonicnet.com (May 8, 2001).
"Latin Grammys' Fallout: Increased Sales, Lingering Controversy," Sonicnet.com, http://www.sonicnet.com (May 8, 2001).
"Review: Shakira Returns to U.S.," Sonicnet.com, http://www.sonicnet.com (May 8, 2001).
"Shakira: Biography," Sonicnet.com, http://www.sonicnet.com (May 7, 2001).

—Don Amerman

Joanne Shenandoah

Singer, songwriter

Photograph by Michael Okoniewski. AP/Wide World Photos. Reproduced by permission.

Singing in her native Iroquois language, Joanne Shenandoah has become one of the most critically acclaimed Native American singers, finding crossover success with her ethereal voice and blend of traditional melodies and contemporary styles. Her appeal has been broadened by performances at events such as the Olympics, Woodstock, President Bill Clinton's and President George W. Bush's inaugurals, and at a private tea party for Tipper Gore and Hillary Clinton. Shenandoah has been compared to Irish chanteuse Enya and is devoted to Native American causes, taking the stage at countless gatherings across the country in support of those causes. Voted Best Female Artist of the Year at the Native American Music Awards (NAMMYS) two years in a row, Shenandoah—and all Native American musicians—were vindicated by the mainstream music industry in 2001. The Grammy Awards debuted a new category, Best Native American Album, for which Shenandoah was nominated. Singer Robbie Robertson, with whom Shenandoah has recorded, told the *Observer-Dispatch,* "She weaves you into a trance with her beautiful Iroquois chants."

Shenandoah grew up on the Oneida Iroquois Territory in central New York in a large house without running water. A descendent of Revolutionary War hero Chief John Shenandoah, she was raised by her mother, Maisie, an Oneida Wolf Clan mother, and her father, Clifford Shenandoah. Music was commonplace in her upbringing; Shenandoah's parents would sing the songs of Billie Holliday, Hank Williams, and Patsy Cline to her and her four siblings. Shenandoah's father, a jazz guitarist, was interested in jazz and early rock 'n' roll. In *Native Peoples,* Shenandoah wrote, "singing was as natural to me as breathing." Her native name, given to her before she could talk, is Tekaiawahway (pronounced De-gal-la-wha-wha), which means "she sings."

As the only Native American student at the private Union Springs Academy in New York, she threw herself into music. She experimented with various musical instruments, including French horn, cello, clarinet, and flute. She spent hours practicing piano and learning to read and write music while developing her talent for singing and composing original music. In the early 1970s, there were few Native American performers for Shenandoah to look up to. Her childhood idols included Rita Coolidge, Buffy Saint-Marie, Floyd Westerman, Paul Ortega, Jim Pepper, and the rock bands Redbone and XIT.

Shenandoah did consider the idea of a professional career as a performer before taking a job in the corporate world as a computer specialist in Washington D.C. "I was working very hard and was doing all the things I thought were important in life," she said in an interview with the *Observer-Dispatch.* But that quickly changed. She released her debut album, *Joanne Shenandoah,* in 1989, and only months later was

Born c. 1958; member of the Wolf Clan, Iroquois Confederacy, Oneida Indian Nation; married Doug George-Kanentiio; children: Leah.

Released debut album, *Joanne Shenandoah*, on Canyon Records, 1989; performed at President Bill Clinton's inaugural, 1993, 1997; opened Woodstock '94 at Saugerties, 1994; released *Matriarch*, 1996; released *Orenda*, 1998; released *Peacemaker's Journey*, 2000; released *Warrior in Two Worlds*, 2000; performed at President George W. Bush's inaugural, 2001; published book, *Skywoman: Legends of the Iroquois*, 2001.

Awards: Native American Musician of the Year, First Americans in the Arts Awards, 1994; Native American Woman's Recognition Award, 1996; Native American Woman of Hope for America, Bread & Roses Cultural Foundation, 1997; Outstanding Achievement Award, Post Standard Newspapers, 1997; Best Acoustic Act and Best National Recording, SAMMY Awards (Syracuse Area Music Awards), 1997; Native American Record of the Year, National Association of Independent Record Distributors (NAIRD), 1997; Best Female Artist and Best Children's Recording, NAMMY Awards (Native American Music Awards), 1998; Popular Awards Recipient, American Society of Composers, Authors and Publishers (ASCAP), 1998; Governor's Commission Honoring the Achievements of Women of New York, 1998; SAMMY Award for Best National Recording for *Orenda*, 1999; NAMMY Awards for Best Female Artist and Best Traditional Recording for *Orenda*, 1999; Outstanding Musical Achievement, *Peacemaker's Journey*, First American in the Arts, 2001.

Addresses: *Record company*—Silver Wave Records, P.O. Box 7943, Boulder, CO 80306, website: http://www.silverwave.com/index.html. *Business*—Joanne Shenandoah, Oneida Nation Territory, P.O. Box 450, Oneida, NY 13421, (315) 363-1655. *Website*—Joanne Shenandoah Official Website: http://www.joanneshenandoah.com.

performing on stage at a benefit with Willie Nelson, Jackson Browne, Kris Kristofferson, and Neil Young, who became a long-time supporter. Her early work was a blend of "traditional Native American style with traditional American folk and even country," wrote Mark Bialczak in the *Syracuse Herald American*.

Once committed to life as a performer, Shenandoah did not hold back. She went on to release a total of ten albums in just over ten years, in addition to countless live performances. Some critics suggested her popularity was a result of the crossover power of her music. Though she did not sing in English, but in her native Iroquois language, Shenandoah's music seemed to transcend the language barrier with her voice and message of peace. Alan Bisbort of the *Hartford Advocate* noted that Shenandoah's 1996 release, *Matriarch*, lacked conventional songs and song structure and called it the "Iroquois version of Gregorian chanting," adding, "You don't need to understand the words to feel the spirit." He also noted Shenandoah's "remarkably soothing voice." Her children's record, *All Spirits Sing*, won the Native American Music Award (NAMMY) for Best Children's Album in 1998, and her album *Orenda* won the NAMMY for Best Traditional Album a year later. As of 1999, each of Shenandoah's recordings had sold more than 100,000 copies worldwide.

Billboard, who had dubbed Shenandoah a "Native American version of Enya," admitted she had "evolved beyond that" on her 2000 release, *Peacemaker's Journey*, calling it her "most impressive album yet." The review noted that the album avoided the clichés that some Native American crossover releases fall victim to. "Crossover is good," Shenandoah said in an interview with the *Post-Standard*. "People are looking beyond the Native chant music, to see how much we're talented." Instead of traditional Native American instruments like cedar flutes and tom-tom drums, Shenandoah was accompanied by hand percussion and guitar. Paige La Grone, in an Amazon.com review, said that the record was "pure magic."

In addition to her own releases, Shenandoah also spent time composing music for more mainstream film and television projects. Her music can be heard on television on the *Larry King Show* and *Northern Exposure*, and on television documentaries like the Discovery Channel's *How the West Was Lost*, as well as a number of Public Broadcasting System (PBS) specials, including the award-winning *Warrior in Two Worlds*.

Shenandoah walked down the red carpet at the 2001 Grammy Awards for the debut of a new Grammy category. She was a nominee for the first-ever Best Native American Album Award. The artist was unconcerned with winning. "Winning and bringing the trophy home is not so important as hoping people will get my message," she said in an interview with the *Sunday Sentinel*. "Mine is a message of peace, not only for the Iroquois community, but for everyone."

Shenandoah lives with her husband and daughter in Oneida Castle in central New York on the land where her grandfather lived in the 1800s. The book *Skywoman: Legends of the Iroquois,* which she co-wrote, was published in 2001, and *Eagle Cries,* a collaboration with longtime supporter Neil Young, was due later that year. She has auditioned for a number of film roles and was the subject of an in-the-works PBS documentary.

Though Native American role models in popular music were few for Shenandoah as a girl, she felt things were turning around in the twenty-first century. "Now is, without a doubt, the best time to be a Native musician," she wrote in *Native Peoples.*

Selected discography

Joanne Shenandoah, Canyon Records, 1989.
Loving Ways, Canyon Records, 1991.
Once in a Red Moon, Canyon Records, 1994.
Life Blood, Silver Wave Records, 1995.
Matriarch, Silver Wave Records, 1996.
All Spirits Sing, Music For Little People, 1997.
Freedom Rocks: Elmer & Friends, Featherwind Productions, 1996.
Orenda, Silver Wave Records, 1998.
Peacemaker's Journey, Silver Wave Records, 2000.
Warrior in Two Worlds, Red Feather Records, 2000.

Sources

Periodicals

Akwesasne Notes, Summer 1995, p. 100.
Billboard, January 28, 1995, p. 68; March 11, 2000.
Hartford Advocate (Hartford, CT), October 9, 1997.
Native Peoples, March/April 2001.
Observer-Dispatch, March 17, 1997.
Post-Standard (New York), December 28, 1999; March 2001.
Sunday Sentinel, January 28, 2001.
Syracuse Herald American, December 14, 1997, p. 3.
Syracuse New Times, February 7-14, 2001.

Online

Joanne Shenandoah Official Website, http://www.joanneshenandoah.com (April 18, 2001).
"Peacemaker's Journey," Amazon.com, http://www.amazon.com (May 25, 2001).

Additional materials were provided by Joanne Shenandoah, 2001.

—*Brenna Sanchez*

Wilson Simonal

Singer

Initially rising to prominence in Brazil's music scene of the early 1960s, Wilson Simonal was one of the first Afro-Brazilian musicians to gain mainstream success in that country with his own television show and numerous album releases. In the early 1970s, however, Simonal's career went into a rapid descent after a scandal involving his alleged ties to police corruption and violence. When Simonal was accused of collaborating with Brazil's military regime during the scandal, his fellow musicians ostracized him. Deserted by the musical community at the height of his career, Simonal suffered an artistic decline as well, with his later recordings bearing only a semblance of the energy and personality of his first recordings. By his death in 2000, however, his wife had proven that Simonal had never informed on his colleagues. After his death, two of his sons, Wilson Simoninha and Max de Castro, carried on his legacy as popular performers and recording artists.

Simonal was born in 1938 in a poor district of Rio de Janeiro, Brazil. His mother worked as a laundress, and while young Simonal did not enjoy many advantages, he was fortunate to be raised in one of the most vibrant music scenes in the world. Most notable among its contributions was samba, a combination of Latin and African musical forms. Describing its development into Brazil's most popular musical style from the early twentieth century onward, *World Music: The Rough Guide* noted that "It started as Carnaval music, and horrified Rio's established (and white) society: it was lewd, loud, and the drums were too African, and so the police regularly raided the area to arrest *sambistas*."

By the time of Simonal's birth, however, samba musicians had become part of Brazil's mainstream culture, and a highly creative music scene in Rio de Janeiro fueled samba's popularity.

Completing a stint in the military in the late 1950s, Simonal often entertained his colleagues with his talent as a singer. Discovered by songwriter and entertainer Carlos Imperial, Simonal gained initial exposure through his 1961 appearances at the famed venue Beco das Garrafas, where he sang rock and calypso songs in addition to contemporary Brazilian songs. Through his contact with Imperial, Simonal appeared on television and released his first album, *Tem Algo Mais,* in 1963. His follow-up, 1964's *A Nova Dimensao do Samba,* offered a mix of Brazilian samba and American soul rhythms that contrasted nicely with the dominant musical trend of the day, bossa nova, or "new wave." Whereas bossa nova employed spare, jazz-oriented arrangements that emphasized syncopation and harmony, best exemplified by the global hit "The Girl from Ipanema," Simonal's style was far more energetic and eclectic. Gaining a reputation as a dynamic entertainer based on his up-tempo arrangements and outgoing personality, Simonal toured throughout Latin America as the leader of the Bossa Trio in the early 1960s. By 1966, when he began a two-year run with *The Wilson Simonal Show* on Brazilian television, the singer was a household name in his home country.

To many, Simonal embodied Brazil's optimistic spirit of the 1960s, when the country looked forward to taking its place as a leader on the international stage. With the success of samba and bossa nova, the national soccer team's victory in the World Cup of 1958, the opening of Brazil's new capital city of Brasilia in 1960, and an ambitious government plan for economic development, the country was imbued with national pride and a belief in continued social and economic progress. As the first widely popular Brazilian musician of African descent, Simonal also demonstrated the greater acceptance of diversity in Brazilian society. Although Simonal thought of himself as Brazilian first and foremost, saying that "I don't have this history of 'Mother Africa,'" as reported by Mauro Dias in São Paulo's *Estado,* his popularity further infused Brazil's African descendents with a sense of hope.

With the economic crisis of the mid 1960s brought about by massive government spending and corruption, the years of optimism for Brazil were short-lived, and the impact on Simonal's career would be tragic. In 1964, a military junta overthrew the democratically elected government and instituted a regime that would last 21 years. Quickly taking steps to repress any dissent, military authorities implemented censorship measures that touched upon every aspect of creative life in Brazil, including its music. Any lyrics or statements that criticized the regime would result in imme-

For the Record . . .

Born Wilson Simonal de Castro in 1938 in Rio de Janeiro, Brazil; died on June 25, 2000, in São Paulo, Brazil; married Sandra Manzini Cerqueira (a lawyer and manager); children: three sons.

Started music career during stint in Brazilian army, late 1950s; released first album, 1963; gained wide popularity with Brazilian television show, 1966-68; became a leading "pilantragem," or "rascal;" compilation works released, 1990s.

Addresses: *Record company*—BMG Entertainment, 1540 Broadway, New York, NY 10036, website: http://www.bmg.com.

diate retribution, including blacklisting and sometimes even a jail term or exile. For Simonal, whose music had steered away from social issues, censorship was not immediately restrictive, although many of his colleagues suffered greatly from the repression. Some artists, however, used the repression to fuel their creativity, introducing oblique references into their music that continued to criticize Brazil's rulers. Simonal's style as a "pilantragem," or "rascal," allowed him to offer at least one such sly critique of the political situation in his song "Pais Tropical," or "Tropical Country," which refers to Brazil as a nation "Blessed by God." Soon, Simonal's phrase "pais tropical," shortened to "pa tropi" in everyday conversation, became a way for Brazilians to refer to their country without fear of retaliation.

For the rest of the 1960s, Simonal continued to release albums, make television appearances, and tour throughout Latin America. In 1971, however, his career took an abrupt fall after Simonal was involved in a scandal involving his enlistment of the police to take revenge on a business associate. Suspecting that his accountant had falsified some financial statements and stolen from him, Simonal asked some acquaintences in the police department to abduct the man and beat him up. When the scandal was uncovered, Simonal himself was arrested and served a brief jail term for his role in the kidnapping. The singer did not enhance his public image when he bragged of political contacts with Brazil's infamous Department of Political and Social Order, responsible for some of the worst repression under the country's military regime. Appearing to have been a collaborator with the state and its attacks on Brazil's artistic community, Simonal was immediately ostracized by his fellow musicians. Although no evi-

dence that Simonal ever directly informed on anyone ever emerged, and he was eventually cleared of such accusations by Brazil's Ministry of Justice, his reputation was ruined. For his part, Simonal claimed that jealousy and racism caused his downfall. As Alessandra Dalevi wrote in her obituary of the singer on Brazzil.com, "After all, he was the only Black singer who was a big star in his time, drove expensive foreign cars, was always dating beautiful blonde women and sold more records than anybody else."

Others saw Simonal's fall more as a result of his own artistic decline rather than vengance on the part of the music community. A review of his output during the 1970s on All Brazilian Music.com notes that "Simonal wastes a crystal clear, soul-driven voice with an incoherent repertoire—the true reason for his artistic suicide." A Slipcue.com reviewer agreed, recommending his mid 1970s releases only to give the listener "a good sense of how far Simonal fell creatively speaking, and how it was almost within his grasp to pull himself back." While Simonal experimented with new musical forms, such as disco and other popular formats, his albums were neither critically nor commercially well-received during the remainder of his life.

The last decade of his life saw some of Simonal's work reissued in compilations that recalled his great successes of the 1960s. The singer's wife, Sandra Manzini Cerqueira, worked to clear his name and obtained a statement from the Ministry of Justice that showed Simonal had never collaborated with the military regime, which had been replaced by a democratically elected government in 1985. By the time of his death on June 25, 2000, of cirrhosis of the liver in a São Paulo hospital, however, Simonal's reputation had only begun to be reevaluated. As music historian Zuza Homem de Mello commented to Dalevi in Simonal's obituary, "Simonal was one of the most modern singers in Brazilian music history…. Whatever sin he committed, he paid too steep a price. There was a lack of humanity, and people transformed him into a monster." Simonal's legacy continues to grow, however, as two of his sons, Max de Castro and Wilson Simoninha, are rising stars in Brazil's contemporary music scene. Shortly after their father's death, the two paid tribute to him at the Rock in Rio concert, and both have released critically acclaimed albums that in part pay tribute to their father's musical heritage.

Selected discography

Tem Algo Mais, Odeon, 1963.
A Nova Dimensao do Samba, Odeon, 1964.
Wilson Simonal, Odeon, 1965.
S'Imbora, Odeon, 1965.
Vou Deixar Cair, Odeon, 1966.
Alegria, Alegria!!!, Odeon, 1967.
Alegria, Alegria, Volume 2, Odeon, 1968.
Alegria, Alegria, Volume 3, Odeon, 1969.

Alegria, Alegria, Volume 4, Odeon, 1969.
Se Dependesse de Mim, Phonogram, 1972.
A Vida E So Pra Cantar, RCA Victor, 1977.
Alegria Tropical, Copacabana, 1985.
Brasil, Movieplay, 1995.
Bem Brasil-Estilo Simonal, Happy Sound, 1998.
A Bossa E O Balanco, Warner Music, 1994.
Meus Momentos, EMI, 1999.
Wilson Simonal, BMG, 2001.

Sources

Books

Broughton, Simon, et al., editors, *World Music: The Rough Guide,* The Rough Guides, 1994.

Fausto, Boris, *A Concise History of Brazil,* Cambridge University Press, 1999.

McGowan, Chris, and Ricardo Pessanha, *The Brazilian Sound: Samba, Bossa Nova, and the Popular Music of Brazil,* Billboard Books, 1991.

Skidmore, Thomas E., *Brazil: Five Centuries of Change,* Oxford University Press, 1999.

Online

All Brazilian Music, http://www.allbrazilianmusic.com (April 20, 2001).

Brazzil, http://www.brazzil.com/p07jul00.htm (April 18, 2001).

Editora, http://www.s3editora.com/br/persona/text_e_list/wilsonsimonal.htm (April 19, 2001).

Estadao, http://www.estadao.com.br/divirtase/noticias/2000/jun/25/42.htm (April 19, 2001).

Memorial Online, http://www.memorialonline.com.br/wilson.htm (April 19, 2001).

Observatorio da Imprensa, http://www.observatoriodaimprensa.com.br/artigos/fd20052000.htm (April 19, 2001).

Rock in Rio, http://www.rockinrio.americaonline.com.br/ing_news_arq11.php3 (April 19, 2001).

SlipCue, http://www.slipcue.com/music/brazil/aa_albums/brazilalbums_S.html (April 20, 2001).

Time, http://www.time.com/time/magazine/printout/0,8816,07099,00.html (April 19, 2001).

—*Timothy Borden*

Grace Slick

Singer

Grace Slick made her name as a lead singer for Jefferson Airplane, one of the pre-eminent bands of the 1960s known for their hits "Somebody to Love" and "White Rabbit." As one of rock's first female superstars, she hobnobbed with fellow flower-power generation icons like Jim Morrison, and embodied the "bad girl" persona and rebellion that would define the era. She also embarked on drug- and alcohol-induced antics that led to the self-destruction of many of her colleagues, including Morrison, Janis Joplin, and Jimi Hendrix. Slick survived the 1960s, though, and rode with her band though their ups and downs as Jefferson Starship in the 1970s and back to the top again as they hit the charts with a new incarnation, Starship, in the 1980s. After retiring from the stage, Slick began selling artworks, including paintings and drawings of animals, her fellow musicians, and herself.

Grace Barnett Wing was born on October 30, 1939, in Chicago, Illinois. Her father, Ivan W. Wing, was an investment banker, and her mother, Virginia (Barnett) Wing, had given up a budding career as a singer and actress in order to marry and settle down. Slick's brother Chris was born in 1949, after the family had moved to San Francisco for her father's job transfer.

For the Record . . .

Born Grace Barnett Wing on October 30, 1939, in Chicago, IL; daughter of Ivan W. (an investment banker) and Virginia (Barnett) Wing; married Gerald "Jerry" Robert Slick (a musician), August 26, 1961 (divorced, 1970); married Skip Johnson (a production manager), November 29, 1976 (marriage ended, 1994); children: (with Paul Kantner) China Kantner. *Education*: Attended Finch College, 1957-58; University of Miami, 1958-59.

Worked as a model for I. Magnin's, 1960-63; member of musical groups, including Grace Slick and the Great Society, 1965-66; Jefferson Airplane, 1966-72; Jefferson Starship, 1974-78; and Starship, 1981-88; co-author (with Andrea Cagan) of autobiography, *Somebody to Love?: A Rock-and-Roll Memoir*, Warner Books, 1998; painter, 1990s—.

Addresses: *Home*—Malibu, CA.

They relocated to the suburb of Palo Alto in the early 1950s.

Though Slick was a chubby blonde child, during adolescence her hair turned dark and she slimmed down. Not achieving the "Barbie doll" look that she had hoped for, she turned to sarcasm to fit in with the popular crowd at Jordan Junior High. However, this soon only served to alienate her. By high school, though, she had regained a social circle and was attending parties regularly at a girlfriend's house. She transferred to a private school, Castilleja School for Girls, to be with her friend. In her teens, Slick began encountering problems with consuming too much alcohol.

After graduation, Slick decided to attend Finch College in New York because another friend was attending there and she had always wanted to go to New York. After a year there, she transferred to the University of Miami in Florida. As she wrote in her autobiography *Somebody to Love?: A Rock-and-Roll Memoir*, "Obviously, none of my academic choices were designed to actually further my education. The most important attraction in selecting a school was how much *fun* might be involved."

Upon receiving a letter from another friend about the "hippie" scene in San Francisco, Slick moved back to the West Coast in 1958. Instead of diving into the counterculture, however, she entered a relationship with childhood pal Jerry Slick, whose parents were close friends of her parents. They were married in 1961 in a traditional ceremony. Soon, they moved to San Diego, where he attended college and Slick worked at a department store. They quickly returned to San Francisco, where she found work modeling for the I. Magnin couturier department.

Before long, Slick and her husband were associating with artistic friends, and she wrote her first song. She also wrote the music to accompany her husband's senior thesis at San Francisco State University, a satirical film called *Everybody Hits Their Brother Once*. It won first prize at the Ann Arbor Film Festival.

In 1965, Slick and her friends saw the band Jefferson Airplane at a local nightclub and decided to put together a group of their own. They called it Grace Slick and the Great Society. She wrote in her book that it was meant to "[make] fun of President Lyndon B. Johnson's grandiose moniker for the U.S. population."

The band consisted of Slick on vocals, piano, guitar, and improvisational organ; her husband on drums; his brother Darby on guitar and sitar; and Brad Du Pont on bass. Veering away from the pervasive love-story songs that had been popular for years, the Great Society began to perform original songs with sociopolitical content. One of the band's biggest numbers— "Somebody to Love"—was, in fact, about love, but as she explained in her autobiography, "The lyrics implied that rather than the loving you're whining about *getting* or *not getting,* a more satisfying state of heart might be the loving you're *giving*."

Joined Jefferson Airplane

The Great Society often played the famous Fillmore Ballroom, sharing a bill with bands like Jefferson Airplane and Moby Grape. Slick and the band also began socializing with the Grateful Dead and Neal Cassady, the lead character in Jack Kerouac's *On the Road*. They also began to experiment widely with drugs, including peyote and LSD. After the band played together for about a year, they broke up and Slick joined the Jefferson Airplane when their female singer quit to raise a family. They already had a contract with RCA and had released one album, *Jefferson Airplane Takes Off*. Meanwhile, Slick's marriage was generally over by 1967, though she didn't officially divorce until 1971. She was involved with music and her husband had a film career, so they did not see each other. In addition, Slick noted in her book that the marriage had never been one of passion to begin with.

Jefferson Airplane's hit album, *Surrealistic Pillow*, came out in 1967 and hit number three on the *Billboard* charts. It is regarded as their best effort. In addition to including the song "Somebody to Love" on the album, Slick also added to their repertoire her original tune

"White Rabbit," which blends musical strains of Bolero with lyrics inspired by Lewis Carroll's book *Alice in Wonderland.* Slick penned it to be a diatribe about the hypocrisy of the older generation's derision of drug use.

Throughout the 1960s, Jefferson Airplane was a mainstay of the hippie scene. They played many of the big rock festivals, including Woodstock, Monterey, and the ill-fated Altamont, in which a fan was beaten and stabbed to death by members of the Hell's Angels motorcycle gang, who had regularly served as security guards at concerts. In 1968, the band released its third album, *After Bathing at Baxter's,* but it was banned from radio play due to the stream-of-consciousness tune "rejoyce." Later that year, their third album, *Crown of Creation* went platinum. *Volunteers* came out in 1969.

Slick, meanwhile, had sexual encounters with most of her bandmates (with the exception of fellow vocalist Marty Balin) as well as other musicians like Morrison, the legendary Doors singer. She also underwent three surgeries to remove nodes from her vocal chords, an ailment that was alleviated after her switch from menthol to regular cigarettes. In her autobiography, she also noted that her condition might have improved due to better technology in monitor speakers.

Collaborated with Kantner

After two more albums, the live 1969 *Bless Its Pointed Little Head* and 1970's compilation *The Worst of the Jefferson Airplane,* the group began to break apart. Two of the members started another band, Hot Tuna, and Slick began to collaborate with another bandmate, Paul Kantner. She also embarked on a relationship with Kantner that produced a daughter. They initially put the name "god" on her birth certificate, but her real name is China. They also collaborated on the 1972 album *Sunfighter,* a tribute to their daughter, and *Baron von Tollbooth and the Chrome Nun,* 1973.

Despite the other projects that were keeping band members busy, Jefferson Airplane managed to release 1971's *Bark,* with help from violinist Papa John Creach and drummer John Barbata, who had played with the Turtles and Crosby, Stills, Nash & Young. They followed this with *Long John Silver* in 1972. After that, the original group completely broke up, and Slick and Kantner reformed Jefferson Airplane with some new members and released the live album *Thirty Seconds over Winterland* in 1973, followed by *Early Flight* in 1974. Slick also released the solo project *Manhole* in 1973.

Soon, the band changed its name to Jefferson Starship and added a hot young guitarist, Craig Chaquico, to the lineup. Their debut album, *Dragon Fly,* yielded the hit single "Caroline," written and performed by former

Airplane member Marty Balin, who would soon re-join the group. Following this, they saw their biggest hit ever with 1975's *Red Octopus,* which contained the romantic ballad "Miracles." It surpassed even the success of *Surrealistic Pillow,* with sales of more than two million copies in its first ten months out. It also became one of only a handful of albums in rock history to reach the number one spot on the *Billboard* chart four separate times.

Renewed Success

In the mid 1970s, Slick began having an affair with Skip Johnson, the band's lighting director. They married on November 29, 1976, in Hawaii. She and Kantner parted amicably and continued to share custody of their daughter. Meanwhile, Jefferson Starship's rocket to the top soon crashed following a disastrous tour of Germany in 1978. Slick's drinking problem contributed to the problems. Though she joined Alcoholics Anonymous and went to treatment centers, she did not permanently stay sober and ended up amassing a string of drunk driving arrests and other citations relating to alcohol abuse. In the meantime, Kantner assembled a new version of Jefferson Starship in 1979 without Slick. She was working on solo projects, but after the new lineup released their first album, *Freedom at Point Zero,* they asked her to return. She joined again for their next effort, *Modern Times,* released in 1981, and after this, the group changed its name to simply "Starship." They had two big commercial albums with *Knee Deep in the Hoopla,* 1985; and *No Protection,* 1987, and three number-one hits: "Sara," "Nothing's Gonna Stop Us Now," and "We Built This City."

Despite the success, Slick decided to leave the group again. Her move was sealed when she came down with a debilitating shoulder problem that hindered her movement. She underwent six months of physical therapy before doctors finally gave her a procedure under anesthesia that repaired the shoulder. Following this, her marriage to Johnson began to crumble as he revealed that he had had several affairs. They eventually divorced in 1994.

In 1989, Slick reunited with the original Jefferson Airplane members for an album and tour. She wrote in her autobiography, "Although the tour was not a financial gold mine, it was a good thing. By the time it was over, we'd traded a lot of energy, renewed our friendships, and had closed some uncompleted circles. Nice."

After this, Slick resumed a relatively low-key life of studying biomedical research and getting involved in animal rights causes. Her peace was shattered, however, when a fire destroyed her Marin County home in 1993. Ironically, it was set ablaze by welders erecting a sign reading "Danger/Fire Area." She later moved to Malibu, California, to be near her daughter, who was forging an acting career in Los Angeles. Slick continued to attend Alcoholics Anonymous meetings as did her daughter, who by this time had encountered problems with drinking as well.

Into her fifties, Slick gave up singing in public, citing the fact that she was too old to be a rock 'n' roll queen and because she was tired of performing the same songs all the time. In 1998, she published *Somebody to Love,* cowritten with her friend Andrea Cagan. It revealed much of her rock goddess past and brought readers up to date on her activities, which included her budding art career.

In 2000, Slick sold about 60 pieces, ranging in style, sizes, and mediums, including oil paint, acrylic paint, pencil, and ink, and had an exhibit at Artrock Gallery in San Francisco late that year. Prices for her works ranged from $1,100 to $8,700, and Slick acknowledged that selling them helped pay her bills since she mainly was living off royalties from her music.

In an Associated Press report that ran in the *Charleston Gazette,* Kim Curtis wrote, "She knows that serious art critics probably won't like her work. And they don't." Slick admitted that many people probably buy art works from someone famous even if the work isn't very good, but also noted, "You don't have to be Rembrandt to make something that appeals to somebody else."

Selected discography

Solo and other

(With Paul Kantner) *Sunfighter,* Grunt, 1971.
(With Kantner and David Freiberg) *Baron Von Tollbooth and the Chrome Nun,* Grunt, 1973.
Manhole, Grunt, 1973.
Dreams, RCA, 1980.
Welcome to the Wrecking Ball, RCA, 1981.
Software, RCA, 1984.

With Jefferson Airplane

Jefferson Airplane Takes Off, RCA, 1966.
Surrealistic Pillow, RCA, 1967.
After Bathing at Baxter's, RCA, 1967.
Crown of Creation, RCA, 1968.
Volunteers, RCA, 1969.
Bless Its Pointed Little Head (live), RCA, 1969.
The Worst of Jefferson Airplane (compilation), RCA, 1970.
(With others) *Woodstock,* Cotillion, 1971.
(With others) *Woodstock Two,* Cotillion, 1972.
Bark, Grunt, 1971.
Long John Silver, Grunt, 1972.
Thirty Seconds over Winterland (live), Grunt, 1973.
Early Flight, Grunt, 1974.
Flight Log (compilation), Grunt, 1977.

2400 Fulton Street (compilation), RCA, 1987.
Jefferson Airplane, Epic, 1989.
(With others) *Live at the Monterey Festival* (live), Thunderbolt, 1990.
White Rabbit and Other Hits (compilation), RCA, 1990.
(With others) *Monterey International Pop Festival Volume 3* (live), Rhino, 1992.
Jefferson Airplane Loves You (compilation), RCA, 1992.
Best Of (compilation), RCA, 1993.
(With others) *Woodstock—25th Anniversary Collection* (live), Atlantic, 1994.

With Jefferson Starship

Dragon Fly, RCA, 1974.
Red Octopus, Grunt, 1975.
Spitfire, Grunt, 1976.
Earth, Grunt, 1978.
Gold (compilation), Grunt, 1979.
Modern Times, RCA, 1981.
Winds of Change, Grunt, 1982.
Nuclear Furniture, RCA, 1984.
At Their Best (compilation), RCA, 1992.
Deep Space/Virgin Sky (live), Intersound, 1995.

With Starship

Knee Deep in the Hoopla, RCA, 1985.
No Protection, RCA, 1987.
Love among the Cannibals, RCA, 1989.
Greatest Hits (Ten Years and Change, 1979-1991) (compilation), RCA, 1991.

Sources

Books

Contemporary Musicians, volume 5, Gale Research, 1991.
Slick, Grace, and Andrea Cagan, *Somebody to Love?: A Rock-and-Roll Memoir,* Warner Books, 1998.

Periodicals

Atlanta Journal and Constitution, November 1, 1998, p. L9.
Booklist, September 1, 1998, p. 49.
Charleston Gazette, November 23, 2000, p.3D.
Daily Telegraph, December 29, 1998.
Entertainment Weekly, August 21, 1998, p. 115.
Life, December 1, 1992, p. 70.
New York Daily News, September 24, 1998, p. 2C.
New York Times, October 18, 1998.
Publishers Weekly, August 10, 1998, p. 382.
San Francisco Chronicle, September 6, 1998, p. 3, 34; November 18, 2000, p. B1.

Online

"Grace Slick," Contemporary Authors Online, http://www.gale net.com (December 8, 2000).

—Geri Koeppel

Soulfly

Heavy metal group

A cross between heavy metal and world music, Soulfly is a leader of the "world metal" movement that has gained popularity across Eastern Europe, Latin America, and the United States. Incorporating indigenous musical forms—in Soulfly's case, Brazilian rhythms and chants—with aggressive guitar work and rage-filled lyrics, world metal has crossed boundaries and cultures to become a truly international genre of music. As leader Max Cavalera commented in an interview with the *Orlando Sun,* "I joke around and say I'm the Paul Simon of metal. I will jam with anybody."

Soulfly had its origins with Cavalera's acrimonious departure from Sepultura, a Brazilian heavy metal group that had released several albums throughout the 1980s and 1990s. With a name that literally meant "grave" in Portuguese, the band attracted a dedicated death-metal following in its own country and toured extensively to promote its work in Eastern Europe and America. Its fans were shocked by Cavalera's departure in late 1996; not only was he one of the band's founders, but its primary singer and songwriter as well. In an open letter posted on This Swirling Sphere website, Cavalera criticized the band for listening to "'outsiders' telling everybody what to do, how to act," and for forcing out his wife as Sepultura's manager. "This is not the tribe I believe in anymore. I'm sorry, but I'm faithful and loyal to the people that have been good to me and I won't change my ways for nothing!" After 15 years together in Sepultura, however, Cavalera's brother stayed on with the band.

In addition to the loss of his band, Cavalera also suffered through the death of his stepson, who was murdered in an unsolved slaying that characterized the chaos of Brazilian society. In the 1990s, more than 100 individuals had "disappeared" and were presumed murdered in Cavalera's hometown of Belo Horizonte, and an estimated ten percent of homicides in São Paulo were committed by the police. Cavalera himself had often criticized the role of the police in perpetuating violent crimes in songs such as Sepultura's "Policia," a stand that he claimed resulted in his arrest for supposedly desecrating the Brazilian flag at a 1994 concert in São Paulo. Fed up with the violence and corruption in Brazil, Cavalera relocated to Phoenix, Arizona, in 1991.

Cavalera may have lost his stepson, his band, and his native country, but he retained the musical direction that Sepultura had taken with the release of the last album he completed with the band, *Roots,* in 1996. That album melded Brazilian Indian chants and percussive rhythms with intense guitar feedback and pointed criticisms of Brazil's military establishment as well as the corporate music industry. Forming a new band, Soulfly, Cavalera was joined by drummer Roy Mayorga, guitarist Jackson Banderia, and former Sepultura roadie and bassist Marcelo Rapp, a lineup that later changed to include Mikey Doling on guitar and Joe Nunez on drums. Continuing the direction he had taken with *Roots* while coping with the series of losses he had faced during the past year gave Cavalera the opportunity to complete "the most personal and diverse [album] of my career," as the front man told *Las Vegas Weekly.* "I had to use all the tragedy around me and turn it into a positive thing. The experimentation and tribal rhythms heard on this album are a cry of celebration and rebirth." Released in 1998, *Soulfly* was "even harder and more aggressive" than anything Sepultura had recorded, as a *Q* magazine review noted, praising its accomplished blend of indigenous and metal influences.

Soulfly underwent a number of personnel changes as Cavalera sought members who could share his commitment "to give it all," as he told *NY Rock* online in 1999. "I think we're on our way somewhere. We're building something. At the moment we sow, later on we can bring the harvest in. But anybody who wants to harvest has to make sacrifices and has to work hard for it, like playing in dingy little clubs and not having a lot of money." Cavalera's dedication included an extensive concert schedule that took the band to Germany, England, America, and Russia, where the audiences were especially receptive to Soulfly's mix of rage and hope. In order to give local bands some exposure, Soulfly tried whenever possible to give them a spot as an opening act. The group also made room for anti-censorship booths to distribute information on its 1999 United States tour. For Cavalera, such deeds demonstrated the possibility of retaining his integrity even while enjoying a successful career. Soulfly's leader was not above commercial endorsements, however,

For the Record . . .

Members include **Max Cavalera** (born Massimiliano Cavalera on August 4, 1968, in Belo Horizonte, Brazil), lead vocals, guitar; **Mikey Doling**, guitar; **Joe Nunez**, drums; **Marcelo D. Rapp** (born Marcelo Dias), bass.

Band formed by Max Cavalera after departing death-metal band Sepultura, late 1996; first album recorded the following year and released as *Soulfly*, 1998; toured extensively based on large international following in America and Europe; released follow-up album, *Primitive*, 2000.

Addresses: *Record company*—Roadrunner Records, 550 Madison Avenue, New York, NY 10022-3297, website: http://www.roadrunnerrecords.com. *Website* —Soulfly Official Website: http://www.soulflytribe. com.

writing a song for a Sprite soft drink commercial that aired in Brazil.

With one well-received album and a string of successful concert tours behind the band, Cavalera and Soulfly looked forward to entering the studio for their second album. Although the band's membership was still changing, Cavalera emphasized the collaborative aspects of Soulfly's creative process. Discussing his musicianship in *Guitar Player*, Cavalera explained, "If everything is completely tight, the band sounds like a machine—yet if everything is too loose, the music sounds sloppy. In our case, when you put Mikey [Doling] and me together, the groove sounds very fresh and loose, without being sloppy." Soulfly also enlisted musicians as diverse as Sean Lennon, Tom Araya of Slayer, and Chino Moreno of the Deftones for its second album, released as *Primitive* in 2000. With elements of Brazilian, gospel, and reggae music incorporated into the band's speed-metal format, the album contained highlights such as "Soulfly II," which *NY Rock* hailed as "a gorgeous example of what [Cavalera] can accomplish with his sense of melody and Brazilian rhythm."

Although most of the lyrics of *Primitive* were less overtly angry than those on Soulfly's debut album, songs like "Terrorist" and "The Prophet" showed Cavalera continuing to vent his rage. The front man hoped, however, that his music served a greater purpose. As

Cavalera commented on his record company's website, "With this album, it's about turning anger into something positive.... The average Soulfly fan deals with a lot of sh** every day, and I think my music helps." As well, the newfound maturity reflected in *Primitive* further completed the separation of Cavalera's Soulfly work from that of Sepultura, which had continued to record and tour with a new singer after Cavalera's departure. Indeed, experimenting with collaborations of guest musicians and taking a musically eclectic approach, Soulfly's first two albums had expanded the heavy metal genre to the extent that the label "heavy metal" seemed too limiting a term to apply to the band.

The completion of *Primitive* and the collaborative efforts of Soulfly also helped Cavalera put the disillusionment of his final Sepultura days behind him. Continuing to live in Phoenix with his wife and son, Cavalera enjoyed a measure of peace that renewed his commitment to his music and Soulfly's fans. Retaining his integrity remained his paramount mission. As Cavalera told *Las Vegas Weekly*, "Too many people in this industry are so worried about money, fame, and security they forget about the real meaning of it all." He concluded, "But things will be all right as long as you don't lose the fire inside of you. I've never lost the fire."

Selected discography

Soulfly, Roadrunner, 1998.
Primitive, Roadrunner, 2000.

Sources

Books

Levine, Robert M., *The History of Brazil,* Greenwood Press, 1999.

Periodicals

Amusement Business, August 8, 1999.
Billboard, March 5, 1994.
Guitar Player, January 2001.
Las Vegas Weekly, September 2000.
Rolling Stone, March 21, 1996.
Orlando Sentinel, April 4, 2001.
Q, May 1998.

Online

All Music Guide, http://www.allmusic.com/cg/amg.dll (April 19, 2001).
CMJ, http://www.cmjmusic.com/articles/ (April 27, 2001).
NY Rock, http://www.nyrock.com/interviews/soulfly_int.htm (April 27, 2001).
Roadrunner Records, http://www.roadrunnerrecords.com/ artists/soulfly (April 21, 2001).

Rough Edge, http://www.roughedge.com/cdreviews/soulfly
.htm (April 27, 2001).
This Swirling Sphere, http://www.thei.aust.com/isite/max.ht
ml (April 27, 2001).

—*Timothy Borden*

Jimmy Sturr

Clarinetist, bandleader

It would be hard to imagine a less likely ambassador for polka than Jimmy Sturr. He describes himself as "100 percent Irish," yet he has managed to lead his polka orchestra to eleven Grammy Awards for Best Polka Album and spread enthusiasm for polka into some quarters where one would never expect to see it. He even managed to wrangle a spot for his group at the Grand Ole Opry in 1995, becoming the first polka band to make an appearance in one of country music's most hallowed venues. Of course, not every young man has formed his own band by the age of eleven, so many people have come to expect the unexpected from Sturr.

Sturr was born and raised in an upstate New York community with the unlikely name of Florida. Located in the Catskills region, the Orange County town is in the heart of onion-growing country. Most of the people in and around Florida are farmers, the majority of whom are descended from immigrants who came to the region from Poland and Germany. "And they brought all their traditions with them," Sturr told the *Washington Post.* "So our high school dances were played by polka bands. The local radio station played polkas every day. Those three-day Polish weddings? They had those every weekend. And every Saturday night I would tune in to the *Lawrence Welk Show,* and I would just sit there until [accordionist] Myron Floren played his polka. And that was enough for me."

In the third grade, Sturr started taking lessons on the clarinet and saxophone, which he continued throughout his school years. Before long, he was good enough to join the school band, and by the age of eleven he had formed his first band, which he dubbed the Melody Makers. The group played its first show at a PTA meeting, an engagement booked for them by Sturr's mother. In his early teens, he won a full scholarship to attend Valley Forge Military Academy in Wayne, Pennsylvania. Sturr continued to work on his music while attending the private military school. He graduated from Valley Forge in 1960 and later attended the University of Scranton, from which he received his bachelor's degree. After a brief stint in the United States Army, Sturr returned to his hometown where he continued to play with his band whenever possible, while working during the day at a bank. After 12 years of splitting his life between the daytime bank job and his band at night, he decided to see if he could make a living with his music alone.

Over the past few decades, Sturr and his orchestra have played in cities all across the United States as well as a number of dates abroad. Touring within the United States, the band travels in its own customized tour bus. Some of the more memorable concert appearances for Sturr and his orchestra have included six sold-out performances at Carnegie Hall, two standing-room-only performances at Avery Fisher Hall in New York's Lincoln Center, and an appearance at the Palace of Culture in Warsaw, Poland. The Warsaw engagement was particularly memorable because the orchestra received seven standing ovations. So impressed was the Cable News Network (CNN) with the immense popularity of Sturr's orchestra that they taped a 15-minute interview with the bandleader that was later broadcast worldwide. Ad agencies, struck by the group's drawing power, decided to use them in a few television commercials, most notably for Pontiac, Budweiser, and Mrs. T's Pierogies.

Of all his accomplishments, Sturr is perhaps proudest of his successful campaign to win a broader audience for the polka music he loves so much. The breakthrough appearance of his orchestra on the Grand Ole Opry was just the beginning of an effort to get country fans more interested in polka music. The first Opry appearance was followed by several return trips and multiple appearances on the Nashville Network. Country superstars Willie Nelson and the Oak Ridge Boys have contributed guest tracks to some of Sturr's polka recordings, and a number of country stars have guested on Sturr's 15-minute syndicated radio show. Among those making appearances have been Bill Anderson, Johnny Paycheck, and Mel Tillis. Appearing in concert with Sturr's orchestra have been such country notables as George Jones, Alan Jackson, Dwight Yoakum, and Nelson.

Early in 2001, Sturr discussed with the *Washington Post* his lifelong mission to get the listening public to at least give polka a chance. He acknowledged that polka music would never achieve the broad popularity of rock

For the Record . . .

Born c. 1942 in Florida, NY. *Education*: Bachelor's degree, University of Scranton.

Formed first polka band at the age of 15; has since recorded more than 100 albums; blends polka with country, pop, Tex-Mex, and Cajun influences.

Awards: Grammy Award, Best Polka Album, 1987-92, 1996-99, 2001.

Addresses: *Record company*—Rounder Records Corporation, 1 Camp Street, Cambridge, MA 02140. *Booking*—United Polka Artists, Box 1, Florida, NY 10921. *Website*—Jimmy Sturr and His Orchestra Official Website: http://www.jimmysturr.com.

and some other musical genres. "And that's what makes me work constantly at this, trying to always gain popularity, not just for the band, but for the word 'polka.' A lot of people think they've nailed the word 'polka.' They feel it's just for old people, that it's only done in a beer hall—and that's just not true."

Sturr's collaborations with some of ethnic music's most popular performers have also helped to expose a broader audience to polka. He recorded a few songs with Flaco Jimenez, one of Tex-Mex music's best-known performers, and Cajun singer Jo-El Sonnier. *Touched by a Polka,* which Sturr released on the Rounder label in 2000, features a Cajun-polka blend on Jimmy C. Newman's "Thibodeaux and His Cajun Band," not to mention a "St. Patty's Polka Medley." In an interview with the *Washington Post,* Sturr pointed out that it is easy enough to convert anything in a two-beat rhythm into a polka. "Take that Cajun music, that Tejano music, some of that western swing—it's nothing more than a polka played a little slower, or a little bit faster. You can't get away from that lively sound of a polka."

High on the list of those who needed to be won over to polka was the National Academy of Recording Arts and Sciences (now known as the Recording Academy), which until 1986 had no polka category at all. In the years since the Grammy Award for Best Polka Album has been offered, Sturr's orchestra has been nominated every year and has won the award eleven times. With a record like that, you might expect Sturr to become rather blasé about the honor. But in late February of 2001, as he waited in his winter home on Singer Island, Florida, to hear who had won the polka Grammy, he was "a nervous wreck," according to the *Palm Beach Post.* "You never get used to it, the waiting," he said. "There are some great bands in the polka field, and they're all over the country. Polka music is like underground music.... People are afraid to say they like polka, especially the young people."

For all his success, Sturr remains fiercely loyal to his hometown of Florida. He maintains an office just across from the school he attended as a boy, and he lives in the home in which he grew up. In addition to his successful musical enterprises, he operates a number of businesses from there, including a travel agency, recording studio, publishing company, and his syndicated radio show. Among the non-musical honors of which he is most proud was his selection by Valley Forge Military Academy in 1995 as "Man of the Year." The military school honored Sturr with a full dress parade in front of the academy's Corps of Cadets.

Selected discography

When It's Polka Time at Your House, Vanguard, 1991.
Live at Gilley's, Vanguard, 1992.
A Jimmy Sturr Christmas, Ranwood, 1992.
Sturr It Up, Vanguard, 1993.
Polka Christmas, Delta, 1993.
Polka Your Troubles Away, Rounder, 1994.
I Love to Polka, Rounder, 1995.
Saturday Night Polka, Ranwood, 1995.
Polka! All Night Long, Rounder, 1996.
Living on Polka Time, Rounder, 1997.
Dance with Me, Rounder, 1998
Life's a Polka, Polka City, 1998.
Polkapalooza, Rounder, 1999.
Touched by a Polka, Rounder, 2000.

Sources

Periodicals

Billboard, August 2, 1997, p. 10.
Palm Beach Post, March 3, 2001, p. 1D.
Washington Post, March 30, 2001, p. T15.

Online

"Jimmy Sturr," *All Music Guide,* http://allmusic.com/cg/x.dll?p=amg&sql=B34629 (May 10, 2001).
"Jimmy Sturr: Biography," Jimmy Sturr and His Orchestra, http://www.jimmysturr.com/bio/ (April 23, 2001).
"Jimmy Sturr," Rounder Records, http://www.rounder.com/rounder/artists/sturr_jimmy/profile.html (May 10, 2001)

—*Don Amerman*

Tan Dun

Composer

Photograph by Reed Saxon. AP/Wide World Photos. Reproduced by permission.

Chinese composer Tan Dun's ethnically diverse and innovative compositions have been performed in the major concert halls of the world and have earned prestigious awards. He has been called on to score music for some the major events of his time, including the reunification of Hong Kong with China and the world's celebration of the new millennium. Tan grew up planting rice during Mao Zedong's Cultural Revolution, but his music has taken him to Manhattan, New York, and on tour around the globe. He came into the Hollywood spotlight in 2001 when his score for the soundtrack to Ang Lee's film *Crouching Tiger, Hidden Dragon* won an Academy Award. He has become one of most prominent composers in the "world classical" genre, but Tan insists that he is not an ambassador between East and West. His goal, rather, is to "create my own unity," he told *Time.*

Born on August 18, 1957 in Si Mao, in China's central Hunan province, Tan was raised by his grandmother. Recruited to "re-education," or forced labor, as a child, Tan planted rice during China's Cultural Revolution. He grew up among peasants in a shamanistic culture that bore a distinct linguistic and folk identity. Tan kept his ears open to the music of village folk songs, and then to occupy his mind, arranged fantastic compositions of the music with any instrument he could find. In addition to traditional folk instruments like the erhu, or one-string Chinese fiddle, he played on woks and agricultural implements. At 17, he was the village musician, playing at parties, weddings, and funerals. At 19, he heard his first piece of Western classical music, Beethoven's Fifth Symphony, while playing violin in a Beijing opera company. In 1978, he was selected over thousands of applicants for a spot at Beijing's Central Conservatory of Music where he earned his bachelor's and master's degrees in composition.

At age 22, Tan was recognized as the leader of an emerging "New Wave" art movement when he wrote the symphony *Li Sao,* based on a fourth-century Hunan lament, to be played by a Western symphony orchestra. In 1983, Tan was the first Chinese composer to win an international prize since the start of the Communist Revolution in 1949. With his string quartet *Feng Ya Song,* Tan was awarded the Weber Prize from Dresden, Germany. Subsequently, performances and broadcasts of his work were banned by the Communist Party for six months as "spiritual pollution." The composer's orchestral work *On Taoism* was noted for its Chinese feel though written for a Western orchestra. Inspired by the death of his grandmother, the work was Tan's first international breakthrough in 1985.

Tan accepted a fellowship at Columbia University in 1986 to work on his doctorate in music. He studied with Chou Wen-Chung, Mario Davidovsky, and George Edwards and made New York City his home. As a student, he wrote in an "international atonal style," according the *All Classical Guide* online. His truly

For the Record . . .

Born on August 18, 1957, in Si Mao, Hunan, China. *Education:* Bachelor's and master's degrees, Central Conservatory of Music, Beijing, China; also studied at Columbia University, New York.

Listened to village songs and played on folk instruments while working in rice fields as a boy; heard first piece of Western classical music at age 19, while playing violin in a Beijing opera company; entered Beijing's Central Conservatory, 1978; first Chinese composer since 1949 to win an international prize for *Fen Ya Song*, 1983; work was then banned in China; was recognized internationally for *On Taoism*, 1985; accepted fellowship at Columbia University, 1986; composed *Heaven Earth Mankind* for Chinese-Hong Kong reunification ceremony, 1997; *2000 Today: A World Symphony for the Millennium,* accompanied New Year's celebrations worldwide, 1999; composer for *Crouching Tiger, Hidden Dragon* film soundtrack, 2000.

Awards: Weber Prize, Dresden, Germany, 1983; Suntory Prize Commission, 1992; *Marco Polo* named Opera of the Year by German opera magazine *Oper,* 1996; Grawemeyer Prize for *Marco Polo,* 1996; elected by Toru Takemitsu for City of Toronto-Glenn Gould Prize in Music and Communication, 1996; Classical Musician of the Year, *New York Times,* 1997; Academy Award for Best Original Soundtrack for *Crouching Tiger, Hidden Dragon,* 2001.

Addresses: Record company—Sony Classical, 550 Madison Ave., New York, NY 10022-3211, (212) 833-8000. *Website*—Tan Dun at Sony Classical: http://www.tandun.com/index.html.

innovative flair became apparent in *Eight Colors* for string quartet in 1988, and the next year in *9 Songs,* which employed the sounds of 50 newly created ceramic instruments. In 1992, Tan became the youngest composer to win the Suntory Prize Commission, and in 1996, was the youngest to be awarded the Grawemeyer Prize for his opera *Marco Polo.*

Tan's first taste of mainstream Western success came with his *Ghost Opera,* which he wrote for the avant-garde Kronos Quartet in 1994. Tan wove a Bach prelude, a Chinese folk song, chanting monks, and the words of Shakespeare into the work. *Marco Polo,* which was commissioned by the Edinburgh Festival and debuted at the Munich Biennale in 1996, was also voted Opera of the Year by the German magazine *Oper.* Among the composer's 14 film scores for American and Chinese films is a jazz-edged score for 1998's *Fallen* starring Denzel Washington. His score for director Ang Lee's 2000 film *Crouching Tiger, Hidden Dragon* featured famed cellist Yo-Yo Ma and Asian pop star CoCo Lee. For the work, which was a blend of ethnic and symphonic music, Tan won an Academy Award for Best Original Score. To the delight of the audience, Tan's Oscar acceptance speech was fast-paced and spoken mostly in Chinese.

Tan has been called on to score music for some of the major events of his time. To celebrate the reunification of China and Hong Kong, Tan composed the 72-minute *Symphony 1997 (Heaven Earth Mankind),* which featured a bianzhong—a set of 65 ceremonial bronze chimes from China's Hubei province from 433 B.C. that had been unearthed by archaeologists. Tan conducted the Hong Kong Philharmonic orchestra in the key of D major—the same as Beethoven's *Ode to Joy*—to an African beat. *Time* critic Terry Teachout called the piece "both frankly romantic and immediately accessible—Beethoven's Ninth boldly recast for postmoderns," and a "seductively savory multi-cultural stew," which featured Ma on cello. Tan composed the symphony in 13 short movements instead of fewer, longer ones. Despite the cultural and political importance of the July 1 changeover ceremony, Teachout declared it "the classical-music event of the summer" of 1997. The minute the musicians had set down their instruments, a recording of the event was rushed into print by Tan's record company, Sony Classical, and debuted at number five on the *Billboard* classical chart.

2000 Today: A World Symphony for the Millennium, was commissioned by the British Broadcasting Corporation (BBC), Public Broadcasting System (PBS) Television, and Sony Classical to debut New Year's Day 2000. A "mosaic" symphony, *2000 Today* was a sampling of Tan's ideas for music in the new millennium. The symphony was heard on 27 hours of New Year's coverage by more than 55 television networks worldwide as midnight reached each successive time zone.

Though his embrace of many cultures is reflected clearly in his work, Tan cringes whenever he is likened to a musical ambassador bringing together the East and the West. "No East anymore, no West anymore," he told *Time.* "My purpose is to be flexible and freely flying around among all kinds of experience. Not to be driven by the wave of culture—fashion, trends, isms, schools—but to create my own unity."

Selected compositions

Five Pieces in Human Accent, piano, 1978.
Li Sao, symphony, 1979-80.
Feng Ya Song, string quartet, 1982.
Fu, for sopranos, bass, and ensemble, 1982.
On Taoism, orchestral work, 1985.
In Distance, for piccolo, harp, and bass drum, 1987.
Out of Beijing, opera for violin and orchestra, 1987.
Eight Colours, for string quartet, 1989.
9 Songs, ritual opera for 20 singers/performers, 1989.
Silk Road, for soprano and percussion, 1989.
Elegy: Snow in June, concerto for cello and four percussionists, 1992.
Death and Fire: Dialogue with Paul Klee, for orchestra, 1993.
Lament: Autumn Wind, for any six instruments, any voice, and conductor, 1993.
CAGE, piano, 1993.
Marco Polo, opera, 1994.
Yi, cello concerto, 1994.
Ghost Opera (written for Kronos Quartet), 1994.
Symphony 1997 (*Heaven Earth Mankind*), 1997.
2000 Today: A World Symphony for the Millennium, 1999.

Selected discography

Snow in June, Composers Recordings Inc., 1993.
Ghost Opera, Wea/Atlantic/Nonesuch, 1997.
Marco Polo, Sony Classical, 1997.
Symphony 1997 (Heaven Earth Mankind), Sony Classical, 1997.
Death and Fire, Ondine, 1998.
Bitter Love, Sony Classical, 1999.
2000 Today: A World Symphony for the Millennium, Sony Classical, 1999.
Crouching Tiger, Hidden Dragon (soundtrack), Sony Classical, 2000.

Sources

Books

Slonimsky, Nicolas, *Baker's Biographical Dictionary of Twentieth-Century Classical Musicians,* Schirmer Books, 1997.

Periodicals

Time, August 11, 1997, p. 76.

Online

"Tan Dun," *All Classical Guide,* http://www.allclassical.com (March 30, 2001).
"Tan Dun," G. Schirmer, Inc. and Associated Music Publishers, http://www.schirmer.com/composers/tan_bio.html (March 30, 2001).

—Brenna Sanchez

Buddy Tate

Saxophonist

Photograph by Delvac. © Bettmann/Corbis. Reproduced by permission.

For more than seven decades, Texas-bred George "Buddy" Tate graced the American jazz scene with his hard-blowing tenor saxophone style. A resilient tone with high register inflections in the so-called "Texas tenor" sound distinguished Tate among his swing era colleagues. He was a member of the Count Basie Orchestra during the late 1930s and 1940s and later became a bandleader in his own right. A legend in his own time, Tate was heard with progeny saxophone player James Carter on *Conversin' with the Elders* in 1996 in what was Tate's final recorded appearance just five years before his death at the age of 87.

By most accounts, Tate was born George Holmes Tate on February 22, 1913, in Sherman, Texas. (He might have been born as late as 1915, and some sources report his birthplace as Fordham, Texas.) True to his heritage, Tate became accomplished in playing Texas tenor saxophone, a robust horn style that was popular during the swing era of jazz. Tate began performing in 1925 while still in his teens when his brother handed him an instrument and asked him to play tenor saxophone with the family quartet called McCloud's Night Owls. Tate and the Night Owls learned to play largely by listening to recordings by Louis Armstrong and mimicking the sound. The band toured professionally for the next four years, after which Tate continued to play the horn, performing with a series of territory bands (which played off-road venues) and with circus bands until the early 1930s when he toured the southwestern United States with Nathan Towles' band. During those early years, Tate spent time with Terrence Holder's band from 1930-33 and toured with Andy Kirk's Clouds of Joy in 1934-35.

In 1934 Tate filled in briefly with Count Basie's Orchestra as a replacement for Lester Young. Young eventually returned to the band, and Tate joined up with Towles for another four years beginning in 1935. Tate worked with Towles until 1939 when Herschel Evans, who was Basie's tenor saxophone player, died. Basie then brought Tate back into the orchestra as a permanent fixture for nearly a decade. Perhaps nowhere was the contention for attention between saxophone players of that era more pronounced than among Basie's sidemen. Among the notables were Illinois Jacquet—also one of the so-called Texas tenors—Lucky Thompson, and Young, all of whom along with Tate transformed moments of the orchestra's performances into full-scale dueling sets between horns. Tate was heard on many recordings by the Basie orchestra during that era, including selected recordings where Tate performed on alto saxophone as well as tenor. He emerged from Basie's band as a seasoned professional. Tate, according to Gene Seymour in *Newsday,* "could howl in one measure and coo in the next ... [He] could climb aboard a 4/4 tempo and ride it straight-backed and resolute without slipping off." After Tate parted ways with Basie in 1949, Tate appeared with Hot Lips Page, Lucky Millinder, and Jimmy Rushing

Born George Holmes Tate on February 22, 1913 (or 1915), in Sherman, TX; died on February 10, 2001, in Chandler, AZ; married Viola (widowed, 1991); four children: Georgette Matthews and Josie Sanabia; two sons (deceased).

Performed with McCloud's Night Owls, 1925-29; with territory and circus bands, late 1920s and early 1930s; with Terence "T" Holder, 1930-33; with Andy Kirk, 1934-35; toured with Nat Towles; with Count Basie Orchestra, 1939-49; house bandleader, Celebrity Club, New York City, 1950s-70s; European tours: 1959, 1961, 1967, 1968; Texas Tenors, with Illinois Jacquet, 1980s; Buddy Tate Sextet, 1993; Lionel Hampton's Statesmen of Jazz, mid-1990s; performed regularly at many jazz festivals; film work included *Choo Choo Swing*, *Reveille with Beverly*, and *Hit Parade of 1943*, 1943; *L'Aventure du Jazz*, 1970; *Born to Swing*, 1973; *Rocky Mountain Jazz Party*, 1977; *To the Count of Basie*, 1979.

until 1952. He then assembled his own house band at Harlem's Celebrity Club in 1953, marking the start of a gig that lasted for 21 years, until the early 1970s.

Tate's European tours brought him largely to France where, in 1967 and 1968, he performed as bandleader in a trio comprised of Milt Buckner on organ and Wallace Bishop on drums. Tate and Buckner recorded a series of tenor saxophone and organ duets in 1967 on the Black and Blue label, including *Buddy Tate with Milt Buckner*, which is revered among Tate's best works. He made two earlier European tours as a sideman for Buck Clayton, in 1959 and 1961 respectively. In 1967 Tate also appeared with John Hammond in a concert program called Spirituals to Swing and toured with the Saints and Sinners. Tate spent time in the 1970s as a sideman in the Benny Goodman Orchestra. In the 1980s, Tate toured extensively with Jacquet's group called the Texas Tenors. The Tenors followed a festival circuit that took the players to the Newport Jazz Festival in 1980 and to the festival in Cork in 1983 and again in 1985. His festival tours with Jacquet in the 1980s included annual visits to the Grande Parade du Jazz in Nice, France. Additionally, Tate's North American agenda included both live and taped performances with Jay McShann and Jim Galloway in Canada.

Tate's 1973 release, *Buddy Tate and His Buddies*, featured his former Basie cohort, Jacquet, pianist Mary Lou Williams, and trumpeter Roy Eldridge. Also numbered among the buddies were guitarist Stan Jordan, drummer Gus Johnson, and Milt Hinton on bass. The album, one of Tate's more popular recordings, was re-issued in 1994. In 1978 Tate taped a collection of recordings for Muse Records under the bill of Buddy Tate & the Muse All Stars. Those albums included *Live at Sandy's, Hard Blowin'*, and *Muse All Stars*. In 1991 Tate joined fellow tenor saxophone player James Moody and a collection of others among his peers on the live recording, *Lionel Hampton and the Golden Men of Jazz*. The 1996 album *Conversin' with the Elders* by saxophonist James Carter marked what would become Tate's final appearance on record.

Tate and his wife, Viola, were married during his years with Count Basie. The couple moved to Massapequa, New York, in 1945 and raised four children. Tate's later career was twice marred by tragedy; in 1981 when he suffered serious scalding in a hotel shower and again in the early 1990s when he suffered fractures in both legs in a car accident. His resilience left his fans to marvel as he rebounded from his burns in particular with remarkable speed. Although both accidents impacted him for a time, neither signaled an end to Tate's career. He remained active and performed with Lionel Hampton and the Statesmen of Jazz in the late 1990s until a bout with cancer left him incapacitated. In January of 2001 Tate moved to Phoenix, Arizona, to live near his daughter. He died in Arizona soon afterward, in a nursing home in Chandler on February 10. The jazz world mourned Tate as the last surviving member of the Count Basie Orchestra of the 1940s. Steve Voce in *Independent* recalled how Tate "played ballads beautifully and … was a consistently interesting soloist who was instantly recognizable."

Of Tate's children, his two daughters, Georgette Matthews and Josie Sanabia survived him along with a number of grandchildren. Viola Tate, founder of the Bayview Rest Home in Babylon, New York, died in 1991.

Selected discography

Buddy Tate and His Orchestra, Halo, 1955.
Swinging Like Tate, London, 1958.
Tate's Date, Swingville, 1959.
Groovin' with Buddy Tate, Swingville, 1959.
Tate-A-Tate, Swingville/OJC, 1960.
Buddy Tate with Milt Buckner, Black & Blue, 1967.
Unbroken, Pausa, 1970.
Broadway, Black & Blue, 1972.
Buddy Tate and His Buddies, 1973; reissued, Chiaroscuro, 1994.
The Count's Men, RCA, 1973.
Kansas City Woman, Black Lion, 1974.

Swinging Scorpio, Black Lion, 1974.
The Texas Twister, New World, 1975.
Jive at Five, Storyville, 1975.
Tate a Tete at La Fontaine, Copenhagen, Storyville, 1975.
Kansas City Joys, Sonet, 1976.
Meets Dollar Brand, Chiaroscuro, 1977.
Sherman Shuffle, Sackville, 1978.
Buddy Tate Quartet, Sackville, 1978.
Hard Blowin', Muse, 1978.
Live at Sandy's, Muse, 1978.
Muse All-Stars, Muse, 1978.
Great Buddy Tate, Concord Jazz, 1981.
Ballad Artistry of Buddy Tate, Sackville, 1981.
Scott's Buddy, Concord Jazz, 1981.
For Sentimental Reasons, Open Sky, 1982.
Just Jazz, Reservoir, 1984.
Long Tall Tenor, Calligraph, 1985.
After Dark, Progressive, 1985.
Jumping on the West Coast, Black Lion, 1993.
(Contributor*) Conversin' with the Elders*, Atlantic, 1996.

Sources

Periodicals

Dallas Morning News, February 14, 2001, p. 26A.
Independent, February 15, 2001, p. 6.
Jet, March 19, 2001, p. 17.
Newsday, February 14, 2001, p. A39; April 6, 2001, p. D23.
Sunday Star Times (New Zealand), February 18, 2001, p. 7.

Online

"Buddy Tate," *All Music Guide,* http://allmusic.com (April 20, 2001).
"Jazz Artists: Buddy Tate," Jazz Canadiana, http://jazz canadiana.on.ca/_TATE.htm (May 18, 2001),
"Tate, Buddy [George Holmes] " Xrefer, http://www.xrefer .com/entry/628264 (May 18, 2001).

—*Gloria Cooksey*

Train

Rock group

Success has been a slow but steady climb for the San Francisco, California, rock group Train. It took more than two years for momentum to build behind the group's self-titled debut and its first single, the melancholy "Meet Virginia," but the story surrounding the group's sophomore effort, *Drops of Jupiter*, is much different. When the premiere single, the title track, began radio play in the spring of 2001, it instantly garnered attention from music fans. The notoriety catapulted the album to number six on the *Billboard* 200 chart within the first week of its release. "It's pretty different because we started off without a record deal, toured and toured and had that hit ['Meet Virginia']. It's been gradual. This record has been well received from the get-go. It's amazing," bassist Charlie Colin told *Contemporary Musicians*.

Extensive touring has been the driving force behind Train since the group's formation in 1994. Train is basically the melding of two Los Angeles-area groups. Guitarists Jimmy Stafford and Rob Hotchkiss as well as Colin performed as The Apostles, who were signed to Polygram in 1991. Meanwhile, singer Pat Monahan fronted the band Exit. When the Apostles broke up in 1993, Colin packed up and moved to Singapore to write commercial jingles while Hotchkiss relocated to San Francisco where he met Monahan. The two founded a folk duo and traveled the coffeehouse circuit playing cover songs and original material.

Wanting to expand the duo into a full-size band, Monahan and Hotchkiss recruited Stafford and called Colin, who had since moved to Colorado. After hearing demo tapes, Colin and his then-drummer, Scott Underwood, headed for San Francisco. "I heard Pat sing once with Rob and Jimmy and I said, 'Forget it.' I packed up my stuff and moved. It was obviously a good thing. The chemistry was immediate. Once we started playing, we immediately started getting good shows. There was no guess work. It was obviously the right band," Colin told *Contemporary Musicians*.

Having experienced dealing with a major label with The Apostles, Colin encouraged his Train bandmates to hone their live skills and build a following before signing a deal. He said it worked out for the best: "We were playing two to three times a week, and we were really prolific. We just focused on playing live shows and writing a lot so we'd try out new songs all the time. We'd rehearse a couple nights a week, so basically we were playing like six nights a week because we were rehearsing and playing live shows," Colin told *Contemporary Musicians*.

Fans responded favorably, allowing Train to become self-sufficient. Within two years, the group had enough original material under its belt to start recording, but money was a problem. The group's family members helped fund the recording of Train's self-titled debut album. To polish songs for their debut, Train recruited Counting Crows' guitarist David Bryson to mix the album. Creating *Train* on its own allowed the band to explore the music without the interference of a record label. Impressed by what it heard, Columbia picked up the group and the album. "We made the album completely unsigned and Columbia bought it from us. We didn't give them the opportunity to let them be the boss. We were completely autonomous. Had I not been signed previously, we would have done it differently. We would have thought we needed to get a record deal and then go [into the studio]. We thought, 'Let's do it ourselves and if people want to hear it, they'll come. If record labels want it, they'll call.' It worked out great for us," Colin told *Contemporary Musicians*.

Train was released by Aware/Red Ink/Columbia Records on February 24, 1998. It received positive reviews, but radio and the record-buying public were slow to make it a hit. In a review for Amazon.com, Jason Josephes compared Train to Georgia's R.E.M., writing, "Ballads like 'If You Leave' and 'Homesick' could be mistaken for early demos by Athens's most beloved sons, but when the guitar solos kick in, it's classic Southern goodness. Luckily Train don't derail themselves by sticking solely to greasy jams and high-wire guitar acrobatics. The San Francisco-based five-piece keep their slice-of-life sound simple and lean, never overdoing what doesn't need to be overdone."

One year later, Train got a boost from Aware Records, a small label that is credited with discovering the likes of Hootie and the Blowfish, the Dave Matthews Band,

Members include **Charlie Colin**, bass, guitars, background vocals; **Rob Hotchkiss**, guitars, bass, background vocals, harmonica; **Pat Monahan**, lead vocals, trumpet, saxophone, percussion; **Jimmy Stafford**, guitars, background vocals, mandolin; **Scott Underwood**, drums, programming, keyboards, percussion.

Group formed in San Francisco, CA, 1994; released debut LP *Train*, 1996; signed with Aware/Red Ink/Columbia/Sony and re-issued *Train*, 1998; contributed to *Aware 5: The Compilation*, 1997; and *Songs From Dawson's Creek Vol. II*, 2000; released *Drops of Jupiter*, 2001.

Awards: U.S. gold certification for *Train*, 1999; U.S. platinum certification for *Train*, 2000.

Addresses: *Record company*—Columbia Records, 550 Madison Avenue, New York, NY 10022-3211; 2100 Colorado Avenue, Santa Monica, CA 90404. *Management*—Bill Graham Management, P.O. Box 31505, Oakland, CA, 94604-1505. *Website*—Train Official Website: http://www.trainline.com.

and Better Than Ezra. It decided to put Train's single "Meet Virginia" on *Aware 5: The Compilation*, part of a series of CDs meant to give fans exposure to new music. It worked, pushing the single into the top ten and eventually helping to drive sales past one million. "The peak moment was when we played this radio show in Philadelphia that summer. We were on after some band I'd never heard of, and before Sean Lennon. Just as we're backstage waiting to go on, we hear thousands of people rushing the stage and chanting, 'Train, Train, Train!' We sort of knew that there was this swelling fan base around the country, but until we had the hit on the radio, we didn't see it in such a ravenous way. That was such a high," Monahan said in Columbia Records press materials.

After three years of supporting *Train*, the band took a six-week break to record its sophomore album, *Drops of Jupiter*, at Atlanta, Georgia's Southern Tracks Studio. The group worked with producer Brendan O'Brien, whose credits include work with Pearl Jam and Stone Temple Pilots. "We're really proud of this album," Monahan explained in Columbia Records press materials. "After years on the road, supporting an album that

we wrote so long ago, we're obviously excited about getting a bunch of new material out there. But beyond that, these songs just have a quality about them. Our songwriting, our relationships, our ability to get our thoughts into songs—all that got stronger after playing in front of a live audience for so many nights."

Fans got their first taste of *Drops of Jupiter* when the song "Respect" appeared on *Songs From Dawson's Creek Vol. II*, released in October of 2000. Like the previous effort, Train wrote the album together, with individual members contributing songs. "It's really interesting how we're extremely close friends and musically, we couldn't do it without each other. There's no way we could have another person come in and be trained. Our drummer, for example, he plays keyboards and writes songs. I play bass predominately and I also play three songs on this record on guitar. We all sing. Everybody writes. Everybody brings in a large amount of material. I don't think we're one of those bands that can afford to lose a member. We wouldn't be a band anymore on any level," Colin told *Contemporary Musicians*.

The plan seems to have worked. In a review for the CDNow website, Paul Semel wrote that "such tunes as 'She's on Fire' and 'Let It Roll' boast just a few simple chords and rhythms, and yet are still solid and infectious. There are occasional variations in the formula; 'Hopeless,' for example, finds Train adopting a stripped-down approach, while the title track finds it employing a sweeping string section and some piano in an impressive impersonation of Elton John."

Just as much as the band missed the road, the fans were yearning for a new record. It became obvious when the single, "Drops of Jupiter," was sent to radio. "There are a lot of people out there who had seen us in small clubs and bars and got to hang out and meet us. We have a really strong grassroots following. They were really eager for the record.... Pat has a way of writing lyrics that are genuine and personal to him. When you listen, you can relate to it. They feel the same way. They kind of attach it to their lives," Colin told *Contemporary Musicians*.

Selected discography

Train (includes "Meet Virginia"), 1996; reissued, Aware/Red Ink/Columbia/Sony, 1998.
(Contributor) *Aware 5: The Compilation,* Aware, 1997.
(Contributor) *Dawson's Creek Soundtrack Volume II*, Columbia, 2000.
(Contributor) *Stoned Immaculate* (includes "Light My Fire"), Elektra, 2000.
Drops of Jupiter (includes "Drops of Jupiter"), Columbia/Sony, 2001.

Sources

Periodicals

Billboard, July 24, 1999, p. 79.
Entertainment Weekly, March 30, 2001, p. 68.
Guitar Player, August 2001, p. 39.
Variety, April 10, 2000, p. 79.

Online

Bill Graham Management, http://www.bgmsf.com (June 4, 2001).
"Train," Amazon.com, http://www.amazon.com (May 28, 2001).
"Train," Sonicnet.com, http://www.sonicnet.com (May 28, 2001).
"Train: Drops of Jupiter," CDNow.com, http://www.cdnow.com (May 29, 2001).

Additional information was provided by Columbia Records publicity materials, 1996 and 2001, and an interview with Charlie Colin on April 27, 2001.

—Christina Fuoco

Dave Valentin

Flutist

It may have been love for a girl that caused former percussionist Dave Valentin to start playing the flute, but it was love for the instrument that has kept him playing. Valentin gained attention early on as a versatile musician who was able to play in Latin jazz groups but found professional success by exploring the sounds of world music with his flute. He was adept at Latin and straight-ahead jazz, but was also known for combining Latin rhythms with pop sounds in his original music. He was the first artist signed to the GRP jazz label in 1978 and released 18 world music albums on the imprint. The son of Puerto Rican parents, he only seriously delved into Latin music on his sixteenth release for GRP called *Tropic Heat* in 1993.

Born on April 29, 1952, in New York's Bronx borough to parents who were from Mayaguez, Puerto Rico, Valentin was surrounded by the music his parents listened to. The Valentin household was filled with the sounds of Tito Rodriguez, Tito Puente, Machito and others. He picked up bongos and congas as a child, and by his early teens, had joined a Latin group as a timbales player. He performed with the group in New York City's Latin nightclubs on the "cuchifrito" circuit, the working-class dance halls of New York. "Oh yes," he said in an interview with Fernando Gonzalez of Knight-Ridder Newspapers, "I've done my three sets for $50 and leave the club at 6 a.m. Sunday morning and seeing the people in Harlem going to church as I'm going home to sleep." He was accepted to New York's High School of Music and Art where he studied percussion, but it was not until Valentin was 18 and in college that he became interested in the flute.

A girl he wanted to meet played the flute, so Valentin borrowed one and asked her to show him a few things. A month later, he played for her, but had become so good that she got jealous, and his plan backfired. He didn't get the girl, but continued to study the flute with Hubert Laws, a popular jazz flutist known for his classical technique, and with a classical player, Hal Bennett. He took up the saxophone for a while, but Laws convinced him to drop the saxophone and focus his energies on the flute. Aside from a few lessons with Laws and Bennett, Valentin is a mostly self-taught flutist. "Sometimes that is best, for it allows one to develop their own style and sound," he was quoted as saying in a Concord Records press release.

The young artist worked as a schoolteacher to pay the bills but continued to play music, becoming one of New York's up-and-coming musicians. In the early 1970s, Valentin was playing with some of the hottest Latin bands in the city, but it was his ability to cross over and play with big-name jazz artists like singer Patti Austin, guitarist Lee Ritenour, and pianist Dave Grusin that got him noticed.

Valentin made his recording debut with Ricardo Marrero's group in 1977. While Valentin was recording a

For the Record . . .

Born David Valentin on April 29, 1952, in Bronx, NY.

Played bongos and congas at age seven, performed at Latin clubs in New York City from age 12; started playing the flute at 18; made recording debut with Ricardo Marrero's group, 1977; first artist to sign with newly formed GRP Records, 1978; released *Red Sun*, 1992; released Latin-themed *Tropic Heat*, 1993; released first album on Concord Records, *Sunshowers*, 1999.

Awards: Named Best Flutist, *Jazziz* Readers Poll, 1989-91.

Addresses: *Record company*—Concord Records, P.O. Box 845, Concord, CA 94522, phone: (925) 682-6770, fax: (925) 682-3508, website: http://www.concordrecords.com.

demo session for violinist Noel Pointer, Pointer became interested in a piece Valentin had written. The session engineer, Larry Rosen, pulled Valentin aside and asked him if he had any other original material. Valentin sent him a tape and a month later was making a record for Rosen and Dave Grusin as the first artist signed to their GRP record label in 1978. Valentin remained with GRP for nearly 20 years to record 18 albums. Valentin continued to teach for a year after the release of his debut album, *Legends,* in 1979.

Though of Puerto Rican descent, Valentin was known for his "willingness to investigate and absorb any style of music," wrote Mark Holston in *Americas.* "I ... consider myself a world artist." He first mastered the common European flute and then experimented with different models in the flute family from around the world. He collected pan pipes from Bolivia, a bamboo bass flute from Peru, a pan flute from Romania and various porcelain and wooden models from Thailand, Japan, and elsewhere, and toured with more than a dozen various flutes. He mastered the charanga, a Cuban music style that featured the flute, after diligently studying the methods of Jose Fajardo, the king of the genre. He often used a Cuban rhythm as the foundation for his take on a pop song, such as "Blackbird" by Paul McCartney and John Lennon. Holston called the flutist "adept at mixing the essence of Afro-Caribbean styles with self-penned songs, jazz standards and world music anthems...."

All Music Guide to Jazz critic Scott Yanow noted that on Valentin's 1991 release, *Musical Portraits,* it was evident that Valentin "could become one of the best jazz flutists," but that he had so far "not quite lived up to his potential." Of Valentin's 1992 release, *Red Sun,* Yanow wrote that Valentin seemed somewhat "controlled," despite some "passionate moments." Over all, he called *Red Sun* a "relatively pleasing" CD.

In 1993, Valentin released *Tropic Heat,* his first Latin jazz album. Though he had always "tried to include some Latin music in some way" on his previous albums, he told Fernando Gonzalez of Knight-Ridder, he added that never wanted to be "pigeonholed" as a strictly Latin artist. The record was a long time coming for Valentin, who felt Puerto Rican rhythms and styles were sorely overlooked by Puerto Rican musicians more clearly influenced by the sounds of Cuba. Valentin teamed up with up-and-coming Latin stars like Dominican saxophonist Mario Rivera, conguero Jerry Gonzalez, trumpeter Charlie Sepulveda, saxophonist David Sanchez, and trombonist Angel "Papo" Vazquez to record. The result was a "mature, seamless blend of jazz and Afro-Caribbean elements," wrote Gonzalez. On the album, Valentin paid tribute to his childhood hero, bandleader and vocalist Tito Rodriguez, with a version of the song "Bello Amanecer." Yanow called *Tropic Heat* "one of [Valentin's] best," and proof that Valentin "continues to grow as a player."

In addition to his usual position as leader and front man, Valentin has also been sideman to some legendary jazz musicians. He was musical director for Tito Puente, his childhood idol, and considered playing with McCoy Tyner "like being in heaven," he said in his Concord Records biography. He played at Dizzy Gillespie's seventieth birthday party and has been a guest with Machito, Ray Barretto, Celia Cruz, Michel Camilo, and Herbie Mann.

In 1999, Valentin released his debut with Concord Records, called *Sunshower.* "On *Sunshower,*" Valentin said in comments included in his Concord biography, "we went for a slightly more commercial sound.... By 'commercial' I mean music that I love to play live and that is quite accessible." The release prompted one *Los Angeles Times* writer to point out that Valentin was an "underrated" artist. Valentin seemed hungry to continue exploring the world of music with his flute. In his Concord biography he said, "I want to continue playing music until the day I drop dead! I want to play until I can play no more...."

Selected discography

Legends, GRP, 1979.
I Got It Right This Time, Arista, 1981.
Mind Time, GRP, 1987.

Live at the Blue Note, GRP, 1988.
Two Amigos, GRP, 1990.
Musical Portraits, GRP, 1991.
Red Sun, GRP, 1992.
Tropic Heat, GRP, 1993.
Primitive Passions, RMM, 1996.
Sunshower, Concord Jazz, 1999.

Sources

Books

All Music Guide to Jazz, Miller Freeman Books, 1998.
Feather, Leonard and Ira Gitler, *Biographical Encyclopedia of Jazz,* Oxford University Press, 1999.
Kernfeld, Barry, *New Grove Dictionary of Jazz,* Macmillan Press Ltd., 1998.

Periodicals

Americas, March/April 1992, p. 56.
Knight-Ridder/Tribune News Service, August 19, 1994.
Los Angeles Times, September 19, 1999.

Online

Concord Records, http://www.concordrecords.com (April 18, 2001).
"Dave Valentin," *All Music Guide,* http://www.allmusic.com (April 17, 2001).

—*Brenna Sanchez*

Vertical Horizon

Rock group

Boston-based Vertical Horizon is the epitome of the do-it-yourself work ethic. Like the Dave Matthews Band and Hootie and the Blowfish, Vertical Horizon did not rely on the backing of a record company to further its career. It took it upon itself, releasing three independent albums before signing a contract with RCA/BMG. "From the beginning, we've always had a grassroots approach," singer-guitarist Keith Kane told Frank Tortorici of Sonicnet.com.

Kane and singer-guitarist Matt Scannell met as Georgetown University students in Washington, D.C. in 1991 when they were recruited to perform acoustically during a party. The two took turns at the microphone, slowly winning over the small crowd. Impressed at what they could achieve, Kane invited Scannell to join him for a weekly series of acoustic shows at a downtown coffeehouse as Vertical Horizon. According to the band's official website, "their sound was anchored in folk music and harmonized vocals, and their catalog consisted of mostly covers and a few originals." The duo's cover song choices—ranging from America to Duran Duran—reflected Scannell and Kane's own musical tastes.

Photograph by Jeffrey Mayer. Wireimage.com. Reproduced by permission.

For the Record . . .

Members include **Sean Hurley** (joined group, 1998), bass; **Keith Kane**, singer, guitarist, songwriter; **Matt Scannell**, singer, guitarist; **Ed Toth** (joined group, 1996), drums.

Group formed in Washington, D.C., 1991; released debut LP *There and Back Again* on own Rythmic Records, 1993; signed with RCA, released *Everything You Want*, 1999; contributed to *Vol. 1 Stop Handgun Violence*, 2000.

Awards: U.S. platinum certification for *Everything You Want*, 2000; Boston Music Awards, Single of the Year for "Everything You Want," 2001; Radio Music Awards, Song of the Year: Pop Alternative Radio for "Everything You Want," 2000.

Addresses: *Record company*—RCA Records, 1540 Broadway, Times Square, New York, NY 10036. *Management*—Metropolitan Entertainment Group, 7 North Mountain Avenue, P.O. Box 1566, Montclair, NJ 07042-1840. *Website*—Vertical Horizon Official Website: http://www.verticalhorizon.com.

Upon graduating in 1992, Scannell and Kane relocated to Cape Cod near Scannell's hometown of Deerfield, Massachusetts. In the summer of 1993, the duo recorded its first CD, *There and Back Again*, at the studio in Scannell's former high school. "I went to a boarding school up in Massachusetts, and they got a recording studio after I had graduated," Scannell told VH1.com. "I called up the headmaster, because we had no money at the time. And I said, 'We'd love to make a record, is it possible for us to break in your new studio?' They let us come in, and we spent 12 days there and recorded the thing." As they completed the record, the duo stayed at the home of Scannell's history teacher and on the studio floor. Upon completion, Vertical Horizon pressed 1,000 copies. "We were pretty sure we'd never be able to sell them all but we'd give them away to family members when we were old and gray and say, 'Hey, your grandfather was a rock star.' But people actually bought them, so we made more," Scannell told VH1.com.

Kane and Scannell then returned to the Washington, D.C. area where they met Cary Pierce and Jack O'Neill of the now-defunct Jackopierce. Like Jackopierce, Vertical Horizon was rooted in acoustic rock, which

made for the perfect touring package. The two acts performed together for three weeks and the experience gave Vertical Horizon the connections it needed to embark on its own jaunt. Wishing to fill out its sound, Vertical Horizon hired back-up musicians. Tortorici quoted Kane as saying that the hired hands made it easier for him to write "rock songs." "They need to have that noise. [Going electric has] opened up my mind a little bit, [because] it's rare that I can hear distortion when I write. Even though our style has changed drastically, we stake everything on songwriting." Kane's songwriting piqued the interest of the Dave Matthews Band, the Allman Brothers Band, Train, Shawn Colvin, and Third Eye Blind, all of whom recruited Vertical Horizon as their opening band.

The Dave Matthews Band tour proved beneficial. Drummer Carter Beauford offered to lend a hand on Vertical Horizon's sophomore effort, 1995's *Running on Ice*. After *Running on Ice* hit stores, Vertical Horizon continued to tour religiously. Then-future drummer Ed Toth met up with Vertical Horizon after Scannell's mother came into the Borders Books and Music store in which he was working to look for her son's CD. Toth, along with the bookstore's manager, caught a Vertical Horizon performance at Aerosmith's Mama Kin club in Boston. When the touring drummer left Vertical Horizon, Toth stepped in. Before the 1996 release of the live album *Live Stages*, Toth became a permanent member of the group.

The relentless touring paid off. Vertical Horizon sold more than 70,000 copies of its three independently released albums. The success led to a frenzy of record company interest but the band opted to sign with RCA, which had inked a deal with the Dave Matthews Band. In 1998, Vertical Horizon recorded its major-label debut *Everything You Want*, which focused on "strong songwriting, vocal harmonies and impressive guitar work," according to the group's official website. To advance promotion of the forthcoming record, RCA repackaged and re-released Vertical Horizon's *There and Back Again*, *Running on Ice* and *Live Stages*. Shortly before the new album's June of 1999 release, bassist Sean Hurley, a veteran of Arlo Guthrie and Mark Curry's bands, became a permanent member of the group. He was the first person to audition for the bass player position.

"When I joined, I got a real taste of the hard work that everyone had done," Hurley told Wall of Sound online. "They had sold 70,000 copies of those first three albums—it's probably closer to 100,000 now—and they probably saw every CD, touched every one of them as it passed from them to the fan. Everybody had their hand in everything and knew what was going on. Now we can appreciate doing the things we want to do and having people that will work for us and with us to do the things that we don't."

Everything You Want went largely unnoticed for six months until the title track hit the radio. The success of another single, "You're a God," pushed *Everything You Want* past platinum status, which marks sales of one million copies or more. To promote its record, Vertical Horizon performed as part of Woodstock 1999 and appeared on the Fox television show *Party of Five* in January of 2000.

Vertical Horizon has continued its non-stop touring both as an opening and headlining band. Scannell told VH1.com that the grassroots approach helped solidify the band's reputation: "It helped us to get our live show down. I think there are a lot of bands out now who don't spend a whole lot of time figuring out how to play stuff live. We really knew how to do a live show. Another thing is, just grassroots organization. Kids just talking about us, college kids trading tapes, encouraging kids to record our shows."

Selected discography

There and Back Again, Rythmic, 1993; reissued, RCA, 1999.
Running on Ice, Rythmic, 1995; reissued, RCA, 1999.
Live Stages, Rythmic, 1996; reissued, RCA, 1999.
Everything You Want (includes "Everything You Want," "You're a God," "Best I Ever Had"), RCA, 1999.

Sources

Periodicals

Billboard, September 25, 1999; February 12, 2000; July 15, 2000.
Entertainment Weekly, June 16, 2000.

Online

Billboard, http://www.billboard.com (May 28, 2001).
"Going Electric Pays Off for Vertical Horizon," Sonicnet.com, http://www.sonicnet.com/artists/ai_singlestory.jhtml?id=61917&ai_id=510063 (May 28, 2001).
"Having Words With … Vertical Horizon," Detroit.citysearch.com, http://detroit.citysearch.com/feature/21938 (May 28, 2001).
"Vertical Horizon," ARTISTDirect, http://imusic.artistdirect.com/showcase/modern/verticalhorizon.html (May 29, 2001).
"Vertical Horizon," CDNow, http://www.cdnow.com (May 28, 2001).
"Vertical Horizon: Working Their Way toward Stardom," VH1.com, http://www.vh1.com/thewire/news/vertical/;$sessionid$QZHZ2FAAAATQECQBAFHCFEQ (May 28, 2001).
Vertical Horizon Official Website, www.verticalhorizon.com (June 4, 2001).
"Vertical Horizon's Long Road," Wall of Sound, http://wallofsound.go.com (May 29, 2001).

—*Christina Fuoco*

Vitamin C

Singer

Vitamin C is a pop singer whose colorful image, talent for reinvention and several chart-toppers has earned her a place among the abundance of teen pop divas in the year 2001. Her catchy vocals and dynamic presence have linked her musically with the likes of young starlets Britney Spears and Christina Aguilera. However, her career, which included a stint as the vocalist for alternative pop-punk band Eve's Plum and several acting roles in major motion pictures has been likened to that of Madonna's. Both women have been acknowledged for their firm multi-media presence. Ironically, the vocalist whose hit single "Graduation (Friends Forever)," made her a favorite among teen music fans, was hardly a teenager when her breakthrough occurred. The singer holds an approximate ten-year age jump over her musical contemporaries as well as the majority of her audience.

Vitamin C was born Colleen Fitzpatrick on July 20, 1969, in Old Bridge, New Jersey, the youngest of three children. While the vocalist denies coming from a creative family, it may have been obvious from an early age she was destined for a career in the arts. As Vitamin C explained to *Interview*'s Vivian Golden, "From the time I was a little girl I was just one of those kids that would grab the typewriter and try to write a play or a novel." As a preteen, Fitzpatrick, diagnosed with a foot problem, began dancing as a form of physical therapy. Much to the dismay of her parents, by the age of 13 she was already securing professional jobs in the field. The talented youngster proceeded to sign with an agent and subsequently performed in several music videos and commercials.

During high school, Fitzpatrick had a fortunate break when she landed a part in eccentric director John Water's 1988 film *Hairspray.* Despite having a substantial role playing the part of Amber Von Tussle, archenemy to (now talk-show host) star Ricki Lake's character Tracey Turnblad, she continued with her education at New York University (NYU). Initially it may have seemed the ambitious teenager had her feet firmly planted in the possibility of a dance or acting career. However, Fitzpatrick expressed that she had always been interested in music. "I used to take a tennis racquet and pretend that I was playing guitar," she explained to *Interview* magazine. "I saw music as a vehicle to get out all the stuff I couldn't say." While she was inspired early on by mega-groups The Beach Boys and The Beatles and later by grunge rockers such as The Breeders, it wasn't until the early nineties that she chose to utilize music as her main form of self-expression. Fitzpatrick proceeded to implement herself in the New York City club scene and began performing with the New Wave band, Pure Liquid.

In 1991, several months prior to graduating from NYU, Fitzpatrick answered an ad in New York paper *The Village Voice* which sought a vocalist. She was surprised to find the advertisement had actually been

Born Colleen Fitzpatrick on July 20, 1969, in Old Bridge, NJ; daughter of Gerard (a communications executive) and Vita (a legal secretary). *Education*: Bachelor of arts degree, New York University, 1991.

Began dancing as a child and by age 13 was securing professional jobs in the field; prior to career in music, landed several small acting rolls; played Amber Von Tussle in *Hairspray*, 1988; appeared in *Naked Gun 2 1/2*, 1991; appeared in *The Mambo Kings*, 1992; formed pop-punk band, Eve's Plum, 1991; group signed to Sony Music, 1992; released *Envy*, 1993; released *Cherry Alive*, 1995; left Eve's Plum, 1996; signed development deal with Elektra Records and began working under the name Vitamin C, 1998; released *Vitamin C*, 1999; had top ten single "Graduation (Friends Forever)," 1999; released *More*, 2000; played Lucy in *Dracula 2000*, 2000.

Addresses: *Record company*—Elektra Entertainment, 75 Rockefeller Plaza, 15th floor, 10019. *Website*—Vitamin C at Elektra Records: http://www.vitamincis good4u.com.

placed by Michael Kotch, one of her college classmates. Impressed by her ability, Kotch along with his twin brother, Ben (drums), asked Fitzpatrick to join their group. With the addition of bassist Theo Mack, the four aspiring musicians conjointly evolved into pop punk outfit, Eve's Plum. The group was named for the actress who played often-troubled middle child Jan Brady on the family sitcom *The Brady Bunch*. After establishing a grassroots following, Eve's Plum soon found themselves in the midst of a record label bidding war, culminating with the group signed to Sony Music in 1992. The band subsequently put forth their debut *Envy* in 1993 and a second album, *Cherry Alive*, two years later. Both were received to moderate success. Unfortunately, the band failed to make the impact in which the record label expected. In 1996, the group was dropped by Sony Music. Fitzpatrick, frustrated with her bandmates' unwillingness to experiment with a new sound amicably parted ways with the group, thereafter traveling to Los Angeles in order to contemplate her next move.

In the midst of a bad depression, Fitzpatrick wrote the song "Smile." It invariably lightened her spirits and pointed her interests in a more positive direction. She returned to New York with the intentions to reinvent herself. The result: the once-edgy vocalist emerged as pop star Vitamin C, a move criticized by many as selling out. However, Fitzpatrick proudly defends her position. "People need to see the sense of humor in it," she explained to *Gear* magazine, "With Vitamin C, I wanted to do 'no rules' pop. Everything is all about branding now, everything has to come back to this one image and I've never seen myself as that. When I was growing up artists challenged you, they were more creative." Fitzpatrick landed a development deal with Elektra Records in 1998 and for the next year worked with a series of collaborators and producers to develop her 1999 self-titled debut. Vitamin C's syrupy high-school anthem "Graduation (Friends Forever)" which *Entertainment Weekly* described as "destined to become as much a June perennial as Alice Cooper's 'School's Out,'" helped turn the album platinum and in turn parlayed Vitamin C into a pop icon.

Despite being in her late twenties at the time, Vitamin C was grouped into a set of teen heroes including Britney Spears, Christina Aguilera, and Mandy Moore. This could be attributed to the saccharine hooks of her first effort, but most notably to her popular image. The attractive blonde singer maintains a dramatic visual appeal, frequently sporting stylish clothes and a bright, multi-colored head of hair. Her trendsetting look has proven to be widely admired by fans and the fashion conscious alike. According to *Cosmopolitan* magazine, "In an era of cookie-cutter music video presences, her catchy tunes and ever-changing Day-Glo locks have made her refreshingly one of a kind." In August of 2000, the Mattel toy company issued a Vitamin C doll, complete with interchangeable hair extensions, a microphone and platform shoes. Additionally, Tommy Hilfiger, a popular clothing designer, named an exclusive shade of lipstick "Vitamin C" in the colorful singer's honor.

At the end of 2000, Vitamin C released her sophomore effort *More*. Due to the success of her first album, on *More* the prolific singer had the assistance of many notable collaborators, including Billy Steinberg (a co-writer on Madonna's "Like a Virgin"), Billy Mann (who had worked with Jennifer Lopez) and Andy Marvel (who had worked with Celine Dion and the Cover Girls.) The record was a catchy, slightly more mature offering. While it comfortably maintained Vitamin C's pop appeal, it definitely held a more adult edge than its predecessor. This is evidenced particularly by two notable tracks on the album: "Sex Has Come Between Us" and the indiscreetly flirtatious "The Itch." A&R guru Josh Deutsch, who worked with Vitamin C on her debut, explained in a 2000 press release, "I think this record is more charged all the way around. Lyrically it's more challenging and I think it's musically more dangerous—a little more risk taking going on. Vitamin C has an incredible ability to go in different directions and still be true to herself."

Refusing to stick with one medium, shortly after releasing her second album, the pop songstress made several appearances on the silver screen. She played the part of the infamous Lucy, a good girl gone bad, in famed horror director Wes Craven's *Dracula 2000* and also had a role in *Get Over It*, a movie starring popular teen actress Kirsten Dunst. In 2001, Vitamin C continued to be a successful, multi-dimensional artist, one whose talent for reinvention enables her to successfully transform from icon to actress to musician without missing a beat.

Selected discography

Singles

"Smile" (CD5/cassette single), Elektra/Asylum, 1999.
"Smile" (vinyl single), Elektra/Asylum, 1999.
"Me Myself and I" (CD5/cassette single), Elektra/Asylum, 1999.
"Itch" (CD5/cassette single), 2000.
"Graduation/Itch" (CD5/single), Warner/Elektra/Atlantic, 2001.

Albums

Vitamin C, Elektra/Asylum, 1999.
More, Elektra/Asylum, 2000.

Sources

Periodicals

Cosmopolitan, February 2001.
Entertainment Weekly, June 30, 2000; January 26, 2001.
Gear, April 2001.
Interview, December 2000.
People, January 29, 2001.
Rolling Stone, February 1, 2001.
Teen People, December 2000/January 2001.
US Weekly, March 26, 2001.

Online

Hip Online, http://www.hiponline.com (April 14, 2001).
Imusic, http://www.imusic.artistdirect.com (April 17, 2001).
Vitamin C, http://www.vitamincfan.com (April 14, 2001).
Throttlebox, http://www.throttlebox.com (April 16, 2001).
Ultimate Band List, http://www.ubl.com (April 14, 2001).

Additional information was provided by Elektra Entertainment publicity materials, 2000.

—*Nicole Elyse*

William Warfield

Singer

American bass-baritone William Warfield is an accomplished concert performer who is best known for the roles he played on stage in *Porgy and Bess* and *Showboat*. Warfield's successful career took off when he debuted at a triumphant recital at New York City's Town Hall in 1950. At the time, opportunities were scarce for African American singers, but Warfield came to be known as a "national treasure," according to the *Los Angeles Times*.

William Caesar Warfield was born in Helena, Arkansas, on January 22, 1920, the oldest of five sons of Robert Warfield, a Baptist minister, and Bertha McCamey. Warfield remembers singing in his father's choir as a child, and he studied piano at an early age. He attended primary and secondary school in Rochester, New York, where Robert Warfield had moved the family in search of better educational and employment opportunities. Warfield was a good student and pursued his vocal studies in high school. Unexcited by the prospect of suffering the life of a singer in New York, Warfield originally aspired to teach music, not perform it.

After winning a vocal competition in his senior year, for which the prize was a scholarship to the music school of his choice, Warfield majored in voice at the Eastman School of Music in Rochester, New York, graduating in 1942. He took four years off from his musical studies to serve in military intelligence in the U.S. Army during World War II, but returned to Eastman to begin work on a master's degree and become a teacher. His academic plans were cut short when he landed a role in the hit Broadway musical *Call Me Mister*. That role led

to another in Heywood's *Set My People Free* in 1948 and Blitzstein's *Regina* in 1950. Warfield continued his vocal training during this time under the American Theatre Wing's Professional Training Program, studying with Yves Tinayre and pianist Otto Herz.

Warfield sung his triumphant debut recital at New York's Town Hall in 1950 to critical raves. It was with this concert that his career as a concert singer took off in earnest. A career singing opera was closed to him at the time as African Americans had yet to secure starring operatic roles. But by the time African American singer Marian Anderson had broken that barrier and made her operatic debut at the Metropolitan Opera in 1955, Warfield was already well on his way as an oratorio singer. Warfield's wildly successful debut led to an invitation from the Australian Broadcasting Company to tour the continent and perform 35 concerts.

While on tour in Australia, Warfield signed on to star as Joe the dock hand in MGM's 1951 film version of *Showboat,* which would forever associate him with the song "Ol' Man River." Moved as a teen by Paul Robeson's performance of the song in the 1936 film version of *Showboat,* Warfield quickly learned the song. For the film, Warfield recorded the song in one take, which brought tears to the eyes of MGM mogul Louis B. Mayer. Warfield later joked that Mayer wept not for how well Warfield performed the song, but because of the money that was saved on repeat takes. Warfield reprised the role on a 1992 recording of *Showboat.* A *People* magazine critic wrote that the baritone sung "Ol' Man River" with "equal parts rage and resignation." Warfield once determined that he first sang "Ol' Man River" at age 16 in a high school vocal combo. Though he has sung it countless times, "It's different every time," he told the *Chicago Tribune,* depending on his feelings the day of the performance. "Sometimes there's a sadness to it, sometimes it's really laid back, and sometimes it's even angry." The most difficult time he had singing it, he recalled, was four days after the assassination of Martin Luther King Jr. "I had to hold back my emotion somewhat to keep from breaking down altogether," he said.

Warfield then agreed to star in *Porgy and Bess* alongside soprano Leontyne Price; the parts became signature roles for them both. They began performing together in 1952 and were married that year. Soon their careers began taking off in different directions. Warfield pursued his career in the musical theater while Price followed a course that would lead her to a serious operatic career. They separated in 1958 and divorced in 1972. "The problem was two careers. That's all it was," Warfield told the *Chicago Tribune*. The two remained close friends and neither of them has remarried. "I guess we both figured we had the best," he said.

During the 1950s, Warfield's career reached new heights. He toured as a soloist with the Philadelphia

For the Record . . .

Born William Caesar Warfield on January 22, 1920, in Helena, AK; married Leontyne Price, 1952; separated, 1958; divorced, 1972. *Education*: Bachelor of music degree, Eastman School of Music, Rochester, NY, 1942.

Served four years in the U.S. Army; debut recital at New York's Town Hall, 1950; starred in MGM's film version of *Showboat*, 1951; starred in *Porgy and Bess* with soprano Leontyne Price; toured West Africa, the Near East, Europe, Asia, Australia, and Cuba sponsored by the U.S. State Department, 1956, 1958, 1959; appeared on the television show *Green Pastures*, 1957, 1959; revived Porgy in *Porgy and Bess*, 1961, 1964, 1965-72; revived Joe in *Showboat*, 1966, 1971-72; professor, University of Illinois' School of Music in Urbana, 1974-90; celebrated the twenty-fifth anniversary of his Town Hall debut at Carnegie Hall, 1975; narrated Aaron Copland's *A Lincoln Portrait*, 1984; published *William Warfield: My Music and My Life* (with Alton Miller), 1991; professor of music, Northwestern University, 1994—.

Awards: Grammy Award, Best Spoken Word Recording for *A Lincoln Portrait*, 1984; Governors' Award, State of Illinois; induction into the Lincoln Academy (Illinois' highest honor bestowed upon a citizen); numerous honorary degrees.

Addresses: *Office*—Northwestern University, School of Music, 711 Elgin Road, Evanston, IL 60208.

Orchestra in 1955 and performed in West Africa, the Near East, Europe, Asia, Australia, and Cuba on tours sponsored by the U.S. State Department in 1956, 1958, and 1959. He also appeared on television as De Lawd on NBC's Hallmark Hall of Fame presentation of *Green Pastures* in 1957 and 1959. Warfield recorded frequently during this time and began to study technique with Rosa Ponelle, a singer with the Metropolitan Opera.

The 1960s and 1970s saw Warfield reviving his signature roles in *Porgy and Bess* and *Showboat*. He played Porgy in 1961 and 1964 productions by the New York City Opera Company and again at the Volksoper in Vienna from 1965 to 1972. He appeared as Joe in a 1966 production of *Showboat* at Lincoln Center in New York City and at the Vienna Volksoper in 1971 and 1972. He performed and traveled heavily during this time, appearing at the Casals Festival in Puerto Rico in 1962 and 1963, at the Athens Festival in 1966, and at the Pacem in Terra II Convocation in Geneva in 1967. He sang in a staging of Puccini's *Gianni Schicchi* in Central City, Colorado, in 1972. Warfield celebrated the twenty-fifth anniversary of his Town Hall debut with a recital at New York's Carnegie Hall for the Duke Ellington Center in 1975.

Warfield's strong dramatic presence led him to narrate Aaron Copland's *A Lincoln Portrait*, a speaking part which incorporated portions of President Abraham Lincoln's speeches. He narrated Copland's work many times over the years and won a 1984 Grammy Award in the spoken word category for his recording with the Eastman Philharmonia Orchestra. Warfield delivered the narration from memory years later in a live performance at a 1991 Copland memorial concert at Lincoln Center. At the event, Warfield, "with poise, eloquent phrasing and exceptional dramatic timing," according to one *Los Angeles Times* critic, "turned political speech into inspiring poetry." Warfield also spoke from Martin Luther King Jr.'s "I Have a Dream" speech when he narrated Jonathan Brace Brown's *Legacy of Vision* at the Nashville Symphony's annual Martin Luther King, Jr. 1997 tribute concert.

Warfield did pursue his original teaching aspirations and balanced those with his performance demands beginning in 1974 when he started as a music professor at the University of Illinois School of Music in Urbana. He retired as chairman of the voice faculty there in 1990 and went on to become a visiting professor at Eastern Illinois University and an adjunct professor at Northwestern University in 1994. While he taught, he maintained a demanding touring schedule, narrating the Jim Cullum Jazz Band's concert performance of *Porgy and Bess* and performing at countless concerts. He also found time to serve on the boards of the Lyric Opera Center Board in Chicago, the National Music Council, and support the National Association of Negro Musicians. He has received honorary degrees including an honorary Doctor of Laws degree from the University of Arkansas in 1972; an honorary degree from Boston University in 1982; an honorary Doctor of Human Letters degree from Augustana College in 1983; and an honorary Doctor of Music degree from Milliken University in 1984.

At 80, Warfield was still garnering attention and critical reviews for his work. At an age when most performers have long since retired, Warfield saw no reason to slow down. "Age has nothing to do with anything," he told the *Chicago Tribune*, "as long as this old voice holds out and I still enjoy it, I'll never stop singing."

Selected discography

Appears on

Show Boat (1951 soundtrack), MGM, 1951; reissued, Metro, 1966; reissued, Sony, 1990; reissued, Columbia, 1992.
Show Boat (1996 Broadway revival cast), RCA, 1966; reissued, RCA, 1992.
(With the Eastman Philharmonia Orchestra) *Copland: Lincoln Portrait*, 1984.
Broadway Greatest Hits, Sony Classics, 1996.
Gershwin: Porgy and Bess Scenes, BCA, 1999.

Sources

Books

Baker, Theodore, *Baker's Biographical Dictionary of Musicians,* Schirmer Books, 1992.
Smith, Jessie Carney, editor, *Notable Black American Men,* Gale Research, 1998.

Warfield, William (with Alton Miller), *William Warfield: My Music and My Life,* Sagamore, 1991.

Periodicals

Chicago Tribune, October 26, 2000.
Los Angeles Times, November 17, 2000, p. F2.
People, September 7, 1992, p. 26.

Online

Riverwalk, Live from the Landing, http://www.riverwalk.org/profiles/warfield.htm (April 24, 2001).
"William Warfield," *All Music Guide,* http://www.allmusic.com (April 24, 2001).

Additional material was provided by Northwestern University, 2001.

—Brenna Sanchez

Warren G

Rap musician

Warren G ushered in what became known as the "G funk" sound of hip-hop, which *Rolling Stone* writer S.H. Fernando Jr. defined as "that fat-bottomed, mellowed-out sound" with "bouncing bass lines and hypnotic, high-end melodies" that was perfect driving music and suited the Southern California climate. As the younger stepbrother of famed West Coast rapper and producer Dr. Dre, Warren G worked to stay out of Dre's shadow and build his own name in hip-hop music. He did so with the hit singles "Regulate" and "This D.J.," and his 1994 debut album *Regulate...G Funk Era.* Warren's streak of success slowed with his follow-up releases *Take a Look Over Your Shoulder* and *I Want It All,* but he still earned a place on the all-star Up In Smoke Tour in 2000.

Warren G was born Warren Griffin III on November 10, 1971, the only son of airplane mechanic Warren Griffin Sr. and his wife, Ola, a dietitian. His parents divorced when he was four, and Warren grew up with his mother and three sisters, Felicia, Traci, and Mitzi, in East Long Beach, California. He moved to North Long Beach before junior high school in 1982 to live with his father and his second wife, Verna, whose three children from a previous marriage included Andre Young (Dr. Dre). Warren's early teen years were consumed by school, football, and hanging out with his friends, including Calvin Broadus (Snoop Dogg). Warren soon got involved with gangs and landed in jail at age 17 for gun possession.

By this time, Dre was already an established rapper and producer with his group N.W.A., and he showed Warren how to program a drum machine. "I'd show him everything he wanted to know," Dre told *People.* "He'd come up with corny beats, and I'd tell him, 'Get back in the lab.' [But] he kept practicing...." Warren and friends Broadus and Nathaniel (Nate Dogg) Hale formed the hip-hop crew 213, which was named after their telephone area code. The trio practiced and recorded in a back room of Long Beach's V.I.P. record store. Warren watched his group fall apart after he played Snoop's demo, "Super Duper Snooper," for Dre, and Snoop embarked on what would become a wildly successful solo career with the more experienced producer. Warren left Jordan High School in 1988 and spent time in jail for selling drugs before working in the Long Beach shipyards. "It was all about peer pressure, kids finding themselves," Warren's father, Warren Griffin Sr. told *People.* "I was angry, but I just knew he would do something positive eventually."

In 1993, Warren met director John Singleton at Dre's studio and produced "Indo Smoke" for the soundtrack to Singleton's film *Poetic Justice* starring Janet Jackson. The song turned out to be a hit, and Warren signed to record label Def Jam, a decision based solely on the sound of "Indo Smoke," Warren maintained, and not because of his famous stepbrother. Though he did contribute to Snoop's recordings with Dre, Warren

For the Record . . .

B orn Warren Griffin III on November 10, 1971; stepbrother to Andre Young (a.k.a. Dr. Dre).

Grew up in Long Beach, CA, with future rappers Calvin Broadus (a.k.a. Snoop Dogg) and Nathaniel Dawayne Hale (a.k.a. Nate Dogg); formed rap group 213 as a teen; single "Indo Smoke" appeared on *Poetic Justice* film soundtrack, 1993; single "Regulate" appeared on *Above the Rim* soundtrack and peaked at number two on *Billboard* chart, 1994; debut album, *Regulate...G Funk Era,* entered at number two on the *Billboard 200* album chart, 1994; released *Take a Look Over Your Shoulder,* 1997; released *I Want It All,* 1999; appeared on Up In Smoke Tour, 2000.

worked for the most part on his own, avoiding his stepbrother's shadow. His next single, for the *Above the Rim* soundtrack, was "Regulate," which peaked at number two on the *Billboard* charts in 1994 and became the "hottest hip-hop single of the summer," according to *Rolling Stone* writer Jonathan Gold.

Fueled by the success of "Regulate," Warren's 1994 debut album *Regulate...G Funk Era* sold one million copies in its first three days, debuted at number two on the *Billboard* album chart, and remained in the top ten long after that. The sound of *Regulate...G Funk Era* was based on vintage R&B rhythms with gangsta-lifestyle lyrics. Warren was both producer and rapper on the album, and his sound was smoother and more melodic than most rap. It was a plush sound that seemed "a little insidious, as if it's turning violence into easy listening," according to *Entertainment Weekly* critic David Browne. Warren employed the talents of several underground rappers, namely Nate Dogg—for whom the appearance generated interest on the hip-hop scene—but Snoop Dogg was conspicuously absent. *Rolling Stone* critic S.H. Fernando Jr. noted that, at the time of *Regulate...G Funk Era*'s release, the market was saturated with like-sounding productions, but the album still had something to offer. Fans agreed as the single "This D.J." became Warren's second top ten single, and the album was soon certified multi-platinum.

People writer Jeremy Helligar wrote that Warren contradicted the posturing of gangsta rap "by offering a kinder, gentler hip-hop attitude and by balancing scenes depicting street violence with tales that celebrate the camaraderie that survives even in crime-infested neighborhoods." Warren had had about

enough with the "gangsta" label, he told *People.* "Gangsta this. Gangsta that," he said. "They label us animals, but that ain't me. If you gotta label me, then label me Warren Griffin Jr., an all-around cool guy."

Three years after Warren introduced the G-funk sound with *Regulate...G Funk Era,* the artist released his follow-up, *Take a Look Over Your Shoulder.* The release showcased Warren's "talent for springy beats and jazzily conversational rapping," wrote *Entertainment Weekly* critic Ken Tucker. *Rolling Stone* critic Kevin Powell likened Warren to 1970s R&B talent Donny Hathaway in that neither artist was as charismatic or controversial as his contemporaries and, as a result, both were highly underrated. Powell stated that *Take a Look* had what it took to turn the spotlight on Warren. The album was built on Warren's strengths, namely "sugary, melodic hooks; snippets of street sounds; rubbery bass lines; and lyrics that flow like a river...," Powell wrote. Most reviews were not as positive, however, and record sales were weak.

Warren released his 1999 album *I Want It All* on his own G-Funk label, an imprint of Restless Records. As president and CEO of G-Funk, Warren's approach to making a successful record was "to do every song as if it's going to be a single," he told *Billboard,* but *I Want It All* left something to be desired, according to critics. The album paled commercially and critically in the shadow of its predecessors because it did not "push much beyond the pop-soul hooks" that drove *Regulate,* wrote Matt Diehl in *Entertainment Weekly.* Warren kept the album's tempo up and relied heavily on hot-name talents like Jermaine Dupri, Slick Rick, Snoop Dogg, Nate Dogg, Eve, El DeBarge, Drag-On, Memphis Bleek, and the Mary Jane Girls' Val Young, among others.

The lack of response to *I Want It All* did not stop Warren from appearing on the 2000 Up In Smoke Tour with rap stars Dr. Dre, Snoop Dogg, Eminem, Nate Dogg, Xzibit, and Kurupt. One *Chicago Tribune* critic suggested that Warren—with only two hits to his credit and a relative dry spell since—was on the tour to "wave the flag of nepotism" as headliner's Dre's stepbrother. But Up In Smoke was the first major gangsta rap tour to hit the road in more than a decade and was a box-office success.

Selected discography

Regulate...G Funk Era, Def Jam, 1994.
Take a Look Over Your Shoulder, Def Jam, 1997.
I Want It All, Restless/G-Funk, 1999.

Sources

Periodicals

Atlanta Constitution, August 6, 2000, p. D5.
Billboard, September 25, 1999, p. 26.
Chicago Tribune, July 10, 2000, p. 5.1.
Entertainment Weekly, July 29, 1994, p. 56; September 23, 1994, p. 70; September 8, 1995, p. 51; October 15, 1999, p. 82; March 28, 1997, p. 69.
Los Angeles Times, November 7, 1999, p. 88.
People, January 30, 1995, p. 71; April 14, 1997, p. 26.
Rolling Stone, August 11, 1994, p. 69; September 8, 1994, p. 94; March 20, 1997, p. 86.

Online

"Warren G," *All Music Guide,* http://www.allmusic.com (May 3, 2001).

—Brenna Sanchez

Gillian Welch

Singer, songwriter

Moving with ease from bluegrass to folk and from country to blues, Gillian Welch (pronounced with a hard "g") has confounded those who like to place musicians in a tidy category. Her growing success as a singer-songwriter, however, is easy to understand. With her strong, clear voice and her honest, unadorned songs, Welch evokes the simple, traditional tunes emanating from the rural Appalachian region in the American Southeast. But while the inspiration for her songs is rooted in the high lonesome sound of early twentieth-century mountain music, Welch imbues her work with a timeless, genre-bending quality. Her songwriting partnership with David Rawlings, who accompanies Welch with vocals and guitar, as well as a fruitful relationship with legendary producer T-Bone Burnett, have yielded two successful albums and launched a career that promises to contribute as much as it borrows from the roots music tradition.

Born in 1968 in Los Angeles, California, Welch grew up with an appreciation for many kinds of music and an intimate knowledge of the songwriting craft. Her parents wrote music for the television program *The Carol Burnett Show,* and the family would occasionally break out their numerous instruments for impromptu sing-alongs. Welch began playing guitar at age eight, learning the music her parents listened to—standards from the 1940s and 1950s and pop hits from the 1960s and 1970s. As her own musical tastes developed, she found herself drawn to acoustic folk and alternative rock.

It wasn't until Welch attended the University of California Santa Cruz (UC Santa Cruz) to study photography that she discovered her passion for bluegrass music. After her first exposure to this music, she realized not only that she liked the way it sounded, but that her voice and playing style were well suited to the genre. She recalled in an interview on the ARTISTdirect website: "I started devouring as much bluegrass as I could. The Stanley Brothers were at the top of the list along with Norman and Nancy Blake and the Delmore Brothers…. I was attracted more to the darker stuff, the brother teams like the Blue Sky Boys." Before graduating from UC Santa Cruz and while eagerly absorbing musical influences and playing in a cover band, Welch determined that music would be more than a hobby for her. In the late 1980s she enrolled at the prestigious Berklee College of Music in Boston. While listening to such alternative Boston groups as the Pixies and the Breeders, Welch was learning traditional country music—and writing her own material—to perform in local clubs. During her second year at Berklee she met David Rawlings; discovering a kindred approach to performing and songwriting, they began working together.

While still a student at Berklee, Welch traveled with her fellow students for the school's annual trip to Nashville for pep talks and career advice from established artists

Born in 1968 in Los Angeles, CA. *Education*: Graduated from the University of California Santa Cruz; graduated from Berklee College of Music, Boston, MA, 1992.

Moved to Nashville, TN, 1992; began performing in local clubs and writing music that would later be recorded by Emmylou Harris and the Nashville Bluegrass Band; signed with Almo Sounds, released *Revival*, 1996; released *Hell among the Yearlings*, 1998; contributed to several high-profile soundtracks and compilations including *The Horse Whisperer* soundtrack, 1998; *Return of the Grievous Angel: A Tribute to Gram Parsons*, 1999; and the *O Brother, Where Art Thou?* soundtrack, 2000; started own label, Acony Records, with David Rawlings, 2001.

Addresses: *Management*—DS Management, 1017 16th Avenue S., Nashville, TN 37212. *Publicity*—Jim Merlis, Big Hassle Media, New York, NY 10011, (212) 366-4492. *Booking*—Keith Case & Associates, 1025 17th Avenue S., Nashville, TN 37212, (615) 327-4646. *Website*—Gillian Welch Official Website: http://www.gillianwelch.com/home.html.

and producers. While known primarily as the home of mainstream, radio-friendly country music—which resides at the opposite end of the country spectrum from Welch's style—Nashville struck Welch as a land of opportunity for practitioners of a wide range of roots music. In 1992, after graduating from Berklee, Welch moved with Rawlings to Music City to begin her slow-but-sure ascent to a recording contract. She adhered to a demanding schedule, participating in songwriters' contests and open-mic competitions at local bars and clubs several nights a week. She developed a dedicated local following, though one of her first breakthroughs came at an event outside Nashville.

In 1993 Welch won the Chris Austin Songwriting Contest at the Merle Watson Memorial Festival in Wilkesboro, North Carolina. Soon after, some of her songs were recorded by the Nashville Bluegrass Band and the brother-sister bluegrass duo Tim and Mollie O'Brien. In 1995 Emmylou Harris released her groundbreaking album *Wrecking Ball*, which featured Welch's song "Orphan Girl." After playing a set at Nashville's

Station Inn one night in the mid 1990s, Welch and Rawlings encountered Burnett, who expressed an interest in producing their work. Welch recalled in an ARTISTdirect interview: "I spent almost a year meeting with other producers, but it came back to T-Bone. I felt like he wanted to make the same first record that I wanted to make." That debut, called *Revival,* was released to widespread critical acclaim in 1996.

Singing in her spare, mournful way, Welch tells stark, powerful stories about such things as the death of a child ("Annabelle") and a bootlegger's dying request for his still to be destroyed ("Tear My Stillhouse Down"). In a review of *Revival* on the Salon website, Lori Leibovich wrote that "Welch mesmerizes with her emotional range; she can sing with the vulnerability of a child, the sass of an adolescent, the dignity of an old woman or the flat-out sex appeal of a nightclub chanteuse...." High praise came from Emmylou Harris, whose appraisal of *Revival* appears on Welch's website: "Gillian writes with what at first seems to be childlike simplicity, but on closer listening, you realize you are in the presence of an old soul, one who knows the blue highways of the heart.... It is a gift to all of us who need music to be more than just background noise."

With assistance from Burnett, Welch achieved an old-fashioned, pared-down sound that, according to Michael McCall of the *All Music Guide* website, "could be lifted from some long lost Depression Era folk recording." Using vintage equipment that had once been wielded by country legend Hank Williams, Welch deliberately avoided the clean, high-fidelity sound that is the hallmark of modern recordings, opting instead for what she felt was a richer, more authentic sound. Not typical fare for mainstream radio stations, *Revival* nonetheless built a strong following based primarily on the strength of Welch's live shows and rave reviews in the press. The album's success was capped off by a Grammy Award nomination for Best Contemporary Folk Artist. While Welch has expressed ambivalence about the "folk" label, she was quoted by Country.com as saying, "I just don't feel like a folk singer." Welch felt reassured by such past winners in that category as Johnny Cash and Bob Dylan. "If they put them in as contemporary folk," she suggested, "you know maybe I am contemporary folk."

Two years later, again collaborating with Rawlings on the songwriting and performance end and with Burnett on the production end, Welch released *Hell among the Yearlings*. The title comes from an old fiddle tune that, like many such tunes, has multiple titles. The other titles for that tune—including "Trouble amongst the Bovine" and "Ox in the Mud"—made "Hell among the Yearlings" the obvious choice for the album's title. While *Revival* is not exactly cheerful, *Hell among the Yearlings* goes even further into the somber, rustic traditions of the traditional music Welch admires. Beginning with "Caleb Meyer," a song about a woman killing her attacker with a broken bottle, and including "One Morning," about a woman who sees her son riding home from battle only to realize it is a lifeless body strapped to the horse, *Hell among the Yearlings* embraces the bleak aspects of life. The album's spare instrumentation—generally consisting only of Rawlings on guitar and Welch playing banjo or guitar—emphasizes the melancholy beauty of Welch and Rawling's two-part harmonies. While some critics questioned whether Welch had submerged too much of her own identity to achieve authentic recreations of an old-time sound, others praised her ability to tap into a rich vein of traditional country and bluegrass music and infuse it with her own modern sensibilities. That ability results in occasionally odd juxtapositions, like a song about drug addiction ("My Morphine") featuring some good old-fashioned yodeling.

In the years following the release of *Hell among the Yearlings,* Welch worked with Rawlings on material for her next album while also contributing to several critically acclaimed compilations, including the soundtracks for *The Horse Whisperer* and *O Brother, Where Art Thou?* A highlight for Welch was being asked to sing on *Clinch Mountain Country,* a star-studded album made by her idol and biggest influence, bluegrass hero Ralph Stanley. In addition to their duet of the Carter Family song "Gold Watch and Chain," the album features Stanley performing with Bob Dylan, George Jones, Dwight Yoakam, and Ricky Skaggs. Some observers have criticized Welch for her devotion to a musical tradition that is worlds away from her modern-day upbringing in Los Angeles. Others dismiss such concerns; as Daniel Durchholz asserted in a Wall of Sound review, "Welch has internalized this stuff, and her songs betray nary a hint of fakery or affectation." Welch herself shrugs off such criticism, acknowledging to Tim Kenneally of *Guitar Player* that her fans care about her music, not where she was born. "We go to these bluegrass festivals," Welch explains, "and I don't get any grief. There, people say, 'Wow, I haven't heard stuff like that since my granddad died.'"

In an effort to escape the hit-driven, highly corporate climate of the major record labels, Welch formed her own label with partner David Rawlings after leaving Almo Sounds when its parent company, Geffen, merged with Interscope in 1999. Acony Records, named after a flower, will issue Welch's third album, slated for release in July of 2001. Acony will also reissue Welch's first two albums.

Selected discography

Revival, Almo Sounds, 1996.
Hell among the Yearlings, Almo Sounds, 1998.
(Contributor) *The Horse Whisperer* (soundtrack), MCA, 1998.
(Contributor) *Clinch Mountain Country* (Ralph Stanley and others), Rebel, 1998.
(Contributor) *Return of the Grievous Angel: A Tribute to Gram Parsons* (various artists), Almo Sounds, 1999.
(Contributor) *O Brother, Where Art Thou?* (soundtrack), Mercury, 2000.
(Contributor) *Concerts for a Landmine Free World* (various artists), Vanguard, 2001.

Sources

Periodicals

Billboard, July 4, 1998, p. 12.
Entertainment Weekly, July 24, 1998, p. 72.
Guitar Player, November 1996, p. 57.
Los Angeles Times, May 13, 2001.
Newsweek, July 15, 1996, p. 57.

Online

All Music Guide, http://www.allmusic.com (April 19, 2001).
"The Birth of a Crossover Star," Salon, http://www.salon.com/weekly/welch1.html (April 19, 2001).
"Gillian Welch," ARTISTdirect, http://imusic.artistdirect.com/showcase/contemporary/gillianwelch.html (April 19, 2001).
"Gillian Welch," Country.com, http://www.country.com/gen/music/artist/gillian-welch.html (April 19, 2001).
"Gillian Welch: Hell among the Yearlings," Wall of Sound, http://wallofsound.go.com/archive/reviews/stories/3651_74Index.html (April 24, 2001).
Gillian Welch Official Website, http://www.gillianwelch.com/home.html (April 19, 2001).

—Judy Galens

Westlife

Pop group

Within a matter of a few years, members of the Irish pop group Westlife went from singing in their school's performance of the musical *Grease* to selling more than 10 million records worldwide. This was not an easy feat considering that the United Kingdom is filled with burgeoning talents trying to replicate the success of boy groups like Take That and Boyzone, which spawned solo artists Robbie Williams and Ronan Keating, respectively. Westlife has been able to rise above other spotlight seekers, though, to find record-setting success.

Shane Filan, Kian Egan, and Mark Feehily formed the backbone of Westlife while the three were attending school in the mid 1990s and performing around Dublin, Ireland, as IOU. Like the Backstreet Boys and O-Town, an entertainment manager had a hand in the formation of Westlife. When IOU appeared on a Dublin television show, the group piqued the attention of Louis Walsh, a pop "Svengali" who also managed the similar-sounding Boyzone. To showcase the group, Walsh offered IOU a spot opening for the Backstreet Boys at the Dublin club The Point.

After the group came together as Westlife in 1998, Walsh took them under his wing and introduced them

Photograph by Sam Levi. Wireimage.com. Reproduced by permission.

For the Record . . .

Members include **Nicky Byrne**; **Kian Egan**; **Mark Feehily**; **Shane Filan**; **Bryan McFadden**, vocalists.

Group formed in Dublin, Ireland, 1998; released *Westlife*, 1999; in U.S., 2000; released *Coast to Coast* worldwide (except for U.S.), 2000.

Awards: BRIT Award, Best Pop Act, 2001.

Addresses: *Record company*—Arista Records (U.S.), 6 West 57th St., New York, 10019, (800) 6-ARISTA. *Website*—Westlife Official Website: http://www.westlife.co.uk.

to Nicky Byrne, an ex-soccer apprentice, and Bryan McFadden, who was attending a local stage school. According to Westlife's record company biography, RCA Records signed the group immediately after seeing a performance. "When showcasing them, I instantly knew they were going to be a very successful band. They have surpassed my expectations. The great thing is that after all of their achievements, they have remained down-to-earth. They are a great bunch of guys to work with," said RCA Records A&R consultant Simon Cowell.

The deal also brought onboard a co-manager, Ronan Keating, who is best known in the United States for his appearance on the *Notting Hill* film soundtrack. Westlife's first single, "Flying Without Wings" debuted at number one on the British charts in 1999. The same success followed with "Seasons in the Sun" and "Swear It Again" in 2000.

The group's self-titled debut album was released in November of 1999 and became the fastest-selling album in Irish music history. It has since gone quadruple platinum in the United Kingdom and sold more than five million copies worldwide. In Indonesia, *Westlife* has been dubbed the biggest-selling international release. The album offered five British number one singles including "Swear It Again," "If I Let you Go" and "Flying Without Wings."

Following in the general practice of saturating the market with an influx of singles to drive sales and broaden exposure for a group, Westlife sent their covers of "I Have a Dream"/"Seasons in the Sun" and later the fifth single, "Fool Again," to stores. The group also earned a *Guinness World Records 2001* listing as

the most successful new chart act of all time for achieving consecutive number one spots on the British charts with its first seven singles.

After finding success in Britain, Westlife moved on to the United States where "Swear It Again" peaked at number two on the *Billboard* sales chart. While Boyzone paired with U2 for the song "The Sweetest Thing," Westlife collaborated with American favorite Mariah Carey on the song "Against All Odds" in September of 2000. Like the group's previous singles, "Against All Odds" hit number one in the United Kingdom. Feehily was thrilled to work with Carey: "It was beyond all my wildest expectations," he said in the RCA biography.

In between touring and making several guest appearances, Westlife traveled to Stockholm, Sweden, and London, England, in the summer of 2000 to record its second album, *Coast to Coast*, which includes the Carey-Westlife piece "Against All Odds" and a cover of Billy Joel's "Uptown Girl." Working with two different sets of producers—the single-named Cheiron in Stockholm, and Steve Mac and Wayne Hector in London—allowed the members of Westlife to indulge in their pop sensibilities. "We're very happy to be working with both sets of producers again. They keep impressing us with their ideas and we're comfortable with how they work—it's like we've grown up together," RCA Records quoted Filan as saying. "On the whole, this album is a big step up for us, both vocally and musically."

The first single, "My Love," achieved the same success as previous releases, reaching number one in October of 2000. British magazine *New Musical Express* (*NME*) panned *Coast to Coast*, however, implying that its lyrics were shallow. "'Angel's Wings' includes the line, 'You make everything that used to seem so big seem to be small'—surely an excuse that ranks up there with 'Sorry love, it's a bit cold' and one which shatters the few illusions we had left of Kian [Egan]."

The popularity of *Coast to Coast* helped the album top its rivals on the charts and at the MTV Europe Music Awards. Westlife beat out Robbie Williams, Craig David, Travis, and Sonique for the Best United Kingdom and Ireland Act prize. The group also won a BRIT Award for Best Pop Act in 2001.

As of the summer of 2001, Westlife had begun work on a collaborative single with Canadian rocker Bryan Adams, whom *NME* called a "serial collaborator." Egan told *NME* that the song is "very much like Bryan Adams' old stuff rather than his new stuff. It's in the same kind of style as '(Everything I Do) I Do It For You.' We're really excited because he's got a great voice and it's a brilliant opportunity for us."

Fame reportedly started wearing on the group after newspapers shared accounts of Westlife's drinking sprees. During a press conference in Kuala Lumpur, Malaysia, in May of 2001, Westlife told journalists that they just want to be normal guys. "We make good music and we're successful all over the world but when it comes to having a private life we got to have a private life. If one of us goes to a bar and is photographed coming out of it, that's not his fault," Filan is quoted as saying in a Reuters news service story on the Yahoo! News website.

Still, fans have flocked to see Westlife. Sixteen fans were injured on May 25, 2001, at Soemantri Bodjonegoro sports stadium in Jakarta, Indonesia, when the audience of 15,000 surged toward the stage at the end of the show. Two months earlier, four fans were crushed to death during an autograph signing at a shopping mall in the same city.

Despite speculation that the group's reign at the top of the pop charts was coming to an end, Westlife planned for continued success with at least four more records on BMG as part of the group's contract with the label. Westlife—who made history in May of 2001 for becoming the first boy band to play in South Africa—planned to record songs in Spanish as its next musical venture.

Selected discography

Westlife (includes "Swear It Again," "If I Let You Go," "Flying Without Wings," "I Have a Dream," "Fool Again"), RCA (U.K), 1999; released in U.S., Arista, 2000.
Coast to Coast (includes "My Love," "Angel's Wings," "Against All Odds"), RCA (U.K.), 2000.

Sources

Periodicals

Time International, April 16, 2001.

Online

BRIT Awards, http://www.britawards.co.uk (June 28, 2001).
"Just Let Us Be Normal Lads," Yahoo! News, http://uk.news.yahoo.com/010525/80/brnac.html (May 28, 2001).
"'Life and Bryan!," *New Musical Express*, http://www .nme-.com (May 28, 2001).
"Westlife Become First Modern-Day Boy Band to Play South Africa," Yahoo! News, http://uk.news.yahoo.com/010519/4/bqq5f.html (May 28, 2001).
"Westlife: Coast to Coast," *New Musical Express*, http://www.nme.com/NME/External/Reviews/Reviews_Story/0,1069,6246,00.html, (May 29, 2001).
"Westlife Fans Injured at Gig," Yahoo! News, http://uk.music.yahoo.com/010525/92/brnz3.html (May 28, 2001).
Westlife Official Website, http://www.westlife.co.uk (May 28, 2001).
"What a Difference a Dane Makes," Yahoo! Music, http://uk.music.yahoo.com/010522/92/br3wq.html (May 28, 2001).

Additional information was provided by Arista Records publicity materials, 2001.

—*Christina Fuoco*

Lee Ann Womack

Singer, songwriter

Photograph by Jeffrey Mayer. Wireimage.com. Reproduced by permission.

After working in the music industry as a promoter and songwriter for a number of years, country music singer Lee Ann Womack released a debut album of her own in 1997. With one-half million records sold in the first year, Womack ranked as a solid hit-maker by the end of the decade, with three albums and several hit singles to her credit. By the end of the decade, Womack had collected an impressive cache of awards from major music associations, including best new female vocalist of 1997, favorite new country artist of 1998, and single of the year along with song of the year in 2000. She had barely exceeded the status of a newcomer, yet already she had amassed a battery of attentive fans, attracted by her fresh talent. Critics hailed her forthright and traditional approach to country music. The younger generation of country musicians identified with her uncluttered singing style and her capable guitar playing. Womack's twangy vocals further imbued her recordings with a sense of nostalgia, reminiscent of great country music crooners, and her songwriting efforts have brought her into collaborations with some of the classic country artists of the late twentieth century.

Womack was born on August 19, 1966, in Jacksonville, Texas. She was the second of two daughters of Ann and Aubrey Womack. Her mother was a schoolteacher; her father was a full-time high school principal and a part-time disc jockey. As a young child, Womack's love of music was apparent. She studied piano and enjoyed her many trips to the radio station with her father. Womack in fact harbored a steadfast dream of going to Nashville and might otherwise have grown discontented with life in her small Texas town. Instead, she was attracted to the local celebrity status of her father in his radio career at KEBE-AM Jacksonville, and she resolved to emulate his success in her own way by joining the ranks of country musicians whose voices drifted across the radio waves all day long.

After graduation from Jacksonville High School in 1984, Womack enrolled in a country music curriculum at South Plains Junior College in Levelland, Texas, against the advice of her parents and counselors. As a college student she toured as a vocalist with the school band, County Caravan, yet by the end of her first year at South Plains—overpowered by her own eagerness—she abandoned the associate degree program and quit the junior college. At 18 years of age and determined to head for Nashville, she made a compromise with her parents and enrolled at Tennessee's Belmont University (then Belmont College) in Nashville for the following school year. At Belmont she studied commercial aspects of the music business and lived in a dormitory at the insistence of her parents.

Womack entered Belmont as a sophomore and was beside herself with enthusiasm at being in Nashville. She wasted little time in securing a student internship in the A&R department at MCA Records, a job geared

For the Record . . .

Born on August 19, 1966, in Jacksonville, TX; daughter of Aubrey and Ann Womack; married Jason Sellers, 1990; divorced, 1997; married, Frank Liddell, November, 1999; daughters, Aubrie Lee (with Sellers), Anna Lise (with Liddell). *Education*: South Plains Junior College, Levelland, TX, 1984; Belmont College (now Belmont University), 1985-90.

Student intern with MCA Records, late 1980s; songwriter, Sony/ATV Tree Publishing, 1995-96; signed with Decca Records, 1996; released debut album, *Lee Ann Womack*, 1997; released *Some Things I Know*, 1998; signed with MCA Nashville, 1999; released *I Hope You Dance*, 2000.

Awards: Best New Female Vocalist, Academy of Country Music, 1997; Favorite New Country Artist, American Music Awards, 1998; Single of the Year, Country Music Association, 2000; Song of the Year, Country Music Association, 2000.

Addresses: *Manager*—The Erv Woolsey Company, 1000 18th Ave. South, Nashville, TN 37212, phone: (615) 329-2402. *Bookings*—Buddy Lee Attractions, 38 Music Square, Suite #300, Nashville, TN 37203, phone: (615) 244-4336, fax: (615) 726-0429. *Website*—Lee Ann Womack Official Website: http://www.leeannwomack.com.

to upper classmen, but one that she secured nonetheless through unflappable persistence. Although she continued her studies until 1990, she left school shortly before securing a degree. She was in fact on the verge of graduation when she quit her final class requirements to pursue an affair of the heart; that same year she married her college sweetheart, musician Jason Sellers. As a newlywed, Womack worked as a waitress, and for a brief time, at a day care center following the birth of her first child. Overall, though, Womack remained focused in pursuit of her career. In 1995, she signed with Sony/ATV Tree Publishing as a songwriter. There she co-wrote songs both for and with some of the prominent personalities in country music. She collaborated with Whisperin' Bill Anderson on occasion, and Ricky Skaggs picked up one of her songs, "I Don't Remember Forgetting," for inclusion on an album.

Ultimately it was the breakup of her young marriage that left Womack as a single mother in the mid 1990s and spurred her to pursue her aspiration in earnest. She held tenaciously to her desire to sing and secured a simple, acoustic audition for MCA Nashville chairman Bruce Hinton. Hinton spoke nothing but praise for the promising talent of the young Womack, according to *Billboard*'s Chet Flippo, and soon afterward Womack accepted a contract offer from Decca Records.

Early in 1997, Womack appeared live in her debut in which she was introduced by her father via videotape at the Country Radio Seminar in Nashville. The introduction by her own father left Womack emotionally charged for her performance at the seminar with attendees numbering approximately 2,500 industry members, many of which were disc jockeys. Thus, by the release of her debut album on Decca in the following May, her advance single, "Never Again, Again" had made playlists and charts already since early March. Advance play of a subsequent single, "The Fool," generated a renewed swell of anticipation mere weeks before the ultimate release of the self-titled album.

The traditional country-style inflection of Womack's singing struck a chord with country music lovers and earned her the title of Best New Female Vocalist of 1997 from the Academy of Country Music (ACM). She was nominated as the Horizon Breaking Artist at the Country Music Awards (CMA), and *Billboard* named her the top new artist that year. Womack's debut album produced a bevy of hit singles, including "A Little Past Little Rock" in addition to "The Fool" and "Never Again, Again." The single "The Fool" secured a spot at number one on the charts. David Hajdu cited her debut album among the top three country albums of 1997 in *Entertainment Weekly*. The following year Womack secured the title of Favorite New Country Artist at the American Music Awards (AMA) and released a follow-up album, *Some Things I Know*. Sales of her earlier album meanwhile topped 500,000 units that year.

When Decca Records shut down in 1999, Womack migrated to the MCA Nashville label. Her third album was released on the new label in 2000 and met with instant success. The recording, *I Hope You Dance*, made its debut at number one on the *Billboard* country music chart. *I Hope You Dance* and its popular title track earned Womack an impressive six CMA award nominations that year; she won two of them: Single of the Year and Song of the Year. Soon afterward, early in 2001, the announcement was made that *I Hope You Dance* had earned six additional award nominations from the Academy of Country Music. The nominations included Best Album, Best Single and Best Song for the title track by Mark D. Sanders and Tia Sillers, and Best Video, also for the title track. Additionally, "I Hope You Dance" received a nomination for Best Vocal

Event for the title track performance with Sons of the Desert. Womack received a sixth nomination for Best Female Vocalist.

According to *Time*, Womack's professional tenacity had earned her the status of a permanent fixture in country music. Her unmistakably countrified voice has been compared to Tammy Wynette. In 2000, *People*'s Ralph Novak called her an "erstwhile Texas firebrand" and declared *I Hope You Dance* as Womack's best effort at that point. Hinton called the record "a career record," according to Deborah Price and Chuck Taylor in *Billboard*. Jamie Schilling Fields noted in *Texas* that Womack "works a sob" with her "cake-sweet soprano that sings like it talks in small-town cain't's and git's," and commented candidly that, "her songs are great." Although Womack admits that much of her music presents an underlying theme relating to so-called cheating hearts, she voiced disapproval at such a lifestyle and earned a reputation for moralizing to her band and entourage about marital fidelity.

From the first appearance of her debut album in 1997, Womack created a stir among established country music superstars. Among them, Loretta Lynn was inspired to write possible songs for her, and Womack received a gift of a trademark red, white, and blue guitar from cowboy crooner Buck Owens. Other popular singers eagerly collaborated with Womack as word of her talent rippled throughout the country music industry. She has made recordings with Vince Gill, Ricky Skaggs, George Strait, and Mark Chesnutt.

Selected discography

Singles

"Never Again, Again," Decca, 1997.
"The Fool," Decca, 1997.
"A Little Past Little Rock," Decca, 1998.
"I Hope You Dance," MCA Nashville, 2001.

Albums

Lee Ann Womack, Decca, 1997.
Some Things I Know (includes "If You're Ever Down in Dallas" and "The Man Who Made My Mama Cry"), Decca, 1998.
I Hope You Dance, MCA Nashville, 2000.

As songwriter

"If You're Ever Down in Dallas" (with Jason Sellers), Sony/ATV Tree Publishing, 1998.
"The Man Who Made My Mama Cry" (with Billy Lawson and Dale Dodson), Sony/ATV Tree Publishing, 1998.

Sources

Books

World Almanac & Book of Facts, 2000, World Almanac Education Group, Inc.

Periodicals

Billboard, April 5, 1997, p. 1; August 23, 1997, p. 100; August 22, 1998, p. 25; May 31, 2000, p. 5; July 1, 2000, p. 68; March 10, 2001, p. 6.
Entertainment Weekly, January 2, 1998, p. 162.
People, June 19, 2000, p. 45; July 31, 2000, p. 129.
Texas, October 1998, p. 80; October 2000, p. 24.
Time, August 14, 2000, p. 80.

Online

"Lee Ann News and Facts," Country.tzo.com, http://www.country.tzo.com/public/law_news.htm (April 10, 2001).
"Lee Ann Womack: I Hope You Dance," MCA Nashville, http://mca-nashville.com/leeannwomack/bio.htm (April 9, 2001).

—*Gloria Cooksey*

Cumulative Subject Index

Volume numbers appear in **bold**

A cappella
Brightman, Sarah **20**
Bulgarian State Female Vocal Choir, The **10**
Golden Gate Quartet **25**
Nylons, The **6**
Sweet Honey In The Rock **26**
　Earlier sketch in CM **1**
Take 6 **6**
Zap Mama **14**

Accordion
Buckwheat Zydeco **6**
Chenier, C. J. **15**
Chenier, Clifton **6**
Queen Ida **9**
Richard, Zachary **9**
Rockin' Dopsie **10**
Simien, Terrance **12**
Sonnier, Jo-El **10**
Yankovic, "Weird Al" **7**

Ambient/Rave/Techno
Aphex Twin **14**
Basement Jaxx **29**
Chemical Brothers **20**
Clark, Anne **32**
Deep Forest **18**
808 State **31**
Front Line Assembly **20**
Gus Gus **26**
Holmes, David **31**
KMFDM **18**
Kraftwerk **9**
Lords of Acid **20**
Man or Astroman? **21**
Mouse On Mars **32**
Neu! **32**
Oakenfold, Paul **32**
Orb, The **18**
Propellerheads **26**
Shadow, DJ **19**
Sheep on Drugs **27**
Tobin, Amon **32**
2 Unlimited **18**
Underworld **26**
Van Helden, Armand **32**

Bandoneon
Piazzolla, Astor **18**
Saluzzi, Dino **23**

Banjo
Boggs, Dock **25**
Bromberg, David **18**
Clark, Roy **1**
Crowe, J.D. **5**
Fleck, Bela **8**
　Also see New Grass Revival, The
Hartford, John **1**
McCoury, Del **15**
Piazzolla, Astor **18**
Scruggs, Earl **3**
Seeger, Pete **4**
　Also see Weavers, The

Skaggs, Ricky **5**
Stanley, Ralph **5**
Watson, Doc **2**

Bass
Brown, Ray **21**
Carter, Ron **14**
Chambers, Paul **18**
Clarke, Stanley **3**
Collins, Bootsy **8**
Dixon, Willie **10**
Fell, Simon H. **32**
Fender, Leo **10**
Haden, Charlie **12**
Hinton, Milt **33**
Holland, Dave **27**
Kaye, Carol **22**
Kowald, Peter **32**
Laswell, Bill **14**
Love, Laura **20**
Mann, Aimee **22**
McBride, Christian **17**
McCartney, Paul **32**
　Earlier sketch in CM **4**
　Also see Beatles, The
Mingus, Charles **9**
Ndegéocello, Me'Shell **18**
Parker, William **31**
Sting **19**
　Earlier sketch in CM **2**
Sweet, Matthew **9**
Was, Don **21**
　Also see Was (Not Was)
Watt, Mike **22**
Whitaker, Rodney **20**

Big Band/Swing
Andrews Sisters, The **9**
Arnaz, Desi **8**
Asleep at the Wheel **29**
　Earlier sketch in CM **5**
Atomic Fireballs, The **27**
Bailey, Pearl **5**
Basie, Count **2**
Beiderbecke, Bix **16**
Bennett, Tony **16**
　Earlier sketch in CM **2**
Berrigan, Bunny **2**
Blakey, Art **11**
Brown, Lawrence **23**
Calloway, Cab **6**
Carter, Benny **3**
Chenille Sisters, The **16**
Cherry Poppin' Daddies **24**
Clooney, Rosemary **9**
Como, Perry **14**
Cornell, Don **30**
Cugat, Xavier **23**
DeFranco, Buddy **31**
Dorsey Brothers, The **8**
Eckstine, Billy **1**
Eldridge, Roy **9**
Ellington, Duke **2**
Ferguson, Maynard **7**
Fitzgerald, Ella **1**

Fountain, Pete **7**
Getz, Stan **12**
Gillespie, Dizzy **6**
Goodman, Benny **4**
Henderson, Fletcher **16**
Herman, Woody **12**
Hines, Earl "Fatha" **12**
Jacquet, Illinois **17**
James, Harry **11**
Jones, Spike **5**
Jordan, Louis **11**
Krupa, Gene **13**
Lavay Smith and Her Red Hot Skillet Lickers **32**
Lee, Peggy **8**
Madness **27**
McGuire Sisters, The **27**
McKinney's Cotton Pickers **16**
Miller, Glenn **6**
Norvo, Red **12**
O'Farrill, Chico **31**
Parker, Charlie **5**
Prima, Louis **18**
Puente, Tito **14**
Ray Condo and His Ricochets **26**
Rich, Buddy **13**
Rodney, Red **14**
Roomful of Blues **7**
Royal Crown Revue **33**
Scott, Jimmy **14**
Setzer, Brian **32**
Severinsen, Doc **1**
Shaw, Artie **8**
Sinatra, Frank **23**
　Earlier sketch in CM **1**
Squirrel Nut Zippers **20**
Stafford, Jo **24**
Strayhorn, Billy **13**
Teagarden, Jack **10**
Torme, Mel **4**
Vaughan, Sarah **2**
Welk, Lawrence **13**
Whiteman, Paul **17**

Bluegrass
Auldridge, Mike **4**
Bluegrass Patriots **22**
Clements, Vassar **18**
Country Gentlemen, The **7**
Crowe, J.D. **5**
Flatt, Lester **3**
Fleck, Bela **8**
　Also see New Grass Revival, The
Gill, Vince **7**
Grisman, David **17**
Hartford, John **1**
Krauss, Alison **10**
Louvin Brothers, The **12**
Martin, Jimmy **5**
　Also see Osborne Brothers, The
McCoury, Del **15**
McReynolds, Jim and Jesse **12**
Monroe, Bill **1**
Nashville Bluegrass Band **14**
New Grass Revival, The **4**

Sixpence None the Richer **26**
Smith, Michael W. **11**
St. James, Rebecca **26**
Stryper **2**
Taylor, Steve **26**
Velasquez, Jaci **32**
Waters, Ethel **11**
Winans, BeBe and CeCe **32**

Clarinet
Adams, John **8**
Bechet, Sidney **17**
Braxton, Anthony **12**
Brötzmann, Peter **26**
Byron, Don **22**
DeFranco, Buddy **31**
Fountain, Pete **7**
Goodman, Benny **4**
Herman, Woody **12**
Russell, Pee Wee **25**
Scott, Tony **32**
Shaw, Artie **8**
Stoltzman, Richard **24**
Sturr, Jimmy **33**
Vandermark, Ken **28**

Classical
Abbado, Claudio **32**
Ameling, Elly **24**
Anderson, June **27**
Anderson, Marian **8**
Argerich, Martha **27**
Arrau, Claudio **1**
Ashkenazy, Vladimir **32**
Austral, Florence **26**
Baker, Janet **14**
Barenboim, Daniel **30**
Beecham, Thomas **27**
Beltrán, Tito **28**
Berio, Luciano **32**
Bernstein, Leonard **2**
Bonney, Barbara **33**
Boulez, Pierre **26**
Boyd, Liona **7**
Bream, Julian **9**
Britten, Benjamin **15**
Bronfman, Yefim **6**
Canadian Brass, The **4**
Carter, Elliott **30**
Carter, Ron **14**
Casals, Pablo **9**
Chang, Han-Na **33**
Chang, Sarah **7**
Chanticleer **33**
Church, Charlotte **28**
Clayderman, Richard **1**
Cliburn, Van **13**
Copland, Aaron **2**
Davis, Anthony **17**
Davis, Chip **4**
Davis, Colin **27**
DuPré, Jacqueline **26**
Dvorak, Antonin **25**
Emerson String Quartet **33**
Fiedler, Arthur **6**
Fleming, Renee **24**
Galway, James **3**
Gardiner, John Eliot **26**
Gingold, Josef **6**
Glennie, Evelyn **33**
Gould, Glenn **9**
Gould, Morton **16**
Hahn, Hilary **30**
Hamelin, Marc-André **33**
Hampson, Thomas **12**
Harrell, Lynn **3**
Hayes, Roland **13**

Heifetz, Jascha **31**
Hendricks, Barbara **10**
Herrmann, Bernard **14**
Hinderas, Natalie **12**
Horne, Marilyn **9**
Horowitz, Vladimir **1**
Isbin, Sharon **33**
Ives, Charles **29**
Jarrett, Keith **1**
Kennedy, Nigel **8**
Kissin, Evgeny **6**
Kremer, Gidon **30**
Kronos Quartet **5**
Kunzel, Erich **17**
Lemper, Ute **14**
Levine, James **8**
Liberace **9**
Ma, Yo Yo **24**
  Earlier sketch in CM **2**
Marsalis, Wynton **6**
Mascagni, Pietro **25**
Masur, Kurt **11**
McNair, Sylvia **15**
McPartland, Marian **15**
Mehta, Zubin **11**
Menuhin, Yehudi **11**
Midori **7**
Mutter, Anne-Sophie **23**
Nancarrow, Conlon **32**
Nyman, Michael **15**
Oregon **30**
Ott, David **2**
Parkening, Christopher **7**
Pavarotti, Luciano **20**
  Earlier sketch in CM **1**
Penderecki, Krzysztof **30**
Perahia, Murray **10**
Perlman, Itzhak **2**
Phillips, Harvey **3**
Pires, Maria João **26**
Quasthoff, Thomas **26**
Rampal, Jean-Pierre **6**
Rangell, Andrew **24**
Rieu, André **26**
Rostropovich, Mstislav **17**
Rota, Nino **13**
Rubinstein, Arthur **11**
Salerno-Sonnenberg, Nadja **3**
Salonen, Esa-Pekka **16**
Schickele, Peter **5**
Schuman, William **10**
Segovia, Andres **6**
Shankar, Ravi **9**
Shaw, Robert **32**
Solti, Georg **13**
Starker, Janos **32**
Stern, Isaac **7**
Stoltzman, Richard **24**
Sutherland, Joan **13**
Takemitsu, Toru **6**
Tan Dun **33**
Temirkanov, Yuri **26**
Thibaudet, Jean-Yves **24**
Tilson Thomas, Michael **24**
Toscanini, Arturo **14**
Turnage, Mark-Anthony **31**
Upshaw, Dawn **9**
Van Hove, Fred **30**
Vanessa-Mae **26**
Vienna Choir Boys **23**
Volodos, Arcadi **28**
von Karajan, Herbert **1**
von Otter, Anne Sofie **30**
Weill, Kurt **12**
Wilson, Ransom **5**
Yamashita, Kazuhito **4**

York, Andrew **15**
Zukerman, Pinchas **4**

Composers
Adams, John **8**
Adamson, Barry **28**
Adderley, Nat **29**
Adès, Thomas **30**
Allen, Geri **10**
Alpert, Herb **11**
Anderson, Fred **32**
Anderson, Wessell **23**
Anka, Paul **2**
Arlen, Harold **27**
Atkins, Chet **26**
  Earlier sketch in CM **5**
Bacharach, Burt **20**
  Earlier sketch in CM **1**
Badalamenti, Angelo **17**
Barry, John **29**
Beiderbecke, Bix **16**
Benson, George **9**
Berio, Luciano **32**
Berlin, Irving **8**
Bernstein, Leonard **2**
Blackman, Cindy **15**
Blegvad, Peter **28**
Bley, Carla **8**
Bley, Paul **14**
Boulez, Pierre **26**
Branca, Glenn **29**
Braxton, Anthony **12**
Brickman, Jim **22**
Britten, Benjamin **15**
Brown, Carlinhos **32**
Brubeck, Dave **8**
Burrell, Kenny **11**
Byrne, David **8**
  Also see Talking Heads
Byron, Don **22**
Cage, John **8**
Cale, John **9**
Carter, Elliott **30**
Casals, Pablo **9**
Clarke, Stanley **3**
Coleman, Ornette **5**
Connors, Norman **30**
Cooder, Ry **2**
Cooney, Rory **6**
Copeland, Stewart **14**
  Also see Police, The
Copland, Aaron **2**
Crouch, Andraé **9**
Curtis, King **17**
Davis, Anthony **17**
Davis, Chip **4**
Davis, Miles **1**
de Grassi, Alex **6**
Dorsey, Thomas A. **11**
Dvorak, Antonin **25**
Elfman, Danny **9**
Ellington, Duke **2**
Eno, Brian **8**
Enya **32**
  Earlier sketch in CM **6**
Eskelin, Ellery **31**
Esquivel, Juan **17**
Evans, Bill **17**
Evans, Gil **17**
Fahey, John **17**
Fell, Simon H. **32**
Foster, David **13**
Frisell, Bill **15**
Frith, Fred **19**
Fröhlich, Frank **32**
Galás, Diamanda **16**
Garner, Erroll **25**

Cahn, Sammy **11**
Cliff, Jimmy **8**
Copeland, Stewart **14**
  Also see Police, The
Copland, Aaron **2**
Crouch, Andraé **9**
Dibango, Manu **14**
Dolby, Thomas **10**
Donovan **9**
Eddy, Duane **9**
Elfman, Danny **9**
Ellington, Duke **2**
Ferguson, Maynard **7**
Froom, Mitchell **15**
Gabriel, Peter **16**
  Earlier sketch in CM **2**
  Also see Genesis
Galás, Diamanda **16**
Gershwin, George and Ira **11**
Gould, Glenn **9**
Grusin, Dave **7**
Guaraldi, Vince **3**
Hamlisch, Marvin **1**
Hancock, Herbie **25**
  Earlier sketch in CM **8**
Harrison, George **2**
Hayes, Isaac **10**
Hedges, Michael **3**
Herrmann, Bernard **14**
Isham, Mark **14**
Jones, Quincy **20**
  Earlier sketch in CM **2**
Kander, John **33**
Knopfler, Mark **25**
  Earlier sketch in CM **3**
  Also see Dire Straits
Lennon, John **9**
  Also see Beatles, The
Lerner and Loewe **13**
Loesser, Frank **19**
Mancini, Henry **20**
  Earlier sketch in CM **1**
Marsalis, Branford **10**
Mayfield, Curtis **8**
McCartney, Paul **32**
  Earlier sketch in CM **4**
  Also see Beatles, The
Menken, Alan **10**
Mercer, Johnny **13**
Metheny, Pat **26**
  Earlier sketch in CM **2**
Montenegro, Hugo **18**
Morricone, Ennio **15**
Nascimento, Milton **6**
Newman, Randy **27**
  Earlier sketch in CM **4**
Nilsson **10**
Nyman, Michael **15**
Parks, Van Dyke **17**
Peterson, Oscar **11**
Porter, Cole **10**
Previn, André **15**
Reznor, Trent **13**
  Also see Nine Inch Nails
Richie, Lionel **2**
Robertson, Robbie **2**
Rollins, Sonny **7**
Rota, Nino **13**
Sager, Carole Bayer **5**
Sakamoto, Ryuichi **18**
Schickele, Peter **5**
Schütze, Paul **32**
Shankar, Ravi **9**
Taj Mahal **6**
Tan Dun **33**

Waits, Tom **27**
  Earlier sketch in CM **12**
  Earlier sketch in CM **1**
Weill, Kurt **12**
Williams, John **28**
  Earlier sketch in CM **9**
Williams, Paul **26**
  Earlier sketch in CM **5**
Willner, Hal **10**
Young, Neil **15**
  Earlier sketch in CM **2**

Flugelhorn
Bowie, Lester **29**
Mangione, Chuck **23**
Sandoval, Arturo **15**

Flute
Galway, James **3**
Jethro Tull **8**
Lateef, Yusef **16**
Mangione, Chuck **23**
Mann, Herbie **16**
Najee **21**
Nakai, R. Carlos **24**
Rampal, Jean-Pierre **6**
Ulmer, James Blood **13**
Valentin, Dave **33**
Wilson, Ransom **5**

Folk/Traditional
Altan **18**
America **16**
Anonymous 4 **23**
Arnaz, Desi **8**
Axton, Hoyt **28**
Baca, Susana **32**
Baez, Joan **1**
Battlefield Band, The **31**
Belafonte, Harry **8**
Belle and Sebastian **28**
Black, Mary **15**
Blades, Ruben **2**
Bloom, Luka **14**
Blue Rodeo **18**
Boggs, Dock **25**
Brady, Paul **8**
Bragg, Billy **7**
Brave Combo **31**
Bromberg, David **18**
Brown, Carlinhos **32**
Buckley, Tim **14**
Buffalo Springfield **24**
Bulgarian State Female Vocal Choir, The **10**
Byrds, The **8**
Campbell, Sarah Elizabeth **23**
Caravan **24**
Carter Family, The **3**
Carthy, Eliza **31**
Chandra, Sheila **16**
Chapin, Harry **6**
Chapman, Tracy **20**
  Earlier sketch in CM **4**
Chenille Sisters, The **16**
Cherry, Don **10**
Chesnutt, Vic **28**
Chieftains, The **7**
Childs, Toni **2**
Clannad **23**
Clegg, Johnny **8**
Cockburn, Bruce **8**
Cohen, Leonard **3**
Collins, Judy **4**
Colvin, Shawn **11**
Cotten, Elizabeth **16**

Crosby, David **3**
  Also see Byrds, The
Cruz, Celia **22**
  Earlier sketch in CM **10**
Curtis, Catie **31**
de Lucia, Paco **1**
DeMent, Iris **13**
Donovan **9**
Dr. John **7**
Drake, Nick **17**
Driftwood, Jimmy **25**
Dylan, Bob **21**
  Earlier sketch in CM **3**
Elliot, Cass **5**
Elliott, Ramblin' Jack **32**
Enya **32**
  Earlier sketch in CM **6**
Estefan, Gloria **15**
  Earlier sketch in CM **2**
Fahey, John **17**
Fairport Convention **22**
Feliciano, José **10**
Frogs, The **31**
Gabriel, Juan **31**
Galway, James **3**
Germano, Lisa **18**
Gibson, Bob **23**
Gilberto, João **33**
Gilmore, Jimmie Dale **11**
Gipsy Kings, The **8**
Gorka, John **18**
Gray, David **30**
Griffin, Patty **24**
Griffith, Nanci **3**
Grisman, David **17**
Gurtu, Trilok **29**
Guthrie, Arlo **6**
Guthrie, Woody **2**
Hakmoun, Hassan **15**
Hardin, Tim **18**
Harding, John Wesley **6**
Harper, Roy **30**
Hartford, John **1**
Havens, Richie **11**
Haza, Ofra **29**
Henry, Joe **18**
Hinojosa, Tish **13**
Hussain, Zakir **32**
Ian and Sylvia **18**
Ian, Janis **24**
  Earlier sketch in CM **5**
Iglesias, Julio **20**
  Earlier sketch in CM **2**
Incredible String Band **23**
Indigenous **31**
Indigo Girls **20**
  Earlier sketch in CM **3**
Ivers, Eileen **30**
Ives, Burl **12**
Khaled **33**
Khan, Nusrat Fateh Ali **13**
Kingston Trio, The **9**
Klezmatics, The **18**
Kottke, Leo **13**
Kuti, Fela **7**
Kuti, Femi **29**
Ladysmith Black Mambazo **1**
Lamond, Mary Jane **33**
Larkin, Patty **9**
Lavin, Christine **6**
Leadbelly **6**
Les Négresses Vertes **30**
Lightfoot, Gordon **3**
Los Lobos **2**
MacNeil, Rita **29**
Makeba, Miriam **8**
Mamas and the Papas **21**

Carter, Ron 14
Chambers, Paul 18
Chanticleer 33
Charles, Ray 24
  Earlier sketch in CM 1
Cherry, Don 10
Christian, Charlie 11
Clarke, Stanley 3
Clements, Vassar 18
Clooney, Rosemary 9
Cole, Holly 18
Cole, Nat King 3
Coleman, Ornette 5
Coltrane, John 4
Connick, Jr., Harry 4
Connors, Norman 30
Corea, Chick 6
Crawford, Randy 25
Davis, Anthony 17
Davis, Miles 1
DeFranco, Buddy 31
DeJohnette, Jack 7
Di Meola, Al 12
Dietrich, Marlene 25
Dirty Dozen 23
Douglas, Dave 29
Eckstine, Billy 1
Edison, Harry "Sweets" 29
Eldridge, Roy 9
  Also see McKinney's Cotton Pickers
Elling, Kurt 31
Ellington, Duke 2
Ellis, Herb 18
Eskelin, Ellery 31
Evans, Bill 17
Evans, Gil 17
Fell, Simon H. 32
Ferguson, Maynard 7
Ferrell, Rachelle 17
Fitzgerald, Ella 1
Five Iron Frenzy 26
Flanagan, Tommy 16
Fleck, Bela 8
  Also see New Grass Revival, The
Flying Luttenbachers, The 28
Fountain, Pete 7
Frisell, Bill 15
Fröhlich, Frank 32
Gaillard, Slim 31
Galway, James 3
Garbarek, Jan 30
Garner, Erroll 25
Garrett, Kenny 28
Getz, Stan 12
Gillespie, Dizzy 6
Goodman, Benny 4
Gordon, Dexter 10
Grappelli, Stephane 10
Green, Benny 17
Green, Grant 14
Guaraldi, Vince 3
Hackett, Bobby 21
Haden, Charlie 12
Hampton, Lionel 6
Hancock, Herbie 25
  Earlier sketch in CM 8
Hardcastle, Paul 20
Hargrove, Roy 15
Harrell, Tom 28
Harris, Barry 32
Harris, Eddie 15
Harris, Teddy 22
Hawkins, Coleman 11
Hawkins, Erskine 19
Haynes, Roy 33
Hedges, Michael 3
Henderson, Fletcher 16

Henderson, Joe 14
Herman, Woody 12
Hines, Earl "Fatha" 12
Hinton, Milt 33
Hirt, Al 5
Holiday, Billie 6
Holland, Dave 27
Horn, Shirley 7
Horne, Lena 11
Humes, Helen 19
Hunter, Alberta 7
Hunter, Charlie 24
Ibrahim, Abdullah 24
Incognito 16
Isham, Mark 14
Jackson, Milt 15
Jacquet, Illinois 17
Jamal, Ahmad 32
James, Boney 21
James, Harry 11
Jarreau, Al 1
Jarrett, Keith 1
Jensen, Ingrid 22
Jobim, Antonio Carlos 19
Johnson, J.J. 33
Johnson, James P. 16
Johnson, Lonnie 17
Jones, Elvin 9
Jones, Hank 15
Jones, Philly Joe 16
Jones, Quincy 20
  Earlier sketch in CM 2
Jones, Thad 19
Jordan, Marc 30
Jordan, Stanley 1
Kang, Eyvind 28
Kennedy, Nigel 8
Kenny G 14
Kent, Stacey 28
Kenton, Stan 21
Kirk, Rahsaan Roland 6
Kitt, Eartha 9
Klugh, Earl 10
Konitz, Lee 30
Kowald, Peter 32
Krall, Diana 27
Kronos Quartet 5
Kropinski, Uwe 31
Krupa, Gene 13
Laine, Cleo 10
Lambert, Hendricks and Ross 28
Lateef, Yusef 16
Lee, Peggy 8
Lewis, John 29
Lewis, Ramsey 14
Lincoln, Abbey 9
Lloyd, Charles 22
London, Julie 32
Lopez, Israel "Cachao" 14
Los Hombres Calientes 29
Lovano, Joe 13
Mahavishnu Orchestra 19
Mahogany, Kevin 26
Malone, Russell 27
Mancini, Henry 20
  Earlier sketch in CM 1
Mangione, Chuck 23
Manhattan Transfer, The 8
Mann, Herbie 16
Marsalis, Branford 10
Marsalis, Ellis 13
Marsalis, Wynton 20
  Earlier sketch in CM 6
Martino, Pat 17
Masekela, Hugh 7
McBride, Christian 17
McCorkle, Susannah 27

McFerrin, Bobby 3
McKinney's Cotton Pickers 16
McLaughlin, John 12
McPartland, Marian 15
McRae, Carmen 9
Medeski, Martin & Wood 32
Metheny, Pat 26
  Earlier sketch in CM 2
Mingus, Charles 9
Monheit, Jane 33
Monk, Thelonious 6
Montgomery, Wes 3
Morgan, Frank 9
Morton, Jelly Roll 7
Mulligan, Gerry 16
Murray, Dave 28
Najee 21
Nascimento, Milton 6
Navarro, Fats 25
Northwoods Improvisers 31
Norvo, Red 12
O'Day, Anita 21
O'Farrill, Chico 31
O'Rourke, Jim 31
Oliver, King 15
Oregon 30
Oxley, Tony 32
Palmer, Jeff 20
Palmieri, Eddie 15
Parker, Charlie 5
Parker, Evan 28
Parker, Leon 27
Parker, Maceo 7
Parker, William 31
Pass, Joe 15
Paul, Les 2
Payton, Nicholas 27
Pepper, Art 18
Perez, Danilo 25
Peterson, Oscar 11
Ponty, Jean-Luc 8
Powell, Bud 15
Previn, André 15
Professor Longhair 6
Puente, Tito 14
Pullen, Don 16
Ralph Sharon Quartet 26
Rampal, Jean-Pierre 6
Redman, Dewey 32
Redman, Joshua 25
  Earlier sketch in CM 12
Reeves, Dianne 16
Reid, Vernon 2
  Also see Living Colour
Reinhardt, Django 7
Ribot, Marc 30
Rich, Buddy 13
Rivers, Sam 29
Roach, Max 12
Roberts, Marcus 6
Robillard, Duke 2
Rodney, Red 14
Rollins, Sonny 7
Roney, Wallace 33
Russell, Pee Wee 25
Saluzzi, Dino 23
Sanborn, David 28
  Earlier sketch in CM 1
Sanders, Pharoah 28
  Earlier sketch in CM 16
Sandoval, Arturo 15
Santamaria, Mongo 28
Santana, Carlos 19
  Earlier sketch in CM 1
Schuur, Diane 6
Scofield, John 7
Scott, Jimmy 14

Doobie Brothers, The **3**
Doors, The **4**
Dreamtheater **23**
Drivin' N' Cryin' **31**
Dropkick Murphys **26**
Duran Duran **4**
Durutti Column, The **30**
Dylan, Bob **3**
Eagles, The **3**
Echo and the Bunnymen **32**
Echobelly **21**
Eddy, Duane **9**
Einstürzende Neubauten **13**
Electric Light Orchestra **7**
Elf Power **30**
Elliot, Cass **5**
Emerson, Lake & Palmer/Powell **5**
Eminem **28**
Emmet Swimming **24**
English Beat, The **9**
Eno, Brian **8**
Erickson, Roky **16**
Escovedo, Alejandro **18**
Etheridge, Melissa **16**
  Earlier sketch in CM **4**
Eurythmics **31**
  Earlier sketch in CM **6**
Eve 6 **31**
Everclear **18**
Ex, The **28**
Extreme **10**
Faces, The **22**
Fairport Convention **22**
Faith No More **7**
Faithfull, Marianne **14**
Fall, The **12**
Fastbacks, The **29**
Fastball **32**
Faust **32**
Fear Factory **27**
Felt **32**
Ferry, Bryan **1**
Filter **28**
fIREHOSE **11**
Fishbone **7**
Five Iron Frenzy **26**
Fixx, The **33**
Flaming Lips **22**
Fleetwood Mac **5**
Flores, Rosie **16**
Flying Luttenbachers, The **28**
Flying Saucer Attack **29**
Fogelberg, Dan **4**
Fogerty, John **2**
  Also see Creedence Clearwater Revival
Folk Implosion, The **28**
Foo Fighters **20**
Ford, Lita **9**
Foreigner **21**
Fountains of Wayne **26**
Four Seasons, The **24**
Fox, Samantha **3**
Frampton, Peter **3**
Frankie Lymon and The Teenagers **24**
Franti, Michael **16**
Frey, Glenn **3**
  Also see Eagles, The
Frogs, The **31**
Front 242 **19**
Froom, Mitchell **15**
Fu Manchu **22**
Fuel **27**
Fugazi **13**
Gabriel, Peter **16**
  Earlier sketch in CM **2**
  Also see Genesis
Galaxie 500 **33**

Gang of Four **8**
Garcia, Jerry **4**
  Also see Grateful Dead, The
Gatton, Danny **16**
Gene Loves Jezebel **27**
Genesis **4**
Geraldine Fibbers **21**
Ghost **24**
Giant Sand **30**
Gift, Roland **3**
Gin Blossoms **18**
Girls Against Boys **31**
Glitter, Gary **19**
Go-Betweens, The **28**
God Is My Co-Pilot **29**
Godsmack **30**
Golden Palominos **32**
Gomez **33**
Goo Goo Dolls, The **16**
Gorky's Zygotic Mynci **30**
Graham, Bill **10**
Grant Lee Buffalo **16**
Grapes of Wrath, The **33**
Grateful Dead **5**
Grebenshikov, Boris **3**
Green Day **16**
Griffin, Patty **24**
Guess Who **23**
Guided By Voices **18**
Guns n' Roses **2**
Gus Gus **26**
Guster **29**
Gwar **13**
Hagar, Sammy **21**
Hagen, Nina **25**
Hall & Oates **6**
Hammill, Peter **30**
Harper, Ben **17**
Harper, Roy **30**
Harrison, George **2**
  Also see Beatles, The
Harry, Deborah **4**
  Also see Blondie
Hart, Beth **29**
Harvey, Polly Jean **11**
Hassman, Nikki **26**
Hatfield, Juliana **12**
  Also see Lemonheads, The
Hawkins, Screamin' Jay **29**
  Earlier sketch in CM **8**
Healey, Jeff **4**
Heart **1**
Helmet **15**
Hendrix, Jimi **2**
Henley, Don **3**
  Also see Eagles, The
Henry, Joe **18**
Hiatt, John **8**
Hodgson, Roger **26**
  Also see Supertramp
Hole **14**
Holland-Dozier-Holland **5**
Hoodoo Gurus **33**
Hooters **20**
Hootie and the Blowfish **18**
Houston, Penelope **28**
Idol, Billy **3**
Imperial Teen **26**
Indigenous **31**
INXS **21**
  Earlier sketch in CM **2**
Iron Maiden **10**
Isaak, Chris **33**
  Earlier sketch in CM **6**
Jackson, Joe **22**
  Earlier sketch in CM **4**
Jackyl **24**

Jagger, Mick **7**
  Also see Rolling Stones, The
Jam, The **27**
Jane's Addiction **6**
Jars of Clay **20**
Jawbox **31**
Jayhawks, The **15**
Jefferson Airplane **5**
Jesus and Mary Chain, The **10**
Jesus Lizard **19**
Jethro Tull **8**
Jett, Joan **3**
Jimmie's Chicken Shack **22**
Joel, Billy **12**
  Earlier sketch in CM **2**
Johansen, David **7**
John, Elton **20**
  Earlier sketch in CM **3**
Jon Spencer Blues Explosion **18**
Joplin, Janis **3**
Journey **21**
Joy Division **19**
Judas Priest **10**
Kansas **32**
Keene, Tommy **31**
Kelly, Jeff **31**
Kennedy, Nigel **8**
Kid Rock **27**
Kidjo, Anjelique **17**
Killing Joke **30**
King Crimson **17**
King Missile **22**
Kinks, The **15**
Kiss **25**
  Earlier sketch in CM **5**
KMFDM **18**
Knopfler, Mark **25**
  Earlier sketch in CM **3**
  Also see Dire Straits
Korn **20**
Kravitz, Lenny **26**
  Earlier sketch in CM **5**
La Ley **33**
Lambchop **29**
Landreth, Sonny **16**
Lanternjack, The **31**
Led Zeppelin **1**
Lee, Ben **26**
Leiber and Stoller **14**
Lemonheads, The **12**
Lennon, John **9**
  Also see Beatles, The
Lennon, Julian **26**
  Earlier sketch in CM **2**
Les Négresses Vertes **30**
Less Than Jake **22**
Letters to Cleo **22**
Limp Bizkit **27**
Lindley, David **2**
Linkous, Mark **26**
Lit **27**
Little Feat **4**
Little Texas **14**
Live **14**
Living Colour **7**
Lofgren, Nils **25**
Logan, Jack **27**
Loggins, Kenny **20**
  Earlier sketch in CM **3**
Los Lobos **2**
Loud Family, The **31**
Love and Rockets **15**
Love Spit Love **21**
Lowe, Nick **25**
  Earlier sketch in CM **6**
L7 **12**
Luna **18**

Crosby, David **3**
　Also see Byrds, The
Crow, Sheryl **18**
Crowe, J. D. **5**
Crowell, Rodney **8**
Curtis, Catie **31**
Dahl, Jeff **28**
Dalton, Nic **31**
Daniels, Charlie **6**
Davies, Ray **5**
　Also see Kinks, the
de Burgh, Chris **22**
DeBarge, El **14**
DeMent, Iris **13**
Denver, John **22**
　Earlier sketch in CM **1**
Des'ree **24**
　Earlier sketch in CM **15**
Diamond, Neil **1**
Diddley, Bo **3**
Diffie, Joe **27**
　Earlier sketch in CM **10**
DiFranco, Ani **17**
Dion **4**
Dixon, Willie **10**
DMX **25**
Doc Pomus **14**
Domino, Fats **2**
Donovan **9**
Dorsey, Thomas A. **11**
Doucet, Michael **8**
Drake, Nick **17**
Dube, Lucky **17**
Dulli, Greg **17**
　Also see Afghan Whigs, The
Dury, Ian **30**
Dylan, Bob **21**
　Earlier sketch in CM **3**
Earle, Steve **16**
Edmonds, Kenneth "Babyface" **12**
Elfman, Danny **9**
Ellington, Duke **2**
Elliott, Ramblin' Jack **32**
Emmanuel, Tommy **21**
English, Michael **23**
Enigma **32**
　Earlier sketch in CM **14**
Enya **32**
　Earlier sketch in CM **6**
Erickson, Roky **16**
Ertegun, Ahmet **10**
Escovedo, Alejandro **18**
Estefan, Gloria **15**
　Earlier sketch in CM **2**
Etheridge, Melissa **16**
　Earlier sketch in CM **4**
Evans, Sara **27**
Everlast **27**
Faithfull, Marianne **14**
Ferry, Bryan **1**
Flack, Roberta **5**
Flatt, Lester **3**
Fogelberg, Dan **4**
Fogerty, John **2**
　Also see Creedence Clearwater Revival
Fordham, Julia **15**
Foster, David **13**
Frampton, Peter **3**
Franti, Michael **16**
Frey, Glenn **3**
　Also see Eagles, The
Fripp, Robert **9**
Frizzell, Lefty **10**
Gabriel, Juan **31**
Gabriel, Peter **16**
　Earlier sketch in CM **2**
　Also see Genesis

Garcia, Jerry **4**
　Also see Grateful Dead, The
Gaye, Marvin **4**
Geldof, Bob **9**
Gershwin, George and Ira **11**
Gibson, Bob **23**
Gibson, Deborah **24**
　Earlier sketch in CM **1**
　Also see Gibson, Debbie
Gift, Roland **3**
Gill, Vince **7**
Gilley, Mickey **7**
Goffin-King **24**
Gold, Julie **22**
Goodman, Benny **4**
Gordy, Berry, Jr. **6**
Gorka, John **18**
Grant, Amy **7**
Gray, David **30**
Gray, Macy **32**
Green, Al **9**
Greenwood, Lee **12**
Griffin, Patty **24**
Griffith, Nanci **3**
Guthrie, Arlo **6**
Guthrie, Gwen **26**
Guthrie, Woodie **2**
Guy, Buddy **4**
Hagen, Nina **25**
Haggard, Merle **2**
Hall, Tom T. **26**
　Earlier sketch in CM **4**
Hamlisch, Marvin **1**
Hammer, M.C. **5**
Hammill, Peter **30**
Hancock, Herbie **25**
　Earlier sketch in CM **8**
Hardin, Tim **18**
Harding, John Wesley **6**
Harley, Bill **7**
Harper, Ben **17**
Harper, Roy **30**
Harris, Emmylou **4**
Harrison, George **2**
　Also see Beatles, The
Harry, Deborah **4**
　Also see Blondie
Hart, Beth **29**
Hartford, John **1**
Hatfield, Juliana **12**
　Also see Lemonheads, The
Hawkins, Screamin' Jay **29**
　Earlier sketch in CM **8**
Hayes, Isaac **10**
Healey, Jeff **4**
Hedges, Michael **3**
Hendrix, Jimi **2**
Henley, Don **3**
　Also see Eagles, The
Henry, Joe **18**
Hiatt, John **8**
Hill, Lauryn **25**
　Also see Fugees, The
Hinojosa, Tish **13**
Hitchcock, Robyn **9**
Holly, Buddy **1**
Hornsby, Bruce **25**
　Earlier sketch in CM **3**
Houston, Penelope **28**
Howard, Harlan **15**
Ian, Janis **24**
　Earlier sketch in CM **5**
Ice Cube **10**
Ice-T **7**
Idol, Billy **3**
Imbruglia, Natalie **27**

Isaak, Chris **33**
　Earlier sketch in CM **6**
Jackson, Alan **25**
　Earlier sketch in CM **7**
Jackson, Janet **16**
　Earlier sketch in CM **3**
Jackson, Joe **22**
　Earlier sketch in CM **4**
Jackson, Michael **17**
　Earlier sketch in CM **1**
　Also see Jacksons, The
Jackson, Millie **14**
Jagger, Mick **7**
　Also see Rolling Stones, The
James, Rick **2**
Jarreau, Al **1**
Jennings, Waylon **4**
Jett, Joan **3**
Jewel **25**
Jimmy Jam and Terry Lewis **11**
Joel, Billy **12**
　Earlier sketch in CM **2**
Johansen, David **7**
John, Elton **20**
　Earlier sketch in CM **3**
Johnson, Lonnie **17**
Jones, George **4**
Jones, Quincy **20**
　Earlier sketch in CM **2**
Jones, Rickie Lee **4**
Joplin, Janis **3**
Jordan, Marc **30**
Jordan, Montell **26**
Kane, Big Daddy **7**
Kee, John P. **15**
Keene, Tommy **31**
Keith, Toby **17**
Kelly, Jeff **31**
Kelly, R. **19**
Ketchum, Hal **14**
Khan, Chaka **19**
　Earlier sketch in CM **9**
King, Albert **2**
King, B. B. **24**
　Earlier sketch in CM **1**
King, Ben E. **7**
King, Carole **6**
King, Freddy **17**
Knopfler, Mark **25**
　Earlier sketch in CM **3**
　Also see Dire Straits
Kottke, Leo **13**
Kravitz, Lenny **26**
　Earlier sketch in CM **5**
Kreviazuk, Chantal **33**
Kristofferson, Kris **4**
L.L. Cool J **5**
Landreth, Sonny **16**
lang, kd **25**
　Earlier sketch in CM **4**
Larkin, Patty **9**
Lauderdale, Jim **29**
Lavin, Christine **6**
LeDoux, Chris **12**
Lee, Ben **26**
Lee, Peggy **8**
Lehrer, Tom **7**
Leiber and Stoller **14**
Lennon, John **9**
　Also see Beatles, The
Lennon, Julian **26**
　Earlier sketch in CM **2**
Lewis, Huey **9**
Lightfoot, Gordon **3**
Linkous, Mark **26**
Little Richard **1**
Loeb, Lisa **23**

Straw, Syd **18**
Streisand, Barbra **2**
Stuart, Marty **9**
Styne, Jule **21**
Summer, Donna **12**
Summers, Andy **3**
  Also see Police, The
Sure!, Al B. **13**
Sweat, Keith **13**
Sweet, Matthew **9**
Taj Mahal **6**
Taupin, Bernie **22**
Taylor, James **25**
  Earlier sketch in CM **2**
Taylor, Kate **30**
Taylor, Koko **10**
Taylor, Steve **26**
Terrell **32**
Thompson, Richard **7**
Thornton, Big Mama **18**
Tikaram, Tanita **9**
Tillis, Mel **7**
Tillis, Pam **25**
  Earlier sketch in CM **8**
Tippin, Aaron **12**
Tone-Loc **3**
Torme, Mel **4**
Tosh, Peter **3**
Toussaint, Allen **11**
Townshend, Pete **1**
  Also see Who, The
Travis, Merle **14**
Travis, Randy **9**
Treadmill Trackstar **21**
Tricky **18**
Tritt, Travis **7**
Trynin, Jen **21**
Tubb, Ernest **4**
Twain, Shania **17**
Twitty, Conway **6**
2Pac **17**
Vai, Steve **5**
  Also see Whitesnake
Van Ronk, Dave **12**
Van Shelton, Ricky **5**
Van Zandt, Steven **29**
Van Zandt, Townes **13**
Vandross, Luther **24**
  Earlier sketch in CM **2**
Vega, Suzanne **3**
Wachtel, Waddy **26**
Wagoner, Porter **13**
Wainwright, Rufus **29**
Waits, Tom **27**
  Earlier sketch in CM **12**
  Earlier sketch in CM **1**
Walden, Narada Michael **14**
Walker, Jerry Jeff **13**
Walker, T-Bone **5**
Waller, Fats **7**
Walsh, Joe **5**
  Also see Eagles, The
Wariner, Steve **18**
Warren, Diane **21**
Waters, Crystal **15**
Waters, Muddy **24**
  Earlier sketch in CM **4**
Watley, Jody **26**
  Earlier sketch in CM **9**
Watt, Mike **22**
Webb, Jimmy **12**
Weill, Kurt **12**
Welch, Gillian **33**
Weller, Paul **11**
West, Dottie **8**
Westerberg, Paul **26**
White, Karyn **21**

White, Lari **15**
Whitley, Chris **16**
Whitley, Keith **7**
Wildhorn, Frank **31**
Williams, Dar **21**
Williams, Deniece **1**
Williams, Don **4**
Williams, Hank, Jr. **1**
Williams, Hank, Sr. **4**
Williams, Lucinda **24**
  Earlier sketch in CM **10**
Williams, Paul **26**
  Earlier sketch in CM **5**
Williams, Victoria **17**
Wills, Bob **6**
Wilson, Brian **24**
  Also see Beach Boys, The
Winbush, Angela **15**
Winter, Johnny **5**
Winwood, Steve **2**
  Also see Spencer Davis Group
  Also see Traffic
Womack, Bobby **5**
Wonder, Stevie **17**
  Earlier sketch in CM **2**
Wray, Link **17**
Wyatt, Robert **24**
Wynette, Tammy **24**
  Earlier sketch in CM **2**
Yearwood, Trisha **25**
  Earlier sketch in CM **10**
Yoakam, Dwight **21**
  Earlier sketch in CM **1**
Young, Neil **15**
  Earlier sketch in CM **2**
Zappa, Frank **17**
  Earlier sketch in CM **1**
Zevon, Warren **9**

Trombone

Anderson, Ray **7**
Bauer, Johannes **32**
Bishop, Jeb **28**
Brown, Lawrence **23**
Johnson, J.J. **33**
Mandel, Johnny **28**
Miller, Glenn **6**
Rudd, Roswell **28**
Teagarden, Jack **10**
Turre, Steve **22**

Trumpet

Alpert, Herb **11**
Armstrong, Louis **4**
Baker, Chet **13**
Berigan, Bunny **2**
Blanchard, Terence **13**
Bowie, Lester **29**
Brown, Clifford **24**
Cherry, Don **10**
Coleman, Ornette **5**
Davis, Miles **1**
Douglas, Dave **29**
Edison, Harry "Sweets" **29**
Eldridge, Roy **9**
  Also see McKinney's Cotton Pickers
Ferguson, Maynard **7**
Gillespie, Dizzy **6**
Hargrove, Roy **15**
Harrell, Tom **28**
Hawkins, Erskine **19**
Hirt, Al **5**
Isham, Mark **14**
James, Harry **11**
Jensen, Ingrid **22**
Jones, Quincy **20**
  Earlier sketch in CM **2**

Jones, Thad **19**
Loughnane, Lee **3**
Mandel, Johnny **28**
Marsalis, Wynton **20**
  Earlier sketch in CM **6**
Masekela, Hugh **7**
Matthews, Eric **22**
Mighty Mighty Bosstones **20**
Miles, Ron **22**
Minton, Phil **29**
Navarro, Fats **25**
Oliver, King **15**
Payton, Nicholas **27**
Rodney, Red **14**
Roney, Wallace **33**
Sandoval, Arturo **15**
Severinsen, Doc **1**
Shaw, Woody **27**
Terry, Clark **24**

Tuba

Phillips, Harvey **3**

Vibraphone

Burton, Gary **10**
Hampton, Lionel **6**
Jackson, Milt **15**
Norvo, Red **12**

Viola

Menuhin, Yehudi **11**
Zukerman, Pinchas **4**

Violin

Acuff, Roy **2**
Anderson, Laurie **25**
  Earlier sketch in CM **1**
Bell, Joshua **21**
Bromberg, David **18**
Carter, Regina **22**
Carthy, Eliza **31**
Chang, Sarah **7**
Clements, Vassar **18**
Coleman, Ornette **5**
Cugat, Xavier **23**
Daniels, Charlie **6**
Doucet, Michael **8**
Germano, Lisa **18**
Gingold, Josef **6**
Grappelli, Stephane **10**
Hahn, Hilary **30**
Hartford, John **1**
Heifetz, Jascha **31**
Kang, Eyvind **28**
Kennedy, Nigel **8**
Krauss, Alison **10**
Kremer, Gidon **30**
Lamb, Barbara **19**
Marriner, Neville **7**
Menuhin, Yehudi **11**
Midori **7**
Mutter, Anne-Sophie **23**
O'Connor, Mark **1**
Perlman, Itzhak **2**
Ponty, Jean-Luc **8**
Rieu, André **26**
Sahm, Doug **30**
  Also see Texas Tornados, The
Salerno-Sonnenberg, Nadja **3**
Schroer, Oliver **29**
Skaggs, Ricky **5**
Stern, Isaac **7**
Vanessa-Mae **26**
Whiteman, Paul **17**
Wills, Bob **6**
Zukerman, Pinchas **4**

Cumulative Musicians Index

Volume numbers appear in **bold**

A-ha **22**
Aaliyah **21**
Aaron
  See Mr. T Experience, The
Abba **12**
Abbado, Claudio **32**
Abbott, Jacqueline
  See Beautiful South
Abbott, Jude
  See Chumbawamba
Abbruzzese, Dave
  See Pearl Jam
Abdul, Paula **3**
Abercrombie, Jeff
  See Fuel
Abercrombie, John **25**
Aboitiz, Rodrigo
  See La Ley
Abong, Fred
  See Belly
Abrahams, Mick
  See Jethro Tull
Abrams, Bryan
  See Color Me Badd
Abrantes, Fernando
  See Kraftwerk
AC/DC **4**
Ace of Base **22**
Achor, James
  See Royal Crown Revue
Ackerman, Will **3**
Acland, Christopher
  See Lush
Acuff, Roy **2**
Acuna, Alejandro
  See Weather Report
Adam Ant **13**
Adamendes, Elaine
  See Throwing Muses
Adams, Bryan **20**
  Earlier sketch in CM **2**
Adams, Clifford
  See Kool & the Gang
Adams, Craig
  See Cult, The
Adams, Donn
  See NRBQ
Adams, John **8**
Adams, Johnny **33**
Adams, Mark
  See Specials, The
Adams, Oleta **17**
Adams, Terry
  See NRBQ
Adams, Tim
  See Swell
Adams, Victoria
  See Spice Girls
Adams, Yolanda **23**
Adamson, Barry **28**
Adcock, Eddie
  See Country Gentleman, The
Adderley, Cannonball **15**
Adderley, Nat **29**

Adderly, Julian
  See Adderley, Cannonball
Adé, King Sunny **18**
Adès, Thomas **30**
Adkins, Trace **31**
Adler, Steven
  See Guns n' Roses
Ævar, Ágúst
  See Sigur Rós
Aerosmith **22**
  Earlier sketch in CM **3**
Afanasieff, Walter **26**
Afghan Whigs **17**
Afonso, Marie
  See Zap Mama
AFX
  See Aphex Twin
Agius, Alfie
  See Fixx, The
Agnew, Rikk
  See Christian Death
Aguilera, Christina **30**
Agust, Daniel
  See Gus Gus
Ainge, Gary
  See Felt
Air **33**
Air Supply **22**
Airport, Jak
  See X-Ray Spex
Aitchison, Dominic
  See Mogwai
Ajile
  See Arrested Development
Akingbola, Sola
  See Jamiroquai
Akins, Rhett **22**
Akita, Masami
  See Merzbow
Alabama **21**
  Earlier sketch in CM **1**
Alan, Skip
  See Pretty Things, The
Alarm **22**
Alatorre, Eric
  See Chanticleer
Albarn, Damon
  See Blur
Alber, Matt
  See Chanticleer
Albert, Nate
  See Mighty Mighty Bosstones
Alberti, Dorona
  See KMFDM
Albini, Steve **15**
Albuquerque, Michael de
  See Electric Light Orchestra
Alder, John
  See Gong
  Also see Pretty Things, The
Alex
  See Mr. T Experience, The
Alexakis, Art
  See Everclear
Alexander, Arthur **14**

Alexander, Tim "Herb"
  See Primus
Alexander, Tim
  See Asleep at the Wheel
Ali
  See Tribe Called Quest, A
Alice in Chains **10**
Alien Sex Fiend **23**
Alkema, Jan Willem
  See Compulsion
All Saints **25**
All-4-One **17**
Allcock, Martin
  See Fairport Convention
  Also see Jethro Tull
Allen, April
  See C + C Music Factory
Allen, Chad
  See Guess Who
Allen, Daevid **28**
  Also see Gong
Allen, Dave
  See Gang of Four
Allen, Debbie **8**
Allen, Duane
  See Oak Ridge Boys, The
Allen, Eric
  See Apples in Stereo
Allen, Geri **10**
Allen, Jeff
  See Mint Condition
Allen, Johnny Ray
  See Subdudes, The
Allen, Papa Dee
  See War
Allen, Peter **11**
Allen, Red
  See Osborne Brothers, The
Allen, Rick
  See Def Leppard
Allen, Ross
  See Mekons, The
Allen, Verden "Phally"
  See Mott the Hoople
Allen, Wally
  See Pretty Things, The
Allison, Luther **21**
Allison, Mose **17**
Allison, Verne
  See Dells, The
Allman Brothers, The **6**
Allman, Chris
  See Greater Vision
Allman, Duane
  See Allman Brothers, The
Allman, Gregg
  See Allman Brothers, The
Allsup, Michael Rand
  See Three Dog Night
Almond, Marc **29**
Alpert, Herb **11**
Alphonso, Roland
  See Skatalites, The
Alsing, Pelle
  See Roxette

Atkinson, Sweet Pea
  See Was (Not Was)
Atomic Fireballs, The **27**
ATR
  See Boredoms, The
Audio Adrenaline **22**
Auf Der Maur, Melissa
  See Hole
Augustyniak, Jerry
  See 10,000 Maniacs
Auldridge, Mike **4**
  Also see Country Gentlemen, The
  Also see Seldom Scene, The
Austin, Cuba
  See McKinney's Cotton Pickers
Austin, Dallas **16**
Austral, Florence **26**
Autry, Gene **25**
  Earlier sketch in CM **12**
Avalon **26**
Avalon, Frankie **5**
Avery, Eric
  See Jane's Addiction
Avery, Teodross **23**
Avory, Mick
  See Kinks, The
  Also see Rolling Stones, The
Axton, Hoyt **28**
Ayers, Kevin
  See Gong
Aykroyd, Dan
  See Blues Brothers, The
Ayler, Albert **19**
Ayres, Ben
  See Cornershop
Azorr, Chris
  See Cherry Poppin' Daddies
Aztec Camera **22**
B, Daniel
  See Front 242
B-52's, The **4**
B-Real
  See Cypress Hill
Baah, Reebop Kwaku
  See Can
  Also see Traffic
Babatunde, Don
  See Last Poets
Babes in Toyland **16**
Babjak, James
  See Smithereens, The
Babyface
  See Edmonds, Kenneth "Babyface"
Baca, Susana **32**
Bacchus, Richard
  See D Generation
Bacharach, Burt **20**
  Earlier sketch in CM **1**
Bachman, Eric
  See Archers of Loaf
Bachman, Randy
  See Guess Who
Backstreet Boys **21**
Bad Brains **16**
Bad Company **22**
Bad Livers, The **19**
Bad Religion **28**
Badalamenti, Angelo **17**
Badfinger **23**
Badger, Pat
  See Extreme
Badly Drawn Boy **33**
Badoux, Gwen
  See Les Négresses Vertes
Badrena, Manola
  See Weather Report
Badu, Erykah **26**

Baez, Joan **1**
Baha Men **32**
Bailey, Keith
  See Gong
Bailey, Mildred **13**
Bailey, Pearl **5**
Bailey, Phil
  See Earth, Wind and Fire
Bailey, Victor
  See Weather Report
Bain, Pete
  See Spacemen 3
Baker, Anita **9**
Baker, Arthur **23**
Baker, Bobby
  See Tragically Hip, The
Baker, Brian
  See Bad Religion
Baker, Chet **13**
Baker, Dale
  See Sixpence None the Richer
Baker, David
  See Mercury Rev
Baker, Ginger **16**
  Also see Cream
Baker, James
  See Hoodoo Gurus
Baker, Janet **14**
Baker, Jon
  See Charlatans, The
Baker, Josephine **10**
Baker, LaVern **25**
Balakrishnan, David
  See Turtle Island String Quartet
Balch, Bob
  See Fu Manchu
Balch, Michael
  See Front Line Assembly
Baldes, Kevin
  See Lit
Baldursson, Sigtryggur
  See Sugarcubes, The
Baldwin, Donny
  See Starship
Baliardo, Diego
  See Gipsy Kings, The
Baliardo, Paco
  See Gipsy Kings, The
Baliardo, Tonino
  See Gipsy Kings, The
Balin, Marty
  See Jefferson Airplane
Ball, Ian
  See Gomez
Ball, Marcia **15**
Ballance, Laura
  See Superchunk
Ballard, Florence
  See Supremes, The
Ballard, Hank **17**
Balsley, Phil
  See Statler Brothers, The
Baltes, Peter
  See Dokken
Balzano, Vinnie
  See Less Than Jake
Bambaataa, Afrika **13**
Bamonte, Perry
  See Cure, The
Bananarama **22**
Bancroft, Cyke
  See Bevis Frond
Band, The **9**
Bangalter, Thomas
  See Daft Punk
Bangles, The **22**

Banks, Nick
  See Pulp
Banks, Peter
  See Yes
Banks, Tony
  See Genesis
Baptiste, David Russell
  See Meters, The
Barbarossa, Dave
  See Republica
Barbata, John
  See Jefferson Starship
Barber, Don
  See Northwoods Improvisers
Barber, Keith
  See Soul Stirrers, The
Barbero, Lori
  See Babes in Toyland
Barbieri, Gato **22**
Barbot, Bill
  See Jawbox
Bardens, Peter
  See Camel
Bardo Pond **28**
Barenaked Ladies **18**
Barenboim, Daniel **30**
Bargeld, Blixa
  See Einstürzende Neubauten
Bargeron, Dave
  See Blood, Sweat and Tears
Barham, Meriel
  See Lush
Barile, Jo
  See Ventures, The
Barker, Andrew
  See 808 State
Barker, Paul
  See Ministry
Barker, Travis Landon
  See Aquabats, The
  Also see Blink 182
Barksdale, Charles
  See Dells, The
Barlow, Barriemore
  See Jethro Tull
Barlow, Bruce
  See Commander Cody and His Lost Planet
    Airmen
Barlow, Lou **20**
  See Dinosaur Jr.
  Also see Folk Implosion, The
  Also see Sebadoh
Barlow, Tommy
  See Aztec Camera
Barnes, Danny
  See Bad Livers, The
Barnes, Jeffrey
  See Brave Combo
Barnes, Jeremy
  See Neutral Milk Hotel
Barnes, Micah
  See Nylons, The
Barnes, Neil
  See Leftfield
Barnes, Prentiss
  See Moonglows, The
Barnes, Roosevelt "Booba" **23**
Barnett, Mandy **26**
Barnwell, Duncan
  See Simple Minds
Barnwell, Ysaye Maria
  See Sweet Honey in the Rock
Barocas, Zach
  See Jawbox
Barr, Al
  See Dropkick Murphys

Barr, Ralph
  See Nitty Gritty Dirt Band, The
Barradas, Miggy
  See Divine Comedy, The
Barre, Martin
  See Jethro Tull
Barrere, Paul
  See Little Feat
Barret, Charlie
  See Fixx, The
Barrett, (Roger) Syd
  See Pink Floyd
Barrett, Dicky
  See Mighty Mighty Bosstones
Barrett, Mike
  See Lettermen, The
Barrett, Robert "T-Mo"
  See Goodie Mob
Barron, Christopher
  See Spin Doctors
Barrow, Geoff
  See Portishead
Barry, John **29**
Barson, Mike
  See Madness
Bartels, Joanie **13**
Bartholomew, Simon
  See Brand New Heavies, The
Bartoli, Cecilia **12**
Barton, Lou Ann
  See Fabulous Thunderbirds, The
Barton, Rick
  See Dropkick Murphys
Bartos, Karl
  See Kraftwerk
Basehead **11**
Basement Jaxx **29**
Basher, Mick
  See X
Basia **5**
Basie, Count **2**
Bass, Colin
  See Camel
Bass, Lance
  See 'N Sync
Bass, Ralph **24**
Bastida, Ceci (Cecilia)
  See Tijuana No!
Batchelor, Kevin
  See Big Mountain
  Also see Steel Pulse
Batel, Beate
  See Einstürzende Neubauten
Bates, Stuart "Pinkie"
  See Divine Comedy, The
Batiste, Lionel
  See Dirty Dozen Brass Band
Batoh, Masaki
  See Ghost
  Also see Pearls Before Swine
Battin, Skip
  See Byrds, The
Battle, Kathleen **6**
Battlefield Band, The **31**
Bauer, Johannes **32**
Bauer, Judah
  See Jon Spencer Blues Explosion
Bauhaus **27**
Baum, Kevin
  See Chanticleer
Baumann, Peter
  See Tangerine Dream
Bautista, Roland
  See Earth, Wind and Fire
Baxter, Adrian
  See Cherry Poppin' Daddies

Baxter, Jeff
  See Doobie Brothers, The
Bayer Sager, Carole
  See Sager, Carole Bayer
Baylor, Helen **20**
Baynton-Power, David
  See James
Bazilian, Eric
  See Hooters
Beach Boys, The **1**
Beale, Michael
  See Earth, Wind and Fire
Beard, Annette
  See Martha and the Vandellas
Beard, Frank
  See ZZ Top
Beasley, Paul
  See Mighty Clouds of Joy, The
Beastie Boys **25**
  Earlier sketch in CM **8**
Beat Farmers **23**
Beat Happening **28**
Beatles, The **2**
Beauford, Carter
  See Dave Matthews Band
Beautiful South **19**
Beauvoir, Jean
  See Wendy O. Williams and The Plasmatics
Beaver Brown Band, The **3**
Bechdel, John
  See Fear Factory
Bechet, Sidney **17**
Beck **18**
Beck, Jeff **4**
  Also see Yardbirds, The
Beck, William
  See Ohio Players
Becker, Joseph
  See Loud Family, The
Becker, Margaret **31**
Becker, Walter
  See Steely Dan
Beckford, Theophilus
  See Skatalites, The
Beckley, Gerry
  See America
Bedford, Mark
  See Madness
Bee Gees, The **3**
Beech, Wes
  See Wendy O. Williams and The Plasmatics
Beecham, Thomas **27**
Beenie Man **33**
Beers, Garry Gary
  See INXS
Begs
  See Les Négresses Vertes
Behler, Chuck
  See Megadeth
Beiderbecke, Bix **16**
Belafonte, Harry **8**
Belanger, George
  See Christian Death
Belew, Adrian **5**
  Also see King Crimson
Belfield, Dennis
  See Three Dog Night
Belitsky, Mike
  See Pernice Brothers
Belk, Darren
  See Wedding Present, The
Bell, Andy
  See Erasure
Bell, Brian
  See Weezer
Bell, Burton C.
  See Fear Factory

Bell, Carl
  See Fuel
Bell, Chris
  See Gene Loves Jezebel
Bell, Derek
  See Chieftains, The
Bell, Eric
  See Thin Lizzy
Bell, Jayn
  See Sounds of Blackness
Bell, Joshua **21**
Bell, Melissa
  See Soul II Soul
Bell, Robert "Kool"
  See Kool & the Gang
Bell, Ronald
  See Kool & the Gang
Bell, Taj
  See Charm Farm
Bell, Trent
  See Chainsaw Kittens, The
Belladonna, Joey
  See Anthrax
Bellamy Brothers, The **13**
Bellamy, David
  See Bellamy Brothers, The
Bellamy, Howard
  See Bellamy Brothers, The
Belle and Sebastian **28**
Belle, Regina **6**
Bello, Elissa
  See Go-Go's, The
Bello, Frank
  See Anthrax
Belly **16**
Belove, David
  See Oakland Interfaith Gospel Choir
Beltrán, Tito **28**
Belushi, John
  See Blues Brothers, The
Ben Folds Five **20**
Benante, Charlie
  See Anthrax
Benatar, Pat **8**
Benckert, Vicki
  See Roxette
Bender, Ariel
  See Mott the Hoople
Benedict, Scott
  See Pere Ubu
Benét, Eric **27**
Bengry, Peter
  See Cornershop
Benitez, Jellybean **15**
Benjamin, Andre "Dre"
  See OutKast
Bennett, Brian
  See Shadows, The
Bennett, Tony **16**
  Earlier sketch in CM **2**
Bennett-Nesby, Ann
  See Sounds of Blackness
Benoit, Tab **31**
Benson, George **9**
Benson, Ray
  See Asleep at the Wheel
Benson, Renaldo "Obie"
  See Four Tops, The
Bentley, Jay
  See Circle Jerks
  Also see Bad Religion
Bentley, John
  See Squeeze
Benton, Brook **7**
Bentyne, Cheryl
  See Manhattan Transfer, The

Berenyi, Miki
    See Lush
Berg, Matraca 16
Bergeson, Ben
    See Aquabats, The
Berggren, Jenny
    See Ace of Base
Berggren, Jonas
    See Ace of Base
Berggren, Linn
    See Ace of Base
Bergman, Alan and Marilyn 30
Bergmark, Christina
    See Wannadies, The
Berigan, Bunny 2
Berio, Luciano 32
Berkely, Anthony (Poetic the Grym Reaper)
    See Gravediggaz
Berlin, Irving 8
Berlin, Liz
    See Rusted Root
Berlin, Steve
    See Los Lobos
Bernal, Steve
    See Poi Dog Pondering
Berndt, Jay
    See Kilgore
Bernstein, Leonard 2
Berry, Bill
    See R.E.M.
Berry, Chuck 33
    Earlier sketch in CM 1
Berry, Jan
    See Jan & Dean
Berry, John 17
Berry, Robert
    See Emerson, Lake & Palmer/Powell
Berryhill, Bob
    See Surfaris, The
Berryman, Guy
    See Coldplay
Bert, Bob
    See Sonic Youth
Beschta, Scott
    See Promise Ring, The
Bessant, Jack
    See Reef
Best, Nathaniel
    See O'Jays, The
Best, Pete
    See Beatles, The
Beta Band, The 27
Betha, Mason
    See Mase
Bethea, Ken
    See Old 97's
Bettencourt, Nuno
    See Extreme
Better Than Ezra 19
Bettie Serveert 17
Bettini, Tom
    See Jackyl
Betts, Dicky
    See Allman Brothers, The
Bevan, Bev
    See Black Sabbath
    Also see Electric Light Orchestra
Bever, Pete
    See Workhorse Movement, The
Bevis Frond 23
Bezozi, Alan
    See Dog's Eye View
Bhag-dad-a, Omar
    See Lane, Fred
Biafra, Jello 18
    Also see Dead Kennedys
Big Audio Dynamite 18

Big Head Todd and the Monsters 20
Big Mike
    See Geto Boys, The
Big Money Odis
    See Digital Underground
Big Mountain 23
Big Paul
    See Killing Joke
Biger, Guenole
    See Les Négresses Vertes
Bigham, John
    See Fishbone
Bill Wyman & the Rhythm Kings 26
Bin Hassan, Umar
    See Last Poets
Bingham, John
    See Fishbone
Binks, Les
    See Judas Priest
Biondo, George
    See Steppenwolf
Birchfield, Benny
    See Osborne Brothers, The
Bird
    See Parker, Charlie
Birdsong, Cindy
    See Supremes, The
Birdstuff
    See Man or Astroman?
Birgisson, Jón Pór
    See Sigur Rós
Biscuits, Chuck
    See Circle Jerks
    Also see D.O.A.
    Also see Danzig
    Also see Social Distortion
Bishop, Jeb 28
    Also see Flying Luttenbachers, The
Bishop, Michael
    See Gwar
Bishop, Steven
    See Powderfinger
Bitney, Dan
    See Tortoise
Bixler, Cedric
    See At The Drive-In
Biz Markie 10
BizzyBone
    See Bone Thugs-N-Harmony
Bjelland, Kat
    See Babes in Toyland
Björk 16
    Also see Sugarcubes, The
Bjork, Brant
    See Fu Manchu
Black, Bobby
    See Commander Cody and His Lost Planet
    Airmen
Black, Clint 5
Black Crowes, The 7
Black Flag 22
Black Francis
    See Black, Frank
Black, Frank 14
Black, Jet
    See Stranglers, The
Black, Jimmy Carl "India Ink"
    See Captain Beefheart and His Magic Band
Black, Mary 15
Black Sabbath 9
Black Sheep 15
Black Uhuru 12
Black, Vic
    See C + C Music Factory
Blackburn, Paul
    See Gomez
BlackHawk 21

Blackman, Cindy 15
Blackman, Nicole
    See Golden Palominos
Blackman, Tee-Wee
    See Memphis Jug Band
Blackmore, Ritchie
    See Deep Purple
Blackstreet 23
Blackwell, Chris 26
Blackwood, Sarah
    See Dubstar
Bladd, Stephen Jo
    See J. Geils Band
Blades, Ruben 2
Blair, Ron
    See Tom Petty and the Heartbreakers
Blake, Eubie 19
Blake, Norman
    See Teenage Fanclub
Blake, Tim
    See Gong
Blakely, Paul
    See Captain Beefheart and His Magic Band
Blakey, Art 11
Blakey, Colin
    See Waterboys, The
Blanchard, Terence 13
Bland, Bobby "Blue" 12
Blatt, Melanie
    See All Saints
Blegen, Jutith 23
Blegvad, Peter 28
Blessid Union of Souls 20
Bley, Carla 8
    Also see Golden Palominos
Bley, Paul 14
Blige, Mary J. 15
Blind Melon 21
Blink 182 27
Bloch, Alan
    See Concrete Blonde
Bloch, Kurt
    See Fastbacks, The
Block, Norman
    See Rasputina
Block, Rory 18
Blonde Redhead 28
Blondie 27
    Earlier sketch in CM 14
Blood, Dave
    See Dead Milkmen
Blood, Johnny
    See Magnetic Fields, The
Blood, Sweat and Tears 7
Bloodhound Gang, The 31
Bloom, Eric
    See Blue Oyster Cult
Bloom, Luka 14
Blount, Herman "Sonny"
    See Sun Ra
Blue, Buddy
    See Beat Farmers
Blue Oyster Cult 16
Blue Rodeo 18
Bluegrass Patriots 22
Blues, "Joliet" Jake
    See Blues Brothers, The
Blues Brothers, The 3
Blues, Elwood
    See Blues Brothers, The
Blues Traveler 15
Bluetones, The 29
Blunstone, Colin
    See Zombies, The
Blunt, Martin
    See Charlatans, The
Blur 17

Brooker, Nicholas "Natty"
  See Spacemen 3
Brookes, Jon
  See Charlatans, The
Brookes, Steve
  See Jam, The
Brooks & Dunn 25
  Earlier sketch in CM 12
Brooks, Baba
  See Skatalites, The
Brooks, DJ
  See Citizen King
Brooks, Garth 25
  Earlier sketch in CM 8
Brooks, Leon Eric "Kix" III
  See Brooks & Dunn
Brooks, Meredith 30
Brooks, Stuart
  See Pretty Things, The
Broonzy, Big Bill 13
Brotherdale, Steve
  See Joy Division
  Also see Smithereens, The
Brötzmann, Caspar 27
Brötzmann, Peter 26
Broudie, Ian
  See Lightning Seeds
Broussard, Jules
  See Lavay Smith and Her Red Hot Skillet
  Lickers
Brown, Amanda
  See Go-Betweens, The
Brown, Bobby 4
Brown, Brooks
  See Cherry Poppin' Daddies
Brown, Bundy K.
  See Tortoise
Brown, Carlinhos 32
Brown, Clarence "Gatemouth" 11
Brown, Clifford 24
Brown, Dan K.
  See Fixx, The
Brown, Dan
  See Royal Trux
Brown, Dennis 29
Brown, Donny
  See Verve Pipe, The
Brown, Duncan
  See Stereolab
Brown, Foxy 25
Brown, George
  See Kool & the Gang
Brown, Greg
  See Cake
Brown, Harold
  See War
Brown, Heidi
  See Treadmill Trackstar
Brown, Ian
  See Stone Roses, The
Brown, James 16
  Earlier sketch in CM 2
Brown, Jimmy
  See UB40
Brown, Junior 15
Brown, Lawrence 23
Brown, Marty 14
Brown, Melanie
  See Spice Girls
Brown, Mick
  See Dokken
Brown, Morris
  See Pearls Before Swine
Brown, Norman 29
Brown, Norman
  See Mills Brothers, The

Brown, Paula
  See Giant Sand
Brown, Rahem
  See Artifacts
Brown, Ray 21
Brown, Ruth 13
Brown, Selwyn "Bumbo"
  See Steel Pulse
Brown, Steven
  See Tuxedomoon
Brown, Tim
  See Boo Radleys, The
Brown, Tony 14
Browne, Jackson 3
  Also see Nitty Gritty Dirt Band, The
Brownstein, Carrie
  See Sleater-Kinney
Brownstone 21
Brubeck, Dave 8
Bruce, Dustan
  See Chumbawamba
Bruce, Jack
  See Cream
Bruce, Jack
  See Golden Palominos
Bruce, Joseph Frank
  See Insane Clown Posse
Bruford, Bill
  See King Crimson
  Also see Yes
Bruno, Gioia
  See Exposé
Bruster, Thomas
  See Soul Stirrers, The
Bryan, David
  See Bon Jovi
Bryan, Karl
  See Skatalites, The
Bryan, Mark
  See Hootie and the Blowfish
Bryant, Elbridge
  See Temptations, The
Bryant, Jeff
  See Ricochet
Bryant, Junior
  See Ricochet
Bryson, Bill
  See Desert Rose Band, The
Bryson, David
  See Counting Crows
Bryson, Peabo 11
Buchanan, Wallis
  See Jamiroquai
Buchholz, Francis
  See Scorpions, The
Buchignani, Paul
  See Afghan Whigs
Buck, Mike
  See Fabulous Thunderbirds, The
Buck, Peter
  See R.E.M.
Buck, Robert
  See 10,000 Maniacs
Buckingham, Lindsey 8
  Also see Fleetwood Mac
Buckland, John
  See Coldplay
Buckler, Rick
  See Jam, The
Buckley, Betty 16
  Earlier sketch in CM 1
Buckley, Jeff 22
Buckley, Tim 14
Buckner, David
  See Papa Roach
Buckner, Richard 31
Buckwheat Zydeco 6

Budgie
  See Siouxsie and the Banshees
Buerstatte, Phil
  See White Zombie
Buffalo Springfield 24
Buffalo Tom 18
Buffett, Jimmy 4
Built to Spill 27
Bulgarian State Radio and Television Female
Vocal Choir
  See Bulgarian State Female Vocal Choir, The
Bulgarian State Female Vocal Choir, The 10
Bulgin, Lascelle
  See Israel Vibration
Bulloch, Martin
  See Mogwai
Bullock, Craig "DJ Homicide"
  See Sugar Ray
Bumbry, Grace 13
Bumpus, Cornelius
  See Doobie Brothers, The
Bunford, Huw "Bunf"
  See Super Furry Animals
Bunker, Clive
  See Jethro Tull
Bunkley, John
  See Atomic Fireballs, The
Bunnell, Dewey
  See America
Bunskoeke, Herman
  See Bettie Serveert
Bunton, Emma
  See Spice Girls
Burch, Curtis
  See New Grass Revival, The
Burchill, Charlie
  See Simple Minds
Burden, Ian
  See Human League, The
Burdon, Eric 14
  Also see War
  Also see Animals, The
Burgess, Paul
  See Camel
Burgess, Tim
  See Charlatans, The
Burke, Clem
  See Blondie
Burkum, Tyler
  See Audio Adrenaline
Burnel, J.J.
  See Stranglers, The
Burnett, Carol 6
Burnett, T Bone 13
Burnette, Billy
  See Fleetwood Mac
Burnham, Hugo
  See Gang of Four
Burning Spear 15
Burns, Barry
  See Mogwai
Burns, Bob
  See Lynyrd Skynyrd
Burns, Joey
  See Calexico
  Also see Giant Sand
Burns, Karl
  See Fall, The
Burr, Clive
  See Iron Maiden
Burrell, Boz
  See Bad Company
Burrell, Kenny 11
Burrell, Raymond "Boz"
  See King Crimson
Burroughs, William S. 26

Carter, Betty **6**
Carter, Carlene **8**
Carter, Deana **25**
Carter, Elliott **30**
Carter Family, The **3**
Carter, Helen
  See Carter Family, The
Carter, James **18**
Carter, Janette
  See Carter Family, The
Carter, Jimmy
  See Five Blind Boys of Alabama
Carter, Joe
  See Carter Family, The
Carter, Johnnie
  See Dells, The
Carter, June Cash **6**
  Also see Carter Family, The
Carter, Laura
  See Elf Power
Carter, Maybell
  See Carter Family, The
Carter, Nell **7**
Carter, Nick
  See Backstreet Boys
Carter, Regina **22**
Carter, Ron **14**
Carter, Sara
  See Carter Family, The
Carter USM **31**
Carthy, Eliza **31**
Carthy, Martin
  See Steeleye Span
Caruso, Enrico **10**
Cary, Justin
  See Sixpence None the Richer
Casady, Jack
  See Jefferson Airplane
Casale, Bob
  See Devo
Casale, Gerald V.
  See Devo
Casals, Pablo **9**
Case, Peter **13**
Casey, Ken
  See Dropkick Murphys
Cash, Johnny **17**
  Earlier sketch in CM **1**
Cash, Rosanne **2**
Cashdollar, Cindy
  See Asleep at the Wheel
Cashion, Doc "Bob"
  See Lane, Fred
Cassidy, Ed
  See Spirit
Castellano, Torry
  See Donnas, The
Cat Power **30**
Catallo, Chris
  See Surfin' Pluto
Catallo, Gene
  See Surfin' Pluto
Catatonia **29**
Catching, Dave
  See Queens of the Stone Age
Cates, Ronny
  See Petra
Catherall, Joanne
  See Human League, The
Catherine Wheel **18**
Catlin, Fritz
  See 23 Skidoo
Caustic Resin **31**
Caustic Window
  See Aphex Twin
Cauty, Jimmy
  See Orb, The

Cavacas, Chris
  See Giant Sand
Cavalera, Igor
  See Sepultura
Cavalera, Max
  See Sepultura
  Also see Soulfly
Cavanaugh, Frank
  See Filter
Cave, Nick **10**
Cavoukian, Raffi
  See Raffi
Cazares, Dino
  See Fear Factory
Cease, Jeff
  See Black Crowes, The
Cervenka, Exene
  See X
Cetera, Peter
  See Chicago
Chad, Dominic
  See Mansun
Chadbourne, Eugene **30**
Chainsaw Kittens, The **33**
Chamberlin, Jimmy
  See Smashing Pumpkins
Chambers, Guy
  See Waterboys, The
Chambers, Jimmy
  See Mercury Rev
Chambers, Martin
  See Pretenders, The
Chambers, Paul **18**
Chambers, Terry
  See XTC
Champion, Eric **21**
Champion, Will
  See Coldplay
Chan, Spencer
  See Aqua Velvets
Chance, Slim
  See Cramps, The
Chancellor, Justin
  See Tool
Chandler, Chas
  See Animals, The
Chandler, Knox
  See Golden Palominos
Chandra, Sheila **16**
Chandrasonic
  See Asian Dub Foundation
Chaney, Jimmy
  See Jimmie's Chicken Shack
Chang, Han-Na **33**
Chang, Sarah **7**
Channing, Carol **6**
Chanticleer **33**
Chapin Carpenter, Mary **25**
  Earlier sketch in CM **6**
Chapin, Harry **6**
Chapin, Tom **11**
Chapman, Gary **33**
Chapman, Steven Curtis **15**
Chapman, Tony
  See Rolling Stones, The
Chapman, Tracy **20**
  Earlier sketch in CM **4**
Chaquico, Craig **23**
  Also see Jefferson Starship
Charlatans, The **13**
Charles, Ray **24**
  Earlier sketch in CM **1**
Charles, Yolanda
  See Aztec Camera
Charm Farm **20**
Charman, Shaun
  See Wedding Present, The

Chasez, Joshua Scott "JC"
  See 'N Sync
Chastain, Paul
  See Velvet Crush
Che Colovita, Lemon
  See Jimmie's Chicken Shack
Chea, Alvin "Vinnie"
  See Take 6
Cheap Trick **12**
Cheatam, Aldolphus "Doc"
  See McKinney's Cotton Pickers
Checker, Chubby **7**
Cheeks, Julius
  See Soul Stirrers, The
Chemical Brothers **20**
Cheng, Chi
  See Deftones
Chenier, C. J. **15**
Chenier, Clifton **6**
Chenille Sisters, The **16**
Cher **1**
  Also see Sonny and Cher
Cherise, Cyd
  See Lane, Fred
Cherone, Gary
  See Extreme
  Also see Van Halen
Cherry, Don **10**
Cherry, Neneh **4**
Cherry Poppin' Daddies **24**
Chesney, Kenny **20**
Chesnutt, Mark **13**
Chesnutt, Vic **28**
Chess, Leonard **24**
Chesters, Eds D.
  See Bluetones, The
Cheung, Jacky **33**
Chevalier, Maurice **6**
Chevron, Phillip
  See Pogues, The
Chicago **3**
Chieftains, The **7**
Child, Desmond **30**
Childish, Billy **28**
Childress, Ross
  See Collective Soul
Childress Saxton, Shirley
  See Sweet Honey in the Rock
Childs, Euros
  See Gorky's Zygotic Mynci
Childs, Megan
  See Gorky's Zygotic Mynci
Childs, Toni **2**
Chilton, Alex **10**
Chimes, Terry
  See Clash, The
Chin, Tony
  See Big Mountain
Chin
  See Quickspace
Chipperfield, Sheila
  See Elastica
Chisholm, Melanie
  See Spice Girls
Chopmaster J
  See Digital Underground
Chris
  See Apples in Stereo
Chrisman, Andy
  See 4Him
Chrisman, Paul "Woody Paul"
  See Riders in the Sky
Christ, John
  See Danzig
Christian, Charlie **11**
Christian Death **28**

Colomby, Bobby
   See Blood, Sweat and Tears
Color Me Badd 23
Colt, Johnny
   See Black Crowes, The
Colthart, Chris
   See Papas Fritas
Coltrane, John 4
Colvin, Shawn 11
Colwell, David
   See Bad Company
Coma, Franche
   See Misfits, The
Combs, Sean "Puffy" 25
   Earlier sketch in CM 16
Comess, Aaron
   See Spin Doctors
Commander Cody and His Lost Planet Airmen
30
Commander Cody
   See Commander Cody and His Lost Planet
   Airmen
Commodores, The 23
Common 23
Como, Perry 14
Compulsion 23
Concrete Blonde 32
Condo, Ray
   See Ray Condo and His Ricochets
Confederate Railroad 23
Congo Norvell 22
Conneff, Kevin
   See Chieftains, The
Connelly, Chris
   See KMFDM
   Also see Pigface
Conner, Gary Lee
   See Screaming Trees
Conner, Van
   See Screaming Trees
Connick, Jr., Harry 4
Connolly, Pat
   See Surfaris, The
Connor, Chris 30
Connors, Marc
   See Nylons, The
Connors, Norman 30
Conti, Neil
   See Prefab Sprout
Convertino, John
   See Calexico
   Also see Giant Sand
Conway, Billy
   See Morphine
Conway, Dave
   See My Bloody Valentine
Conway, Gerry
   See Pentangle
Cooder, Ry 2
   Also see Captain Beefheart and His Magic
   Band
Cook, David Kyle
   See Matchbox 20
Cook, Greg
   See Ricochet
Cook, Jeffrey Alan
   See Alabama
Cook, Jesse 33
Cook, Paul
   See Sex Pistols, The
Cook, Stuart
   See Creedence Clearwater Revival
Cook, Wayne
   See Steppenwolf
Cooke, Mick
   See Belle and Sebastian

Cooke, Sam 1
   Also see Soul Stirrers, The
Cool, Tre
   See Green Day
Cooley, Dave
   See Citizen King
Coolio 19
Coombes, Gary
   See Supergrass
Coomes, Sam
   See Quasi
Cooney, Rory 6
Cooper, Alice 8
Cooper, Jason
   See Cure, The
Cooper, Martin
   See Orchestral Manoeuvres in the Dark
Cooper, Michael
   See Third World
Cooper, Paul
   See Nylons, The
Cooper, Ralph
   See Air Supply
Coore, Stephen
   See Third World
Cope, Julian 16
Copeland, Stewart 14
   Also see Police, The
Copland, Aaron 2
Copley, Al
   See Roomful of Blues
Coppola, Donna
   See Papas Fritas
Corea, Chick 6
Corella, Doug
   See Verve Pipe, The
Corgan, Billy
   See Smashing Pumpkins
Corina, Sarah
   See Mekons, The
Cornelius, Robert
   See Poi Dog Pondering
Cornell, Chris
   See Soundgarden
Cornell, Don 30
Cornershop 24
Cornick, Glenn
   See Jethro Tull
Cornwell, Hugh
   See Stranglers, The
Corr, Andrea
   See Corrs, The
Corr, Caroline
   See Corrs, The
Corr, Jim
   See Corrs, The
Corr, Sharon
   See Corrs, The
Corrigan, Brianna
   See Beautiful South
Corrs, The 32
Cosper, Kina
   See Brownstone
Costanzo, Marc
   See Len
Costanzo, Sharon
   See Len
Costello, Elvis 12
   Earlier sketch in CM 2
Coté, Billy
   See Madder Rose
Cotoia, Robert
   See Beaver Brown Band, The
Cotrubas, Ileana 1
Cotten, Elizabeth 16
Cotton, Caré
   See Sounds of Blackness

Cotton, Jeff "Antennae Jimmy Siemens"
   See Captain Beefheart and His Magic Band
Cougar, John(ny)
   See Mellencamp, John
Coughlan, Richard
   See Caravan
Counting Crows 18
Country Gentlemen, The 7
Coury, Fred
   See Cinderella
Coutts, Duncan
   See Our Lady Peace
Coverdale, David
   See Whitesnake
Cowan, Dennis
   See Bonzo Dog Doo-Dah Band
Cowan, John
   See New Grass Revival, The
Cowboy Junkies, The 4
Cows, The 32
Cox, Andy
   See English Beat, The
   Also see Fine Young Cannibals
Cox, Terry
   See Pentangle
Coxon, Graham
   See Blur
Coxon, John
   See Spring Heel Jack
Coyne, Mark
   See Flaming Lips
Coyne, Wayne
   See Flaming Lips
Crack, Carl
   See Atari Teenage Riot
Cracker 12
Cracknell, Sarah
   See Saint Etienne
Cragg, Jonny
   See Spacehog
Crahan, Shawn
   See Slipknot
Craig, Albert
   See Israel Vibration
Craig, Carl 19
Crain, S. R.
   See Soul Stirrers, The
Cramps, The 16
Cranberries, The 14
Craney, Mark
   See Jethro Tull
Crash Test Dummies 14
Crawford, Dave Max
   See Poi Dog Pondering
Crawford, Ed
   See fIREHOSE
Crawford, Michael 4
Crawford, Randy 25
Crawford, Steve
   See Anointed
Crawford-Greathouse, Da'dra
   See Anointed
Cray, Robert 8
Creach, Papa John
   See Jefferson Starship
Creager, Melora
   See Rasputina
Cream 9
Creed 28
Creedence Clearwater Revival 16
Creegan, Andrew
   See Barenaked Ladies
Creegan, Jim
   See Barenaked Ladies
Crenshaw, Marshall 5
Cretu, Michael
   See Enigma

Davis, Anthony **17**
Davis, Brad
    See Fu Manchu
Davis, Chip **4**
Davis, Clive **14**
Davis, Colin **27**
Davis, Gregory
    See Dirty Dozen Brass Band
Davis, Jody
    See Newsboys, The
Davis, John
    See Superdrag
Davis, John
    See Folk Implosion, The
Davis, Jonathan
    See Korn
Davis, Linda **21**
Davis, Michael
    See MC5, The
Davis, Miles F.
    See Northwoods Improvisers
Davis, Miles **1**
Davis, Norman
    See Wailing Souls
Davis, Reverend Gary **18**
Davis, Sammy, Jr. **4**
Davis, Santa
    See Big Mountain
Davis, Skeeter **15**
Davis, Spencer
    See Spencer Davis Group
Davis, Steve
    See Mystic Revealers
Davis, Zelma
    See C + C Music Factory
Davol, Sam
    See Magnetic Fields, The
Dawdy, Cheryl
    See Chenille Sisters, The
Dawn, Sandra
    See Platters, The
Day, Doris **24**
Dayne, Taylor **4**
dc Talk **18**
de Albuquerque, Michael
    See Electric Light Orchestra
de Burgh, Chris **22**
de Coster, Jean Paul
    See 2 Unlimited
de Grassi, Alex **6**
de Jonge, Henk
    See Willem Breuker Kollektief
de la Rocha, Zack
    See Rage Against the Machine
de Lourcqua, Helno Rota
    See Les Négresses Vertes
de Lucia, Paco **1**
de Prume, Ivan
    See White Zombie
de Young, Joyce
    See Andrews Sisters, The
De Borg, Jerry
    See Jesus Jones
De Gaia, Banco **27**
De La Luna, Shai
    See Lords of Acid
De La Soul **7**
De Lisle, Paul
    See Smash Mouth
De Meyer, Jean-Luc
    See Front 242
De Oliveria, Laudir
    See Chicago
Deacon, John
    See Queen
Dead Can Dance **16**
Dead Kennedys **29**

Dead Milkmen **22**
Deakin, Paul
    See Mavericks, The
Deal, Kelley
    See Breeders
Deal, Kim
    See Breeders
    Also see Pixies, The
Dean, Billy **19**
Dean, Paul
    See X-Ray Spex
Death in Vegas **28**
DeBarge, El **14**
Dee, Mikkey
    See Dokken
    Also see Motörhead
Deebank, Maurcie
    See Felt
Deee-lite **9**
Deep Forest **18**
Deep Purple **11**
Def Leppard **3**
DeFrancesco, Joey **29**
DeFranco, Buddy **31**
DeFreitas, Pete
    See Echo and the Bunnymen
Deftones **22**
DeGarmo, Chris
    See Queensryche
Deibert, Adam Warren
    See Aquabats, The
Deily, Ben
    See Lemonheads, The
DeJohnette, Jack **7**
Del Amitri **18**
Del Mar, Candy
    See Cramps, The
Del Rubio Triplets **21**
Del the Funky Homosapien **30**
Delaet, Nathalie
    See Lords of Acid
DeLeo, Dean
    See Stone Temple Pilots
DeLeo, Robert
    See Stone Temple Pilots
Delgados, The **31**
Delirious? **33**
Dells, The **30**
Delonge, Tom
    See Blink 182
DeLorenzo, Victor
    See Violent Femmes
Delp, Brad
    See Boston
DeMent, Iris **13**
Demeski, Stanley
    See Luna
Deming, Michael
    See Pernice Brothers
DeMone, Gitane
    See Christian Death
Demos, Greg
    See Guided By Voices
Dempsey, Michael
    See Cure, The
Denison, Duane
    See Jesus Lizard
Dennis, Garth
    See Black Uhuru
Dennis, Rudolph "Garth"
    See Wailing Souls
Denny, Sandy
    See Fairport Convention
Densmore, John
    See Doors, The
Dent, Cedric
    See Take 6

Denton, Sandy
    See Salt-N-Pepa
Denver, John **22**
    Earlier sketch in CM **1**
Depeche Mode **5**
Depew, Don
    See Cobra Verde
Derakh, Amir
    See Orgy
Derosier, Michael
    See Heart
Des'ree **24**
    Earlier sketch in CM **15**
Desaulniers, Stephen
    See Scud Mountain Boys
Deschamps, Kim
    See Blue Rodeo
Desert Rose Band, The **4**
Desjardins, Claude
    See Nylons, The
Desmond, Paul **23**
Destiny's Child **33**
Destri, Jimmy
    See Blondie
Dettman, John
    See Swell
Deupree, Jerome
    See Morphine
Deurloo, Hermine
    See Willem Breuker Kollektief
Deutrom, Mark
    See Melvins
Deutsch, Stu
    See Wendy O. Williams and The Plasmatics
DeVille, C. C.
    See Poison
Devito, Nick
    See Four Seasons, The
Devito, Tommy
    See Four Seasons, The
Devlin, Adam P.
    See Bluetones, The
Devo **13**
Devoto, Howard
    See Buzzcocks, The
DeWitt, Lew C.
    See Statler Brothers, The
Dexter X
    See Man or Astroman?
di Fiore, Vince
    See Cake
Di Meola, Al **12**
Di'anno, Paul
    See Iron Maiden
Diagram, Andy
    See James
Diamond, "Dimebag" Darrell
    See Pantera
Diamond, Mike "Mike D"
    See Beastie Boys, The
Diamond, Neil **1**
Diamond Rio **11**
Dibango, Manu **14**
Dick, Coby
    See Papa Roach
Dick, Magic
    See J. Geils Band
Dickens, Little Jimmy **7**
Dickerson, B.B.
    See War
Dickerson, Lance
    See Commander Cody and His Lost Planet Airmen
Dickinson, Paul Bruce
    See Iron Maiden
Dickinson, Rob
    See Catherine Wheel

Dube, Lucky **17**
Dubstar **22**
Duce, Adam
  See Machine Head
Dudley, Anne
  See Art of Noise
Duffey, John
  See Country Gentlemen, The
  Also see Seldom Scene, The
Duffy, Billy
  See Cult, The
Duffy, Martin
  See Primal Scream
Dufresne, Mark
  See Confederate Railroad
Duggan, Noel
  See Clannad
Duggan, Paidraig
  See Clannad
Duke, John
  See Pearls Before Swine
Dukowski, Chuck
  See Black Flag
Dulli, Greg
  See Afghan Whigs
Dumont, Tom
  See No Doubt
Dunbar, Aynsley
  See Jefferson Starship
  Also see Journey
  Also see Whitesnake
Dunbar, Sly
  See Sly and Robbie
Duncan, Bryan **19**
Duncan, Gary
  See Quicksilver Messenger Service
Duncan, Steve
  See Desert Rose Band, The
Duncan, Stuart
  See Nashville Bluegrass Band
Dunckel, Jean-Benoit
  See Air
Dunham, Nathanel "Brad"
  See Five Iron Frenzy
Dunlap, Slim
  See Replacements, The
Dunlop, Andy
  See Travis
Dunn, Donald "Duck"
  See Booker T. & the M.G.'s
Dunn, Holly **7**
Dunn, Larry
  See Earth, Wind and Fire
Dunn, Ronnie Gene
  See Brooks & Dunn
Dunning, A.J.
  See Verve Pipe, The
DuPré, Jacqueline **26**
Dupree, Champion Jack **12**
Dupree, Jesse James
  See Jackyl
Dupri, Jermaine **25**
Duran Duran **4**
Durante, Mark
  See KMFDM
Duritz, Adam
  See Counting Crows
Durrill, Johnny
  See Ventures, The
Durst, Fred
  See Limp Bizkit
Durutti Column, The **30**
Dury, Ian **30**
Dust Brothers **32**
Dutt, Hank
  See Kronos Quartet

Dutton, Garrett
  See G. Love
Dutton, Lawrence
  See Emerson String Quartet
Dvorak, Antonin **25**
Dyble, Judy
  See Fairport Convention
Dylan, Bob **21**
  Earlier sketch in CM **3**
Dylan, Jakob
  See Wallflowers, The
Dyrason, Orri Páll
  See Sigur Rós
E., Sheila
  See Sheila E.
Eacrett, Chris
  See Our Lady Peace
Eagles, The **3**
Earl, Ronnie **5**
  Also see Roomful of Blues
Earle, Steve **16**
Early, Ian
  See Cherry Poppin' Daddies
Earth, Wind and Fire **12**
Easton, Elliot
  See Cars, The
Easton, Sheena **2**
Eazy-E **13**
  Also see N.W.A.
Echeverria, Rob
  See Helmet
Echo and the Bunnymen **32**
Echobelly **21**
Eckstine, Billy **1**
Eddy, Duane **9**
Eden, Sean
  See Luna
Eder, Linda **30**
Edge, Graeme
  See Moody Blues, The
Edge, The
  See U2
Edison, Harry "Sweets" **29**
Edmonds, Kenneth "Babyface" **12**
Edmonton, Jerry
  See Steppenwolf
Edmunds, Dave **28**
Edson, Richard
  See Sonic Youth
Edward, Scott
  See Bluetones, The
Edwards, Dennis
  See Temptations, The
Edwards, Edgar
  See Spinners, The
Edwards, Gordon
  See Kinks, The
  Also see Pretty Things, The
Edwards, John
  See Spinners, The
Edwards, Johnny
  See Foreigner
Edwards, Leroy "Lion"
  See Mystic Revealers
Edwards, Mark
  See Aztec Camera
Edwards, Michael James
  See Jesus Jones
Edwards, Mike
  See Electric Light Orchestra
Edwards, Nokie
  See Ventures, The
Edwards, Skye
  See Morcheeba
Edwardson, Dave
  See Neurosis
eels **29**

Efrem, Towns
  See Dirty Dozen Brass Band
Egan, Kian
  See Westlife
Ehart, Phil
  See Kansas
Ehran
  See Lords of Acid
Eid, Tamer
  See Emmet Swimming
808 State **31**
Einheit
  See Einstürzende Neubauten
Einheit, F.M.
  See KMFDM
Einstürzende Neubauten **13**
Einziger, Michael
  See Incubus
Eisenstein, Michael
  See Letters to Cleo
Eisentrager, Thor
  See Cows, The
Eitzel, Mark
  See American Music Club
Ekberg, Ulf
  See Ace of Base
Eklund, Greg
  See Everclear
El Hefe
  See NOFX
El-Hadi, Sulieman
  See Last Poets
Elastica **29**
Eldon, Thór
  See Sugarcubes, The
Eldridge, Ben
  See Seldom Scene, The
Eldridge, Roy **9**
  Also see McKinney's Cotton Pickers
Electric Light Orchestra **7**
Elf Power **30**
Elfman, Danny **9**
Elias, Hanin
  See Atari Teenage Riot
Elias, Manny
  See Tears for Fears
Ellefson, Dave
  See Megadeth
Elling, Kurt **31**
Ellington, Duke **2**
Elliot, Cass **5**
  Also see Mamas and the Papas
Elliott, Dennis
  See Foreigner
Elliott, Doug
  See Odds
Elliott, Joe
  See Def Leppard
Elliott, Missy **30**
Elliott, Ramblin' Jack **32**
Ellis, Arti
  See Pearls Before Swine
Ellis, Bobby
  See Skatalites, The
Ellis, Herb **18**
Ellis, Ingrid
  See Sweet Honey in the Rock
Ellis, John
  See Stranglers, The
Ellis, Rob
  See Swell
Ellis, Terry
  See En Vogue
Ellis, Warren
  See Dirty Three
Ellison, Rahsaan
  See Oakland Interfaith Gospel Choir

Feedback, Captain
  See Rube Waddell
Feehily, Mark
  See Westlife
Fehlmann, Thomas
  See Orb, The
Fehn, Chris
  See Slipknot
Feinstein, Michael **6**
Fela
  See Kuti, Fela
Felber, Dean
  See Hootie and the Blowfish
Felder, Don
  See Eagles, The
Feldman, Eric Drew
  See Pere Ubu
  Also see Captain Beefheart and His Magic
  Band
Feliciano, José **10**
Fell, Simon H. **32**
Felt **32**
Fender, Freddy
  See Texas Tornados, The
Fender, Leo **10**
Fennell, Kevin
  See Guided By Voices
Fennelly, Gere
  See Redd Kross
Fent-Lister, Johnny
  See Lane, Fred
Fenwick, Ray
  See Spencer Davis Group
Ferguson, Doug
  See Camel
Ferguson, Jay
  See Sloan
Ferguson, Jay
  See Spirit
Ferguson, Keith
  See Fabulous Thunderbirds, The
Ferguson, Maynard **7**
Ferguson, Neil
  See Chumbawamba
Ferguson, Steve
  See NRBQ
Fernandes, John
  See Olivia Tremor Control
Ferrell, Rachelle **17**
Ferrer, Frank
  See Love Spit Love
Ferry, Bryan **1**
Ficca, Billy
  See Television
Fiedler, Arthur **6**
Fielder, Jim
  See Blood, Sweat and Tears
Fields, Johnny
  See Five Blind Boys of Alabama
Fieldy
  See Korn
Fier, Anton
  See Golden Palominos
  Also see Pere Ubu
Filan, Shane
  See Westlife
Filter **28**
Finch, Adrian
  See Elf Power
Finch, Carl
  See Brave Combo
Finch, Jennifer
  See L7
Finck, Robin
  See Nine Inch Nails
Finckel, David
  See Emerson String Quartet

Fine Young Cannibals **22**
Finer, Jem
  See Pogues, The
Finestone, Peter
  See Bad Religion
Fink, Jr., Rat
  See Alien Sex Fiend
Finn, Micky
  See T. Rex
Finn, Neil
  See Crowded House
Finn, Tim
  See Crowded House
fIREHOSE **11**
Fischer, Matt
  See Minty
Fish, Pat
  See Jazz Butcher, The
Fishbone **7**
Fisher, Brandon
  See Superdrag
Fisher, Eddie **12**
Fisher, Jerry
  See Blood, Sweat and Tears
Fisher, John "Norwood"
  See Fishbone
Fisher, Morgan
  See Mott the Hoople
Fisher, Phillip "Fish"
  See Fishbone
Fisher, Roger
  See Heart
Fishman, Jon
  See Phish
Fitzgerald, Ella **1**
Fitzgerald, Kevin
  See Geraldine Fibbers
Five Blind Boys of Alabama **12**
Five Iron Frenzy **26**
Fixx, The **33**
Flack, Roberta **5**
Flaming Lips **22**
Flanagan, Tommy **16**
Flanagin, Craig
  See God Is My Co-Pilot
Flannery, Sean
  See Cherry Poppin' Daddies
Flansburgh, John
  See They Might Be Giants
Flash, Flying Johnny
  See Lanternjack, The
Flatt, Lester **3**
Flavor Flav
  See Public Enemy
Flea
  See Red Hot Chili Peppers, The
Fleck, Bela **8**
  Also see New Grass Revival, The
Fleetwood Mac **5**
Fleetwood, Mick
  See Fleetwood Mac
Fleischmann, Robert
  See Journey
Fleisig, Alexis
  See Girls Against Boys
Fleming, Renee **24**
Flemion, Dennis
  See Frogs, The
Flemion, Jimmy
  See Frogs, The
Flemons, Wade
  See Earth, Wind and Fire
Flesh-N-Bone
  See Bone Thugs-N-Harmony
Fletcher, Andy
  See Depeche Mode

Fletcher, Guy
  See Dire Straits
Flint, Keith
  See Prodigy
Flores, Rosie **16**
Floyd, Heather
  See Point of Grace
Fluoride, Klaus
  See Dead Kennedys
Flür, Wolfgang
  See Kraftwerk
Flying Luttenbachers, The **28**
Flying Saucer Attack **29**
Flynn, Pat
  See New Grass Revival, The
Flynn, Robert
  See Machine Head
Fogelberg, Dan **4**
Fogerty, John **2**
  Also see Creedence Clearwater Revival
Fogerty, Thomas
  See Creedence Clearwater Revival
Folds, Ben
  See Ben Folds Five
Foley
  See Arrested Development
Folk Implosion, The **28**
Foo Fighters **20**
Foote, Dick
  See Lane, Fred
Forbes, Derek
  See Simple Minds
Forbes, Graham
  See Incredible String Band
Ford, Frankie
  See Pretty Things, The
Ford, Lita **9**
Ford, Marc
  See Black Crowes, The
Ford, Maya
  See Donnas, The
Ford, Penny
  See Soul II Soul
Ford, Robert "Peg"
  See Golden Gate Quartet
Ford, Tennessee Ernie **3**
Fordham, Julia **15**
Foreigner **21**
Foreman, Chris
  See Madness
Forrester, Alan
  See Mojave 3
Forsi, Ken
  See Surfaris, The
Forster, Robert
  See Go-Betweens, The
Forte, Juan
  See Oakland Interfaith Gospel Choir
Fortune, Jimmy
  See Statler Brothers, The
Fortus, Richard
  See Love Spit Love
Fossen, Steve
  See Heart
Foster, David **13**
Foster, Malcolm
  See Pretenders, The
Foster, Paul
  See Soul Stirrers, The
Foster, Radney **16**
Fountain, Clarence
  See Five Blind Boys of Alabama
Fountain, Pete **7**
Fountains of Wayne **26**
4Him **23**
Four Seasons, The **24**
Four Tops, The **11**

Garrett, Peter
  See Midnight Oil
Garrett, Scott
  See Cult, The
Garrison, Chuck
  See Superchunk
Garvey, Steve
  See Buzzcocks, The
Garza, Rob
  See Thievery Corporation
Gaskill, Jerry
  See King's X
Gaston, Asa
  See Lane, Fred
Gates, Jimmy Jr.
  See Silk
Gatton, Danny **16**
Gaudio, Bob
  See Four Seasons, The
Gaudreau, Jimmy
  See Country Gentlemen, The
Gaugh, IV, "Bud" Floyd
  See Sublime
Gavurin, David
  See Sundays, The
Gay, Marc
  See Shai
Gayden, Mac
  See Pearls Before Swine
Gaye, Marvin **4**
Gayle, Crystal **1**
Gaynor, Adam
  See Matchbox 20
Gaynor, Mel
  See Simple Minds
Gayol, Rafael "Danny"
  See BoDeans
Geary, Paul
  See Extreme
Geddes, Chris
  See Belle and Sebastian
Gedge, David
  See Wedding Present, The
Gee, Rosco
  See Traffic
Gee, Rosko
  See Can
Geffen, David **8**
Geils, J.
  See J. Geils Band
Gelb, Howe
  See Giant Sand
Geldof, Bob **9**
Gendel, Keith
  See Papas Fritas
Gene Loves Jezebel **27**
Genensky, Marsha
  See Anonymous 4
Genesis **4**
Gentling, Matt
  See Archers of Loaf
Gentry, Teddy Wayne
  See Alabama
George, Lowell
  See Little Feat
George, Rocky
  See Suicidal Tendencies
George, Stephen
  See Swervedriver
Georges, Bernard
  See Throwing Muses
Georgiev, Ivan
  See Tuxedomoon
Geraldine Fibbers **21**
Gerber, Scott
  See Giant Sand
Germano, Lisa **18**

Gerrard, Lisa
  See Dead Can Dance
Gershwin, George and Ira **11**
Gessle, Per
  See Roxette
Geto Boys, The **11**
Getz, Stan **12**
Ghost **24**
Ghostface Killah **33**
  Also see Wu-Tang Clan
Giammalvo, Chris
  See Madder Rose
Gianni, Angelo
  See Treadmill Trackstar
Giant Sand **30**
Gibb, Barry
  See Bee Gees, The
Gibb, Maurice
  See Bee Gees, The
Gibb, Robin
  See Bee Gees, The
Gibbins, Mike
  See Badfinger
Gibbons, Beth
  See Portishead
Gibbons, Billy
  See ZZ Top
Gibbons, Ian
  See Kinks, The
Gibbons, John
  See Bardo Pond
Gibbons, Michael
  See Bardo Pond
Giblin, John
  See Simple Minds
Gibson, Bob **23**
Gibson, Debbie
  See Gibson, Deborah
Gibson, Deborah **24**
  Earlier sketch in CM **1**
Gibson, Wilf
  See Electric Light Orchestra
Gifford, Alex
  See Propellerheads
  Also see Electric Light Orchestra
Gifford, Katharine
  See Stereolab
Gifford, Peter
  See Midnight Oil
Gift, Roland **3**
  Also see Fine Young Cannibals
Gil, Gilberto **26**
Gilbert, Bruce
  See Wire
Gilbert, Gillian
  See New Order
Gilbert, Nick
  See Felt
Gilbert, Nicole Nicci
  See Brownstone
Gilbert, Ronnie
  See Weavers, The
Gilbert, Simon
  See Suede
Gilberto, João **33**
Giles, Michael
  See King Crimson
Gilkyson, Tony
  See X
Gill, Andy
  See Gang of Four
Gill, George
  See Wire
Gill, Janis
  See Sweethearts of the Rodeo
Gill, Johnny **20**

Gill, Ped
  See Frankie Goes To Hollywood
Gill, Pete
  See Motörhead
Gill, Vince **7**
Gillan, Ian
  See Deep Purple
  Also see Black Sabbath
Gillard, Doug
  See Cobra Verde
Gillespie, Bobby
  See Jesus and Mary Chain, The
  Also see Primal Scream
Gillespie, Dizzy **6**
Gilley, Mickey **7**
Gillies, Ben
  See Silverchair
Gillingham, Charles
  See Counting Crows
Gillis, Steve
  See Filter
Gilmore, Jimmie Dale **11**
Gilmore, Mike
  See Northwoods Improvisers
Gilmour, David
  See Pink Floyd
Gilvear, Marcus
  See Gene Loves Jezebel
Gin Blossoms **18**
Gingold, Josef **6**
Ginn, Greg
  See Black Flag
Ginsberg, Allen **26**
Gioia
  See Exposé
Gipp, Cameron "Big Gipp"
  See Goodie Mob
Gipsy Kings, The **8**
Giraudy, Miquette
  See Gong
Girls Against Boys **31**
Gittleman, Joe
  See Mighty Mighty Bosstones
Glabicki, Michael
  See Rusted Root
Glamorre, Matthew
  See Minty
Glascock, John
  See Jethro Tull
Glaser, Gabby
  See Luscious Jackson
Glass, Daniel
  See Royal Crown Revue
Glass, David
  See Christian Death
Glass, Eddie
  See Fu Manchu
Glass, Philip **1**
Glasscock, John
  See Jethro Tull
Glenn, Gary
  See Silk
Glennie, Evelyn **33**
Glennie, Jim
  See James
Glitter, Gary **19**
Glover, Corey
  See Living Colour
Glover, Roger
  See Deep Purple
Gnewikow, Jason
  See Promise Ring, The
Go-Betweens, The **28**
Go-Go's, The **24**
Gobel, Robert
  See Kool & the Gang

Goble, Brian Roy
See D.O.A.
God Is My Co-Pilot 29
Godchaux, Donna
See Grateful Dead, The
Godchaux, Keith
See Grateful Dead, The
Goddess, Tony
See Papas Fritas
Godfrey, Paul
See Morcheeba
Godfrey, Ross
See Morcheeba
Godin, Nicolas
See Air
Godsmack 30
Goettel, Dwayne Rudolf
See Skinny Puppy
Goffey, Danny
See Supergrass
Goffin, Gerry
See Goffin-King
Goffin-King 24
Gogin, Toni
See Sleater-Kinney
Goh, Rex
See Air Supply
Gold, Julie 22
Golden Gate Quartet 25
Golden Palominos 32
Golden, William Lee
See Oak Ridge Boys, The
Golding, Lynval
See Specials, The
Goldsmith, William
See Foo Fighters
Also see Sunny Day Real Estate
Goldstein, Jerry
See War
Golson, Benny 21
Gomez 33
Gong 24
Gonson, Claudia
See Magnetic Fields, The
Goo Goo Dolls, The 16
Gooden, Ramone Pee Wee
See Digital Underground
Goodie Mob 24
Goodman, Benny 4
Goodman, Jerry
See Mahavishnu Orchestra
Goodridge, Robin
See Bush
Googe, Debbie
See My Bloody Valentine
Googy, Arthur
See Misfits, The
Gordon, Dexter 10
Gordon, Dwight
See Mighty Clouds of Joy, The
Gordon, Jay
See Orgy
Gordon, Jim
See Traffic
Gordon, Kim
See Sonic Youth
Gordon, Mike
See Phish
Gordon, Nina
See Veruca Salt
Gordy, Berry, Jr. 6
Gordy, Emory, Jr. 17
Gore, Martin
See Depeche Mode
Gorham, Scott
See Thin Lizzy
Gorka, John 18

Gorky's Zygotic Mynci 30
Gorman, Christopher
See Belly
Gorman, Steve
See Black Crowes, The
Gorman, Thomas
See Belly
Gorter, Arjen
See Willem Breuker Kollektief
Gosling, John
See Kinks, The
Gossard, Stone
See Brad
Also see Pearl Jam
Goswell, Rachel
See Mojave 3
Gotobed, Robert
See Wire
Gott, Larry
See James
Goudreau, Barry
See Boston
Gould, Billy
See Faith No More
Gould, Glenn 9
Gould, Morton 16
Goulding, Steve
See Gene Loves Jezebel
Grable, Steve
See Pearls Before Swine
Gracey, Chad
See Live
Gradney, Ken
See Little Feat
Graffety-Smith, Toby
See Jamiroquai
Graffin, Greg
See Bad Religion
Graham, Bill 10
Graham, Glen
See Blind Melon
Graham, Johnny
See Earth, Wind and Fire
Graham, Larry
See Sly & the Family Stone
Gramm, Lou
See Foreigner
Gramolini, Gary
See Beaver Brown Band, The
Grandmaster Flash 14
Grant, Amy 7
Grant, Bob
See The Bad Livers
Grant, Colyn "Mo"
See Baha Men
Grant, Gogi 28
Grant Lee Buffalo 16
Grant, Lloyd
See Metallica
Grapes of Wrath, The 33
Grappelli, Stephane 10
Grateful Dead, The 5
Gratzer, Alan
See REO Speedwagon
Gravatt, Eric
See Weather Report
Gravediggaz 23
Graves, Alexander
See Moonglows, The
Graves, Denyce 16
Graves, Michale
See Misfits, The
Gray, David 30
Gray, David
See Spearhead
Gray, Del
See Little Texas

Gray, Ella
See Kronos Quartet
Gray, F. Gary 19
Gray, James
See Spearhead
Gray, James
See Blue Rodeo
Gray, Luther
See Tsunami
Gray, Macy 32
Gray, Paul
See Slipknot
Gray, Tom
See Gomez
Gray, Tom
See Country Gentlemen, The
Also see Seldom Scene, The
Gray, Walter
See Kronos Quartet
Gray, Wardell
See McKinney's Cotton Pickers
Greater Vision 26
Grebenshikov, Boris 3
Grech, Rick
See Traffic
Greco, Paul
See Chumbawamba
Green, Al 9
Green, Benny 17
Green, Carlito "Cee-lo"
See Goodie Mob
Green, Charles
See War
Green, David
See Air Supply
Green Day 16
Green, Douglas "Ranger Doug"
See Riders in the Sky
Green, Grant 14
Green, James
See Dru Hill
Green, Jeremiah
See Modest Mouse
Green, Peter
See Fleetwood Mac
Green, Susaye
See Supremes, The
Green, Willie
See Neville Brothers, The
Greenall, Rupert
See Fixx, The
Greene, Karl Anthony
See Herman's Hermits
Greenfield, Dave
See Stranglers, The
Greenhalgh, Tom
See Mekons, The
Greensmith, Domenic
See Reef
Greenspoon, Jimmy
See Three Dog Night
Greentree, Richard
See Beta Band, The
Greenwood, Al
See Foreigner
Greenwood, Colin
See Radiohead
Greenwood, Gail
See Belly
Greenwood, Jonny
See Radiohead
Greenwood, Lee 12
Greenwood,Colin
See Radiohead
Greer, Jim
See Guided By Voices

Gregg, Dave
  See D.O.A.
Gregg, Paul
  See Restless Heart
Gregory, Bryan
  See Cramps, The
Gregory, Dave
  See XTC
Gregory, Keith
  See Wedding Present, The
Gregory, Troy
  See Prong
Greller, Al
  See Yo La Tengo
Grey, Charles Wallace
  See Aquabats, The
Grice, Gary "The Genius"
  See Wu-Tang Clan
Griffin, A.C. "Eddie"
  See Golden Gate Quartet
Griffin, Bob
  See BoDeans, The
Griffin, Dale "Buffin"
  See Mott the Hoople
Griffin, Kevin
  See Better Than Ezra
  Also see NRBQ
Griffin, Mark
  See MC 900 Ft. Jesus
Griffin, Patty **24**
Griffin, Rodney
  See Greater Vision
Griffith, Nanci **3**
Grigg, Chris
  See Treadmill Trackstar
Grisman, David **17**
Grohl, Dave
  See Nirvana
  Also see Foo Fighters
Grossman, Rick
  See Hoodoo Gurus
Grotberg, Karen
  See Jayhawks, The
Groucutt, Kelly
  See Electric Light Orchestra
Grove, George
  See Kingston Trio, The
Grover, Charlie
  See Sponge
Grundy, Hugh
  See Zombies, The
Grusin, Dave **7**
Guaraldi, Vince **3**
Guard, Dave
  See Kingston Trio, The
Gudmundsdottir, Björk
  See Björk
  Also see Sugarcubes, The
Güereña, Luis
  See Tijuana No!
Guerin, John
  See Byrds, The
Guess Who **23**
Guest, Christopher
  See Spinal Tap
Guided By Voices **18**
Gun, John
  See X-Ray Spex
Gunn, Trey
  See King Crimson
Guns n' Roses **2**
Gunther, Cornell
  See Coasters, The
Gunther, Ric
  See Bevis Frond
Gurewitz, Brett
  See Bad Religion

Gurtu, Trilok **29**
  Also see Oregon
Guru
  See Gang Starr
Gus Gus **26**
Guss, Randy
  See Toad the Wet Sprocket
Gustafson, Steve
  See 10,000 Maniacs
Guster **29**
Gut, Grudrun
  See Einstürzende Neubauten
Guthrie, Arlo **6**
Guthrie, Gwen **26**
Guthrie, Robin
  See Cocteau Twins, The
Guthrie, Woody **2**
Guy, Billy
  See Coasters, The
Guy, Buddy **4**
Guy, Geordie
  See Killing Joke
Guyett, Jim
  See Quicksilver Messenger Service
Gwar **13**
H.R.
  See Bad Brains
Hacke, Alexander
  See Einstürzende Neubauten
Hackett, Bobby **21**
Hackett, Steve
  See Genesis
Haden, Charlie **12**
Hadjopulos, Sue
  See Simple Minds
Hagar, Regan
  See Brad
Hagar, Sammy **21**
  Also see Van Halen
Hagen, Nina **25**
Hagerty, Neil
  See Royal Trux
Haggard, Merle **2**
HaHa, Jimi
  See Jimmie's Chicken Shack
Hahn, Hilary **30**
Hajjar, Tony
  See At The Drive-In
Hakim, Omar
  See Weather Report
Hakmoun, Hassan **15**
Hale, Simon
  See Incognito
Haley, Bill **6**
Haley, Mark
  See Kinks, The
Haley, Paige
  See Orgy
Halford, Rob
  See Judas Priest
Hall & Oates **6**
Hall, Bruce
  See REO Speedwagon
Hall, Daryl
  See Hall & Oates
Hall, John S.
  See King Missile
Hall, Lance
  See Inner Circle
Hall, Randall
  See Lynyrd Skynyrd
Hall, Terry
  See Specials, The
Hall, Tom T. **26**
  Earlier sketch in CM **4**
Hall, Tony
  See Neville Brothers, The

Halliday, Toni
  See Curve
Halliwell, Geri
  See Spice Girls
Halstead, Neil
  See Mojave 3
Ham, Pete
  See Badfinger
Hamelin, Marc-André **33**
Hamer, Harry
  See Chumbawamba
Hamilton, Arnold (Frukwan da Gatekeeper)
  See Gravediggaz
Hamilton, Frank
  See Weavers, The
Hamilton, Katie
  See Treadmill Trackstar
Hamilton, Milton
  See Third World
Hamilton, Page
  See Helmet
Hamilton, Tom
  See Aerosmith
Hamlisch, Marvin **1**
Hammer, Jan **21**
  Also see Mahavishnu Orchestra
Hammer, M.C. **5**
Hammerstein, Oscar
  See Rodgers, Richard
Hammett, Kirk
  See Metallica
Hammill, Peter **30**
Hammon, Ron
  See War
Hammond, John **6**
Hammond, Murry
  See Old 97's
Hammond-Hammond, Jeffrey
  See Jethro Tull
Hampson, Sharon
  See Sharon, Lois & Bram
Hampson, Thomas **12**
Hampton, Lionel **6**
Hancock, Herbie **25**
  Earlier sketch in CM **8**
Handley, Jerry
  See Captain Beefheart and His Magic Band
Handsome Family, The **30**
Handy, W. C. **7**
Hanley, Kay
  See Letters to Cleo
Hanley, Steve
  See Fall, The
Hanna, Jeff
  See Nitty Gritty Dirt Band, The
Hannan, Patrick
  See Sundays, The
Hanneman, Jeff
  See Slayer
Hannibal, Chauncey "Black"
  See Blackstreet
Hannon, Frank
  See Tesla
Hannon, Neil
  See Divine Comedy, The
Hansen, Mary
  See Stereolab
Hanson **20**
Hanson, Isaac
  See Hanson
Hanson, Paul (Prince Paul A.K.A. Dr. Strange)
  See Paul, Prince
  Also see Gravediggaz
Hanson, Taylor
  See Hanson
Hanson, Zachary
  See Hanson

Hearn, Kevin
　　See Barenaked Ladies
Heart **1**
Heath, James
　　See Reverend Horton Heat
Heaton, Paul
　　See Beautiful South
Heavy D **10**
Hecker, Robert
　　See Redd Kross
Hedford, Eric
　　See Dandy Warhols
Hedges, Eddie
　　See Blessid Union of Souls
Hedges, Michael **3**
Heggie, Will
　　See Cocteau Twins, The
Heidorn, Mike
　　See Son Volt
Heifetz, Jascha **31**
Heitman, Dana
　　See Cherry Poppin' Daddies
Helfgott, David **19**
Helium, Bryan
　　See Elf Power
Hell, Richard
　　See Television
Hellauer, Susan
　　See Anonymous 4
Hellerman, Fred
　　See Weavers, The
Hellier, Steve
　　See Death in Vegas
Helliwell, John
　　See Supertramp
Helm, Levon
　　See Band, The
　　Also see Nitty Gritty Dirt Band, The
Helmet **15**
Hemingway, Dave
　　See Beautiful South
Hemmings, Paul
　　See Lightning Seeds
Henderson, Andy
　　See Echobelly
Henderson, Billy
　　See Spinners, The
Henderson, Fletcher **16**
Henderson, Joe **14**
Henderson, Stewart
　　See Delgados, The
Hendricks, Barbara **10**
Hendricks, Jon
　　See Lambert, Hendricks and Ross
Hendrix, Jimi **2**
Henley, Don **3**
　　Also see Eagles, The
Henrit, Bob
　　See Kinks, The
Henry, Bill
　　See Northern Lights
Henry, Joe **18**
Henry, Kent
　　See Steppenwolf
Henry, Nicholas "Drummie"
　　See Mystic Revealers
Hensley, Ken
　　See Uriah Heep
Hepcat, Harry **23**
Hepner, Rich
　　See Captain Beefheart and His Magic Band
Heppner, Ben **23**
Herdman, Bob
　　See Audio Adrenaline
Herman, Maureen
　　See Babes in Toyland

Herman, Tom
　　See Pere Ubu
Herman, Woody **12**
Herman's Hermits **5**
Hernandez, Alfredo
　　See Queens of the Stone Age
Hernandez, Bubba
　　See Brave Combo
Hernandez, Phil
　　See Brave Combo
Herndon, John
　　See Tortoise
Herndon, Mark Joel
　　See Alabama
Herndon, Ty **20**
Heron, Mike
　　See Incredible String Band
Herrema, Jennifer
　　See Royal Trux
Herrera, Mike
　　See MxPx
Herrera, R. J.
　　See Suicidal Tendencies
Herrera, Raymond
　　See Fear Factory
Herrlin, Anders
　　See Roxette
Herrmann, Bernard **14**
Herron, Cindy
　　See En Vogue
Hersh, Kristin
　　See Throwing Muses
Hester, Paul
　　See Crowded House
Hetfield, James
　　See Metallica
Hetson, Greg
　　See Bad Religion
　　Also see Circle Jerks, The
Heveroh, Ben
　　See Oakland Interfaith Gospel Choir
Hewitt, Bobby
　　See Orgy
Hewitt, Steve
　　See Placebo
Hewson, Paul
　　See U2
Hexum, Nick
　　See 311
Hiatt, John **8**
Hibbard, Bill
　　See Paul Revere & The Raiders
Hickey, Kenny
　　See Type O Negative
Hickman, Johnny
　　See Cracker
Hicks, Chris
　　See Restless Heart
Hicks, Sheree
　　See C + C Music Factory
Hidalgo, David
　　See Los Lobos
Hield, Nehemiah
　　See Baha Men
Hield, Omerit
　　See Baha Men
Higgins, Jimmy
　　See Altan
Higgins, Terence
　　See Dirty Dozen Brass Band
Highway 101 **4**
Hijbert, Fritz
　　See Kraftwerk
Hilah
　　See Boredoms, The
Hill, Brendan
　　See Blues Traveler

Hill, Brian "Beezer"
　　See Frogs, The
Hill, Dave
　　See Cobra Verde
Hill, Dusty
　　See ZZ Top
Hill, Faith **18**
Hill, Ian
　　See Judas Priest
Hill, John
　　See Apples in Stereo
Hill, Lauryn **25**
　　Also see Fugees, The
Hill, Scott
　　See Fu Manchu
Hill, Stuart
　　See Shudder to Think
Hillage, Steve
　　See Orb, The
　　Also see Gong
Hillier, Steve
　　See Dubstar
Hillman, Bones
　　See Midnight Oil
Hillman, Chris
　　See Byrds, The
　　Also see Desert Rose Band, The
Hilton, Eric
　　See Thievery Corporation
Hinderas, Natalie **12**
Hinds, David
　　See Steel Pulse
Hines, Earl "Fatha" **12**
Hines, Gary
　　See Sounds of Blackness
Hinojos, Paul
　　See At The Drive-In
Hinojosa, Tish **13**
Hinton, Milt **33**
Hirst, Rob
　　See Midnight Oil
Hirt, Al **5**
Hitchcock, Robyn **9**
Hitchcock, Russell
　　See Air Supply
Hitt, Bryan
　　See REO Speedwagon
Hobson, Motor
　　See Lane, Fred
Hodge, Alex
　　See Platters, The
Hodges, Johnny **24**
Hodgson, Roger **26**
　　Also see Supertramp
Hodo, David
　　See Village People, The
Hoenig, Michael
　　See Tangerine Dream
Hoerig, Keith
　　See Five Iron Frenzy
Hoerner, Dan
　　See Sunny Day Real Estate
Hoffman, Ellen
　　See Oakland Interfaith Gospel Choir
Hoffman, Guy
　　See BoDeans, The
　　Also see Violent Femmes
Hoffman, Kristian
　　See Congo Norvell
Hoffman, Sam
　　See Captain Beefheart and His Magic Band
Hoffs, Susanna
　　See Bangles, The
Hogan, Mike
　　See Cranberries, The
Hogan, Noel
　　See Cranberries, The

Jones, Michael
  See Kronos Quartet
Jones, Mick
  See Foreigner
Jones, Mick
  See Clash, The
Jones, Orville
  See Ink Spots
Jones, Paul
  See Elastica
Jones, Paul
  See Catatonia
Jones, Philly Joe **16**
Jones, Quincy **20**
  Earlier sketch in CM **2**
Jones, Randy
  See Village People, The
Jones, Richard
  See Stereophonics
Jones, Rickie Lee **4**
Jones, Robert "Kuumba"
  See Ohio Players
Jones, Robin
  See Beta Band, The
Jones, Rod
  See Idlewild
Jones, Ronald
  See Flaming Lips
Jones, Russell "Ol Dirty Bastard"
  See Wu-Tang Clan
Jones, Sandra "Puma"
  See Black Uhuru
Jones, Simon
  See Verve, The
Jones, Spike **5**
Jones, Stacy
  See Letters to Cleo
  Also see Veruca Salt
Jones, Steve
  See Sex Pistols, The
Jones, Teren
  See Del the Funky Homosapien
Jones, Terry
  See Point of Grace
Jones, Thad **19**
Jones, Tom **11**
Jones, Vincent
  See Grapes of Wrath, The
Jones, Will "Dub"
  See Coasters, The
Jonsson, Magnus
  See Gus Gus
Joplin, Janis **3**
Joplin, Scott **10**
Jordan, Lonnie
  See War
Jordan, Louis **11**
Jordan, Marc **30**
Jordan, Montell **26**
Jordan, Stanley **1**
Jordison, Joey
  See Slipknot
Jorgenson, John
  See Desert Rose Band, The
Jos
  See Ex, The
Joseph, Charles
  See Dirty Dozen Brass Band
Joseph, Kirk
  See Dirty Dozen Brass Band
Joseph-I, Israel
  See Bad Brains
Josephmary
  See Compulsion
Jourgensen, Al
  See Ministry
Journey **21**

Joy Division **19**
Joy Electric **26**
Joyce, Don
  See Negativland
Joyce, Mike
  See Buzzcocks, The
  Also see Smiths, The
Juanita
  See Les Négresses Vertes
Judas Priest **10**
Judd, Naomi
  See Judds, The
Judd, Wynonna
  See Judds, The
  Also see Wynonna
Judds, The **2**
Judy, Eric
  See Modest Mouse
Juhlin, Dag
  See Poi Dog Pondering
Jukebox
  See Geto Boys, The
Julot
  See Les Négresses Vertes
Jungle DJ "Towa" Towa
  See Deee-lite
Junior, Marvin
  See Dells, The
Jupp, Tim
  See Delirious?
Jurado, Jeanette
  See Exposé
Jurgensen, Jens
  See Boss Hog
Justman, Seth
  See J. Geils Band
Jym
  See Mr. T Experience, The
K-Ci
  See Jodeci
Kabongo, Sabine
  See Zap Mama
Kaczor, Neil
  See Minty
Kaczynski, Ray
  See Northwoods Improvisers
Kahlil, Aisha
  See Sweet Honey in the Rock
Kain, Gylan
  See Last Poets
Kaiser, Henry
  See Golden Palominos
Kakoulli, Harry
  See Squeeze
Kale, Jim
  See Guess Who
Kalligan, Dick
  See Blood, Sweat and Tears
Kamanski, Paul
  See Beat Farmers
Kaminski, Mik
  See Electric Light Orchestra
Kamomiya, Ryo
  See Pizzicato Five
Kanal, Tony
  See No Doubt
Kanawa, Kiri Te
  See Te Kanawa, Kiri
Kand, Valor
  See Christian Death
Kander, John **33**
Kane, Arthur
  See New York Dolls
Kane, Big Daddy **7**
Kane, Keith
  See Vertical Horizon

Kane, Kevin
  See Grapes of Wrath, The
Kane, Nick
  See Mavericks, The
Kang, Eyvind **28**
Kannberg, Scott
  See Pavement
Kansas **32**
Kantner, Paul
  See Jefferson Airplane
Kaplan, Ira
  See Yo La Tengo
Karajan, Herbert von
  See von Karajan, Herbert
Karges, Murphy
  See Sugar Ray
Karlsson, Gunnar
  See Wannadies, The
Karoli, Michael
  See Can
Kath, Terry
  See Chicago
Kato, Nash
  See Urge Overkill
Katrin
  See Ex, The
Katunich, Alex
  See Incubus
Katz, Mike
  See Battlefield Band, The
Katz, Simon
  See Jamiroquai
Katz, Steve
  See Blood, Sweat and Tears
Kaukonen, Jorma
  See Jefferson Airplane
Kavanagh, Chris
  See Big Audio Dynamite
Kavanaugh, Lydia
  See Golden Palominos
Kay Gee
  See Naughty by Nature
Kay, Jason
  See Jamiroquai
Kay, John
  See Steppenwolf
Kaye, Carol **22**
Kaye, Tony
  See Yes
Kaylan, Howard
  See Turtles, The
Keaggy, Phil **26**
Kean, Martin
  See Stereolab
Keane, Sean
  See Chieftains, The
Kee, John P. **15**
Keefe, Dylan
  See Marcy Playground
Keelor, Greg
  See Blue Rodeo
Keenan, Maynard James
  See Tool
Keene, Barry
  See Spirit
Keene, Tommy **31**
Keifer, Tom
  See Cinderella
Keitaro
  See Pizzicato Five
Keith, Jeff
  See Tesla
Keith, Toby **17**
Keithley, Joey "Sh**head"
  See D.O.A.
Kelly, Betty
  See Martha and the Vandellas

Knox, Richard
  See Dirty Dozen Brass Band
Knudsen, Keith
  See Doobie Brothers, The
Konietzko, Sascha
  See KMFDM
Konishi, Yasuharu
  See Pizzicato Five
Konitz, Lee **30**
Konto, Skip
  See Three Dog Night
Kontos, Chris
  See Machine Head
Kool & the Gang **13**
Kool Moe Dee **9**
Kooper, Al
  See Blood, Sweat and Tears
Koppelman, Charles **14**
Koppes, Peter
  See Church, The
Korn **20**
Koster, Julian
  See Neutral Milk Hotel
Kottke, Leo **13**
Kotzen, Richie
  See Poison
Kowalczyk, Ed
  See Live
Kowald, Peter **32**
Koz, Dave **20**
Kraftwerk **9**
Krakauer, David
  See Klezmatics, The
Krall, Diana **27**
Kramer, Amanda
  See Golden Palominos
Kramer, Joey
  See Aerosmith
Kramer, Wayne
  See MC5, The
Krasnow, Bob **15**
Krause, Bernie
  See Weavers, The
Krauss, Alison **10**
Krauss, Scott
  See Pere Ubu
Kravitz, Lenny **26**
  Earlier sketch in CM **5**
Krawits, Michael
  See Pearls Before Swine
Krayzie Bone
  See Bone Thugs-N-Harmony
Krazy Drayz
  See Das EFX
Kremer, Gidon **30**
Kretz, Eric
  See Stone Temple Pilots
Kreutzman, Bill
  See Grateful Dead, The
Kreviazuk, Chantal **33**
Krieger, Robert
  See Doors, The
Kriesel, Greg "Greg K."
  See Offspring
Kris Kross **11**
Kristofferson, Kris **4**
Krizan, Anthony
  See Spin Doctors
Kronos Quartet **5**
Kropinski, Uwe **31**
Kropp, Mike
  See Northern Lights
KRS-One **8**
Krukowski, Damon
  See Damon and Naomi
  Also see Galaxie 500

Krummenacher, Victor
  See Monks of Doom
Krupa, Gene **13**
Krusen, Dave
  See Pearl Jam
Kruspe, Richard
  See Rammstein
Kuba
  See D.O.A.
Kulak, Eddie
  See Aztec Camera
Kulick, Bruce
  See Kiss
Kunkel, Bruce
  See Nitty Gritty Dirt Band, The
Kunzel, Erich **17**
Kurdziel, Eddie
  See Redd Kross
Kurihara, Michio
  See Ghost
Kuti, Fela **7**
Kuti, Femi **29**
L.L. Cool J. **5**
L7 **12**
La Ley **33**
LaBar, Jeff
  See Cinderella
LaBelle, Patti **8**
LaBour, Frederick "Too Slim"
  See Riders in the Sky
LaBrie, James
  See Dream Theater
Labrum, Jerry
  See Paul Revere & The Raiders
Lachey, Drew
  See 98 Degrees
Lachey, Nick
  See 98 Degrees
Lack, Steve
  See Veruca Salt
LaCroix, Dimples
  See Lane, Fred
Lacy, Steve **23**
Lady Miss Kier
  See Deee-lite
Ladybug
  See Digable Planets
Ladysmith Black Mambazo **1**
Lafalce, Mark
  See Mekons, The
Lagerburg, Bengt
  See Cardigans, The
Laine, Cleo **10**
Laine, Denny
  See Moody Blues, The
Laing, Corky
  See Mountain
Laird, Rick
  See Mahavishnu Orchestra
Lake, Greg
  See Emerson, Lake & Palmer/Powell
  Also see King Crimson
LaKind, Bobby
  See Doobie Brothers, The
Lally, Joe
  See Fugazi
LaLonde, Larry "Ler"
  See Primus
Lamb, Barbara **19**
Lamb, Michael
  See Confederate Railroad
Lambchop **29**
Lambert, Ben
  See Carter USM
Lambert, Dave
  See Lambert, Hendricks and Ross
Lambert, Hendricks and Ross **28**

Lamble, Martin
  See Fairport Convention
Lamm, Robert
  See Chicago
Lamond, Mary Jane **33**
Lampkin, Troy
  See Oakland Interfaith Gospel Choir
Lancaster, Brian
  See Surfin' Pluto
Landers, Paul
  See Rammstein
Landreth, Sonny **16**
Lane, Fred **28**
Lane, Jani
  See Warrant
Lane, Jay
  See Primus
Lane, Ronnie
  See Faces, The
Lanegan, Mark
  See Screaming Trees
lang, k. d. **25**
  Earlier sketch in CM **4**
Lang, Jonny **27**
Langan, Gary
  See Art of Noise
Langdon, Antony
  See Spacehog
Langdon, Royston
  See Spacehog
Langford, Jon
  See Mekons, The
Langford, Willie
  See Golden Gate Quartet
Langley, John
  See Mekons, The
Langlois, Paul
  See Tragically Hip, The
Langosch, Paul
  See Ralph Sharon Quartet
Langston, Leslie
  See Throwing Muses
Lanier, Allen
  See Blue Oyster Cult
Lanker, Dustin
  See Cherry Poppin' Daddies
Lanois, Daniel **8**
Lanternjack, The **31**
LaPread, Ronald
  See Commodores, The
Larkin, Patty **9**
Larkins, Tom
  See Giant Sand
Larson, Chad Albert
  See Aquabats, The
Larson, Nathan
  See Shudder to Think
Lash, Tony
  See Sunset Valley
Last Poets **21**
Laswell, Bill **14**
  Also see Golden Palominos
Lataille, Rich
  See Roomful of Blues
Lateef, Yusef **16**
Latimer, Andrew
  See Camel
Lauderdale, Jim **29**
Laughner, Peter
  See Pere Ubu
Lauper, Cyndi **11**
Laurence, Lynda
  See Supremes, The
Lava, Larry
  See Lanternjack, The
Lavay Smith and Her Red Hot Skillet Lickers **32**

Lindsay, Mark
  See Paul Revere & The Raiders
Linkous, Mark **26**
Linna, Miriam
  See Cramps, The
Linnell, John
  See They Might Be Giants
Lippok, Robert
  See To Rococo Rot
Lippok, Ronald
  See To Rococo Rot
Lipsius, Fred
  See Blood, Sweat and Tears
Lisa, Lisa **23**
Lisher, Greg
  See Monks of Doom
Lit **27**
Little Feat **4**
Little, Keith
  See Country Gentlemen, The
Little, Levi
  See Blackstreet
Little Richard **1**
Little Texas **14**
Little Walter **14**
Littrell, Brian
  See Backstreet Boys
Live **14**
Livgren, Kerry
  See Kansas
Living Colour **7**
Livingston, Edwin
  See Los Hombres Calientes
Llanas, Sam
  See BoDeans
Lloyd, Charles **22**
Lloyd, Mick
  See Felt
Lloyd, Richard
  See Television
Lloyd Webber, Andrew **6**
Lo Fidelity All Stars **27**
Locke, John
  See Spirit
Locking, Brian
  See Shadows, The
Lockley, Jayne
  See Wedding Present, The
Lockwood, Robert, Jr. **10**
Lodge, John
  See Moody Blues, The
Loeb, Lisa **23**
  Earlier sketch in CM **19**
Loesser, Frank **19**
Loewe, Frederick
  See Lerner and Loewe
Loewenstein, Jason
  See Sebadoh
Lofgren, Nils **25**
Logan, Jack **27**
Loggins, Kenny **20**
  Earlier sketch in CM **3**
Logic, Laura
  See X-Ray Spex
Lohner, Danny
  See Nine Inch Nails
Lombardo, Dave
  See Slayer
Lonberg-Holm, Fred
  See Flying Luttenbachers, The
London, Frank
  See Klezmatics, The
London, Julie **32**
Lonestar **27**
Lopes, Lisa "Left Eye"
  See TLC
Lopez, Israel "Cachao" **14**

Lopez, Jennifer **27**
Lord, Jon
  See Deep Purple
Lords of Acid **20**
Lorenz, Flake
  See Rammstein
Loria, Steve
  See Spirit
Lorimer, Roddy
  See Waterboys, The
Lorson, Mary
  See Madder Rose
Los Hombres Calientes **29**
Los Lobos **2**
Los Reyes
  See Gipsy Kings, The
Loud Family, The **31**
Loughnane, Lee
  See Chicago
Louison, Steve
  See Massive Attack
Louris, Gary
  See Jayhawks, The
Louvin Brothers, The **12**
Louvin, Charlie
  See Louvin Brothers, The
Louvin, Ira
  See Louvin Brothers, The
Lovano, Joe **13**
Love and Rockets **15**
Love, Courtney
  See Hole
Love, Gerry
  See Teenage Fanclub
Love, Laura **20**
Love, Mike
  See Beach Boys, The
Love, Rollie
  See Beat Farmers
Love Spit Love **21**
Loveless, Patty **21**
  Earlier sketch in CM **5**
Lovering, David
  See Cracker
  Also see Pixies, The
Lovett, Lyle **28**
  Earlier sketch in CM **5**
Lowe, Chris
  See Pet Shop Boys
Lowe, Nick **25**
  Earlier sketch in CM **6**
Lowe, Victoria
  See Tuxedomoon
Lowell, Charlie
  See Jars of Clay
Lowery, David
  See Cracker
Lozano, Conrad
  See Los Lobos
Luc
  See Ex, The
Luca, Nick
  See Giant Sand
Lucas, Gary
  See Captain Beefheart and His Magic Band
Lucas, Kirk
  See Northwoods Improvisers
Lucas, Trevor
  See Fairport Convention
Luccketta, Troy
  See Tesla
Lucero, Nick
  See Queens of the Stone Age
Lucia, Paco de
  See de Lucia, Paco
Luciano, Felipe
  See Last Poets

Luckett, LaToya
  See Destiny's Child
Luke
  See Campbell, Luther
Lukin, Matt
  See Mudhoney
Lulu **32**
Luna **18**
Lunsford, Bret
  See Beat Happening
Lupo, Pat
  See Beaver Brown Band, The
LuPone, Patti **8**
Luscious Jackson **27**
  Earlier sketch in CM **19**
Lush **13**
Luster, Ahrue
  See Machine Head
Luttell, Terry
  See REO Speedwagon
Lydon, John **9**
  Also see Sex Pistols, The
Lydon, John
  See Golden Palominos
Lyfe, DJ
  See Incubus
Lymon, Frankie
  See Frankie Lymon and The Teenagers
Lynch, David
  See Platters, The
Lynch, Dermot
  See Dog's Eye View
Lynch, Edele
  See B*Witched
Lynch, George
  See Dokken
Lynch, Keavy
  See B*Witched
Lynch, Laura
  See Dixie Chicks
Lynch, Stan
  See Tom Petty and the Heartbreakers
Lyngstad, Anni-Frid
  See Abba
Lynn, Lonnie Rashid
  See Common
Lynn, Loretta **2**
Lynne, Jeff **5**
  Also see Electric Light Orchestra
Lynne, Shelby **29**
  Earlier sketch in CM **5**
Lynott, Phil
  See Thin Lizzy
Lynyrd Skynyrd **9**
Lyons, Leanne "Lelee"
  See SWV
Lyons, Richard
  See Negativland
M People **27**
  Earlier sketch in CM **15**
M.C. Hammer
  See Hammer, M.C.
M.C. Ren
  See N.W.A.
Ma, Yo-Yo **24**
  Earlier sketch in CM **2**
Mabry, Bill
  See Asleep at the Wheel
MacColl, Kirsty **12**
MacDonald, Barbara Kooyman
  See Timbuk 3
MacDonald, Eddie
  See Alarm
MacDonald, Iain
  See Battlefield Band, The
MacDonald, Pat
  See Timbuk 3

Martsch, Doug
 See Built to Spill
Marvin, Hank B.
 See Shadows, The
Marx, Richard **21**
 Earlier sketch in CM **3**
Mascagni, Pietro **25**
Mascis, J
 See Dinosaur Jr.
Masdea, Jim
 See Boston
Mase **27**
Masekela, Hugh **7**
Maseo, Baby Huey
 See De La Soul
Masi, Nick
 See Four Seasons, The
Mason, Dave
 See Traffic
Mason, Nick
 See Pink Floyd
Mason, Stephen
 See Beta Band, The
Mason, Steve
 See Jars of Clay
Mason, Terry
 See Joy Division
Masse, Laurel
 See Manhattan Transfer, The
Massey, Bobby
 See O'Jays, The
Massey, Graham
 See 808 State
Massi, Nick
 See Four Seasons, The
Massive Attack **17**
Mastelotto, Pat
 See King Crimson
Master D
 See Asian Dub Foundation
Master P **22**
Masur, Kurt **11**
Matchbox 20 **27**
Material
 See Laswell, Bill
Mathis, Johnny **2**
Mathus, Jim
 See Squirrel Nut Zippers
Matlock, Glen
 See Sex Pistols, The
Mattacks, Dave
 See Fairport Convention
Mattea, Kathy **5**
Matthews, Cerys
 See Catatonia
Matthews, Chris
 See Shudder to Think
Matthews, Dave
 See Dave Matthews Band
Matthews, Donna Lorraine
 See Elastica
Matthews, Eric **22**
Matthews, Ian
 See Fairport Convention
Matthews, Quinn
 See Butthole Surfers
Matthews, Scott
 See Butthole Surfers
Matthews, Simon
 See Jesus Jones
Matthews, Winston "Pipe"
 See Wailing Souls
Mattock, John
 See Spacemen 3
Maunick, Bluey
 See Incognito

Maurer, John
 See Social Distortion
Mavericks, The **15**
Maxwell **22**
Maxwell, Charmayne
 See Brownstone
Maxwell, Tom
 See Squirrel Nut Zippers
May, Brian
 See Queen
May, Phil
 See Pretty Things, The
Mayall, John **7**
Mayfield, Curtis **8**
Mayfield, Irvin
 See Los Hombres Calientes
Mays, Odeen, Jr.
 See Kool & the Gang
Mazelle, Kym
 See Soul II Soul
Mazibuko, Abednigo
 See Ladysmith Black Mambazo
Mazibuko, Albert
 See Ladysmith Black Mambazo
Mazzola, Joey
 See Sponge
Mazzy Star **17**
MC Breed **17**
MC Clever
 See Digital Underground
MC Eiht **27**
MC Eric
 See Technotronic
MC Lyte **8**
MC 900 Ft. Jesus **16**
MC Serch **10**
MC5, The **9**
MCA
 See Yauch, Adam
McAloon, Martin
 See Prefab Sprout
McAloon, Paddy
 See Prefab Sprout
McArthur, Keith
 See Spearhead
McBay, Clint
 See Chainsaw Kittens, The
McBoutie, Rip
 See Lane, Fred
McBrain, Nicko
 See Iron Maiden
McBrayer, Jody
 See Avalon
McBride, Christian **17**
McBride, Martina **14**
McCabe, Nick
 See Verve, The
McCabe, Zia
 See Dandy Warhols
McCall, Renee
 See Sounds of Blackness
McCandless, Paul
 See Oregon
McCann, Lila **26**
McCarrick, Martin
 See Siouxsie and the Banshees
McCarroll, Tony
 See Oasis
McCartney, Paul **32**
 Earlier sketch in CM **4**
 Also see Beatles, The
McCarty, Jim
 See Yardbirds, The
McCary, Michael S.
 See Boyz II Men
McCaughan, Mac
 See Superchunk

McCaughey, Scott **31**
McClain, Dave
 See Machine Head
McClary, Thomas
 See Commodores, The
McClennan, Tommy **25**
McClinton, Delbert **14**
McCloud, Scott
 See Girls Against Boys
McCluskey, Andy
 See Orchestral Manoeuvres in the Dark
McColgan, Mike
 See Dropkick Murphys
McCollum, Rick
 See Afghan Whigs
McCombs, Doug
 See Tortoise
McConnell, Page
 See Phish
McCook, Jack
 See Superchunk
McCook, Tommy
 See Skatalites, The
McCorkle, Susannah **27**
McCoury, Del **15**
McCowin, Michael
 See Mighty Clouds of Joy, The
McCoy, Neal **15**
McCracken, Chet
 See Doobie Brothers, The
McCrea, John
 See Cake
McCready, Mike
 See Pearl Jam
McCready, Mindy **22**
McCullagh, John
 See Divine Comedy, The
McCulloch, Andrew
 See King Crimson
McCulloch, Ian **23**
 Also see Echo and the Bunnymen
McCullough, Danny
 See Animals, The
McCuloch, Ian **23**
McCurdy, Xan
 See Cake
McCusker, John
 See Battlefield Band, The
McCutcheon, Ian
 See Mojave 3
McD, Jimmy
 See Jimmie's Chicken Shack
McDaniel, Chris
 See Confederate Railroad
McDaniels, Darryl "D"
 See Run DMC
McDermott, Brian
 See Del Amitri
McDonald, Ian
 See Foreigner
 Also see King Crimson
McDonald, Jeff
 See Redd Kross
McDonald, Lloyd "Bread"
 See Wailing Souls
McDonald, Michael
 See Doobie Brothers, The
McDonald, Richie
 See Lonestar
McDonald, Steven
 See Redd Kross
McDorman, Joe
 See Statler Brothers, The
McDougall, Don
 See Guess Who
McDowell, Hugh
 See Electric Light Orchestra

Messina, Jo Dee **26**
Metallica **33**
 Earlier sketch in CM **7**
Meters, The **14**
Methembu, Russel
 See Ladysmith Black Mambazo
Metheny, Pat **26**
 Earlier sketch in CM **2**
Method Man **31**
 Also see Wu-Tang Clan
Metzger, Mark
 See Chainsaw Kittens, The
Mew, Sharon
 See Elastica
Meyer, Eric
 See Charm Farm
Meyers, Augie
 See Texas Tornados, The
Mhaonaigh, Mairead Ni
 See Altan
Michael, George **9**
Michaels, Bret
 See Poison
Michel, Luke
 See Emmet Swimming
Michel, Prakazrel "Pras"
 See Fugees, The
Michiles, Malcolm
 See Citizen King
Middlebrook, Ralph "Pee Wee"
 See Ohio Players
Middleton, Darren
 See Powderfinger
Middleton, Malcolm
 See Arab Strap
Middleton, Mark
 See Blackstreet
Midler, Bette **8**
Midnight Oil **11**
Midori **7**
Mighty Clouds of Joy, The **17**
Mighty Mighty Bosstones **20**
Mike & the Mechanics **17**
Mike D
 See Diamond, Michael
Mikens, Dennis
 See Smithereens, The
Mikens, Robert
 See Kool & the Gang
Milchem, Glenn
 See Blue Rodeo
Miles, Chris
 See Northern Lights
Miles, Richard
 See Soul Stirrers, The
Miles, Ron **22**
Millar, Deborah
 See Massive Attack
Miller, Buddy **31**
Miller, Charles
 See War
Miller, David
 See Asleep at the Wheel
Miller, Glenn **6**
Miller, Jacob "Killer"
 See Inner Circle
Miller, Jerry
 See Moby Grape
Miller, Kevin
 See Fuel
Miller, Mark
 See Sawyer Brown
Miller, Mitch **11**
Miller, Rhett
 See Old 97's
Miller, Rice
 See Williamson, Sonny Boy

Miller, Robert
 See Supertramp
Miller, Roger **4**
Miller, Ryan
 See Guster
Miller, Scott
 See Loud Family, The
Miller, Steve **2**
Milli Vanilli **4**
Mills Brothers, The **14**
Mills, Bryan
 See Divine Comedy, The
Mills, Donald
 See Mills Brothers, The
Mills, Fred
 See Canadian Brass, The
Mills, Harry
 See Mills Brothers, The
Mills, Herbert
 See Mills Brothers, The
Mills, John, Jr.
 See Mills Brothers, The
Mills, John, Sr.
 See Mills Brothers, The
Mills, Mike
 See R.E.M.
Mills, Sidney
 See Steel Pulse
Mills, Stephanie **21**
Milsap, Ronnie **2**
Milton, Doctor
 See Alien Sex Fiend
Mingus, Charles **9**
Ministry **10**
Minnelli, Liza **19**
Minns, Danielle
 See Minty
Minogue, Kylie **32**
Minott, Sugar **31**
Mint Condition **29**
Minton, Phil **29**
Minty **32**
Minutemen, The **31**
Misfits, The **32**
Miskulin, Joey "The Cowpolka King"
 See Riders in the Sky
Miss Kier Kirby
 See Lady Miss Kier
Mitchell, Alex
 See Curve
Mitchell, Bruce
 See Durutti Column, The
Mitchell, John
 See Asleep at the Wheel
Mitchell, Joni **17**
 Earlier sketch in CM **2**
Mitchell, Keith
 See Mazzy Star
Mitchell, Mitch
 See Guided By Voices
Mitchell, Roscoe
 See Art Ensemble of Chicago, The
Mittoo, Jackie
 See Skatalites, The
Mize, Ben
 See Counting Crows
Mizell, Jay "Jam Master Jay"
 See Run DMC
Mo', Keb' **21**
Moby **27**
 Earlier sketch in CM **17**
Moby Grape **12**
Modeliste, Joseph "Zigaboo"
 See Meters, The
Modest Mouse **30**
Moerlen, Pierre
 See Gong

Moffat, Aidan
 See Arab Strap
Moffatt, Katy **18**
Moginie, Jim
 See Midnight Oil
Mogwai **27**
Mohan, John
 See Felt
Mohr, Todd
 See Big Head Todd and the Monsters
Mojave 3 **26**
Molko, Brian
 See Placebo
Molla, Chris
 See Monks of Doom
Molland, Joey
 See Badfinger
Molloy, Matt
 See Chieftains, The
Moloney, Paddy
 See Chieftains, The
Monahan, Pat
 See Train
Monahan, Thom
 See Pernice Brothers
Monarch, Michael
 See Steppenwolf
Monch, Pharoahe **29**
Money B
 See Digital Underground
Money, Eddie **16**
Monheit, Jane **33**
Monica **26**
Monifah **24**
Monk, Meredith **1**
Monk, Thelonious **6**
Monkees, The **7**
Monks of Doom **28**
Monroe, Bill **1**
Monster, Drunkness
 See Len
Montana, Country Dick
 See Beat Farmers
Montand, Yves **12**
Montenegro, Hugo **18**
Montgomery, John Michael **14**
Montgomery, Ken "Dimwit"
 See D.O.A.
Montgomery, Little Brother **26**
Montgomery, Wes **3**
Monti, Steve
 See Curve
Montoya, Craig
 See Everclear
Montrose, Ronnie **22**
Moody Blues, The **18**
Moon, Doug
 See Captain Beefheart and His Magic Band
Moon, Keith
 See Who, The
Mooney, Malcolm
 See Can
Mooney, Tim
 See American Music Club
Moonglows, The **33**
Moore, Alan
 See Judas Priest
Moore, Angelo
 See Fishbone
Moore, Archie
 See Velocity Girl
Moore, Chante **21**
Moore, Glen
 See Oregon
Moore, Johnny "Dizzy"
 See Skatalites, The

Nashville Bluegrass Band **14**
Nasta, Ken
  See Royal Trux
Nastanovich, Bob
  See Pavement
Naughty by Nature **11**
Navarro, David
  See Jane's Addiction
  Also see Red Hot Chili Peppers
Navarro Fats **25**
Nawasadio, Sylvie
  See Zap Mama
Ndegéocello, Me'Shell **18**
Ndugu
  See Weather Report
Near, Holly **1**
Neel, Johnny
  See Allman Brothers, The
Negativland **30**
Negron, Chuck
  See Three Dog Night
Negroni, Joe
  See Frankie Lymon and The Teenagers
Neil, Chris
  See Less Than Jake
Neil, Vince
  See Mötley Crüe
Nelson, Brett
  See Built to Spill
Nelson, Brian
  See Velocity Girl
Nelson, David
  See Last Poets
Nelson, Errol
  See Black Uhuru
Nelson, Gabe
  See Cake
Nelson, Nate
  See Platters, The
Nelson, Rick **2**
Nelson, Shara
  See Massive Attack
Nelson, Willie **11**
  Earlier sketch in CM **1**
Nero, Peter **19**
Nesbitt, John
  See McKinney's Cotton Pickers
Nesmith, Mike
  See Monkees, The
Ness, Mike
  See Social Distortion
Netson, Brett
  See Built to Spill
  Also see Caustic Resin
Neu! **32**
Neufville, Renee
  See Zhane
Neumann, Kurt
  See BoDeans
Neurosis **28**
Neutral Milk Hotel **31**
Nevarez, Alfred
  See All-4-One
Neville, Aaron **5**
  Also see Neville Brothers, The
Neville, Art
  See Meters, The
  Also see Neville Brothers, The
Neville Brothers, The **4**
Neville, Charles
  See Neville Brothers, The
Neville, Cyril
  See Meters, The
  Also see Neville Brothers, The
Nevin, Brian
  See Big Head Todd and the Monsters
New Grass Revival, The **4**

New Kids on the Block **3**
New Order **11**
New Rhythm and Blues Quartet
  See NRBQ
New York Dolls **20**
Newman, Colin
  See Wire
Newman, Randy **27**
  Earlier sketch in CM **4**
Newmann, Kurt
  See BoDeans, The
Newsboys, The **24**
Newsham, Sean
  See Quickspace
Newson, Arlene
  See Poi Dog Pondering
Newsted, Jason
  See Metallica
Newton, Colin
  See Idlewild
Newton, Paul
  See Uriah Heep
Newton, Wayne **2**
Newton-Davis, Billy
  See Nylons, The
Newton-John, Olivia **8**
Nibbs, Lloyd
  See Skatalites, The
Nichol, Al
  See Turtles, The
Nicholas, James Dean "J.D."
  See Commodores, The
Nicholls, Geoff
  See Black Sabbath
Nichols, Chad
  See Lettermen, The
Nichols, Eddie
  See Royal Crown Revue
Nichols, Gates
  See Confederate Railroad
Nichols, Todd
  See Toad the Wet Sprocket
Nickerson, Charlie
  See Memphis Jug Band
Nicks, Stevie **25**
  Earlier sketch in CM **2**
  Also see Fleetwood Mac
Nico
  See Velvet Underground, The
Nicol, Simon
  See Fairport Convention
Nicolette
  See Massive Attack
Nielsen, Rick
  See Cheap Trick
Nielsen, Tim
  See Drivin' N' Cryin'
Nijholt, Nico
  See Willem Breuker Kollektief
Nikleva, Steven
  See Ray Condo and His Ricochets
Nile, Willie **31**
Nilija, Robert
  See Last Poets
Nilsson **10**
Nilsson, Birgit **31**
Nilsson, Harry
  See Nilsson
Nine Inch Nails **29**
98 Degrees **32**
Nirvana **8**
Nisbett, Steve "Grizzly"
  See Steel Pulse
Nishino, Kohji
  See Ghost
Nitty Gritty Dirt Band, The **6**
Nixon, Mojo **32**

No Doubt **20**
Nobacon, Danbert "The Cat"
  See Chumbawamba
Nocentelli, Leo
  See Meters, The
NOFX **28**
Nolan, Jerry
  See New York Dolls
Nomiya, Maki
  See Pizzicato Five
Nono
  See Les Négresses Vertes
Noone, Peter "Herman"
  See Herman's Hermits
Norica, Sugar Ray
  See Roomful of Blues
Norman, Jessye **7**
Norman, Jimmy
  See Coasters, The
Norman, Patrick
  See Rusted Root
Norris, Jean
  See Zhane
Northern Lights **19**
Northey, Craig
  See Odds
Northwoods Improvisers **31**
Norton, Butch
  See eels
Norum, John
  See Dokken
Norvell, Sally
  See Congo Norvell
Norvo, Red **12**
Notorious B.I.G. **20**
Nova, Heather **30**
Novoselic, Chris
  See Nirvana
Nowell, Bradley James
  See Sublime
NRBQ **12**
Nugent, Ted **2**
Nunez, Joe
  See Soulfly
Nunn, Bobby
  See Coasters, The
Nutter, Alice
  See Chumbawamba
Nylons, The **6**
Nyman, Michael **15**
Nyolo, Sally
  See Zap Mama
Nyro, Laura **12**
O'Brien, Brien
  See D.O.A.
O'Brien, Danny
  See Brave Combo
O'Brien, Darrin Kenneth
  See Snow
O'Brien, Derek
  See Social Distortion
O'Brien, Dwayne
  See Little Texas
O'Brien, Ed
  See Radiohead
O'Brien, Marty
  See Kilgore
O'Bryant, Alan
  See Nashville Bluegrass Band
O'Carroll, Sinead
  See B*Witched
O'Ciosoig, Colm
  See My Bloody Valentine
O'Connell, Chris
  See Asleep at the Wheel
O'Connor, Billy
  See Blondie

Pandit G
  See Asian Dub Foundation
Pankow, James
  See Chicago
Panter, Horace
  See Specials, The
Pantera 13
Papa Roach 30
Papach, Leyna
  See Geraldine Fibbers
Papas Fritas 29
Pappalardi, Felix
  See Mountain
Pappas, Tom
  See Superdrag
Parazaider, Walter
  See Chicago
Paris, Twila 16
Park, Cary
  See Boy Howdy
Park, Larry
  See Boy Howdy
Parkening, Christopher 7
Parker, Charlie 5
Parker, Evan 28
Parker, Graham 10
Parker, Jeff
  See Tortoise
Parker, Kris
  See KRS-One
Parker, Leon 27
Parker, Maceo 7
Parker, Tom
  See Animals, The
Parker, William 31
Parkin, Chad
  See Aquabats, The
Parks, Van Dyke 17
Parnell, Lee Roy 15
Parsons, Alan 12
Parsons, Dave
  See Bush
Parsons, Gene
  See Byrds, The
Parsons, Gram 7
  Also see Byrds, The
Parsons, Ted
  See Prong
Parsons, Tony
  See Iron Maiden
Partch, Harry 29
Partington, Darren
  See 808 State
Parton, Dolly 24
  Earlier sketch in CM 2
Partridge, Andy
  See XTC
Parvo, Carpella
  See Rasputina
Pascale, Nina
  See Quickspace
Pasemaster, Mase
  See De La Soul
Pash, Jim
  See Surfaris, The
Pasillas, Jose
  See Incubus
Pass, Joe 15
Passons, Michael
  See Avalon
Pastorius, Jaco
  See Weather Report
Paterson, Alex
  See Orb, The
Patinkin, Mandy 20
  Earlier sketch CM 3

Patrick, Richard
  See Filter
Patti, Sandi 7
Pattinson, Les
  See Echo and the Bunnymen
Patton, Antwan "Big Boi"
  See OutKast
Patton, Charley 11
Patton, Mike
  See Faith No More
Paul, Alan
  See Manhattan Transfer, The
Paul III, Henry
  See BlackHawk
Paul, Les 2
Paul, Prince 29
  Also see Gravediggaz
Paul Revere & The Raiders 30
Paul, Vinnie
  See Pantera
Paulo, Jr.
  See Sepultura
Paulus, Jean-Marie
  See Les Négresses Vertes
Pavarotti, Luciano 20
  Earlier sketch in CM 1
Pavement 14
Pavia, John
  See Four Seasons, The
Paxton, Tom 5
Payne, Bill
  See Little Feat
Payne, Dougie
  See Travis
Payne, Richard
  See Bluetones, The
Payne, Scherrie
  See Supremes, The
Payton, Denis
  See Dave Clark Five, The
Payton, Lawrence
  See Four Tops, The
Payton, Nicholas 27
Pea, Planet
  See Len
Peacock, Olly
  See Gomez
Pearce, David
  See Flying Saucer Attack
Pearl Jam 32
  Earlier sketch in CM 12
Pearl, Minnie 3
Pearls Before Swine 24
Pearson, Dan
  See American Music Club
Peart, Neil
  See Rush
Pedersen, Chris
  See Monks of Doom
Pedersen, Herb
  See Desert Rose Band, The
Peduzzi, Larry
  See Roomful of Blues
Peebles, Ann 30
Peek, Dan
  See America
Peeler, Ben
  See Mavericks, The
Peeples, Philip
  See Old 97's
Pegg, Dave
  See Fairport Convention
  Also see Jethro Tull
Pegrum, Nigel
  See Steeleye Span
Peligro, Darren H.
  See Dead Kennedys

Pelletier, Mike
  See Kilgore
Pence, Jeff
  See Blessid Union of Souls
Penderecki, Krzysztof 30
Pendergrass, Teddy 3
Pendleton, Brian
  See Pretty Things, The
Pengilly, Kirk
  See INXS
Peniston, CeCe 15
Penn, Michael 4
Penner, Fred 10
Pennywise 27
Pentangle 18
Pentland, Patrick
  See Sloan
Pepper, Art 18
Perahia, Murray 10
Pere Ubu 17
Peretz, Jesse
  See Lemonheads, The
Perez, Danilo 25
Perez, Louie
  See Los Lobos
Perkins, Carl 9
Perkins, John
  See XTC
Perkins, Percell
  See Five Blind Boys of Alabama
Perkins, Stephen
  See Porno for Pyros
Perkins, Steve
  See Jane's Addiction
Perko, Lynn
  See Imperial Teen
Perlman, Itzhak 2
Perlman, Marc
  See Jayhawks, The
Pernice, Bob
  See Pernice Brothers
Pernice Brothers 33
Pernice, Joe
  See Pernice Brothers
  Also see Scud Mountain Boys
Peron, Jean-Hervé
  See Faust
Perry, Brendan
  See Dead Can Dance
Perry, Doane
  See Jethro Tull
Perry, Joe
  See Aerosmith
Perry, John G.
  See Caravan
Perry, Phil 24
Perry, Steve
  See Cherry Poppin' Daddies
Perry, Steve
  See Journey
Perry, Virgshawn
  See Artifacts
Persson, Nina
  See Cardigans
Pet Shop Boys 5
Peter, Paul & Mary 4
Peters, Bernadette 27
  Earlier sketch in CM 7
Peters, Dan
  See Mudhoney
Peters, Joey
  See Grant Lee Buffalo
Peters, Mike
  See Alarm
Petersen, Chris
  See Front Line Assembly

Powell, Kobie
  See US3
Powell, Owen
  See Catatonia
Powell, Paul
  See Aztec Camera
Powell, William
  See O'Jays, The
Powers, Kid Congo
  See Congo Norvell
  Also see Cramps, The
Poynton, Bobby
  See Lettermen, The
Prater, Dave
  See Sam and Dave
Pratt, Awadagin 19
Pratt, Guy
  See Killing Joke
Prefab Sprout 15
Presley, Elvis 1
Preston, Aaron
  See Chainsaw Kittens, The
Preston, Leroy
  See Asleep at the Wheel
Preston, Mark
  See Lettermen, The
Pretenders, The 8
Pretty Things, The 26
Previn, André 15
Price, Alan
  See Animals, The
Price, Leontyne 6
Price, Lloyd 25
Price, Louis
  See Temptations, The
Price, Mark
  See Archers of Loaf
Price, Martin
  See 808 State
Price, Ray 11
Price, Rick
  See Electric Light Orchestra
Pride, Charley 4
Priest, Maxi 20
Prima, Louis 18
Primal Scream 14
Primettes, The
  See Supremes, The
Primrose, Neil
  See Travis
Primus 11
Prince 14
  Earlier sketch in CM 1
Prince Be
  See P.M. Dawn
Prince, Prairie
  See Journey
Prince, Vivian
  See Pretty Things, The
Prine, John 7
Prior, Maddy
  See Steeleye Span
Proclaimers, The 13
Prodigy 22
Professor Longhair 6
Promise Ring, The 28
Prong 23
Propatier, Joe
  See Silver Apples
Propellerheads 26
Propes, Duane
  See Little Texas
Prophet, Chuck 32
Prosper, Marvin
  See Baha Men
Prout, Brian
  See Diamond Rio

Pryce, Guto
  See Super Furry Animals
Psychedelic Furs 23
Ptacek, Rainer
  See Giant Sand
Pte
  See Indigenous
Public Enemy 4
Puccini, Giacomo 25
Puente, Tito 14
Puff Daddy
  See Combs, Sean "Puffy"
Pullen, Don 16
Pulp 18
Pulsford, Nigel
  See Bush
Pusey, Clifford "Moonie"
  See Steel Pulse
Pyle, Andy
  See Kinks, The
Pyle, Artemis
  See Lynyrd Skynyrd
Pyle, Chris
  See Royal Trux
Pyle, Pip
  See Gong
Pyro, Howie
  See D Generation
Q-Ball, D.J.
  See Bloodhound Gang, The
Q-Tip
  See Tribe Called Quest, A
Quaife, Peter
  See Kinks, The
Quasi 24
Quasthoff, Thomas 26
Quaye, Finley 30
Queen 6
Queen Ida 9
Queen Latifah 24
  Earlier sketch in CM 6
Queens, Hollis
  See Boss Hog
Queens of the Stone Age 31
Queensryche 8
Querfurth, Carl
  See Roomful of Blues
Quicksilver Messenger Service 23
Quickspace 30
Quinn, Mickey
  See Supergrass
Qureshi, Ustad Alla Rakha 29
R.E.M. 25
  Earlier sketch in CM 5
Raaymakers, Boy
  See Willem Breuker Kollektief
Rabbitt, Eddie 24
  Earlier sketch in CM 5
Rabin, Trevor
  See Yes
Race, Tony
  See Felt
Radalj, Rod
  See Hoodoo Gurus
Radiohead 24
Raekwon
  See Wu-Tang Clan
Raffi 8
Rage Against the Machine 18
Raheem
  See Geto Boys, The
Rainey, Ma 22
Rainey, Sid
  See Compulsion
Rainford, Simone
  See All Saints

Rainwater, Keech
  See Lonestar
Raitt, Bonnie 23
  Earlier sketch in CM 3
Rakim
  See Eric B. and Rakim
Raleigh, Don
  See Squirrel Nut Zippers
Ralph Sharon Quartet 26
Ralphs, Mick
  See Mott the Hoople
Ralphs, Mick
  See Bad Company
Rammstein 25
Ramone, C. J.
  See Ramones, The
Ramone, Dee Dee
  See Ramones, The
Ramone, Joey
  See Ramones, The
Ramone, Johnny
  See Ramones, The
Ramone, Marky
  See Ramones, The
Ramone, Ritchie
  See Ramones, The
Ramone, Tommy
  See Ramones, The
Ramones, The 9
Rampage, Randy
  See D.O.A.
Rampal, Jean-Pierre 6
Ramsay, Andy
  See Stereolab
Ranaldo, Lee
  See Sonic Youth
Rancid 29
Randall, Bobby
  See Sawyer Brown
Raney, Jerry
  See Beat Farmers
Rangell, Andrew 24
Ranglin, Ernest
  See Skatalites, The
Ranken, Andrew
  See Pogues, The
Rankin, Cookie
  See Rankins, The
Rankin, Heather
  See Rankins, The
Rankin, Jimmy
  See Rankins, The
Rankin, John Morris
  See Rankins, The
Rankin, Raylene
  See Rankins, The
Ranking, Roger
  See English Beat, The
Rankins, The 24
Rapp, Marcelo D.
  See Soulfly
Rapp, Tom
  See Pearls Before Swine
Rarebell, Herman
  See Scorpions, The
Rasboro, Johnathen
  See Silk
Rasputina 26
Rat Fink, Jr.
  See Alien Sex Fiend
Ratcliffe, Simon
  See Basement Jaxx
Rathbone, Andie
  See Mansun
Ravel, Maurice 25
Raven, Paul
  See Killing Joke

Scherpenzeel, Ton
　See Camel
Schickele, Peter **5**
Schifrin, Lalo **29**
Schlesinger, Adam
　See Fountains of Wayne
Schlitt, John
　See Petra
Schloss, Zander
　See Circle Jerks, The
Schmelling, Johannes
　See Tangerine Dream
Schmid, Daniel
　See Cherry Poppin' Daddies
Schmidt, Irmin
　See Can
Schmit, Timothy B.
　See Eagles, The
Schmoovy Schmoove
　See Digital Underground
Schneider, Christoph
　See Rammstein
Schneider, Florian
　See Kraftwerk
Schneider, Fred III
　See B-52's, The
Schneider, Robert
　See Apples in Stereo
Schneider, Stefan
　See To Rococo Rot
Schnitzler, Conrad
　See Tangerine Dream
Schock, Gina
　See Go-Go's, The
Schoenbeck, Scott
　See Promise Ring, The
Scholten, Jim
　See Sawyer Brown
Scholz, Tom
　See Boston
Schon, Neal
　See Journey
Schönfeldt, Fredrik
　See Wannadies, The
Schönfeldt, Stefan
　See Wannadies, The
Schramm, Dave
　See Yo La Tengo
Schrody, Erik
　See House of Pain
　Also see Everlast
Schroer, Oliver **29**
Schroyder, Steve
　See Tangerine Dream
Schulman, Mark
　See Foreigner
Schulz, Guenter
　See KMFDM
Schulzberg, Robert
　See Placebo
Schulze, Klaus
　See Tangerine Dream
Schuman, William **10**
Schütze, Paul **32**
Schuur, Diane **6**
Schwartz, Will
　See Imperial Teen
Schwartzberg, Alan
　See Mountain
Sclavunos, Jim
　See Congo Norvell
Scofield, John **7**
Scorpions, The **12**
Scott, Andrew
　See Sloan
Scott, George
　See Five Blind Boys of Alabama

Scott, Howard
　See War
Scott, Jimmy **14**
Scott, Mike
　See Waterboys, The
Scott, Ronald Belford "Bon"
　See AC/DC
Scott, Sherry
　See Earth, Wind and Fire
Scott, Tony **32**
Scott-Heron, Gil **13**
Screaming Trees **19**
Scruggs, Earl **3**
Scruggs, Randy **28**
Scud Mountain Boys **21**
Seal **14**
Seales, Jim
　See Shenandoah
Seals & Crofts **3**
Seals, Brady
　See Little Texas
Seals, Dan **9**
Seals, Jim
　See Seals & Crofts
Seaman, Ken
　See Bluegrass Patriots
Sears, Pete
　See Jefferson Starship
Sebadoh **26**
Sebesky, Don **33**
Secada, Jon **13**
Secrest, Wayne
　See Confederate Railroad
Sed, Billy
　See Giant Sand
Sedaka, Neil **4**
Seeger, Peggy **25**
Seeger, Pete **4**
　Also see Weavers, The
Seger, Bob **15**
Seger, David
　See Giant Sand
Segovia, Andres **6**
Seidel, Martie
　See Dixie Chicks
Selberg, Shannon
　See Cows, The
Seldom Scene, The **4**
Selena **16**
Selway, Phil
　See Radiohead
Semisonic **32**
Sen Dog
　See Cypress Hill
Senior, Milton
　See McKinney's Cotton Pickers
Senior, Russell
　See Pulp
Sensi
　See Soul II Soul
Sepultura **12**
Seraphine, Daniel
　See Chicago
Sergeant, Will
　See Echo and the Bunnymen
Sermon, Erick
　See EPMD
Sete, Bola **26**
Setzer, Brian **32**
　Also see Stray Cats, The
Setzer, Philip
　See Emerson String Quartet
Severin, Steven
　See Siouxsie and the Banshees
Severinsen, Doc **1**
Sex Pistols, The **5**
Sexsmith, Ron **27**

Sexton, Chad
　See 311
Seymour, Neil
　See Crowded House
Shabalala, Ben
　See Ladysmith Black Mambazo
Shabalala, Headman
　See Ladysmith Black Mambazo
Shabalala, Jockey
　See Ladysmith Black Mambazo
Shabalala, Joseph
　See Ladysmith Black Mambazo
Shabo, Eric
　See Atomic Fireballs, The
Shade, Will
　See Memphis Jug Band
Shadow, DJ **19**
Shadows, The **22**
Shaffer, James
　See Korn
Shaffer, Paul **13**
Shaggy **19**
Shaggy 2 Dope
　See Insane Clown Possee
Shai **23**
Shakespeare, Robbie
　See Sly and Robbie
Shakira **33**
Shakur, Tupac
　See 2Pac
Shallenberger, James
　See Kronos Quartet
Shamen, The **23**
Shane, Bob
　See Kingston Trio, The
Shanice **14**
Shankar, Ravi **9**
Shannon, Del **10**
Shannon, Sarah
　See Velocity Girl
Shannon, Sharon
　See Waterboys, The
Shanté **10**
Shapiro, Jim
　See Veruca Salt
Shapiro, Lee
　See Four Seasons, The
Shapps, Andre
　See Big Audio Dynamite
Sharon, Lois & Bram **6**
Sharon, Ralph
　See Ralph Sharon Quartet
Sharp, Dave
　See Alarm
Sharp, Laura
　See Sweet Honey in the Rock
Sharpe, Matt
　See Weezer
Sharpe, Trevor
　See Minty
Sharrock, Chris
　See Lightning Seeds
Sharrock, Sonny **15**
Shaw, Adrian
　See Bevis Frond
Shaw, Artie **8**
Shaw, Martin
　See Jamiroquai
Shaw, Robert **32**
Shaw, Woody **27**
Shea, Tom
　See Scud Mountain Boys
Shearer, Harry
　See Spinal Tap
Shearing, George **28**
Sheehan, Bobby
　See Blues Traveler

Sly & the Family Stone **24**
Sly and Robbie **13**
Sly, Randy "Ginger"
  See Atomic Fireballs, The
Small, Heather
  See M People
Smalls, Derek
  See Spinal Tap
Smart II, N.D.
  See Mountain
Smart, Terence
  See Butthole Surfers
Smash, Chas
  See Madness
Smash Mouth **27**
Smashing Pumpkins **13**
Smear, Pat
  See Foo Fighters
Smelly
  See NOFX
Smith, "Legs" Larry
  See Bonzo Dog Doo-Dah Band
Smith, Adrian
  See Iron Maiden
Smith, Allen
  See Lavay Smith and Her Red Hot Skillet
  Lickers
Smith, Bessie **3**
Smith, Brad
  See Blind Melon
Smith, Chad
  See Red Hot Chili Peppers, The
Smith, Charles
  See Kool & the Gang
Smith, Chas
  See Cobra Verde
Smith, Clifford
  See Method Man
Smith, Curt
  See Tears for Fears
Smith, Debbie
  See Curve
  Also see Echobelly
Smith, Elliott **28**
Smith, Fran
  See Hooters
Smith, Fred
  See MC5, The
Smith, Fred
  See Blondie
Smith, Fred
  See Television
Smith, Garth
  See Buzzcocks, The
Smith, James "Smitty"
  See Three Dog Night
Smith, Jimmy **30**
Smith, Jocelyn B. **30**
Smith, Joe
  See McKinney's Cotton Pickers
Smith, Keely **29**
Smith, Kevin
  See dc Talk
Smith, Lavay
  See Lavay Smith and Her Red Hot Skillet
  Lickers
Smith, Mark E.
  See Fall, The
Smith, Martin
  See Delirious?
Smith, Michael W. **11**
Smith, Mike
  See Dave Clark Five, The
Smith, Mike
  See Paul Revere & The Raiders
Smith, Parrish
  See EPMD

Smith, Patti **17**
  Earlier sketch in CM **1**
Smith, Rick
  See Underworld
Smith, Robert
  See Cure, The
  Also see Siouxsie and the Banshees
Smith, Robert
  See Spinners, The
Smith, Shawn
  See Brad
Smith, Simon
  See Wedding Present, The
Smith, Smitty
  See Three Dog Night
Smith, Steve
  See Journey
Smith, Stewart
  See Delirious?
Smith, Tommy **28**
Smith, Tweed
  See War
Smith, Wendy
  See Prefab Sprout
Smith, Will **26**
  Also see DJ Jazzy Jeff and the Fresh Prince
Smith, Zachary
  See Loud Family, The
Smithereens, The **14**
Smiths, The **3**
Smog **28**
Smyth, Gilli
  See Gong
Smyth, Joe
  See Sawyer Brown
Sneed, Floyd Chester
  See Three Dog Night
Snoop Doggy Dogg **17**
Snouffer, Alex "Alex St. Clair"
  See Captain Beefheart and His Magic Band
Snow **23**
Snow, Don
  See Squeeze
Snow, Hank **29**
Snow, Phoebe **4**
Snyder, Richard "Midnight Hatsize Snyder"
  See Captain Beefheart and His Magic Band
Soan, Ashley
  See Del Amitri
Sobule, Jill **20**
Social Distortion **27**
  Earlier sketch in CM **19**
Solal, Martial **4**
Sollenberger, Isobel
  See Bardo Pond
Soloff, Lew
  See Blood, Sweat and Tears
Solowka, Peter
  See Wedding Present, The
Solti, Georg **13**
Sommer, Günter "Baby" **31**
Son Volt **21**
Sondheim, Stephen **8**
Sonefeld, Jim
  See Hootie and the Blowfish
Sonic Youth **26**
  Earlier sketch in CM **9**
Sonnenberg, Nadja Salerno
  See Salerno-Sonnenberg, Nadja
Sonni, Jack
  See Dire Straits
Sonnier, Jo-El **10**
Sonny and Cher **24**
Sorum, Matt
  See Cult, The
Sosa, Mercedes **3**

Sosna, Rudolf
  See Faust
Soucie, Michael
  See Surfin' Pluto
Soul Asylum **10**
Soul Coughing **21**
Soul II Soul **17**
Soul Stirrers, The **11**
Soulfly **33**
Soundgarden **6**
Sounds of Blackness **13**
Sousa, John Philip **10**
Southerland, Bill
  See Kilgore
Spacehog **29**
Spacemen 3 **31**
Spampinato, Joey
  See NRBQ
Spampinato, Johnny
  See NRBQ
Spann, Otis **18**
Sparks **18**
Sparks, Brett
  See Handsome Family, The
Sparks, Chris "Cornbread"
  See Workhorse Movement, The
Sparks, Donita
  See L7
Sparks, Rennie
  See Handsome Family, The
Spear, Roger Ruskin
  See Bonzo Dog Doo-Dah Band
Spearhead **19**
Spears, Britney **28**
Special Ed **16**
Specials, The **21**
Spector, Phil **4**
Spector, Ronnie **28**
Speech
  See Arrested Development
Spellman, Jim
  See Velocity Girl
Spence, Alexander "Skip"
  See Jefferson Airplane
  Also see Moby Grape
Spence, Cecil
  See Israel Vibration
Spence, Skip
  See Spence, Alexander "Skip"
Spencer Davis Group **19**
Spencer, Jeremy
  See Fleetwood Mac
Spencer, Jim
  See Dave Clark Five, The
Spencer, Jon
  See Boss Hog
  Also see Jon Spencer Blues Explosion
Spencer, Thad
  See Jayhawks, The
Sperske, Aaron
  See Pernice Brothers
Spice Girls **22**
Spillane, Scott
  See Neutral Milk Hotel
Spin Doctors **14**
Spinal Tap **8**
Spindt, Don
  See Aqua Velvets
Spinners, The **21**
Spirit **22**
Spiteri, Sharleen
  See Texas
Spitz, Dan
  See Anthrax
Spitz, Dave
  See Black Sabbath
Sponge **18**

Stockman, Shawn
  See Boyz II Men
Stockwood, Kim **26**
Stoll
  See Clannad
  Also see Big Mountain
Stoller, Mike
  See Leiber and Stoller
Stoltz, Brian
  See Neville Brothers, The
Stoltzman, Richard **24**
Stonadge, Gary
  See Big Audio Dynamite
Stone, Curtis
  See Highway 101
Stone, Doug **10**
Stone Roses, The **16**
Stone, Sly **8**
Stone Temple Pilots **14**
Stookey, Paul
  See Peter, Paul & Mary
Story, Liz **2**
Story, The **13**
Stotts, Richie
  See Wendy O. Williams and The Plasmatics
Stradlin, Izzy
  See Guns n' Roses
Strain, Sammy
  See O'Jays, The
Strait, George **5**
Stranglers, The **31**
Stratton, Dennis
  See Iron Maiden
Strauss, Richard **25**
Stravinsky, Igor **21**
Straw, Syd **18**
  Also see Golden Palominos
Stray Cats, The **11**
Strayhorn, Billy **13**
Street, Richard
  See Temptations, The
Streisand, Barbra **2**
Strickland, Keith
  See B-52's, The
Stringer, Gary
  See Reef
Strummer, Joe
  See Clash, The
Stryper **2**
Stuart, Mark
  See Audio Adrenaline
Stuart, Marty **9**
Stuart, Peter
  See Dog's Eye View
Stubbs, Levi
  See Four Tops, The
Sturr, Jimmy **33**
Styne, Jule **21**
Styrene, Poly
  See X-Ray Spex
Sub Commander Ras I Zulu
  See Spearhead
Subdudes, The **18**
Sublime **19**
Such, Alec Jon
  See Bon Jovi
Suede **20**
Sugar Ray **22**
Sugarcubes, The **10**
Suicidal Tendencies **15**
Sulley, Suzanne
  See Human League, The
Sullivan, Jacqui
  See Bananarama
Sullivan, Jeff
  See Drivin' N' Cryin'

Sullivan, Kirk
  See 4Him
Summer, Donna **12**
Summer, Mark
  See Turtle Island String Quartet
Summers, Andy **3**
  Also see Police, The
Summers, Bill
  See Los Hombres Calientes
Sumner, Bernard
  See Joy Division
  Also see New Order
Sun Ra **27**
  Earlier sketch in CM **5**
Sun-J
  See Asian Dub Foundation
Sundays, The **20**
Sunny Day Real Estate **28**
Sunnyland Slim **16**
Sunset Valley **31**
Super DJ Dmitry
  See Deee-lite
Super Furry Animals **28**
Superchunk **29**
Superdrag **23**
Supergrass **30**
Supertramp **25**
Supremes, The **6**
Sure!, Al B. **13**
Surfaris, The **23**
Surfin' Pluto **24**
Sutcliffe, Stu
  See Beatles, The
Sutherland, Joan **13**
Suzuki, Kenji "Damo"
  See Can
Sveinsson, Kjartan
  See Sigur Rós
Svenigsson, Magnus
  See Cardigans
Svensson, Peter
  See Cardigans
Svigals, Alicia
  See Klezmatics, The
Swanson, Dave
  See Cobra Verde
Swarbrick, Dave
  See Fairport Convention
Sweat, Keith **13**
Sweet Honey In The Rock **26**
  Earlier sketch in CM **1**
Sweet, Matthew **9**
Sweet, Michael
  See Stryper
Sweet, Robert
  See Stryper
Sweethearts of the Rodeo **12**
Swell **31**
Swervedriver **31**
Swing, DeVante
  See Jodeci
SWV **14**
Sykes, John
  See Whitesnake
Sykes, Roosevelt **20**
Sylvain, Sylvain
  See New York Dolls
Sylvian, David **27**
T. Rex **11**
Tabac, Tony
  See Joy Division
Tabor, Ty
  See King's X
Tackett, Fred
  See Little Feat
Tacuma, Jamaaladeen
  Golden Palominos

Tadlock, Tom
  See Tuxedomoon
Taff
  See Killing Joke
TAFKAP (The Artist Formerly Known as Prince)
  See Prince
Taggart, Jeremy
  See Our Lady Peace
Tait, Chris
  See Fixx, The
Tait, Michael
  See dc Talk
Taj Mahal **6**
Tajima, Takao
  See Pizzicato Five
Takac, Robby
  See Goo Goo Dolls, The
Takahashi, Maki
  See Blonde Redhead
Takanami
  See Pizzicato Five
Take 6 **6**
Takeda, Clint
  See Bardo Pond
Takemitsu, Toru **6**
Takizawa, Taishi
  See Ghost
Talbot, Ivor
  See Divine Comedy, The
Talbot, Joby
  See Divine Comedy, The
Talbot, John Michael **6**
Talcum, Joe Jack
  See Dead Milkmen
Talk Talk **19**
Talking Heads **1**
Tampa Red **25**
Tan Dun **33**
Tandy, Richard
  See Electric Light Orchestra
Tangerine Dream **12**
Taree, Aerle
  See Arrested Development
Tate, Buddy **33**
Tate, Geoff
  See Queensryche
Tatum, Art **17**
Taupin, Bernie **22**
Taylor, Aaron
  See MC Eiht
Taylor, Andy
  See Duran Duran
Taylor, Billy **13**
Taylor, Cecil **9**
Taylor, Chad
  See Live
Taylor, Corey
  See Slipknot
Taylor, Courtney
  See Dandy Warhols
Taylor, Dan
  See Silver Apples
Taylor, Dave
  See Pere Ubu
Taylor, Dick
  See Rolling Stones, The
Taylor, Earl
  See Country Gentlemen, The
Taylor, Isaiah
  See Baha Men
Taylor, James **25**
  Earlier sketch in CM **2**
Taylor, James "J.T."
  See Kool & the Gang
Taylor, John
  See Duran Duran

Toma, Andi
  See Mouse On Mars
Tone-Loc 3
Tong, Winston
  See Tuxedomoon
Tonic 32
Tontoh, Frank
  See Aztec Camera
Tony K
  See Roomful of Blues
Tony Williams 6
Tony! Toni! Toné! 12
Too $hort 16
Toohey, Dan
  See Guided By Voices
Took, Steve Peregrine
  See T. Rex
Tool 21
Toomey, Jenny
  See Tsunami
Topham, Anthony "Top"
  See Yardbirds, The
Topper, Sharon
  See God Is My Co-Pilot
Tork, Peter
  See Monkees, The
Torme, Mel 4
Torrence, Dean
  See Jan & Dean
Torres, Hector "Tico"
  See Bon Jovi
Torry, Richard
  See Minty
Tortoise 32
Toscanini, Arturo 14
Tosh, Peter 3
Toth, Ed
  See Vertical Horizon
Toure, Ali Farka 18
Tourish, Ciaran
  See Altan
Toussaint, Allen 11
Towner, Ralph 22
Towner, Ralph
  See Oregon
Townes, Jeffery
  See DJ Jazzy Jeff and the Fresh Prince
Towns, Efrem
  See Dirty Dozen Brass Band
Townshend, Pete 1
  Also see Who, The
Traa,
  See P.O.D.
Traffic 19
Tragically Hip, The 18
Train 33
Trammell, Mark
  See Greater Vision
Trautmann, Gene
  See Queens of the Stone Age
Travers, Brian
  See UB40
Travers, Mary
  See Peter, Paul & Mary
Travis 29
Travis, Abby
  See Elastica
Travis, Merle 14
Travis, Randy 9
Traynor, Kevin
  See Divine Comedy, The
Treach
  See Naughty by Nature
Treadmill Trackstar 21
Tremonti, Mark
  See Creed
Trevi, Gloria 29

Tribe Called Quest, A 8
Trick Daddy 28
Tricky 18
  Also see Massive Attack
Trimble, Vivian
  See Luscious Jackson
Trimm, Rex
  See Cherry Poppin' Daddies
Tripp, Art "Art Marimba"
  See Captain Beefheart and His Magic Band
Tristano, Lennie 30
Tritsch, Christian
  See Gong
Tritt, Travis 7
Trotter, Kera
  See C + C Music Factory
Trucks, Butch
  See Allman Brothers, The
Trugoy the Dove
  See De La Soul
Trujillo, Robert
  See Suicidal Tendencies
Truman, Dan
  See Diamond Rio
Trynin, Jen 21
Trytten, Lorre Lynn
  See Willem Breuker Kollektief
Tsunami 21
Tubb, Ernest 4
Tubridy, Michael
  See Chieftans, The
Tucker, Corin
  See Sleater-Kinney
Tucker, Jim
  See Turtles, The
Tucker, Moe
  See Velvet Underground, The
Tucker, Sophie 12
Tucker, Tanya 3
Tucker, William
  See Ministry
  Also see Pigface
Tufnel, Nigel
  See Spinal Tap
Tull, Bruce
  See Scud Mountain Boys
Turbin, Neil
  See Anthrax
Turgon, Bruce
  See Foreigner
Turnage, Mark-Anthony 31
Turnbull, Alex
  See 23 Skidoo
Turnbull, Johnny
  See 23 Skidoo
Turner, Big Joe 13
Turner, Elgin "Masta Killa"
  See Wu-Tang Clan
Turner, Erik
  See Warrant
Turner, Ike
  See Turner, Ike and Tina
Turner, Ike and Tina 24
Turner, Joe Lynn
  See Deep Purple
Turner, Mick
  See Dirty Three
Turner, Mike
  See Our Lady Peace
Turner, Roger 32
Turner, Sonny
  See Platters, The
Turner, Steve
  See Mudhoney
Turner, Tina 29
  Earlier sketch in CM 1
  Also see Turner, Ike and Tina

Turpin, Will
  See Collective Soul
Turre, Steve 22
Turtle Island String Quartet 9
Turtles, The 29
Tutton, Bill
  See Geraldine Fibbers
Tutuska, George
  See Goo Goo Dolls, The
Tuxedomoon 21
Twain, Shania 17
23, Richard
  See Front 242
23 Skidoo 31
Twist, Nigel
  See Alarm
Twitty, Conway 6
2Pac 17
  Also see Digital Underground
2 Unlimited 18
Tyagi, Paul
  See Del Amitri
Tyler, Steve
  See Aerosmith
Tyner, McCoy 7
Tyner, Rob
  See MC5, The
Type O Negative 27
Tyson, Ian
  See Ian and Sylvia
Tyson, Ron
  See Temptations, The
UB40 4
Ulmer, James Blood 13
Ulrich, Lars
  See Metallica
Ulvaeus, Björn
  See Abba
Um Romao, Dom
  See Weather Report
Underwood, Scott
  See Train
Underworld 26
Ungerman, Bill
  See Royal Crown Revue
Unitt, Victor
  See Pretty Things, The
Unruh, N. U.
  See Einstürzende Neubauten
Uosikkinen, David
  See Hooters
Upshaw, Dawn 9
Urge Overkill 17
Uriah Heep 19
US3 18
Usher 23
Utley, Adrian
  See Portishead
Utsler, Joseph
  See Insane Clown Possee
U2 12
  Earlier sketch in CM 2
Vaché Jr., Warren 22
Vachon, Chris
  See Roomful of Blues
Vai, Steve 5
  Also see Whitesnake
Valdès, Chucho 25
Vale, Jerry 30
Valens, Ritchie 23
Valenti, Dino
  See Quicksilver Messenger Service
Valentin, Dave 33
Valentine, Gary
  See Blondie
Valentine, Hilton
  See Animals, The

Wallis, Larry
  See Motörhead
Walls, Chris
  See Dave Clark Five, The
Walls, Denise "Nee-C"
  See Anointed
Walls, Greg
  See Anthrax
Walsh, Joe 5
  Also see Eagles, The
Walsh, Marty
  See Supertramp
Walsh, Steve
  See Kansas
Walsh, Tim
  See Brave Combo
Walter, Tommy
  See eels
Walter, Weasel
  See Flying Luttenbachers, The
Walters, Richard
  See Slick Rick
Walters, Robert "Patch"
  See Mystic Revealers
Walton, Mark
  See Giant Sand
Wanbdi
  See Indigenous
Wannadies, The 29
War 14
Ward, Andy
  See Bevis Frond
  Also see Camel
Ward, Bill
  See Black Sabbath
Ward, Jim
  See At The Drive-In
Ward, Michael
  See Wallflowers, The
Ware, Martyn
  See Human League, The
Wareham, Dean
  See Galaxie 500
  Also see Luna
Warfield, William 33
Wariner, Steve 18
Warmling, Hans
  See Stranglers, The
Warner, Les
  See Cult, The
Warnes, Jennifer 3
Warnick, Kim
  See Fastbacks, The
Warrant 17
Warren, Diane 21
Warren G 33
Warren, George W.
  See Five Blind Boys of Alabama
Warren, Mervyn
  See Take 6
Warwick, Clint
  See Moody Blues, The
Warwick, Dionne 2
Was (Not Was) 6
Was, David
  See Was (Not Was)
Was, Don 21
  Also see Was (Not Was)
Wash, Martha
  See C + C Music Factory
Washington, Chester
  See Earth, Wind and Fire
Washington, Dinah 5
Washington, Grover, Jr. 5
Wasserman, Greg "Noodles"
  See Offspring
Waterboys, The 27

Waters, Crystal 15
Waters, Ethel 11
Waters, Muddy 24
  Earlier sketch in CM 4
Waters, Roger
  See Pink Floyd
Watkins, Christopher
  See Cabaret Voltaire
Watkins, Tionne "T-Boz"
  See TLC
Watley, Jody 26
  Earlier sketch in CM 9
Watson, Doc 2
Watson, Guy
  See Surfaris, The
Watson, Ivory
  See Ink Spots
Watt, Ben
  See Everything But The Girl
Watt, Mike 22
  Also see fIREHOSE
  Also see Minutemen, The
Watters, Sam
  See Color Me Badd
Watts, Bari
  See Bevis Frond
Watts, Charlie
  See Rolling Stones, The
Watts, Eugene
  See Canadian Brass, The
Watts, Lou
  See Chumbawamba
Watts, Pete "Overend"
  See Mott the Hoople
Watts, Raymond
  See KMFDM
Watts, Todd
  See Emmet Swimming
Weather Report 19
Weaver, Louie
  See Petra
Weavers, The 8
Webb, Chick 14
Webb, Jimmy 12
Webb, Paul
  See Talk Talk
Webber, Andrew Lloyd
  See Lloyd Webber, Andrew
Webber, Mark
  See Pulp
Webster, Andrew
  See Tsunami
Wedding Present, The 28
Wedgwood, Mike
  See Caravan
Wedren, Craig
  See Shudder to Think
Ween 30
Weezer 20
Wegelin, Aaron
  See Elf Power
Wehner, Marty
  See Lavay Smith and Her Red Hot Skillet
  Lickers
Weider, John
  See Animals, The
Weiland, Scott
  See Stone Temple Pilots
Weill, Kurt 12
Weir, Bob
  See Grateful Dead, The
Weiss, Janet
  See Sleater-Kinney
  Also see Quasi
Weissman, Marco
  See Waterboys, The

Welch, Bob
  See Fleetwood Mac
Welch, Brian
  See Korn
Welch, Bruce
  See Shadows, The
Welch, Gillian 33
Welch, Justin
  See Elastica
Welch, Mcguinness
  See Lords of Acid
Welch, Sean
  See Beautiful South
Welk, Lawrence 13
Weller, Freddy
  See Paul Revere & The Raiders
Weller, Paul 14
  Also see Jam, The
Wells, Cory
  See Three Dog Night
Wells, Junior 17
Wells, Kitty 6
Welnick, Vince
  See Grateful Dead, The
Welsh, Alan
  See Aztec Camera
Welty, Ron
  See Offspring
Wenberg, Erik
  See Emmet Swimming
Wendy O. Williams and The Plasmatics 26
Wenner, Niko
  See Swell
Werner, Mike
  See Handsome Family, The
Wertz, Jenn
  See Rusted Root
West, Brian
  See Cherry Poppin' Daddies
West, Dottie 8
West, Leslie
  See Mountain
West, Steve
  See Pavement
West Virginia Creeper
  See Commander Cody and His Lost Planet
  Airmen
West-Oram, Jamie
  See Fixx, The
Westerberg, Paul 26
  Also see Replacements, The
Westlife 33
Weston, Randy 15
Weston
  See Orb, The
Wetton, John
  See King Crimson
Wexler, Jerry 15
Weymouth, Tina
  See Talking Heads
Wez
  See Carter USM
Whalen, Katharine
  See Squirrel Nut Zippers
Whalley, Dennis
  See Captain Beefheart and His Magic Band
Wharton, Dianaruthe
  See Sweet Honey in the Rock
Wheat, Brian
  See Tesla
Wheeler, Audrey
  See C + C Music Factory
Wheeler, Caron
  See Soul II Soul
Wheeler, Harriet
  See Sundays, The

Wilson, Brian **24**
  Also see Beach Boys, The
Wilson, Carl
  See Beach Boys, The
Wilson, Carnie
  See Wilson Phillips
Wilson, Cassandra **26**
  Earlier sketch in CM **12**
Wilson, Chris
  See Love Spit Love
Wilson, Cindy
  See B-52's, The
Wilson, Dan
  See Semisonic
Wilson, Dennis
  See Beach Boys, The
Wilson, Don
  See Ventures, The
Wilson, Eric
  See Sublime
Wilson, Gerald **19**
Wilson, Jackie **3**
Wilson, Kim
  See Fabulous Thunderbirds, The
Wilson, Mary
  See Supremes, The
Wilson, Nancy
  See Heart
Wilson, Nancy **28**
  Earlier sketch in CM **14**
Wilson, Orlandus
  See Golden Gate Quartet
Wilson, Patrick
  See Weezer
Wilson Phillips **5**
Wilson, Ransom **5**
Wilson, Ricky
  See B-52's, The
Wilson, Robin
  See Gin Blossoms
Wilson, Ron
  See Surfaris, The
Wilson, Shanice
  See Shanice
Wilson, Sid
  See Slipknot
Wilson, Wendy
  See Wilson Phillips
Wilson-James, Victoria
  See Soul II Soul
  Also see Shamen, The
Wilton, Michael
  See Queensryche
Wimpfheimer, Jimmy
  See Roomful of Blues
Winans, BeBe and CeCe **32**
Winans, Carvin
  See Winans, The
Winans, Marvin
  See Winans, The
Winans, Michael
  See Winans, The
Winans, Ronald
  See Winans, The
Winans, The **12**
Winbush, Angela **15**
Winfield, Chuck
  See Blood, Sweat and Tears
Winston, George **9**
Winter, Johnny **5**
Winter, Kurt
  See Guess Who
Winter, Paul **10**
Winthrop, Dave
  See Supertramp
Winwood, Muff
  See Spencer Davis Group

Winwood, Steve **2**
  Also see Spencer Davis Group
  Also see Traffic
Wire **29**
Wire, Nicky
  See Manic Street Preachers
Wiseman, Bobby
  See Blue Rodeo
Wiseman, Mac **19**
WishBone
  See Bone Thugs-N-Harmony
Wisniewski, Tom
  See MxPx
Withers, Pick
  See Dire Straits
Witherspoon, Jimmy **19**
Wolf, Kurt
  See Boss Hog
Wolf, Peter **31**
Wolf, Peter
  See J. Geils Band
Wolfe, Gerald
  See Greater Vision
Wolstencraft, Simon
  See Fall, The
Womack, Bobby **5**
Womack, Lee Ann **33**
Wonder, Stevie **17**
  Earlier sketch in CM **2**
Woo, John
  See Magnetic Fields, The
Wood, Chris
  See Medeski, Martin & Wood
Wood, Chris
  See Traffic
Wood, Danny
  See New Kids on the Block
Wood, Ron
  See Faces, The
  Also see Rolling Stones, The
Wood, Roy
  See Electric Light Orchestra
Woodgate, Dan
  See Madness
Woods, Adam
  See Fixx, The
Woods, Gay
  See Steeleye Span
Woods, Terry
  See Pogues, The
  Also see Steeleye Span
Woods-Wright, Tomica **22**
Woodson, Ollie
  See Temptations, The
Woodward, Alun
  See Delgados, The
Woodward, Keren
  See Bananarama
Woody, Allen
  See Allman Brothers, The
Woolfolk, Andrew
  See Earth, Wind and Fire
Woomble, Roddy
  See Idlewild
Workhorse Movement, The **30**
Worley, Chris
  See Jackyl
Worley, Jeff
  See Jackyl
Worrell, Bernie **11**
  Also see Golden Palominos
Wozniak, John
  See Marcy Playground
Wray, Link **17**
Wreede, Katrina
  See Turtle Island String Quartet

Wren, Alan
  See Stone Roses, The
Wretzky, D'Arcy
  See Smashing Pumpkins
Wright, Adrian
  See Human League, The
Wright, David "Blockhead"
  See English Beat, The
Wright, Heath
  See Ricochet
Wright, Hugh
  See Boy Howdy
Wright, Jimmy
  See Sounds of Blackness
Wright, Norman
  See Country Gentlemen, The
Wright, Rick
  See Pink Floyd
Wright, Simon
  See AC/DC
Wright, Tim
  See Pere Ubu
Wu-Tang Clan **19**
Wupass, Reverend
  See Rube Waddell
Wurster, Jon
  See Superchunk
Wurzel
  See Motörhead
Wusthoff, Gunter
  See Faust
Wuv
  See P.O.D.
Wyatt, Robert **24**
Wyman, Bill
  See Rolling Stones, The
  Also see Bill Wyman & the Rhythm Kings
Wynette, Tammy **24**
  Earlier sketch in CM **2**
Wynn, Steve **31**
Wynne, Philippe
  See Spinners, The
Wynonna **11**
  Also see Judds, The
Wysocki, Jon
  See Staind
X **11**
X-Ray Spex **31**
Xefos, Chris
  See King Missile
XTC **26**
  Earlier sketch in CM **10**
Xzibit **31**
Ya Kid K
  See Technotronic
Yale, Brian
  See Matchbox 20
Yamamoto, Hiro
  See Soundgarden
Yamamoto, Seichi
  See Boredoms, The
Yamano, Atsuko
  See Shonen Knife
Yamano, Naoko
  See Shonen Knife
Yamashita, Kazuhito **4**
Yamataka, Eye
  See Boredoms, The
Yamauchi, Tetsu
  See Faces, The
Yamazaki, Iwao
  See Ghost
Yang, Naomi
  See Damon and Naomi
  Also see Galaxie 500
Yankovic, "Weird Al" **7**
Yanni **11**